Why Do We Still Have the Electoral College?

Why Do We Still Have the Electoral College?

Alexander Keyssar

 Harvard University Press

CAMBRIDGE, MASSACHUSETTS

LONDON, ENGLAND

2020

Cataloging-in-Publication Data available from the Library of Congress

ISBN: 978-0-674-66015-1 (alk. paper)

For Rosabelli

Contents

Why Do We Still Have the Electoral College?

INTRODUCTION

The institution that Americans now call the "Electoral College" has been a source of discontent for more than 200 years. As early as the 1790s, political leaders began pointing to flaws in their new Constitution's blueprint for selecting presidents, and by the 1820s even James Madison—the principal "father" of the Constitution—was voicing support for significant reform.[1] The nineteenth and twentieth centuries each witnessed recurrent, broadly supported efforts to transform the presidential election system, and the twenty-first century began with a new wave of criticism after George W. Bush became president despite losing the popular vote. Hundreds of books and countless articles have debated the virtues and defects of the unique American method of choosing a chief executive.

For many citizens of the twenty-first century, the problematic features of the Electoral College are not far to seek. Most obviously, the institution makes it possible for the winner of the popular vote to lose the electoral count and not become president—an outcome that violates conventional expectations about the workings of electoral democracy. This has happened five times in our history, most recently in 2016, and it has come close to happening on numerous other occasions, including 2004.[2] A related issue is that the Electoral College does not conform to the widely accepted principle of "one person, one vote." Because electoral votes are allocated to each state based on the size of its congressional delegation in the Senate and the House combined, the votes of residents of small states carry more weight, per capita, than do the votes of large-state residents. In 2016, for example, Wyoming cast one electoral vote for every 190,000 residents; in California, an electoral vote represented 680,000 people.[3]

Equally troublesome is the practice, in every state but Maine and Nebraska, of awarding all of a state's electoral votes to the winner of its popular vote. This long-standing, but not constitutionally mandated, feature of presidential elections leaves millions of voters feeling that their votes do not really count, especially if they live in states where one political party is dominant. It also has a profound impact on election campaigns, which are now conducted almost entirely in "swing" or "battleground" states, while those that are less competitive are largely ignored except for fund-raising.[4] The use of "winner-take-all" in the states also contributes to the possibility that someone other than the winner of the national popular vote could become president.

It is largely for these reasons that a majority of Americans since the 1940s—when modern, scientific polls on the subject were first conducted—have consistently expressed a preference for changing the presidential election system. (See Appendix Tables A.1 and A.2.) In the late 1960s and 1970s, 65 to 80 percent of voters favored amending the Constitution to replace the Electoral College with a national popular vote; during the first decade of the twenty-first century, the figure hovered just above 60 percent, including majorities of both Democrats and Republicans. Indeed, from the 1940s to the present, no national opinion poll reported that a majority of Americans preferred to keep the Election College. (Republican support for the Electoral College did rise sharply after the 2016 election, but it remains to be seen whether that shift will prove to be durable.) Polls also indicate that many Americans are confused about what the Electoral College is and how it works.[5]

Historically, unhappiness with the Electoral College has had multiple origins and shifting emphases; at one time or another, serious criticism has been aimed at every distinctive feature of the institution. The ink on the Constitution was barely dry when detractors began to argue that the complex apparatus of choosing obscure individuals as intermediaries to cast a state's electoral votes was unnecessary; that view became increasingly common as the "colleges" of electors that convened in every state showed no sign of deliberating in the manner envisioned by the framers of the Constitution. Other early critics concluded that electors also posed a risk to popular government because they were legally free to vote for whomever they wished. The presence of "agents to execute the will of the people" heightened the "danger" of the people's "wishes being frustrated," observed President Andrew Jackson. Worries about "faithless electors" (as the problem came to be called) have persisted into the twenty-first century, although no faithless elector has yet determined the outcome of an election.[6]

Criticism of winner-take-all—originally labeled the "general ticket" and sometimes called the "unit rule"—also began in the early years of the republic.[7] The practice first appeared, rather benignly, in a few states in the 1790s, yet within a decade it was being attacked, with reason, as a partisan maneuver at variance with the intentions of the Constitution's authors— an "illegitimate offspring of faction," one newspaper called it in 1804. Despite such criticism, and despite repeated congressional efforts to ban the practice through a constitutional amendment, the general ticket became nearly universal by the early 1830s.[8] Since that time, politicians and political observers of diverse stripes have lamented the impact of this practice on presidential elections and repeatedly pressed for reforms that would get rid of it. If the general ticket were eliminated, predicted former Pennsylvania senator Charles Buckalew in 1877, "popular disfranchisement within a state will be swept away, while the supporters of no candidate will control more than their due share of electoral power." Fifty years later, Clarence Lea, a respected California congressman, declared that "our system of electing the president . . . lacks the inherent quality of political justice, and the fundamental defect is in the unit-voting system."[9]

Even more widely disparaged than winner-take-all has been the "contingent election system"—the constitutional procedure for deciding an election when no candidate has won a majority of the nation's electoral votes. If that happens, the president is chosen by the House of Representatives, with each state delegation casting one vote. This would permit an election to be decided by states with a relatively small minority of the nation's population (less than 20 percent in 2020), an outcome so inconsistent with republican principles that Thomas Jefferson in 1823 denounced the provision as "the most dangerous blot in our constitution."[10] The contingent election system has been utilized only twice, in 1800 and in 1824, leading to controversy on both occasions. After the 1820s the emergence of durable two-party systems greatly reduced the odds of an election ending up in the House of Representatives, and the shortcomings of the constitutional procedure have receded from view. Yet even the occasional possibility that a third party could garner enough votes to prevent any candidate from gaining a majority—as occurred in 1948, 1968, and 1992— has prompted analysts and politicians alike to demand reform.[11]

Other, less well-known features of the electoral system have also drawn fire. One is that the Constitution permits state legislatures to choose electors by itself, without holding popular elections; numerous states did so between 1790 and 1830, and the Florida legislature threatened to resurrect this power as recently as December 2000. (See Appendix B for the relevant constitutional texts.) Relatedly, states can change the manner in which they select electors from one election to the next, making it possible for states to alter the rules in pursuit of partisan advantage. (This happened repeatedly in the early nineteenth century.) A third flaw, from at least some perspectives, is that the complex apparatus of the Electoral College—requiring slates of electors in each state—has discouraged independent candidacies and given an unfair advantage to well-funded party organizations. It was in part for this reason that George Norris, Nebraska's five-term progressive senator (1913–1943), concluded that the electoral system was "unnecessary . . . confusing . . . and with no merit whatsoever."[12]

Over the last two centuries, Electoral College reform, or abolition, has been advocated not only by iconoclasts like Norris but also by a long roster of mainstream political leaders with disparate political interests and ideologies. Jefferson, Madison, Jackson, and Missouri senator Thomas Hart Benton were among the prominent political leaders who favored changes in the early nineteenth century. In 1872 Massachusetts Republican senator Charles Sumner denounced the institution as "highly artificial . . . cumbersome . . . radically defective, and unrepublican."[13] Five years later, after the disputed election of 1876, Sumner's influential Republican colleague Oliver Morton of Indiana concluded that "experience, as well as reason, now suggests that the rubbish of the Electoral College be brushed away entirely."[14] Between 1950 and the late 1970s, reform was advocated by Republicans Henry Cabot Lodge Jr., Bob Dole, and Gerald Ford, as well as by liberal Democrats like Hubert Humphrey, Edward Kennedy, Indiana senator Birch Bayh, and the esteemed Senate majority leader, Mike Mansfield. Somewhat more grudgingly (or less enthusiastically), Presidents Lyndon Johnson, Richard Nixon, and Jimmy Carter also signaled their support for changes to the electoral system.

Although there have been recurrent efforts to do away with winner-take-all at the state level (which is possible because state legislatures control the "manner" in which electors are chosen), movements to abolish or significantly reform the Electoral College have generally focused on amending Article II, section 1, of the U.S. Constitution, a section that spells out the procedure for choosing a president.[15] (The recent drive for an interstate compact to institute a national popular vote is a notable exception.)[16] Between 1800 and 2016, members of Congress introduced more than 800 such amendments, and the tally grows every few years.[17] The Congressional Research Service concluded in 2004 that "more proposed constitutional amendments have been introduced in Congress regarding Electoral College reform than on any other subject." According to one estimate, roughly 10 percent of all amendments introduced into Congress have been aimed at the presidential election system.[18] On six occasions, election reform amendments were approved, by the requisite two-thirds vote, in one branch of Congress; the most recent was in 1969 when the House passed an amendment calling for a national popular vote.[19] The only proposal to become law, however, was the Twelfth Amendment, ratified in 1804. It required electors to differentiate their votes for president from their votes for vice president and made a small alteration in the procedure to be followed if the election ended up in the House.[20] The Twelfth Amendment had a significant impact on the conduct of elections, but it left untouched most of the core features of the electoral system.

Americans in recent years have tended to equate Electoral College reform with the adoption of a national popular vote, but that has not always been the case: a majority of the reform amendments introduced in Congress since 1787 had different goals. In the nineteenth century and into the twentieth, the most frequent proposal was to require states to choose their electors in district elections. After the Civil War and periodically ever since, some reformers have preferred a "proportional" system, through which a state's electoral votes would be distributed to candidates based on the proportion of the popular vote that they received. The possibility of replacing the Electoral College with a national popular vote, first introduced in Congress in 1816, moved to the forefront of public debate only in the second half of the twentieth century. Nearly all proposed amendments have also tried to alter the contingent election process: by having the decision revert to a vote by all members of Congress; by holding a runoff election; or by permitting a plurality winner. Numerous resolutions in the nineteenth and twentieth centuries provided for the elimination of electors, instructing state governments to calculate their electoral vote totals without input from intermediaries.[21]

Despite these numerous and highly varied initiatives, the presidential electoral system today operates much as it has since the early 1830s, when a few holdout states reluctantly adopted the general ticket. Electoral votes are awarded to each state according to the number of seats it holds in the House of Representatives plus two (for its senators). A plurality popular vote in each state selects a slate of electors who are pledged to a particular presidential candidate; those pledged electors convene briefly in their state capitals roughly a month later and cast their electoral votes, without debate or discussion. The state electoral vote tallies are then forwarded to Washington, where they are counted at a joint session of Congress presided over by the sitting vice president. If no candidate receives a majority of the electoral votes, the House of Representatives then chooses among the three top vote getters, with each state delegation getting one vote and a majority required for election.

This book is an attempt to explain the survival, the persistence, of this complicated and much-criticized method of electing presidents. Why has the Electoral College endured—despite the hundreds of proposed amendments, scores of congressional hearings, thousands of books and articles, and a growing handful of disputed and unpopular election outcomes? Why has this institution remained unchanged since the early nineteenth century despite its awkward fit with democratic values, the weight of modern public opinion, and its failure to ever function in the deliberative manner envisioned by the framers of the Constitution? These are historical questions, yet they are prompted not only by curiosity about the past but also by contemporary voices, the voices of countless American citizens who straightforwardly ask every four years: Why do we elect our presidents this way? Such questions, remarkably, have received very little attention from historians, perhaps because they invert the historian's customary intellectual burden. What begs for explanation here is not change, but its absence, over the course of two centuries.[22]

Framing the inquiry in this way, of course, implicitly suggests that the reasons for the survival of the Electoral College are not self-evident—that it is not the case, for example, that the institution is still with us because it is undeniably the best way to elect a president or because the claims made in its support have always been more compelling than the arguments for reform or abolition. This study does not directly join contemporary debates about the merits and flaws of the Electoral College—there would be little to add to the work of previous writers—but it does proceed from the judgment that the flaws have been sufficiently salient that the institution's survival requires explanation. Although there are, and always have been, defenders of the Electoral College, few have maintained that the institution was unproblematic; and even a cursory glance at the historical record makes plain that the system has not survived because of the shattering brilliance of the arguments made in its behalf.[23]

Nor can the survival of the Electoral College be explained by a simple proposition that has circulated as conventional wisdom in recent decades: that small states have stood as an effective, even impenetrable, roadblock against change because the Electoral College enhances their political influence (by granting them more electoral votes per capita than large states). That argument is plausible but historically untrue, as the chapters that follow will demonstrate. For one thing, most proposals for reform, from the early 1800s into the 1950s, would not have eliminated the small-state advantage: they aimed to abolish winner-take-all and/or the apparatus of having electors, but they would not have altered the allocation of electoral votes to the states. Among the common reform proposals, only a national popular vote would have terminated the per capita advantage in electoral votes that accrues to the small states.[24]

Members of Congress from small states, moreover, have not been predictable or reliable opponents of a national popular vote. Senator John Pastore of Rhode Island, for example, was a staunch advocate of precisely such a reform in the 1950s and 1960s. "I want to do away with the Electoral College," Pastore declared. "I say that when the people go to the polls the man who receives the greatest number of votes should be elected President of the people. . . . It makes no difference to me how many electoral votes the people of Rhode Island have."[25] The evidence is more than anecdotal: analyses of roll call votes on national popular vote proposals in the 1960s and 1970s make clear that there was no small-state bloc, that representatives of the smallest states were divided on the issue in both the House and the Senate.[26] Public opinion polls also indicate that residents of small states have generally favored abolition of the Electoral College.[27]

Indeed, for key periods of our history, the prevailing view—put forward by politicians and commentators alike—has been that large states, not small states, have been the primary beneficiaries of the Electoral College. In 1956 Senator Price Daniel of Texas insisted in congressional debate that it was large states like New York and Ohio that "have undue weight . . . under our present system."[28]

The reasons for the failure of Electoral College reform are, in fact, complex, and most of them have varied in significance over time. The one important historical constant has been the difficulty of amending the U.S. Constitution. Changing the nation's fundamental law requires the support of two-thirds of each branch of Congress, followed by the approval of three-quarters of the states. These are high procedural hurdles, and it is possible, perhaps likely, that some reform proposals would have cleared even slightly lower barriers. (A prime example is the 1969–1970 proposal for a national popular vote that sailed through the House but fell short of the two-thirds threshold in the Senate.) Still, the difficulty of the process cannot, in itself, account for the long track record of failure. Despite the challenge of attaining supermajorities, Congress and the states have, in fact, passed ten amendments that altered electoral processes and procedures. Some of these addressed relatively minor procedural matters (such as the date on which the winner of a presidential election assumes office); but six have dealt with consequential issues of voting rights, and the Seventeenth Amendment mandated the direct election of senators. The amendment process has been an impediment, but not an insuperable obstacle, to the reform of electoral institutions.[29]

Presidential election reform has also been hindered by the simple, if often unrecognized, fact that the Electoral College is not a stand-alone institution. In its design and operation, the Electoral College is intertwined with other facets and features of the nation's political structure and organization, complicating efforts at reform and sometimes sparking resistance that had little to do with ideas about electoral systems. The Electoral College has always, for example, been embedded in the web, and thus the tensions, of federalism. Although the presidency is a national office, the electoral blueprint drawn up by the framers called for the president to be chosen through procedures largely determined by the states. According to Article II, section 1, Congress has the power to determine the date on which electors will be chosen and the date on which they "shall give their votes," but everything else was left to the states—including the breadth of the franchise, the rules governing the allocation of electoral votes among candidates, how candidates got on the ballot, and whether there would even be a popular election to choose electors. The autonomy of the states in these matters, their control over the electoral process, would almost inevitably be diminished by federal reform. "Abolition of the electoral college would mean the taking over of presidential elections by the national government," observed the *Washington Post* in 1916 in response to a surge of sentiment in favor of a national popular election. As the editors of the *Post* knew well, states had long been reluctant to cede any of their powers to the federal government, and that reluctance has often surfaced during debates over electoral reform.[30]

Other sources of resistance have been more fluid, shifting over time as political contexts have evolved. Proposals to choose electors by congressional district, for example, have long had a straightforward appeal, but they seemed more problematic in eras—like the late nineteenth century or the early twenty-first—when gerrymandering has been particularly rampant.[31] Prior to a series of critical Supreme Court decisions in the early 1960s, moreover, congressional districts did not reliably conform to the principle of "one person, one vote," and many states, particularly in the first half of the twentieth century, drew district boundaries that heavily favored rural areas. As a result, urban members of Congress sometimes displayed little sympathy for this alternative, whatever their views of the Electoral College.[32]

Efforts to replace the Electoral College with a national popular vote have run up against a more troubling obstacle: slavery and its legacy. Before the Civil War, as is well known, the "three-fifths clause" gave the slave states of the South congressional seats, and therefore electoral votes, in proportion to their white populations plus three-fifths of their slaves (who, of course, could not vote). This arrangement effectively gave southern whites influence in presidential elections disproportionate to their numbers, an advantage they would have surrendered with a national popular vote. In the late nineteenth century, after the "redemption" of the South barred free African-Americans from the ballot box, this pattern reemerged in stronger form. From the 1890s into the 1960s, an undeclared "five-fifths clause" (with

African-Americans counting fully for representation but still unable to vote) permitted southern whites to wield far more power through the Electoral College than they would have in a national popular election. As *Washington Post* columnist Drew Pearson observed in 1944, the "Southern States now have 25.2 percent of the nation's vote in the Electoral College" while casting "only 12 percent of the popular vote." This was an advantage that white southerners welcomed and fought to keep; they also knew that a national vote would create pressures to broaden the franchise in their states. The design of the Electoral College was such that states did not lose any influence in presidential elections by imposing restrictions on the right to vote.[33]

Partisan politics, of course, has also played a role in debates over electoral reform. Even in the early years of the republic, before a durable party system had taken shape, politicians were bending their views about the electoral system to suit their preferred electoral outcomes; unsurprisingly, they have continued to do so ever since. Party interests (or perceived interests) have, however, been highly malleable, and different parties, factions, and individual leaders have frequently shifted their stances toward particular reforms. Some Republican leaders in the 1870s, for example, pressed hard for changes that were opposed by their successors a generation later. Democrats in the mid-twentieth century were regionally, and ideologically, divided over an array of proposals that came before Congress. In 1950 Texas congressman Ed Lee Gossett, a conservative Democrat, led a campaign in favor of proportional elections because the "Electoral College" gave "the American Labor Party and the Communist Party in the State of New York . . . power . . . out of all proportion to their numbers." Twenty years later, a national popular vote was embraced not only by most liberal Democrats but also by the American Bar Association and the United States Chamber of Commerce.[34] Party interests have not always been clear or paramount, and most amendment resolutions that made headway in Congress have had bipartisan support. Only in the last forty years has presidential election reform been squarely identified with one party (the Democrats), but there is little reason to regard that pattern as immutable.[35]

It is for reasons like these that there has never been a simple, enduring answer to the question: Why do we still have the Electoral College? Although the question might seem to invite a broad structural explanation, grappling with it requires instead a series of historical probes—into key episodes in the long chain of failed reform efforts, into those critical moments when change seemed most possible, and into the shifting contours of the political landscape in which the presidential election system has always been embedded. What these probes yield is a story that is not only about the weight of the past but also about the particular difficulty—widespread in democracies—of altering electoral institutions once they are already in place. It is a multilayered tale of idealism and dedication, missed opportunities, mistaken predictions, ingenious yet disingenuous arguments, an ever-present tension between democratic values and partisan advantage, and, as in so many dimensions of American life, the difficult-to-transcend legacy of slavery and racial discrimination.

✳   ✳   ✳

A few words about the plan of this book may be helpful to readers, particularly given that the sequence of chapters is a blend of the thematic and the chronological. This roadmap may prove especially useful to those who are less interested in the contours of nineteenth-century history than they are in more recent developments.

The book begins with the Constitutional Convention of 1787, where the framers of the Constitution struggled to figure out the best way for a new kingless nation to choose a chief executive. After much "tedious and reiterated" debate (as James Madison described it), the convention tossed the problem to a committee, which came up with the basic blueprint for the Electoral College. How and why the framers arrived at this design is an issue at the heart of Chapter 1. This chapter also recounts the problems with the new electoral system that cropped up as early as the 1790s—problems that led to the adoption of the Twelfth Amendment in 1804 and to a strong but unsuccessful effort to amend the Constitution to require states to choose electors by district.[36]

Part II picks up this latter thread and traces the recurrent efforts to get rid of the "general ticket" from the early nineteenth century into the 1950s. Chapter 2 focuses on the years between 1810 and 1830, when Congress repeatedly wrestled with proposals to mandate district elections, revamp the contingent election process, and dispense with electors. Several of these proposals won approval in the Senate, and one came very close to passage in the House as well. Most members of Congress, often prodded by their constituents, appeared to favor change during this period, but—in a harbinger of things to come—they had difficulty reaching agreement about the best path forward. Had they managed to do so, had a handful of representatives voted differently at key junctures, the subsequent history of presidential elections would have been different—perhaps very different.

Chapter 3 brings this story forward in time, spotlighting three important episodes in the effort to abolish winner-take-all between the Civil War and the mid-twentieth century. The first occurred during Reconstruction, when interest in democratic reform again ran high but ended up being diverted by the electoral (and Electoral College) crisis generated by the disputed election of 1876. The second transpired in Michigan in the 1890s, when a recently elected Democratic legislature took it upon itself to abandon winner-take-all and institute district elections. The Democrats' initiative provoked a ferocious reaction from Republicans in Michigan and throughout the Midwest, including from Indiana's Benjamin Harrison, who was then serving as president of the United States (although he had not won the popular vote in 1888). The political conflict also prompted a legal battle that made its way with extraordinary speed to the Supreme Court. The third episode unfolded in Washington in 1950 when an unusual—even bizarre—coalition of northern moderates and liberals (led by Republican Henry Cabot Lodge Jr.) and southern conservatives (led by Texas Democrat Ed Lee Gossett) succeeded in getting the Senate to approve a constitutional amendment requiring states to allocate their electoral votes on a proportional basis. Within weeks of that Senate vote, however, northern liberals—who had apparently been asleep at the switch—realized that such a measure would likely have devastating consequences for civil rights (as well as other causes they held dear), and the House rejected the amendment by a large margin. Soon thereafter, the appeal of district and proportional plans began to diminish in Washington, although individual states—as described in subsequent chapters—have resurrected such proposals from time to time.

In Part III the thematic focus shifts to the idea of replacing the Electoral College with a national popular vote, a reform that would have brought an end to the "unit rule" and done much else besides. Chapter 4 opens with a return to the early nineteenth century, when the first proposal for a national ballot was put before Congress, only to be dismissed after a brief, yet revealing, debate. The remainder of the chapter, which reaches chronologically into the 1950s, attempts to explain why the idea of a national popular vote—which now seems so plausible an alternative to the Electoral College—was essentially a nonstarter until the second half of the twentieth century. The answer has a lot to do with race.

Chapter 5 contains what is perhaps the dramatic high point of this long saga. It examines how and why the idea of a national popular vote moved to the center of political debate in the 1960s, tracing both the events and the shifting ideological currents that culminated in the passage of an amendment resolution in the House of Representatives in 1969. The chapter also explores the obstacle-strewn path followed by the same resolution as it became embattled in the Senate in 1969–1970, with liberals led by Indiana senator Birch Bayh squaring off against an opposition largely led by southern senators, including South Carolina's Strom Thurmond and North Carolina's Sam Ervin. The core analytic thrust of the chapter is to explain both why a national vote came so close to passage at this historical moment and why it ultimately failed.

Chapter 6 focuses on the 1970s, particularly the years 1976–1979, when Senate liberals, again led by Birch Bayh, sought to resurrect a national popular vote amendment. They were prompted to do so partly by the 1976 election, which came perilously close to keeping President Gerald Ford in the White House despite a decisive popular vote victory by Jimmy Carter. In the wake of that election, optimism about the prospects for reform was widespread, but Bayh and his allies were obliged to navigate through two and a half years of procedural delays before they were able to bring their resolution up for a vote in the Senate in the summer of 1979. Once again, the amendment was defeated—although the political lineups were intriguingly different from what they had been a decade earlier.

Part IV (Chapter 7) brings the tale up to date, tracing what did and (importantly) did not happen between 1980 and 2019, a still-ongoing era during which the issue of Electoral College reform has been encased in partisan politics. At the center of the chapter (and inviting explanation) is the remarkable fact that Congress has paid almost no attention to presidential election reform despite "wrong winner" elections in 2000 and 2016; until November 2000 it was widely believed that any such event would surely spur change and perhaps precipitate a legitimacy crisis. The chapter also traces the ways in which the silence in Washington generated activity elsewhere in the nation: numerous attempts at reform surfaced at the state level, as did a variety of innovative ideas, and initiatives, for altering the system without going through Congress. (The most substantial of these has been the National Popular Vote Interstate Compact.) The recent history, consequently, may not be quite as deflating for the reform-minded as it might appear at first glance.

The Conclusion sums things up and reflects on their meaning: that's what conclusions do. By then, I hope, the reader will have come to appreciate the wisdom of J. Hampden Dougherty, an early twentieth-century writer on the Electoral College. "Every attempt to solve the problem," Dougherty observed in 1906, "should be predicated upon the teaching of history."[37]

PART I

Origins

ONE

FROM THE CONSTITUTION TO THE TWELFTH AMENDMENT

The Electoral College did not spring full-grown from the head of Zeus—or James Madison. The delegates to the Constitutional Convention in Philadelphia in 1787 had difficulty designing a system for choosing the chief executive of their new nation, and they reached agreement on a plan only as the Convention was coming to an end. The first three presidential elections, conducted in accordance with the constitutional blueprint, proceeded fairly smoothly, although they revealed some wrinkles in the electoral process, suggesting a potential lack of alignment between the Constitution's directives and the emerging practice of presidential politics. The fourth contest, between John Adams and Thomas Jefferson in 1800, precipitated a severe and messy electoral crisis that was resolved in the House of Representatives only after prolonged public and behind-the-scenes drama. In its wake, members of Congress, seeking to avoid a repeat of that crisis and to address other issues as well, pursued two different amendments to the Constitution, one of which was adopted as the Twelfth Amendment in 1804. To use modern parlance, the rollout of the presidential election system was bumpy.

Creating the Electoral System

In September 1787, as the Constitutional Convention was drawing to a close, James Wilson of Pennsylvania observed that "in truth the most difficult" issue that the framers had encountered was designing a method for choosing the nation's chief executive. The "subject has greatly divided" the Convention, Wilson observed, and "will also divide the people out of doors." One of the most active and influential participants in Philadelphia, Wilson further acknowledged that "he had never made up an opinion on it entirely to his own satisfaction."[1]

Wilson's words were telling, all the more so because they were echoed by other prominent framers, including James Madison and his Virginia colleague, George Mason.[2] When the delegates assembled in late May 1787 to revise the Articles of Confederation—a task that quickly segued into drafting an entirely new Constitution—they had rapidly agreed that the government they were designing would possess an executive branch. (There was a Congress but no separate executive under the Articles of Confederation that had loosely bound the states together since 1781.) In the deliberations that followed, stretching out over several months, they also settled on the powers to be vested in the chief executive and by mid-August had determined that he would hold the title "president."[3]

But the delegates struggled with the process of choosing a president. A key source of their difficulty was the absence of models: history offered few precedents for the selection of a republican chief executive, and in their own colonial experience executive power was wielded by men who had attained their positions through either heredity or appointment by a higher authority. To be sure, the recently formed American states (other than Pennsylvania) had governors, but the states themselves were still experimenting with their institutions. Most governors were chosen by state legislatures for one-year terms and consequently had little independence from their legislatures; the governors of New York and Massachusetts, in contrast, were popularly elected and wielded more power. It was not evident that either of these models could or should be replicated in a national, and federal, government. The framers faced the challenge of having to invent something, almost from scratch.[4]

When the Convention began, the most readily available option (the "default" in twenty-first-century argot) was selection by the legislature. That was the method proposed in the Virginia Resolutions that shaped the early weeks of deliberation, and some delegates regarded it as the obvious choice. Roger Sherman of Connecticut, for example, "considered the Executive magistracy as nothing more than an institution for carrying the will of the Legislature into effect," and the executive thus "ought to be appointed by and accountable to the Legislature only." In the first vote taken on the issue, the delegates clearly signaled their approval of legislative selection, with the president to serve a term of seven years. They would reach the same decision—with variations in the details—three more times in the course of the summer.[5]

Yet these decisions did not stick, and the delegates reopened the issue again and again, sometimes voting on one day to reverse a decision made a day or two earlier. Straightforward as legislative, or congressional, selection may have appeared—permitting, as it did, the nation's political leaders to choose the executive—the method nonetheless had a cluster of troubling defects: it made the executive dependent on the legislature, undercut the executive's capacity to check legislative power, and seemed likely to encourage "cabal and corruption" in the selection process. Elbridge Gerry of Massachusetts was adamant that "an election at all by the National Legislature was radically and incurably wrong." The executive "will be the mere creature of the Legislature if appointed and impeachable by that body," insisted Pennsylvania's Gouverneur Morris. He also warned of "the danger of intrigue and faction if the appointment should be made by the Legislature." "If the Executive be chosen by the National Legislature," Morris maintained, "he will not be independent on it; and if not independent, usurpation and tyranny on the part of the Legislature will be the consequence."[6]

Madison, the most influential of the framers, put forward a broader, more theoretical argument, spelling out his view that the executive branch, in fact, did not exist simply to carry out "the will of the Legislature." It was "a fundamental principle of free government that the Legislative, Executive, and Judiciary powers should be *separately* . . . and *independently* exercised," he observed. "It is essential then that the appointment of the Executive should either be drawn from some source, or held by some tenure, that will give him a free agency with regard to the Legislature. This could not be if he was to be appointable from time to time by the Legislature."[7] Defenders of congressional election tried to meet some of these objections by proposing that presidents hold office for lengthy terms and not be eligible for reelection.[8]

The early rounds of debate included substantial discussion of the possibility of choosing the president through a national popular election. James Wilson spoke repeatedly "in favor of an appointment by the people," claiming that popular elections would render different branches of the government "as independent as possible of each other, as well as of the States." George Mason agreed in principle although he thought it "impracticable." When the issue came up for extended consideration in the middle of July—after a critical three-week period during which the Convention finally resolved thorny issues regarding representation in Congress—several key figures voiced support for a popular election. Gouverneur Morris insisted that the executive "ought to be elected by the people at large, by the freeholders of the Country." (For nearly all of the framers, election "by the people" meant election by adult men who owned some property or paid taxes.) He acknowledged that "difficulties attend this mode," but "they have been found superable in New York and in Connecticut" and could be overcome for the nation as a whole. Morris also insisted that a national election was the surest way for a worthy man to be chosen. "If the people should elect, they will never fail to prefer some man of distinguished character, or services; some man . . . of continental reputation."[9] Morris, as well as other prominent advocates of popular election, favored both a strong executive and a strong national government. Direct popular election—a method that bypassed the states and created one national constituency for the presidency—seemed likely to further those aims.[10]

Notably, Madison also endorsed "election by the people or rather by the qualified part of them." He reached that conclusion not from an *a priori* commitment to democratic values or processes but by surveying the logically possible alternatives. "The election must be made either by some existing authority under the National or State Constitutions—or by some special authority derived from the people—or by the people themselves. The two Existing authorities under the National Constitution would be the Legislative and the Judiciary," he noted. Madison had steadfastly objected to legislative selection, and the judiciary, he concluded, "was out of the question." Equally powerful arguments were raised against selection of the national executive by governors or state legislatures, possibilities that had also been raised at the Convention. "The Option before us then lay between an appointment by Electors chosen by the people" (another idea that had surfaced in debate) "and an immediate appointment by the people." Electors, Madison believed, would be vastly preferable to a decision by the legislature, but "with all its imperfections," election by the people would be "best."[11]

Among the "imperfections" that Madison perceived, one touched directly on the hot-coal issue that most profoundly divided the states and had already come close to derailing the constitutional project: slavery. If the executive were selected through "an immediate choice by the people," then the influence of each state—or region—would be determined entirely by the number of votes that its residents cast. This was a "difficulty," Madison observed on July 19, because "the right of suffrage was much more diffusive in Northern than the Southern States; and the latter could have no influence in the election on the score of the Negroes." Madison and his colleagues, of course, were particularly sensitive to this issue in the mid-July debates because they had just finished hammering out the "three-fifths" compromise, a provision that resolved a deep-rooted, potentially fatal conflict between the North and the South by counting each slave as three-fifths of a person in determining the number of seats a state would have in Congress. (The Convention had simultaneously forged a compromise between the large and small states by deciding that representation in the House, but not the Senate, would reflect a state's population.) If the president were to be chosen in a national popular election, the southern states would gain no comparable political advantage from their slaves. Nonetheless, Madison—who consistently maintained that the fundamental division in the country was between the North and the South, not between small and large states—concluded on July 25 that "local considerations must give way to the general interest." As a southerner, he was "willing to make the sacrifice" and accept a national popular vote.[12]

Most of Madison's colleagues—and nearly all of his fellow southerners—found the arguments for a national election to be less compelling than he did. Sherman worried that the people "will never be sufficiently informed of characters" and would simply vote for someone from their home state, making it likely that the executive would always come from a large state. Charles Pinckney of South Carolina concurred, adding his apprehension that the people would end up being "led by a few active and designing men." (The notion that the "people" were subject to manipulation by unscrupulous or charismatic demagogues was a commonly expressed reason both for restricting the franchise and for preferring indirect, multitiered elections to direct balloting by the people.) George Mason compared a popular election to "a trial of colors" by "a blind man"—because "the extent of the Country renders it impossible that the people can have the requisite capacity to judge" the candidates. Gerry was more intemperate, insisting that "the ignorance of the people" would render a popular election "radically vicious."[13]

Importantly, the Convention debates regarding popular election did not revolve around—or even directly address—political rights. There were few suggestions (Morris and Wilson may have come closest) that the people had an inherent *right* to choose their chief executive; nor were there direct assertions that the people were inherently unqualified to participate or that their doing so would pose a threat to the social order, although hints of that perspective were present.[14] The debate, which was publicly joined by only a minority of the delegates, was not about democracy or republicanism or the political values of the new nation but about institutional balance and efficacy. Most of the stated opposition to a national popular vote emphasized the advantage it would give to the large states and the difficulty of acquainting a national electorate with the candidates. What limited the support for a single national election, thus, was not antagonism to popular participation but an array of other apprehensions: that such an election would be too conducive to a national, rather than federal government; that it would be too "impractical" (the term that Wilson and Madison ascribed to the views of the opposition during the ratification debates); and that it could threaten the balance of influence between free and slave, as well as small and large, states. Formal proposals for a direct national election never garnered broad support and on several occasions were voted down by large margins.[15]

A similar lack of enthusiasm—and unanimity—greeted the numerous other ideas that bobbed up over the summer: selection by the governors of the states or by state legislatures; election by a committee of fifteen legislators chosen by lot (and obliged to act as soon as they were chosen, to avoid intrigue); a popular election in which each voter cast ballots for two or three candidates, only one of whom could be from his own state: nomination of one candidate by the people of each state, with the winner to then be chosen by the national legislature.[16] As the summer wore on, the

Convention also considered several proposals mandating that the chief executive be chosen by specially designated "electors" who could be chosen and apportioned among the states in a variety of ways. Although the use of electors could avoid some of the problems attributed to congressional selection (executive dependence on the legislature) or a national ballot (lack of acquaintance with the candidates), no single proposal gained traction for very long.[17] As a result, and in the absence of an agreed-upon alternative, the Convention kept returning, reluctantly and halfheartedly, to its original position of authorizing the legislature to choose the president for a single term (most likely lasting seven years).[18]

It was against this backdrop—months of indecision, disagreement, and "reiterated discussions"—that the weary delegates, at the end of August, finally turned the issue over to a committee on "postponed parts" (also called the Committee of Eleven, reflecting the presence of one representative from each state), chaired by David Brearley of New Jersey.[19] In less than a week, that committee, which counted Madison and Morris among its members, returned with a proposal for the institutional configuration that, with slight revision, would come to be called "the Electoral College." Each state would be entitled to a number of electors equivalent to its total membership in Congress (thus replicating the hard-fought compromises over representation that had been reached in July), and the legislature of each state would determine the manner in which those electors would be chosen (giving state governments significant influence in the process while allowing for the possibility of a popular vote to choose electors). The electors would meet to cast their ballots in their respective state capitals on the same date (thus avoiding "the great evil of cabal" as Gouverneur Morris put it), and they would each cast two votes, one of which had to be for an inhabitant of a state other than their own.[20] The electoral votes would be tallied in Congress; if no candidate received a majority of the nation's electoral votes, the Senate would decide among the top five vote-getters. After the president was chosen, the candidate who had the next largest number of electoral votes would become vice president. The president and vice president would serve for four years and be eligible for reelection.[21]

The Convention was receptive to the proposal, which included numerous ideas and elements that had surfaced earlier in the summer. Gouverneur Morris, known as an advocate of popular election, ably explained and defended the proposal on behalf of the committee. Wilson, Mason, and Pierce Butler of South Carolina quickly labeled it "a valuable improvement" on choice by the legislature—although some of their colleagues pointedly disagreed.[22] Most of the criticism of the committee's handiwork, some of it harsh, centered on the role of the Senate in choosing among candidates in the event that no candidate won a majority of the electoral votes: the issue loomed large because many delegates believed that this would be a routine occurrence. ("Nineteen times in twenty the President would be chosen by the Senate," declared George Mason.)[23] Giving the Senate the power to frequently choose the president, it was feared, would undercut the executive's independence, forge a dangerous "coalition" between the president and the Senate, and enhance the Senate's tendency toward "aristocracy," particularly given that chamber's anticipated role in approving treaties as well as appointments to executive and judicial offices.[24] After an energetic debate (and an impressive display of collective problem-solving), the Convention decided to transfer that power from the Senate to the House of Representatives—where each state delegation would cast one vote, thus maintaining the equality of influence among small and large states.[25] To further safeguard the process from political intrigue, the Convention also inserted a proviso that electors not be members "of the Legislature of the United States" or persons holding "any office of profit or trust under the United States."[26]

This brief nativity story makes clear that the presidential election system enshrined in the Constitution embodied a web of compromises, spawned by months of debate among men who disagreed with one another and were uncertain about the best way to proceed. For many, perhaps most, of the framers, the "Electoral College" was not their first choice or preferred option. Madison, among others, consistently favored a national popular vote, while numerous delegates persisted in supporting legislative selection. Indeed, as historian Jack Rakove has pointed out, the key to the outcome in the Convention was not that the Electoral College had great and unmistakable virtues but that it had fewer perceived disadvantages than the leading alternatives.[27] It was, in effect, a consensus second choice, made acceptable, in part, by the remarkably complex details of the electoral process, details that themselves constituted compromises among, or gestures toward, particular constituencies and convictions.[28]

At heart, the architecture of the electoral system represented a compromise between those who favored selection by Congress and those who insisted that such a process had fatal flaws. In its composition, the Electoral College was (and is) a temporary replica of Congress populated by "electors" (chosen by the states) who would assemble only once (in their home states) and who would have no ongoing dealings with the national government. It was, in effect, a temporary legislature, an assembly that could not legislate and thus could not wield ongoing influence or be corrupted. It also would disband as soon as it had carried out its one function. The ingenious stroke of the Committee of Eleven's proposal was to satisfy the objections of those who opposed legislative selection while still apportioning power and influence to the states according to the same principles that governed representation in Congress.[29]

This impressively clever design, however, came with costs—or side effects. The proposal adopted by the Convention carried over into presidential selection the advantages that had been granted to small and slave states with respect to representation in Congress; in so doing, it gave both groups influence in presidential elections disproportionate to their free (or voting) populations. This disproportionate power could affect the outcome of elections, as would soon become clear when electoral votes attributable to slaves provided Thomas Jefferson's margin of victory over John Adams in 1800; it remained clear in 2000 when George W. Bush became president despite losing the popular vote, thanks to his having won most of the smallest states in the nation. Another significant consequence of this design—unforeseen and probably unforeseeable at the time—was that it laid the groundwork for an alliance between small states and the South that would, in future decades and centuries, be a potential source of resistance to reforms of the electoral system.[30]

Ingenious as the blueprint for choosing a president may have been, the framers had little shared understanding of how it would actually work in practice. Many, perhaps most, believed that the electors, scattered among the states, would serve as a kind of nominating board, picking the five candidates who would then be vetted by the House of Representatives. Others, including Madison and Alexander Hamilton, believed or hoped that this would not be the norm, that elections would only occasionally end up in the House. Whether the electors would deliberate, or just cast ballots, when they met in their state capitals was also unclear; nor was there certainty about whether there would be popular elections at all—given that the Constitution left it up to state legislatures to determine how electors would be chosen. The constitutional blueprint, in effect, did not offer or reflect a coherent vision of how candidates would compete for the highest office in the land.[31] (The framers, on the whole, did not believe that political parties would, or should, become part of the institutional landscape.) As would quickly become apparent, moreover, the delegates also failed to anticipate the complications that could flow from a system in which electors did not distinguish their votes for president from their votes for vice president.[32]

Such issues likely seemed remote to the forty-two delegates who remained in Philadelphia in the middle of September 1787. They were eager to bring their summer's work to a close and were increasingly convinced that however flawed their handiwork might be, it was the best they could do "at this time." The framers were buoyed by the conviction that the Constitution they had drafted was vastly superior to the Articles of Confederation and that whatever defects it possessed—no one thought it perfect—would be tested over time and could be rectified through the amendment process built into the document.[33]

Notably, the presidential election system attracted relatively little attention during the sometimes ferocious debates over ratification that unfolded in the states in the months after the draft Constitution was circulated to the public. Hamilton, writing in March 1788 (in *Federalist 68*), observed that "the mode of appointment of the Chief Magistrate of the United States is almost the only part of the system, of any consequence, which has escaped without severe censure." He attributed this to the virtues of the design: "If the manner of it be not perfect, it is at least excellent."[34] Hamilton's view, widely cited by modern defenders of the Electoral College, must be taken with a generous helping of salt: *Federalist 68*, after all, was a polemic written to promote ratification in New York. In fact, there was criticism—much of it focused on the complexity of the apparatus and the distance separating the people from the ultimate decision, particularly if the House were called upon to make the final decision. That the criticism was not more abundant likely stemmed less from any widely recognized excellence than from the presence of much larger, more compelling objections to the draft Constitution, including the centralization of power in a distant, potentially "aristocratic" national government and the absence of a bill of rights. Then too, Federalists and Anti-Federalists alike, in the fall of 1787 and the spring of 1788, may have been less focused on "the mode of appointment of the Chief Magistrate" because they all knew that—however the electoral system actually worked—George Washington would be their first president.[35]

The First Elections

The ratification of the Constitution in June 1788 opened a critical period of experimentation with the new electoral system. Washington's election may have been a foregone conclusion, but there was much to be discovered—and determined—during the first handful of presidential contests; no one could confidently predict how the complicated mechanism crafted by the founders would operate in practice. Because the Constitution specified only that the electors of each state would be appointed "in such Manner as the Legislature thereof may direct," key decisions shaping the presidential selection process were still to be made by the states. Each legislature would have to devise rules and procedures for choosing electors, apportioning electoral votes, and conducting elections. The laws and rules, moreover, would be only part of the story, because they would inescapably interact with, shape, and be shaped by an emergent political culture and by diverse political actors who would explore, probe, and exploit the incentives and opportunities that—wittingly or not—were embedded in the institutional arrangements.

The first presidential election—begun in 1788 and completed in 1789—offered a few preliminary answers to the questions that hung in the air.[36] It quickly became clear, for example, that the legislatures of the states would adopt diverse methods of choosing electors. (See Table 1.1.) After substantial debate, Pennsylvania and Maryland opted for statewide popular elections to select slates of electors (a method known as the "general ticket"); two states preferred elections by district; and three legislatures, with less debate, decided to appoint electors by themselves. Both Massachusetts and New Hampshire devised mixed systems that permitted the legislature to choose electors from the highest vote-getters in elections, while New Jersey entrusted the selection of electors to its governor and privy council.[37] Particularly in those states that held popular elections, no small amount of political jockeying preceded the selection of electors. Despite the framers' oft-stated aversion to "factions," these contests were shaped by the divide between Federalists and Anti-Federalists (many of whom were intent on amending the Constitution).[38] On the whole, the men who became electors were a distinguished group, with ample political experience, suggesting that they were expected to exercise judgment in casting their electoral votes.[39]

The 1788–1789 election also brought to the surface a problem latent in the process of selecting both the president and the vice president with a single set of ballots. The Constitution instructed each elector to vote for two candidates for president: the person receiving the largest number of votes (if a majority) would become president, while the runner-up would assume the vice presidency. Once the electors had been chosen, in early January 1789, there was little doubt about the identities of the men who would hold these two offices. George Washington had long been the consensus choice for president, despite his reluctance to signal his willingness to serve, and after months of maneuvering, Federalist leaders had coalesced around John Adams for the vice presidency. With the Federalists performing strongly in most states, support for Adams was so widespread that he seemed likely to garner nearly as many electoral votes as Washington.[40]

That posed a problem—or at least a potential problem: electors had no way to rank their two votes, to distinguish their choice for president from their choice for vice president. It consequently could arise, as the ever-vigilant Alexander Hamilton put it, that "a few votes insidiously withheld from Washington" would usher Adams into the presidency. "Everybody is aware of that defect in the Constitution," Hamilton noted, "which renders it possible that the man intended for Vice President may in fact turn up President." Hamilton, Tench Coxe, and other Federalists appear to have dodged that bullet by arranging for a handful of electors to cast ballots for candidates other than Adams, but the potential for future trouble was clear.[41]

The next three presidential elections—in 1792, 1796, and 1800—offered a more ample demonstration of the system's distinctive, and sometimes problematic, properties. The outcomes of these elections have, in retrospect, acquired an aura of orderly inevitability, with a procession of eminences holding the nation's highest office. Washington and Adams were reelected in 1792; Adams was victorious in 1796, with Thomas Jefferson, the runner-up, becoming vice president; and Jefferson ascended to the presidency in 1801 (albeit with the less celebrated Aaron Burr as his vice president). Yet much was stirring beneath the surface, both in the tone of political life and in the process through which the nation was choosing its chief executive.

Most importantly, these years witnessed the sharpening of political divisions and the emergence of state and national organizations that increasingly resembled parties. In the course of the 1790s the tensions between Federalists and Anti-Federalists, born in the struggle over ratification of the Constitution, morphed into a broader ideological cleavage between Federalists and Republicans, or Democratic-Republicans, the labels adopted by political clubs or "societies" that began to organize in 1793.[42] The Federalists, centered in the northeastern states, were advocates of a strong central government, a national bank (as well as other features of Treasury Secretary Hamilton's economic program), and close ties to Britain. Some were hostile to slavery, and most were skeptical about the desirability of non-elite participation in public affairs. The Democratic-Republicans (or, hereafter, Republicans) were less elite, more popular in the South, wary of granting too much power to the national government, antagonistic to Hamilton's economic program, and sympathetic with the wave of democratic sentiments unleashed by the French Revolution. The gulf between the Federalists and the Republicans widened in the 1790s, while relations among their leaders grew testier. In 1797, Jefferson, writing from Philadelphia, observed that "men who have been intimate all their lives cross the streets to avoid meeting, and turn their heads another way, lest they should be obliged to touch their hats."[43]

By the middle of the 1790s the men who adhered to these two ideological tendencies were actively constructing state and national alliances whose purpose was to win elections. They were also intent on distinguishing themselves from their adversaries—sometimes with venom and with the aid of a newly created partisan press. That both sides repeatedly blamed their rivals for the increasingly partisan atmosphere (and even for the need to organize at all) was a telling sign that political parties were not yet an accepted feature of the political landscape, that the anti-party convictions so often voiced by the framers retained normative weight. Yet parties, or proto-parties, were taking shape, even if there was no presumption that they, or a two-party system, would be permanent.[44]

For the leaders and builders of these alliances, no prize was greater than the presidency, and the efforts to win that office—through the complex electoral system—contributed substantially to the development of national parties. Although the system had been designed to hinder organized political competition (and parties), the leading candidates for president, as early as the 1790s, were selected by their party's congressional caucus.[45] Winning the presidency and the vice presidency, moreover, required strategic coordination across state lines, coalescing behind preferred candidates, and discouraging local favorites who could end up handing the election to an opponent or into the House of Representatives. It also meant monitoring a complicated electoral calendar (there was no single date on which all states chose their electors) and keeping track of not only the "first" but also the "second" vote that each elector might cast.[46] In addition, competition for the presidency put a premium on winning control of state legislatures, which sometimes chose electors by themselves or, at the least, could decide how electors would be chosen: in many states the decisive elections were those that determined the makeup of the legislature months before the casting of presidential ballots.[47] The men who organized state campaigns also had to generate lists of reputable electors, make sure that those electors were reliable supporters, and prepare handbills informing voters how to cast ballots for their candidates' electors.[48] (Presidential candidates themselves did not visibly campaign for the office.) Accomplishing these tasks—which seem routine in the twenty-first century and have been routine since the 1820s—demanded organizations of a type that would surely have been frowned upon by the framers, who had done their utmost in Philadelphia to mitigate the influence of faction. Yet by 1796 such organizations existed in every state, in at least rudimentary form, and with each passing year the parties became more skilled at electioneering.[49]

Indeed, thanks to the emergence of political parties, the electoral system, by 1800 or even 1796, was functioning in ways quite different than the framers had envisioned.[50] The men who became electors, for example, continued to be local notables, but increasingly often they were chosen not to offer independent judgments but to cast ballots for candidates that they were known to support.[51] As early as 1792 some aspiring electors pledged in advance to cast their "second" vote for John Adams or, alternatively, George Clinton.[52] In 1796 Samuel Adams, the redoubtable old revolutionary and Anti-Federalist, campaigned for the office of elector in Massachusetts by signaling clearly that he would vote against his cousin, John, and for Republican Thomas Jefferson. In northern Virginia, Leven Powell, a wealthy landowner and businessman, actively sought the post of elector in a heated contest against S. T. Mason, a nephew of prominent Anti-Federalist George Mason. Powell barely disguised his support of Adams and was overt in his antagonism to Jefferson.[53]

Most electors, moreover, were selected not in hotly contested elections but by small groups of legislators and political leaders who were aware of the electors' political sympathies.[54] A Virginia pamphlet highlighted the shrinking role of the elector by noting that "talents are not necessary, and even experience is not required. It cannot therefore be material who the elector is, providing his character assures us, that he will give the vote which his constituents appointed him to bestow." When a Federalist elector from Pennsylvania cast one of his votes for Jefferson rather than Adams in 1796, he became the target of a public rebuke: "I chose him to act, not to think," complained a Federalist voter, providing the first recorded remonstrance against a "faithless" elector. By 1800 there had ceased to be any expectation that electors would deliberate when they gathered in their respective state capitals.[55]

LEGISLATURES, DISTRICTS, OR THE GENERAL TICKET

More consequentially, partisan impulses were influencing state legislatures as they made decisions about methods of choosing electors. In 1792, 1796, and 1800, electors in some states were chosen through district elections, while elsewhere they were elected through the general ticket or by the legislature itself. (See Table 1.1.) But the lineup of states and selection methods was not fixed: states took advantage of the flexible constitutional architecture to switch procedures from one election to the next. Delaware, for example, shifted from district elections to legislative selection between 1789 and 1792; Maryland and North Carolina adopted the district method in 1796; four states turned the matter over to their legislatures in 1800, while

TABLE I.I: METHODS OF SELECTING PRESIDENTIAL ELECTORS, BY STATE, 1789–1836

State	1789	1792	1796	1800	1804	1808	1812	1816	1820	1824	1828	1832	1836
Alabama	–	–	–	–	–	–	–	–	L	G	G	G	G
Arkansas	–	–	–	–	–	–	–	–	–	–	–	–	G
Connecticut	L	L	L	L	L	L	L	L	G	G	G	G	G
Delaware	D	L	L	L	L	L	L	L	L	L	L	G	G
Georgia	L	L	G	L	L	L	L	L	L	L	G	G	G
Illinois	–	–	–	–	–	–	–	–	D	D	G	G	G
Indiana	–	–	–	–	–	–	–	L	L	G	G	G	G
Kentucky	–	D	D	D	D	D	D	D	D	D	G	G	G
Louisiana	–	–	–	–	–	–	L	L	L	L	G	G	G
Maine	–	–	–	–	–	–	–	–	C	D	D	G	G
Maryland	G	G	D	D	D	D	D	D	D	D	D	D	G
Massachusetts	C	C	C	L	C	L	D	L	C	G	G	G	G
Michigan	–	–	–	–	–	–	–	–	–	–	–	–	G
Mississippi	–	–	–	–	–	–	–	–	G	G	G	G	G
Missouri	–	–	–	–	–	–	–	–	L	D	G	G	G
New Hampshire	C	C	C	L	G	G	G	G	G	G	G	G	G
New Jersey	L	L	L	L	G	G	L	G	G	G	G	G	G
New York	–	L	L	L	L	L	L	L	L	L	D	G	G
North Carolina	–	L	D	D	D	D	L	G	G	G	G	G	G
Ohio	–	–	–	–	G	G	G	G	G	G	G	G	G
Pennsylvania	G	G	G	L	G	G	G	G	G	G	G	G	G
Rhode Island	–	L	L	G	G	G	G	G	G	G	G	G	G
South Carolina	L	L	L	L	L	L	L	L	L	L	L	L	L
Tennessee	–	–	C	C	D	D	D	D	D	D	D	G	G
Vermont	–	L	L	L	L	L	L	L	L	L	G	G	G
Virginia	D	D	D	G	G	G	G	G	G	G	G	G	G

	1789	1792	1796	1800	1804	1808	1812	1816	1820	1824	1828	1832	1836
Number of States	10	15	16	16	17	17	18	19	24	24	24	24	26
General ticket	2	2	2	2	7	6	5	7	9	12	18	22	25
Legislature	4	9	7	10	6	7	9	9	9	6	2	1	1
District	2	2	4	3	4	4	4	3	4	6	4	1	0
Combination	2	2	3	1	0	0	0	0	2	0	0	0	0

Key: L (chosen by the legislature)   G (chosen by popular vote on a general ticket)

    D (chosen by popular vote in districts) C (chosen by a combination of methods)

Sources: Compiled from the following sources: Lisa Thomason, "Jacksonian Democracy and the Electoral College: Politics and Reform in the Method of Selecting Presidential Electors, 1824–1833" (PhD diss., University of North Texas, 2001), 19, 20, 23, 31, 133–135, 147;

Virginia abandoned district elections in favor of the general ticket. As Table 1.1 indicates, the most evident trend between 1789 and 1800 was the increase in the number of states in which the legislatures themselves chose the electors. In 1800 popular elections of any type were held in only six out of sixteen states.[56]

These shifts reflected something more than an impulse to experiment with a new institution: electoral strategizing was clearly at work. Although popular elections by district were often heralded, especially by Republicans, as the method most consistent with the principles of republican government,

---

Andrew E. Busch, "The Development and Democratization of the Electoral College," in *Securing Democracy: Why We Have an Electoral College,* ed. by Gary L. Gregg II (Wilmington, DE, 2001), 34; Tadahisa Kuroda, *The Origins of the Twelfth Amendment: The Electoral College in the Early Republic, 1787–1804* (Westport, CT, 1994), 59, 67, 71, 94, 95, 164, 179; Jeffrey Pasley, *The First Presidential Contest:1796 and the Founding of American Democracy* (Lawrence, KS, 2013), 346; Jerrold G. Rusk, *A Statistical History of the American Electorate* (Washington, DC, 2001), 131; Stephen G. Kurtz, *The Presidency of John Adams: The Collapse of Federalism, 1795–1800* (Philadelphia, 1957), 409; Charles O. Paullin, *Atlas of the Historical Geography of the United States* (Washington, DC, 1932), 93; Merrill Jensen and Robert A. Becker, eds., *The Documentary History of the First Federal Elections, 1788–1790,* vol. 1 (Madison, WI, 1976), 232.

Primary sources consulted when there was disagreement among the authors above: "Defence of the Legislature of Massachusetts," *Early American Imprints,* 2nd ser., no. 6136 (1804); "Resolve Prescribing the Mode for the Choice of Electors of President and Vice-President of the United States," passed on June 15, 1804, chap. 21, in *Acts and Laws, Passed by the General Court of Massachusetts, at the Session Begun and Held at Boston, in the County of Suffolk, on Wednesday, the Thirtieth Day of May, Anno Domini, 1804,* ed. Secretary of the Commonwealth (Boston, 1804, 1898), 296; "An Act Providing for the Election of Electors to Elect a President and Vice President of the United States," passed on Aug. 8, 1796, in *Acts Passed at the Second Session of the First General Assembly of the State of Tennessee* (Knoxville, TN, 1796), chap. 4, pp. 9–11; *Congressional Quarterly's Guide to U.S. Elections* (Washington, DC, 1975), 202, 948, 949n14; "A New Nation Votes: American Election Returns, 1787–1825," accessed June 25, 2014, http://elections.lib.tufts.edu; "An Act Directing the Time, Places and Manner of Holding Elections for Representatives of this State in the Congress of the United States and for Appointing Electors on the Part of This State for Choosing a President and Vice-President of the United States," passed on Oct. 4, 1788, in *The Statutes at Large of Pennsylvania from 1682 to 1801,* vol. 13, *1787–1790,* ed. James T. Mitchell and Henry Flanders (Harrisburg, PA, 1908), 143; *Resolves of the Twelfth Legislature of the State of Maine* (Augusta, ME, 1832), 392–393; *The Age* (Augusta, ME), Mar. 6, 1832, 3, online at *Readex: America's Historical Newspapers.*

it quickly became evident to all participants that a party with majority support in a state or its legislature would gain an advantage if it utilized the general ticket or had the legislature itself choose electors. That way, all of a state's electoral votes could be cast for the party's preferred candidate. Conversely, a minority party had instrumental reasons for preferring district elections—although precisely because of its minority status it could not impose that preference on the legislature. In Pennsylvania in 1796 the Republicans, who were pessimistic about their chances of winning the state, tried to get the Federalist legislature to agree to district elections; not surprisingly, the Federalists refused, insisting on retention of the general ticket. Four years later, when the state's Republicans were more upbeat about their prospects, they altered their stance and declared themselves to be in favor of the general ticket.[57]

New York also offered a vivid example of the partisan maneuvers infusing decisions about the methods of choosing electors. In the late winter of 1800 the Federalist-dominated legislature rejected Republican proposals to choose electors by district and decided to retain that power for itself. Two months later, the Republicans scored a surprising victory in state legislative elections, thanks to working-class discontents with Federalist elitism in New York City and an energetic legislative campaign choreographed by Aaron Burr. The shift in control of the legislature, to the chagrin of Federalists, promised to deliver all of New York's electoral votes to Jefferson. Unwilling to accept defeat, Hamilton then promoted a Machiavellian scheme (justified in the name of "public safety") to have Federalist governor John Jay call the outgoing legislature back into session to pass a law requiring an election by districts—which would rescue some electoral votes (and perhaps the election) for Adams. Jay, demonstrating that personal honor could still occasionally outweigh political partisanship, rebuffed Hamilton's entreaty. "Proposing a measure for party purposes," Jay scrawled on the back of the letter he had received from Hamilton, "would not become me to adopt."[58]

Most famously, of course, partisan advantage was the motive behind Virginia's decision to switch from district elections to the general ticket in 1800. (It was one of six states to change its method of choosing electors leading up to that election.) Jefferson had lost the election of 1796 by three electoral votes, one of which had come from the Virginia district that had chosen Federalist Leven Powell as an elector. Jefferson's supporters were determined that this scenario not be repeated in 1800, and a legislative committee that included Madison, an eloquent advocate of district elections, recommended a switch to the general ticket. Notably the legislature formally acknowledged that the change was grounded in political pragmatism rather than principle, declaring that such action was warranted "until some uniform mode for choosing a President and Vice President . . . shall be prescribed by an amendment to the Constitution." Despite the apologetic rationale and to no one's surprise, Adams's home state of Massachusetts reacted to Virginia's decision by retaliating: it abandoned district elections in favor of choice by the legislature.[59]

The frequent changes in procedure were accompanied by noisy, sometimes strident, public debates about the virtues and defects of different methods of choosing electors. There were two axes to these debates, which played out in newspapers, pamphlets, state legislatures, and taverns across the country. The first was whether the choice of electors ought to be in the hands of the people or the legislature. Advocates of popular election, numerous in both parties—although the Republicans were more united and boisterous about it—were adamant that the people had the right to choose their "chief magistrate" and that legislative selection smacked of aristocracy. The "independent freemen of this state," argued a member of New Jersey's legislature in 1799, should "exercise a right which, by the federal constitution, and by the nature and spirit of a republican government, is guaranteed to them." The constitutional argument was grounded in a slightly tortured parsing of the wording of Article II, section 1: by declaring that "*each state* shall appoint" (rather than "each state legislature shall appoint") electors, it was claimed, the framers intended to give the people, rather than the legislature, the right to choose electors.[60]

Defenders of legislative decision rejected these arguments, insisting that the words *state* and *legislature* were synonymous, that the Constitution left the choice of method entirely to the legislatures, and that state legislators were best equipped to choose electors who would express the wishes of the state. Some New York Federalists even maintained that an election by the people would violate the constitutional requirement that "each state shall *appoint*" electors. As early as 1792, advocates of legislative selection also maintained that elections were costly, inconvenient (especially in "an inclement season of the year"), difficult to organize in the short temporal window mandated by Congress, and likely to create "tumult and disorder." District elections were criticized as particularly burdensome because district lines would have to be redrawn after each census and could not coincide with congressional district boundaries (because there were more electors than members of Congress). Usually in private but occasionally in public, overtones of Federalist elitism crept into the defense of legislative authority. "Representatives have more expanded minds," claimed a Federalist from Albany, New York. "Popular elections are bad, because the electors get misinformed by wicked and designing men."[61]

The second axis of debate pitted advocates of district elections against proponents of the general ticket. (In many states there were similar and parallel debates regarding the best method for electing members of the House of Representatives.)[62] The arguments for district elections, which were favored by most Republicans and some Federalists, were straightforward: voters in districts would be more knowledgeable about candidates for elector than they possibly could be in a statewide election; minority opinions would be represented (with the general ticket "one half of the people are reduced to a cipher"); and the views of the people would be more accurately reflected in the electoral tally. Jefferson himself, writing in 1800, endorsed this perspective: "It is merely a question whether we will divide the United States into sixteen or one hundred and thirty-seven districts," Jefferson observed. "The latter being more checquered, and representing the people in smaller sections, would be more likely to be an exact representation of their diversified sentiments." Proponents of district elections commonly sought to claim the mantle of the founding fathers, asserting that the framers had district elections in mind when they devised the electoral system. Direct evidence for that assertion was skimpy, but James Madison, writing in the 1820s, recollected that "the district mode was mostly, if not exclusively in view when the Constitution was framed and adopted." Madison, who always (or almost always) had an eye on the big picture, also deepened the argument, maintaining that district elections could serve as a counterweight to the formation of regional political blocs. Some district advocates took a more aggressive stance, attacking the general ticket as "aristocratic" (a damning accusation) because it obliged the people to cast ballots for electors whom they did not know and gave real power to the coteries of political leaders who nominated the electors.[63]

Advocates of the general ticket dismissed such criticisms, arguing that it was the method "most likely to accomplish the wishes of a majority of the people" and was perfectly consistent with "republican principles." They pointed out that under the district system a candidate could win a majority of a state's electoral votes without winning the popular vote, and they claimed that only men chosen in a statewide election could truly represent the interests of the entire state. "Crito," who penned a South Carolina polemic urging that both electors and members of Congress be chosen by the general ticket, insisted that statewide elections would help to unify his politically divided state. "District elections foster and nourish local attachments" that were "frequently incompatible with the general good," Crito claimed. The general ticket, in contrast, would "melt down the hitherto discordant opinions of Carolina into the great mass of public interest and general happiness" and "obliterate those invidious lines of demarcation ... between the upper and lower divisions of the state." A pamphlet offering an impassioned, if overwrought, defense of Virginia's switch to the general ticket in 1800 maintained that statewide elections were needed to preserve the influence of the large states—which would be dissipated if states were divided into districts. (Large states, the author asserted, were already disadvantaged by the allocation of electoral votes and by the contingent election procedure.) Even worse, the pamphlet argued, with more than a touch of sophistry, district elections could deprive a state of all influence if half of its electors went to each candidate![64]

The rhetorical battles were sharp-witted and sometimes fierce, yet by 1800 it was clear that the virtues or defects of different systems were somewhat beside the point. The issues were completely enmeshed in partisan politics, and both the pamphlet wars and the jousting in state legislatures were heavily laced with partisan interests and accusations. The *Washington Federalist* claimed that Republicans supported district elections only when they were in the minority, and Virginia's switch to the general ticket in 1800 was widely denounced as an unprincipled maneuver designed to help elect Jefferson. That denunciation had merit, of course, and Republican attempts to justify the move on principled grounds rang hollow and defensive.[65]

Yet there was also truth to Virginia Republicans' claim that it would be foolish for them to maintain a district system while so many Federalist-leaning states utilized legislative selection or the general ticket—both of which guaranteed to deliver all of a state's electoral votes to the Federalist candidate.[66] As Jefferson put it,

> On the subject of an election by a general ticket, or by districts, most persons here seem to have made up their minds. All agree that an election by districts would be best, if it could be general; but while ten States choose either by their legislatures or by a general ticket, it is folly and worse than folly for the other six not to do it. In these ten States the minority is certainly unrepresented; and their majorities not only have the weight of their whole State in their scale, but have the benefit of so much of our minorities as can succeed at a district election.[67]

Such views were not unique to Virginians. Politically active citizens in many states expressed the opinion that district elections would be best but that "as long as some of the states choose their electors ... by a general vote either of their legislatures or the people at large, the other states must in their own defense either adopt the same method or submit to be unequally represented in the election."[68]

That opinion may well have been shared by a majority of Americans in the months leading up to the sharply contested election of 1800. Although three states (Kentucky, Maryland, and North Carolina) held district elections in 1800, thirteen embraced the pragmatic and partisan logic of winner-take-all. As long as some states were choosing electors through the general ticket or legislative action, others—or, to be precise, their dominant parties—could maximize their influence only by following suit. The combination of a close election and an acrid partisan climate, moreover, lent urgency and a sense of legitimacy to efforts by state party leaders to do everything in their power to elect their preferred candidate. The 1800 election, after all, was portrayed as pitting an elitist with monarchical tendencies, who had sought to suppress dissent and a free press through the Sedition Act, against an "infidel" slave owner with radical democratic, even Jacobin, leanings. With so much at stake, the niceties of republican principles took a back seat to victory.[69]

DUAL VOTES AND THE 1800 ELECTION

The 1796 and 1800 elections also returned the spotlight to the problems that could arise from the requirement that each elector cast two votes for president. If Alexander Hamilton had learned in 1789 that a bit of maneuvering could prevent the "dual" or "double" vote system from having an unintended outcome, by 1796 he was also alert to its other strategic possibilities. Although a Federalist, Hamilton did not welcome the prospect of an Adams presidency, and he worked hard behind the scenes to elect instead the younger and more malleable Thomas Pinckney of South Carolina. Pinckney was generally regarded as his party's choice for vice president, but Hamilton hoped to persuade a smattering of Federalists, particularly in the South, to cast their two ballots for Pinckney and someone other than Adams, thereby giving Pinckney the edge in total electoral votes. The scheme backfired (handing the Republican Jefferson the vice presidency), in part because some of Adams's supporters, alert to Hamilton's maneuvers, also engaged in strategic voting, casting their second ballots for men other than Pinckney. Remarkably, in the final tally forty-eight electoral votes were recorded for persons other than the four quasi-official candidates (Adams, Pinckney, Jefferson, and Burr).[70]

Four years later, with this history fresh in mind, the Republican congressional caucus, while nominating Jefferson and Burr for national office, specified that Jefferson was its candidate for president, with Burr implicitly assigned to the vice presidency. The Federalists, however, did not take a similar step, opening the door for the tireless Hamilton to engage in a new round of electoral machinations designed to unseat Adams and elevate Charles Coatsworth Pinckney (Thomas's older brother) to the presidency. (C. C. Pinckney, the "second" Federalist on the ballot, was a distinguished lawyer who had fought in the Revolutionary War and served as a delegate to the Constitutional Convention.) Hamilton failed once again, with the Republicans edging out the Federalists in the electoral vote tally. Notably, the electors of both parties displayed far greater party discipline than they had in 1796. All of the electors except one (a Federalist from Rhode Island) cast their votes for the two chosen candidates of their party.[71]

What resulted was an election that was tied, with both Jefferson and Burr receiving seventy-three electoral votes while Adams garnered sixty-five and Pinckney sixty-four. As the Constitution instructed, the choice between Jefferson and Burr (they alone remained in the running because each had a majority) was turned over to the House of Representatives, where the Republican caucus's designation of Jefferson as the party's presidential candidate carried no legal weight. On February 11, 1801, immediately after the electoral vote tally was announced at a joint session of the lame-duck Congress, the House convened and began polling the state delegations, each of which was entitled to one vote. The Republicans controlled eight delegations in the lame-duck House, all of which voted for Jefferson. The six delegations dominated by Federalists cast their ballots for Burr, while two delegations were evenly split and abstained. Nine votes (a majority of the sixteen states) were needed to elect a president. The House remained in session deep into the evening, conducting nineteen roll call votes, with the outcome the same each time.[72]

The electoral system had produced a major crisis a dozen years after its creation. The Republican candidate who was preferred by Republicans was locked in a tie with the party's "second candidate." The tie could be broken only with Federalist votes, and many Federalists were so hostile to Jefferson that they favored Burr despite his reputation as an unscrupulous schemer—a reputation fortified by Burr's odd public silence and alleged private maneuvers in the winter of 1800–1801. (Hamilton, significantly, could not bring himself to support Burr, a fellow New Yorker and longtime antagonist whom Hamilton characterized as "morally bankrupt" and "unprincipled.") Adding urgency to the drama, if the tie persisted until March 4 (the end of Adams's term and the term of the sitting Congress), there would be no way to elect a president until the new Congress convened nine months later. Meanwhile, either there would be no chief executive or the office would be filled by the president pro tem of the Senate or the Speaker of the House of Representatives, both of whom were Federalists. As the standoff dragged on, rumors proliferated that Virginia would secede, that Republicans would take up arms if Jefferson were not elected, and that armed men had seized the arsenal in Philadelphia and were preparing to march on Washington. Calls for a new constitutional convention were widespread. Equally persistent were rumors and suggestions (some of them apparently true) that Federalists were offering deals to both Jefferson and

Burr, hoping to trade votes for policy concessions. This unseemly, potentially dangerous deadlock was surely not what the founding fathers had in mind when they imagined the House of Representatives solemnly choosing the best man to be president.[73]

The logjam was finally broken in mid-February when Federalist James Bayard, Delaware's only congressional representative, signaled his willingness to change his vote for Burr to an abstention, which would effectively deliver the election to Jefferson. On February 17, after several more days of internal Federalist wrangling, coupled with claims that concessions had been wrung from Jefferson, a handful of Federalist congressmen, including Bayard, abstained on the thirty-sixth ballot, giving Jefferson the votes of ten states. Chaos had been averted (John Adams later said that he had feared a "civil war"), the Republicans were victorious, and the Federalists, already in decline as an organized political force, had avoided the stain of having deliberately thwarted the will of the people.[74]

But the flaws in the system had been laid bare. The constitutional design that permitted states to vary their methods of choosing electors had transformed the long electoral campaign into a procedural free-for-all—with changes made for largely partisan reasons and the people excluded from direct participation in nearly two-thirds of the states. (Pennsylvania came close to not casting any electoral votes at all because the two chambers of its legislature could not agree on a method of choosing electors.) The dual-vote requirement, meanwhile, had given rise to endless scheming, and the presidential electors themselves played no constructive role, casting their ballots without even pretending to deliberate. Once the election landed in the House of Representatives, moreover, the nation faced the prospect of a risky, prolonged deadlock, with the political party that had lost the election wielding the power to decide which Republican would become president. The electoral system designed by the framers had, in sum, proven to be a poor fit with the partisan political realities that obtained at the turn of the century. Thanks to the system's cascading problems, Aaron Burr—perhaps the most distrusted politician of his era, and the candidate with the least popular support among the official four—came within a whisker of the presidency.[75]

The Challenges of Reform

As one would expect, the elections of 1796 and 1800 gave rise to widespread calls for reform of the electoral system. Two proposals, in particular, garnered significant support and attention. The first was for the passage of a constitutional amendment that would compel states to choose electors through popular elections in districts. The second—also requiring an amendment—was to solve the dual-vote problem by instituting "discrimination" or "designation" in the balloting: each elector would be obliged to cast one vote for president and a separate vote for vice president. This change, it was argued, would prevent a repeat of the 1800 debacle and ensure that a president would have majority support.[76] A third proposal, which attracted far less notice, called for abolishing the office of elector and allowing the "immediate suffrage" of the people to determine the candidate (or candidates) for whom a state's electoral votes would be cast. This last idea gained little traction—in part, no doubt, because the existence of electors per se had played no role in the crisis of 1800—but it made clear that electors had begun to be regarded as superfluous.[77] Both the consideration and the fate of these proposals shed early light on the challenges of altering the electoral system, challenges that would bedevil reform efforts for more than two centuries.

DISTRICT ELECTIONS

Proposals for constitutionally mandated district elections were a direct outgrowth of the machinations and debates that figured so prominently in the long campaign of 1800. The idea, which bubbled up out of state legislatures before reaching the floor of Congress, was favored not only by those who had consistently supported district elections in the 1790s but also by political leaders who—echoing Jefferson—had defended their states' adoption of other methods while acknowledging their preference for district elections if they could be held everywhere. By 1801 it was widely recognized that if the decisions were left up to individual states, the partisan advantages of winner-take-all would generally triumph over the reputed virtues of district elections. "Bystander" (the pen name of Federalist Robert Goodloe Harper) wrote to his fellow citizens of Maryland in 1800, in the midst of that state's heated partisan debate about the mode of choosing electors, that "district elections are, in themselves, the fairest mode," but "they must be general and permanent," a condition that could be achieved "only by an amendment of the constitution." Such an amendment would permit states to enjoy the benefits of district elections without losing electoral clout, guarantee that the people would choose their chief magistrate, and put an end to the unseemly spectacle of states altering their rules to suit the interests of political parties. Most of the active supporters of a district amendment were Republicans, but they were joined by prominent Federalists, including Hamilton and Gouverneur Morris, who had returned to his native New York from Pennsylvania and served in the Senate from 1800 to 1803.[78]

Formal congressional consideration of mandatory district elections began in March 1800 when John Nicholas, a Virginia Republican, submitted a resolution to the House of Representatives to amend the Constitution so that every state would be divided "into a number of districts equal to the number of Electors, to be chosen in such States." In each district, one elector would be chosen "by the persons . . . who shall have the qualifications requisite" to vote "for the most numerous branch of the Legislature of such state." (The suffrage provision replicated the constitutional requirement for voting in elections to the House of Representatives.) Nicholas's timing was infelicitous—with the election campaign well under way and his own state having recently switched to the general ticket—and the resolution received no formal consideration. But Nicholas reintroduced his proposal in late November, and it was referred to a committee composed of three Federalists and two Republicans, including Nicholas himself.[79]

The committee report, delivered to the House in January 1801, pointedly rejected the amendment, concluding that it would be "inexpedient to change the Constitution of the United States, in the manner proposed." The report offered two rationales for that verdict. The first was that it was premature to start tinkering with the Constitution. "The provisions of the Constitution of the United States can, in no instance, be reasonably considered as mere pleonasms or inadvertencies," the committee claimed, and it should be presumed that they were adopted after "due consideration" and for good reason. (The archaic, yet still valuable, word *pleonasm* is defined as "the use of more words than are necessary to express an idea.") That the

Constitution did not impose upon the states any one method of choosing electors indicated that the framers wanted the states to experiment with different modes and thereby gain "the advantages of experience," a process the proposed amendment would short-circuit. With only a few elections having been held, the committee considered it "foreign to their duty to enter into a comparative view of the merits and demerits of the various modes which have been or may be adopted."[80]

After sounding these sober cautionary notes, the committee report then veered in a more combative direction, insisting that district elections were "liable to serious abuses of most dangerous consequence to the public peace." It laid out the problems in remarkable detail. District elections would require the appointment of officers to preside over every district (and every "sub-division of every electoral district"), and some of these officers would inevitably have "a liability to the deviations of error, if not to those of a worse nature." The results from every district would have to be gathered, counted, transmitted, and transported, which would open the door to further "suppressing the polls" or other corruptions. Such actions, in turn, would inevitably yield disputes over the legitimacy of electors, yet Congress had no means of "discriminating between the votes of those who shall have been duly appointed . . . and those . . . defectively appointed." The eventual upshot could easily be "a disputed election to the Presidency," which might be "calamitous." In the end, the committee report, although eerily prescient regarding the disputed elections that would occur in 1876 and 2000, seemed less a rejection of the specific amendment than of popular elections—and the messiness of democracy. Its tone made clear that apprehensions about popular rule remained strong, at least among Federalists, even as (and perhaps because) Jefferson approached the presidency.[81]

Despite the vehemence of the House report (which was issued just as the electoral crisis was unfolding in Washington), the issue was brought up again in Congress, with more formally organized political support, the following winter. By February 1802 the House had received resolutions for a district elections amendment from the legislatures of New York, Vermont, North Carolina, and Maryland, the last of which had begun circulating its proposal to other states a year earlier.[82] Several of these resolutions, also submitted to the Senate, coupled the district elections issue with a proposed amendment to require that "in all future elections of President and Vice President, the persons voted for shall be particularly designated, by declaring which is voted for as President and which as Vice President." A similar view, advocating both district elections and "designation," was put forward in September 1801 in a letter to Jefferson from Treasury secretary Albert Gallatin, who argued that the two measures combined would effectively prevent a repeat of the 1800 election.[83] A designation amendment had first been brought before Congress in January 1797 by Federalist William Smith of South Carolina, but it had attracted little support.[84] After the near-debacle of 1800, the issue appeared more ripe for action.

Yet even as these proposed amendments were being introduced and considered, the politics of reform—and the political climate more broadly—were shifting. Republicans had not only won the presidency for the first time in 1800, but they had also posted significant gains in Congress and state legislatures. After the midterm elections of 1802, they would hold large majorities in both the House and the Senate and control legislatures in three-quarters of the states. As a result, Republicans were increasingly confident of their ability to retain the presidency in 1804 no matter how electors were chosen. While many continued to proclaim their support for district elections, most Republicans found the issue to be less compelling than they had a year or two earlier. Reform, moreover, had a potential downside: district elections would permit Federalists to pick up some electoral votes in states where the Republican Party was in the majority. What had begun to loom as a far more pressing matter to many Republicans was the need to prevent a replay of the final stages of the 1800 election. They could all too easily imagine scenarios in which a Federalist minority could prevent Jefferson's reelection either through the strategic casting of electors' second votes or in the House of Representatives.[85]

DESIGNATION

The upshot of these political shifts was that congressional Republicans started to place greater priority on securing a designation amendment than on achieving their oft-mentioned, and ideologically justified, goal of district elections. This change was manifest as early as the spring of 1802. On May 1, at the very close of the congressional session, Republicans in the House insisted on taking up the constitutional amendments that had been introduced months earlier, but they quickly shelved the district elections issue to focus entirely on a designation amendment. (There were objections to this move by both Federalists and some Republicans.) After a brief debate regarding the propriety of considering such an important matter when there was little time for discussion and many members had already left Washington, the Republicans succeeded in passing the revised resolution by the requisite two-thirds majority (of those present). The vote was forty-seven to fourteen on a straight-line party vote.[86] In the Senate, a parallel set of developments fell one vote short of two-thirds, dooming the resolution. Nearly all of the negative votes came from northeastern Federalists.[87]

More than a year later—with some skirmishing in the interim—the Republicans, holding comfortable majorities in both branches of Congress, launched their final push for a designation amendment. Although there was no certainty that they could muster the necessary majorities, they were determined to try to change the Constitution before the 1804 election. (By this time the issue of district elections was firmly consigned to a back burner, despite the protests of dissident Republicans as well as a growing number of Federalists who, now in the minority, were coming to appreciate the shortcomings of winner-take-all.) In October 1803 the House passed an awkwardly written draft of what would become the Twelfth Amendment to the Constitution. It required electors to separately designate their votes for president and vice president; in the event that no candidate received a majority, the House, under the procedure already outlined in the Constitution, would choose among the five candidates with the largest number of votes; if no vice-presidential candidate garnered a majority, the Senate would decide between the top two vote-getters. The Senate then clarified the language, reduced the number of candidates to be considered by the House from five to three, and introduced a clause specifying that if no president had been chosen by March 4 of the year after the election, the vice-president-elect would assume the presidency. The Senate resolution was passed with no votes to spare (twenty-two to ten); nine of the negative votes were cast by Federalists. In early December, the House, after an exegetical debate over the changes introduced by the Senate, voted to accept that chamber's version by a precise two-thirds majority of eighty-four to forty-two. (Seven Republicans joined the Federalists in opposition.) The amendment was quickly dispatched to the states, and by the late summer of 1804 it had been ratified, with only the Federalist strongholds of Delaware, Massachusetts, and Connecticut voting negatively. Electors in 1804 would, and did, cast separate ballots for president and vice president.[88]

Designation, thus, became a part of the Constitution, but it was not an easy, or automatic, sell, even as a stand-alone measure detached from the district elections issue to which it had once been joined. From the vantage point of later decades, the Twelfth Amendment may appear to have been a straightforward correction of a (rare) mistake committed by the framers, an almost clerical reconciling of constitutional language with procedural necessity. But in fact it was perceived differently by many contemporaries, and its narrow approval by Congress came only after sharp debate and skillful negotiations.[89]

The opposition to designation had multiple sources. Prominent among them were the short-run political interests of the Federalists: if ballots for president were clearly distinguished from ballots for vice president, the Federalists would have little chance, in 1804 or the foreseeable future, of affecting the outcome of presidential elections or of electing one of their own candidates as vice president. The Republicans, with popular and legislative majorities in most states, would have a clear electoral path to both executive offices. Designation consequently would reinforce the Federalists' new, and unwelcome, status as a minority party wielding little power in Washington. "The members from New England, even when united," grumbled a pamphleteer, "have no more influence in Congress than they have over the Conservative Senate of France." Some complained that what really needed to be changed in the Constitution was not designation but the three-fifths clause, which was widely believed to have won the election for Jefferson. Many Federalists, indeed, portrayed the Twelfth Amendment as a partisan measure aimed at them, proof that Jefferson and his allies were willing to adopt extreme measures—even tinkering with the Constitution—to bolster their power and subdue the opposition. "The Amendment . . . secures to Mr. Jefferson his election to the Presidency for life," lamented one Massachusetts Federalist.[90]

Other, less partisan concerns were also at play, including a broadly felt reluctance to make alterations to a still-new Constitution. South Carolina

Federalist Benjamin Huger, for example, "confessed that he trembled at the idea of altering" the Constitution and worried that "we should not lose more than we should gain" with any changes.[91] Of at least equal importance, designation would upset the balance of small-state and large-state interests that was built into the constitutional design. With designation, elections would be significantly less likely to end up in the House of Representatives, and consequently the influence of small states would be diminished—because they wielded more power in contingent elections than they did in the Electoral College.[92] There were partisan undercurrents to this claim, given the Federalists' dominance of many small states, but small-state Republicans also voiced concern. Writing many years later, Henry Adams, in his magisterial history of Jefferson's administration, concluded that the Twelfth Amendment "swept away one of the checks on which the framers had counted to resist majority rule by the great States ... stripping the small States of an advantage which had made part of their bargain."[93]

Resistance to the Twelfth Amendment also stemmed from an uneasy awareness that this ostensibly small shift in procedure would effectively institutionalize a conception of presidential elections that departed from the vision embedded in the Constitution. Instead of a contest among prominent individuals—possibly numerous individuals—presidential elections would become contests between candidates identified with political parties. Greater emphasis, accordingly, would be placed on program, ideology, and organization than on the character and virtues of individual leaders. Designation would also have a profound impact on the vice presidency: a politician would occupy the nation's second highest office not because he had wide support for the presidency but because he was the designated ally of his party's presidential candidate. Numerous critics maintained that this would place men of inferior talents in the vice presidency (a claim borne out for much of the nation's subsequent history). With impressive foresight, Connecticut's Roger Griswold predicted that "the only criterion which will be regarded as a qualification for the office of Vice-president will be the temporary influence of the candidate over the electors of his State." Gouverneur Morris quipped that "the vice-presidency would hereafter be but as a bait to catch State gudgeons." His fellow framer in Philadelphia, Senator Jonathan Dayton of New Jersey, maintained that the best solution to the dual-vote problem would be to abolish the office of vice president altogether.[94]

These objections did not carry the day, but the debate over the Twelfth Amendment nonetheless offered a telling illustration, and an augury, of the difficulties that would confront proponents of electoral reform for more than two centuries. Although the framers' dual-vote design was widely recognized as a serious problem by 1801, there was no evident solution to that problem that did not have real or perceived negative consequences for some constituencies or groups of political actors. Many Federalists thus opposed passage of the amendment not because they thought that designation itself was a bad idea but because they believed that it would harm their short-run prospects for wielding influence in Washington. The complexity of the electoral system's design, moreover, meant that tinkering with one piece of the apparatus could have repercussions elsewhere. This critical fact was clearly manifested in the congressional debates, which included few objections to designation per se; most of the clamor was about the impact of designation on the likelihood of contingent elections and therefore the influence of the small states. An alteration to one feature of the elaborate electoral system could spawn opposition because it might disturb the intricate balances built into the system, the compromises forged in 1787 that were well remembered in 1803.

Similar—and equally far-reaching—dynamics contributed to the failure of Congress to enact an amendment mandating district elections. Here too, the compromises of 1787 came into play. In the eyes of its supporters, the district elections amendment was not simply a means of institutionalizing a particular conception of the best way to choose electors; it would also correct a flaw in the constitutional architecture that had been exposed by a decade of elections. By permitting electors to be appointed by each state "in such Manner as the Legislature thereof may direct," the Constitution had unwittingly opened the door not just to experimentation but also to partisan jockeying and manipulation of the electoral process. As "Bystander" observed, "The truth of the whole matter is, and it need not be concealed, that while the mode of choosing electors remains on its present footing, variable according to the will of the state legislatures, variations will be made, in some states, to serve the candidate who may happen to be the favorite there."[95] The framers, presumably, had adopted their formulation as one of several gestures, or concessions, to the autonomy of the states, granting to each the power to decide how to express its voice in choosing a national executive. But this gesture had consequences that the framers did not foresee: in the absence of a national set of ground rules for selecting electors, the Constitution tacitly encouraged state legislatures, or the political factions that controlled them, to alter the rules in order to game the system.

The most straightforward solution to that problem was, indeed, an amendment to the Constitution. But to impose on the states a "uniform mode for the choice of Electors" (in the words of the Vermont resolution) was to undercut a constitutionally assigned prerogative of the states, and, unsurprisingly, states' rights arguments against the proposed amendment took shape quickly. In Connecticut, for example, Federalists justified their antagonism to the proposed amendment by invoking the need for diversity among the states and by pointing out that the amendment stripped power from the legislatures that were a critical bulwark of state sovereignty. Such sentiments also seemed to undergird the 1801 House committee's opposition to "the exclusive establishment of any particular mode" of choosing electors. As reformers of many types would discover again and again in American history, any threat to the balance of power between the states and the national government was likely to generate resistance. In this instance, the wording of the Constitution created both a constituency and a handy rationale for opposition to change.[96]

The potential infringement on the prerogatives of the states, however, was not the most important factor leading to the defeat of the district elections amendment. That distinction belonged to the growing influence of political parties, the deepening of partisan sentiments, and the increasing willingness of political actors to let party interests guide their decision-making. Partisan factors, of course, had been prominent in the conflicts over district elections from the beginning. From the early 1790s through 1800, Republicans in state legislatures had generally advocated district contests for reasons of both principle and party advantage. Federalists had often rejected the idea for an analogous mix of reasons, including the well-being of their party, a lack of commitment to popular elections, and the desire not to diminish their states' clout by splitting the electoral vote.

It was a bit later, in 1802–1804, that party interests scored their clearest triumph over principle and ideology. This was a period when the Republicans held the presidency, had two-thirds majorities in both branches of Congress, and controlled a majority of state governments. Memories of the 1800 election were vivid, and popular interest in reforming the electoral system remained strong. After the elections of 1800 and 1802, moreover, a growing number of Federalists had become sympathetic to the cause of district elections, for their own pragmatic reasons. (The presence of Federalist support, indeed, suggested that a districting amendment might have passed more easily than the designation resolution.) The Republicans, thus, had an excellent opportunity to pass an amendment that would secure a reform that they had championed for a decade, that would achieve the goal that Jefferson had articulated in 1800 when he wrote that "an election by districts would be best if it could be general." It is at least arguable, and perhaps likely, that Republicans could have successfully promoted a Twelfth Amendment that addressed both designation and district elections, precisely as some state resolutions had advocated in 1802.[97]

But the Republican leadership chose not to do so. Enjoying their recent electoral victories, yet still feeling politically embattled, the Republicans calculated that their political interests, in the short run at least, would best be served by maintaining the status quo. Given their control of a majority of state legislatures, either the general ticket or legislative selection would work to their advantage; implementing district elections would probably cost them more votes than they would gain. Although many Republicans continued to profess their support for district elections in principle, the party's congressional leaders, with Jefferson's backing, retreated from their advocacy of an amendment, effectively dooming the measure. Tellingly, a similar retreat unfolded at the state level. In New York, where Republicans had fought so vigorously for district elections on numerous occasions, they declined to implement them after they had gained majorities in both houses of the legislature. Three states that the Republicans controlled (Pennsylvania, New Jersey, and New Hampshire) did change their method of choosing electors for the 1804 elections—from legislative selection to the general ticket. The switch burnished the Republicans' credentials as advocates of popular government while still guaranteeing that they would win every electoral vote. In the new state of Ohio, in 1803, Republican governor Edward Tiffin urged the legislature to decide whether Ohio should choose its electors by a general ticket election or a joint ballot of the legislature. He did not mention district elections as an option.[98]

On March 2, 1804, Representative David Thomas, a Republican from New York, took the floor of the House of Representatives to move "that the resolution proposing an amendment to the Constitution districting the States for the choices of Electors of President and Vice President be committed to a Committee of the Whole House on the state of the Union." Thomas reminded his colleagues that this issue had been before Congress "some time ago," and he believed that it was appropriate to reconsider it during the current session, now that the Twelfth Amendment had been sent to the states and was gaining approval. The House did not discuss Thomas's proposal, and, in the words of the official proceedings, "the motion was lost."[99]

*   *   *

By the end of Thomas Jefferson's first term in office, the initial era of experimentation with the presidential electoral system had drawn to a close. The blueprint drawn up by the framers had been fleshed out by state legislatures and transformed into a set of practices. Questions posed in 1788 had been answered, at least provisionally, by 1804. Candidates for president and vice president were put forward by political parties, centered in Congress; the parties also coordinated the election campaigns. Nearly everywhere the strategic goal of these campaigns was to win legislative or popular majorities within entire states—since all but four (out of seventeen) delivered their full complement of electoral votes to one candidate. Those votes were physically cast by electors who gathered in state capitals and served simply as messengers: they did not deliberate, discuss, or "think." Political actors had repeatedly tested the structures and the rules in search of advantage, and their actions had helped to change the mechanics of the system.

These early years of experimentation yielded one significant change to the Constitution: the Twelfth Amendment. Its passage testified to the failure of the framers to discern or imagine how presidential elections would actually work, and it altered forever the conduct of those elections. Instead of a nonpolitical process among notable individuals that would produce a consensus chief executive (as the founders had envisioned), the Twelfth Amendment encouraged organized political competition that aimed at mustering popular or state legislative majorities. By effectively requiring that candidates run in teams or "tickets," the amendment—as many contemporaries recognized—strengthened the national political parties whose formation, and behavior, had made the original electoral design unworkable. The amendment took some of the mischief and scheming out of the system while demoting the vice president to the role of junior partner in national election campaigns.[100]

At least as important as the Twelfth Amendment was the emergence of winner-take-all as the dominant method of allocating the electoral votes of the states. This practice was implemented by state legislatures in response to national partisan competition, and, in the eyes of numerous contemporaries, it violated the spirit and intent of the Constitution. The general ticket, as many noted, muffled the voices of minorities within states, while legislative decision-making went a step further, denying the people any say in choosing among presidential candidates. The institutionalization of winner-take-all was far from complete by 1804—that would take another generation—but the practice was already shaping the ways in which political leaders thought about, and approached, contests for the presidency.

In retrospect, the failure of Congress to enact a district elections amendment during Jefferson's first term looms large. Choosing electors by district was the most readily available alternative to winner-take-all in this era, and the years from 1801 to 1804 constituted an uncommon political moment in which district elections might well have become the national norm.[101] The congressional supermajorities needed for an amendment were within plausible reach; public opinion had been aroused by the 1800 election; another amendment altering the electoral system was moving forward; and the Constitution itself had not yet become so sacralized as to be an impediment to reform. Republican leaders, of course, did not know, and could not have known, that conditions so favorable to an amendment would prove hard to replicate, but their decision to place short-run political advantage ahead of their own principles and ideas certainly ran the risk of squandering an opportunity. Stalwart advocates of district elections resurrected the issue during Jefferson's second term, but the movement for electoral reform had lost steam after Jefferson's landslide reelection and the government became preoccupied with other matters, particularly foreign affairs.[102] Proposals for district elections would be introduced into Congress again and again, throughout the nineteenth century and for much of the twentieth, but rarely, if ever, in circumstances as propitious as those that prevailed during Jefferson's first term.

It is, of course, ironic that responsibility for this missed opportunity lies largely at the doorstep of the Republicans. The political party that manifestly represented the emergent forces of democracy in the United States of 1800 failed to pursue a reform that, in critical respects, would have democratized presidential elections, both by requiring elections and by giving greater influence to political minorities. That said, one ought not be too harsh in judging the Republicans: neither feckless nor unprincipled, they had been seared by a half-dozen years of nasty political combat. The once-dominant Federalists had, after all, enacted the Sedition Act (1798) that brought criminal charges against Republican editors and sympathizers; they had tried mightily to block Jefferson's election in the House of Representatives; and just as John Adams was leaving office, they had packed the judiciary with Federalists and passed a law designed to prevent Jefferson from making an appointment to the Supreme Court. Since the early 1790s, Federalists in the states had repeatedly rigged the rules for presidential elections to benefit their own candidates. After 1800 they intimated that there was a whiff of illegitimacy to Jefferson's election because his victory could be attributed to the electoral votes that slave states wielded thanks to the three-fifths clause. "The Negro votes made Mr. Jefferson president," wrote Senator William Plumer of New Hampshire.[103]

Against this backdrop, it is understandable that the Republicans found it difficult to rise above the partisan fray, that they were reluctant to institute a reform that, in the short run, might have advantaged the Federalists in the electoral vote count. The unfortunate truth was that the nation's early years of experimentation with the new electoral system—years when adjustments or reforms might have been expected and relatively easy to promulgate—overlapped with an era of acrimonious partisanship, an era when the two parties were not merely rivals but distrustful adversaries, when they perceived one another as threats to core values as well as their own political viability.[104] The first window of opportunity for reform happened to open at a moment when the political winds were shifting but the atmosphere remained thick with distrust and recrimination.

PART II

The Long Struggle to Abolish Winner-Take-All

The district system is the true system; that to which the people are attached, because it renders their elective franchise efficient and gives to every portion of the State its legitimate influence. But, as long as some of the States adhere to the general ticket system, all the rest will be compelled, in self defence, to adopt it, and, in this manner the very worst plan will prevail, from a sort of State necessity, in opposition to the deliberate sentiments of the community.

—Representative George McDuffie, South Carolina, 1824

Discontent with winner-take-all (through either general-ticket elections or the choice of electors by legislatures) did not evaporate after Thomas Jefferson left the White House in 1809. For the next 200 years (and counting), the practice of casting all of a state's electoral votes for one candidate would be regarded—by reformers and politicians of diverse persuasions—as perhaps the most insidious feature of the Electoral College. It stripped all influence from political minorities within states, seriously deformed electoral campaigns, distorted the expression of political preferences, and occasionally helped to deliver the presidency to candidates who did not win the popular vote. The indictment was powerful, and, not surprisingly, it gave rise to recurrent efforts to adopt some other method of allocating a state's electoral votes.

In the nineteenth century the most commonly proposed alternative to the "general ticket" was to choose electors in district elections; that idea, already popular in 1800, retained substantial support into the 1950s. A somewhat different approach, which first surfaced in the mid-nineteenth century and became more prominent in the twentieth, called for a "proportional" system in which a state's electoral votes would be allocated in arithmetic proportion to a candidate's popular vote. A third possibility, of course, was that of instituting a nationwide popular vote, but, for reasons to be explored in later chapters, that option was regarded as politically implausible—and something of a nonstarter—until the second half of the twentieth century.

Part II focuses on the history of efforts to institute district or proportional elections during the long era—a century and a half—in which they constituted the principal alternatives to winner-take-all. When the period began, in the early nineteenth century, only a handful of states were choosing electors by district, and that remained the case into the late 1820s. Maryland, in 1833, was the last state to shift from district to general-ticket elections. Thereafter, occasional state experiments with district elections did occur, notably in Michigan in the 1890s, Maine (beginning in 1972), and Nebraska (starting in 1992). Organized attempts to replace winner-take-all with district elections were also mounted in a variety of other states between 1990 and 2015.[1]

Despite these scattered state efforts, those who hoped to eliminate winner-take-all generally understood that they would need a national mandate to do so. Accordingly, hundreds of proposals were put forward in Congress for constitutional amendments that would require all states to either hold district elections or allocate electoral votes in proportion to a candidate's popular vote. Many of these efforts had widespread backing among political leaders, and several, as early as 1813 and as late as 1950, had enough support to be approved by one branch of Congress.

That all of these proposals failed to become law reflected, in part, the critical fact that the Constitution did not offer the states, or the American people, an evenhanded choice among different methods of allocating electoral votes. Whatever the framers may have intended when they left it to the states to determine the "manner" in which electors were chosen, the constitutional blueprint turned out to be biased in favor of winner-take-all—something the framers surely did not intend.[2] As the developments of the 1790s had suggested, and as would become evident by the 1820s, the pressures of partisan competition meant that each state, left to its own devices, would be likely to adopt the general ticket; and if some states did so, the rest would almost inevitably follow. District or proportional elections, in contrast, could become, and remain, part of the national landscape only if they were imposed through an amendment to the Constitution.

This asymmetry in the choice of methods placed two significant obstacles in the path of those who sought to abolish winner-take-all. The first, of course, was the high bar for constitutional amendments: approval by two-thirds of the members of each branch of Congress and by three-quarters of the states. The second obstacle was more ideological and political: any proposed national mandate was likely to encounter resistance grounded in a reluctance to disturb the balance of power between the national government and the states. An amendment *requiring* any system of allocating electors would effectively limit the autonomy of the states, depriving them of a choice, or right, granted in the Constitution. Those who zealously guarded the prerogatives of the states were likely to balk at an amendment mandating national uniformity, and those who—for whatever reason—wished to preserve winner-take-all had a ready-made, ideologically defensible argument for opposing reform. The only system of allocating electoral votes that could operate nationally without encountering objections on federalism grounds was the general ticket.

The many efforts to jettison winner-take-all were also shaped by the evolution of political parties—as the fledgling organizations of the "first party system" gave way to the stronger, if more fluid and mutable, parties of the nineteenth century and eventually to the institutionalized two-party system of the twentieth. The presidential election system encouraged the formation of national party organizations in the early years of the republic, and once national parties were firmly implanted, the Electoral College (and especially its winner-take-all feature) influenced their strategies and policies. Partisan interests often helped to define the content of proposed electoral reforms, while party leaders and members commonly viewed prospective changes to the electoral system through the prism of their own political reckonings.[3]

The impulse, or desire, to abolish winner-take-all has been something of a constant in the history of presidential politics. But there were several periods after the passage of the Twelfth Amendment when congressional efforts to institute district or proportional elections were particularly strong and visible. The first stretched from roughly 1812 to 1830, largely overlapping the "Era of Good Feelings," a period when the fledgling republic had only one fully functioning national party but numerous competing political factions. The second took place from the end of the Civil War into the early 1890s, when the nation's political direction and party alignments were being recast. The third arose after World War II and lingered into the early 1960s. The dynamics of reform were different in each of these periods, as befitted a rapidly changing nation still governed by its eighteenth-century Constitution.

TWO

ELECTORAL REFORM IN THE ERA OF GOOD FEELINGS

Significant efforts to alter the presidential election system reappeared a few years after the end of Thomas Jefferson's second term and continued into the presidency of Andrew Jackson. Critics of the Electoral College, even as modified by the Twelfth Amendment, mounted prolonged and sometimes passionate attacks on the shortcomings of the general ticket; they also deplored the inclination of some state legislatures to choose electors by themselves and to opportunistically switch electoral methods from one election to the next. Some reform advocates derided presidential electors as, at best, unnecessary and, at worst, as vehicles for thwarting the will of the people. Many found the contingent election system to be deeply flawed, particularly after the House of Representatives in 1824 denied the presidency to Jackson and delivered it instead to John Quincy Adams.[1]

Reform of the electoral system occupied a prominent place on the agenda of Congress during these years. Scores of resolutions calling for constitutional amendments, some of them originating in state legislatures, were introduced in the House and the Senate, and more than a few were debated at great length. At the outset these proposals focused on requiring states to choose electors in district elections; resolutions to that effect, varying in their details, were introduced in nearly every Congress from 1813 to 1835. (Some of them also sought the same mandate for elections to the House of Representatives.)[2] Beginning in the 1820s, members of Congress gravitated toward other issues as well, including eliminating presidential electors, the imposition of term limits for presidents, and, most urgently, transforming the contingent election system.

These proposals did not emanate from marginal political figures or factions: they enjoyed substantial support in Congress. A half dozen of the

FIGURE 2.1: CONGRESSIONAL VOTING ON DISTRICT ELECTIONS
RESOLUTIONS, 1813–1822

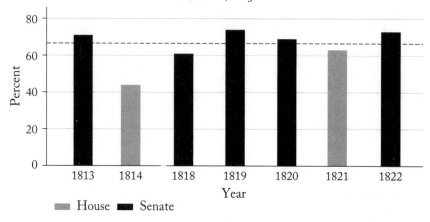

Percentage of favorable votes[a] on constitutional amendments to require district elections for presidential electors, 1813–1822.[b]

---Two-thirds (percentage required for passage of a constitutional amendment)

Sources: Roll call data obtained from Howard Rosenthal and Keith T. Poole, *United States Congressional Roll Call Voting Records, 1789–1990* (Pittsburgh, PA, 2000), http://doi .org/10.3886/ICPSR09822.v2; 26 Annals of Cong. 828–844, 1198–1199 (1813–1814).

a. Percentage among those who cast votes.

b. The 1813 and 1814 proposals specified that there were to be as many districts in each state as there were electoral votes. The proposals for 1818–1821 provided that the number of districts would match the number of representatives in the House, with the two additional electors per state to be appointed as the legislature directed. The 1822 variant specified that the two additional electors would be chosen by qualified voters in a manner to be determined by the legislature.

district elections resolutions gained majority votes in at least one branch of Congress, and the Senate, on four occasions, passed resolutions by more than the two-thirds vote needed to amend the Constitution. In the Sixteenth Congress (1819–1821), a district elections resolution was approved by a two-thirds vote in the Senate and received 63 percent of the vote in the House: a shortfall of only a few votes prevented the amendment from being sent to the states for ratification.[3] (See Figure 2.1.) Five years later, 73 percent of the House voted in favor of eliminating any role for Congress in choosing a president, a stance that would have upended the contingent election procedure. Reform was in the air—and seemed, to many, to be within reach.[4]

Political Parties in Flux

Political parties are always central to matters of electoral reform, and this period was an unusual one, a transition or interregnum, in the evolution of American parties. Republicans from Virginia won all of the presidential contests from 1800 through 1820, and after 1802 the Republican Party held large majorities in both branches of Congress. The Federalists remained strong only in New England and some pockets of the mid-Atlantic region, although they had sufficient strength in Congress to square off repeatedly against the administrations of Jefferson and his successor, James Madison, particularly over international issues. Briefly, if modestly, resurgent in the congressional elections of 1812 and 1814, the Federalists then spiraled into terminal decline in national politics in the wake of their ill-judged maneuvers in opposition to the war with Britain. Despite retaining considerable strength in local and state elections, the Federalists contested the presidency for the last time in 1816 when their candidate, Rufus King, won only three states.[5]

By that time the country had effectively entered a period of one-party rule, with its new Republican president, James Monroe, celebrating national unity as well as the war's conclusion, and a Massachusetts newspaper heralding the arrival of an "Era of Good Feelings." Monroe, reflecting the hegemony of the Republicans, was reelected without opposition in 1820. The unity of his party, however, soon began to unravel, as sharp disagreements surfaced over questions of policy and politics. Reflecting those divisions, five candidates, all nominally Republicans, sought the presidency in 1824. In the aftermath of that hard-fought and bitterly concluded election, many politicians, in and out of Congress, identified less with the Republican Party than with its pro-Jackson and pro-Adams wings.[6]

While these events were unfolding, political leaders were wrestling ambivalently with the theory and reality of political parties. Even as the Republicans and (less successfully) the Federalists built national parties, they professed to see little virtue in such organizations and no enduring need for them. The anti-party apprehensions that were so prevalent in the 1790s—dramatically memorialized in George Washington's Farewell Address—remained widespread into the 1820s.[7] The dominant Republicans never regarded the Federalists as having a constructive role to play in governance, and the concept of a "legitimate opposition" was foreign to the thinking of most, if not all, political practitioners. Indeed, when the Federalist Party collapsed, some leading Republicans concluded that partisan contestation had come to an end and that the new nation was returning to a more natural state of party-less politics. James Monroe, to cite a prominent example, was convinced that parties were both unnecessary and undesirable. He wrote to Jefferson in 1822 that "surely our government may go on and prosper without the existence of parties. I have always considered their existence as the curse of the country, of which we had sufficient proof, more especially in the late war." Others were less sanguine or perhaps more realistic, particularly as conflicts and factions emerged among Republicans. Madison came to conclude that "parties, under some denominations or other," were inevitable, and he strongly hoped that such parties would not be sectional, exacerbating the always-present tensions between North and South.[8]

The ambivalence about parties began to fade in the later 1820s, thanks in part to the rise of a new generation of political leaders, including New York's Martin Van Buren. Van Buren had cut his political teeth fighting against the highly personalized Republican network of DeWitt Clinton, a patrician who held offices in city and state government from 1798 until his death in 1828. Beginning in 1817, Van Buren and his allies formed a competing organization, rooted in the premise that politicians and officeholders ought to be loyal, not to prominent notables like Clinton, but to the Republican Party itself. Shedding the views of the founding generation, Van Buren insisted that parties performed valuable functions and that competition between parties was salutary. "Political parties," he wrote in his autobiography, "are inseparable from free governments." National political parties, he believed, could also perform the essential function of muting sectional conflict and divisive debates over slavery. After the election of 1824, Van Buren played a critical role both in advancing the presidential ambitions of Andrew Jackson and in building the Democratic Party, history's first mass national party, officially founded in 1828. (Van Buren himself was elected president in 1836, after having served as a senator, ambassador to England, secretary of state, and vice president.) In response, an array of other factions (including supporters of Adams and Kentucky's Henry Clay) came together in 1834 to form a conservative counterpart, the

Whig Party. The Democrats and the Whigs constituted the nation's second party system, which lasted into the 1850s.[9]

It was not a coincidence that this era of unsettled, fluid party arrangements witnessed sustained congressional efforts to reform an electoral system that many had regarded as problematic since at least 1800. Between 1810 and 1830 the nation lacked a competitive two-party system (or even two competitive national parties), and not until 1824 was there a closely contested presidential election. As a result, partisan animosities were minimized, and it was possible for reform ideas and proposals to be imagined, developed, and circulated without being reflexively measured by a gauge of partisan advantage. The interlude in two-party competition, in effect, opened the space for new schemes and for new variations on old themes, for legislators to think out loud, for resolutions to be improved from one legislative session to the next. At the same time, reinvigorated anti-party sentiments quieted the voices of those state legislative leaders who instinctively thought it best to keep the choice of electors in their own hands or to maximize their influence through the general ticket. South Carolina representative Benjamin Huger grasped the import of the moment in December 1816 when he insisted that the Era of Good Feelings was precisely the right time for Congress to turn its attention to the problems with the presidential election system.

> It had been objected, that this was not the proper time to do anything, inasmuch as there was no excitement in the public mind, and our national concerns were progressing smoothly and prosperously. . . . On the contrary, it would seem, for these very reasons, the most proper time to investigate and act upon subjects of this kind. . . . All those passions and domestic feuds which had unfortunately divided and agitated the good people of these United States since the Constitution had been adopted, had subsided. . . . Party feelings were altogether extinct; or, if perchance any latent sparks still remained, there was nothing on the present occasion to rouse them into a flame. . . . Surely no more favorable moment could be imagined, or asked for, to take up and decide upon the expediency of making a change . . . in the great national compact.[10]

Discontents and Districts, 1813–1822

THE CASE FOR CHANGE

Agitation for reform was first triggered by an unseemly spate of partisan maneuvers that occurred during the election campaign of 1812, a campaign heated both by war and by Federalist opposition to war. In North Carolina, which had utilized a district system since 1796, the legislature announced that it would choose electors by itself: its majority feared that Madison might lose the state to DeWitt Clinton, who ran with the support of both Federalists and dissident Republicans. Massachusetts, continuing a dispute that had begun in 1808, found itself with a Republican senate and a Federalist lower house that could not agree on either a method of choosing electors or a map for congressional districts; in the end, an extra legislative session had to be convened to save the state from losing its electoral votes altogether. Most dramatically, the Federalist legislature in New Jersey announced, just days before the election, that it was canceling the scheduled balloting and appointing electors on its own. In all three states (and beyond), the legislatures' actions ignited firestorms of protest and recrimination.[11] *Niles' Weekly Register,* an influential national newsweekly published in Baltimore, declared its support for a district elections amendment "to prevent abuses, and in strict obedience to the generous spirit of the constitution itself."[12] North Carolina's James W. Clark, a legislator who had voted in favor of the change in method, felt obliged to publish a nineteen-page "address" to his constituents defending himself against "the charge of having, willfully and maliciously ... deprived the good people of this county of a certain portion of their rights."[13]

Indeed, the North Carolina legislature, responding to the public outcry, quickly reversed itself after the 1812 election. It not only returned to its citizens the right to vote for presidential electors (by general ticket) but took the further step of forwarding to Congress a resolution for a constitutional amendment that would require presidential electors, as well as members of the House of Representatives, to be chosen through district elections. The districts were to be "composed of contiguous territory, and contain, as nearly as may be, an equal number of inhabitants." According to Hezekiah Niles, the adoption of the general ticket by North Carolina's Republican legislature arose out of "necessity" (given the use of winner-take-all

TABLE 2.1: CONGRESSIONAL VOTES ON DISTRICT ELECTIONS
BY POLITICAL PARTY, 1813–1822

Year (chamber)	Federalist		Democratic-Republican	
	Percentage (number) voting in favor[a]	Number not voting	Percentage (number) voting in favor[a]	Number not voting
1813 (Senate)	20 (1)	(1)	81 (21)	(4)
1814 (House)	26 (15)	(9)	54 (49)	(24)
1818 (Senate)	56 (5)	(3)	63 (15)	(3)
1819 (Senate)	70 (7)	(2)	75 (21)	(2)
1820 (Senate)	90 (9)	(0)	63 (20)	(2)
1821 (House)	68 (17)	(5)	62 (75)	(32)
1822 (Senate)	50 (2)	(1)	75 (27)	(6)

Sources: Roll call data obtained from Howard Rosenthal and Keith T. Poole, *United States Congressional Roll Call Voting Records, 1789–1990* (Pittsburgh, PA, 2000), http://doi .org/10.3886/ICPSR09822.v2; 26 Annals of Cong. 828–844, 1198–1199 (1813–1814); party affiliations based on the Congressional Biographical Directory (http://bioguide .congress.gov). If no party affiliation was listed in the Congressional Biographical Directory, then party affiliation was taken from the roll call vote database.

a. Percentage among those who cast votes.

in other states), but its true preference, in the wake of the 1812 controversy, was for district elections.[14]

The North Carolina resolution was introduced on the Senate floor on January 20, 1813. It was referred to a committee that quickly amended the resolution, striking all reference to congressional elections. Less than a month later the Senate approved the amended resolution by a vote of twenty-two to nine, slightly above the two-thirds mark. More than 80 percent of Republicans voted favorably, with strong support in both the North and the South. The tiny bloc of Federalists who remained in the Senate opposed the resolution, but they were too few in number to be consequential.[15] (See Table 2.1.)

The rapid action of the Senate signaled the presence of broad support for reform. The progress of the resolution in the House of Representatives, however, was far more halting, suggesting a more complex political picture. The resolution was introduced in the House on January 18, 1813, yet even after the Senate had acted, the House still balked, perhaps because it was soon to recess. Serious debate on the amendment appears (based on incomplete congressional records) to have begun only a year later, in January 1814.[16]

The case for the amendment was spearheaded by Israel Pickens, an ambitious North Carolina Republican who later moved to Alabama (where he served as governor while becoming a wealthy planter and banker).[17] Clearly troubled by the recent tumult in his state ("which caused more agitation . . . than had been witnessed since the Government commenced"), he believed that it was imperative for the nation to adopt "some uniform method of appointing Electors." As long as state legislatures were free to decide the mode of selection, parties would quarrel over the issue, and "at the eve of our elections sudden changes will be made or attempted." The upshot would be "much crimination and recrimination, which naturally produce an irritation in the public feelings, always unpleasant and often dangerous." District elections, according to Pickens, were preferable to the general ticket or legislative selection because they best matched the "maxim that all legitimate power is derived from the people" and because they would sharply reduce the odds that "a man may be elected to the first office of the nation by a minority of votes of the people." District contests would also produce "less sectional" political parties than any winner-take-all scheme. Finally, Pickens noted that district elections would eliminate the practice of "a caucus or self-appointed committee" choosing a slate of electors and thereby prevent the "intrigue and corruption" that could arise when critical decisions were left in the hands of a small number of legislators.[18]

Pickens's argument was dramatically seconded by his fellow North Carolinian, Federalist William J. Gaston. Gaston, a Catholic (the first student ever enrolled at Georgetown College and, soon after, its first dropout), was a widely respected attorney and a slave-owning opponent of slavery who later became an influential justice of the North Carolina Supreme Court. Nationally known for his eloquence, Gaston opened his floor speech by declaring his "reverence'" for the "sacred character" of the Constitution (an invocation that was *de rigueur* by 1814) while insisting that an amendment was needed "to rescue it from perversion and abuse." (The rhetorical challenge confronting all amendment advocates was to make a compelling case for change without appearing to disparage the judgment of the framers.) "It is well known," Gaston observed, "that no part of the plan of a Federal Government presented greater difficulties to the illustrious men who framed it, than that which relates to the appointment of the executive." He then sketched, with considerable accuracy, the reasoning that had led the founders to devise the complex electoral system, including their desire to avoid "cabal, intrigue, and corruption" by making the electors "transient" and by barring members of Congress (and other federal officeholders) from serving as electors. "It was contemplated that the people from each state should select from among the wisest and most virtuous of their neighbors, the persons best qualified to vote for a President," and those electors would convene "under circumstances the most favorable to deliberation." Gaston presumed that the framers had left it to state legislatures to determine how electors should be chosen because they anticipated a period of experimentation after which the method "which should ultimately be found most judicious ... would generally be adopted."[19]

"Thus beauteous smiled the theory," Gaston intoned, but "how hideous the deformity of the practice!" Despite the wise "outlines" provided by the framers, what had emerged was a "monstrous" process dominated by self-seeking politicians and parties. The discretion granted to states had given rise to "perpetual fluctuation," to recurrent "struggles between contending parties to render the mode of appointment subservient to their immediate" partisan interests. These struggles undermined the stability of the nation's institutions and were so blatantly unprincipled that members of the same political party sometimes advocated district elections in one state and legislative selection in another. In addition, the growing use of winner-take-all meant that a president could be chosen who "obtained the support of a little more than one-fourth of the nation!" This was contrary to the intentions of the founders and "revolting to our republican notions."[20]

Nor was that all. Gaston, who had begun fighting for reform in the legislature in November 1812, was particularly incensed that the practice of presidential politics had undermined the framers' key goal of minimizing "intrigue" and "cabal." Members of Congress, who were to have been kept at arm's length from the choice of a chief magistrate, were instead gathering in partisan caucuses to nominate the candidates. Similarly, state legislatures had taken it upon themselves to directly choose the electors or, in general-ticket states, to construct slates of electors known to be sup-porters of particular candidates. As a result, "pre-existing bodies of men, and not the people, make the appointment" of the chief magistrate. ("The right of election is virtually exercised by the Legislatures, and only for-mally by the people," concluded one of Gaston's colleagues.) An amend-ment guaranteeing that all electors would be chosen through district elec-tions would restore influence to the people and, in so doing, help to realize the original vision of the founders.[21]

The arguments advanced by Pickens and Gaston were powerful, fusing widely accepted Republican principles with evidence drawn from recent elections and well-known events. Notably, their adversaries seem not to have presented an equally forceful case: the frustratingly incomplete records of the debates hint that the amendment's opponents did not offer extensive rationales for their position, and Gaston himself commented that he wished that "some of the gentlemen who were averse to its adoption would have fully stated the grounds upon which their opposition was founded."[22] The champions of rhetoric, however, did not carry the day: on January 31, 1814, the House voted its "disagreement" with the Senate's resolution, by a solid margin.[23] As had been true in the Senate, most Republicans appeared to favor district elections, and a large majority of Federalists were opposed—but Federalists were proportionately more numerous in the House and thus had a greater impact on the tally. Foreshadowing later patterns, many large-state representatives also tended to oppose the amendment, and they constituted nearly 60 percent of the House.[24] (See Tables 2.1 and 2.3.)

Proponents of an amendment were undeterred by their defeat in the House and buoyed by their victory in the Senate. From 1816 into the mid-1820s, district elections resolutions were introduced into every Congress, often at the behest of state legislatures. In addition to North Carolina, formal proposals for amendments came from the legislatures of New Jersey, Massachusetts, New York, Virginia, Connecticut, Pennsylvania, and, later, Illinois.[25] Governors also weighed in: New Hampshire's William Plumer asserted in a speech to his legislature that the "most equal and proper" mode of choosing electors was through district elections. In Congress, leading advocates, such as Senator Mahlon Dickerson of New Jersey, shared Benjamin Huger's view that the period after the 1816 election was particu-larly propitious for reform. Pickens observed that when the House had considered the issue two years earlier, it had been "at a moment . . . not favorable to a mature deliberation." In contrast, "if ever there was a period favorable to a proper amendment of the Constitution, it was the present moment, when we are literally at peace, at home and abroad."[26]

When the congressional debates resumed—and as they continued year after year—advocates of change echoed, extended, and broadened the arguments put forward in 1813–1814. Their point of departure was, as New York's Federalist senator Rufus King put it, that "the election of the President of the United States is no longer that process the Constitution contemplated." (King spoke with some authority since he had been a delegate to the Constitutional Convention in 1787.)[27] Members of both chambers offered harsh portraits of recent elections, often rivaling the apocalyptic rhetoric of Pickens and Gaston. Dickerson, a dedicated Jeffersonian and former governor of New Jersey who led the campaign for change in the Senate from 1818 into the mid-1820s, observed that the historical record offered "the most deplorable proofs of the imbecility of our system." (Dickerson had witnessed firsthand his state's electoral shenanigans in 1812.) A House member claimed that the process of choosing a president "might be called a political farce, but for the importance of the actors, and the weight of the results." Although he opposed an amendment, the acerbic Representative John Randolph of Virginia acknowledged, in words frequently cited, that what unfolded every four years was "a mockery, the shadow of a shade of an election."[28]

The reformers had an array of specific complaints. One was the lack of "uniformity" or "permanence" in the manner of choosing electors: practices not only varied from state to state but could change from one election to the next, usually for partisan reasons. Huger, in 1816, alluded to the "various turns, and twists, and quirks, which had alternately been adopted by different states or rather predominant factions in different states, to insure a result of the election of the day favorable to their wishes and views." Five years later, Representative Ezra Carter Gross of New York voiced his objection to "the present variety of modes, adopted by the different States, and the power of change to suit the times." To Huger, Gross, and many others, there was something corrupt, even illegitimate, about a system that permitted partisan actors to change the electoral rules as an election approached. That such actions were legal offered evidence of a flaw in the constitutional structure that opened "a boundless field . . . for the intrigues of ambitious men and ambitious states." New York representative Jabez Hammond (later a prominent historian) declared that "the power of the states to choose . . . the manner of choosing Electors . . . is a rotten, a gangrenous part of our Constitution, which if not removed will infect and poison the body politic."[29]

An equally important target of the reformers was the practice of allocating all of a state's electoral votes to one candidate, through either the general ticket or legislative selection. By 1816, winner-take-all operated in sixteen out of nineteen states, and its predominance, reformers pointed out, was itself the consequence of partisan jockeying: Virginia in 1800 was only the most famous example. The defects of winner-take-all, moreover, were numerous. It deprived political minorities of any voice in the electoral colleges, as Representative James Strudwick Smith of North Carolina observed in 1820. Majority parties "resort to that mode of electing Electors that would promise most effectually to stifle the voice of the minority, and . . . give the greatest majority in favor of the dominant party."[30] Winner-take-all also heightened the risk of installing a president who was supported by only a minority of the population: numerous speakers conjured up hypothetical examples of such an occurrence, complete with detailed arithmetic.[31] In addition, statewide blocs of votes had "the effect of encouraging sectional feelings and divisions," which could easily tend toward "disunion."[32] Some critics took a further step, holding winner-take-all elections responsible for exacerbating partisan strife by raising the stakes of each contest, especially in the larger states. "Everything is put to hazard," noted Dickerson in 1819. "A party must gain or lose all: there is no intermediate point on which to rest." Despite the collapse of the Federalist Party, winner-take-all "tends to create and keep alive that party animosity, that political warfare, which almost constantly agitates and distracts the larger states."[33]

Both legislative selection and the general ticket were attacked on democratic grounds as well. (The words *democracy* and *democratic* appeared rarely in these debates, although references to "the people" and "popular government" were plentiful.) Legislative selection was "the worst possible system of choosing Electors," according to Dickerson, because it "usurped the power of appointing electors," departing "from the spirit if not from the letter of the Constitution." His New Jersey colleague, Representative John Linn, noted succinctly that in some states, "the legislatures choose the electors and the people have nothing to do with it."[34]

The general ticket was better but still deeply flawed. It permitted the people to cast ballots, but their choices were limited to slates of electors chosen by legislative committees and caucuses. The process of selection was often secretive and subject to "the most extensive intrigues," and because slates were prepared for an entire state, voters could have little acquaintance with the electors. "The people, instead of having a personal knowledge of those for whom they vote, must take their characters on trust," complained Republican senator (and former House Speaker) Nathaniel Macon of North Carolina in 1816. Dickerson was more emphatic: a process "where the voters can know nothing of the characters of four-fifths of the candidates for whom they vote" was "a total dereliction of every principle of republicanism."[35] "General tickets . . . are a great evil," wrote Hezekiah Niles in 1816, referring to both presidential and congressional elections, because they undermined the "principle . . . of representation," and turned elections into matters "of prejudice or party" rather than "reason or judgment."[36] Such vehement criticism made it clear that, in some circles at least, the general ticket was regarded not as a legitimate alternative to district elections but as a mechanism that improperly relocated power from citizens to legislators and party managers. Little wonder that John Marshall, the Chief Justice of the Supreme Court, stopped voting in presidential elections after Virginia adopted the general ticket—and believed that he "never should vote during its continuance."[37]

Many of these arguments were infused with anti-party sentiments. The core narrative of reformers was that the constitutional process for electing presidents had been deformed, even hijacked, by what Dickerson in 1819 referred to as "the disorganizing spirit of party."[38] Individual politicians, political parties, and factions within parties were routinely doing all they could to win presidential elections, and that included exploiting loopholes or ambiguities in the law or even bending the rules altogether.[39] According to Huger, presidential campaigns and the legislative elections that preceded them included "a train of abuses, which had sprung up of late years, and been introduced by artful and intriguing men, to influence elections and take them virtually, if not nominally, out of the hands of" the people.[40] If the constitutional framework had been designed to shield the selection of the chief executive from congressional and factional scheming, it had failed: candidates were nominated by partisan congressional caucuses and the electors who cast the ballots were chosen by equally partisan state legislators.[41] Senator Jeremiah Mason of New Hampshire feared that Congress and the state legislatures, acting in concert, "would forever give a President to the United States."[42]

The advocates of reform, however, did not believe that the solutions to these grave problems were to be found in a revival of the political order imagined by the framers or in President Monroe's vision of a future without parties. Tacitly accepting the presence of parties, they pursued a change to the Constitution that would circumscribe the ability of parties and factions to engage in "intrigue" or "mischief." (No word was deployed more often in these debates than *intrigue*.) Dickerson, in a grand peroration delivered in the Senate in January 1819 (it would not be his last) declared that "the proposed amendment" would not "afford a remedy for all of the evils complained of; but it will afford a remedy for part of them. It will not eradicate the principles of ambition, but it will retard their progress."[43] If a district elections amendment were adopted, methods of choosing electors would become uniform across the country and consistent from one election to the next. Such a change would, as James Smith put it, "give the minority as well as the majority of the people of every State, a chance of being heard," and the odds of a president being chosen without the support of a national majority would be greatly reduced. As an added bonus, "sectional feelings will, in some degree, be broken down, and union and harmony will be effectually preserved."[44]

Of equal importance, district elections promised to decentralize the process of selecting a president and, in so doing, to strengthen the sinews of popular government. "All power is declared to be derived from the people," Jabez Hammond reminded his colleagues in 1816. The key step, asserted Mason, was to put each elector "within the sphere of the personal knowledge of those who are to choose him," a goal that was not implausible in a nation that counted one representative in Congress for every 40,000 inhabitants. The people in each district could choose as an elector "a man with whom they are acquainted, on whose intelligence and virtue they can rely," Smith noted.[45] Mason and Smith were not proposing that electors deliberate in the manner envisioned by the framers—although that perspective was suggested by some who viewed district elections for members of the House and presidential electors as closely parallel endeavors. Yet embedded in their remarks was something deeper than a strategy for avoiding mischief: a conception of politics more tightly binding the local to the national, coupled with a vision of an engaged people, rather than states or parties, taking the lead in choosing a president. "You will bring the election near to the people," Smith continued, "and, consequently you will make them place more value on the elective franchise, which is all-important in a republican form of Government."[46]

DEFENDING THE SYSTEM (AND A FEW REBUTTALS)

Members of Congress who preferred to retain the status quo, perhaps sensing that the tide of public opinion was flowing against them, fought back hard against the reformers and their crusading rhetoric. In 1816 Senator James Barbour of Virginia, a prominent Republican (and a friend of Jefferson) denied that a serious problem existed. There was, he maintained, "no danger to the liberties of the people from the present mode of electing a President." He found it appropriate that caucuses nominated candidates, because members of Congress had "knowledge" of "public sentiment," and electors chosen through the general ticket were a fair reflection of "public opinion." "The electors," he observed, "are only the organs of that public sentiment which has been long and unequivocally made up." Several years later Barbour, a shrewd and vocal opponent, shifted ground, acknowledging that abuses had taken place but arguing that it was "vain to argue against a system because bad men, when in power, occasionally abuse it."[47]

The most pointed, and perhaps most resonant, argument against an amendment was that it would deprive the states of a right granted to them in the Constitution and thereby disturb the carefully negotiated balance of power between the states and the federal government. Jefferson's curmudgeonly cousin, John Randolph, who was always a fierce defender of states' rights and often at odds with his own party, opened a lengthy speech in 1816 by declaring that "he was opposed to this resolution for the simple reason that it contemplated an abridgment of the powers of the States— that was enough for him." The amendment before Congress struck "at the very root of the Constitution," and it was "his duty to oppose any proposition which" might "diminish the actual existing powers of the States." Randolph, a self-described "aristocrat" who spoke disparagingly of "popular government" while also condemning slavery, offered a withering critique of Virginia's use of the general ticket, but insisted that Virginians, and not the federal government, ought to address that problem. Congress should not "dare to think itself competent to interfere between the Legislature and the people of Virginia."[48]

Other members of Congress, many with less extreme views of states' rights, also regarded the amendment as endangering the "federative" structure of the government. Thomas Grosvenor of New York, for example, saw it as a giant step toward "a consolidated popular government" that would "strip the states of their dignity and sovereignty" and strike "at the very root of our safety." Opponents also argued that states as entities—and not just the people inhabiting them—were intended to have a role in selecting presidents, a claim that lent legitimacy to both the general ticket and the right of legislatures to decide how electors would be chosen. "In the choice of electors," according to Barbour, "the people and the sovereignty of a State are represented." Less abstractly, Joseph Brevard of South Carolina inclined "in favor of preserving the power which the several states now have" rather than "vesting it in the Congress."[49]

Randolph also gave voice to another oft-repeated objection to the proposed amendment: it would "change the actual existing compromise of weight and influence in this government, between the greater and small States." This was so because district elections would likely divide the electoral votes of large states and thus reduce their power in choosing a president. To Randolph, such an outcome meant that the "great" states would cease to have influence in proportion to their populations, undermining another compromise built into the Constitution. A large state that shared its electoral votes evenly between two candidates would find "its influence ... completely neutralized."[50] Barbour, among others, spotted a further disadvantage for the large states: choosing electors by district, he alleged, would increase the likelihood that elections would end up in the House of Representatives, where all states, large and small, would have only one vote. If the House were to decide elections more often, small states would gain influence at the expense of larger ones. Not for the first—or last—time, the complex compromises woven into the electoral system presented an obstacle to reform.[51]

In the spring of 1816, New York's Grosvenor, a Federalist, attacked the district elections proposal on still other grounds. He acknowledged that "in many of the States the managers of a party have converted the right of election into a farce, by intrigues and violence, without precedent or parallel." But he insisted that the proposed amendment would not alleviate these problems. Abuses and manipulation would still occur, in congressional caucuses as well as state legislatures, and it would still be possible for a minority of the people to "elect a chief Magistrate."[52] Grosvenor also pointed squarely at a serious potential defect of district elections: "gerrymanders." (This new word, imported from Massachusetts, had quickly entered the political language.) He recounted his own experience with the process of drawing district boundaries for New York's legislature:

> Counties were cut and slashed in every direction; districts, single, double, and treble, of every shape and of every size, were manufactured; cities were sundered, and the parts whose political character was not of the right sort were connected with counties at the distance of an hundred miles; towns were cut out of the very heart of a county, and annexed to other counties. In short, no device, however shameful, was omitted to obtain the result, and the result was obtained.

If presidential electors were chosen by district, he insisted, gerrymanders would abound, and "each district . . . will become the victim of caucus influence, State intrigue, and Executive patronage." "With these facts in full view," Grosvenor concluded, "can gentleman hope any good from their district plan?"[53]

These criticisms may have given some representatives pause, but the amendment's principal backers were not swayed, responding with counterarguments and a modest alteration of the amendment itself. Huger acknowledged that mandatory district elections might reduce the influence of the large states, but this, he maintained, would simply restore the constitutional balance that had prevailed before the passage of the Twelfth Amendment (which had made it less likely that elections would go to the House).[54] Others opined that a minor diminution in the influence of large states was a small price to pay to rescue elections from the maneuvers that robbed the people of their rightful power. Hammond, thus, was "willing . . . that the influence of the great States . . . should be diminished. While I say this, I do not forget that I come from a great state." Ezra Gross, a fellow New Yorker, foreshadowed views that would become common in the mid-twentieth century. "What matters it," he pleaded, "whether the Electors of this or that state be divided or in the minority, so long as the majority of the people of the United States prevail?"[55]

Advocates of district elections also addressed the sensitive, even combustible, federalism issue that Randolph, Barbour, and others had raised. There was no denying that an amendment would take from state legislatures a power that they had wielded since the nation's birth. But this was "no violation of first principles," declared North Carolina's Smith in 1820, emphasizing that the number of electoral votes allotted to each state would not change. Ezra Gross believed that the loss to the states was minimal. The amendment "exchanged the insignificant State right of altering, from year to year, the mode of choosing Electors, for the permanent benefit of enabling the voice of the people to be heard." Others claimed that the framers had never intended to permit legislatures to choose electors by themselves and that therefore the amendment was consistent with "the true spirit and intention of the original constitution."[56]

Sponsors of the measure also offered a concession to the defenders of states' rights: they modified the proposed amendment so that two of each state's electors would be selected in a fashion to be determined by the state legislature while the remainder would be chosen in elections to be held in each congressional district. This idea was first put forward in the House in 1816 by Erastus Root of New York, and by 1818 it had become the standard text of amendment proposals. Root maintained that this arrangement fairly embodied the competing principles that shaped the Constitution: the people would choose electors equal in number to their state's representation in the House while "the other two in each State, who were to represent the State sovereignties, ought to continue to be chosen as the Legislature might direct." It would also be very "inconvenient," he added, to create two sets of districts, one for House elections and the other for electors. Barbour, always argumentative, dismissed the proposal as "an insult" to the large states that stripped away their real strength and left them with only an "effigy" of their "former power."[57]

These arguments cycled through Congress from 1813 to 1822, with some drama and much repetition, as successive iterations of the amendment resolution made their way through the Senate and the House. By January 1819, Dickerson lamented that "the subject is old and hacknied." Three years later he declared that there were "no new arguments" to offer, and there was "probably not a man in the Union . . . whose mind was not fully made up on the subject."[58] Whether the views of members of Congress accurately mirrored the opinions of men "in the Union" is, of course, impossible to determine. Nor, unfortunately, is there any way to judge how influential these debates may have been—whether members of Congress, or the public, were persuaded by particular arguments, by the soaring rhetoric and inventive examples, by the visions of calamity proffered by both friends and foes of the amendment. There is also no way to readily distinguish between arguments that stemmed from firm convictions and those that were mobilized as debating points or masked more self-interested motives. Presumably, some of each were present on both sides of the debate.

What the years of debate do make clear is that the impetus to mandate district elections emerged from profound and widespread concerns about the practice of presidential politics. It also tapped into significant disagreements about the appropriate limits of federal power, the proper organization of politics in a republic, and the wisdom of altering the Constitution (which was not amended at all between 1804 and 1865). The debates were framed—and the issues understood—largely as a set of conflicts, or trade-offs: between the right of the people to actively participate in choosing electors and the right of states to determine how electors would be chosen; between the desire of political minorities within states to have their preferences count and the desire of states (or majorities within states) to maximize their influence; between the palpable need to bring uniformity and stability to the election process (and thus avoid partisan manipulation) and a reluctance to begin unraveling the compromises entwined in the details of the electoral system; between the democratic virtues of localized, district elections and the awkward truth that such elections could be ensured only by augmenting the power of the central government in Washington. Coursing through the discourse was also considerable unease about the role of legislators in choosing a chief executive and about the extent to which electoral competition itself was being managed and choreographed by politicians, factions, and parties.

FALLING SHORT

The outcome of these multiyear debates is not a secret: no amendment resolutions were approved by both branches of Congress and forwarded to the states for ratification. Nonetheless, the strength and breadth of support for mandatory district elections were notable. More than 60 percent of the Senate favored constitutional change throughout the decade from 1813 through 1822. District elections amendments were approved by the requisite two-thirds votes in 1813, 1819, 1820, and 1822; in 1818 the approval figure was 61 percent (two votes short of passage), and procedural votes suggest that there was strong support in 1816 as well.[59] (See Figure 2.1.)

In the House, the story was more complicated. After the decisive defeat in 1814, support for the measure began to climb. In December 1816 a resolution was tabled after it received a positive vote (on a second reading) of eighty-seven to fifty-one (63 percent), just shy of the two-thirds necessary "to sanction the proposition eventually." In 1819 a resolution forwarded by the Senate was read twice but then thwarted by procedural maneuvering, never receiving a final vote.[60]

Thanks both to the Senate's persistence and to an ongoing flow of resolutions from the states, the pressure on the House mounted, with the drama coming to a head in the winter of 1820–1821. In January 1820 the Senate had again approved a district elections amendment (both for presidential electors and for the House of Representatives) and sent it forward to the House. The House debate opened in the spring, but the issue was tabled until Congress reconvened in the fall. In late November, James Smith of North Carolina relaunched the debate, imploring his colleagues to pass the resolution and thus "allow the question to be submitted to the people of the United States, as represented in the several state legislatures."[61] On December 5 the House voted 103–59 (64 percent) to print a final copy of the resolution and have it read a third time (in preparation for the decisive vote). With the margin expected to be close, both sides engaged in a few additional weeks of legislative jockeying: postponing votes, tabling the resolution, offering modifications (including the possible excision of the provision aimed at elections to the House), and encouraging speaker after speaker to take the floor.[62] Finally, on January 25, 1821, the House voted 92–54 in favor of the resolution, six votes short of the two-thirds majority that would have sent the amendment to the states for ratification.[63]

Breakdowns of the roll call votes in Congress make clear that support for district elections was broad and not confined to any party or region. (See Tables 2.1 and 2.2.) Although Federalists had strongly opposed an amendment in 1813–1814, their views shifted thereafter, with most voting favorably starting in 1818, a stance befitting a shrinking minority party that had something to gain from ending winner-take-all. More consequentially, at least 60 percent of Republicans favored an amendment in every congressional vote from 1813 thru 1822, except that of 1814 (when 54 percent favored it). Ample support could also be found in both the North and the South, although northern preferences were weaker before 1819: the figures for the two regions were nearly identical in the decisive House vote of 1821.[64] Unsurprisingly, members of Congress from the handful of states that

TABLE 2.2: CONGRESSIONAL VOTES ON DISTRICT ELECTIONS
BY REGION, 1813–1822

	North[a]		South[a]	
Year (chamber)	Percentage (number) voting in favor[b]	Number not voting	Percentage (number) voting in favor[b]	Number not voting
1813 (Senate)	60 (9)	(3)	81 (13)	(2)
1814 (House)	22 (19)	(17)	74 (45)	(16)
1818 (Senate)	50 (8)	(3)	71 (12)	(3)
1819 (Senate)	81 (17)	(1)	65 (11)	(3)
1820 (Senate)	80 (16)	(2)	59 (13)	(0)
1821 (House)	63 (52)	(22)	63 (40)	(15)
1822 (Senate)	76 (16)	(3)	68 (13)	(4)

Source: Roll call data obtained from Howard Rosenthal and Keith T. Poole, *United States Congressional Roll Call Voting Records, 1789–1990* (Pittsburgh, PA, 2000), http://doi.org /10.3886/ICPSR09822.v2; 26 Annals of Cong. 828–844, 1198–1199 (1813–1814).

a. North: Connecticut, Massachusetts, New Hampshire, New Jersey, New York, Ohio, Pennsylvania, Rhode Island, Vermont, Indiana (first represented in Congress in 1818), Maine (first represented in Congress in 1822). South: Delaware, Georgia, Kentucky, Louisiana, Maryland, North Carolina, South Carolina, Tennessee, Virginia, Mississippi (first represented in Congress in 1818), and Missouri (first represented in Congress in 1822).

b. Percentage among those who cast votes.

already utilized district elections tended to favor the amendment resolutions by large margins (above 80 percent), but they had plenty of company: beginning in 1818 a majority of those from winner-take-all states also voted positively.[65]

The roll call votes also indicate that a key factor influencing the tallies was the size of the state from which a member of Congress came. (See Table 2.3.) This was the only consistently significant variable, and it matched the content of the debates.[66] Senators and House members who came from small states generally voted in high proportions for the amendments; those from medium-sized states also tended to vote favorably, but by smaller margins; and the percentages were lowest for members of Congress who hailed from the largest states. To be sure, there was ample support for district elections even in the large states, particularly in some years, but the levels of support were generally below (and sometimes well below) the critical threshold of 67 percent.

The relationship between state size and favorable votes sheds light on why the amendments fared better in the Senate than in the House: there were proportionately more votes from large states in the House. In 1820–1821, for example, only 10 of the 44 senators (23 percent) came from the largest states (Virginia, New York, Pennsylvania, Massachusetts, and North Carolina); in the House, in contrast, 106 representatives (58 percent) came from those states. A slim majority of those representatives (52 percent) voted favorably in the roll call vote of 1821, but the proportion was low enough to prevent passage of the amendment.[67]

That said, not too much weight should be given to state size alone as a determinant of an elected official's stance toward reform. Although representatives from large states were, on the whole, less receptive to change than were their colleagues from smaller states, the votes cast by the delegations from the five largest states were far from uniform.[68] In 1821, for example, strong majorities from Virginia and Pennsylvania did vote against the amendment in the House, but the opposite was true for the delegations from New York, North Carolina, and Massachusetts. That North Carolina's congressmen unanimously favored district elections likely reflected popular sentiments still aroused by the machinations that took place in 1812; New York's split, but positive, vote surely had roots in the incessant skirmishing between Van Buren and DeWitt Clinton. Most importantly, the variations from state

TABLE 2.3: CONGRESSIONAL VOTES ON DISTRICT ELECTIONS
BY STATE SIZE, 1813–1822[a]

Year (chamber)	Small Percentage (number) voting in favor[b]	Small Number not voting	Medium Percentage (number) voting in favor[b]	Medium Number not voting	Large Percentage (number) voting in favor[b]	Large Number not voting
1813 (Senate)	80 (8)	(4)	64 (7)	(1)	70 (7)	(0)
1814 (House)	50 (2)	(1)	51 (25)	(20)	39 (37)	(12)
1818 (Senate)	60 (6)	(0)	67 (10)	(4)	50 (4)	(2)
1819 (Senate)	75 (9)	(0)	75 (12)	(4)	70 (7)	(0)
1820 (Senate)	77 (10)	(1)	68 (13)	(1)	60 (6)	(0)
1821 (House)	100 (7)	(0)	76 (41)	(16)	52 (44)	(21)
1822 (Senate)	93 (13)	(2)	72 (13)	(3)	38 (3)	(2)

Sources: Roll call data obtained from Howard Rosenthal and Keith T. Poole, *United States Congressional Roll Call Voting Records, 1789–1990* (Pittsburgh, PA, 2000), http://doi.org/10.3886/ICPSR09822 .v2; 26 Annals of Cong. 828–844, 1198–1199 (1813–1814). State size based on U.S. Census Bureau, *2000 Census of Population and Housing, Population and Housing Unit Counts PHC-3-1, United States Summary* (Washington, DC, 2004).

a. State size as measured by number of representatives in the House. Categories were adjusted after 1820 census:

   1813–1820: Small, 1–4 representatives; medium-sized, 5–11 representatives; large, 12 or more representatives

   1821–1822: Small, 1–4 representatives; medium-sized, 5–12 representatives; large, 13 or more representatives

b. Percentage among those who cast votes.

to state underscored the presence of diverse factors that could, and did, influence the votes of representatives from large (and all other) states.[69]

SOURCES OF DEFEAT

Leading reform advocates like Dickerson, Huger, and Pickens proved to have been correct in gauging that the Era of Good Feelings would be an auspicious time to press for presidential election reform. After years of intermittent debate, Congress came extremely close to approving an amendment that would have significantly—and probably permanently—transformed the conduct of presidential elections. It would not get that close again until the late 1960s.

That the effort fell short was due, in good part, to the constitutional requirement that amendments be approved by supermajorities in both branches. The sponsors of reform measures repeatedly convinced a majority of their colleagues to join them, but they could not quite get to the two-thirds mark in the House. Their inability to clear that high hurdle had multiple sources, as is always the case when the switch of a handful of votes could have reversed the outcome. Certainly the pockets of self-interested resistance in the large states (especially Virginia and Pennsylvania) played an important role. In addition, some members of Congress surely embraced the states' rights arguments put forward by Randolph and others; wary of federal authority, they voted against the amendment because they did not want their states to surrender any right, or power, granted to them by the Constitution. It also seems likely that there were leaders of state parties or factions who preferred to stick with winner-take-all for partisan reasons that would probably not be voiced in congressional debates. As Dickerson pointed out in 1819, the reform amendment "proposes to the dominant parties in the respective States, without whose aid it cannot succeed, to give up a portion of their power. Such applications are always unwelcome, and but rarely attended with success, whether made to individuals, to States, or to political parties."[70]

Factors other than perceived self-interest were also in play, difficult as they may be to weigh. Some members may have found compelling Thomas Grosvenor's vivid depiction of gerrymandering in New York and thus shared his skepticism that district elections would put an end to partisan abuses. Others were loath to tinker with the Constitution, leading Dickerson to conclude that "there is . . . a sort of sanctity attached to this instrument, that leads many to . . . consider any attempt to alter it as a sort of political profanation; a sacrilege against the palladium of our liberties."[71] More hypothetically, the inclusion of a districting requirement for elections to the House in 1821 may have generated just enough opposition to doom the entire resolution.[72] Finally, one cannot rule out—for this period or any other—the presence of a temperamental bias in favor of the status quo. It is not difficult to imagine some of James Brevard's colleagues nodding in agreement when he observed, during the final arguments in the House in 1821, that "it is better . . . to bear those ills we have than to fly to others that we know not of."[73]

In retrospect, the House vote in January 1821 looms as an inflection point, an early high-water mark in the history of efforts to transform the Electoral College. For contemporary reformers, however, that near victory was one more measure of their strength: the issue retained its urgency, and having come so close to victory, advocates were not about to abandon the fight. Amendment resolutions, accordingly, were reintroduced in both the Senate and the House in December 1821. The Senate, after a brief discussion, approved an amendment by a very decisive vote of twenty-nine to eleven in March 1822. It then forwarded its resolution (once again) to the House, where it was read twice and "committed to the committee of the whole House on the state of the Union." The House took no further action in 1822.[74]

Then things got complicated.

1823–1824: A New Equation for Reform

You have probably noticed that the manner in which the Constitution as it stands may operate in the approaching election of President is multiplying projects for amending it. If Electoral Districts, and an eventual decision by joint ballot of the two Houses of Congress could be established it would I think be a real improvement; and as the smaller states would approve the one and the larger the other, a spirit of compromise might adopt both.

—James Madison to Thomas Jefferson, January 14, 1824

By the winter of 1822–1823, the eyes of political leaders were already fixed on the next presidential election. Unlike its predecessor, the coming contest promised to be highly competitive, and the early field of likely candidates was crowded with notables: Secretary of War John Calhoun; Henry Clay, the Speaker of the House; Treasury Secretary William Crawford; New York potentate DeWitt Clinton; Secretary of State John Quincy Adams; and General Andrew Jackson. All were nominally Republicans, but each had his own personal, factional, and geographic sources of support. The campaign began early because it was essential for candidates and their allies to acquire supporters in state legislatures the year before presidential ballots were cast.[75]

The impending election did not bring an immediate pause to reform efforts, but it did reshape them in three ways. The first was that some political leaders began to assess national proposals in terms of their potential impact on the prospects of individual candidates. The second unfolded within several key states, as different factions jockeyed to arrange a mode of choosing electors that would favor their candidates. The third was a direct consequence of the size of the contending field: with multiple candidates in the running, it seemed likely that no one would capture an electoral vote majority. As a result, renewed attention was focused on the constitutional provision for deciding such elections in the House of Representatives.

Indeed, the first amendment resolution filed in early 1823 called for an overhaul of the contingent election system. It was presented in the Senate by John Taylor of Caroline, a Virginian who had been active in public life since the late 1770s and was one of the era's most highly regarded political writers. Taylor proposed that, in the absence of an electoral vote majority for any candidate, the electors should vote a second time, choosing between the top two contenders (or more if there were a tie). If that second round of balloting failed to produce a majority winner, the decision would revert to a joint session of Congress (which would give states influence roughly in proportion to their populations). Taylor argued, at length and with passion, that his proposal would "prevent almost" the selection of the executive by the legislative branch, which he believed was "an unnatural and illegitimate connection of distinct powers and duties." He also made clear that he opposed district elections because they would increase the likelihood of a contingent election and contribute to the domination of the nation by "an aristocracy of small states."[76]

Within two days, Mahlon Dickerson rose to offer a substitute to Taylor's resolution. The New Jersey senator predictably insisted on district elections as an essential ingredient of electoral reform. But this time he added two new features to the proposal that he had championed for years. One was to limit presidents to two terms in office. The second was to transform the contingent election process in a manner similar to what Taylor had proposed. Dickerson opposed a second round of balloting by electors (because it invited "intrigue and corruption") but agreed with Taylor that, in the absence of a majority vote among electors, the decision should be made by all members of Congress, with each getting one vote.[77]

Dickerson's new proposal was designed not only to address multiple problems but to forge a political bargain, to enlist support from large and small states alike. The New Jerseyan, an astute political analyst little known to history, knew well that some large-state leaders continued to oppose district elections, and he could not deny that if electors were chosen by district, large states would often be unable to deliver sizable blocs of electoral votes to a candidate. But he was now offering the "great" states something in return for the influence they might surrender: significantly increased power if the election ended up in Congress. To the small states, he offered the inverse. A districting system would likely enhance their influence in the Electoral College, but they would end up with less clout if the decision went to Congress. As Senator John Holmes of Maine put it, Dickerson's proposal "increases the power of the small states in the *original* and reduces it in the *final* vote." This reconfigured compromise between large and small states appeared to offer Dickerson and his allies a path to the victory in Congress that had so far eluded them. It also had the virtue of doing away with a contingent process that departed sharply from the principle of majority rule and seemed out of step with the rising democratic ethos of the period. (The shortcomings of this process were becoming more salient as new small states were added to the nation and the gap in size between the largest and smallest states grew larger.) Dickerson's multipronged proposal was taken up and championed in the House by Representative George McDuffie of South Carolina, a sometime ally of Calhoun and Jackson.[78]

When the Eighteenth Congress convened in December 1823, additional reform ideas burst forward. The first—and most long-lived—came from recently elected senator Thomas Hart Benton, the dominant figure in Missouri politics from the 1820s into the 1850s. (Benton was also well known for having wounded Andrew Jackson in a brawl, although the two later became political allies.) Benton proposed, as he would do almost annually for twenty years, abolishing the office of elector and holding district elections in which the people would cast ballots directly for president and vice president. Each state would have as many districts as it had electoral votes, and the "person having the greatest number of votes for President" in each district would receive one electoral vote. A candidate would gain the presidency if he won a majority of the electoral votes.[79] Benton's brief for district elections added one new element to a roster of familiar claims: that only district elections could give voice to the diversity of economic interests (commerce, agriculture, and manufacturing) frequently present within a state.[80]

The distinctive feature of Benton's proposal was his plan to eliminate electors and have the people themselves cast ballots directly for president and vice president. The system created by the framers, he insisted, "has wholly failed in the execution." "The Electors," he claimed, "are not independent ... not useful" and "dangerous to the liberties of the people." This critique was common by the 1820s, but Benton went a step further, criticizing the framers for an institutional design that was inherently undemocratic. "Intermediate electors," he pointed out, "are the peculiar and favorite institution of aristocratic republics, and elective monarchies," while "a direct vote by the people" is the favored "institution of democratic republics." "This machinery," he maintained, "was introduced into our Constitution for the purpose of softening the action of the democratic element," and such buffers lessened citizens' interest in elections and placed "them at too great a distance from their first servant."[81]

Benton presented his proposal as a democratic one (he often used that word), and the arguments he made in its behalf celebrated the ways in which it would empower the people and heighten popular involvement with politics. There were, however, limits to the democratic polity that he envisioned. For one thing, Benton opposed making any changes to the contingent election system, defending it as necessary to protect the interests of small states like Missouri. A president, consequently, could still be chosen by men who represented a relatively small minority of the people. Benton also emphasized repeatedly—in response to apprehensions that arose about the meaning of "direct elections"—that his plan would not alter the allocation of electoral votes among the states. This coded assertion meant that the three-fifths clause (as well as the two "senatorial" electoral votes granted to each state) would be preserved. Benton acknowledged that the objections to a direct popular vote would "be fatal if the votes were to be consolidated in one general return" for the entire nation. But his direct elections system would avoid that pitfall. Benton's plan was designed to enhance democratic participation without jeopardizing the interests of the slave states.[82]

Other amendment resolutions were also introduced, signaling the presence of diverse perspectives and inventive legislators. South Carolina senator Robert Hayne was so eager to avoid congressional involvement in the choice of a president that he sought to require electors to keep balloting until one candidate achieved a majority. Such a step was urgent, he believed, because the growth of the country meant that "the probability of effecting an election at the first balloting of the electors will continue to diminish." (*Niles' Register* found Hayne's proposal to be "reasonable and rightful" as a means of keeping the legislative and executive branches "independent of the other.") Elijah Hunt Mills of Massachusetts advocated a return to the pre–Twelfth Amendment method of electing presidents and vice presidents. Martin Van Buren, then in the Senate, favored an amalgam of Dickerson's district plan with Taylor's scheme for a second round of balloting by the electors; this could be accomplished "in a spirit of mutual concession" between the large and small states. Maine's John Holmes endorsed Dickerson's proposal and also presciently, if unsuccessfully, argued that the Constitution needed a clear mechanism for adjudicating disputed presidential elections. In the House, Edward Livingston of Louisiana pressed for a direct vote and districting plan not unlike Benton's but added a new wrinkle: voters, in each district, would also cast ballots for electors who would convene only if no candidate received a majority of the electoral votes in the direct-vote election.[83]

Even James Madison joined in the fray—although he did so only in private correspondence. The seventy-two-year-old former president sketched out his ideas in response to inquiries from Virginia lawyer and politician, George Hay, and from South Carolina's McDuffie, who had sent Madison a copy of a committee report on electoral reform. Madison stressed to both men that he did not wish his views "to be brought into any public discussion," in part because it was "the propensity of the moment to view everything, however abstract" from the perspective of the forthcoming election. In his August 1823 letter to Hay, the son-in-law of President Monroe, Madison acknowledged that there were flaws in the constitutional design, attributing them to "the hurrying influence produced by fatigue and impatience" during the final weeks of the convention in Philadelphia. He explained why the framers had arrived at their formulation for a contingent election in the House but unhesitatingly declared it to have been a mistake. "The present rule of voting for President by the House of Representatives is so great a departure from the Republican principle of numerical equality . . . that an amendment of the Constitution on this point is justly called for by all its considerate and best friends." Madison recommended replacing the existing procedure with "a joint vote of the two Houses of Congress, restricted to the two highest names on the Electoral lists."[84]

Madison also made clear to Hay that he favored district elections for electors (which he believed to have been the intent of the framers) and that he thought it "very proper" to pursue this reform while also revamping the contingent election system. "A constitutional establishment" of district elections "will doubtless aid in reconciling the smaller States to the other change which they will regard as a concession on their part." Five months later, he commended McDuffie's committee report for "linking the amendments together, as a compromise between States who may mutually regard them as concessions." The foremost architect of the Constitution was, in effect, endorsing the idea of a revised contract between large and small states, one that would make both phases of presidential elections more democratic.[85]

Madison, who was following the public debates closely, also offered his opinions about other suggested reforms. He thought it unwise to choose a president by a plurality, rather than majority, vote, and he opposed abolishing the office of elector. He was also skeptical about any scheme that would have the electors meet and vote twice (or more), because such a process opened the door to "extraneous management and intrigue." As an alternative means of reducing the odds of an election ending up in Congress, Madison proposed a different mechanism: each elector would cast two ballots for president, one for his first-choice candidate and the other for his second choice. A candidate would become president if he received a majority of the votes on the "first choice" list or (if that did not occur) on the "second choice" list. "Such a process," Madison wrote, "would avoid the inconvenience of a second resort to the Electors; and furnish a double chance of avoiding an eventual resort to Congress."[86]

Madison's innovative idea of having each elector cast two ranked ballots never made its way into the congressional debates, but his worries about presidential elections being decided by Congress were widely shared. The presence of a large handful of candidates in the current campaign, coupled with the steady rise in the number of states, led many to conclude that electoral vote majorities would henceforth be difficult to achieve and that elections therefore would often be decided by the contingent mechanism. (Not for the last time in this story, short-term developments were mistakenly projected into long-term trends.) As a result, the debates during the key winter months of 1823–1824 focused less on districting (the arguments were familiar anyway) than on ways to modify contingent elections. The two issues, however, were not altogether separable—because some members of Congress, like John Taylor, believed that districting would make it significantly more difficult for any candidate to win an electoral vote majority. Robert Hayne also maintained that "under the district system," majorities would fail to be achieved "in nine cases out of ten," and thus the "substance" of Dickerson's resolution "would be to provide for the election of the Chief Magistrate by Congress and not by the people." Dickerson emphatically rejected that assertion, but he had no more evidence to support his rebuttal than Hayne had for his claim.[87]

Despite such disagreements, the House and the Senate moved forward with resolutions that would transform both phases of presidential elections beginning in 1828. (By midwinter it was widely acknowledged that no amendment could become law in time for the 1824 balloting.) In the House, a committee chaired by McDuffie recommended district elections to be followed, if necessary, by a second, runoff round of balloting by the electors. If that second round failed to produce a majority, the decision would pass to a joint session of Congress. A month later, the House postponed further consideration of this recommendation, seemingly to await developments in the Senate.[88]

In the upper chamber, a divided select committee, with Benton and Hayne dissenting, endorsed Dickerson's proposal for district elections and, if necessary, voting by a joint session of Congress.[89] Most speakers in the ensuing debate accepted the premise that it was imperative to alter a contingent election process that would permit small states with only 20 percent of the country's population to elect a president. (Senators from the smallest states were notably quiet.) They also seemed to agree that an electoral reform amendment could be successful only with a package of mutual concessions by the large and small states. The floor debate, moreover, contained promising signals that key players were prepared to negotiate and compromise. Van Buren announced that he would support a resolution even if he did not agree with all of its details; Hayne indicated that he would support district elections if the resolution included "a second ballot by the electors"; and Dickerson declared that he was not wedded to the idea of a joint ballot of the two houses of a Congress "if some better plan can be suggested."[90] Dickerson's proposal was similar enough to McDuffie's that action by both chambers seemed within reach.

The stage seemed to be set for a breakthrough—but none was forthcoming. By early March, it was apparent that no consensus had formed regarding the best approach to contingent elections. That fact, coupled with concerns about the "excitement" of the election campaign, prompted calls in the Senate to postpone further consideration until "a time when the public mind was not so much agitated on the subject of an election." (According to Senate rules, then as now, a motion for indefinite postponement had to be considered and decided before returning to the issue at hand.) One of the advocates of postponement, New York's elderly senator, Rufus King, then proceeded to derail the debate and shatter the decorum of the Senate by launching into a fierce attack on caucuses and the men who participated in them. Before amending the Constitution, King insisted, the Senate needed to recognize the presence of a "new, extraordinary, self-created central power . . . which . . . has assumed the direction and control of the fundamental provisions of the Constitution, relative to the election of the President." The members of Congress who composed this "central power," King maintained, were conspiring, dangerously and perhaps illegally, "to nominate the President of the United States eight months before his election." His angry, detailed indictment filled eight pages of the Annals of Congress and included the charge that caucus members spent more time politicking than "on the ordinary and regular business of Congress." King's views were not idiosyncratic. Criticism of caucuses was widespread, both within and outside of Washington; so too was the notion that members of Congress were overly preoccupied with "electioneering."[91]

King's barbs were felt by numerous colleagues who had participated in nominating caucuses, but his most obvious target was Van Buren, his fellow New Yorker, who had spent much of the winter trying, with limited success, to organize a caucus that would endorse the candidacy of William

Crawford. Ironically, King's attack came as the caucus system was already crumbling: Van Buren's gathering was attended by barely one quarter of members of Congress, and 1824 proved to be the last year in which a nominating caucus was held.[92] Nonetheless, King's charges provoked a storm of objections and counterattacks that went on for days, diverting the Senate's attention from the proposed amendments while souring the chamber's mood and perhaps the possibility of compromise. The venerable Nathaniel Macon, who had served in Congress since 1791, lamented the "extremely unfortunate circumstance, that a subject which had nothing to do with the real question before the Senate . . . was about to destroy all chance of considering the amendments to the Constitution." Macon pleaded with his colleagues to press forward for a solution ("there must be a concession of opinion somewhere"), but his pessimistic prediction proved to be well-founded. On March 22, the Senate voted thirty to thirteen to postpone "the whole subject indefinitely." The package of reforms that had seemed so promising was shelved until after the election.[93]

THE MELEE IN NEW YORK

Nowhere were the links between electoral reform and presidential politics in the 1820s played out more dramatically—even melodramatically—than in New York. For several years political life in the Empire State was roiled by the interplay between factional support for different presidential candidates and a widely popular effort to change the state's method of choosing electors. At stake were New York's thirty-six electoral votes, a grand prize that could easily, and probably did, determine the outcome of the 1824 election.[94] What unfolded was a bewilderingly complex, even zany, episode that vividly demonstrated both the need for reform and the difficulty of achieving it.[95]

The story began with Martin Van Buren, as did most things in New York politics during these years. After the elections of 1822, Van Buren appeared to be in firm control of the state. His arch nemesis, DeWitt Clinton, had left the governor's office, replaced by a Van Buren ally, Joseph Yates, and Van Buren's Bucktail faction (also called the Regency) was dominant in both houses of the state legislature. From his seat in the Senate, Van Buren could focus on national politics: he welcomed the opportunity to find a successor to James Monroe and expected to play a major role in the presidential contest. New York had more electoral votes than any other state, and its electors had always been chosen by the legislature.[96]

By the early months of 1823, Van Buren had decided to back Crawford, not least because Crawford's views about party, caucuses, and patronage were close to his own. He traveled extensively promoting the Georgian's candidacy, hoping to cement an alliance between New York and Virginia that would seal Crawford's nomination in a caucus. This prompted John Calhoun, a long-standing antagonist of Crawford's, to make a counter-move. He encouraged some of his allies in New York to launch a news-paper, the *New York Patriot*, that would openly criticize Van Buren for his many intrigues, including his support for caucuses. One proposal promi-nently put forward by the *Patriot* was to change New York's electoral law so that electors would be chosen not by the legislature but by the people, voting in districts.[97]

The idea caught fire, encouraged not only by Calhoun's supporters but by Clinton's forces, who relished the prospect of undermining the Regency. (Clinton himself had endorsed general-ticket, but not district, elections in 1820.) District elections were also, quite simply, a popular idea, and an overdue reform, in a state where a constitutional convention in 1821 had already taken key steps toward democratizing the polity. By the summer of 1823 the varied political groups endorsing electoral reform, including supporters of John Quincy Adams, formed the People's Party, which ran candidates in the November legislative elections. Many of these challengers defeated Republican candidates, while some Bucktails hung on to their of-fices by breaking with the Regency and pledging to support electoral re-form. Van Buren was sensitive to the dilemma faced by his allies in the legislature (it was "an awkward affair," he later reminisced), but he also knew that a popular election would render it difficult to deliver the state's elec-toral votes to Crawford.[98]

It was against this backdrop that Van Buren had risen on the floor of the Senate, on December 29, 1823, to endorse a federal amendment for district elections and to offer his own variant of such an amendment. The argu-ments he put forward were cogent and carefully phrased, yet the timing of Van Buren's intervention suggests that it was prompted more by his political problems in Albany than by his preference for district elections— which he was opposing in New York even as he celebrated their virtues in Washington. By embracing a federal amendment, which could not take effect for the 1824 election, Van Buren was identifying himself with the cause of reform while creating a democratic-sounding rationale for opposing change in New York: it would be better to have a nationally uniform mode of choosing electors than for a state to act on its own. Roughly a week later, in a message to the newly convened legislature, Governor Yates made precisely that argument. Pointing out that "the subject has recently been brought before congress," and asserting that it was a "propitious" moment for a federal amendment, Yates questioned "whether, under existing circumstances, the present manner of choosing electors ought, at this time, to be changed" in New York. Yates's circuitously worded message was widely interpreted as a recommendation that the legislature retain the power to select electors, and it offered legislators a plausible reason for doing so. Van Buren, in memoirs written decades later, professed to have been shocked by Yates's "unexpected" stance. At least a few others, including Rufus King, believed that the Crawford camp had dangled the vice presidency in front of Yates to induce him to oppose electoral reform.[99]

The legislature itself was too divided to pass a reform bill. In the assembly, where reform forces were strong, a bill was passed in early February 1824, but it was so watered down that it seemed unlikely to have much impact. The popular elections that it provided for would be binding only if a slate of electors received a majority of all the votes cast. If no slate received a majority (the likely result in 1824), the choice of electors would revert to the legislature. In the state senate, the reform forces were weaker: the assembly bill was referred to a committee, which reported, in early March, that it "would not be expedient" to pass such a measure as long as Congress was still considering a constitutional amendment on the subject. (Van Buren, at precisely this time, was arguing against an indefinite postponement of the amendment resolution in Washington.) After some tussling, further consideration of the measure was put off until November.[100]

Van Buren and his allies thus succeeded in blocking reform and keeping the selection of electors in the hands of the legislature. But victory had political costs: Governor Yates's role in the affair rendered him so unpopular that the Regency dumped him as a candidate for reelection, and many

Bucktail legislators, especially those who had reneged on their campaign promises to support reform, feared for their political futures. Above all, the Regency worried that its opposition to a popular measure was strengthening an alliance between Clintonites and the other political forces that had formed the People's Party. In an effort to strain that alliance and to punish the Clintonites, leaders of the Regency (apparently without Van Buren's knowledge) introduced a bill to remove DeWitt Clinton as president of the Erie Canal Commission, an unpaid position that he had held for fourteen years in recognition of his leadership in promoting the canal. Roger Skinner, the Bucktail lieutenant who devised this scheme, believed that the proposal would offer an unpalatable choice to legislators from the People's Party: either publicly support Clinton (who was unpopular in many quarters) or vote for his removal and create a rift with the Clintonites.[101]

The plan backfired—to say the least. The legislature did vote to remove Clinton from office, but that decision provoked an enormous public outcry, in part because Clinton's role in building the canal (a godsend to the western portions of the state) was widely appreciated. The public, moreover, saw through Skinner's maneuver and blamed the Bucktails, not the People's Party, for "this most glaring outrage . . . this act of violence and ingratitude." Making matters even worse, the outpouring of sympathy for Clinton led him to enter the gubernatorial race, which he won easily in November 1824, running as a champion of democratic causes (a new identity for him), including popular voting for electors and an end to legislative caucuses. Clinton's supporters and the People's Party also routed the Regency in legislative elections, taking control of the assembly and winning three-quarters of the contested senate seats. It was in the immediate aftermath of those elections that Van Buren famously berated Skinner that "there is such a thing in politics as *killing a man too dead*."[102]

Meanwhile, the shape of the presidential contest had changed significantly since the early winter of 1823–1824. Calhoun had withdrawn as a candidate (opting for the vice presidency) and signaled his support for Andrew Jackson, who was also popular in the South. Crawford's candidacy had grown weaker, in part because of a medical condition that raised questions about his capacity to serve. By the fall of 1824, most informed observers believed that the House would decide the election and that Jackson and

Adams were likely to be among the top three vote-getters whose names would be forwarded to the House. What was unclear was whether they would be joined by Crawford or by Henry Clay—who, as Speaker of the House, would have been well positioned to round up congressional votes. New York's electoral votes were key to the outcome.[103]

Fortunately for Van Buren and other supporters of Crawford, it was the lame duck legislature in New York, rather than the newly elected one, that chose presidential electors. Yet even that body was too fragmented for the Regency to control. The senate quickly generated a slate of thirty-six electors dominated by Clay supporters, but the assembly was splintered into different factions. What followed, over a period of weeks, was a labyrinthine sequence of maneuvers by all parties in both chambers, including deals made and unmade, lies, misrepresentations, dissembling, clandestine meetings, arguments over whether blank votes counted in the total, a double cross followed by a "double double cross," culminating in the selection by the legislature of twenty-five Adams electors, seven for Clay, and four for Crawford. The scheming did not end even there: somehow (threats were rumored), when the New York College of Electors finally met on December 1, Crawford ended up with five votes and Clay four. This belated shift in the totals proved to be just large enough to ensure that Crawford would be the third candidate considered by the House of Representatives. Precisely the kind of "intrigue" and manipulation that reformers in Congress had been denouncing for a decade helped to shape the election's outcome.[104]

* * *

In March 1825, New York's legislature did finally pass a law requiring that presidential electors be chosen in district elections. It was supported by both Clintonites and by the Regency and was ratified in a popular referendum the following November. As a result, the citizens of New York cast ballots in a presidential election for the first time in 1828. Andrew Jackson, strongly supported by Van Buren, narrowly outpolled President Adams that year and received twenty of the state's thirty-six electoral votes. Several months before the election, the Jackson camp had asked Van Buren if the choice of electors could be returned to the legislature, so that Jackson could capture all of the Empire State's electoral votes. Van Buren, having learned a hard lesson, dismissed the request. But the "Little Magician," as Van Buren was called, remained well aware of the advantages, to a party leader and power broker, of winner-take-all. DeWitt Clinton died in February 1828, and Van Buren was elected governor the following November. In the first and only formal message he delivered as governor (he resigned in March 1829, to become secretary of state), Van Buren asked the legislature to again change the electoral vote law so that electors would be chosen in a general-ticket election rather than by districts. The legislature quickly obliged.[105]

After 1824: Getting the Election Out of the House

If we refer to the number of resolutions, and the variety of opinions, it is clear that there is no unity of sentiment on the subject; and if gentlemen bring here the sentiments of their constituents, the People would appear to be as much divided as they are.

—Representative Dutee J. Pearce of Rhode Island, March 14, 1826

The 1824 election provided ample grist for the mills of electoral reformers. Once again the mode of choosing electors had been far from uniform: twelve states utilized the general ticket, six held district elections, and in six others the legislatures acted on their own. In addition, partisan battles over the mode of selection had erupted not only in New York but in Alabama and Indiana; and a new source of discontent emerged in several states (including North Carolina, Louisiana, and Missouri) when citizens complained that their representatives in the House cast ballots in the contingent election that did not reflect the views of their constituents.[106] For most political leaders, however, such issues were overshadowed by the controversial outcome of the election. Backers of Andrew Jackson were convinced that their candidate, rather than John Quincy Adams, ought to have been chosen by the House, because Jackson had garnered pluralities of both the electoral and the popular votes. Reports that the House's decision stemmed from a "corrupt bargain" between Adams and Speaker Henry Clay only heightened the sense of injustice. (The alleged bargain was that Clay threw his support to Adams in return for being appointed secretary of state, a common stepping stone to the presidency.) Such reports, although never verified, appeared to confirm fears that the contingent election process was corruptible—that there were dangers in permitting the legislature to choose the chief executive.[107]

The campaign for reform consequently resumed soon after the election was settled, propelled in part by a flood of resolutions from state legislatures.[108] In December 1825, George McDuffie set the terms for discussion in the House with a resolution calling for "a uniform system of voting by Districts" and, more vaguely, an amendment that "will prevent the election ... from devolving upon the respective Houses of Congress." In the Senate, Benton asked for a select committee to consider direct, district elections, and Hayne requested that the committee also look into amending the Constitution "to secure the election of President and Vice President ... without the intervention of the Senate or House of Representatives." The committee was appointed by Vice President Calhoun and included, among its nine members, Benton (as chair), Van Buren, Dickerson, Macon, and Hayne.[109]

The Senate committee delivered its report a month later. The nine members were unanimous in recommending "a uniform mode of election, by districts," the abolition of "the institution of electors" so that the people would vote directly for president and vice president, and a runoff election between the two highest vote-getters if no candidate received a majority of the electoral votes. (In the extremely unlikely event that a runoff ended in a tie, the election would revert to the House.) The report was written by Benton and bore his imprint, not least in its bombastic rhetoric and extended forays into Roman history. Much of it rehearsed arguments that he and others had put forward for years, including the claim that the defects of the electoral system were dampening turnout in presidential contests.[110]

What was new—and most noteworthy—about the report was its endorsement of a runoff election if no candidate received an electoral vote majority. That proposal had surfaced in 1823 without garnering much support, and Benton himself had opposed any change to the contingent election system. The recent election, however, had convinced the select committee that "it is almost a vain hope that the election of President can ever again be effected on the first trial," and the existing contingent procedure, although perhaps acceptable on rare occasions, would be intolerable as a regular occurrence. Despite coming from a very small state (Missourians cast fewer than 3,500 votes in 1824), Benton was now ready to relinquish the substantial influence wielded by small states in the contingent process. His committee's report implicitly recognized that Congress would never approve a district plan without changes to contingent elections and that a runoff election of some kind was the most plausible alternative to a decision made by Congress.[111]

Many of Benton's colleagues, however, were reluctant to enlist in his project, and discussion of the report was repeatedly postponed, effectively leaving the issue in the hands of the House. In that chamber, a passionate debate over McDuffie's resolution stretched out over four months, eventually filling hundreds of pages of congressional records. It was marked by numerous long speeches, many of which dissected and rebutted other long speeches. The arguments mattered because the issues were complex and the outcome was not a foregone conclusion.

The debate had several distinctive features. Prominent among them was a broad rhetorical consensus in favor of changing the contingent election system. No one disputed the claim of Romulus M. Saunders of North Carolina that "the election of President must, and will, hereafter, most usually devolve upon this House," and nearly all speakers endorsed the objective of keeping Congress from deciding presidential elections. (The idea of having elections decided by a joint session, popular before 1824, retreated from view.) We must "sunder," Churchill C. Cambreleng of New York insisted, "this unnatural union between the Legislator and his patron, the Executive." If they failed to do so, McDuffie and others argued, their personal reputations would be in jeopardy and instead of "the making of laws ... we shall be exclusively engrossed in making Presidents."[112] Notably, the felt urgency about altering the contingent election system turned upside down the arguments that had been made in 1823–1824 for a reform package affecting both phases of elections. At that time, changes to the contingent process were commonly presented as strategically necessary for reformers to achieve their primary goal of mandating district elections. In 1826, in contrast, district elections were often presented as a concession needed to induce the small states to agree to alter the contingent procedure, which was "the most important branch of the amendment." "The small States will never consent to give up their eventual equality in voting for the President, in this House," McDuffie insisted at the end of his major speech on the resolution, "unless the large States will consent to break their power of concentration and combination, by the establishment of the District System."[113]

The pervasive interest in disentangling Congress from presidential elections did not, however, yield a clear path forward. McDuffie's resolution provided a formal framework to the deliberations, but its only specific recommendation was for district elections, and therefore the door was open to a plethora of alternative schemes, particularly with regard to contingent elections. (McDuffie personally preferred a runoff election, but he was not adamant about it.) Those alternatives included awarding the presidency to the plurality winner of the electoral vote; retaining electors for the first ballot but having a direct-vote second round if no one gained a majority; holding a direct vote by districts in the first round and a vote by electors in the second round; repealing the Twelfth Amendment, with the provision that if no candidate received a majority of electoral votes, the states would choose among the two highest vote-getters, in a manner to be determined by each legislature (sponsored by future president James Buchanan); having a direct vote, by districts or by general ticket, with the proviso that the mode of election in any state would be unchangeable for eight years and never could be "changed within three years of any Presidential election"; and instituting a national popular vote (a "general vote, per capita through the United States") by white men only.[114] Variations on these themes were abundant.

In addition to spotlighting the contingent election process, the 1824 election left a legacy of rancor that suffused the debates in 1826 and hindered the formation of consensus. The Era of Good Feelings came to a resounding end in 1824–1825, and the factional cleavages that had emerged during the election campaign remained salient, in good part because of the election's contentious outcome. Jacksonian politicians and newspapers, as well as Old Hickory himself, never relented in their charge that the election had been stolen (or bought). They steadfastly opposed the Adams administration, began to organize a new party, and made it clear that Jackson planned to unseat the president in 1828. Backers of Adams and Clay, of course, angrily rejected all claims of impropriety, and the Adams administration itself had little interest in reforms sponsored by the likes of Benton and McDuffie. The intemperate McDuffie—who had been wounded in two duels in 1822—raised the temperature on the House floor by insulting Adams and describing Clay as "the skulking manager who moves the wires of this whole concerted operation." Two friends of Adams responded to McDuffie's insults by challenging him to a duel; it never took place, reportedly because McDuffie's second refused to recognize rifles as legitimate dueling weapons.[115] A less violent, but equally telling, expression of antagonism emerged in an exchange between Adams supporter Edward Everett, an outspoken opponent of electoral reform, and John H. Bryan, a Jacksonian ally of McDuffie. Everett, a noted orator who had taught classical literature at Harvard, delivered an erudite speech rebutting every step of McDuffie's lengthy argument in favor of reform. Bryan responded by mocking the "rich classical repast" that Everett had offered the House. Citing his own origins in "the cotton fields of North Carolina," Bryan then defended McDuffie's resolution as being in tune with "the wishes and . . . the rights of the People."[116]

This acrimony colored the many references to the need to change the contingent system because of the potential corruptibility of the House. Concerns about political corruption had been present for decades, but they now appeared against the backdrop of the 1824 election and were voiced most frequently by Jackson supporters, including McDuffie, whose long, fiery speech on the subject was still being read by schoolchildren after the Civil War.[117] "If this election shall frequently devolve upon Congress . . . a door will be opened to corruption, intrigue, and to office hunters," declared the newly elected Tennessee representative, Jackson protégé, and future president, James K. Polk. Responding to objections that such statements cast aspersions on members of the House, Polk asked his interlocutors whether "immaculate purity" is "to be found within these walls, and in no other corner of the earth?" James C. Mitchell, also from Tennessee, described how the corruption might work, imagining an emissary from a presidential candidate approaching a member of Congress to say, "You have gained a little reputation; you are now getting old; if you could now get some snug office, how nice a thing it would be—and it would smooth the pillow of your old age." Adams and Clay supporters, not surprisingly, took umbrage at such disquisitions. Everett dismissed out of hand "this whole argument of corruption."[118]

Mounting sectional tensions—which would become clearly visible in the election of 1828—also infiltrated the debate. Most pointedly, references to slavery and the three-fifths clause punctuated the deliberations far more frequently than they ever had in the past. New York's Henry Storrs, an Adams backer and reform opponent, opined that if McDuffie were truly interested in uniformity and equality among the states, he ought to "propose to establish a popular election within the states, and apportion the electoral power equally between them according *to their respective numbers of free citizens.*" The three-fifths clause, Storrs maintained, contradicted the democratic principles that McDuffie was so enthusiastically celebrating.[119] Storrs's agenda ran deeper than scoring points about inconsistency or hypocrisy. He was suggesting that if Congress refashioned the compromises between large and small states and between the states and the federal government, then it might just as well reconsider the compromises regarding slavery. Numerous northern representatives shared Storrs's perspective, rejecting the efforts of pro-slavery southerners like McDuffie to claim the mantle of democracy and making clear that they had little interest in amending the Constitution while leaving intact the increasingly consequential three-fifths clause.[120] Ichabod Bartlett of New Hampshire declared that he saw no reason for the small states to make concessions to broader principles if the slave states did nothing analogous. Pennsylvania's Charles Miner pointed out that citizens of nonslave states could accept the "jarring" fact that "five slaves give as much political weight ... as three of our farmers," because they recognized it as a "compromise, necessary to union, under our excellent Constitution, which brings with it so many blessings." But if the people began to see the Constitution as "imperfect" and "constantly needing amendment," the three-fifths clause "will be felt to gall like a neck chain."[121]

At least one southerner heard the warning. Responding to McDuffie's threat to call a constitutional convention to enact electoral reform if Congress failed to do so, Andrew Stevenson of Virginia, an opponent of district elections soon to become Speaker of the House, declared that he saw good reason to leave the Constitution alone. "Do you believe, Mr. Chairman, or does the honorable gentleman from South Carolina," Stevenson asked, "that if this Constitution were now to be abrogated another could be formed, upon those principles of *compromise* and concession, and equality, upon which this was based?"[122] Other southerners were more assertive, justifying the three-fifths clause as having been necessary to the formation of a national government. Polk sharply criticized Storrs and Everett for raising "this unfortunate subject of slavery," claiming it had no relevance to the electoral debate. Thomas Mitchell, a Jacksonian from South Carolina—a slaveholder who nonetheless stated that slavery was a "curse"—voiced anger that "no topic of debate can arise in this House … but our negroes must be hauled into the question, and made a black hook for gentlemen to hang upon?" Reform of presidential elections was not in itself a sectional issue, but as Hezekiah Niles observed, sectional distrust had become an obstacle to the construction of the congressional majorities needed to pass a resolution.[123]

The debate in the House came to a close on April 1, 1826. At McDuffie's request, the two parts of his resolution were voted on separately. On the proposal to amend the Constitution "in such manner as will prevent the election" of the president and vice president "from devolving upon Congress," the House voted favorably, 138 to 52, thereby announcing its extraordinary intention of relinquishing a power granted by the Constitution. The chamber then voted down the district elections provision by the decisive margin of 102 (nays) to 90. (Passage would have required 128 yea votes.) Immediately thereafter, a select committee of twenty-four members was appointed to further consider and report on the generically worded resolution that had passed.[124]

The strong vote (73 percent) in favor of preventing any congressional involvement in presidential selection confirmed the presence of wide-ranging discontent with the contingent system. Sizable majorities from states of all sizes favored the resolution, with the largest states, unsurprisingly, leading the way. (See Table 2.4.) Region and party, however, appear to have mattered in the balloting, much as they had in the debates. (No real national parties existed in 1826, but there were political groupings identified with Adams and Jackson, both of whom would compete for the presidency again in 1828.)[125] More than 90 percent of southerners and Jackson allies voted in favor of changing the contingent election mechanism; in contrast, northerners and Adams backers were split, with nearly half opposing change. Support for reform was still substantial in the North

TABLE 2.4: HOUSE OF REPRESENTATIVES ROLL CALL VOTES ON
PROPOSALS TO CREATE DISTRICT ELECTIONS AND TO REMOVE
CONTINGENT ELECTIONS FROM THE HOUSE, 1826

	District elections	Remove contingent elections from the House
	Percentage (number) of yes votes[a]	Percentage (number) of yes votes[a]
All House members who cast ballots	47 (91)[b]	73 (138)
Party affiliation[c]		
Adams	37 (34)	52 (48)
Jackson	60 (53)	97 (84)
Other	36 (4)	55 (6)
Region		
North	35 (39)	57 (62)
South	63 (52)	94 (76)
State size[d,e]		
Small (1–5 Reps)	29 (5)	63 (10)
Medium (6–14 Reps)	46 (47)	63 (64)
Large (22–34 Reps: NY, PA, VA)	53 (39)	88 (64)
or		
Small (1–5 Reps)	29 (5)	63 (10)
Medium (6–9 Reps)	43 (23)	64 (33)
Large (12–34 Reps: NY, PA, VA, OH, NC, MA, KY)	51 (63)	78 (95)

Source: Roll call data obtained from Howard Rosenthal and Keith T. Poole, *United States Congressional Roll Call Voting Records, 1789–1990* (Pittsburgh, PA, 2000), http://doi.org/10.3886/ICPSR09822.v2.

a. Percentage among those who cast votes.

b. The *Congressional Record* records the vote as 90 yeas, 102 nays; the *Journal of the House of Representatives* records the vote as 91 yeas, 101 nays.

c. Regarding party affiliation, see Chapter 2, note 125.

d. State size as measured by number of representatives in the House.

e. Two different breakdowns regarding state size are presented, largely because there was a considerable size gap between the three largest states (New York, Pennsylvania, and Virginia) and others that were relatively large but notably smaller than the big three. The voting patterns proved to be similar in both breakdowns.

(and among Adams men), but the House vote nonetheless had the ear-marks of a retrospective referendum on the fairness of the 1824 election.

Regional and partisan patterns were also visible in the vote on district elections, but the decisive defeat of that proposal had many sources: there was less support for district elections than for reform of the contingent process in states of all sizes, both party groupings, and the South as well as the North.[126] Shaping those roll-call tallies were an array of politically cross-cutting interests and beliefs. Numerous representatives from large states opposed district elections (as they had in the past) because they feared a diminution of their states' influence.[127] Staunch advocates of states' rights, from all regions, continued to regard a district elections requirement as an unwelcome effort "to diminish or impair the relative rights and powers of the States." Many Adams men, as well as some Jacksonians, embraced the principle that presidents ought to be chosen by the states (rather than the citizenry) and that the general ticket, accordingly, was the appropriate means of choosing electors. Then too, the Adams administration was hostile to McDuffie for partisan reasons (which were becoming increasingly pronounced), and the antagonisms spawned by the 1824 election had created a climate of distrust not conducive to building alliances. After taking a final jab at southerners over slavery and the three-fifths clause, Charles Miner urged Congress to be guided by the maxim "Let Well Enough Alone." The net impact of these diverse factors was that, in sharp contrast to the vote tallies from 1819 to 1822, only a third of northern representatives favored district elections.[128]

A month after the House vote, the Senate agreed to table the issue until the next session of Congress. Benton was grumpy, even petulant, but he pledged to continue the fight because he was convinced that "an immense majority of the American people" favored his proposals for district and direct elections. He also suggested that if Congress did not act, he would turn to "the theatre of the People themselves" and call for a "national convention." Van Buren professed optimism about the future passage of an amendment because the people were "perfectly united" in wanting to take "the election of President from the House of Representatives." Nathaniel Macon voiced regret that Congress had rejected the district proposal and urged Benton to be patient because "on such a mighty question . . . it could hardly be expected, that in a Government like this, it could be done at

once." "Only leave the People alone to their good sense," Macon coun-
seled reassuringly, "and they will set the thing right themselves."[129]

Two weeks later, McDuffie reported to the House on behalf of the
select committee that had been appointed to devise a means of implementing the resolution "to prevent the election of President and Vice
President from devolving upon Congress." The committee, he reported,
had "not been able to agree upon any specific plan for carrying" the resolution into effect. It therefore asked "to be discharged from the further
consideration of the subject." Five months of impassioned debate ended
with a whimper.[130]

The select committee left no records of its deliberations, but presumably its twenty-four members encountered the same problem that had con-
founded the House: despite the widely shared view that the existing
system was profoundly flawed, no alternative method had broad support.
Each of the many options proposed for keeping the election out of
Congress—generally involving either a plurality victor or some form of
runoff election—had its detractors and defects (as all electoral arrangements do). *Niles' Weekly Register,* observing that the outcome of the committee's deliberations was "almost universally expected," concluded that
"however generally it may be agreed that the election of presidents and
vice-presidents of the United States *ought* not to devolve on congress, there
is a serious difficulty in establishing any other power upon which such elections may devolve; and it is very possible that the twenty-four gentlemen
who were on the committee ... entertained not less than eight or ten different opinions as to the details of such proposed alteration."[131]

What made these differences of opinion hard to bridge was that nearly
all alternatives to the existing system bumped into knotty issues that had
arisen in the debates over district elections and the abolition of electors. If
the president had to be chosen by a majority (and there was little discernible
support for a plurality election), then there had to be a runoff mechanism of
some type. But what rules would govern a runoff? Would the electors who
had already been chosen decide the election by choosing among the top two
vote-getters? If a second popular election were held, would voting be by
general ticket or by district—and with or without electors? Would each
state legislature decide on the mode of election or would there be a national
mandate? The most obvious approach would have been to hold a runoff

election utilizing the first-round election rules already in existence, but those rules were already unpopular in many quarters. The district elections resolution had been defeated, but ninety representatives (47 percent) had endorsed it, and it was unlikely that many of them would embrace a constitutional amendment that doubled down on the existing system, with all its shortcomings.[132] Nor was it likely that relatively small states would surrender their influence in the contingent process if they would not get a district election scheme in return. Years of debate had, in fact, made it clear that there was no set of electoral rules—whether for the initial balloting or a runoff—that had the support of two-thirds of Congress. Little wonder, then, that McDuffie's committee gave up so quickly! The contingent election problem, serious as it may have been, could not be solved without settling other outstanding issues. The vote in the House had, in effect, been a statement of principle or aspiration that had little chance of being translated into institutional change. The always-shrewd Van Buren was on target when he pointed out that it was "in vain . . . for gentlemen to be, or to affect to be, in favor of taking the election from the House" unless they also agreed to district elections: "Without that, all is empty profession."[133]

The collapse of the reform initiative in 1826 was closely linked to the diversity of its supporters' goals. For district elections advocates, the 1826 effort continued a campaign that had been ongoing for a dozen years; for Benton and his allies, it was an occasion to renew their drive to eliminate electors (among other reforms); for many others, disturbed by what had transpired in 1824, the only important goal was to keep presidential elections out of the hands of Congress. The overarching case for change was strong, particularly given the prevailing belief that most elections henceforth would not be settled by a majority vote in the Electoral College. But pursuing several reforms at once had its challenges, not least because the leading proponents of reform were not united in their priorities. As Van Buren had intimated, success could be attained only through compromise and coalition building.

The failure to achieve any reform at all in 1826 also attested to the difficulty of revamping an electoral system as intricate and multifaceted as the one bequeathed by the framers. Alterations to any one part of the system could easily throw off the balance of interests so carefully distributed across the system's different features—between small states and large,

slave states and free, the national government and the states. In an era when
state size loomed important, large states were reluctant to agree to district
elections unless the small states gave up their disproportionate power if
the election went to the House. Conversely, the blatantly undemocratic
contingent procedure could not be jettisoned without some concession
from large states that wielded power by casting electoral votes in a bloc.
While the hopeful view was that the desirability of reforming both phases
of the election created an opportunity for a bargain, the imperative of acting
on multiple fronts also created more potential obstacles, sources of disagreement, and veto points: the absence of a two-thirds majority for either
reform could kill both. The complexity of the electoral structure could, and
did, stymie an attempt to fix a system that was widely believed, in and out
of Congress, to be badly in need of repair.

Aftermath

The impasse reached in Congress in 1826 marked the end of a remarkable
period of engagement with electoral reform. Never again in the nineteenth
century would a proposal to reform the electoral system attract the level
of congressional support present from 1813 into the mid-1820s. Not until
the middle of the twentieth century would a branch of Congress again approve an amendment that aimed to abolish winner-take-all.

Interest in reform, of course, did not disappear after the House votes
in 1826. Dickerson put forward yet another district elections resolution
barely a month later, and McDuffie submitted a direct-vote district elections motion (with no involvement by Congress) in December 1827. Benton
continued to introduce his preferred proposal (for districts, a direct vote,
and a popular runoff) into the 1840s, and representative (later president)
Andrew Johnson advocated a similar plan in 1851 and 1852. (By 1860 Johnson
had changed his mind, concluding that it would be best for the North and
South to alternate in choosing presidents.) In 1848 a new option was added
to the mix when William Lawrence, a New York Whig, introduced a plan
to end winner-take-all by allocating a state's electoral votes in proportion
to the percentage of the popular vote that each candidate received. These
proposals, and others like them, received limited attention in Congress, and
none were brought to a final vote.[134]

Indeed, the movement for district elections, already weaker in 1826 than it had been a few years earlier, lost additional steam in the late 1820s and 1830s. That it did so stemmed not only from weariness with the issue but from changes taking place in numerous states.[135] Thanks to grassroots pressure and the growing conviction that the "people" ought to choose the president, legislative selection was abandoned in one state after another in the 1820s. Nine states (out of twenty-four) had utilized this method in 1820, but only two were still doing so by 1828, and thereafter the practice was confined to South Carolina.[136] The eight states that switched between 1820 and 1832 all adopted the general ticket, although both Missouri and New York had brief experiments with district elections. (See Chapter 1, Table 1.1.)

For different reasons, five of the six states that had utilized district elections in 1824 converted to the general ticket by 1832. Most often, the publicly stated rationale for such shifts was to increase the influence of the state in presidential elections. In 1833, when Maryland finally came around, the preamble to its new electoral law declared that the district system, which had long been in use, deprived the state's citizens "of their just weight in the choice of the Chief Magistrate, as compared with the majority of the citizens of most of the other states."[137] For many politicians, to be sure, increasing their state's influence was indistinguishable from gaining electoral votes for their party (or faction); a thorough state-by-state account leaves little doubt that partisan impulses and factional fighting figured prominently in most of the changes.[138] Yet whatever the mix of motives, the upshot was that district elections were no longer in use by 1836. In 1832 Erastus Root of New York proposed a constitutional amendment requiring general-ticket elections by a direct vote—both to guarantee that popular elections be held and to bring the federal Constitution in line with the practices of the states. Root had been a strong advocate of district elections in 1816.[139]

These changes meant that by 1832, or even 1828, there was substantial uniformity in the methods that states deployed to choose electors. With uniformity, moreover, came the promise of stability. By the late 1820s, state legislatures were unlikely to risk popular wrath by reclaiming the power of choosing electors by themselves, and there were few imaginable circumstances in which a state would switch back to district elections for partisan purposes.[140] Two key arguments for nationally mandated district elections were therefore undermined: the method of choosing electors was now the same almost everywhere, and opportunistic partisan changes to the method were unlikely. "What more do we want, as far as uniformity goes?" Edward Everett had asked a bit prematurely in 1826. "If the States will all adopt the General Ticket system . . . then the only evil which I admit to exist, is remedied."[141] Some committed advocates of district elections, like Benton and McDuffie, were far from satisfied: they believed deeply that district elections were more democratic than the general ticket, that they gave more power to the people and less to party leaders. But many others who had embraced the cause chose to cease fighting a battle that had been partially won and had diminished prospects of advancing further.[142]

Proposals for eliminating electors and prohibiting congressional involvement in the choice of presidents carried more momentum into the 1830s. Both ideas were strongly promoted by President Jackson whose unhappy memories of the 1824 election reinforced his democratic convictions. In his first annual address, in December 1829, Jackson declared that the "right of electing their Chief Magistrate" belongs to "the people," and it was

> never designed that their choice should in any case be defeated, either by the intervention of electoral colleges or by . . . the House of Representatives. Experience proves that in proportion as agents to execute the will of the people are multiplied there is danger of their wishes being frustrated. . . . I would therefore recommend such an amendment of the Constitution as may remove all intermediate agency in the election of the President and Vice-President. The mode may be so regulated as to preserve to each State its present relative weight in the election.[143]

Although Jackson reiterated these views in nearly all of his annual messages, he never issued an exact blueprint for change. By calling for the maintenance of each state's "relative weight," he was endorsing the preservation of electoral votes (even without electors), and his silence on the matter suggested that he had no preference between the general ticket and district elections. More striking was the absence of a concrete plan for keeping elections out of the hands of Congress. Like the House of Representatives in 1826, Jackson was far more clear about what he opposed than what he supported.[144]

Numerous state legislatures and members of Congress also endorsed proposals to eliminate electors and hold a "direct vote of the people," usually specifying that the existing "weight of the States, and the present basis of representation be retained."[145] Even amendment resolutions calling for the mandatory use of the general ticket in the 1830s sometimes included the requirement that elections be direct and without electors.[146] Such proposals were popular, both because they meshed well with the democratic ethos of the period and because there seemed to be little point in having electors who served only as messengers. Nonetheless, they made little headway in Congress, in part because the issue lacked urgency: the presence of electors had not created any noteworthy problems. More importantly perhaps, any amendment that insisted on maintaining the "present basis of representation" would implicitly constitute an endorsement of the three-fifths clause, and sectional tensions made it increasingly improbable that such a step would be approved by two-thirds of Congress.[147]

The desire to change the contingent procedure also remained strong into the 1830s. Resolutions were passed in the legislatures of Ohio (1827), Alabama (1828), and Indiana (1837) favoring an amendment that would prevent the election from "devolving on the House of Representatives" (or Congress itself.)[148] Specific schemes for improving the process (including runoff elections, a vote by both branches of Congress, or a popular vote to determine how each state would cast its one vote in the House) popped up throughout the late 1820s and the first half of the 1830s.[149] Agreement, however, remained elusive: resolutions from the states urging that elections not "devolve" upon Congress did not offer solutions, and Congress itself seemed disinclined to wrestle anew with the complexities of designing a runoff procedure.[150]

Meanwhile, the alarm bells rung by the 1824 election quieted down when the elections of 1828 and 1832 failed to produce another multi-candidate train wreck. Those two elections, in fact, suggested that a new framework of party politics was taking shape. Although not firmly in place by the early 1830s, a second two-party system was emerging, as the nation's political leaders began to line up either behind Jackson and Van Buren's Democratic Party or in opposition to it. (The opposition coalesced as the Whig Party in 1834.) Once presidential contests were again contested by two large national parties—and two major candidates—the likelihood of an election ending up in the hands of Congress was greatly diminished. The formation of a two-party system, moreover, was encouraged and reinforced by the now-universal use of winner-take-all—since third-party or independent candidates could no longer win any of a state's electoral votes without capturing a plurality of the popular vote. Indeed, national politics and presidential elections would henceforth be dominated by two-party systems, greatly lessening the pressure on Congress to come up with a better—and more democratic—contingent mechanism than the framers had devised.

✳   ✳   ✳

The burst of reform activity in the early decades of the nineteenth century was the product of specific historical developments interacting with problematic features of the constitutionally mandated electoral system. The Constitution's silence regarding the methods that states should use to choose electors commanded attention because it was producing disparities among the states as well as unseemly partisan manipulations that could thwart the public will. It also permitted more than a third of the states to select electors without holding a popular vote, a pattern that seemed inconsonant with republican or democratic values. Similarly, the wisdom of the contingent election provision had been questioned since the near debacle of 1800–1801, but those questions became insistent only when a multi-candidate race approached in 1824—and even more insistent after its outcome! Meanwhile, the temporary absence of national parties and partisan competition for the presidency facilitated and enabled wide-ranging public debates about reform in Congress and in state legislatures.

These circumstances fostered a reform effort of remarkable breadth. Not only did the Senate on four occasions approve amendment resolutions, but a few more votes (or different absences) in the House would have sent a district election amendment to the states for ratification in 1821. Three years later, key actors in the Senate seemed on the verge of forging a muscular compromise that would have simultaneously ended winner-take-all and transformed the contingent procedure. Two years after that, in 1826, the

House voted overwhelmingly to remove Congress from the process of electing presidents. Notably, many of the congressmen and senators who backed these changes did so more out of principle, or conviction, than from any readily apparent calculus of political self-interest. Party boundaries were permeable, even in 1826 when partisan identifications were regaining importance. Numerous large-state representatives voted repeatedly in favor of district elections; most House members from small states voted to do away with the contingent system. The records of congressional debate clearly document a widespread distaste for the workings of the existing system, as well as a search to figure out a better, and fairer, way to choose a president. With roots in both a nostalgic vision of party-less politics and a forward-looking democratic temper, the proposed reforms sought to empower citizens, albeit modestly, at the expense of parties, leaders, and managers.

Although the reform endeavor succeeded in altering practices in numerous states, it failed to achieve its goal of amending the Constitution and restructuring the electoral system. That failure had multiple sources, including the need for supermajorities to change the Constitution, the complexity of the electoral system itself, and disagreements regarding the appropriate remedies for acknowledged problems. Inertia also played a role, as did the divisive partisanship that surfaced after the 1824 election. The relative weights of these different factors varied over time between 1812 and the late 1820s.

The defeat of reform further demonstrated the difficulty of modifying an electoral system once it was implanted in the political landscape. All electoral institutions create constituencies that resist changes to the rules, and the early American system was no exception. Among the supporters of the status quo were some who were defending interests, or even beliefs, generated by the system itself. Numerous small-state politicians, for example, sought to retain the contingent procedure, although few, by the 1820s, would have argued that their states ought to possess the outsized influence they had been granted by the Constitution. Similarly, some leaders in large states had come to view their state's ability to cast sizable, and possibly decisive, blocs of electoral votes as an entitlement—even if it was never mentioned in the Constitution. Virginia's legislature was apologetic when it first adopted the general ticket in 1800, but within two decades most of the commonwealth's elected leaders were adamant in its defense. The carefully constructed reform packages that were put forward repeatedly between 1823 and 1826 would almost certainly have made presidential elections more democratic, but they could not overcome the misgivings—the reluctance to relinquish familiar advantages—of a sufficient number of political leaders and elected officials. Gaining influence in the contingent process was not necessarily adequate recompense for the political leader of a large, or medium-sized, state who was accustomed to choosing slates of electors and being courted by national candidates.

Despite Congress's failure to approve an amendment, presidential elections became more procedurally orderly, more stable, and in some respects more democratic by the mid-1830s than they had been in the 1810s. By 1836, presidential candidates were selected by party conventions rather than by congressional caucuses. All states except South Carolina held popular elections to choose electors, and every state cast all of its electoral votes for the candidate who had won its popular vote. States were no longer altering their processes in search of short-term partisan advantage, and the reappearance of a two-party system kept the contingent procedure on a back burner. A new equilibrium had been reached, and it would endure—more or less intact—into the twenty-first century.

Yet many of the underlying problems with the system remained unsolved. The defects of winner-take-all not only persisted but had been extended to all states—which meant (among other things) that the voices of political minorities continued to be stifled and a president could still be elected without the support of a majority of voters. Electoral votes were cast by electors who could, and would, occasionally prove to be "faithless." The often-disparaged contingent procedure (which even the House had sought to replace) remained in the Constitution, ignored except in rare moments when a third-party candidate seemed strong enough to potentially disrupt the Electoral College. These issues, and others, would prompt later generations of political reformers to take up the mantle once carried by dedicated, if now largely forgotten, men like Israel Pickens, Mahlon Dickerson, George McDuffie, and Thomas Hart Benton.

THREE

THREE UNEASY PIECES, 1870–1960

Between the Civil War and the early twenty-first century, hardly a decade went by without a member of Congress or an influential journal of opinion strongly advocating the abolition of the general ticket. Despite vast changes in the practice of politics (and much else) over the last century and a half, the Electoral College has remained unpopular in many quarters, and winner-take-all has been the institution's most unpopular feature. (In some periods, it was rivaled in unpopularity by electors, who were generally viewed as "useless, if not pernicious.")[1] As had been true in the Era of Good Feelings, unhappiness with the general ticket gave rise to recurrent attempts to amend the Constitution.

In contrast to the reform efforts of the early nineteenth century, however, later attempts to dispense with winner-take-all did not focus exclusively on district elections and the design of a new contingent mechanism. Although districting had its advocates, many proponents of reform preferred a system that would allocate a state's electoral votes in proportion to a candidate's share of the popular vote. (In addition, a growing number favored a national popular vote, as recounted in Chapters 4 and 5.) A proportional system would serve many of the same purposes as direct, district elections: it would eliminate slates of electors, give some influence to political minorities, and bring the electoral vote tallies more in line with the popular vote. If coupled with a provision for a plurality victor (as was often the case), proportional elections would also put an end to the contingent system. As its supporters repeatedly pointed out, a proportional system had the immense advantage of not importing the problem of gerrymandering into the process of selecting a president.[2]

Not surprisingly, many of the early nineteenth-century arguments, for and against reform, were reiterated, and even cited, in later decades. (Thomas Hart Benton and Andrew Jackson were particular favorites of late nineteenth-century reformers.) Yet there were differences, several of them worthy of note. One was that state size ceased to be a significant axis of conflict: perhaps because of the growing salience of other differences (urban-rural, industrial-agricultural, and regional), and perhaps because the number of states grew rapidly, the contrast between the interests of large and small states never dominated debates over electoral reform after the Civil War. A second difference was that parties and partisan interests shaped the fate of legislative proposals far more decisively than had been the case between 1812 and 1830. This began to be true in the last quarter of the nineteenth century, when partisan competition was intense and presidential elections were often decided by very narrow margins; it remained true for most, but not all, of the twentieth century. An additional contrast with the early nineteenth century was that proponents of reform put increasing weight on elementary democratic values. "The rule of the majority is the fundamental principle of popular government," claimed attorney Roger Pryor, a former Confederate soldier who became active in Democratic politics in New York after the war.[3]

Three episodes in the history of presidential election reform illumine the path traversed. The first unfolded in the 1870s and 1880s, as Congress once again considered jettisoning the general ticket, only to see those discussions enmeshed in the crisis over vote counting that followed the disputed 1876 election. The second took place in (and around) Michigan in the early 1890s, when the state legislature decided to replace the general ticket with district elections. The third came later, in the mid-twentieth century, when an unusual coalition of partisan and sectional interests mounted a strong campaign to replace winner-take-all with a proportional system. Taken together, these three episodes go a long way toward explaining why the general ticket is still with us in the twenty-first century—even if its name has changed.

Postbellum Reform, Crisis, and Stasis

After every Presidential election there is more or less discussion of the defects of the Electoral system and of the desirability of a change in the method of choosing the President and Vice President.... It is in fact very desirable that a change should be made, but the amendment of the Constitution of the

United States is a difficult matter to accomplish, unless it is forced by some
great emergency, and it requires a degree of sustained interest which this
Electoral question does not seem to inspire. Another difficulty is to find a substantial agreement among those who advocate a change as to what the
change ought to be. Hardly any one thinks the present system a desirable one
to retain, but there is no clear and generally-accepted opinion as to what
should take its place.

—*New York Times*, December 29, 1892

Within a few years after the end of the Civil War, members of Congress
were once again raising the prospect of overhauling the presidential election system. They did so in a political environment shaped not only by
the Civil War and the challenges of Reconstruction but also by the political realignments of the 1850s. The Whig Party had collapsed early in that
decade, putting an end to the second party system and setting the stage
for a brief spell of multiparty competition that eventuated in the rise of
the recently founded antislavery Republican Party. The Republicans, based
in the Northeast and the Midwest, dominated northern (and thus national)
politics during the Civil War and Reconstruction, but the Democrats—
stronger in the South and parts of the West—gradually regained strength
in the 1870s, thanks in part to the readmission to the Union of the former
states of the Confederacy. By 1876 the two parties were evenly matched
in national elections, which would be hotly contested for the remainder
of the century. In many states, third and fourth parties also played significant roles.

These developments influenced the impulse to reform, in several ways.
The first was that the political shifts of the 1850s served as a reminder, if any
were needed, of the problems that could arise under the existing electoral
system. The demise of the Whigs led to multi-candidate elections in 1856
and 1860, and in the latter year Abraham Lincoln was elected with less than
40 percent of the national popular vote. Had New York not voted Republican, the election would have landed in the House.[4] In addition, the process
of readmitting the southern states raised anew the concern that the general
ticket could reinforce the formation of regional blocs in presidential elections. Most importantly, both the war and Reconstruction led many
Republicans—particularly in the party's more radical wing—to espouse,

and pursue, far-reaching reforms not only in the South but in the nation as a whole. The cascading democratic convictions that yielded the Fourteenth and Fifteenth Amendments also fostered a desire to democratize presidential elections, both by eliminating winner-take-all and by reducing the role of parties in structuring electoral contests.

Republican representative James Ashley of Ohio, for example, proposed several variants of a national popular vote amendment between 1866 and 1868.[5] Ashley, who played a key role both in shepherding the Thirteenth Amendment into law and in the impeachment proceedings against Andrew Johnson, then shifted ground in 1869, promoting a proportional system that he believed had a better chance of gaining the approval of Congress. Johnson himself (hardly a radical) embraced direct district elections and an end to contingent elections in the House, quoting extensively from Andrew Jackson in a message sent to Congress in 1868. He also sharply criticized political parties for limiting the choices available to the people through the use of conventions, caucuses, and control over slates of electors.[6] A few years later the influential Massachusetts senator Charles Sumner denounced the electoral system as "radically defective and unrepublican," in part because it permitted parties and political managers to dictate the choices available to the people.[7]

The foremost advocate of reform in these years was Senator Oliver P. Morton of Indiana, the formidable wartime governor of his conflict-torn state, a staunch proponent of universal (male) suffrage, and an energetic Republican stalwart who was a vigorous presence in the Senate despite being partially paralyzed from a stroke he had suffered in 1865. Morton was a committed opponent of the general ticket and was also presciently alert to the potentially dangerous absence of a constitutional mechanism for resolving disputes over electoral votes reported by the states, an issue that rose to the fore during Reconstruction. He was a harsh critic of the Twenty-Second Joint Rule adopted by Congress in 1865, which permitted either branch of Congress to reject a state's electoral votes, and in 1873, as chair of the Committee on Privileges and Elections, he was charged with investigating disputes over the electoral votes of Louisiana and Arkansas in the 1872 election.[8]

That same year, at Morton's instigation, the Senate passed a resolution instructing the Committee on Privileges and Elections to "examine . . . the best and most practicable mode of electing the President and Vice-President, and providing a tribunal to adjust and decide all contested questions" arising from presidential elections. The committee delivered its report in the spring of 1874. Declaring that the "electoral colleges have turned out to be wholly useless," the report called for direct elections in congressional districts, with the winner of each district gaining one "presidential" vote; the statewide winner would receive two additional presidential votes. The candidate with the most presidential votes nationally (not necessarily a majority) would become president, thereby eliminating the need for any contingent or runoff procedure. The electoral process, accordingly, would be greatly simplified. "The more complicated the machinery is," the committee concluded, "the more liable it is to get out of order."[9]

Morton's proposal resembled those put forward a half century earlier, and so did some of the arguments in its behalf. Whatever the framers of the Constitution might have intended at a time when "the theory of democratic government was . . . imperfectly understood," it was argued, electors in practice served no constructive purpose, and district elections offered a far better gauge of public opinion than the general ticket. The committee further noted that, without an amendment, state legislatures would retain the potentially hazardous authority to change the mode of choosing electors whenever they wished. Morton's report also placed new emphasis on the capacity of district elections to reduce fraud. Where "fraud will only affect the vote of a single district" rather than an entire state, "the temptations to commit it are greatly diminished," the report concluded.[10] Like Sumner and Johnson, moreover, Morton stressed an issue that had been tangential to the debates of the 1820s: the general ticket made it impossible for citizens to vote for candidates whose parties were not able to organize a full slate of electors in their states. (An example cited was the 1856 election, in which many southerners had no opportunity to vote for Republicans John Fremont and William Dayton.) Giving voice to a strand of anti-partyism that surfaced frequently in this period, Morton claimed that no system should be called "free or republican" that "does not enable the individual voter to cast his vote for the men of his choice whether anybody else in the same State votes for them or not."[11]

Morton's committee report also insisted that Congress find some method of adjudicating disputes over the legitimacy, or validity, of electoral votes—a subject that two years later would land at the center of a national political crisis. The issue had arisen sporadically before the Civil War, notably in early 1857 when a snowstorm prevented Wisconsin's electors from gathering on the appointed date. It gained new force after 1865 as Congress considered whether individual southern states had regained the right to cast electoral votes. To address such questions the Senate and the House in 1865 had agreed to the Twenty-Second Joint Rule, which effectively gave each branch veto power over the electoral tallies submitted by the states. (A joint rule, in contrast to legislation, did not require the agreement of the president.) That rule guided congressional action in the conflicts that emerged after the 1868 and 1872 elections.[12]

But Morton, among others, believed that there was no constitutional basis for the Twenty-Second Joint Rule and that it gave to Congress a power that it ought not possess.[13] The joint rule, Morton and his allies maintained, inescapably subjected the process of counting electoral votes to partisan manipulation and conflict. Even worse, it created the possibility that a partisan House could reject enough electoral votes to deny any candidate a majority, thus sending the election to the House itself, where small states would have the same power as large states. Morton's committee decried the absence, both in the states and in Washington, of mechanisms for settling electoral vote disputes, asserting that there was "imminent danger of revolution" if an election outcome hinged on state returns tainted by "fraud or violence." Despite such danger, the report's recommendations were vague: it urged only that the states take action and that Congress create some form of "machinery or tribunal" that could settle electoral disputes in advance of the date on which the Senate president counted the votes. The committee further observed that conflicts over electoral votes would become less likely and less heated if its recommendations for changing the electoral system were adopted.[14]

Well before the election of 1876, thus, the desire to reform the electoral system was tied to concerns about the electoral vote count and the resolution of disputes. Many of the Republicans who sought to abolish the general ticket and alter the contingent process also feared that the suppression of newly enfranchised black voters in the South would yield electoral returns of doubtful integrity favoring the Democrats. Morton sought to separate the two issues early in 1875 when he proposed a constitutional amendment calling for district elections and other substantive reforms and several days later introduced a bill to regulate the counting of votes. (He believed that the vote-counting issues should be handled through legislation rather than amendment.) Almost simultaneously, the House Committee on Elections proposed an amendment, favorably reported by the *New York Times*, that called for direct, district elections, a plurality victor, and the involvement of the Supreme Court in settling "contests." Morton's amendment proposal generated some support in the Senate, but it never came to a vote because it was eclipsed by a sharp, multipronged debate over his vote-counting bill. That bill advocated replacing the Twenty-Second Joint Rule with legislation that would permit Congress to reject a state's electoral returns only if both chambers agreed to do so. The measure was endorsed by the Senate in February 1875 but died in the House. The following winter the Senate unilaterally rescinded the Twenty-Second Joint Rule but was unable to decide on a new procedure for settling disputes. This left Congress with no agreed-upon mechanism to cope with the crisis that erupted after the 1876 election.[15]

That well-known crisis—dramatic and consequential as it surely was—warrants only a brief summary here. The outcome of the election hinged on disputes over the electoral votes of three southern states (Florida, Louisiana, and South Carolina) and one electoral vote in Oregon. In each case, multiple, and conflicting, certificates of election were sent to the president of the Senate. The Republican candidate, Rutherford B. Hayes, would become president if all of the disputes were resolved in his favor; otherwise the victor would be the Democrat, Samuel Tilden of New York. Coloring the dispute was the fact that Tilden appeared to have won the national popular vote, bolstering Democratic claims of victory. At the same time, abundant evidence indicated that (Republican) African-American voters had been suppressed in large numbers in the South.[16]

The absence of an established process for resolving disputes left ample room for partisan skirmishing over procedure. If, as some Republicans claimed, the president of the Senate had the right to judge the validity of election certificates, the election would likely go to Hayes, because the Senate president was Republican senator Thomas Ferry of Michigan. (Ferry was serving as president pro tem because Vice President Henry Wilson had died in 1875 and the Senate had a Republican majority.) In contrast, most Democrats asserted that the Senate president had no such power but that Congress (and particularly the House) did. They sought to invoke the Twenty-Second Joint Rule (despite the Senate's rescission) and threatened to block or delay the count so that the election would devolve upon the Democratic-controlled House. Amid widespread threats of violence and disorder—even fears of a renewed civil war—the two chambers of Congress agreed to create an extraordinary electoral commission (of questionable constitutionality) composed of five senators, five members of the House, and five Justices of the Supreme Court. That commission (which included Oliver Morton, although he had opposed its creation) eventually awarded all of the disputed electoral votes to Hayes, in a series of straight (eight to seven) party-line votes. It was (and is) widely believed that the Democrats acquiesced in this outcome in part because Hayes agreed to remove all remaining troops from the South after he took office.[17]

The election was settled and the nation had—more than metaphorically, perhaps—dodged a bullet. But the underlying issue endured: there was still no agreed-upon mechanism for dealing with disputed electoral votes. The crisis, moreover, left in its wake a climate of intense partisan hostility and distrust.[18] Democratic newspapers commonly referred to Hayes as "His Fraudulency," and the House even passed a resolution declaring that Tilden, in fact, was the "duly elected President."[19] The Republicans, in turn, raised the volume of their denunciations of the ongoing "fraud and violence practiced by" Democrats in southern elections.[20] In that climate, and despite the palpable urgency of the issue—presidential elections were expected to be close for the foreseeable future—it took Congress another decade to agree on even a weak, heavily compromised, and confusing procedural law, the Electoral Count Act of 1887.[21]

Not surprisingly, the crisis of 1876 also gave rise to calls for transformation of the electoral system in both the North and the South. Shortly after election day, Atlanta's *Daily Constitution* commented that newspapers everywhere were "demanding the abolition of the electoral college," approvingly quoting a Philadelphia publication's assertion that "the whole system of the electoral college is clumsy, inefficient, and dangerous." The lack of agreement between the popular and the electoral votes, the *Constitution* noted, was even boosting support for a national popular vote "disregarding state lines."[22] Similarly, *Harper's Weekly* observed in early 1877 that "by common consent the present system of Presidential election is too perilous to endure."[23] The Republican-leaning *Chicago Daily Tribune* urged that attention be focused less on vote-counting issues than on "the machinery of the Electoral College, which machinery is at present the source of all the trouble in regard to these contested cases, and which promises to be of still more trouble in the future."[24]

Oliver Morton, of course, agreed. Convinced that his plan would cure the defects of the system and greatly alleviate the vote-counting problem, he reintroduced his amendment in December 1876, insisting that "public opinion" now supported his view that "this electoral college is a total failure, that it is dangerous, and that it ought to be abolished." It was also, he claimed, "antirepublican, antidemocratic in the true sense of the word." As Congress tried to figure out a path forward in the winter of 1876–1877, Morton maintained that the American people would find unacceptable any response that did not include ending winner-take-all and preventing the election from devolving on the House.[25] Most of his colleagues demurred, but Morton (described by one of his Senate adversaries as a man of "untiring energy" and "indomitable will") continued to press the case even after the immediate crisis had subsided—despite the deterioration of his health following a second stroke.[26] In the summer of 1877 he published a forceful essay in the *North American Review,* a prominent national journal, declaring that "experience, as well as reason, now suggests that the rubbish of the electoral college be brushed away entirely." Reiterating arguments that he had made for years (while reminding readers that he had predicted the recent "shipwreck"), Morton maintained that governments needed to utilize the "power of amendment" to remedy "demonstrated imperfections" in their institutions. Such an amendment would ideally implement a national popular vote ("a direct vote of the people, as one great community"), but Morton feared that "the smaller States will never consent to it." His district elections plan was thus the "best" that could be achieved.[27] Morton seemed prepared for a lengthy legislative campaign, but he died in November 1877, at age fifty-four, depriving the reform effort of one of its most dedicated and forceful leaders.[28]

Other members of Congress picked up the torch. More often than not, they advocated replacing the general ticket, not with district elections, but with a proportional distribution of a state's electoral votes. That preference stemmed from a desire to avoid both the evils of gerrymandering and disputes over the outcomes of district elections—which were all too common in contests for House seats. Proponents believed that proportional elections would also greatly reduce fraud—because there would be little incentive to stuff ballot boxes simply to achieve a fractional increase in a candidate's electoral vote. One widely noticed proposal was introduced in the House in 1877 by Democrat Levi Maish of Pennsylvania and reported favorably (with slight modifications) by a select committee in 1878. It called for direct elections, a proportional calculation of each state's electoral votes (to three decimals!), and a plurality victor. In the highly unlikely event of a tie, the election would revert to the House. The proposal also outlined a procedure for settling disputes about the validity of electoral votes.[29]

A bipartisan majority of the select committee, chaired by Democrat Milton Southard of Ohio, maintained that the measure would solve the problems associated with the general ticket while producing electoral outcomes that would closely match the people's wishes. At the same time, it would treat "each state as a separate political community" (by leaving suffrage laws to the states) and protect the interests of small states (by retaining the existing formula for allocating electoral votes).[30] The proposal, in its broad principles if not in all its details, attracted substantial support in and outside of Congress. Democrat Charles R. Buckalew, a former senator and future representative from Pennsylvania, as well as the nation's foremost advocate of proportional representation, sang its praises in the *North American Review*, emphasizing that the "Maish amendment" would "almost extinguish the chances of a disputed election," keep the election out of the House, and "greatly discourage and prevent unfairness and fraud."[31] An essay in *The Independent* (which tilted Republican) applauded Maish's proposal for getting rid of "the cumbersome, useless" Electoral College—although it faulted the measure for leaving too much control in the hands of the states and for not altogether abolishing the contingent election system.[32]

Despite the favorable committee recommendation, its amendment resolution was never brought to a vote in the House, just as the Senate never voted on Morton's district measure. That fate was shared by all of the reform proposals, for both proportional and district elections, that came before Congress in the 1870s and 1880s.[33] This legislative stasis persisted, as was frequently noted in the press, despite a series of extremely close presidential elections that advertised the hazards of winner-take-all as well as other flaws in the system. In 1880 Republican James Garfield defeated Winfield Hancock by 0.1 percent of the popular vote (while the Greenback candidate won 3 percent); had Garfield lost New York, which was close, he would have been defeated by one electoral vote. Similarly, in 1884 Democrat Grover Cleveland, who led the popular vote by a very narrow margin, triumphed in the Electoral College only because he won New York by 1,149 votes (out of 1.2 million cast). Four years later Cleveland again gained a narrow popular vote plurality (at least officially), but Benjamin Harrison won the electoral vote and the presidency, an outcome that produced little outcry among Democrats.[34] That the general ticket could easily keep the popular vote winner from becoming president was increasingly obvious, as was the danger that electors could engage in consequential mischief. The close elections, coupled with the presence of third parties, also heightened the odds that an election would land in the House, a feature of the existing system that was almost universally criticized as "anti-republican."[35]

Nonetheless, Congress proved unable, or unwilling, to press forward with any of the proposed alternatives, even as they continued to be introduced, usually to favorable notice in the press, in the 1880s and into the early 1890s. A fitting, if unwitting (or perhaps snarky), emblem of the legislative pattern was offered by the *New York Times* in 1881 as it reported on a district elections plan offered by Pennsylvania's Democratic senator William A. Wallace. The article quoted at length from a speech given by Wallace and then concluded: "These and many other arguments Mr. Wallace advanced in favor of his proposition, and when he had closed his speech the Senate went on with the consideration of the Post Office Appropriation bill."[36]

The inertia in Congress begs for explanation, in part because the arguments put forward by advocates of direct district and proportional elections were intellectually compelling. A proportional allocation of electoral votes would indeed have significantly lessened the chances of a candidate winning the popular vote but not becoming president. It would also have enlarged and invigorated election campaigns beyond the "doubtful" states (as swing or "battleground" states were then called); and with a plurality winner, it would have dispensed with the dreaded possibility of an election going to the House. The reformers were correct too that their proposals would help diminish the vote-counting problems that seemed so urgently in need of solution. In addition to reducing the incentives for fraud, proportional or direct district elections would eliminate other potential sources of dispute stemming from the apparatus of the system, such as the eligibility of individuals to be electors or whether electoral votes were cast on the correct day.[37] Finally, of course, these proposed reforms offered each major party the chance to gain electoral votes in states or regions where they were in the minority.

Why, then, was there so little progress, so little forward movement—particularly in the wake of the severe political crisis of 1876–1877? Although the reasons prompting congressional leaders not to bring particular issues to a vote are often hidden from view, several factors seem clearly to have played a role. The most immediate was that reform of the electoral system remained entangled in the ongoing debates over vote counting and the resolution of disputes. As long as those issues remained on the table (which they did until 1887), Congress was reluctant to separate and prioritize district or proportional election proposals—as Oliver Morton had learned in the mid-1870s. Some reform advocates, like Maish, Southard, Wallace, and Thomas Browne of Indiana, tried to circumvent that obstacle by incorporating approaches to dispute resolution into substantive amendment resolutions, but that strategy enmeshed their amendments in the complicated, sometimes heated, disagreements (constitutional, theoretical, and partisan) that bedeviled attempts to resolve the vote-counting problem.[38] Although critics of the general ticket rightly claimed that reform would lessen the likelihood of disputes, the leadership of Congress believed that the vote-counting problems had to be remedied before embarking on a lengthy debate about reforming the Electoral College. Democrat Abram Hewitt of New York, a close ally of Samuel Tilden and a former chair of the Democratic National Committee, stated the case emphatically in 1882 in response to a reform measure put forward by Indiana Republican Thomas Browne. Once the dispute resolution issue is settled, Hewitt maintained, "I am ready to go hand in hand with my friend from Indiana and with other gentlemen to mature such an amendment to the Constitution . . . as will remove the manifest evils of the electoral system. But in the mean time let us do all we can to prevent a recurrence of such a condition of affairs as that which threatened this country with such disasters in 1877. That should be the highest object and aim of Congress." As had been true in 1802–1804 and in the 1820s, efforts to abolish the general ticket were impeded by the perceived need to address other flaws in the electoral system.[39]

Of equal importance, neither of the major political parties was united in support of electoral reform. (The issue was not mentioned in their quadrennial platforms at any point in the nineteenth century.)[40] Among Democrats, the splits fell largely on regional lines. Some northern Democrats like Maish, Wallace, and Southard (the chair of the 1878 committee) endorsed, and even sponsored, amendments for proportional or district voting.[41] That they did so reflected their conviction, often eloquently voiced in speeches, that the electoral system was profoundly flawed. Yet partisan considerations were present as well: district or proportional systems would have political payoffs for northern Democrats who lived in states commonly carried by Republicans in presidential elections. In Pennsylvania, the home state of Maish, Buckalew, and Wallace, the Republicans were victorious in every presidential election from 1876 through 1888, although in each of those elections the Democratic candidate won 43 to 48 percent of the vote. If a proportional or district system replaced winner-take-all, the Democrats would gain a sizable slice of the state's twenty-nine electoral votes. Similar patterns were apparent elsewhere in the Northeast and Midwest.[42]

At the same time there was vocal opposition from southern Democrats, who feared any change to the Constitution that might deepen federal involvement in elections.[43] Early in 1878, for example, Congressman Alexander Stephens of Georgia, the former vice president of the Confederacy, published an essay arguing that there was no need to alter the electoral system, other than by fixing the vote-counting procedure. That view was shared by the three southern Democrats (H. A. Herbert of Alabama, John F. House of Tennessee, and Eppa Hunton of Virginia) who filed a long, angry dissent from the House committee report that had recommended a proportional allocation of electoral votes. They attacked the report's criticism of the existing system as based on "the false assumption that our government was intended to represent the will of the majority of the whole people of the United States." If national majorities were to rule, they argued, "we must . . . destroy the whole Constitution, tear down the whole fabric, stamp it under foot and build anew." The election system was designed to capture "the will of the States" rather than "the will of the people of the whole of the United States." The majority's plan, they maintained, would threaten the "right of local self government" and lead to the imposition of national suffrage requirements. Although "the late war" and Republican reconstruction policies had given "a powerful impetus to centralization," the minority insisted that the states needed to retain the right to decide how their presidential balloting would be conducted. The *Atlanta Daily Constitution* cited the dissenting minority report approvingly.[44]

Republicans too were divided—although not regionally and not quite so visibly. Sumner and Morton, of course, were prominent party leaders, and both favored eliminating the general ticket. Similarly, all of the Republicans on the 1878 House committee, including one from North Carolina, supported the proposal for proportional elections. Mugwump elements in the party endorsed an end to the general ticket both because it was more democratic and because it would reduce the power of "electioneering managers from a few great States" who were debasing political life and wielding disproportionate power.[45] In addition, some Republicans believed that district or proportional elections would give them a better shot at gaining electoral votes in the South, where they had won six states in 1872 with significant help from African-American voters. As late as 1889 a contributor to the *Atlantic Monthly* optimistically claimed that with a proportional system "the solid South, that bugbear of our politics . . . would immediately disappear, together with many of the attending evils of sectional hatred and race prejudice."[46]

Republican leaders in some northern states, however, believed that winner-take-all served their immediate interests well, giving them reliable blocs of electoral votes that would be fragmented by district or proportional elections. (The fragmentation could come at the hands of third-party movements—which were numerous—as well as the Democrats.)[47] After 1876, as Republican strategies to win votes in the South failed to bear fruit and the country gradually settled into a new electoral map featuring a largely Republican North and a Democratic South, hanging on to as many electoral votes as possible in reliably Republican states came to seem more important, and safer, than transforming the Electoral College.

This partisan perspective was not solidified or loudly voiced until the late 1880s and the 1890s, but it played a role in stymieing congressional action even in the late 1870s.[48]

The obstacles to reform were thus substantial: a high level of antagonism between the two major parties; divisions within each party that rendered a two-thirds vote for reform unlikely; the existence of a range of different proposals; and the inability of Congress to rapidly settle the vote-counting issues. These obstacles were significant enough to slow and divert the wave of bipartisan reform energy set in motion by the political crisis of 1876–1877, a crisis that originated not only in the turmoil of Reconstruction and the lack of a mechanism for dispute resolution but also in the architecture of the electoral system itself.

Notably, one of the impediments to change was tied to the crisis itself and, perhaps, intrinsic to electoral crises: the sharpening of partisan animosities. Less than two years before the 1876 election, the *New York Times* had observed that "the question of changing the method of election is not a partisan question, and ... there is some probability that both Democrats and Republicans may unite in action."[49] But that probability dropped precipitously once the disputed election erupted into months, indeed years, of nasty partisan recriminations. In this atmosphere, with national elections decided by razor-thin margins, both parties became more distrustful and defensive, more protective of their electoral flanks, less likely to take the risks that would come with a reconfigured electoral system—however compelling the arguments for reform might have been. The congressional leadership consequently narrowed its focus to the one issue that seemed essential—creating a mechanism for settling disputes—and it took a decade to accomplish even that. It is worthy of note that a not-dissimilar dynamic unfolded after the 2000 election when early outcries about the Electoral College were deflected and Congress ended up focusing its energies on new voting technology.

The aftermath of the 1876 election also revealed another common feature of political crises. Although some elected officials, party stalwarts, and intellectuals remained exercised about the systemic problems underlying the drama, public interest in the subject faded, particularly after the next presidential contest was (rather luckily) settled without dispute.[50] By 1885 the *Chicago Daily Tribune,* asserting that the electoral system remained "dangerous," lamented that "the public apparently takes no interest" in the matter except during a dispute. "It is exactly like the old story of the man who did not mend his roof when it was raining for fear he would get wet, and when it didn't rain it did not need mending." An institution that was put to use once every four years and that severely malfunctioned only occasionally was unlikely to galvanize the public for very long, however unsatisfactory its routine functioning may have been to many voters.[51]

As had been true in 1824–1825, thus, an unpopular and disputed election outcome failed to produce changes to the electoral system. That failure led one contemporary scholar of Electoral College reform, Herman V. Ames (later a professor of constitutional history at the University of Pennsylvania) to conclude pessimistically that prospects for reform were bleak, largely because the Constitution was so difficult to amend. In a monograph published by the American Historical Association in the 1890s, Ames surveyed all of the amendments to the Constitution that had ever been proposed. "The fact that it was impossible" for Congress to take action "in the years succeeding the contested election of 1876," Ames wrote, "indicates that the adoption of a new system of electing the Chief Magistrate is improbable before the present method of amending the Constitution is itself changed."[52]

A Partisan Storm: The Miner Law in Michigan

The failure of Congress to act on electoral reform in the 1870s and 1880s set the stage for a remarkable, if little-known, drama that unfolded in the early 1890s. Its focal—and flash—point was the passage in Michigan, in 1891, of a law abolishing the general ticket and requiring electors to be chosen in district elections. By enacting this law (which was called the Miner Law, after its author, John Miner, a one-term state representative), the state of Michigan adopted a practice that had been common before 1830 and embraced an idea that enjoyed support for much of the nineteenth century. Michigan was the first state to switch to district elections since the 1820s.

But the Miner Law, passed by a Democratic majority in the legislature, was greeted not as a routine, or even legitimate, change in electoral procedure; nor as a cross-party embrace of Republican Oliver Morton's proposal of the 1870s; and certainly not as the resurrection of a plan favored by James Madison. Instead it provoked a fierce partisan storm, both political and legal, that engulfed political life in Michigan and rumbled loudly across the nation. Democrats in many states celebrated its passage (some sought to emulate it), while Republicans denounced the Miner Law as an act of "Democratic piracy," that conferred "unfair and . . . unnatural advantages" on Democratic candidates—and was unconstitutional to boot. President Benjamin Harrison joined the fray, offering his own counterproposal in a major address to Congress, and the U.S. Supreme Court ended up ruling on the law just weeks before the 1892 presidential election.[53]

The storm had been brewing at least since the election of 1876, which had left members of both parties convinced that their political adversaries were willing to game or pervert electoral laws and the Constitution for partisan advantage. In states throughout the nation, the political rancor was intensified, year after year, by the widespread use of gerrymanders and malapportionment in drawing district boundaries for legislative and congressional seats. As historian Peter Argersinger has established in rich detail, this was a golden age of partisan gerrymandering, prompted in part by socioeconomic changes, population growth in urban areas, immigration, and—in the South—the enfranchisement of black citizens. With the laws governing districting in flux and sometimes contradictory, majority parties in legislatures commonly created districts that were not only bizarrely shaped but of highly unequal size. In Iowa in 1882, for example, state house districts ranged in population from 7,448 to 25,201; a few years later in Wisconsin, the largest district had nearly six times as many voters as the smallest. Such practices enabled a party that controlled a legislature after a census to draw maps that would significantly increase its odds of remaining in power and winning seats in Congress. Because state legislatures chose U.S. senators, such maneuvers, of course, reverberated further into national politics and policies. It was not only in the South—where these methods were complemented by the removal of black voters from the electorate—that political parties ignored norms of fair competition and changed electoral rules to suit their own interests.[54]

Nowhere were these practices more common than in the Midwest, a key battleground in national politics.[55] Both major parties had strength in the Midwest, but the Republicans had an edge—which they sought to keep through districting schemes that advantaged older agricultural counties at the expense of the rapidly growing manufacturing centers that were attracting large numbers of immigrants. This was clearly the pattern in Michigan, where the Republicans had enacted severe partisan gerrymanders in 1881 and again (after a state census) in 1885.[56] But the tables were turned in the Wolverine State in 1890 when the Democrats, with some help from the Prohibitionists and the Patrons of Industry (a recently founded farmers' organization), rode a wave of agrarian discontent, coupled with antagonism toward Republican tariff policies, to gain majorities in the legislature. (Democrats made similar gains in several other midwestern states.) To cement their victory and optimize their chances in subsequent elections, Michigan's Democrats proceeded to draw new, lopsided maps for both legislative and state senatorial districts; they also redrew the boundaries of congressional districts. Republicans howled in protest, denouncing the legislature's actions and challenging the districting plans in the courts. The new map of state senate districts, they claimed, was a "monstrous outrage perpetrated on the good people of Michigan by the thieving Democracy."[57]

Once the redistricting was accomplished, Michigan's Democrats turned their attention to presidential elections and the Electoral College. Here too, resentment and a sense of unfairness had built up over decades. In 1876, 1884, and 1888, the Democratic presidential candidate had won at least 44 percent of the state's popular vote, but, thanks to the general ticket, had garnered no electoral votes; in the latter two years, the Republicans received all of Michigan's electoral votes without even winning a majority of the state's popular vote. The pattern was similar elsewhere in the large, economically diverse states of the Midwest. In 1888, for example, Republican Benjamin Harrison defeated Grover Cleveland by less than 3 percent of the popular vote in Illinois, Indiana, and Ohio, but Harrison pocketed fifty electoral votes and the election, despite having lost the national popular vote. It is little wonder, then, that Michigan's Democrats, once they gained power, seized the opportunity to discard the general ticket and adopt the Miner Law in April 1891. They rightly gauged that they could not count on consistently winning the popular vote (and thus benefit from the general ticket), but a district system would permit them to pick up some electoral votes—possibly enough to swing the 1892 election.

The Miner Law provided that one elector would be chosen from each congressional district; to select the two additional electors, the state was divided into eastern and western mega-districts, one of which the Democrats hoped to control.[58]

Democrats throughout the North applauded the Miner Law as a reform that brought presidential elections closer to the people and gave minority parties the influence that their numbers warranted. They also acknowledged, and sometimes crowed, that it would enhance the odds of electing a Democratic president. Legislators in Ohio and Wisconsin considered taking similar action, while the Detroit *Evening News* predicted that widespread adoption of Miner-type laws would "revolutionize American politics." (In pursuit of that goal, a Pennsylvania Democrat introduced an amendment proposal in Congress.) The national press also gave favorable notice. Soon after the Miner Law was passed, the *Washington Post* noted that it contained "an element of fairness which may lead to its adoption by other States." The *Post* cautioned, however, that the use of districts would be "unwieldy," leading to many contested elections, and that laws like Michigan's would prove to be way stations on the road from the "present electoral-college method" toward a much-preferable national popular vote. The *New York Times* also saw the virtues of district elections, although it preferred proportional schemes. Third parties, like the rapidly growing Populists, voiced support for district election laws because they believed that such laws would give them a chance to gain influence in presidential elections.[59]

Republicans, in contrast, attacked the law as a purely partisan maneuver that would reduce Michigan's influence in presidential contests and infect presidential elections with the evil of gerrymandering. Rarely, if ever, did they engage the substantive arguments in favor of district elections or acknowledge that leading members of their own party had recently endorsed similar reforms. They also departed from their party's opposition to states' rights claims to insist that each state had a right to cast its electoral votes as a unit and express its choice "through a majority of the voters." Worried that other northern states would become "Michiganized" and thus jeopardize their chances of winning the presidency, Republicans further claimed that the Democrats were hypocrites who were pressing for Miner-type laws in the North but not in the South, where they were the dominant party.

The *Chicago Daily Tribune*, without even a nod at its support for district and proportional schemes in the 1870s and 1880s, decried the Miner Law for turning Michigan into a "bob to the Southern kite." With the backing of some prominent legal authorities, the Republicans also declared that the Miner Law was unconstitutional—despite the Constitution's quite explicit statement that electors in each state would be chosen "in such manner as the legislature thereof may direct."[60]

President Benjamin Harrison assumed a prominent role in the anti-Miner cause, a natural outgrowth of his own history of combat against Democratic electoral stratagems. In 1885 in Harrison's home state of Indiana, a politically divided state that was consistently "doubtful" in presidential elections, Democrats gained control of the legislature and passed a highly partisan redistricting bill to help keep themselves in power at the next election. (That the Republicans had engaged in similar maneuvers goes without saying.) If they succeeded, Harrison was certain to lose his seat in the Senate. Harrison then embarked on a highly publicized campaign to regain control of the legislature for his party, denouncing gerrymanders and linking Democratic redistricting policies to the growing suppression of black votes in the South. His campaign narrowly failed, but it helped bring him to national prominence and to the White House as a crusader for fair elections.[61]

In December 1891, in his third annual address to Congress, Harrison laid out his case against district elections and Michigan's recent "departure . . . from the method which had become uniform in all the States." He acknowledged that states had experimented with different modes of choosing electors until the 1830s but asserted that they had inexorably gravitated toward the general ticket because "uniformity was desirable" and "a general election in territorial divisions not subject to change was most consistent with the popular character of our institutions." Rewriting the history through the prism of his own preoccupations, Harrison inaccurately ascribed the triumph of the general ticket to the desire of the states to remove "the choice of President from the baneful influence of the 'gerrymander.'" The Miner Law, accordingly, was a step in the wrong direction and a "danger" to the nation. The remedy that Harrison put forward was a constitutional amendment to make the general ticket "permanent" as well as universal. He also proposed the creation of a nonpartisan national commission charged with developing "some plan for removing or miti-gating" the "evils connected with our election system" in order to protect the right of suffrage and ensure "an equality of value in each ballot cast."[62]

Nothing came of Harrison's proposals. Although many welcomed his focus on the compelling problem of gerrymandering, the partisan subtext to his address was far too visible—and Congress was too divided—to galva-nize any serious movement toward an amendment. (A bishop of the Meth-odist Episcopal Church concluded that Harrison's objections to district elections were "as weighty as can be made, but ... not formidable.")[63] The general ticket was widely viewed as a flawed and not particularly democratic institution, and, as the *New York Times* noted, even gerrymandered districts gave more "value" to the votes cast by supporters of minority parties than did the winner-take-all system that Harrison was defending.[64] The intense hostility of many Republicans to the Miner Law, moreover, made clear that they saw the general ticket working to their advantage in presidential elec-tions, particularly in the Midwest. Indeed, Harrison arguably owed his own election to the general ticket—he had become president while losing the national popular vote—and with a reelection battle looming, his stance could not shed its self-serving aura. Viewed in historical perspective, Har-rison's position, shared by many Republicans, was notable for its reversal of arguments put forward in the first third of the nineteenth century. De-fenders of the general ticket had then fought proposals for a district elec-tions amendment on federalism grounds: states had the constitutionally guaranteed right to determine their own method of choosing electors. In the very different political context of the early 1890s, a Republican president was seeking to override states' rights and deploy the power of the federal government in order to impose the general ticket everywhere.[65]

The governor of Michigan, Democrat Edwin B. Winans, published a response to Harrison and other critics in the spring of 1892. Writing in the *North American Review,* Winans sought to dispel the "impression" that Michigan had adopted a "dangerous innovation." He sketched the history of district elections from the 1790s into the 1830s, cited James Madison's 1823 letter to John Hay favoring district elections, and offered his own suc-cinct explanation of the adoption of the general ticket. "As the people di-vided into parties," Winans wrote, "the majorities in certain States, having control of the legislatures, decided to shut the mouths of their opponents."

Turning to the present, he pointed out that political views were rarely uniform across a state and that district elections would consequently yield "a more exact expression of the preferences" of the people. They would, in addition, have the positive consequence of "destroying the commanding importance of pivotal States," like Indiana and New York, which every four years became potentially corrupt scenes of partisan warfare and "debauchery." Responding to the claim that district elections would reduce the influence of a state in the "selection of a President," he opined that "if popular sentiment in a State is divided, her electoral vote ought to be divided, be the result what it may." Finally, taking dead aim at Harrison, Winans acknowledged that gerrymandering was a widespread (and bipartisan) problem and that it was an "undoubted wrong." But, he noted, "its injustice lies in the fact that it lessens the representation to which the political minority, by reason of their numbers, are justly entitled. But if we condemn the gerrymander because it lessens the representation of the minority, what is to be said of a system which excludes the minority from any representation whatever? Yet this is the exact result attained by choosing Presidential electors on a general ticket."[66]

With a presidential election approaching and a national debate under way, Michigan's Republicans took to the courts to rid themselves of the Miner Law in the spring of 1892. Their first stop was the Michigan Supreme Court, where they alleged that the law was unconstitutional for eleven different reasons, most of them minor or even trivial. The most important were claims that that the Constitution had always required a state to "act as a unit in appointing presidential electors" and that the Miner Act violated the Fourteenth Amendment. The latter argument—clearly designed to circumvent the undeniable fact that district elections had been utilized in the early nineteenth century—rested on the dubious assertion that the Fourteenth Amendment, ratified in 1868, granted to Michigan's citizens (as one of the "privileges" of citizenship) the right to vote for all of the state's electors. Although the legal case was thin, many observers, including Governor Winans, believed that the Republicans stood a fair chance of winning because Michigan's judges were elected and three of the five members of the state's supreme court were Republican. During a hearing that lasted nearly twelve hours, in a courtroom packed with lawyers and raucous partisans, the Republicans pressed their claims in detail, while the Democrats insisted that the Constitution plainly gave the legislature the authority to decide how to choose electors. (In an effort to give the legal combat a less partisan cast, each legal team included one member from the opposing party, yet, as the *Chicago Daily Tribune* reported, "politics is here and in it just the same.") The Democrats also derided the notion that the Fourteenth Amendment had altered the constitutional process of choosing a president without anyone having mentioned it or known about it. On June 17 the court unanimously ruled that "the statute must stand as the lawful edict of the Legislature." Although it lamented the "injustice of any other than a uniform system of electing the President," the court concluded that it lacked the constitutional authority to substitute its judgment for the legislature's.[67]

The Republicans then appealed the state court's verdict to the U.S. Supreme Court, requesting an expedited review in light of the forthcoming election. The Supreme Court agreed to hear the case on the first possible date, October 11. Both sides added nationally prominent attorneys to their Michigan legal teams, with the Republicans—reflecting their sense of urgency and desperation—fielding a battery of lawyers that included a former U.S. attorney general, two assistant attorneys general, the solicitor general, and the sitting attorney general (Harrison's former law partner), who was acting as a private citizen. (In so doing, he had "laid aside his dignity," according to the *New York Times*.) But neither the size nor the prestige of the Republican legal team could compensate for the weakness of its legal position. A bare six days after the oral arguments, the Supreme Court issued a unanimous ruling, written by Chief Justice Melville Fuller, upholding the Miner Law. The Court concluded that the overwhelming weight of contemporary and historical evidence made clear that the framers of the Constitution intended to entrust the "mode of appointment of electors . . . exclusively to the states." Nor was the Court "able to discover any conflict between" the Miner Law and the Fourteenth Amendment, the object of which was "not to radically change the whole theory of the relations of the state and federal governments to each other, and of both governments to the people." The legal case, in effect, was open and shut, and the Supreme Court stood aside from the partisan fray.[68]

Predictably, Democrats celebrated the Court's ruling while Republicans resumed their denunciations of the Miner Law as an unscrupulous, even if legal, outgrowth of partisan gerrymandering. (Many Republicans knew that their legal claims were a stretch; even President Harrison, by proposing a constitutional amendment, had appeared to concede that Michigan's law did not violate the Constitution.) Both parties then turned their full attention to the November elections, which delivered another blow to the Grand Old Party. Grover Cleveland defeated Harrison in the popular vote by a larger margin (3 percent) than he had in 1888, but this time he won a decisive majority in the Electoral College. Cleveland won five of Michigan's fourteen electoral votes (the first to go to a Democrat since the Civil War), but contrary to some early predictions, those votes had no impact on the outcome. The unusual twist in the national election was the success of the Populists, whose presidential candidate won more than 8 percent of the popular vote and twenty-two electoral votes.[69]

The Republicans fared better in Michigan's state elections, paving the way for retaliation against the Democrats. Although the Miner Law had passed muster in all courts, in July 1892 the state's supreme court rejected the Democratic districting plan for the state legislature, which eventually led to a new map more favorable to the Republicans. The Republicans campaigned ferociously against the "gerrymandering" Democrats and in November were able to regain control of the legislature, thanks in part to a lack of full cooperation between the Democrats and the Populists. (The Republicans actually polled fewer votes than did the other parties combined.) When the new legislature convened in January 1893, the first item on the Republicans' agenda was repeal of the Miner Law. Over the loud protests of Populists, Democrats, Prohibitionists, and Patrons of Industry, the Republican majorities rammed the repeal through both branches of the legislature on straight party-line votes. In early November, just days before the election, the *New York Times* had observed that "in Michigan the voters can come nearer to voting directly for President and Vice President than they can anywhere else in the United States." That proved to be true for one, and only one, election.[70]

The Republicans, moreover, were not finished. To help ensure their future dominance of the legislature, they altered the system of electing state representatives in the cities, giving Republican candidates a better chance of winning seats in Democratic strongholds. Even before the next census, they attempted to redraw the state's congressional districts, failing to do so only because they could not agree among themselves on a new map. (Three of their state senators even criticized a Republican house bill as an "outrageous gerrymander.") On another party-line vote, the Republicans approved a constitutional amendment to repeal the state's "alien intent" law, which for decades had enfranchised (predominantly Democratic) immigrants who had been in the state for several years and declared their intention to become citizens. Between 1893 and 1895, they also took steps toward instituting an "anti-fusion" law that would hinder an electoral alliance between the Democrats and the Populists. In the latter year the legislature instituted an educational requirement for voting as well as a vote-suppressing registration law that was particularly targeted at the city of Detroit. Republicans remained in control of the Michigan legislature until 1933.[71]

Michigan's experience with the Miner Law was a vivid and disturbing illustration of the immense difficulty of reforming electoral institutions in an era of intense partisanship and close elections. What transpired was not a debate regarding the merits of different modes of choosing electors but partisan warfare grounded in assessments of the electoral impact of abandoning the general ticket. (In that respect it resembled the battles between the Federalists and the Democratic-Republicans in the early 1800s.) Michigan's Democrats, to be sure, did have principled and long-standing arguments on their side, but their partisan interests were undeniable, and given the ruthless actions of their party colleagues in the South, the Democrats were in no position to be overly righteous about democratic values or fair electoral processes. Similarly (but not too similarly), the Republicans had a point about district elections being subject to the "baneful" and all-too-common evil of gerrymandering, but, as they surely knew, that problem could be circumvented by holding statewide proportional elections. The tenacious Republican embrace of the general ticket stemmed from fear of the political consequences of district or proportional elections, not from objections to the principles or ideas undergirding them. Republicans were surely aware that prominent members of their own party, like Oliver Morton, had trumpeted those principles, eloquently supporting district elections in the 1870s. They likely also knew that in 1880 Republicans in New York and New Jersey had advanced schemes much like the Miner Law.[72]

But the national political terrain had shifted in important ways between the 1870s and 1891, thanks to the deepening dominance of the Demo-

cratic Party in the South and its increasingly evident intention of removing African-Americans from the region's political life. The fate of
the South—and the Republican Party in the South—had still appeared
to be in play in the 1870s, and Republican leaders, including Presidents
Rutherford Hayes and Chester Arthur, had pursued various strategies to
draw targeted segments of the white electorate to their party in the 1870s
and 1880s. Hayes even made two trips of symbolic conciliation to the
South in 1877. Yet these efforts met with little success, and in one state
after another the party's loyal African-American supporters were losing
access to the polls.[73]

In 1890 President Harrison and congressional Republicans—who controlled both the Senate and the House—made a final effort to stem that
political tide. Alarmed at the violations of the Fifteenth Amendment, the
blatant electoral manipulations in the South, and the violence perpetrated
against African-Americans, the Republicans put forward the Federal Elections Bill (also known as the Lodge Force Bill) which would have deployed the power of the federal government to protect the voting rights of
African-Americans. But a prolonged Democratic filibuster, aided by divisions among Republicans, led to the defeat of the Federal Elections Bill
in the Senate in January 1891, after it had been narrowly approved by the
House. That defeat came just months before the passage of the Miner Law,
and it signaled that the federal government would not impede the South's
transformation into a one-party region.[74] Although the Republicans retained some electoral strength in the upper South and the Populists briefly
flourished in Alabama, Georgia, and a few other states, there was little
doubt that the Democrats henceforth would control the vast majority of
electoral votes in the South, with or without the general ticket.[75]

The fervor of Republican hostility to Electoral College reform was
rooted, thus, in both a political calculus and a passionate conviction, im-
bued with moral certainty, that the general ticket in the northern states
was a needed counterweight to the unconstitutional assault on democracy
taking place in the South. The *Chicago Daily Tribune,* once a strong voice
in favor of reform, opposed a pending constitutional amendment for proportional elections because it "would prevent Republican States making
their controlling majorities count, while it would not have that result in
the South, and hence would cut down on Republican Electoral strength

heavily and give the Democracy the victory every time." Without winner-take-all, the Democrats would be rewarded with the presidency for having disenfranchised African-Americans and established a one-party regime in the states of the former Confederacy. The general ticket had acquired democratic virtues.[76]

What transpired in Michigan also pointed to the particular challenges facing any effort to eliminate winner-take-all on a state-by-state basis. As Governor Winans had pointed out in 1892, the cumbersome procedures and supermajorities needed to amend the U.S. Constitution could be circumvented because "it is within the power of each state legislature to give every section of its state a fair representation in the Electoral College."[77] The dynamics of party competition, however, made such a step unlikely. Any political party that had (or believed it had) a secure hold on a state's legislature was also likely to have a secure hold on the state's electoral votes; it would therefore have no political incentive to abandon the general ticket. The same was true of any political party that came to power in a legislature and was convinced that it would remain ascendant in the state.[78] In contrast, a minority party that gained a temporary legislative majority might well have an incentive to institute district or proportional elections, but even if it succeeded, its victory could prove to be short-lived and reversible, as happened in Michigan. Only if the political parties in a state were evenly matched might they both perceive it to be in their interest to share the state's electoral votes, and even then both would have to be willing to shed the potential influence that came from being a battleground in presidential elections. Durable reform could also occur in a state if the parties agreed that some system other than winner-take-all was more consistent with their professed values and principles; but in the late nineteenth century, at least, democratic values, although proclaimed by all, rarely took precedence over partisan interests.[79]

It was, then, not surprising that no other states were "Michiganized" in the 1890s. Circumstances favorable to state action were uncommon, and Michigan's unhappy experience surely served as a warning to reformers elsewhere that disturbing the status quo could be hazardous. Notably, only two states have adopted district elections in the 125 years since the Miner Law. Maine did so with bipartisan support in 1969, partly in response to George Wallace's third-party candidacy and the possibility that all of the state's electoral votes might be awarded to a plurality victor.[80] Nebraska took a similar step in 1991, although the Republicans tried several times to repeal or undermine the law, particularly after Barack Obama won one of Nebraska's districts in 2008.[81] In recent years, efforts to replace winner-take-all with district elections have periodically been launched by minority parties—Republicans in California, for example—but such efforts were generally doomed by their overt partisan intent and the minority status of the parties proposing them.

The uproar over the Miner Law marked the effective end of efforts to abolish the general ticket in the nineteenth century. Constitutional amendments favoring a proportional system continued to be introduced in Congress, but they were never brought to a vote and never attracted much attention. With the Republican Party increasingly committed to protecting winner-take-all, it was apparent to nearly all observers that a district or proportional amendment could not be passed.[82] Nonetheless, critics of the electoral system continued to speak out: one of them, John G. Carlisle, a (Democratic) Speaker of the House in the 1880s and Grover Cleveland's treasury secretary in the 1890s, insisted that the system was "the source of all the greatest dangers to which we are now subject." He was particularly concerned that the rise of new parties, such as the Populists, would permit "a mere plurality of the popular vote to control the entire electoral vote" in each state and increase the likelihood that elections would end up in the House of Representatives. Yet, as the century came to a close, the critics sounded more resigned than impassioned. Writing in the *American Journal of Politics* in 1893, attorney Norman T. Mason observed that attempts to amend the Constitution to abolish the deeply flawed Electoral College had met "with so little success that the effort seems to have been finally abandoned." He worried that it would be "a national calamity if the discouragement of the older shall become, as now seems likely, the apathy of the younger generation of statesmen."[83]

Interlude: 1900–1944

The late nineteenth-century pessimism about the prospects for presidential election reform proved to be warranted. Although criticism of the Electoral College continued to appear in the press, particularly in election years (in 1904 the *Washington Post* called the institution "curious and un-republican"), it was more subdued after 1900 than it had been in the 1870s and 1880s. There was also less editorializing or published commentary in favor of district or proportional elections.[84] Similarly, constitutional amendments to alter the election process were proposed in Congress but in reduced numbers and with little impact; between 1899 and 1911 none were introduced at all.[85] Both the Progressive era and the New Deal, of course, were periods of significant social and political reform, but the conduct of presidential elections never ranked high on the agenda of reformers. The issue was, in effect, politically frozen, largely because the Republican Party (which won seven of the nine presidential elections from 1896 through 1928) was well known to oppose any scheme that would undermine winner-take-all.[86] Only once between 1900 and 1950 did such an amendment resolution come up for a vote in either branch of Congress, and that was on a proposal, put forward by progressive Republican senator George Norris in 1934, that was so watered down that little would have changed even if it had passed.

Indeed, Norris's experience during the four decades he served in Congress (1903–1943) encapsulated many of the challenges facing those who favored electoral reform. As early as 1913, when he entered the Senate after five terms in the House, he declared himself to be in favor of abolishing the Electoral College, in part because he believed that the complex apparatus of the institution gave too much power to established political parties and made it nearly impossible for independent candidates to mount serious campaigns for the presidency.[87] (His stance paralleled that of Thomas Hart Benton a century earlier.) He later maintained that the Electoral College was "as useless politically as the human appendix." In the early 1920s Norris sponsored amendment resolutions that would have eliminated electors in favor of direct voting in each state, a method that came to be called the "automatic system" because electoral votes would be cast automatically, without the intervention of electors. But the fiercely independent senator from Nebraska could not sell that option to his Republican colleagues who dominated both branches of Congress. A decade later, with Democrats in control, he proposed a more ambitious amendment that called for the proportional allocation of electoral votes, the elimination of electors, and a plurality winner; it also mandated that, subject to state law, the names of independent candidates had to appear on the ballot. This resolution reached the Senate floor but only after the Judiciary Committee, with Norris's assent, transformed the measure so that it would have permanently institutionalized winner-take-all, required a majority winner, and retained the existing contingent process. This eviscerated proposal—which would have eliminated electors and enhanced the prospects of independent candidates—still fell two votes short of passage. Most of its support came from Democrats, joined by a handful of progressive Republicans.[88]

A more steadfast advocate of proportional elections was Representative Clarence Lea, a long-serving and highly respected Democrat from northern California. First in 1928 and again in subsequent years, Lea put forward amendment resolutions calling for proportional elections with a plurality victor. "Our system of electing the President is archaic, crude, cumbersome, and, above all, lacks the inherent quality of political justice," he observed, and "the fundamental defect is in the unit-voting system." (For reasons that remain obscure, the general ticket had come to be called the "unit rule," a phrase borrowed from political conventions.) Lea's arguments closely tracked those of late nineteenth-century advocates of proportional plans, and he took pains to distinguish his proposal from the idea of a national popular vote. At the same time, he placed unusual emphasis on the ethical shortcomings of the existing system. There is, Lea declared, "no political morality in the unit vote. It is against good morals to take the votes that are intended for one man and count them for the other." In 1933 his proposal was twice reported favorably by House committees, but it never reached a floor vote or debate. Despite the lack of success, Lea continued to introduce resolutions for a proportional vote almost annually until shortly before his retirement from the House in 1949.[89]

Mr. Lodge and Mr. Gossett

Political pressures to reform or abolish the Electoral College mounted once again in the mid-1940s, giving rise to public and congressional debates that continued, on and off, for more than three decades. At the heart of this resurgence were regional tensions emanating from the uneasy coexistence of the one-party, conservative, Democratic South with an urban pro-civil-rights liberalism that had gained strength during the New Deal and was centered in the more pluralist and competitive states of the North. These tensions, which touched Republicans as well as Democrats, intersected with long-standing discontents to generate a wide variety of proposals for revamping the electoral system. One of these proposals, in 1950, suffered the unusual fate of gaining the approval of more than two-thirds of the Senate and then being resoundingly defeated in the House. It also occasioned a paradoxical sequence of debates in which reform ideas that were regarded as intrinsically progressive and democratizing encountered opposition from liberals who feared that they would have profoundly undemocratic and conservative consequences.

The saga began with the "Southern revolt" within the Democratic Party in 1944. Tensions between the northern and southern wings of the party had been mounting since the 1930s, with many southerners opposing the New Deal's social legislation as well as its support for organized labor and a stronger federal government. Even more disturbing and potentially divisive was the increasingly visible support of northern Democrats for measures aimed at ending racial discrimination. The party platform of 1940 pledged to support the principle of equal protection of the laws regardless of race, and in June 1941 Franklin Roosevelt issued Executive Order 8802, which banned discrimination in hiring for government or defense industry jobs. Although southerners wielded considerable power in Congress, thanks to the seniority system and their longevity as legislators (a byproduct of single-party dominance), they chafed at their exclusion from the presidency itself, a sentiment strengthened in 1940 by Roosevelt's decision to seek a third term, dashing the presidential hopes of Vice President John Nance Garner of Texas.[90]

By the spring of 1944, many southerners were in open rebellion against Roosevelt and the liberal wing of the party. The Democratic state convention in Texas named a slate of presidential electors and instructed them to vote for a candidate other than Roosevelt if the national convention were to adopt platform planks opposing the right of states to segregate schools or to set their own qualifications for voting. Mississippi took a similar step, adding poll taxes to the litmus test. At the national convention in July, delegates from seven southern states cast their ballots for Virginia senator Harry F. Byrd, an outspoken critic of the New Deal and desegregation. The liberal wing of the party, however, stood firm on the issues, making only a few procedural gestures toward the dissidents, and the revolt faded quickly after the national convention—largely because the southerners had no realistic alternative to remaining within the Democratic Party. In the November election, Franklin Roosevelt won all of the South's electoral votes.[91]

Although unsuccessful, the revolt set off alarm bells. The possibility that Democratic electors would not cast their ballots for the nominee of the Democratic Party reawakened a long-standing, yet long-submerged, concern about the dangers inherent in a system that relied on intermediaries. Soon after the Texas convention had issued its instructions to electors (which, if adhered to, would have meant that Texas would cast no electoral votes for Franklin Roosevelt), Emanuel Celler, a liberal Democrat from New York, introduced an amendment resolution to abolish the Electoral College and replace it with a proportional allocation of electoral votes in each state, with a plurality victor. "What is the real necessity of retaining a mechanism," Celler asked, "that is—at best—a useless, cumbersome, expensive automaton, and—at worst—a dangerous weapon that has within itself the possibilities of thwarting the popular will?" (The use of the word *cumbersome* to describe the Electoral College had successfully migrated from the nineteenth century to the twentieth.) Within a few weeks Senator Joseph Guffey of Pennsylvania presented a companion resolution in the Senate, reciting the well-known defects of the unit rule and arguing that the Electoral College itself was "an unnecessary go-between between the will of the people" and the choice of a president. The Celler-Guffey amendment caused a stir in Congress and briefly suggested that Electoral College reform might be imminent. In December 1944, New York's secretary of state opened the quadrennial convening of his state's electoral college with the announcement that this method of electing a president might soon be coming to an end.[92]

Things quieted down after the 1944 election—but not for long. The fissures in the Democratic Party widened in the later 1940s, giving rise to a renewed and better organized southern revolt in 1948. After the party adopted a fairly strong civil rights plank at its convention, thirty-five southern delegates walked out and headed to Birmingham, Alabama, where they joined 6,000 compatriots to found the States' Rights Democratic Party. The Dixiecrats, as they came to be called, nominated South Carolina governor Strom Thurmond as their presidential candidate and Mississippi governor Fielding Wright as his running mate. Single-mindedly devoted to preserving segregation and white supremacy, the Dixiecrats hoped to win enough electoral votes to throw the election into the House, where they could trade their support for policy commitments. At the least, Dixiecrats believed, a show of strength would enlarge their influence within the Democratic Party. The strategy was plausible, but it did not pan out: in the November election, most southerners stuck with the Democrats. Thurmond won four states and thirty-nine electoral votes, too few to derail President Truman's unexpected victory over New York governor Thomas Dewey.[93]

The events of 1948 further heightened concerns about the electoral system. The possibility of the election being decided in the House of Representatives was a jarring reminder that the Constitution retained a contingent election mechanism that was almost universally regarded as undemocratic and corruptible. The Dixiecrats' strategy, moreover, made clear that the unit rule could easily transform a regional candidate into a kingmaker. In January 1949 Arthur Krock, Washington bureau chief of the *New York Times*, recalled the uncertainties of election night when the "wobbling" counts in Ohio and California suggested that the decision might end up in the House. He then sketched in detail the complex horse trading that could have unfolded in the House as inauguration day approached. "This nightmare vision of a might-have-been," Krock concluded, "furnishes another reason for . . . electoral reform."[94]

Enter Henry Cabot Lodge and Ed Lee Gossett, a political odd couple who sponsored the most widely supported electoral reform proposal of the first half of the twentieth century. Lodge, a Harvard-educated Republican scion of a distinguished New England family, had returned to the Senate in 1946 after having given up his seat to fight in World War II. The grandson of a famous senator (who had proposed the ill-fated Federal Elections Bill of 1890), Lodge was an ambitious, principled politician who adhered to the moderate and internationalist wing of his party and fought openly against the crusty, and sometimes isolationist, conservatism of midwesterners like Ohio senator Robert Taft. Gossett, in contrast, was a Democrat who had grown up on a farm in central Texas and worked as a small-town lawyer and district attorney before being elected to the House of Representatives in 1938. An ardent segregationist and antagonist of the left, with undisguised anti-Semitic proclivities, Gossett was one of the leaders of Texas's rebellion against the national Democratic Party and its civil rights stance in 1948.[95]

Lodge and Gossett teamed up to promote a resolution that would abolish the Electoral College and allocate each state's electoral votes in proportion to the popular vote tallies in that state; the candidate who received a plurality of the national electoral vote would become president. (In the course of the Senate debates in 1950, Lodge accepted an amendment requiring that the winning candidate receive at least 40 percent of the electoral vote.) The Lodge-Gossett proposal was, of course, similar to the Celler-Guffey resolution and to dozens of other proportional measures that had been put forward in Congress since the Civil War. But the political climate in the late 1940s—for a moment at least—was more receptive to the idea than had ever been true before.[96] The Democratic Party held majorities in the Senate as well as the House, and both its northern and southern wings were expressing interest in altering the system. Democrats were also well aware that Electoral College dynamics threatened to fracture their party. In addition, Lodge's presence as a sponsor of the resolution suggested that cracks were emerging in the Republican Party's long-standing opposition to eliminating winner-take-all.

Lodge, who first introduced the proposal in May 1948, was the leading spokesman in its behalf, repeatedly presenting detailed, cogent arguments in favor of proportional elections; with great patience, he even responded in writing to a list of skeptical questions posed by Republican senator Homer Ferguson of Michigan.[97] Senate Joint Resolution 2 (S.J. Res. 2), Lodge argued, would prevent elections from devolving on the House and greatly reduce the odds of choosing a president who had lost the popular vote, two dangers that had loomed large in 1948. It would also put an end to concerns about "faithless" electors or state legislatures deciding not to hold popular elections. The electoral vote—which would be retained "purely as a counting device"—would closely mirror the popular vote, the influence of small states would be preserved, "sure" states would no longer be ignored, and "doubtful" states would cease receiving the lion's share of attention. With the unit rule abolished, political parties would be also be freer to nominate candidates from locales other than large swing states. Six of the last ten presidents had come from either New York or Ohio, both of which were competitive in presidential elections.[98]

Lodge also voiced a less traditional argument for eliminating winner-take-all. Proportional elections, he maintained, would not only diminish the influence of the largest states; they would also take power from the organized "voting minorities in those States." The genteel senator from Massachusetts left it to Gossett and others to itemize those "voting minorities," but Lodge himself warned that if a close election hinged on the outcome in New York, then "the Communist Party in the State of New York alone could determine who was to be President of the United States." That eventuality, of course, was unlikely, but the potential influence of the Communist Party and other radicals of the left emerged as a new leitmotif in these early Cold War debates. Jettisoning the unit rule would help protect the political mainstream against disruptions from the organized left, which was strongest in urban states like New York.[99]

While most of Lodge's case was constructed to appeal to liberals and moderates of both parties who deplored the undemocratic features of the Electoral College, he also offered a partisan rationale targeted at his fellow Republicans. Proportional elections, he maintained, would tend "to break up so-called solid or one-party areas"—by which he meant the South—and, in so doing, improve the fortunes of the GOP. (The phrase "solid states" was a common political euphemism for the South, a way of talking about the region without appearing to single it out.) His party had effectively written off the South for the first half of the twentieth century, but Lodge believed that Republicans could win electoral votes in the region and, in so doing, reverse the string of losses they had suffered in presidential elections from 1932 through 1948. "This reform," he insisted, "would definitely encourage the two-party system in the so-called one-party sections of the country."[100] While acknowledging that such an outcome "involves a change as to the future," he intimated that proportional elections would gradually bring traditionally Republican African-Americans into the polity and alter "the voting complexion in the so-called politically solid areas." Lodge declined, however, to expressly mention the racial barriers that kept millions of African-Americans from voting in the South, and he touted as a virtue of his plan that it would leave suffrage requirements in the hands of the states. Race was rarely mentioned in either the committee hearings or the floor debates in the Senate, and when questions arose about the unusual

scope of voting rights in the South, the example invoked almost invariably was the atypical voting age of eighteen in Georgia.[101]

Lodge, like Clarence Lea, was careful to distinguish his plan from a
national popular vote, a proposal for which was also before the Senate. Unlike Lea, however, the Massachusetts senator acknowledged that he had
supported a national election in the past and would still prefer it; he believed, however, that such an amendment would never pass because small
and sparsely populated states would not agree to a proposal that would
lessen their influence.[102] Lodge accordingly sought to portray S.J. Res. 2 as
a bipartisan, centrist measure, a reasonable compromise between inaction,
which would leave a flawed system in place, and the more radical alternative
of a national popular vote. When he reintroduced it in 1949, the resolution
had ten co-sponsors in the Senate (most of them Democrats, six from the
South or border states) and abundant, if sometimes qualified, support from
newspapers and magazines around the country.[103] Buttressing the case for S.J.
Res. 2, a Gallup poll in August 1948 indicated that 58 percent of Americans
favored the proposed change while only 15 percent preferred to retain the
unit rule. (See Appendix Table A.2.)

Meanwhile, in the House Ed Gossett was telling a somewhat different
story. He introduced House Joint Resolution 2 (H.J. Res. 2) in January 1949,
and committee hearings were held the following month. (Former representative Clarence Lea was the first witness.) In those hearings, Gossett
provided a detailed list of the problems with the Electoral College and
maintained that proportional elections would solve most of them. He sup-
plemented these routine arguments, however, with a lengthy, excited ex-
position of the claim that the unit rule had to be abolished because it gave
excessive influence to minority groups in pivotal states. "The electoral college," he maintained, "permits and invites irresponsible control and domination by small organized minority groups, within the large pivotal States."
He then proceeded, "at the danger of stepping on some toes," to "get down
to specific cases." Gossett's first example was the support by both major
parties in 1948 for legislation making permanent the Fair Employment
Practice Committee, a wartime agency mandated to prevent discrimination in government and defense industry hiring. This was, according to
Gossett, a "dangerous and radical proposal" that was supported "as a bid
for the Negro vote. There are enough Negroes in New York city, when

voting in bloc, to determine often how the entire electoral vote of the State of New York is cast." His second target was "the radical wing of organized labor," which could also tip the electoral votes of states like New York, Pennsylvania, Illinois, and Michigan.[104]

He then turned to Jews ("with all due deference to our many fine Jewish citizens"). According to Gossett, the presence of two and a half million Jews in New York had led both political parties to illegitimately and dangerously meddle in British foreign policy by supporting a resolution calling for unrestricted Jewish immigration to Palestine. The Italians, the Irish, the Poles, and "other large racial groups" were also guilty of acting as pressure groups in the "large pivotal states," as were the American Labor Party and the Communist Party, which might "some day soon" determine who will become president of the United States. "Strange to say," Gossett noted, the Communist Party has "its greatest following . . . in the aforesaid large pivotal States." Lest his audience misconstrue his remarks, Gossett summarized his central concern:

> Now, please understand, I have no objection to the Negro in Harlem voting and to his vote being counted, but I do resent the fact that both parties will spend a hundred times as much money to get his vote, and that his vote is worth a hundred times as much in the scale of national politics as is the vote of a white man in Texas. I have no objection to a million folks who cannot speak English, voting, or to their votes being counted, but I do resent the fact that because they happen to live in Chicago, or Detroit, or New York, that their vote is worth a hundred times as much as mine.[105]

Gossett's comments, remarkably, received little attention in 1949. Press coverage of the hearings was sparse and focused more on Lea's careful presentation than on Gossett's reactionary polemic. Less than two months later the House Judiciary Committee, although divided, reported the resolution favorably. Its rambling majority report itemized the shortcomings of the Electoral College and denounced the "gross and outstanding evil" of the unit rule; the minority report agreed that the Electoral College was flawed but sharply dissented from the recommendation. The House then put the issue on hold, waiting for the Senate to act.[106]

In the Senate, S.J. Res. 2 gained support between 1948 and 1950—although few predicted that the resolution would be approved. If Gossett's anti-civil-rights, anti-labor, and anti-ethnic perspective registered at all, it was overshadowed by Lodge's steady moderation and by the strong desire of many members to find some workable alternative to the existing system. For liberals and moderates, Lodge's proportional system promised to make presidential elections more democratic and to solve, or at least ameliorate, long-standing problems with the Electoral College that had become acute in 1944 and 1948. Some liberals, like Minnesota Democrat Hubert Humphrey, a passionate civil rights advocate, strongly preferred a national popular vote, but they were willing to back Lodge's resolution as a politically pragmatic "step in the direction of greater democratization."[107] Meanwhile, most southern Democrats, although worried that proportional elections would encourage "a multiplicity of parties" and give African-Americans more incentive to vote, were convinced that the South would benefit by a breakup of the blocs of votes cast by large, northern states. The South's voting patterns would change little, they believed, whereas competition for the electoral votes of New York, Illinois, and Ohio would decline. Gossett's rhetoric may have been extraordinary, but his views were widely shared in the region.[108]

The strongest opposition in the Senate came from conservative Republicans, who raised a host of objections to Lodge's plan. Michigan's Homer Ferguson feared that Lodge's proposal could lead to the "break-down of the two-party system" that "has been so instrumental in preserving political stability and responsible government." Correctly pointing out that the "electoral system itself" contributed to the durability of two-party dominance, he maintained that proportional elections would lead to the "continental curse of European politics," with parties proliferating, countries governed by unstable coalitions, and radical groups gaining a foothold in governments. (Lodge and others protested that this would not occur because no one was advocating proportional elections to Congress.)[109] Ferguson also raised a more traditional objection by claiming that S.J. Res. 2 would infringe on the sovereignty of the states and lead to a federal takeover of elections. Ohio's Senator Taft joined in that line of attack, hoping to soften southern support for the resolution. "If this amendment is adopted," Taft warned, a bit deviously, "then inevitably the Congress will enact national legislation to regulate the voting, doing so in such a manner that every person of voting age in every State in the southern part of the country will have an absolute, clear, and free right to vote.... I do not say it would not be a good result, but ... I think it would be the inevitable result."[110]

Republican opponents also dismissed as mere "speculation" Lodge's assertion that proportional elections would lead to a resuscitation of their party in the South. There was no evidence that "dissatisfied voters will turn only from one major party to the other," Ferguson argued, pointing out that southern politicians in 1948 fled the Democratic Party not to join the GOP but to form "their own party, a splinter party, the Dixiecrat Party." When Democratic senator Estes Kefauver of Tennessee, a strong supporter of the resolution, suggested that Republicans did not fare well in the South because they did not tailor their platforms to attract southern voters, Ferguson caustically replied that "the Senator from Tennessee knows of a much better reason for the situation in the South." Implied but unspoken was the widely shared belief that white southerners were unlikely to embrace the party of Lincoln or enfranchise African-Americans, the two paths that could lead to increased Republican strength in the region. Ferguson's adamant rejection of Lodge's prediction of inroads in the South was, in effect, a reaffirmation of the Republican calculus that had prevailed since the early 1890s: ending winner-take-all was more likely to benefit Democrats in the North than Republicans in the South. That calculus may have been out of date by 1950, but Ferguson was undeterred. Resurrecting the stance that Benjamin Harrison had adopted in 1891, the Michigan senator proposed, as a replacement for Lodge's plan, an amendment that would eliminate the machinery of the Electoral College but require all states to utilize the unit rule in allocating electors.[111]

The Senate voted on the Lodge-Gossett resolution, as well as several alternatives, on February 1, 1950. Two proposals for a national popular vote were considered first, and both were defeated by two to one margins. Ferguson's resolution, which would have eliminated electors and mandated winner-take-all, fared less well, attracting only twenty favorable votes, almost all from conservative Republicans. Finally, S.J. Res. 2 was brought to a vote, and, to the surprise of many observers, it passed by a vote of sixty-four to twenty-seven, more than the two-thirds necessary for a constitutional amendment. Nearly all of the Senate's Democrats voted favorably, and they were joined by a substantial number of Republican moderates and liberals; the measure was supported by more than two-thirds of senators from both small and large states. It was the first time since the 1820s that a branch of Congress had approved a constitutional amendment calling for a change in the method of electing presidents.[112] (See Table 3.1.)

Then things ground to a halt. In the House, the next procedural stop for the resolution was the powerful Rules Committee, which served as a gatekeeper for the consideration of legislation by the full chamber. In the weeks following the Senate vote, Gossett pressed the Rules Committee to clear the resolution for floor action. But the committee, chaired by Democrat Adolph Sabath of Chicago, the longest-serving member of the House, voted against issuing a rule that would permit the resolution to go forward— despite the urgings of President Truman, who had recently endorsed the proposal. Indeed, only four of the committee's eleven members favored sending H.J. Res. 2 to the floor: three southern Democrats and Christian Herter, a moderate Massachusetts Republican with ties to Lodge. The remaining three Republicans and all four northern Democrats voted against the measure. Sabath noted that he was "fearful" of the proposal, and another Democrat declared it to be "dangerous." It was a widely noted irony that the Rules Committee, well known for bottling up civil rights legislation and keeping it from the floor of the House, was now giving the same treatment to a resolution strongly supported by southern Democrats.[113]

Why this reversal of fortune in the span of five short weeks? Put most simply, the Senate's action prompted northern liberals, mostly Democrats but also some Republicans, to take a closer look at the Lodge-Gossett resolution, and they did not like what they saw. Despite the ostensible democratic appeal of proportional elections, the proposed amendment seemed likely, upon closer scrutiny, to move the nation in a conservative, antidemocratic direction—enhancing the political power of southern Democrats at the expense of northern liberals as well as Republicans. With northern Democrats unable to deliver large-state blocs of electoral votes in presidential elections, analysts argued, the party would be increasingly dependent on its southern wing and thus more vulnerable to political pressure and threats from Dixiecrats.[114] Critics also believed that H.J. Res. 2 would not lead to real two-party competition in the South or to an expansion of the voting rights of African-Americans; it could instead further entrench reactionary forces in the South. Another danger was that the measure could generate splinter parties formed by progressives (such as those that supported Henry Wallace in 1948) who would no longer feel at home in a Democratic Party dominated by the South.

This shift in perspective did not just happen: it was actively promoted by a handful of liberals who were alarmed by the prospect of the Lodge-Gossett resolution becoming law. The key actor, perhaps, was Representative (later senator) Clifford P. Case of New Jersey, a liberal Republican whose views on most issues were close to those of Lodge. Case, a strong progressive on civil rights issues, led the opposition to H.J. Res. 2 in the Judiciary Committee and authored its minority report, in which he had argued that enactment of the measure would be a "most grievous error" that would have "far-reaching and, quite likely, disastrous effects." Case agreed that the office of elector ought to be abolished and that the contingent election system needed to be overhauled. But he disagreed sharply with the contention—voiced by Gossett and many of his allies—that winner-take-all ought to be eliminated because minority groups in the "pivotal states" had an "undue voice" in determining national policy. That such groups had influence, Case maintained, was normal and appropriate in a pluralist, two-party system. Indeed, he cautioned, "some of those who advocate the Lodge-Gossett resolution do so, not because they want the major parties freed from the necessity to give undue recognition to minority groups, but because they wish the major parties to give such groups no recognition whatever."[115]

In the 1949 report Case had also challenged the majority's claim that proportional elections would lead to increased electoral participation, political liberalization, and healthy two-party competition in the "sure" or "solid" states that were dominated by one political party. (Remarkably, the majority report included a circuitous, slightly bizarre definition of "solid states.")[116] In fact, the opposite would occur: faced with competition, the dominant parties in states that had restricted the franchise "by statute and by extra-legal practices" would likely limit voting rights further in order to remain in power. Case further maintained that it was chimerical to believe that the Republican Party could get very far with the existing electorate in the South, particularly if Republicans advocated civil and voting rights for the party's most evident constituency, disenfranchised African-Americans. Only if H.J. Res. 2 were to be significantly amended, Case concluded, could proportional elections have anything close to the desired consequences. The amendment that he proposed (echoing the Fourteenth Amendment) specified that a state's electoral votes in each election be reduced in proportion to the percentage of persons of voting age who did not cast ballots.[117]

After the Senate approved the Lodge resolution, Case did his utmost to try to block the measure in the House. He approached two long-standing allies, James Loeb and Charles M. LaFollette of Americans for Democratic Action (ADA), a liberal lobbying and activist group, and quickly persuaded them that H.J. Res. 2, by enhancing the power of southern Democrats, would weaken the civil rights movement, the labor movement, and the progressive wing of the Democratic Party. Although the president of ADA, Hubert Humphrey, had voted for the resolution, the two officials—emphasizing that they were acting as individuals and not on behalf of their organization—sprang into action, writing letters and memos, contacting members of Congress, reaching out to prominent leaders of organized labor, and (later) testifying against the measure. "Whereas there now is competition between the two major parties for liberal support, under the amendment the competition will be for the conservative Southern vote," LaFollette declared. "This could set back the liberal cause a generation."[118]

Meanwhile, after some initial ambivalence about the proposal, African-Americans mobilized.[119] Ten days after the Senate vote, the *Baltimore Afro-American* published an article under the headline "Planned Amendment Held Threat to Us." It claimed that proportional elections would "wipe out the influence of colored voters in States where they now held the balance of power in elections." The story may have originated with Clarence Mitchell Jr., head of the Washington Bureau and labor secretary of the NAACP, who launched a tireless lobbying campaign against the measure and circulated a critical memo prepared by Lincoln University professor John A. Davis.[120] He also arranged for Davis to address a gathering of members of Congress in early March. Tacitly agreeing with Gossett about the importance of blacks as swing voters, Davis noted that the migration of African-Americans to the large industrial states of the North had, in fact, given them significant, sometimes critical, leverage in those states—which they very much needed. "The only offset the Negro has had to disfranchisement in the South and the southern filibuster," he argued, "has been his political influence in the northern pivotal states. The Lodge proposal will rob him of this political influence without enfranchising him in the South." Davis and Mitchell further maintained that if Lodge-Gossett were to be enacted, "the importance of the South will grow in the councils of the Democratic Party and in the nation as a whole." Strategically, they insisted that the measure had to be blocked in the House, where the nation's urban population had representation proportional to its numbers; if the resolution proceeded to the states, it was likely to be ratified.[121]

In making their case to liberals, Mitchell, Case, and their allies were equipped with ammunition drawn directly from public statements made by southern advocates of the amendment. A newspaper in Vernon, Texas, for example, editorialized that the "Gossett-Lodge" resolution, if adopted and ratified, "will put an end to the bipartisan contest for Negro votes in pivotal States and eliminate the so-called civil rights issue from national politics." A Macon, Georgia, paper boasted that the measure "would take from Walter White [the executive secretary of the NAACP] his ability to manipulate the votes of the mere 3,000,000 Negroes living outside the South" to control the presidency. More judiciously, Gladstone Williams, a columnist for the *Atlanta Constitution,* observed that southern Democrats were not embracing the Lodge-Gossett proposal because they supported Lodge's goal of breaking down the South's one-party system. What attracted southern backing was the hope that the amendment would stop both major parties from "catering to special minority interest groups in presidential elections." "The genesis of the President's civil rights program, vigorously opposed by Southern Democrats," Gladstone wrote, "is to be found in these minority groups."[122]

Gossett himself, moreover, must have made northern liberals more than a little uneasy. Once it received more attention, Gossett's racially loaded, red-baiting language—which was extreme but not altogether foreign to the discourse of southern Democrats—lent credence to the arguments of men like Case, Mitchell, and LaFollette that the resolution posed a danger to numerous causes that liberals, and moderates, held dear. Marquis Childs, a highly respected columnist for the *Washington Post,* described the Texas congressman in 1950 as someone "who has always taken a narrowly reactionary view, particularly on any issue involving race or color." Evidence mounted that liberals ought to be cautious about embracing a measure sponsored by Ed Gossett; at a minimum, it required a second look.[123]

Once the evidence was assembled and the arguments aggressively pressed in Washington, it took little time for the liberals and moderates on the Rules Committee to join forces with conservative Republicans to put a brake on the resolution's forward motion. (President Truman told Lodge, in a private meeting, that he was puzzled by that alliance of Democrats and Republicans.) After the Rules Committee vote, Emanuel Celler, the Brooklyn Democrat who was chair of the Judiciary Committee and an initial supporter of the measure, announced that he was not likely to try to circumvent the Rules Committee's action. The resolution itself would need to be reexamined. "The opposition that has developed in connection with the Lodge-Gossett resolution," he noted, "cannot be taken lightly. It comes from important sources."[124]

The resolution then remained in limbo for several months, with both the House and liberal opinion divided. The quandary for liberals was that even though the Lodge-Gossett measure would create an electoral system with more intrinsically democratic features, proportional elections also seemed likely to serve the interests of political forces that opposed universal suffrage and civil rights.[125] The *New York Times,* which had endorsed proportional elections in 1940, chastised both liberal and conservative opponents of the measure for taking into account potential political consequences that ought to be deemed "immaterial." The paper loftily suggested that the amendment "should stand on its own merits as a genuine and democratic improvement" that could "bring our constitutional structure more in line with modern conditions." The left-liberal *Nation* acknowledged that "Gossett and his fellow-Dixiecrats may have, from our point of view, the worst of motives," but its editors believed that opponents were taking too "static" a perspective: the South was changing "under the pressure of industrialization" and "the long-range result would be a marked advance in democracy and good sense." The magazine also cautioned liberal

Democrats that they would be subject to the charge of hypocrisy if, for partisan reasons, they were to "oppose a reform they have long espoused."[126]

The *New Republic* also insisted that "the sands are shifting in the South." The Dixiecrats had already loosened the grip of the Democratic Party on the region; Republicans had won almost two million (out of seven million) votes in the South in 1948; and African-Americans were gradually gaining the franchise. Lodge's optimistic vision, therefore, was not unrealistic. But the magazine's editors then hedged, arguing that Congress had to accept Case's amendment calling for a reduction in a state's electoral votes in "the proportion that the number of persons actually voting is less than the total number of citizens of voting age." This provision was needed "to discourage further restrictions on the franchise ... until the necessary national legislation can be passed to assure a full electorate." That southerners were exceedingly unlikely to agree to Case's amendment was not mentioned. In early April the national convention of ADA adopted the same ambivalent posture, favoring the Lodge-Gossett proposal "but only if it includes the Case amendment."[127]

In July 1950, after additional months of public debate and backroom maneuvering, Gossett and his allies finally succeeded in getting H.J. Res. 2 to the floor of the House. Majority leader John W. McCormack, a Massachusetts Democrat, announced that the measure would be brought up under a motion to suspend the rules, a procedure that allowed very limited time for debate and did not permit amendments to be offered. The pro-resolution forces, thus, would get a vote on the measure but under circumstances unfavorable to passage.[128]

The truncated floor debate, which took place on July 17, had a *pro forma* quality, with several participants openly indicating that the measure had little chance of passage. Gossett launched the debate, largely repeating the testimony he had given to the Judiciary Committee in 1949.[129] He presented an episodic history of "how badly" the Electoral College "has worked" and outlined the advantages that would flow from the adoption of proportional elections. He also noted that, in its final form, H.J. Res. 2 provided for an improved contingent election process that would entrust the decision to a joint session of Congress if no candidate received more than 40 percent of the electoral vote.[130] Then, seemingly oblivious to the controversy that had swirled around the resolution for months, Gossett put forward a verbatim replica of his 1949 testimony indicting the power of "small organized minority groups," including African-Americans, organized labor, Jews, Italians, and Communists. He also repeated his earlier equation of expanded voting rights with states being reduced to the "lowest common denominator." Gossett made no attempt to address the concerns of liberals or win over skeptics. In the end he limply asked that any colleagues who had "doubts" about the "merits of this resolution" vote for it anyway and let the states decide whether to ratify. It was the speech of a man who knew he had been defeated.[131]

Several of his allies did try to reach cross the ideological and regional divide. Brooks Hays of Arkansas, a self-styled "southern moderate" who accepted the need for some civil rights legislation, announced that he supported the resolution, despite its imperfections, because it was a "tremendous improvement." Distancing himself from Gossett, he commented that he had "no complex against any of the new blocs" of voters and "had never knowingly said anything to prejudice their rights." Christian Herter of Massachusetts, the one Republican who had voted favorably at the Rules Committee, acknowledged that many of the objections to the resolution had "a certain degree of validity," but he believed that the "very able arguments presented by Senator Lodge on behalf of this bill override the objections."[132]

The opposition was led by Case, who succinctly argued that he agreed with many of the objectives of the resolution but believed proportional elections would have "disastrous" consequences, including reducing the Republican Party to "impotence," delivering the Democratic Party into the control of its "conservative southern wing," and destroying any chance of implementing a federal civil rights program. Case then passed the baton to his colleagues. Chet Holifield, a California Democrat, declared the Lodge-Gossett proposal to be "dangerous" and "only seemingly a democratic reform." If the proponents of the resolution were serious about making the nation more democratic, he insisted, they would not be opposing the repeal of poll taxes or endorsing other measures that kept African-Americans from voting. Harlem's Adam Clayton Powell Jr., one of two African-Americans in Congress, recited almost verbatim the major points made in John Davis's memo. Joe Martin, the House Republican leader, blasted the resolution's backers for pretending that it would "make everybody happy" and attacked the Democratic leadership for bringing a constitutional amendment to the floor under a rule that permitted so little deliberation or debate.[133]

The final vote on the resolution was 134 ayes, 210 nays, and 86 members not voting. Sizable majorities of both Republicans and Democrats voted against the measure; support was strong only among southerners. (See Table 3.1.) Opposition was almost uniform among Democrats from the Northeast and Midwest, while 75 percent of the numerous representatives from seven "pivotal" states voted negatively.[134] The *Dallas Morning News* reported that the defeat of Gossett's effort had come at the hands of "a coalition of left-wing administration Democrats and Republican standpatters." The *Cleveland Call and Post,* an African-American newsweekly, reported on the vote with an article headlined "Dixie Attempt to Reduce Negro Vote Power Fails."[135]

The rise and fall of the Lodge-Gossett proposal can be understood, at one level of analysis, as yet another example of the difficulty of reforming an existing electoral system. In the late 1940s nearly everyone in Congress, as well as a majority of the American people, agreed that the Electoral College was in need of a major overhaul. (See Appendix A for public opinion polls.) The fallible and unnecessary network of electors ought to be eliminated; the archaic contingent procedure had to be replaced with something more democratic; the unit rule had severe defects. But in the end—as had so often happened—there was no consensus about the structure or shape of a new electoral system.

This episode was also historically specific, with roots stretching back into the nineteenth century. The Lodge-Gossett proposal, spearheaded by a Republican, was an attempt to end the stalemate on Electoral College reform that had prevailed since the early 1890s, when Republicans had determined that any system other than winner-take-all would be damaging to their interests as long as the South remained a one-party region. Lodge was willing to shake up that long-standing partisan position, in part because of his own democratic values and also because, seeking to enlarge and liberalize his party, he was willing to risk some losses on the electoral map in the North in exchange for the prospect of long-term, significant gains in

TABLE 3.1: CONGRESSIONAL VOTES ON THE LODGE-GOSSETT
RESOLUTION, 1950

Senate: percentage[a] (number)		
	Voting in favor	Number not voting
Republicans	44 (18)	1
Democrats (all)	92 (46)	4
Democrats (South[b])	89 (25)	3
Democrats (non-South)	95 (21)	1
Total	70 (64)	5
House: percentage[a] (number)		
	Voting in favor	Number not voting
Republicans	34 (48)	29
Democrats (all)	43 (86)	57
Democrats (South[b])	76 (68)	36
Democrats (non-South)	16 (18)	21
Total	39[c] (134)	86[d]

Source: 96 Cong. Rec. 1276–1279, 10427–10428 (1950).

a. Percentage of those voting. Senators Bourke Hickenlooper (R-IA), Russell Long (D-LA), and James Murray (D-MT) are included as "not voting" although the Congressional Record noted that they intended to vote favorably if they did vote.

b. South based on the U.S. census definition: TX, OK, AR, LA, MS, AL, GA, FL, SC, TN, NC, KY, VA, WV, MD, DE. For the sake of comparability with later tables, percentages were also calculated using a narrower definition of South, excluding WV, MD, and DE; the results were very similar.

c. Two third-party representatives voted "Nay" on the Lodge-Gossett resolution, Rep. Vito Marcantonio (American Labor Party, NY) and Rep. Franklin Roosevelt Jr. (Liberal Party, NY). They are included in the percentage calculated for "total" representatives.

d. Fifty-six of the eighty-six members not voting were paired.

the South. That Democrats from all regions initially jumped on Lodge's bandwagon was not surprising: northern Democrats, after all, had embraced the Miner Law's abolition of winner-take-all in Michigan; Clarence Lea's proposals for proportional elections had significant Democratic support in the 1930s and early 1940s; liberal Democrats like Emanuel Celler had voiced sharp criticism of the Electoral College; and southerners saw in Lodge's proposal a means of weakening the civil rights movement, with few political risks to themselves. What was dramatic and unusual about the events of 1950 was the shift in posture of northern Democrats between the Senate and the House votes—the rapid, if belated, abandonment of the reform effort by liberals and moderates who had begun to doubt the validity of Lodge's analysis and to shrink from the embrace of white supremacists like Gossett. For at least some liberals, the conclusion reached was sobering, both intellectually and politically: an institutional reform that, in itself, had long been regarded as democratic, might well have anti-democratic consequences in a nation containing a large region that lacked universal suffrage. James Loeb of the ADA made the point vividly, and with a jarring international comparison, in a statement submitted to Congress in 1951. "The theory of the Lodge amendment breaks down completely, so long as a substantial section of the country maintains what amounts to a one-party political system," Loeb wrote. "If a united Germany were achieved under present political controls, would Senator Lodge suggest the application of his system, with Western Germany having democratic elections and with Eastern Germany under one-party rule?"[136]

Coda

The defeat of the Lodge-Gossett resolution in 1950 did little to dampen interest in reform, although different factions in Congress retained their own preferences about how best to proceed. Among liberals from both parties, support was mounting for a national popular vote, a position shared by a majority of the American people. (See Chapter 4 and Appendix Table A.1.) Many were also willing to endorse a proportional plan (which had the political advantage of preserving the small-state bonus and state control of elections), with the proviso that it include the "Case amendment." Southern Democrats, in contrast, continued to favor the Lodge-Gossett approach (without the Case amendment), although many were sympathetic as well with a revived district elections proposal promoted by conservative Republican Frederic Coudert of New York. At the far end of the spectrum were other Republican conservatives like Taft, who wanted to get rid of the machinery of the Electoral College but retain the unit rule.

The diversity of stances did not bode well for passage of an amendment, but the problem was not simply the presence of different ideas and preferences. Slicing across the spectrum of policy proposals was a red line, a fundamental divide, that had come to the surface in the debates over Lodge-Gossett and that stood squarely in the way of constitutional change. On one side of that divide were southerners who would not accept any reforms—such as a national popular vote or the Case amendment—that would create legal or political pressures to enfranchise African-Americans or deepen federal involvement in elections. On the other side were northern liberals who would not endorse any changes that might politically strengthen southern Democrats without promoting civil and voting rights for the region's large minority population. The partisan lineups were no longer what they had been in 1890, but race remained at the heart of the impasse.

The Lodge-Gossett resolution itself did not fade into oblivion after the debacle in the House. It remained before Congress, in different iterations, even after Gossett resigned from the House in 1951 and Lodge was defeated for reelection in 1952 by John F. Kennedy. In mid-1951, a version of the proposal was reported favorably by the judiciary committees of both branches of Congress, but neither chamber took any further action. In 1955, after several additional rounds of hearings, a measure identical to the original Lodge-Gossett resolution, now labeled S.J. Res. 31 and sponsored by Democratic senators Estes Kefauver (Tennessee) and Price Daniel (Texas), was reported by the Senate Judiciary Committee, reaching the floor in 1956. Kefauver was an independent-minded, border-state liberal, a nationally known figure, and a serious contender for the Democratic presidential nomination in both 1952 and 1956. Daniel was an ardent segregationist who had signed the "Southern Manifesto" declaring the Supreme Court's landmark 1954 decision desegregating schools to be unconstitutional. The arguments that they voiced for proportional elections were much the same as those advanced by Lodge and Gossett in 1949–1950—although the inflammatory rhetoric was considerably dialed down.[137]

Other approaches also remained on the congressional menu. North Dakota senator William Langer and New York's Herbert Lehman advocated versions of a national popular vote, and Minnesota Democrat Hubert

Humphrey concocted an ingenious compromise plan that combined a national popular vote with state control over some electoral votes.[138] (It went nowhere.) More influential, in the short run, was a resolution for district elections put forward by Representative Coudert and Senator Karl Mundt, a conservative Republican from South Dakota. The Mundt-Coudert plan, strikingly similar to nineteenth-century proposals, called for electors to be chosen in congressional districts, with the winner of each state's popular vote gaining two additional electors. In the absence of a majority, the president would be chosen by a joint session of Congress.[139]

Backers of district elections put forward a variety of reasons for preferring their approach to proportional elections. Some moderate commentators—like Walter Lippmann, an influential journalist, and Lucius Wilmerding, an expert on the electoral system—were acutely aware of the defects of winner-take-all, but they, like Homer Ferguson, worried that any scheme for proportional elections would soon spill over into legislative elections, encourage parties of the extreme left and right, and endanger the two-party system. Europe's experience in the interwar years was much on their minds (and they were not alone). District elections, they believed, were a safer option.[140] Conservatives like Mundt shared those concerns but also had a more partisan, or ideological, agenda. Mundt believed that district elections would give greater voice and influence to conservative rural voters, particularly those who lived in states with large urban centers, like New York, Pennsylvania, and Illinois. Under his plan, the voices of such voters would cease to be drowned out by the metropolitan areas; indeed, they would be magnified by the common practice of creating congressional districts that were apportioned and gerrymandered to advantage rural areas.[141] (The principle of "one person, one vote" would be mandated by the Supreme Court only in the 1960s.) Mundt believed similarly that rural and small-town Republicans were more conservative than their urban counterparts and that district elections, therefore, would strengthen the conservative wing of his party against the likes of Henry Cabot Lodge and Clifford Case. The roster of district election supporters included some Dixiecrats who gauged that such a system could achieve much the same goals as Lodge-Gossett.[142]

While Coudert, Mundt, and their allies were stressing the reasons district elections would be preferable to any version of the Lodge-Gossett plan, proponents of proportional elections were returning the fire. The Mundt-Coudert plan, they argued, retained (potentially faithless) electors; districts would be subject to gerrymandering; and district elections were just as likely as the unit rule to yield a minority president or toss the decision to Congress. Despite this critical cross-fire, which went on for several years, backers of the two schemes temporarily joined forces in 1956, a marriage of convenience propelled by the shared goal of getting rid of the unit rule. Recognizing that the proportional plan (S.J. Res. 31) originally reported by the Judiciary Committee lacked sufficient support for passage, Price Daniel, after extensive negotiations with Mundt and with South Carolina senator Strom Thurmond, proposed a substitute—a hybrid that would give each state the option of choosing either district or proportional elections. Supporters of this proposal insisted that the scheme would come as close to a popular vote as possible while maintaining states' rights and the principles of federalism.[143]

Critics, both in and out of Congress, derided the measure as incoherent and shortsighted: the *Washington* Post called it "a constitutional smog" and "an invitation to chaos."[144] In the Senate the fight against the hybrid plan (and S.J. Res. 31) was led by urban liberals, most notably Democrats Paul Douglas of Illinois and John F. Kennedy of Massachusetts, with Clifford Case, now in the Senate, playing an important supporting role. Their arguments against proportional elections recapitulated the criticism made in the House in 1950, and they attacked the Mundt option as an effort to extend to presidential elections the conservative, anti-urban bias already baked into many states' districting practices. The nation's cities, according to Douglas, were "grossly underrepresented" in state legislatures and in Congress, and advocates of district elections were now seeking to eradicate the only electoral counterweight possessed by urban areas: their influence in presidential elections. The net effect of the hybrid plan, critics believed, would be to concentrate political power in the one-party states of the South and rural portions of the Midwest.[145] During the debate, Douglas took the rare step of referring explicitly to racial restrictions on voting in the South and their impact on the region's low turnout. "I know that out of deference to our good Southern friends, we usually skirt around the issue, and do not mention it, and do not bring the skeletons out of the closet. However, we should speak frankly, because this is a very important issue."[146]

Kennedy focused his criticism on the internal contradictions embedded in the "hybrid monstrosity" introduced by Daniel. "The two schemes joined together by this shotgun wedding," Kennedy insisted, "are wholly incompatible, the sponsors of each having thoroughly and accurately assailed the merits of the other over the years."

> The Mundt proposal multiplies the general ticket system; the Daniel proposal abolishes it. The Mundt proposal continues the importance of states as units for electoral purposes; the Daniel proposal reduces it. The Mundt plan keeps the electoral college; the Daniel plan abolishes it. And yet it is now proposed that the Senate, being unable to give its approval to either system, should lump them together and give each state its choice. No surer method of introducing confusion and loss of public confidence in our electoral system could be devised.

Kennedy further observed that if the hybrid scheme were adopted, state legislatures could change the mode of election every four years—which would return the electoral system to the instability that had prevailed in the early nineteenth century.[147] Kennedy's arrows were deftly aimed, but the Massachusetts senator likely had concerns in addition to the illogic of the hybrid proposal. Already eyeing a presidential run, he may well have gauged that the unit rule would serve his own electoral interests; late in the senate debates, he signaled a willingness to accept an amendment that did away with the apparatus of the Electoral College but preserved winner-take-all.[148] Four years later, Kennedy was narrowly elected to the presidency, thanks in part to the blocs of electoral votes cast by most of the large battleground states of the Northeast and Midwest.

Despite the objections of Kennedy, Douglas, and numerous others, the Senate accepted the hybrid plan as an amendment to S.J. Res. 31 by a vote of forty-eight to thirty-seven. Almost all of the favorable votes came from southerners and conservative, rural-state Republicans. (A half-dozen of the original co-sponsors of S.J. Res. 31 did not back the hybrid idea.) Although the vote was positive, the tally made clear to the proposal's backers that they lacked the two-thirds majority needed for passage. Daniel consequently moved to recommit the resolution to the Judiciary Committee "for further study" rather than face defeat in a final vote. The Texas senator and his allies were hoping that either a proportional or a hybrid measure could be successfully resurrected during a subsequent session of Congress. That hope was never fulfilled: 1956 proved to be the last year in which either branch of Congress voted on a proposal for district or proportional elections.[149]

The congressional proceedings from 1949 through 1956 thus constituted the high-water mark of twentieth-century efforts to replace winner-take-all with either district or proportional elections. Both approaches had dedicated backers and substantial support, but they also had opponents who were numerous and determined. That remained the case into the 1960s. After the close election of 1960 (in which fifteen unpledged or faithless electors cast ballots for Virginia senator Harry Byrd), Estes Kefauver, among others, revived the case for proportional elections—which would have brought an end to problems with electors. Extensive hearings were held in 1961, but strong opposition came from various quarters, including northern liberals and those who feared the emergence of splinter parties.[150] Mundt also reintroduced his district elections proposal in 1961 and in every Congress thereafter into the early 1970s. After the Supreme Court's 1964 ruling that congressional districts had to be of equal size, Mundt claimed, with reason, that criticism of his plan rooted in concerns about malapportionment was no longer relevant. He could not, however, assuage similar worries about gerrymandering. Nor could he satisfy critics who claimed that district elections could yield a minority president, that they would dilute the influence of competitive states but not single-party ones, and that they would unbalance the system by preserving the "small state advantage" while stripping large states of the extra edge that they enjoyed through the unit rule.[151] After midcentury, in sum, the votes for proportional or district plans were not to be found in the Senate. The House, where northern liberals were proportionately more numerous, posed an even greater obstacle.

The mid-twentieth-century debates over district and proportional elections were suffused with historical echoes and ironies. For much of the nineteenth century, proposals to abolish the general ticket had been at the heart of efforts to reform the Electoral College; they had been championed by progressive political leaders, including Jacksonians and Radical Republicans, who sought to make the electoral system more democratic, more egalitarian, more responsive to popular sentiments. Those goals were shared by some of the prominent supporters of proportional elections after World War II: Henry Cabot Lodge, Clarence Lea, Estes Kefauver, Emanuel Celler, and Hubert Humphrey all believed that winner-take-all had significant democratic shortcomings that could be remedied, or ameliorated, by dividing up each state's electoral votes.[152] When they endorsed legislative action on those beliefs, however, they found themselves allied with politicians whose goals and values clashed sharply with their own. Ed Gossett and Price Daniel may have agreed with Lodge about some features of the reform effort, but they regarded proportional elections primarily as a means of blunting the drive for civil and political rights for African-Americans. Similarly, Karl Mundt and his supporters regarded district elections not as a means of democratizing the electoral process but as a mechanism for constraining the influence of the nation's rapidly growing, polyglot urban population.

The presence and political strength of these conservative proponents of change compelled postwar liberal leaders to rethink their views, leading many, if not most, to oppose reforms that their ideological progenitors had embraced.[153] In so doing, they were not simply defending partisan interests—although they were doing that, much as Jefferson had in 1802–1803. They were also recognizing, somewhat to their own surprise, that political context mattered in the design of electoral institutions.[154] The thrust of proportional elections was not altogether democratic in a nation that had a sizable one-party region with a disenfranchised minority; district elections did not enhance popular influence in a nation where the boundaries of districts had not kept pace with population movements and a century of urbanization.[155] For those liberals who, like Hubert Humphrey, sought "to perfect our form of democracy," it was becoming increasingly clear that the best, and perhaps only, available option was to replace the Electoral College with a national popular vote.[156]

PART III

A National Popular Vote

The idea of choosing a president through a nationwide popular election dates to the country's founding. It was introduced at the Constitutional Convention in 1787 and had several prominent advocates, including Gouverneur Morris and James Wilson. James Madison noted that a national popular vote would have disadvantages for the slave states, including his own, but he too concluded that it would, on balance, be the best method of selecting a chief executive. Most delegates to the convention did not agree.

The institution that the framers designed instead differed from a national popular vote in three critical respects. The first was that it created a set of state elections and not a single national election; the system was structured to determine the preferences of states rather than those of the citizenry at large. The second was that elections were indirect: the people did not vote for presidential candidates but for intermediaries who then voted for presidential candidates. The third was that the Electoral College was not grounded in the principle that the votes of all individuals should count equally. The framers, acting out of perceived political necessity, chose to give extra weight to the votes of two groups of citizens: inhabitants of small states and white residents of states that had slavery. This last feature meant that, from the outset, the nation contained two sizable constituencies that would lose political influence if a national popular vote were ever adopted.

For many years after the adoption of the Constitution, the possibility of replacing the Electoral College with a national popular vote attracted no more, and perhaps less, political support than Gouverneur Morris's proposal had received in Philadelphia. The idea bobbed up from time to time (and increasingly over time), but it failed to gain many politically influential adherents until the middle of the twentieth century. Between 1787 and the Civil War, reformers, deeply unhappy with the existing system, focused their energies on promoting district elections and altering the contingent mechanism; only at moments was a national popular vote even discussed. During the long period that stretched from Reconstruction through World War II, the notion that a national popular vote could best solve the recurrent problems with the Electoral College became more widespread but encountered sharp resistance. It continued to be an outlier, an idea flatly rejected by many political leaders while regarded by others as attractive in theory but less politically viable than alternative reforms. Only in the mid-twentieth century did proposals for a national popular vote begin to gain traction; support for the idea then mushroomed, almost culminating in congressional passage of a constitutional amendment in 1969–1970. Since that time, a national popular vote has remained the foremost option for replacing the Electoral College.

FOUR

"A POPULATION ANOMALOUS" AND A NATIONAL POPULAR VOTE, 1800–1960

In March 1816 the possibility of electing the president through a national popular vote was formally raised in Congress for the first time. This noteworthy, if little noticed, event occurred in the midst of the Senate's consideration of an amendment resolution to require that both presidential electors and members of the House be chosen through district elections. That resolution, proposed in late February by Joseph Varnum of Massachusetts, was one of numerous district election amendments to come before Congress between 1813 and 1826. As we have seen, this was a period when many political leaders were actively seeking to reform and make nationally uniform the process of selecting presidential electors.

Varnum's amendment was referred on March 1 to a five-member select committee. A week later the committee reported to the Senate, amending and recommending the proposal; debate began in earnest on March 20.[1] It was then that Abner Lacock, a Democratic-Republican from western Pennsylvania, made an alternative motion, to refer the issue back to committee "with instructions to inquire into the expediency of proposing an amendment to the Constitution . . . providing for the election of President and Vice President by the Electors of each State qualified to vote for the most numerous branch of the state legislature."[2] (The word *electors* here referred to all voters rather than the men who would cast ballots in the electoral colleges.) Lacock's motion was at first ignored, as the Senate proceeded to discuss the pros and cons of mandating district elections for both presidential electors and members of the House.[3]

Then Lacock, who had been a member of the select committee, took the floor to support his motion. He began by observing that "there appeared to be a general opinion that there would be an advantage in bringing the question nearer the people." If that were the goal, he could "see no reason why" there should be "agents ... employed between the people and their votes." If these agents "were dispensed with," the voters in each state could simply cast their ballots, which would be gathered together by the "State Executives" and forwarded to the "General Government." The "mode of election" would thus be uniform across the states, and there would be no need for "the machinery of electoral colleges." With "this popular mode of election," moreover, "there could be no fear of corruption" because there would be no intermediaries to corrupt. Lacock's intervention, unlike many Senate speeches, had an air of unpolished spontaneity; he appeared to be thinking on his feet, responding to the unfolding logic of the debate. Although he was an experienced legislator, having served in the House of Representatives and in both branches of the Pennsylvania legislature, he had not worked out the precise wording of a proposal and quickly modified his original formulation at the suggestion of Samuel Dana of Connecticut.[4]

Several of Lacock's colleagues immediately voiced support. Dana announced that he would vote for it, noting that the framers of the Constitution had great difficulty deciding how best to choose a president and that they too had considered a national popular election. He also maintained that such a method was superior to district elections because it was less prone to corruption: in contrast, "the very circumstance of districting a State for ten years at a time" was an invitation to "cabal and intrigue."[5] Rufus King of New York, soon to become the last Federalist candidate for president, was more emphatic in his support, asserting that "nobody is so competent as the great body of the freemen to make a proper selection" of the chief magistrate. An influential figure who had been a delegate to the Constitutional Convention in Philadelphia, King worried that "the course of things under the present mode of choosing a President was in its nature pernicious" and was undermining the Constitution's goal of having "a pure elective magistracy." Lacock's proposed plan would complicate the logistics of gathering and counting votes, he acknowledged, but these objections were not "insuperable." King recognized too that "this proposition, if agreed to, would break down the power of the Great States," including his own. Nonetheless, he "was willing to let the election of the Presidency rest wholly on the people." In key respects, King's comments strongly—and perhaps knowingly—echoed James Madison's speech endorsing a national popular election in Philadelphia in 1787.[6]

Other senators were quick to challenge Lacock's proposal. Elgius Fromentin of Louisiana, a former Catholic priest and a refugee from the French Revolution, argued that it was impractical given the "vast expanse of our country from Maine to Louisiana." He could not imagine how "it would be possible to ascertain the result of such an election." Fromentin favored district elections but would not entertain Lacock's more radical proposition. New Hampshire's Jeremiah Mason objected that the variations in suffrage requirements among the states would make the "whole election . . . unequal."[7] Robert Goodloe Harper of Maryland, who would become King's running mate in the 1816 campaign, agreed with Fromentin that there would be great difficulty carrying out a national election, but he also raised more theoretical objections. If "the election should be *per capita*," he maintained, it would violate "the Federal principle by which the sovereignties of States are represented" in the choice of a president. It "would break in upon the principles of our government, and destroy" the network of compromises laced into the Constitution. In addition, "it would destroy that influence of the smaller States in the Presidential election" because they would each lose the two electoral votes that came from statehood. If Lacock's plan were adopted, he pointed out, a small state like Louisiana would surrender proportionally far more influence than would New York.[8]

Lacock, a man with little formal education but abundant political experience (he was well respected in Washington, including by President Madison), responded by stating that "the objections urged might all be obviated or overcome" and that it would be well worth trying to do so because the potential virtues of the system he proposed were significant and far-reaching. "What could make us so much one people, as to give to all the people this general equal privilege?" It would bring forth "in the national habits, manners, and love of country, more harmony than any other political measure." With the stakes so large, he urged his colleagues to simply let his proposal "go to a committee" to see if they could resolve "the objections of mere detail" that had been raised.[9]

Then a different shoe dropped. William Wyatt Bibb of Georgia (later the first governor of Alabama) indicated that he had "no particular objection" to an inquiry into Lacock's proposal, but he shared Harper's concern that it would unravel the compromises built into the existing electoral system. "What," he asked, "would be the condition of the slave-holding states? They would lose the privilege the Constitution now allows them, of votes upon three-fifths of their population other than freemen? It would be deeply injurious to them."[10] James Barbour of Virginia pressed the issue, clearly alarmed that in the course of debate Lacock's idea "had now risen to a degree of importance far greater than it at first possessed." The proposal, Barbour insisted, "contemplated not merely a change in the mode of election, but a revolution in the Government" that would destroy "the balance of power" among the states. "It had pleased God to give the Southern country a population anomalous, having the double character of persons and property," he observed, and a national vote would deprive the South of the influence that the Constitution gave to the region in recognition of that population. Since there could be no possible remedy "for the evils of this project," Barbour announced that he would vote against even sending it to a committee.[11]

After Bibb and Barbour had spoken, the question was called on Lacock's motion to instruct a committee "to inquire into the expediency" of having presidents elected by "the whole people." Twelve senators voted favorably; twenty-one were opposed.[12] The possibility of holding a national popular vote would not be voted on again in Congress until 1950.

✳   ✳   ✳

This brief Senate debate encapsulated and foreshadowed the issues that for the next century and a half would surround the idea of electing presidents by a national popular vote.[13] As Abner Lacock pointed out, the democratic logic in favor of such an election was simple and straightforward: it would give the people a direct say, and all votes would count equally. That argument would become more compelling in the course of the nineteenth and twentieth centuries, as democratic values were increasingly embraced and celebrated. Yet the objections raised in 1816 would also be heard again and again. (The one exception was the claim that such an election was not logistically feasible, which faded after the 1830s.) Variations in suffrage requirements meant that the people of different states would not really have equal voices. A national popular vote would undermine the federal structure of the government and undo the compromises made at the nation's founding. It would rob states of their sovereignty and unfairly diminish the influence of small states. Above all, a national popular vote would harm the South because it would take from southern whites the added electoral power that they wielded in the Electoral College by virtue of their states' nonvoting African-American populations. This last objection was crucial to consigning the idea of a national vote to the outskirts of public debate for much of our nation's history.

An Idea at the Margins

Between 1816 and the middle of the twentieth century, amendments requiring that presidents be chosen through a direct vote of the people "irrespective of state or district lines" were introduced in Congress numerous times—although far less frequently than were proposals for district or proportional elections.[14] The resolutions tended to come in small waves. The first occurred in the wake of the 1824 election, which bitterly divided the supporters of Andrew Jackson from the backers of John Quincy Adams. The second took place during and soon after Reconstruction, a period when there was substantial interest in reforming electoral institutions; this was also a moment when African-Americans were enfranchised in the South and white southerners gained no distinctive advantage from the structure of the electoral system. A third wave appeared in the late Progressive era, linked to the surge of democratic reform that yielded the Seventeenth and Nineteenth Amendments (providing for the direct election of senators and the enfranchisement of women). A further burst of interest emerged from the mid-1940s into the 1950s when Congress once again was seriously contemplating alternative methods of reforming the Electoral College.

ANTEBELLUM

Despite the seemingly conclusive defeat of Abner Lacock's proposal in 1816, a handful of resolutions for a national popular vote (NPV) were introduced in Congress in the latter 1820s. They were put forward during the contentious debates over reform precipitated by the 1824 election, as Congress considered mandating district elections for presidential electors and removing itself from the contingent election process. District elections were promoted as a democratizing reform and were strongly supported by Jacksonians and southerners; northern allies of President Adams, in contrast, tended to be lukewarm or hostile to the idea. (See Chapter 2.)

Notably then, most—and perhaps all—of the proposals for a national popular vote, an even more democratic reform, came not from Jacksonians but from Adams supporters.[15] In January 1826, Representative William McManus, an Adams backer from New York, called for amending the Constitution so that "citizens themselves, instead of electors," would "elect by ballot" the president and vice president; he maintained that citizens of all states possessed "the same equal and just right to elect" the government's chief officers.[16] Six weeks later, Adams supporter John Sloane of Ohio, expressing the wishes of his state's pro-Adams legislature, put forward an unambiguous proposal "that the Constitution of the United States ought to be so amended, that the free white males of the several States, above the age of twenty-one years, by a general vote, *per capita*, throughout the United States, shall elect the President and Vice President thereof."[17] A variation on this resolution was introduced in 1827 and again in 1829 by another Ohio representative, John Wright. It called for a national popular vote of "all free white male citizens," age twenty-one and over, and further provided for the simultaneous election of electors in each state who would choose among the top two candidates if no candidate received an outright majority of the popular ballots. The Electoral College, in effect, would be transformed into a contingent election mechanism, thereby also achieving the popular goal of preventing elections from devolving on Congress.[18]

There were few signs that the sponsors of these resolutions believed that they had much chance of being enacted. Wright, in fact, indicated that he shared the view of the Ohio legislature that it would be best not to amend the Constitution at all: leaving the existing electoral system in place would be preferable to adopting district elections or any of the other schemes that had been brought forward. But if the Constitution were to be amended, he argued, it should be done "on the basis of political justice . . . if we are to make a new bargain, we must do the best we can for our state."[19] For Wright and his allies, "political justice" meant that all citizens' votes should count equally, which would be possible only by abolishing "the ratio . . . the three-fifths of the colored population held to involuntary service" and "the equal representation . . . of the Senate in the electoral colleges." (Limiting the franchise to white citizens apparently did not violate norms of "political justice." Ohio had done so since 1803, when it became a state, and in the late 1820s most states had racial exclusions.) By advocating a national popular vote, thus, Adams backers were registering their objections to the three-fifths clause and pointing to the hypocrisy of Jacksonians who were promoting district elections in the name of democratic values. They "shrink from the results of their own arguments," declared Thomas Whipple of New Hampshire. Only a national popular vote, which would eliminate the advantages possessed by slave and small states, would actually meet the goals of uniformity and "equal political weight" that the Jacksonians were trumpeting.[20] With uncanny precision, the arguments of the pro-Adams representatives prefigured those that would be put forward by northern liberals against the Lodge-Gossett bill in 1950.

The few NPV proposals that did surface in Congress before the Civil War served primarily to underscore the limits of antebellum approaches to reform. As long as slavery endured and the three-fifths clause was operative, a national popular vote could not be seriously considered as a remedy for the troubling defects of the Electoral College. The era's most persistent and well-known advocate of reform, Thomas Hart Benton, emphasized that his plan for direct, district elections did not call for votes to be combined into a national tally because "in that case the slaveholding states would lose the three votes in five which they now give for their black population."[21] Andrew Jackson's stance was similar, despite his declaring that "the right of electing their Chief Magistrate" belongs "to the people."[22] (Thanks to his embrace of slavery, the disappointed plurality winner of the popular vote in 1824 could not advocate an NPV.) Mahlon Dickerson, who spearheaded reform drives in the 1810s and 1820s, and who, unlike Benton and Jackson, did not reside in a slave state, offered a different perspective but still regarded the idea of a national vote to be outside the realm of the possible. "The election of a President by the people at large would be a preferable mode, if it were practicable," Dickerson observed, "but whoever will look at the situation of our country, with its different kinds of population; different modes of election; different qualifications of voters, must at once perceive that such an election is utterly impracticable." It was likely not by chance that "different kinds of population" was the first item on Dickerson's list.[23]

RECONSTRUCTION AND THEREAFTER

The Civil War and the abolition of slavery transformed the institutional and political landscape, making it possible for a national popular vote to at least be discussed as a credible alternative to the Electoral College. It was not surprising then that NPV proposals appeared in Congress shortly after the war ended and that they continued to appear during and after Reconstruction; these proposals were less numerous than those for district or proportional elections but, for a time at least, they were part of the conversation.[24] The proponents of a national popular vote were most often Republicans whose political views had been shaped by abolitionism, the Civil War, and the challenges of Reconstruction itself. They were intent on strengthening the federal government and committed to the democratic principles that informed the Fourteenth and Fifteenth Amendments.

The first such proposal was put forward in 1866 and again in 1868 by Representative James M. Ashley of Ohio, a Radical Republican, former abolitionist, and point man in the congressional effort to impeach Andrew Johnson.[25] Ashley's resolution called for a national election to be held in April of every fourth year, with a runoff election, among the top five vote-getters, the following October. He also sought to limit presidents to one term and, in an undisguised jab at Johnson, to eliminate the office of vice president; the successor to a president who was impeached or died in office would be chosen by Congress. Ashley's proposal, drafted before the passage of the Fifteenth Amendment outlawed racial restrictions on voting, further provided that every citizen age twenty-one or over be entitled to vote in presidential elections. "I want citizenship and suffrage to be synonymous," he declared.[26]

In a speech accompanying his resolution in May 1868, Ashley acknowledged that his earlier proposals "have slept the sleep which knows no waking in the committees to which, under our rules, they must be referred." He persisted, however, because of the gravity of the issues: "The present mode of electing a President ... seems to me to be violative of the democratic principle and dangerous to the peace and stability of the government." Potentially corrupt party conventions were selecting the candidates, and intermediaries, rather than the people, were choosing among them. Ashley's speech, delivered just days after the conclusion of Johnson's impeachment trial, also referred ominously to Johnson's ascension to the presidency

as evidence that the existing structure offered "temptations" to "conspira-
tors and assassins." Framing electoral reform as a logical outcome of the
Union's victory in the war, he maintained that "but for the existence of
slavery the present indefensible anti-democratic system of electing the
President . . . would long since have been changed, and a system more in
accord with the democratic spirit of the age adopted."[27]

Although Ashley's ideas meshed well with the ideological thrust of
Radical Republicanism, he was not able to prod the House into giving
them a serious hearing. Congress in the late 1860s was preoccupied with
other compelling matters, including the impeachment of a president, the
rights of African-Americans, and the reentry of ex-Confederate states into
the Union. In the autumn of 1868 Ashley was narrowly defeated for reelection, as were several other vocal supporters of equal suffrage for African-
Americans. A few months later, as his congressional career drew to a close
(and the wording of the Fifteenth Amendment was being hammered out
in a conference committee), he introduced two final amendments. The first,
which he preferred, was identical to the NPV proposal he had advocated
a year earlier. The second, tacitly recognizing the lack of adequate support
for a national popular vote, called instead for proportional elections to be
held in each state.[28]

In the Senate, Charles Sumner, the eminent Radical Republican from
Massachusetts, took positions similar to Ashley's. In February 1867
Sumner called for "the election of the President directly by the people," a
process that "would give every individual voter, wherever he might be, a
positive weight in the election." He also advocated a single presidential
term as well as the abolition of the vice presidency—because vice presidents were "selected less with reference to fitness than to transient political considerations." The following day a resolution closely matching
Sumner's ideas was put forward by his colleague Luke Poland of Vermont. Five years later, Sumner himself introduced an amendment calling
for a national popular vote, with a runoff election to be held among the
top three candidates if no candidate gained an outright majority. Such a
system, he believed, would empower the people and eliminate the large role
that caucuses and conventions played in choosing presidential candidates.
By 1872, however, the aging Sumner had lost much of his influence in Congress and in the Republican Party, thanks in part to his attacks on the

Grant administration and his efforts to prevent Grant's reelection. Sumner's proposal, following the itinerary so memorably described by Ashley, disappeared into a committee chaired by Oliver Morton without ever being brought to the floor. Less than two years later the Massachusetts senator died of a heart attack.[29]

Ashley and Sumner were the most prominent, but not the only, post–Civil War advocates of a national popular vote. In 1872–1873 NPV resolutions were introduced in the House by Republican representatives John Lynch (Maine), Nathaniel Banks (Massachusetts), and Charles Porter of Virginia (a New Yorker temporarily living in the South, following a stint in the Union Army). These measures, which varied in their details, were all relegated to committees.[30] A hint of bipartisan support came from Democrat John Storm of Pennsylvania, who took to the floor in February 1873 to endorse Banks's proposal as the best replacement for an existing system that was "cumbersome" and "dangerous" as well as "unjust and unequal in its operations." Storm argued that a national popular vote was superior to district elections both because it avoided the problem of gerrymandering and because it guaranteed that the winner of the popular vote would become president. "Nothing but a direct vote of the people, irrespective of state or district lines, and without the intermediation of electors, will give full and fair expression to the popular will."[31] In the 1880s the NPV banner was held aloft by Richard Townshend from southern Illinois, a six-term Democrat who introduced measures calling for a national popular vote and runoff elections in almost every Congress from 1880 until the end of the decade. Labor and farmers' organizations, as well as radical political parties, voiced similar preferences for national popular elections.[32]

Support for an NPV also surfaced occasionally in the mainstream press and in journals of opinion. In 1875 and again in 1880, the *Chicago Tribune* expressed interest in the idea, and the *Washington Post* in 1884 declared flatly that "the people ought to vote directly for President and Vice President, and a plurality should elect—a plurality of all votes cast in all the states." That endorsement was followed by the *Post*'s approval of the Miner Law in 1891 as "a step toward a consummation in which the present electoral-college method will probably be abandoned, and the President be elected by the popular vote of the nation." In 1892 John Roebling pointed out in the *American Journal of Politics* that only an NPV could prevent election outcomes such as that of 1888 when the Electoral College had put Benjamin Harrison in the White House despite his apparent loss of the popular vote. He further argued (anticipating mid-twentieth-century claims) that an NPV "would quicken the political life of all the states and bring out the greatest part of the latent vote." The *New York Times*, which preferred proportional elections, nonetheless treated the idea of an NPV respectfully, editorializing that the "one serious objection to" a national popular vote was that it could "intensify and make perilous any sectional division that might spring up."[33]

Numerous other objections were raised, both in the press and in Congress. A national popular vote constituted a more radical innovation than either district or proportional elections because it would alter the distribution of power among the states and create a truly national election rather than an aggregation of state elections. Proposals for an NPV accordingly spawned their own lines of resistance in addition to those that had formed in defense of winner-take-all. One was that a national vote would, in the words of Pennsylvania Democratic senator William Wallace, destroy the "federative system," obliterating "state lines" and "state independence and equality." (An ardent proponent of district elections, Wallace also feared that an NPV would permit a few populous states to overwhelm the votes of citizens elsewhere.) Similarly, Republican senator Henry Dawes of Massachusetts, writing in the *North American Review* in 1885, insisted that "while more democratic," an NPV "would be a stride toward centralization at war with the whole theory of the government. It does not admit of discussion." Seven years later, Democratic representative David De Armond of Missouri concluded that a "direct vote . . . will be but another step toward wiping out state lines." "I should oppose," he announced, "anything that tends to an obliteration of the autonomy of the states."[34] Lawyer and writer Richard H. Dana Jr. believed that the nationalization of the election would encourage fraud. "The result of every . . . illegal act would go directly into the aggregate vote of the whole country," he cautioned.[35]

Opponents of an NPV also emphasized the "small-state" argument, a line of criticism that rapidly acquired two somewhat distinct branches. The first was that a national vote was unfair to the small states because it disproportionately reduced their influence (by eliminating the two senatorial electoral votes given to each state) and because it violated the compact between large and small states embedded in the Constitution. This historical and moral argument, although repeated with some frequency, did not go unchallenged. (After all, the three-fifths clause had also been part of the compact among the states.) The *Washington Post*, for example, maintained that the small-state advantage "ought not have been given and it could be surrendered without any apprehension of danger to the smaller commonwealths."[36]

The more common small-state argument was a pragmatic, political one: pursuing an NPV was pointless because the small states would object and would consequently prevent a national popular vote from ever being approved by the requisite supermajorities in Congress and the states. This was the reasoning offered by Oliver Morton in 1874 to justify his advocacy of district elections, despite his personal preference for an NPV, and it was reiterated by other politicians and commentators. Notably, those who pressed this argument did not generally speak as representatives of small states; nor did they produce evidence that the small states would, in fact, line up against a national popular vote. But the claim was increasingly believed to be true. In 1875 the *Chicago Tribune* had been dismissive of the whole notion, certain that the small states would not "dare to defeat a constitutional amendment." Less than two years later, it ruefully concluded that those states would indeed prevent passage of any amendment that took away their "senatorial" electoral votes.[37]

Advocates of a national popular vote during the decades after the Civil War never expressed high hopes about the fate of their proposals. Although abolition of the three-fifths clause permitted the idea of an NPV to enter the national conversation, it remained on the fringes of debate, pressed forward more as a matter of principle than expectation. Two months before he died in 1877, Oliver Morton reminded a lecture audience that his preferred reform was "to elect the president by one great vote of the people," but he wistfully acknowledged that he had "not much hope" that it would be accomplished. Similarly, the pro-NPV *Washington Post* editorialized seven years later that "we have little hope that an amendment so radical as we have suggested will meet with immediate and general favor, but its justice will commend it to all who believe in anything like a close approximation to democratic government."[38]

Of at least equal and perhaps greater importance, obstacles to electoral reform of any type were much in evidence by the late 1870s and 1880s—as proponents of district and proportional elections were also learning. (See Chapter 3.) Congress had its hands full with other matters (recurrent downturns in the business cycle, civil service reform, tariffs, and the money supply, to name a few), and its members' remained preoccupied, after 1876, with the tortuous process of resolving problems with the electoral vote count.[39] In addition, two partisan sources of resistance to change had begun to emerge: the reluctance of the more centrist, pragmatic wing of the Republican Party to relinquish the general ticket; and the strengthening of states' rights politics among southern Democrats.[40] This resistance complicated the path of any reform that sought to bring an end to winner-take-all or to make nationally uniform the processes of presidential elections.

LITTLE FORWARD PROGRESS, 1890–1945

The election of 1888, which brought Benjamin Harrison to the White House despite his having received fewer votes than his opponent, produced no great clamor to replace the Electoral College with a national popular vote. Although the muted response was attributable in part to the uncertain integrity of Grover Cleveland's popular vote margin, it also reflected the absence of strong political interest in altering the electoral system, a condition that would prevail for the next half century.[41] As recounted earlier, the decades stretching from 1890 into the late 1940s constituted a sluggish, even stagnant period for presidential election reform, partly because there were no electoral crises and because the Republican Party was known to oppose any departure from winner-take-all. The idea of holding a national vote gained a small added measure of acceptability during these years, but it was far removed from the central concerns of political practitioners and intellectuals.

Still, amendment resolutions calling for an NPV were occasionally introduced in Congress. Although there were none from 1900 to 1910, they came in spurts between 1911 and 1917, sponsored by both Democrats and Republicans and encouraged by the passage of the Seventeenth Amendment, which provided for the direct election of senators. One advocate was the young Kentucky congressman Alben Barkley, who would become vice president in 1949 and who remained an advocate of a national popular vote throughout his long career.[42] Interest in an NPV was particularly pronounced in the wake of the 1916 election, in which Woodrow Wilson barely eked out an Electoral College victory despite having a clear, if narrow, lead in the popular vote. A half dozen resolutions were rapidly introduced in Congress, and a survey conducted by the *New York World* in late November 1916 found numerous present and former public officials who favored replacing the Electoral College with a "direct popular vote."[43] Between 1920 and 1943 another nine amendment resolutions were proposed, mostly from progressive Republicans, the last from Henry Cabot Lodge Jr.[44] But none of these proposals gained any traction, and a study commissioned by Congress in the late 1920s flatly concluded that any proposal calling "for the popular election of the President with a complete disregarding of state lines would hardly be ratified by the requisite three-fourths of the States." In 1932 and 1933, Massachusetts senator Marcus A. Coolidge (the Democratic Coolidge!) introduced an amendment that the *Boston Globe* characterized as "the same proposal" put forward by Charles Sumner in the 1870s. It was never reported out of committee.[45]

The arguments advanced for a national popular vote during this long period were similar to those put forward in earlier decades. As would always be true, the case emphasized democratic principles, the importance of all votes counting equally, and the desirability of guaranteeing "the election of the candidate receiving the highest number of votes." The *Washington Post,* criticizing the Electoral College as "obsolete and unsatisfactory," stressed in 1904 that a national vote would remove the inequalities built into the electoral system and "make the vote of the citizen in one state as potent as that of the citizen of another." "The electoral college is an undemocratic institution," declared the Pulitzer-owned (and Democratic leaning) *New York World* in November 1916. "The President of the United States ought to be elected like a Governor or a Senator by the voters themselves." The *Washington Herald* echoed that sentiment after observing that Woodrow Wilson had come close to losing his reelection bid in the Electoral College: "The President of this nation should be the man desired by the greatest number of citizens and not a man who receives the greatest number of votes technically under a system devised for a nation in the babyhood of its existence." Several writers pointed out—as did others with regard to proportional elections—that an NPV would have the added virtue of encouraging candidates from a "wider field" of states, an attractive prospect in an era when nearly all candidates came from states with large blocs of electoral votes, like Ohio and New York. Occasionally an advocate even challenged the Republican apprehension that anything other than winner-take-all would lead to consistent Democratic victories thanks to the suppression of black votes in the South. "An unjust method of counting," declared one commentator, "is no proper remedy for an unjust method of voting."[46]

The arguments against an NPV also followed a well-trodden path. The most common were the two variations on the small-state theme: a national vote would harm small states, and it would never be approved because those states would oppose it. An NPV would "decrease the power of the small states" and "thereby affect the dignity and equality of the states," wrote two analysts in 1904.[47] "It may be assumed that the smaller States would object," concluded another.[48] In a slightly different vein, Republican governor James Withycombe of Oregon worried that an NPV would harm small states by giving "the overwhelming preponderance of power to half a dozen thickly populated Eastern states."[49] Such arguments were invoked both by advocates of district or proportional elections, like Congressman Clarence Lea, and by those skeptical about the possibility of any reform.[50] Schemes like a national popular vote, wrote Columbia University law professor Lindsay Rogers in 1937, "even if . . . commendable in theory . . . would have no chance of approval because they would be opposed by the small states, which now have greater weight in the choice of a president than their population warrants."[51] Speaking from within (and to) a small state, the Sioux Falls (South Dakota) *Argus Leader* in the 1930s published a series of editorials about an NPV with headlines such as "Electoral College Helps Us" and "We Would Lose."[52]

Concerns about federalism also persisted. "Shall state independence be so far surrendered as to permit the people of the nation to vote *en masse* for the chief executive?" asked J. Hampden Dougherty, the author of a lengthy 1906 disquisition about the electoral system. "Such a change would be revolutionary." (Dougherty evasively concluded that it was "unnecessary" to answer that question because the requisite number of states would never agree to an NPV.) A decade later, in response to demands to eliminate the Electoral College, the *North American Review* insisted that "merging the entire nation into a single electorate" would constitute an unacceptable departure from the principles of federalism, even if it was desirable to "get rid of the obsolete, cumbersome and actually evil features of the present system." The *New York Times* in 1916 dismissed concerns about state sovereignty as "largely academic" but concluded nonetheless that an NPV would alter "the fundamental basis of our institutions, which have merits with all their faults."[53]

Although most claims about federalism contained more rhetoric than substance, some critics of a national vote did raise a concrete and potent federalism issue: an NPV, they argued, would require presidential elections to be managed not by the states but by the national government. In the fall of 1916 both the *New York Times* and the *Washington Post* (which had lost its affection for an NPV) focused on this concern. "It would require an army of officials exercising functions within the states which most citizens would prefer to have exercised in the present manner, under home control rather than under orders of a distant power," warned the *Times*.[54] Clarence Lea, among others, made the related argument that a national vote would inexorably lead to national suffrage laws, which many states would find objectionable. "The direct election of the President, ignoring State lines," Lea added, could "tend to lower the voting standards of the country."[55] In an exchange on the Senate floor in 1934, Senators Simeon Fess of Ohio and Joseph Robinson of Arkansas agreed that an NPV was the only way to avoid the possibility of a minority victor, but they worried that it "would inject the Federal authority in every State."[56]

Among these recurrent themes were worries that a national popular vote would encourage fraud—because the tallies reported anywhere could potentially tip the entire election. A Progressive-era critic from North Carolina warned that states dominated by one party might be tempted to pad the totals to help its national candidates. This could yield charges of fraud across the nation that could end up as a "provocation of civil war." The Philadelphia *Evening Ledger* agreed, without invoking the prospect of war.[57] A new objection, surfacing in the wake of the 1916 election, was that the outcome of a national popular vote could take days or weeks to determine, a prolonged "suspense" that the American people would be loath to tolerate. In 1936 the editors of the *New York Times* fused these two objections, cautioning that a slow count would yield "suspicion that unscrupulous political managers were tampering with the counting of the votes."[58]

A unique turn in the debate occurred in the late Progressive era, when women were able to vote in some states but not others. Congressional interest in reform was relatively strong during these years, and a spate of NPV resolutions were introduced in Congress from 1913 through 1917. The partial enfranchisement of women, however, created a new barrier to adoption of a national popular vote. As the *New York Times* pointed out, the number of votes cast in 1916 in California, Washington, and Illinois (all of which permitted women to vote) dwarfed the numbers in states of similar size where only men were enfranchised. With the passage of a national suffrage amendment far from assured, the *Times,* among others, concluded that "it is not likely that states which have not yet granted the ballot to women" would agree to a new electoral system that would significantly "decrease their own relative importance" in presidential elections.[59] That issue happily disappeared after the ratification of the Nineteenth Amendment in 1920, but so too did the reform impulses of the Progressive era.

The South and the Electoral College after Redemption

Accompanying these varied arguments, seeping through them, and shaping the political arena in which they were heard was something else: the recognition that the post-Reconstruction political transformation of the South placed an enormous obstacle in the path of a national popular vote. By 1890 the disenfranchisement of African-Americans was well under way, and by the early years of the twentieth century it was complete. The southern electorate had become almost entirely white, the Democratic Party firmly controlled the region, and general elections were usually uncompetitive, with low turnout. Republicans had tried to check these developments in 1890 by pressing for passage of the Federal Elections Bill, but that effort had narrowly failed, with consequences that would endure into the 1960s.

As Republicans somberly noted during the first decades of the twentieth century, white southerners were wielding more influence in national politics than they had before the Civil War. After the abolition of slavery and the "three-fifths" clause, African-Americans counted fully toward representation, and southern states consequently gained additional seats in the House of Representatives and votes in the Electoral College. Yet once blacks were again denied the right to vote, white Democrats effectively became the beneficiaries of an unwritten "five-fifths" clause: they wielded national political power on their own behalf and in the name of the region's entire African-American population.[60]

Northern critics like retired general Henry Edwin Tremain, author of a forceful 1907 book entitled *Sectionalism Unmasked*, blasted this state of affairs, compiling election results to demonstrate that the actual number of votes cast per member of Congress (or electoral vote) in the South was only a fraction of what it was elsewhere in the country. In 1904, for example, Delaware had cast roughly the same number of votes for Congress as Georgia had, but Georgia had eleven representatives while Delaware had only one. Ohio that same year cast as many votes for president as nine southern states together, but those nine states possessed ninety-nine electoral votes in comparison to Ohio's twenty-three. (The 1904 election was no anomaly: in every presidential contest from the 1890s into the 1960s, there were many fewer ballots cast per electoral vote in the South than elsewhere.)[61] Tremain, a Medal of Honor winner and former president of the Republican Club of New York City, demanded that Congress enforce section 2 of the Fourteenth Amendment and thereby reduce the representation of southern states in proportion to the number of citizens that they had disenfranchised. That demand had passionate support among Republicans in parts of the North, but it never came close to being acted upon by Congress.[62]

Similarly, twentieth-century Republican calls for a revived "Force Bill" to impose federal supervision of elections went nowhere. Such a measure was forcefully advocated in December 1916 by Senator Boies Penrose, the conservative boss of Pennsylvania's Republican political machine. He went on to declare that if Congress objected to federal supervision of elections, then he would "work for the elimination of the Electoral College and the election of President of the United States by a popular vote." From Penrose's perspective, the Electoral College reinforced white supremacy in the South and gave southern Democrats unmerited strength in national elections. A national popular vote would eliminate winner-take-all (which most Republicans defended), but it would at least prevent white southerners from casting electoral votes allotted because of the presence of a large population of disenfranchised African-Americans. (In that respect, an NPV was considered preferable to either district or proportional elections.) "Let us have Federal supervision or the popular election of President," Penrose urged.[63] His demands, however, had little chance of being met in a Congress dominated by Democrats. The *New York Times* dismissed them as unrealistic fulminations, emanating from a defeated and fragmented political party. Nonetheless, the paper acknowledged that "the South most certainly does possess an unfair advantage in having its non-voters counted as voters, so that a handful of Southerners are more potent than a great number of Northerners." Governor Withycombe of Oregon, responding to that same "unfair advantage," proposed that electoral votes be apportioned based on the number of votes cast in a state rather than on its population.[64]

What this turn of affairs meant for the prospects of a national popular vote was clear, although most often left unspoken. Under the existing electoral system, each southern state wielded influence in a presidential election in rough proportion to its total population, black and white. With a national popular vote, however, a state's influence would be determined only by the number of votes cast: southern whites would surrender the electoral power that they gained from disenfranchisement and the "five-fifths" clause. White southerners would then be left with a choice between losing clout for their states in presidential elections or eliminating restrictions on the franchise and permitting blacks to vote— which would also limit white influence, if not the region's. That southerners would balk at such a prospect was evident, although they rarely said so in public. Walter M. Clark, a progressive Democrat and long-serving chief justice of the North Carolina Supreme Court, did address the issue candidly in a law review article. Southern states, he wrote in 1917, "would not consent to a system which would deprive them of representation by reason of the negroes . . . not voting at the ballot box."[65] The *Washington Post* was more emphatic, concluding that the South would surely resist an NPV because "the abolition of the electoral college would mean the taking over of presidential elections by the national government. . . . What would the South say to national control of elections? Is the force bill forgotten?"[66]

Twenty years later the *New York Times* offered a similar assessment after noting that the disparity between the electoral and the popular votes in 1936, when Republican Alf Landon garnered only eight electoral votes, made the Electoral College look exceptionally "obsolete." "Why not get rid of the cumbrous and useless piece of old governmental machinery and have the President chosen directly by popular vote?" an editorial asked. The editors offered a multipart answer to their own question, predicting that an NPV would contain "many complexities and will meet with many objections," not least the reluctance of the states to hand over control of presidential elections and suffrage rules to the federal government. In addition, "the Southern States would be almost sure to set up obstacles to the plan. If the Presidential election were to be decided solely by a majority of the popular vote, there would be enormous pressure everywhere to bring all eligible voters to the polls. This would mean in the South a drive to permit Negroes to exercise their right of suffrage. If they did it in a Federal election, they would be encouraged to demand it in State and local elections. Is this a prospect which would seem welcome in the Southern states?"[67]

RICHMOND P. HOBSON: SOUTHERN EXCEPTION

Between 1900 and 1960, only one southern member of Congress introduced an amendment resolution calling for a national popular vote: Richmond Pearson Hobson of Alabama.[68] Hobson, a Democrat, was born and raised in Alabama and then attended the Naval Academy in Annapolis, where he graduated first in his class. After further training in naval architecture and construction, he served in the Spanish-American War, where he led a daring and dangerous mission to block the escape of Spanish warships by sinking an old American collier, the *Merrimac,* in the harbor of Santiago, Cuba. Hobson was captured by the Spanish, who praised his valor, and later returned to the United States in an exchange of prisoners. His wartime exploits earned him a Medal of Honor and transformed him into a nationally celebrated hero, a status that he thoroughly enjoyed. After the war ended, he embarked on a cross-country speaking and greeting tour that earned the handsome, charismatic captain the sobriquet of the "most kissed man in America."[69]

Ambitious, eloquent, self-righteous, and self-promoting, Hobson returned to Alabama several years later and ran for political office. In his second try he won election to the House of Representatives in 1906, defeating ten-term incumbent John Bankhead. Both in his campaign and in Congress he emphasized the need for U.S. naval supremacy while also pressing for regulations to rein in the power of the railroads. Nationally known, mentioned as a possible vice presidential candidate in 1908, he also became a committed champion of temperance and prohibition both within Alabama and nationally. Allying himself with progressives, as did many temperance advocates, he sometimes took controversial stands in defense of the rights of African-Americans and became an ardent promoter of democratic reforms, including the direct election of senators and suffrage for women, neither of which was a popular cause in the South.[70]

Between 1911 and 1913, Hobson also introduced six resolutions calling for the abolition of the Electoral College and the election of presidents through a national popular vote.[71] These resolutions were neither debated in Congress nor reported out of committee, but they did provoke an extraordinarily candid and revealing expression of southern opinion about the dangers of a national popular vote. In 1913 Alabama senator Joseph F. Johnston died in office, and Hobson announced his candidacy to serve out the remainder of Johnston's term. His principal opponent in the all-important Democratic primary was a senior congressional colleague, Oscar Underwood, the House majority leader and chairman of the Ways and Means Committee, framer of an important tariff measure, and recent contender for the Democratic presidential nomination. The campaign—one of the first popular elections for the Senate under the Seventeenth Amendment—was heated and personal, with Hobson passionately advocating prohibition and denouncing Underwood as a "tool" of the liquor interests and Wall Street. Underwood, who could not match Hobson's eloquence and charisma, declined to debate him in person, although they squared off several times on the floor of the House. Underwood's campaign made the case for its candidate and against Hobson largely through the press and through a lengthy pamphlet entitled "The Issue and the Facts," authored primarily by Johnston's son, Forney.[72]

That pamphlet attacked Hobson on numerous grounds, including his advocacy of a national popular vote. "Hobson's plan is to allow the honest vote of a white man in Alabama to be neutralized by the fraudulent and debauched vote which disgraces the larger cities," the pamphlet proclaimed.

The vote of every white male Alabamian "would be paired with that of any negro woman authorized to vote under his female suffrage plan in the Northern or Western States, unless we adopt woman suffrage and negro suffrage to maintain our proportion." Nor was that all:

> Is there a man in Alabama so foolish as to think that the Federal Government would adopt an amendment to the Constitution of the United States providing for direct election of presidents, without providing uniform qualifications for voters . . . how long under this system would we be able to prevent the adoption of a Federal statute authorizing every negro over the age of twenty-one year to vote, and regulating elections in Alabama?

"And suppose," the pamphlet continued,

> we were able to prevent the restoration of the nightmare conditions of the black ballot. With the negro half of our people not voting, our voice in the national elections, which is now based upon total population, would then be based solely on our voting population and, therefore, reduced by half.

Statistics from the 1912 election were offered to give precision to the claim: standing General Tremain's argument on its head, the pamphlet proudly boasted that Alabama contributed more than 2 percent of the nation's electoral votes while casting less than 1 percent of the popular vote. Hobson's plan, in contrast, would "shrink Alabama to the size of Utah."[73]

Underwood won the election decisively. That outcome was hardly surprising, given that he was by far the more seasoned and influential political figure; and it seems unlikely that Hobson's views on presidential election reform played a major role in the younger man's defeat. (His views on prohibition were not universally welcomed either.) Still, the Underwood campaign's strident attacks on Hobson had pulled back the curtain on a partially hidden corner of southern politics, revealing, without disguise or euphemism, the intensity and sources of hostility to the idea of replacing the Electoral College with a national popular vote. An NPV was unacceptable—not because of federalism, state sovereignty, or the needs of the small states but because it was regarded as a direct threat to white supremacy and the influence of white southern Democrats. A national popular vote was simply anathema: for a southerner like Hobson to promote such a reform was a betrayal of southern values. Given that climate of opinion, it was fitting that the only southern sponsor of an NPV resolution in Congress was a maverick, a native Alabamian yet an outsider, a man whose prestige as a war hero permitted him to be elected to Congress without climbing through the ranks of local Democratic politics. Hobson was from Alabama but, in a sense, not *of* Alabama; he was often criticized for spending little time in the state and failing to identify with sectional interests. Although Hobson did make one final run for Congress in 1916, his career as a politician effectively ended with his defeat by Underwood. He spent the next two decades crusading for temperance and prohibition and against narcotics.[74]

Alabamians were hardly unique in taking a dim and hostile view of a national popular vote. Throughout the South, politicians intent on maintaining segregation and white supremacy believed they had nothing to gain and much to lose from abolishing the Electoral College and replacing it with a national ballot. The fourteen southern political leaders (governors, senators, and representatives) who responded to the *New York World*'s inquiry about "directly electing the president by popular vote" in November 1916 were nearly unanimous in opposing such a reform. The only exceptions were House members from the border states of West Virginia and Kentucky. The governors of Virginia, Alabama, and South Carolina, as well as the four southern senators who were polled, were flatly against an NPV. Mississippi's governor, Theodore Bilbo, a notorious white supremacist, declared that he was "unalterably opposed" to a national popular vote, which "would destroy the last vestige of state rights."[75] Southern newspapers did not often editorialize on the subject, but when they did, they commonly favored preservation of the Electoral College.[76] In 1950, when the Senate voted on a national popular vote proposal for the first time since 1816, only one senator from a state that had been part of the Confederacy—the dedicated left-liberal Claude Pepper of Florida—voted favorably.[77]

SMALL STATES AND SOUTHERN STATES

As late as the 1940s, there was little congressional enthusiasm for an NPV, and the mainstream press consequently paid it little heed. That this was so, that a national popular vote remained at the outskirts of public debate, reflected both substantive opposition to the idea and the perception that such a reform could never be implemented. Some of this opposition was broadly ideological or even temperamental. Opponents of an NPV, from diverse locales, worried about the encroachment of the federal government on the autonomy of the states; many felt more comfortable leaving the control of elections in the hands of familiar state officials; politicians were apprehensive about the impact that an NPV would have upon election campaigns. Change was threatening, and an NPV was more threatening than either district or proportional elections.

Of greater salience was the resistance emanating from the two groups, or categories, of states that would lose electoral clout if an NPV were adopted. Southern political leaders, as we have seen, knew well that the Electoral College served their interests: it gave each state influence in proportion to its total population and imposed no penalties on states with large, disenfranchised minorities. An NPV—unlike district or proportional elections—would have reduced the region's electoral weight unless, and until, restrictions on the franchise were lifted. The South's resultant antagonism undergirded the judgment of the nation's opinion leaders that a national popular vote was an unrealistic alternative to the Electoral College. Built-in opposition from the eleven formerly Confederate states (and perhaps a few border states as well) would likely doom a constitutional amendment that required supermajorities in Congress as well as ratification by three-quarters of the states.[78]

Small states also loomed as an apparent obstacle to an NPV because their citizens, under the Electoral College, wielded more electoral votes per capita than did residents of larger states. That slight advantage had not figured at all in antebellum discussions of an NPV: it was eclipsed both by the three-fifths clause and by efforts to alter a contingent election system that gave the small states a far more significant—if occasional—advantage.[79] Only in the 1870s did the edge given to small states in the allocation of electoral votes begin to be invoked as a reason that a national popular vote should not or could not be implemented. The small-state issue was raised frequently thereafter and even more frequently in the twentieth century. An inequality originating in the Constitution stood as a source of resistance to the one reform that would make all votes count equally.

The small-state argument was always a plausible one, and it was surely true that small states, or at least some small states, might seek to prevent adoption of a national popular vote. There was, however, relatively little direct evidence that either the people or the political leaders of small states were systematically or consistently opposed to a national popular vote between Reconstruction and the late 1940s. The politicians and writers who publicly emphasized the issue tended to come from large or medium-sized states. Declarations of hostility to an NPV from leaders of small states did not surface often in the national press or the records of Congress.[80]

A sampling of (digitized) small-state newspapers sheds a bit of additional light on the subject. Some papers, like the Sioux Falls *Argus Leader,* were repeatedly critical of an NPV. "The suggestion of electing Presidents by direct vote of the people contains an intriguing sound," cautioned the paper's editors in 1932. "But South Dakotans, before endorsing it, should realize that it means a curtailment of their voting strength." (The editorial, tellingly, implied that South Dakotans were divided on the issue, and, in fact, one of the state's senators, Edwin S. Johnson, had sponsored an NPV amendment in 1916.)[81] Other papers offered more mixed or tentative opinions, and at least a few favored the replacement of the Electoral College with a national popular vote. "It is hard to get around the argument that the majority should rule," concluded the Republican-leaning Burlington (Vermont) *Free Press* in both 1924 and in 1947.[82] The *Albuquerque Journal,* the leading newspaper in New Mexico, editorialized in favor of a national popular vote in 1933 and applauded Henry Cabot Lodge's 1940 announcement that he would introduce an amendment calling for a national popular vote. Notably, the *Journal* observed that it was not sanguine about the amendment's prospects because it feared that southern states—not other small states like New Mexico—would block its adoption. Thirteen states could block approval of a constitutional amendment, the newspaper pointed out, "and the Solid South contains 13 states, not counting Maryland or Missouri. These 13 states might all refuse to ratify an amendment for popular election of the president, on the ground that it would reduce their present importance in electing a president."[83]

Such evidence suggests that despite the frequent repetition of the small-state argument, there was not a united small-state coalition that stood in the way of a national vote in the first half of the twentieth century. There may have been a tendency for politicians from small states to be more skeptical of an NPV than their counterparts elsewhere, but small states (such as Nevada, Delaware, and Wyoming) were geographically scattered as well as diverse in their interests and political alignments. For residents of these states, the extra weight that their votes received in the Electoral College was presumably a factor in shaping their views of reform, but it was not necessarily an overriding or even significant factor. In the South, in contrast, a national popular vote was regarded as a vital threat to the post-Redemption political order, and southern states constituted a regional bloc unified by the dominance of the Democratic Party and the disenfranchisement of African-Americans.

This contrast inescapably raises a question about why, in congressional debates as well as other arenas, small states were invoked as an impediment to an NPV far more often than were southern states. The South's antagonism to a national vote was known to political actors in Washington and elsewhere, and it created at least as high a hurdle for an NPV as united small-state opposition would have. One possible answer to this question—a hunch derived from reading thousands of pages of documents—is that members of Congress, as well as other commentators, commonly found it to be more decorous and less contentious to attribute the challenges confronting an NPV to the politically bland issue of state size rather than to the historically charged matter of black disenfranchisement in the South. Patterns of coded language in floor debates affirm that it was generally considered impolite or inappropriate to speak in Congress about race and the absence of democracy in the region.[84] The small-state worry was real—even a handful of small states acting in conjunction with the South could easily kill an amendment in the Senate—but it was also an uncontroversial peg on which to hang other concerns.

The paucity of congressional interest in a national popular vote, in sum, was shaped by both southern and, to a far lesser degree, small-state opposition to the idea. While the dominant, conservative wing of the Republican Party was largely responsible for blocking district or proportional elections during the first half of the twentieth century, southern Democrats played that role with respect to a national popular vote. Given their strident resistance (and the possibility that they would be joined by some other states), the notion of replacing the admittedly flawed Electoral College with an NPV seemed to hold no more promise than it had when Abner Lacock was in the Senate.[85] Whatever their personal views, most members of Congress—like Henry Cabot Lodge by the mid-1940s—saw little point in spending their time, or expending their political capital, on a losing cause.

William Langer and John Pastore: 1944–1956

One small-state leader who had no reservations about a national popular vote was Senator William Langer of North Dakota. A Republican, often referred to as a "maverick" and well known for his isolationism in international affairs, Langer had political roots in the Nonpartisan League, an organization launched in 1915 in North Dakota and nearby states to defend the interests of farmers, particularly against predatory banks, railroads, and other large corporations. Langer generally described himself as a "progressive" Republican and was regarded by many contemporaries as being to the left of the New Deal on domestic issues. Before being elected to the Senate in 1940, he had twice served as governor of his state—although he had been removed from office during his first term as the result of a politically entangled financial scandal.[86]

Langer was the flag bearer in Congress for a national popular vote in the 1940s and 1950s. He first introduced an NPV proposal in 1944 and did so again three times in the late 1940s and twice in the 1950s. (His North Dakota colleague, and occasional adversary, William Lemke, introduced a similar resolution in the House in 1945.)[87] Langer's proposals were distinctive in calling not only for a national presidential election but also for national primaries to nominate candidates. Sharing the anti-party sentiments of his fellow maverick, George Norris, Langer sought "to take the selection of our highest executive offices out of the atmosphere of smoke-filled back rooms" and check the power of corporate interests that, he believed, dominated both major parties. Convinced that the Electoral College was "obsolete, dangerous, and completely illogical," he wanted "to make absolutely certain that the man sworn into the Presidency of the United States is the man that the majority of the people want." Langer also believed that the existing winner-take-all system concentrated "too much political power in too few States," especially the large, urban states with "big-city bosses and their political machines." A national popular vote, he claimed, would reduce the influence of the largest states while enhancing the power of citizens of smaller, rural states such as his own. It would have the added virtue of increasing turnout, which in some states had fallen to disturbingly low levels.[88]

A majority of the American people supported Langer's core proposal. The first reliable public opinion polls regarding the desirability of replacing the Electoral College with a national popular vote were conducted by the Gallup organization in 1944 and 1947. They revealed that two-thirds of Americans favored the change while only a fifth preferred to keep the existing system.[89] (See Appendix Table A.1.) The unprecedented surveys pointed not only to the broad appeal of an NPV but also to a remarkably large gap between the views of citizens and the stances of the nation's political leaders and professional analysts. Officials in Washington and elsewhere may have taken note of these polls, but the numbers had no immediate impact in Congress: Langer's proposals (as well as Lemke's) made little headway in the 1940s.[90]

Langer's resolution did, however, gain a floor vote in 1950 as an alternative to the Lodge-Gossett resolution. In the Senate, Langer's views were strongly seconded by (among others) the recently elected senator from Minnesota, Hubert Humphrey. Humphrey, who had catapulted to national attention with an impassioned call for civil rights at the 1948 Democratic Convention, put forward his own NPV resolution, which made no mention of national primaries. He compared the Electoral College to the "human appendix" ("useless, unpredictable, and a possible center of inflammation") and introduced a new theme, and rationale, by insisting that "the American people have a right to elect their President by direct popular vote." Acknowledging that neither his proposal nor Langer's had much chance of succeeding, he nonetheless urged his colleagues to "line up behind the principle of majority rule."[91]

Thirty-one senators voted in favor of Langer's resolution in 1950; a slightly smaller number endorsed Humphrey's alternative. Although the defeat was decisive, Langer's proposal drew bipartisan, if scattered, support from liberal Democrats as well as moderate and conservative Republicans. The twenty Republicans who cast positive votes, an otherwise diverse group, presumably shared the desire to prevent white southern Democrats from wielding electoral strength in the name of disenfranchised African-Americans. Those southern Democrats, unsurprisingly, were nearly unanimous in opposing Langer's amendment.[92] Ten senators from small states (with six or fewer electoral votes) supported Langer's proposal.[93]

Six years later Langer succeeded in getting another floor vote on his resolution, in the midst of the Senate's consideration of proportional and district election plans as well as the ill-fated hybrid promoted by Price

Daniel, Karl Mundt, and Estes Kefauver. (See Chapter 3.) This time Langer's proposal for an NPV and national primaries did less well, garnering only thirteen votes; a straight NPV resolution sponsored by New York liberal Herbert Lehman fared slightly better, with nearly half of its support coming from small-state senators.[94] Notably, Republican support evaporated between 1950 and 1956, at least in part because two-thirds of those who had favored an NPV were no longer in the Senate by 1956. This left Langer and Lehman with the votes of roughly a dozen liberal Democrats, Langer himself, and Oregon's very independent (former Republican) Wayne Morse.[95] Appropriately nicknamed "Wild Bill," Langer was too loose a cannon to be effective at corralling votes or coalition building, but those who voted "yea" were a geographically diverse lot, including Senate notables like Paul Douglas of Illinois, Albert Gore of Tennessee, Dennis Chavez of New Mexico, and Mike Mansfield of Montana. The only senator from an ex-Confederate state who voted favorably (Claude Pepper had been defeated for reelection) was Louisiana's Russell Long—giving voice perhaps to a populist impulse inherited from his legendary father, Huey Long.[96]

In both 1950 and 1956, nearly all of the arguments against NPV proposals were repetitions of those that had circulated earlier in the century. (The one exception, shaped by perceptions of European politics leading up to World War II, was that an NPV would lead to the formation of extremist parties, the demise of the two-party system, and political instability.)[97] Some conservative critics, like Ohio Republican Robert Taft, insisted that an NPV would damage federalism and make it difficult "to maintain the states."[98] Six years later, Massachusetts Democrat John Kennedy agreed, claiming that that "the Langer amendment . . . would break down the Federal system under which most States entered the Union."[99] Exactly how and why that would occur was no more evident in the 1950s than it had been in earlier decades, but the claim was often made.

A linked objection was that a national popular vote could not coexist with "the differences in voting qualifications in the various States," that there could be no truly national election if suffrage laws varied from state to state. Direct elections, it was further argued, would give an advantage to states with an expansive franchise while putting pressure on states elsewhere to enlarge the right to vote. The result, inevitably, would be nationally uniform suffrage laws.[100] Langer, never one to equivocate, confronted this issue head on in

1950 by inserting a provision that Congress would determine the qualifications for voting in presidential elections. That addition was predictably
denounced by southerners.[101] "I would never knowingly support anything
that would fix the age limit at 18 years," maintained Florida senator Spessard Holland in 1956, speaking in the circuitous code that focused on the
age of voting in Georgia rather than the disenfranchisement of millions of
African-Americans. "Nor would I ever want to take away from any State
the privilege of doing it if they saw fit to do it." (Holland was one of many
southern leaders who signed the "Southern Manifesto," promising to resist
the Supreme Court's 1954 decision mandating the integration of public
schools.)[102] More surprisingly, Langer's suffrage provision was applauded
by some Republicans, including Taft and Homer Ferguson. Although often
hostile to federal interventions, they recognized that congressional control
over the franchise would lead to the enfranchisement of African-Americans
in the South, potentially creating favorable conditions for their party even
in the absence of winner-take-all. It would, in addition, fulfill a Republican
promise to African-Americans that dated back to the late 1860s.[103]

Members of Congress, as well as commentators, also invoked both of
the small-state arguments. In 1956 Kennedy, who seemed intent on
blocking Electoral College reform, resurrected the claim that it would be
unfair to deprive small states of the senatorial electoral votes that they had
long possessed. It "would be a breach of the agreement made with the
States when they came into the Union. At that time it was understood that
they would have had the same number of electoral votes as they had Senators and Representatives."[104] (An able and informed debater, Kennedy
surely knew that the same criticism would have applied to the Thirteenth
Amendment, which abolished slavery.) Far more common was the almost-
ritualized assertion that an NPV could never win the support of two-thirds
of Congress or three-quarters of the state legislatures because of the opposition of the small states—Langer's sponsorship of the resolution notwith-
standing. (The liberal New Republic even insisted inaccurately that small-
state opposition had prevented Electoral College reform for 150 years.)[105]
This argument was once again advanced both by firm opponents of an NPV
and by moderates like Henry Cabot Lodge and Tennessee Democrat Estes
Kefauver, who professed support for the idea despite their sponsorship of
other measures. During the floor debates in 1956, Kefauver observed that

if in the beginning the Constitution had been written so that the people of the States could have voted for President and Vice President by popular vote, and if there could have been some uniform requirements or qualifications for the voters, that would have been a good thing. Even now I would support the idea. . . . The reason I do not support the popular vote proposal today, is that the political facts of life make it impossible to secure the approval of such an amendment by three-fourths of the States. About two-thirds of the States secure some benefit because the number of electors is based upon the number of Senators and Representatives, which gives to the small States a little advantage.[106]

Although Kefauver, who had refused to sign the Southern Manifesto, was doubtless sincere in his stated, if theoretical, preference for an NPV, the Tennessee senator surely knew that "the political facts of life" were not limited to the "little advantage" possessed by small states.[107]

More unusual and noteworthy than these incantations of old arguments were the forceful statements of Democratic senator John Pastore debunking the notion that small states would inevitably resist adoption of a national popular vote. Pastore, from the quite-small state of Rhode Island, was the son of working-class immigrants and the first person of Italian-American descent to serve in the Senate; before that he had been the first Italian-American to be elected governor of any state. Pastore began his remarks in 1956 by announcing that he preferred an NPV to the hybrid proposal that was before the Senate.

If we believe that this is a government of the people, by the people, and for the people, and that the President of the United States is President, not of the States, but of the people of the United States, why should we not adopt the principle that the President of the United States ought to be the popular selection of the people, and that the popular vote of the country should count?

Pastore was quickly challenged by Kennedy, a leader of the anti-reform forces in the Senate. Kennedy asserted that under Pastore's preferred plan "Rhode Island would cease to be of any real importance" whereas, under the current system, "Rhode Island is overrepresented in the electoral college today, based upon its population."[108]

Pastore shot back immediately, demanding that Kennedy explain what he meant by "any real importance."

> Why should one citizen in Rhode Island resent the fact that a man who is elected President received 51 percent of the entire vote of the country? Why is it of any importance to Rhode Island, if the man who is elected President is the selection of the majority of the people?
>
> I want to do away with the electoral college. I want to elect my President on election day. I say that when the people go to the polls the man who receives the greatest number of votes should be elected the President of the people. . . . It makes no difference to me how many electoral votes the people of Rhode Island have. What difference does it make?

Kennedy then shifted ground, claiming that the plan favored by Pastore could never get a two-thirds vote and "the smaller States would not accept it." (The future president gave no hint that he grasped the irony of addressing that criticism to Pastore of Rhode Island and Langer of North Dakota.) Pastore retorted that he had "never worried about what gets by and what does not get by. I am concerned with the principle involved." He then lobbed a question at Kennedy: "If we believe in the principle that this is a government of the people, for the people, and by the people, why do we not elect our President by popular vote?" Kennedy dodged, insisting "that the people now have the right of electing their President" and claiming that only once in the last 120 years had the loser of the popular vote become president. Pastore then restated his position:

> I would have the people elect the President of the United States on election day. . . . Let the man that gets the most votes be our President. It is as simple as that. That is my idea of representative government. Everything else beyond that is a gimmick.[109]

Moments later, Paul Douglas, a liberal Democrat from Illinois, intervened. Affirming that he too favored Langer's amendment, Douglas noted appreciatively that "representatives from two relatively small States, North Dakota and Rhode Island, are proposing an amendment which would decrease the power of their respective States." This he found to be "somewhat remarkable and to my mind praiseworthy." (Kennedy chimed in that it was "admirable.") "It is an indication," Douglas continued, "that in the small States, as well as in the large States, people who are like these two Senators put the interests of the Nation first. I believe the Senator from Rhode Island and the Senator from North Dakota ought to be commended for the position they have taken." Pastore, principled to the end, rebuffed the praise (as well as its premises) and denied that he was "making any sacrifice."

> I believe that the power of a Rhode Islander lies in the fact that he has the right of franchise to vote for the President of the United States.... When we talk about the right to elect a President, we are talking about carrying out the popular will of the people.... We are all Americans. We are all one Nation. Our president ought to be chosen by popular votes in an election by all the people.[110]

Neither Pastore's powerful words nor Langer's sponsorship, of course, banished the small-state arguments from public or congressional debate. They did, however, drain some strength from those arguments, making clear by example—and in the roll call votes—that small-state political leaders were not, as a group, committed to preventing the adoption of a national popular vote. In so doing, Pastore and Langer helped to diminish, or at least dilute, the pessimism that had long prevailed regarding the prospects of an NPV. Indeed, despite the decisive defeats on the floor of the Senate in 1950 and (especially) 1956, Langer and his allies succeeded in enhancing the political legitimacy of the notion that a national popular election might be the best way for the United States to choose its presidents. Reputable and respected politicians from both parties and from states of all sizes had spoken out on behalf of a national popular vote; nearly a third of the Senate had voted for an amendment resolution; even Senator Kennedy had acknowledged that Langer's plan offered "many advantages." Then too, there were those public opinion polls indicating that the American people preferred an NPV to the Electoral College. In Congress in the 1950s a national popular vote continued to take a back seat to district and proportional plans, but it had joined the roster of options that had to be considered. William Langer died in office in 1959 before he could witness the fruits of his labor, but his decade and a half of tilting at windmills helped to set the stage for the drama that would unfold in the 1960s.[111]

FIVE

AN IDEA WHOSE TIME HAS COME

A sea change in attitudes toward a national popular vote occurred after 1960, both in Congress and among opinion makers in much of the country. Over the course of the next decade, dissatisfaction with the Electoral College remained widespread, and an NPV (or "direct election") came to be viewed in many quarters as the primary, and most attractive, alternative to an electoral system that was clumsy, out of date, and potentially hazardous.[1] This shift in opinion took place, not coincidentally, as all three branches of the federal government were giving voice to more progressive values and taking major steps to democratize the nation's political institutions. The Supreme Court's embrace of the principle of "one person, one vote" and the passage by Congress of the Voting Rights Act were of particular importance in ushering the idea of a national popular vote onto center stage. What ensued was the most dramatic chapter in the long history of attempts to eliminate the Electoral College—a complex story deeply entangled in the era's highly charged tensions over race, equality, and political rights.

The 1960 Election: "A Game of Russian Roulette"

The election of 1960 did little to quiet critics of the Electoral College. Although remembered afterward as a close contest that brought an articulate and telegenic young leader to the White House, the election also cast a spotlight on several of the more problematic features of the electoral apparatus. Most visibly, machinations in the casting of electoral votes—grounded largely in the mounting antagonism between northern and southern Democrats—served as a reminder of the hazards of a system that relied on intermediaries to select presidents. Some Democratic electors from Alabama and Mississippi were formally "unpledged" and eventually cast their ballots for conservative senator Harry F. Byrd of Virginia; a faithless Republican elector from Oklahoma did the same, after first trying to organize a revolt among electors to deny the presidency to the "labor, Socialist" John F. Kennedy. Meanwhile, other southern Democrats tried to arrange enough defections from Kennedy to throw the election into the House of Representatives. There were also charges of fraud, especially in Illinois, where, thanks to the unit rule, the Democrat's tiny popular vote margin of 8,858 votes gave Kennedy all of the state's twenty-seven electoral votes. The Massachusetts senator ended up winning a clear-cut Electoral College majority, but the election raised once again the specter of a president being elected while losing the popular vote: Kennedy's margin in the national popular vote was either razor-thin or nonexistent, depending on how one counted the results of Alabama's complicated ballot. In either case, a shift of fewer than 12,000 votes in key states would have made Richard Nixon president.[2]

In the wake of the election, extensive hearings on electoral reform were held by the Subcommittee on Constitutional Amendments of the Senate Judiciary Committee. Estes Kefauver, the subcommittee chair, stressed the urgency of the task:

> Defenders of the electoral college are hard to find. No less than twenty members of the U.S. Senate have introduced proposals before us today which are careful attempts to correct the inequities and dangers of this outmoded relic. Originally adopted as a compromise, the electoral college resulted from a distrust of the people and conditions of geography and communications which no longer exist. Despite its confusions and uncertainties, by sheer luck it has managed in most instances to elect a President who reasonably reflected the choice of a majority of the people. But this good fortune has lulled us into inaction after each election and the system has continued from one election to the next. Every four years the electoral college is a loaded pistol pointed at our system of government. Its continued existence is a game of Russian roulette. Once its antiquated procedures trigger a loaded cylinder, it may be too late for the needed corrections.

After that portentous introduction, the committee heard detailed testimony from advocates of district and proportional elections, a minimalist "automatic" plan (eliminating electors but retaining electoral votes and the unit rule), and a national popular vote. Proposals for an NPV had been introduced by Mike Mansfield of Montana, by Republican Kenneth Keating of New York, and jointly by Republican Margaret Chase Smith (Maine) and Democrat Dennis Chavez (New Mexico).[3]

Most members of the subcommittee, as well as several witnesses, maintained that an NPV was not politically viable. They insisted that the small states would oppose a nationwide election—despite the highly visible stances taken by Senators Smith, Chavez, and Mansfield and despite testimony from experts that the Electoral College, in fact, benefited large rather than small states. Opposition was also believed to be strong in states that were described—rather generically—as fearing further federal control over elections and voting rights. One senator, Francis Case, a moderate Republican from South Dakota, broke with decorum by asking aloud whether "any Southern State today would agree to any constitutional amendment which would diminish its voice in the election of a President?"[4]

Although there was widespread agreement within the subcommittee and in the Senate that something ought to be done to eliminate faithless electors and to prevent the election of a "minority" president, there remained little consensus about the best course of action. The lines of cleavage that had marked the debates over district and proportional elections in the 1950s—between the North and the South, rural and urban interests, liberals and conservatives—remained much in evidence in 1961.[5] Faced with these divisions, Smith chastised her colleagues for their unwillingness to unite behind a single proposal, thereby permitting the "standpatters" to preserve the Electoral College; she indicated that she would happily support proportional elections despite her preference for an NPV.[6] In the end, a majority of the subcommittee tepidly endorsed a district elections proposal put forward by Karl Mundt, but the full Judiciary Committee took no action.[7] Congress remained at the same impasse that had halted its efforts in the 1950s.

One Person, One Vote: Moving into the Mainstream

The winds finally began to shift in the mid-1960s, driven and energized by an ascendant liberalism as well as a burst of reforms intended to democratize the nation's electoral institutions. The Twenty-Third Amendment, granting residents of the District of Columbia the right to vote in presidential elections, was ratified in 1961; three years later, poll taxes in federal elections were swept away by the Twenty-Fourth Amendment. More far-reaching and influential were the Supreme Court's decisions, in 1962 and 1964, requiring states to create legislative and congressional districts that had roughly the same number of inhabitants. Those decisions upended long-standing practices that, in many states, had produced districts of widely disparate sizes, greatly favoring rural over urban areas. In California, for example, Los Angeles County had one state senator for its six million inhabitants; elsewhere in the state, a senator represented fewer than 15,000. Disparities were also evident in congressional districts: in Georgia, the district that included Atlanta had twice as many residents as any other district in the state.[8]

The Supreme Court, which had long steered clear of districting and apportionment issues, famously plunged into the "political thicket" in 1962 in the historic case of *Baker v. Carr*. In a series of cases decided over several years, the Court put forward a new democratic yardstick. "The conception of political equality from the Declaration of Independence to Lincoln's Gettysburg Address, to the Fifteenth, Seventeenth, and Nineteenth Amendments can mean only one thing—one person, one vote," declared Justice William Douglas in *Gray v. Sanders*. The Court's actions, unsurprisingly, sparked great controversy, but liberals in Congress applauded the decisions and blocked efforts to significantly delay their implementation or reverse them through constitutional amendment.[9] Urban liberals also knew that the Court's decisions would swell their ranks.

The apportionment decisions lent considerable strength to the arguments for a national popular vote. Although Chief Justice Earl Warren had insisted that "one person, one vote" did not apply to the U.S. Senate (and thus the Electoral College) because of the special historical circumstances surrounding the nation's founding, the Court had articulated and given constitutional sanction to a democratic principle that was powerful, commonsensical, and widely recognized. And that principle, as advocates like John Pastore had pointed out, could be realized in presidential elections only through a national popular vote. If one accepted the Supreme Court's notion that having "a vote . . . worth more in one district than another" ran "counter to our fundamental ideas of democratic government," then the case for eliminating the Electoral College became all the more compelling, and the only proposed reform that gave life to that principle was a national popular vote. "The 'one man, one vote' edict manifestly should apply to the choosing of our highest officials," concluded the *Albuquerque Journal* in 1967.[10]

An equally momentous step forward was the passage of the Voting Rights Act (VRA) of 1965, which aimed to enforce the Fifteenth Amendment and bring an end, at last, to the disenfranchisement of African-Americans in the South. The VRA, of course, was a muscular affirmation of democratic values by Congress, President Lyndon Johnson, and the Supreme Court (which upheld the act in 1966), an insistence that all citizens had the right to participate in elections. Although some white southerners harbored hopes that the act would be declared unconstitutional or that its implementation would be halting or temporary, African-Americans in the region began to register to vote by the hundreds of thousands, and later the millions, permitting them to play a role in casting the electoral votes of the South. What this meant—if the VRA remained in force, something that was not self-evident in the mid-1960s—was that white southerners would no longer benefit from a "five-fifths clause" in presidential elections and the prospect of a national popular vote would no longer pose the same threat to white southerners that it had for the previous 175 years. If African-Americans were fully enfranchised, under the protection of the federal government, then direct elections would no longer confront southern states with the unwelcome, and feared, choice between eliminating barriers to voting or losing electoral power. It would take time—at least a decade—for these implications to sink in, but the landscape of southern politics was never the same once Lyndon Johnson had signed the Voting Rights Act into law. The partisan coloration of that landscape, moreover, was already shifting. In 1964, when both Johnson and congressional Democrats won landslide victories nationally, Republican Barry Goldwater won five southern states (and only one other, his home state of Arizona).

These institutional enlargements of democracy—expressions of a widespread and newly forceful embrace of democratic values during and after World War II—were soon followed by a series of developments announcing the arrival of the NPV idea into the mainstream of public debate. Early in

1966 the United States Chamber of Commerce, after conducting a referendum, announced that more than 90 percent of its members believed that the Electoral College ought to be replaced with a national popular vote or district elections. At the same time, the *New York Times* editorialized that it would be preferable to have an NPV or a proportional plan rather than the "automatic" plan (limited to getting rid of electors) advocated by Lyndon Johnson in 1965 and 1966. Several months later a Gallup poll revealed that 63 percent of a large national sample favored abolishing the Electoral College and instituting an NPV.[11] Then, in February 1967 the American Bar Association (ABA) issued a thorough, careful report calling for a constitutional amendment "to provide for the election of the President and Vice President by direct, nationwide popular vote."[12]

The ABA report proved to be particularly influential, in part because "congressional and executive leaders" had urged the association to examine the subject of presidential election reform, much as it had in developing the Twenty-Fifth Amendment dealing with presidential disability and succession. Early in 1966 the president of the ABA appointed a blue-ribbon Commission on Electoral College Reform that included an array of distinguished attorneys, judges, and academics, as well as two governors, two former members of Congress (one of them Ed Gossett of Texas), and Walter Reuther, president of the United Auto Workers.[13] The commission and its staff worked on the report for nearly a year, emphatically concluding that "the electoral college method of electing a President of the United States is archaic, undemocratic, complex, ambiguous, indirect, and dangerous."[14]

The commission report, endorsed by the ABA House of Delegates, recommended that Congress pass a constitutional amendment abolishing the Electoral College and instituting a national popular vote, with the proviso that a candidate needed to obtain at least 40 percent of the vote to be elected; if no candidate reached that threshold, a runoff election would be held. The report recommended that suffrage requirements for presidential elections be identical to those for congressional elections, which would effectively leave the franchise in the hands of the states. At the same time, it urged that states be permitted to deploy less restrictive residence rules for those voting for president (as some already did) and that Congress be given the "reserve power" to set age and residence qualifications, if necessary.[15]

In making its case for an NPV, the bar association argued that the most commonly voiced objections to a national vote were not persuasive. Its report rebuffed the claim that the Electoral College was necessary to preserve a two-party system while maintaining that the 40 percent plurality rule would encourage "factions and splinter groups to operate . . . within the framework of the major parties." Nor did the ABA find credible the notion that direct elections "would wipe out state lines or destroy our federal system." Of equal importance, the ABA report took aim at the small-state objection that an amendment favoring an NPV could never be passed by Congress or "the necessary number of state legislatures." It pointed out that members of Congress from both large and small states were on record favoring direct elections and called attention to a recent poll of several thousand state legislators indicating that a significant majority, in small states as well as large, endorsed an NPV. "In summary," the report concluded, "direct election of the President would be in harmony with the prevailing philosophy of one person, one vote."[16]

Meanwhile, an unusual legal attack on the Electoral College was launched by the State of Delaware. Explicitly invoking a parallel to the apportionment cases, the "First State" (Delaware's nickname), later joined by twelve other states, filed a motion in the Supreme Court in July 1966 asking that it be permitted to file a complaint against New York State (and all other states) alleging that the laws providing for the "general ticket" or "unit vote" system were unconstitutional. According to Delaware, the "unit system" violated the equal protection and due process clauses of the Fourteenth Amendment "by arbitrarily cancelling" the votes of political minorities "and misappropriating their voting power to assert it for candidates whom they oppose." It also abridged the rights of Delaware's citizens "under the Ninth and Tenth Amendments to engage in national political activity in association with citizens of other states." The motion further asserted that "the state unit system operates to the unfair advantage of the large states and their citizens and denies citizens of Delaware and other small states privileges of United States citizenship, in violation of the Fourteenth Amendment." Delaware acknowledged that a durable solution to these problems could come only through a constitutional amendment; proportional or district elections could offer a remedy, but the "ultimate result might be the submission of a proposed constitutional amendment for direct national election." Meanwhile, the First State asked the Court for interim relief that would "open the door" to change by "requiring each state to appoint its presidential electors by a method reasonably calculated to reflect the will of all the people of the state." Otherwise, "entrenched political interests" would block any reform of the system.[17]

New York's attorney general adamantly rejected Delaware's claims, insisting that any advantages that accrued to the large states from the general ticket were offset by advantages the small states possessed by virtue of the allocation of electoral votes. He also maintained that Delaware lacked standing to bring a suit and that the issues Delaware had raised were not justiciable.[18] The Supreme Court seemed to agree: without explanation, it refused to hear the case.[19] Nonetheless, Delaware's legal action, coupled with the support it received from other states, signaled loudly that the notion that all votes should count equally was gaining traction—for presidential as well as other elections. It also put a few more nails in the coffin of the claim that small states benefited from the Electoral College and would never accept a national popular vote. Among the states that joined tiny Delaware's motion were three other very small states (Wyoming, North Dakota, and South Dakota) and a half dozen medium-sized states. Notably, two large states, Pennsylvania and Florida, also backed Delaware's action, as did two southern states, Arkansas and Kentucky.[20]

THE CONVERSION OF BIRCH BAYH

These cascading expressions of public opinion, backed by establishment organizations and more than a dozen state governments, set the stage for a new surge of activity in Washington. The first key step in Congress was taken by Indiana senator Birch Bayh, a young Democrat first elected to the Senate in 1962, who had become the chair of the Subcommittee on Constitutional Amendments of the Senate Judiciary Committee after the death of Estes Kefauver in 1963. (Bayh played a crucial role in persuading the Judiciary Committee chairman, James Eastland, not to abolish the subcommittee.)[21] In May 1966, after holding two months of hearings on reforming the electoral system, Bayh announced that his views had changed and that he would henceforth promote a constitutional amendment providing for a national popular vote. In so doing, he was dropping his support for, and sponsorship of, the minimalist measure backed by President

Johnson: an "automatic" plan that would eliminate electors and provide for the "automatic" casting of a state's electoral votes, thereby solving the problem of faithless electors.[22] Johnson, who was personally close to Bayh, was not pleased, but Bayh, "after a great deal of soul-searching," had become convinced that simply making changes to the Electoral College was "like shifting around parts of a creaky and dangerous automobile engine, making it no less creaky and no less dangerous." A national popular vote, in contrast, was the "next logical outgrowth of the persistent and inevitable movement toward the democratic ideal" of universal suffrage and all votes counting equally.[23]

Bayh's shift in position was critical. Although he was a first-term senator, he had already garnered respect for his deft handling of the soon-to-be-ratified Twenty-Fifth Amendment, dealing with presidential disability and succession.[24] More importantly, it marked the first time a congressional committee in charge of electoral reform was chaired by an advocate of a national popular vote. Bayh formally introduced a direct election resolution (S.J. Res. 2) in 1966 and again in 1967 in the Ninetieth Congress, the second time with eighteen co-sponsors. His proposal to abolish the "archaic and dangerous electoral college" required a winning candidate to gain at least 40 percent of the national vote; if no one reached that threshold, the election would be decided by a joint session of Congress. Soon after the ABA report was issued, however, Bayh modified his resolution, accepting the ABA's recommendation that a runoff election be held between the top two candidates. The Indiana senator's amendment was backed by majority leader Mike Mansfield, and, in March 1967, by the Republican minority leader, Everett Dirksen of Illinois.[25]

Bayh's subcommittee held extensive hearings in the spring and summer of 1967; before the committee were Bayh's own resolution as well as a district elections proposal sponsored by Karl Mundt and a proportional plan drawn up by Democrat John Sparkman of Alabama. (Similar resolutions were also put forward in the House, which did not hold hearings on them.)[26] Although all three ideas remained under consideration, the dynamics of reform had shifted in favor of an NPV: the district and proportional schemes loomed as vestiges of earlier political moments or rearguard efforts to slow the momentum of a national popular vote. Accordingly, much of the testimony at the hearings came from proponents of direct elections, including representatives of the ABA and the Chamber of Commerce. Support was also offered by academic experts, such as Lucius Wilmerding and Joseph Kallenbach, who were known to have endorsed other plans in the past. Opposition was voiced by groups on the political right (like the American Good Government Society) and by conservative senators from both parties.[27]

The most resonant expert testimony came from John F. Banzhaf III, a lawyer, an MIT-trained electrical engineer, and a specialist in using mathematics and computers to address voting issues, including in apportionment cases. At Bayh's invitation, Banzhaf offered the committee a lengthy "mathematical analysis of the electoral college" in which he assessed the "voting power" ("the ability to affect decisions through the process of voting") of citizens in different states under the Electoral College. Banzhaf concluded that the Electoral College, with the unit rule, "greatly favors the citizens of the most populous states and deprives citizens of the less populous states of an equal chance to affect the election of the President." Each resident of New York, California, Pennsylvania, and Ohio wielded more than twice as much power as a resident of the smallest states. Banzhaf also pointed out that under both proportional and district plans, the large states would lose their advantage but significant inequalities in voting power would persist: residents of Alaska and other small states, for example, would possess a far greater chance of influencing an election outcome than would a resident of New York or California. Only a national popular vote could guarantee "to each citizen the chance to participate equally in the election of the President."[28]

Banzhaf's testimony and an article detailing his analysis attracted a great deal of attention, largely because they seemed to scientifically debunk the long-standing, if already eroding, notion that the Electoral College benefited citizens of small states who would understandably be loath to give it up. As the political editor of *Congressional Quarterly* noted, "Banzhaf has given mathematical proof for a phenomenon which politicians have grasped intuitively since the early nineteenth century: the disproportionate weight of the votes cast by citizens of the large states under a unit-vote . . . system of electoral voting." To be sure, not everyone agreed with Banzhaf's conclusion that an analysis of "voting power" pointed inexorably toward the desirability of direct elections. Mundt believed that

Banzhaf's work was "interesting but ... irrelevant" (based, as it was, "upon a mechanical computer and not the Constitution"), while Sparkman urged that reform be shaped by "broad and long term values" rather than an impulse "to assure an exactly equal value" of every vote for president.[29] Nonetheless, Banzhaf's testimony, as well as the findings of other social and political scientists, appeared to slice analytically through the fog of competing opinions and to widen the strategic path toward a national popular vote.[30]

GEORGE WALLACE AND THE ELECTION OF 1968

One person who was not invited to testify before Bayh's subcommittee—but who was much on the minds of its members—was George C. Wallace of Alabama. By the spring of 1967 it was widely known that Wallace, a former governor and the husband of the sitting governor, would seek the presidency in 1968 as a third-party candidate. His candidacy, and the likelihood that he would run well in southern states roiled by the Voting Rights Act and federally mandated desegregation, lent urgency to the reform cause. Echoing Strom Thurmond's Dixiecrat candidacy in 1948 (although Thurmond himself was backing Richard Nixon), Wallace threatened to win a handful of states and prevent either Nixon or Democrat Hubert Humphrey from winning an electoral vote majority. Wallace could then barter his support—either in the Electoral College or in the House of Representatives—for a commitment, or even an understanding, that the pace of federal intervention in the South would be slowed. The prospect of Wallace as kingmaker was chilling to many and encouraged some leaders in Washington, including Dirksen, to press for rapid action on Bayh's resolution so that the Electoral College could be abolished before the 1968 elections.[31] Bayh and his Democratic allies, however, thought it unrealistic to push forward that fast: they were far from certain that they had the votes to get an amendment through Congress, and time seemed too short to get an amendment ratified by thirty-eight states before November 1968.[32]

As it turned out, the election did not precipitate the crisis that many had feared. Wallace won five states and 45 electoral votes, but that was not enough to block the election of Richard Nixon, who won a clear majority of the electoral vote while besting Humphrey by less than 1 percent of the popular vote. Nonetheless, political leaders in both major parties knew that they had narrowly dodged a bullet: two months before the balloting, Wallace had been running more strongly in the national polls (21 percent) and seemed to have a chance to win more than 100 electoral votes. Only a belated surge by Humphrey, coupled with a fairly predictable melting away of some of the Wallace vote, prevented the Alabamian from securing enough electoral votes to create turmoil. Nixon's margins of victory over Wallace in North Carolina and Tennessee, moreover, were uncomfortably close, and a shift of 53,000 votes from Nixon to Humphrey in three key northern states would have left Nixon short of an electoral vote majority. Adding to the potential confusion, a disgruntled Republican elector from North Carolina chose to be "faithless" and cast his ballot for Wallace. A crisis had been averted, but the hazards of the Electoral College were all too evident, even glaring, to anyone who looked closely at the election returns. The stage was set for a strong, and perhaps final, assault on the "archaic and undemocratic" institution in 1969.[33]

Almost over the Top

It has become a condition of American life that a citizen could always look forward to death, taxes, and electoral college reform. But today, across this land, there breathes a new hope. Perhaps, at long last, electoral college reform is an idea whose time has come.

—William M. McCulloch, House of Representatives, February 5, 1969

When the Ninety-First Congress convened on January 3, 1969, presidential election reform ranked high on its agenda. The recent election intensified concerns that had been building throughout the 1960s, and advocates of change—particularly advocates of direct election—were convinced that the time for action had arrived. The need for reform was foregrounded on January 6, when one of the shortcomings of the Electoral College came into full public view: as the House and Senate met in joint session to count the electoral votes, members of both chambers raised formal objections to the vote cast for George Wallace by Dr. Lloyd Bailey, an ultraconservative Republican elector from North Carolina. Following the procedure spelled out in the 1887 Electoral Count Act, the two chambers then met separately to consider the challenge; after debate, both permitted the vote to be counted, implicitly upholding the right of an elector to be "faithless" and adding strength to calls to amend the Constitution.[34]

Outside of Congress the conviction that something had to be done about the Electoral College was widespread; in late 1968 and early 1969 the nation's newspapers and news magazines were peppered with articles taking sides on different proposals. Alexander Bickel, a Yale Law School professor and prominent opponent of direct elections, quickly leaped into the fray, publishing an essay in *Commentary* in December 1968 that urged Congress to limit itself to solving the faithless elector problem and modifying the contingent election process. An NPV, he believed, would throw off the balance between urban and rural biases that had been built into the Constitution and was sustained through the Electoral College. Bickel also argued strenuously that direct elections would lead to the dissolution of a two-party system that promoted "a politics of coalition and accommodation," as well as moderate, stable governments.[35] Lucius Wilmerding, a one-time adversary of direct elections, weighed in a few weeks later, in the *National Review,* with an impassioned article urging Congress to abolish the Electoral College and adopt an NPV. The *Wall Street Journal* urged caution, warning that "the issue is encrusted with loose thinking." A signed editorial by the editor of the *Charlotte Observer,* C. A. McKnight, declared that electoral reform was an "urgent" task and that the "creaky old system has few defenders left." After surveying various reform options, McKnight, a voice of southern liberalism, indicated that his own preference was for direct elections.[36]

Yet presidential election reform was hardly the only thing on the minds of members of Congress or writers of opinion pieces. The nation was sharply divided as the increasingly unpopular Vietnam War consumed policymakers in Washington, and an energetic antiwar movement prepared to square off against President Nixon. The country was also feeling the aftershocks of race-related riots that had exploded in cities around the country in 1967 and 1968, not to mention the assassinations of Martin Luther King Jr. and Robert Kennedy. Within the government too, divisions and uncertainties abounded. When Nixon took office on January 20, he became the first incoming president in more than a century to face a Congress entirely controlled by an opposing party; and the Democratic Party, despite holding decisive majorities in both the Senate and the House, was far from unified, with tensions high between its southern conservative and northern liberal wings. At the same time, younger and more liberal members of Congress, growing in number, were challenging both the existing leadership and traditional methods of conducting business, including the filibuster rule in the Senate. As the session opened, thirty-six-year-old Edward Kennedy defeated Russell Long of Louisiana for majority whip in the Senate, while the moderate Hugh Scott of Pennsylvania, a staunch civil rights advocate, bested Nebraska conservative Roman Hruska on the Republican side.[37]

THE ROAD TO VICTORY IN THE HOUSE

Congress began its full-fledged consideration of electoral reform soon after Nixon's inauguration. Bayh's Subcommittee on Constitutional Amendments opened hearings on January 23, 1969, while the full Judiciary Committee in the House, chaired by Emanuel Celler, launched its own hearings on February 5. Both sets of hearings were extensive, with long rosters of witnesses, including members of Congress, registering their views about possible reforms. In the House alone, more than fifty proposals were introduced, most of them advocating some version of an NPV, a district plan, a proportional plan, or an "automatic" scheme to solve the problem of faithless electors. Observers found the House hearings particularly notable because the leadership of the Judiciary Committee was not firmly committed to any one proposal and many committee members began the hearings without having staked out positions. Education took place, minds were changed, and the committee frequently dug deep into the details and implications of the different proposals.[38]

Chairman Celler opened the hearings by pointing out that he was sponsoring both H.J. Res. 179, a direct elections proposal identical to Bayh's, and H.J. Res. 181, which was limited to eliminating electors and reforming the contingent process. In a similar spirit, the ranking Republican on the Committee, William McCulloch of Ohio, introduced three resolutions: a district plan, a proportional plan, and a proposal for an NPV. He then rehearsed the "seven defects" of the existing system, all of which made it plain "that reform is necessary." "The disease is clear," McCulloch declared, "the remedy is not.... Each of the plans has its advantages and disadvantages. We must sort them out."[39]

The witnesses who testified, like the committee members themselves, were in nearly universal agreement that something had to be done to reform the contingent procedure and end the threat of faithless electors. (Some states were attempting to address the latter issue, but state laws were widely viewed as thin reeds.)[40] More than a few of the witnesses, backing H.J. Res. 181 or a similar approach, argued that Congress should limit itself to solving these "housekeeping" or "mechanical" matters—that the system worked well enough otherwise and any further changes could prove to be risky and politically contentious. As Republican David Dennis of Indiana put it, "When you start fooling with the basic system, you can't avoid getting into arguments about who is advantaged and who isn't."[41] Most of the testimony, however—including detailed, often probing and fruitful exchanges between witnesses and committee members—took the form of a multipronged debate between those who favored a national popular vote and those who preferred district or proportional elections or other schemes designed to abolish the unit rule.[42]

Advocates of a national popular vote had a relatively simple case to make: only direct elections could solve the most glaring problems and also guarantee that the candidate who won the most votes would become president. "The rule of the majority," declared AFL-CIO president George Meany in lengthy testimony, "is the very essence of democracy." Meany, who deftly parried critical questions, stuck to his democratic guns by also signaling his support for uniform national suffrage laws in presidential elections. Similarly, Margaret Heckler, a Republican congresswoman from Massachusetts (later a member of Ronald Reagan's cabinet) stressed that "philosophically," direct election was "in keeping with the modern concept of one man, one vote" and that it "is meaningful for the simplicity in its approach."[43] Advocates of an NPV almost uniformly emphasized the importance of democratic principles while eschewing discussions of "who is advantaged and who isn't." Proponents did voice some differences among themselves regarding the 40 percent threshold for a plurality victory (some thought it should be higher or lower), the need to give Congress control over suffrage requirements, and the optimal timing of runoff elections. But they kept the spotlight on the values undergirding direct elections while steadfastly avoiding claims about political consequences. An emotional highlight of the hearings was the spirited testimony of eighty-nine-year-old Jeannette Rankin of Montana, who in 1916 had become the first woman ever elected to Congress. She not only endorsed a direct vote but—still forward-looking—urged Congress to take advantage of newly available "computers" and adopt a "preferential" (or ranked-choice) ballot that would obviate the need for a runoff election.[44]

Advocates of other proposed reforms did not have a democratic, or values, argument of equal strength or simplicity. District elections (like the well-known "Mundt plan") or a proportional allocation of electoral votes would likely bring the electoral vote closer to the popular vote, but neither method gave equal weight to the votes of all Americans; nor could they guarantee that the winner of the popular vote would assume office. The advantages of these less "radical" proposals, according to supporters like the National Cotton Council, the American Farm Bureau, and the American Jewish Congress, lay elsewhere: they lacked the defects, or objectionable features, of a national popular vote. The list of alleged defects (most of which had been invoked for decades) included the risk of undermining the two-party system by encouraging third parties, the weakening or destruction of federalism and "state sovereignty," the prospect of widespread fraud, and the unpredictable hazards of election campaigns run according to new rules. Going a step further, a witness from the crankily conservative Liberty Lobby declared that "the United States is not, and was never intended to be a mass democracy." A national vote also drew criticism because of its purported political consequences: a loss of power for small states and rural regions, and the vesting of too much power in large, urban areas (no matter what John Banzhaf might have calculated). Alaska's sole representative in Congress, Howard Pollock, thus preferred district elections because under a "direct popular vote, a candidate need carry only the population centers of the country," and the interests of his constituents were not the same as "those of the nation's urban centers." Like Pollock, numerous advocates of district elections, particularly those from rural areas, also insisted that an NPV would never be ratified by the states. This pessimism about ratification—rooted in the claim that the "less populous" states would inevitably oppose direct elections—led Democrat John Dingell of Michigan, among others, to endorse a proportional plan, despite his personal preference for a national vote.[45]

Supporters of an NPV, of course, countered these charges. Banzhaf re-iterated at length his 1967 Senate testimony, mathematically demon-strating that large, rather than small, states benefited from the existing system. Harvard Law professor Paul Freund, who had served on the ABA panel, observed that "the fraudulently disposed . . . could operate more readily under the present system where a few votes in one or two heavily populated states can swing a decisive electoral bloc." He also maintained that holding a runoff election would deter splinter parties (it would not "be worth the candle" to mount a national campaign just to force a runoff between the major parties) and that the two-party system had numerous institutional buttresses that had nothing to do with presidential elections. His views were strongly seconded by William Gossett, president of the American Bar Association. Representative John B. Anderson, a Republican from Rockford, Illinois (later an independent candidate for president), countered the claim that an NPV could not win ratification by reporting that a poll conducted in his conservative district indicated that 82 percent of his constituents supported direct elections.[46]

Near the end of the hearings, Attorney General John Mitchell appeared before the committee to promote a proposal that President Nixon had in-cluded in a message sent to Congress in late February. Nixon had urged Congress to take prompt action on electoral reform and indicated that he would accept any reform that disposed of electors and brought the elec-toral vote more in line with the popular vote; he also maintained that de-spite his personal preference for an NPV, he did not think it was politi-cally feasible. The president advocated, in its place, a new composite plan calling for eliminating electors, holding district or proportional elections to allocate electoral votes, and conducting a popular vote runoff in the event that no candidate received 40 percent of the electoral votes. Mitchell de-fended both proportional and district plans as "a compromise of sorts" be-tween a national election and the existing "unit vote system." He also lectured supporters of direct elections that if they really wanted to seize the opportunity to enact reform, they would have to back some other plan. Celler and his colleagues—who had become increasingly sympathetic to an NPV—challenged Mitchell to provide evidence to back up his claim that there was little or no chance of passing an NPV resolution. The at-torney general's most concrete response was that there was very little support for direct election "in the southern states." Nixon's message muddied the waters for a short time but in the end attracted very few backers. The president also drew substantial criticism for not speaking out strongly on behalf of the reform that he purportedly favored.[47]

What was going on in the southern states was also at the heart of the troubling testimony offered by Clarence Mitchell Jr., director of the Washington Bureau of the NAACP and one of the key actors in the 1950 effort to block the Lodge-Gossett bill. Mitchell stated that his organization was, in principle, in favor of direct elections but only if there were "adequate safeguards against all forms of discrimination that deny the ballot to our citizens because of race." He acknowledged that progress had been achieved since the passage of the Voting Rights Act but insisted that those gains were neither sufficient nor secure: the proportion of African-Americans who were registered to vote in the South remained well below the figure for whites, and there were still 188 counties in covered jurisdictions that had never received federal examiners. Many southern officials were still trying to "circumvent" the law; and particularly with the VRA up for renewal in 1970, Mitchell feared that things could go "backward," that "the Negro voting population could be reduced to minuscule proportions." Given these circumstances, Mitchell stated that the only reform the NAACP could endorse was an "automatic" plan that would eliminate electors while preserving the swing-vote role of African-Americans in key northern states. Sympathetic committee members like liberal Democrat Abner Mikva of Chicago, as well as Republicans Clark MacGregor and Robert McClory, gently quarreled with Mitchell, urging him to reconsider and to support an electoral process that "would be more representative of the will of the people than the existing system." But the NAACP leader—still influenced perhaps by the battle over Lodge-Gossett—was not yet ready to commit to a reform that, in his eyes, presupposed that systematic racial discrimination in voting had come to an end.[48]

Within weeks after the conclusion of the hearings, the Judiciary Committee began its deliberations, in executive session, and by the end of April it reported out, by a vote of twenty-nine to six, a bill (H.J. Res. 681) hewing closely to Bayh's proposal for a national popular vote with a runoff election, if needed. (Four of the six dissenters were southerners.)[49] The unexpectedly one-sided vote, which marked the first time an NPV resolution had been reported favorably by a congressional committee, was nourished by the strength and simplicity of the core arguments for direct elections. As the committee's majority report emphasized, a direct popular election was "the only electoral reform proposal which would eliminate all of the principal defects in the present system, and guarantee that the popular winner is elected President." The committee also affirmed that the electoral system "should no longer afford favored positions for certain classes of voters" (whether from large or small states or different regions). "No citizen's vote should have more weight than any other's."[50] The *Wall Street Journal* praised the work of the committee for its openness and lack of "emotionalism," noting that some members ended up favoring direct elections because the simplicity of the case made by its supporters stood in such contrast to "the confusing welter of arguments for retaining the Electoral College in some form." Ironically, in light of President Nixon's intervention, some members, including minority leader Gerald Ford, shifted their stances and backed a direct vote in part because they believed it to be the only reform that had a chance of getting through Congress.[51]

The Judiciary Committee's decisive, bipartisan vote energized reform advocates and weakened the resistance of some skeptics. In early May the *New York Times* editorialized that the vote indicated that small states would, in fact, be willing to support direct elections, despite prevailing views to the contrary. *Time* magazine reported that "electoral reform is an idea whose time has come," although it cautioned that an NPV still faced "formidable obstacles" from rural and conservative areas. *Reader's Digest* brought the issue of electoral reform into the homes of its substantial audience by publishing a condensed version of novelist James Michener's *Presidential Lottery;* Michener, who had served as a Pennsylvania elector in 1968, judged the Electoral College to be a "time bomb lodged near the heart of the nation."[52] To be sure, there remained skeptical currents in the national media, not always in predictable places: the *New Republic* dismissed direct elections as "a proposal for simplistic democracy," while the *New Yorker* was reluctant to tinker with "a system that has worked as well as ours." Like many other opponents of reform, the *New Yorker* emphasized that a "wrong winner" scenario was extremely unlikely.[53]

The House committee vote was important also because Bayh's amendment in the Senate had become stalled in his own subcommittee (as discussed below), and action by the House was thus critical to sustaining the momentum of the reform effort. That momentum was slowed slightly in the early summer by the Rules Committee, whose chair, William Colmer of Mississippi, was no friend of direct elections, but by the end of July Celler, a savvy legislative strategist, had succeeded in getting a rule that would permit the Judiciary Committee's measure to come to the full House for a vote. The rule permitted amendments to be made from the floor, a procedure that would allow alternative proposals to be introduced and brought to a vote before the House voted on H.J. Res. 681. The *New York Times* reported that the bill's prospects remained uncertain.[54]

The floor debate in the House began on September 10, with Chairman Celler outlining the defects of the electoral system and characterizing it as "barbarous, unsporting, dangerous, and downright uncivilized." As expected, a host of amendments were introduced, including proposals to substitute district or proportional elections, or an automatic plan, for H.J. Res. 681. As was also expected—by early September both Celler and the Chamber of Commerce had reliable headcounts—all of these amendments were rejected by majority votes. What remained uncertain was whether Celler and his allies could then muster the two-thirds vote necessary to approve a constitutional amendment: reaching that threshold would require the support of representatives who had preferred other plans but were now faced with a choice between an NPV or no reform at all. That such support might be forthcoming was signaled by Virginia Republican Richard Poff, who had announced that if the district plan he co-sponsored failed, he would support an NPV. As the debate came to a close, Celler sentimentally announced that he was nearing his eighty-second birthday ("the abyss awaits me") and that the passage of the resolution "will be a crowning achievement in my own life." This personal appeal did not likely change any votes, but when the roll was finally called on September 18, H.J. Res. 681 was approved by an overwhelming vote of 338 to 70, well above the two-thirds threshold. Eighty-three percent of the representatives who cast ballots favored replacing the Electoral College with a national popular vote.[55]

Strong support in both parties, and in most regions of the country, contributed to what *New Yorker* columnist Richard Rovere labeled "a stunning and quite unanticipated majority."[56] As Table 5.1 indicates, 184 Democrats voted in favor of the resolution, while only 44 were opposed; among

TABLE 5.1: HOUSE OF REPRESENTATIVES VOTE ON H.J. RES. 681,
SEPTEMBER 18, 1969

	Yea	Nay	Not voting
All representatives	338	70	22
Democrats	184	44	15
Republicans	154	26	7
South[a]			
Democrats	42	41	5
Republicans	24	6	1
Total	66	47	6
Non-South			
Democrats	142	3	10
Republicans	130	20	6
Total	272	23	16
Large states[b]			
Democrats	96	8	9
Republicans	84	5	6
Total	180	13	15
Medium-sized states[b]			
Democrats	72	35	4
Republicans	53	14	1
Total	125	49	5
Small states[b]			
Democrats	16	1	2
Republicans	17	7	0
Total	33	8	2

Source: 115 Cong. Rec. 26007–26008 (1969).

a. South includes FL, GA, SC, NC, VA, KY, TN, AL, MS, AR, LA, OK, TX. See Chapter 5, note 57.

b. "Large" includes all states that had fifteen or more electoral votes in the 1968 presidential election; "medium-sized" includes all states that had between seven and fourteen electoral votes in the 1968 presidential election; and "small" includes those with six or fewer electoral votes in the 1968 presidential election.

Republicans, the vote was 154–26. Nearly all northern Democrats voted positively, but southern Democrats were evenly split, with sizable variations from state to state and opposition concentrated in the deep South.[57] (In contrast, more than three-quarters of southern Republicans, including George H. W. Bush of Texas, voted in favor of the amendment.) A majority of the negative votes (41 out of 70) came from southern Democrats, with most of the rest cast by conservative Republicans, particularly from the mountain and plains states. Representatives from states of different sizes had quite similar voting patterns: 93 percent of those from the largest states voted favorably, but so did 80 percent of representatives from small states. (The figure was lowest—but still 72 percent—for medium-sized states, a category that included much of the South.) Importantly, a substantial number of Republicans, as well as some southern Democrats, gave their support to H.J. Res. 681 on the final vote, despite having earlier favored district elections or other proposals.[58]

The scale of the victory in the House unleashed a wave of optimism—unprecedented optimism—among supporters of direct elections. Obstacles remained, to be sure, but successful passage of an amendment seemed, for the first time ever, within reach. This optimism was reinforced, a week after the vote, by the release of a Gallup poll indicating that 81 percent of Americans (a percentage almost identical to the House vote) approved of an amendment to replace the Electoral College with a direct national election. Surely the Senate would not stand in the way of a measure that enjoyed such enormous popular support! At the end of September, President Nixon climbed on the bandwagon, announcing his support for direct elections and urging the Senate to act expeditiously. Early in October the *New York Times* reported that a survey of state legislatures indicated that thirty states seemed certain or likely to ratify an amendment, while six were toss-ups; a similar poll commissioned by Republican senator Robert Griffin found thirty-five states favoring direct elections. Thirty-eight states would be needed, so ratification was no sure thing, but the lineup of states was more promising than many skeptics had anticipated. Critics of direct elections, meanwhile, were dejected, even resigned, although they continued to trumpet their objections; neoconservatives Irving Kristol and Paul Weaver spelled out their views in an op-ed entitled "A Bad Idea Whose Time Has Come."[59]

THE SENATE AND THE SOUTH

The victory in the House tossed the joint resolution back to the Senate, where the sailing was far less smooth than it had been in the larger chamber. Bayh's subcommittee had held hearings beginning in late January 1969 and stretching into the spring. They covered much the same ground as the House hearings, with diverse viewpoints amply represented in the 1,000-page printed record. Howard Baker, a political moderate and a rising Republican star from Tennessee (as well as the son-in-law of Everett Dirksen), endorsed direct elections and insisted that they would not undermine the two-party system for which he had "deep reverence." He also tried to thread a needle (or perhaps square a circle) by arguing that "some national qualifications" for voting would be "proper," although he did not wish to interfere with "the rights of the states to control elections." Sam Ervin of North Carolina, a member of the subcommittee, staked out his position as both an advocate of electoral reform (a proportional plan with a 40 percent threshold for victory) and a staunch adversary of direct elections. Retaining electoral votes, he maintained, would ensure that a state would be represented in the selection of the chief executive by its entire population and not just by those who showed up to vote. Ervin also argued that a direct elections amendment had no chance of passage (because many states would lose influence) and that it "might also result in uniform qualifications for voting" which "could further erode the powers of our States." Perhaps the most revelatory testimony, at least for historians, came from Theodore Sorenson, who had been a close aide to John Kennedy both in the Senate and the White House. Sorenson noted that opponents of direct elections often cited Kennedy's words from the 1956 debates, but he maintained that Kennedy was not, in fact, averse to a national popular vote. His posture in 1956 had been tactical, objecting to all reforms as a means of blocking the district and proportional schemes that had a "real prospect of passage that year." Sorenson also reminded the committee that Kennedy's views were expressed before the Supreme Court's apportionment decisions and before the close elections of 1960 and 1968.[60]

After the hearings had concluded in May 1969, the subcommittee—which included three prominent southern opponents of civil rights—voted six to five to replace Bayh's direct-election amendment with the district plan long advocated by Mundt. The vote was a setback to Bayh and his allies, but the Indiana senator was reasonably confident that the outcome could be reversed in the full Judiciary Committee.[61] That committee, however, took no action in the summer and early fall of 1969, ostensibly waiting to see what would transpire in the House. The committee's agenda was controlled by its powerful chairman, James Eastland, a wealthy planter from Mississippi, who ardently defended segregation (even in the restaurants of Washington) and fought hard to defeat every civil rights bill that came before Congress in the 1950s and 1960s. Eastland was a sharp critic of Bayh's resolution and had no interest in facilitating its passage, but the House vote, and the momentum it created, put pressure on him to allow the Judiciary Committee to begin deliberations. That pressure was partially counterbalanced by Strom Thurmond's repeated threats to filibuster the issue within the Judiciary Committee if Eastland acceded to Bayh's demand that it be brought forward. The Senate had no rule, or procedure, for terminating a filibuster within a committee.[62]

Detours

On November 3, 1969, Eastland announced that the question of electoral reform would be shelved indefinitely, or at least until his committee had finished dealing with the nomination of Clement Haynsworth to the Supreme Court. President Nixon had announced Haynsworth's nomination in mid-August. He was to fill the seat vacated by the resignation of Justice Abe Fortas in the face of a widening financial ethics scandal. (Fortas's earlier nomination to be promoted to chief justice had been rebuffed by the Senate because of similar issues.) Haynsworth, the chief judge of the Virginia-based Fourth Circuit, had strong professional credentials, and his confirmation, at the outset, seemed unproblematic. A South Carolinian, and a friend of Thurmond, Haynsworth was the first southerner nominated to the Supreme Court in three decades. His selection was strongly backed by Attorney General John Mitchell, one of the key architects of the Republican strategy to build electoral strength in the South (and marginalize George Wallace).[63]

Opposition to Haynsworth's nomination appeared quickly. It came first from civil rights and labor groups who believed that Haynsworth's record in school desegregation cases, among others, suggested a disregard for the rights of African-Americans and workers. Haynsworth lacked a "balanced view and a compassionate sensitivity to the needs and feelings of those dispossessed in our country," declared the National Catholic Conference for Interracial Justice. George Meany testified against the nomination, pointing out that Haynsworth's decisions on labor issues had been reversed seven times by the Supreme Court. A statement issued by eight African-American members of the House opposed the confirmation of "a man whose views have been so often at odds with a Supreme Court which achieved distinction through its attack on the malaise of racial discrimination."[64] It then emerged that Haynsworth, as a judge, had participated in decisions affecting firms in which he had financial interests, albeit distant or indirect ones. In the eyes of some senators, Haynsworth had been, at a minimum, insensitive to the appearance of judicial impropriety. Questions about the judge's ethics, moreover, provided a rationale for opposing the confirmation on grounds other than the nominee's political "philosophy" (which was frowned upon at the time). Two Republican leaders of the Senate, Robert Griffin and Margaret Chase Smith, indicated that, having fought the nomination of Fortas, they could not deploy a double standard and endorse Haynsworth.[65]

Despite the mounting opposition, Nixon refused to withdraw the nomination, and in late November the Senate voted fifty-five to forty-five not to confirm Haynsworth. The vote marked the first time that a nominee to the high court had been rejected since 1930 and was regarded as a "stunning" political defeat for Nixon. For those interested in Electoral College reform, the Senate vote and the debate that preceded it held added significance: it sharpened the battle lines between southern and northern Democrats, in particular, and between liberals and conservatives more broadly. Every southern Democrat except Ralph Yarborough of Texas and Albert Gore of Tennessee voted to confirm Haynsworth; all but one of the Democrats from elsewhere in the country voted negatively. Meanwhile, the Republicans were split (twenty-six to seventeen in favor), with conservatives generally backing the president's nominee, while moderates like Ed Brooke, Clifford Case, and minority leader Hugh Scott voted against confirmation. Eastland, furious at the opposition, denounced the "liberal press" for distorting the facts of the case and declared that "the so-called liberal establishment ... does not understand what is in the minds and hearts of the American people." That liberal establishment apparently included Birch Bayh, who had been one of the Senate's leading critics of Haynsworth.[66]

The divisive aftertaste of the failed Haynsworth nomination was soured further by Nixon's subsequent nomination of G. Harrold Carswell in January 1970. Carswell had been a district court judge in northern Florida until

June 1969 when Nixon, with the approval of the Senate, elevated him to the Fifth Circuit Court of Appeals. The White House, announcing his nomination to the Supreme Court, indicated that Carswell had been thoroughly vetted and that his record revealed no trace of the ethical or financial improprieties that had dogged Haynsworth. The Senate was initially receptive, hoping to get past the rancor that had enveloped the Haynsworth nomination. Within days, however, problems emerged. The news media revealed that Carswell, while running for a seat in the legislature in 1948, had delivered a speech defending segregation and white supremacy. This was followed by a steady trickle of information suggesting that Carswell, as a judge, had acted unsympathetically on civil rights issues and antagonistically toward African-American attorneys; as a private citizen, he had also lent support to segregated organizations. Civil rights organizations rapidly declared their opposition to the appointment, as did—strenuously— Republican Ed Brooke of Massachusetts, the only African-American in the Senate.[67]

Criticism of Carswell also came from the legal profession. Scores of attorneys, scholars, and law school deans questioned Carswell's legal and intellectual competence, as did one of the most respected senior judges on the Fifth Circuit. A widely publicized study found that his decisions had been overturned by appeals courts at an exceptionally high rate, and the liberal Republican Ripon Society deemed the nomination "an insult to southern jurisprudence." The case for Carswell was even undercut by one of his defenders, Roman Hruska, the ranking Republican on the Judiciary Committee. In response to criticism of Carswell's abilities, Hruska memorably declared that "even if he was mediocre, there are a lot of mediocre judges and people and lawyers. They are entitled to a little representation, aren't they?"[68]

In early April, Carswell's nomination was voted down by the Senate fifty-one to forty-five; the partisan and regional lineups were similar (but not identical) to the vote on Haynsworth. Nixon, hoping to salvage some political gain from the debacle, immediately issued a statement declaring that the Senate evidently would not confirm any nominee "from the South who believes as I do in the strict construction of the Constitution." He indicated that he would not subject another southerner "to the kind of malicious character assassination" accorded to both Haynsworth and

Carswell. "I understand the bitter feeling of millions of Americans who live in the South about the act of regional discrimination that took place in the Senate," the president concluded.[69]

The theme of "regional discrimination" also figured prominently in another issue that confronted Congress in the latter months of 1969 and the spring of 1970: the renewal of key portions of the Voting Rights Act, which were set to expire in August 1970. In the fall of 1969 the House Judiciary Committee, encouraged by northern liberals and civil rights groups, approved a simple extension of the VRA until 1975. In December, however, the full House voted, by a narrow margin, in favor of a substitute measure supported by President Nixon, Attorney General Mitchell, and most southerners. It extended the ban on literacy tests to all states (not just those in the South with a record of racial discrimination) and, more consequentially, terminated the "preclearance" provision that required many southern states and counties to get the approval of the Justice Department or a federal court in Washington before making changes to their election laws and processes. Liberals like Joseph Tydings of Maryland believed that this substitute would "gut" the VRA, while southern spokesmen, including Ervin, Thurmond, and Eastland, found it to be an improvement on the 1965 act, although they remained convinced that the entire VRA was discriminatory and unconstitutional.[70] (The Supreme Court had concluded otherwise.) Ervin declared the VRA to be an "iniquitous law" that ought to be "allowed to expire quietly."[71]

After some complex procedural maneuvers—largely designed to prevent Ervin and Eastland from bottling up the renewal in committees, a strategy long deployed to thwart civil rights legislation—the administration measure came to the floor of the Senate in March 1970. There, a carefully designed substitute, a compromise crafted by Democrat Philip Hart and Republican leader Hugh Scott, was introduced and subsequently approved, despite the opposition of most southerners, including Ervin and Eastland. The bill retained the national ban on literacy tests while keeping the preclearance provision intact, with a slightly revised triggering formula. In mid-June the House accepted the Senate version, and several days later Nixon signed it into law.[72] For many southerners, the renewal was another painful defeat, reinforcing their conviction that the region was being bullied by unsympathetic liberals who had gained control of the federal

government. In his testimony to Congress, Georgia's flamboyant segregationist governor, Lester Maddox, had proclaimed that the Voting Rights
Act was "ungodly, unworkable, unpatriotic and unconstitutional." When,
he asked, would Congress "stop warring on the South?"[73]

Spring and Summer in the Judiciary Committee

It was against this backdrop that the Senate resumed consideration of Electoral College reform in the spring of 1970. That it did so at all was the result of a hardball parliamentary maneuver carried out by Bayh in early February. Even after the Haynsworth affair had been settled the previous
November, Thurmond's threat to filibuster gave Eastland a rationale for
keeping electoral reform off the Judiciary Committee agenda, and Bayh
feared that the committee might be indefinitely prevented from taking action. The Indiana senator then announced that he would filibuster the
Carswell nomination, which both Eastland and Thurmond supported,
unless the Judiciary Committee consented to discuss Electoral College reform. Bayh's decision to fight fire with fire led to an agreement to hold a
timely committee vote on Carswell in exchange for a commitment that the
Judiciary Committee would consider and vote on the various electoral reform plans by April 24.[74]

Eastland and Ervin made a tactical move of their own in early April by
scheduling, on short notice, hearings with a lopsided witness list that featured well-known opponents of a national popular vote, including Alexander
Bickel, journalist Theodore White, and former Democratic presidential adviser Richard Goodwin. White, the author of widely read books about presidential election campaigns, insisted that an NPV would lead to increased
fraud as well as to political chaos if no candidate won a large plurality.
Goodwin, who believed that the existing system worked well, was convinced
that direct elections would undermine the "two-party system which has
helped make the United States the most able and long-lasting democracy in
the history of the world."[75] The hearings offered an exquisite example of
Ervin's frequently deployed technique of rhetorical "crossquotemanship":
citing or showcasing liberals in defense of conservative causes.[76]

The full Judiciary Committee, in fact, was sharply divided: on April 19
the *New York Times* reported that "direct election" was "in serious trouble."
Nonetheless, Bayh was able to achieve his long-sought objective a few days

later. After a recommendation for a proportional plan had been turned back by the narrowest of margins (eight to nine), the Judiciary Committee voted eleven to six in favor of S.J. Res. 1, a resolution nearly identical to the one passed by the House. (Notably, two key senators who had supported a proportional plan, Republican leader Hugh Scott and Democrat Robert Byrd of West Virginia, voted for S.J. Res. 1 after the proportional option had been defeated.) The Bayh amendment, as it came to be called, would finally get a hearing on the floor of the Senate. The *New York Times* editorialized that there was now "a relatively simple choice between right and wrong . . . the shoddy compromise devised by the founding fathers for the purpose of keeping the union intact . . . must be discarded to avoid risks of chaos, sordid manipulations and defeat of the will of the people."[77]

Six weeks later, the need for reform was underscored, in the eyes of many Democrats and Republicans alike, by George Wallace's come-from-behind victory in the Democratic gubernatorial primary in Alabama. His defeat of Albert Brewer, the sitting governor and a racial moderate supported by Nixon, seemed certain to propel Wallace back into presidential politics, and he appeared capable of winning at least three and perhaps as many as nine states in 1972. The *Washington Post* editorialized that Wallace's election "should be the signal for a full-scale drive in the Senate for enactment of the direct-election amendment." Birch Bayh wholeheartedly agreed.[78]

Still, despite the added spur provided by the revival of Wallace's political fortunes, the repeated delays in the Senate had taken a toll. The passage of seven months between the House vote and the Senate Judiciary Committee's decision had broken the momentum that had built up in the late summer of 1969, dissipating some of the optimistic energy that had been so palpable in the immediate wake of the House's action. The delays also made it less likely that any amendment could be ratified in time for the 1972 election, a development that, for some, lessened the urgency of reform.[79] Just as importantly, the intervening months gave opponents of direct election time to regroup, to focus their arguments, to strategize and organize resistance. The recently founded American Conservative Union was active in this effort, and Ervin tirelessly wrote to his Senate colleagues, suggesting strategies and rationales for blocking Bayh's amendment.[80] Developments in Congress also stiffened the resolve of southerners who identified a national popular vote with the same liberal forces and politicians that had pressed for the renewal of the VRA and defeated the nominations of Carswell and Haynsworth.[81]

In addition, the passage of time had permitted worries and doubts to strengthen among allies of reform and uncommitted senators, particularly regarding the 40 percent threshold for election, the desirability of a runoff, and the risk of weakening the two-party system by encouraging minor-party candidacies. Senators Thomas Eagleton of Missouri and Robert (Bob) Dole of Kansas consequently put forward a complicated alternative plan designed to prevent "fragmentation and polarization" and to make certain that an incoming president had a national mandate. Joseph Tydings and Republican Robert Griffin offered a different proposal that would avoid a runoff by maintaining roles for the Electoral College and Congress. In May 1970, *Time* magazine, while acknowledging that all electoral schemes had potential drawbacks, urged Congress to go "back to the drawing board in pursuit of the best plan possible."[82]

The delays, moreover, had not come to an end. The majority report from the Judiciary Committee, which was supposed to have been written in a week, was completed only five weeks after the late-April committee vote; the minority report took a remarkable sixteen weeks. As a result, S.J. Res. 1 was not formally reported to the full Senate until August 14, and debate began only after Labor Day.

The two committee reports were strikingly different from one another, in content, tone, and length, and they prefigured the debate that would ensue. The majority report, written by Bayh, was concise and matter-of-fact. It enumerated the major flaws in the existing system and sketched the reasons the committee majority preferred direct election to the well-known alternatives that had been presented in committee—emphasizing the importance of all votes counting equally and of ensuring that the candidate who won the most votes would become president. At more length, it justified the choice of a 40 percent threshold for election as "a prudent cutoff point" that would make runoffs infrequent while providing "a sufficient mandate to govern." The report defended the concept of a runoff election—in contrast to other schemes that involved Congress or electoral votes—on the grounds that the "final choice" ought to be made by "the people" and that only a runoff could guarantee that the winner of the popular vote took office. It concluded with a reminder that an NPV had received overwhelming support in the House as well as in public opinion polls and was endorsed by "a formidable array of national organizations."[83]

In a separate statement, Senators Griffin and Tydings endorsed the principle of direct elections but expressed serious reservations about the desirability of a runoff. They feared that the runoff provision would encourage third parties to field candidates in the hope of preventing anyone from reaching the 40 percent threshold; they could then bargain with the major-party candidates, deforming policy decisions and potentially undermining the perceived legitimacy of an election's outcome. Griffin and Tydings proposed instead that, if no candidate received 40 percent of the vote, the popular vote winner would still become president if he also won a majority of the electoral vote; if not, the decision would go to a joint session of Congress, with each member casting one vote. Griffin also favored a provision that would give to Congress the power to establish "uniform election procedures and voter qualifications." Since the premise of an NPV was that all votes should count equally, the Michigan Republican wrote, it was "essential to guard against any device which would tend to dilute the vote of any individual or class of individuals."[84]

The minority report was more than twice as long and mounted an angry, full-throated attack on the idea of direct elections. Signed by four prominent southerners (Eastland, Ervin, Thurmond, and John McClellan of Arkansas), as well as Republicans Roman Hruska and Hiram Fong, the document was a jeremiad, decrying the damage that a national popular vote would inflict upon the republic. Its focus was not on principles but on consequences—or alleged consequences. Direct elections would destroy the two-party system, undermine "the federal system," jeopardize the separation of powers, "radicalize public opinion," "endanger the rights of all minorities," create "an irresistible temptation to electoral fraud," lead to "interminable" recounts and challenges, and "necessitate national direction and control of every aspect of the electoral process." Only the last of these claims was anything other than highly speculative: it was plausible, as Griffin had implied, that a national presidential election would indeed lead to federal regulation of election processes and voting qualifications.[85]

The minority report, in addition, assailed the "invincible innocence" of NPV advocates, accusing them of a "naïve" embrace of "mathematical purity." It dismissed the majority's concern about votes counting equally with the declaration that "'one-man, one-vote' can be bought only at the price of constitutional destruction." The minority defended winner-take-all (although several of its leading members had long championed district or proportional elections) and chided the majority for overreacting to George Wallace: "A constitutional amendment will be with us long after Governor Wallace has disappeared from the scene." They flatly rejected the notion that the Electoral College was "antiquated or outmoded; no more viable institution, nor a more salutary one, will be found today." The report curtly dismissed the Griffin-Tydings proposal—which was seen as a compromise that might satisfy some skeptics of Bayh's plan—as "no cure for the ills of direct election."[86]

The most disingenuous, if not downright hypocritical, claim of the report was that an NPV would "endanger minority rights." The argument buttressing that assertion was a murky and perverse rechanneling of pieces of the debate over the Lodge-Gossett resolution: minorities could more readily make strategic alliances, and thus better protect their interests, under the Electoral College (with winner-take-all and a two-party system) than "under direct election, with its emphasis on mere numbers" (and a multiplicity of parties). The not-so-hidden subtext was to suggest that defenders of the Electoral College, including the four ardent segregationists who signed the report, were sensitive to minority rights and were not simply voicing long-standing southern apprehensions about a national popular vote. Accordingly, the report quoted a brief excerpt from testimony given in the Senate in April by William Clay, an African-American congressman from Missouri. Clay, who had voted against an NPV in the House, had voiced concern that "the direct popular vote would inhibit the political influence of minority groups," particularly African-Americans in urban communities. The report, however, made no mention of Clay's reasoning, which he had spelled out in his testimony. Like Clarence Mitchell, Clay feared that African-Americans would face continued and intensified efforts at disenfranchisement unless there were ongoing and strengthened federal protections of the right to vote. Without such protection, "two and a half million black people" would remain disenfranchised in the South, while direct elections would deprive African-Americans of their swing-vote clout in key northern states. The fact that five of the six authors of the minority report had opposed renewal of the Voting Rights Act (and thus the continuation of federal protection of voting rights) was not mentioned. Nor did the report acknowledge that Clay's testimony was given before the VRA had been renewed or that he was one of only two African-Americans, out of ten, who had voted against the direct election amendment in the House.[87]

Showdown in the Senate

The floor debate in the Senate opened on September 8, with the fate of electoral reform far from certain. Bayh believed that he could count on fifty-five votes, and possibly as many as fifty-eight, in support of S.J. Res. 1; these were sizable numbers but still short of the two-thirds (of those voting) needed for passage. The Indiana senator and his allies—including more than forty co-sponsors—could only hope that the undecided votes, roughly a dozen in all, would break heavily in their favor as the debate proceeded. Alternatively, they might be able to clear the two-thirds threshold by agreeing to replace the runoff provision with some version of the Griffin-Tydings proposal. Hugh Scott, the Republican leader, predicted that the vote would be close but that S.J. Res. 1 would likely be approved if it were voted on after all of the substitute amendments had been considered and rejected—precisely the dynamic that had won the day both in the House and in the Senate Judiciary Committee. In contrast, Strom Thurmond announced that opponents of S.J. Res. 1 "have the votes to beat it outright" and publicly discounted the possibility of a filibuster, although privately he was reported to be preparing for one.[88]

Indeed, the threat of a filibuster hung in the air during the first weeks of September, held aloft in part by the constraints of the Senate calendar. The two parties had agreed to a customary pre-election recess beginning on October 15, and majority leader Mike Mansfield was intent on pushing through key pieces of legislation before that date. The Senate consequently was meeting in double sessions, debating Electoral College reform until mid-afternoon and then turning to other matters. Although the Senate would reconvene after the November elections, the window for passage of Bayh's amendment in the Ninety-First Congress seemed likely to close by mid-October.[89]

Bayh opened the debate with a familiar recitation of the virtues of a national popular vote as "the only system that is truly democratic, truly equitable, and truly responsive to the will of the people." He alluded to the long history of efforts to reform the Electoral College, stretching back to 1816; he underscored the remarkable breadth of support for S.J. Res. 1 as evidenced by the House vote, public opinion polls, and the endorsement of major organizations; and he briefly sketched the shortcomings of the alternative proposals. Bayh also anticipated, and countered, the small-state objection by noting that nine of the co-sponsors of S.J. Res. 1 came from small states. Republican Henry Bellmon of Oklahoma agreed, noting that in the 1968 campaign, sixteen relatively small states had received no visits from a major party candidate. He argued that less-populated states like his own would be helped, rather than hurt, by direct elections. Throughout the opening salvos, Bayh's views were forcefully seconded by Howard Baker, who insisted on keeping the spotlight on the broad principles at stake. While identifying himself as being "from a relatively small state" and "a relatively southern state," Baker declared that "the paramount issue . . . is the fundamental right of every citizen to cast a vote that has no more weight nor no less weight than that of any other citizen." Russell Long, from the unarguably southern state of Louisiana, took a folksier approach. "The average American," he observed, "would think that if the electoral system is going to be reformed, the logical way to do it would be simply to say that the man who gets the most votes wins." Long, who had voted for the Langer amendment in 1956, was the only senator from the deep South to voice support for S.J. Res.1.[90]

Opponents of direct election quickly jumped into the fray, voicing their own (equally familiar) perspectives and, not infrequently, interrupting Bayh and Baker to register objections and score debating points. Nebraska Republican Carl Curtis, for example, baited Baker that his concern for electoral equality led logically to the abolition of the Senate. Eastland claimed that the threshold for election ought to be 50 percent rather than 40 percent; he then acknowledged that he would not support S.J. Res. 1 even if the threshold were raised. Eastland also dismissed Banzhaf's study and challenged the credentials of the American Bar Association panel that had endorsed direct elections.[91] Hruska voiced the fear that farm states would be overwhelmed by urban areas in a national election; he linked the prospect of direct elections to a broad loss of power by the states, decrying their newfound inability (thanks to the Supreme

Court) to determine the composition of their own legislatures. Hruska, Curtis, and Eastland all hammered away at the notion that direct elections would lead to a federal takeover of voting and registration rules, and Thurmond weighed in with his own distinctive argument that direct elections would harm the party system. An NPV, he claimed, would encourage ideological parties, which were divisive, whereas the Electoral College encouraged regional coordination, which was "a healthy development."[92] Two novel considerations were introduced by Florida's Spessard Holland, a Democrat nearing the end of his fourth and final term in the Senate. Holland was disturbed that under S.J. Res. 1 the District of Columbia would have more influence than numerous small but "sovereign" states. He also worried that some states, like Florida, would be disadvantaged by a national popular vote because inclement weather in November could prevent many of their citizens from getting to the polls.[93]

Despite a few highlights, there was a desultory quality to the first week of debate. Although Bayh himself seemed eager (almost too eager) to engage any and all criticisms of S.J. Res. 1, the Senate chamber was often largely empty, and many of the speeches seemed designed to fill the record and use time rather than to gain converts or persuade the undecided. Opponents of reform quoted extensively from statements made by Bickel, Goodwin, Charles Black of Yale, conservative columnist James Kilpatrick, and even their own minority report. The proceedings did not match the classic image of a filibuster—one senator at a time holding the floor to speak for many hours, as Thurmond had famously done for twenty-four hours in 1957—but the debate was moving sideways, or in circles, rather than forward. On September 14, Mansfield convened a lengthy meeting with Bayh as well as other key senators to try to agree on a timetable for voting. In the absence of such an agreement, Mansfield was prepared to introduce a cloture motion, which, if successful, would force an end to the debate.[94]

Meanwhile, one person who was conspicuously absent from the public dialogue was Richard Nixon—who had said little about electoral reform since his endorsement of the House-approved amendment a year earlier. In late August the leaders of five major organizations supporting S.J. Res. 1 (the ABA, the AFL-CIO, the Chamber of Commerce, the United Auto

Workers, and the League of Women Voters) had formally requested a meeting with the president; they heard nothing from the White House until September 10, when they received a telegram that Nixon was unavailable. The following day Nixon issued a message to Congress urging action on a long list of issues, including electoral reform. "Every four years," the president observed, "the American democracy places a large, unacceptable, and unnecessary wager" that the Electoral College "will work one more time." Recalling that he had "originally favored other methods" of changing the system, he nonetheless deemed the House-passed amendment to be a "thoroughly acceptable reform," and he urged the Senate to pass it in time for the 1972 elections, thereby averting "calamity by anticipating it." Nixon's less-than-enthusiastic words were formally welcomed by Bayh and Griffin, but one staff member found the statement "so backhanded that I fear it won't help at all." Of equal importance, Nixon expended no effort to persuade individual senators, even though a majority of the undecided votes belonged to Republicans. "The White House," noted another staffer, was not "putting the hammer on anyone."[95]

Nixon's tepid stance—which some commentators regarded as consequential—was shaped by his own political interests. By endorsing S.J. Res. 1, he was gesturing his support for congressional moderates, particularly those from his own party; by doing little to promote passage, he was placating conservatives. Several observers also believed that Nixon was disinclined to help produce a major policy victory for Birch Bayh, who had spearheaded the campaigns against Haynsworth and Carswell and was a potential, if long-shot, Democratic candidate for president in 1972. Above all, Nixon was trying to thread the needle of his own, and his party's, "Southern Strategy." Obsessed with the threat that Wallace might pose in 1972, Nixon was more than willing to do away with the Electoral College; on the other hand, he did not want to press too publicly for a reform that was widely disliked in the South. Already under fire from Thurmond because he was carrying out long-delayed, court-ordered steps to implement school desegregation, Nixon's primary objective was to keep as many southern states as possible in the Republican column.[96]

On September 15 the Senate proceedings took a turn, perhaps an inevitable one. In the morning, southern Democrats held a private meeting at which they decided that they would oppose any attempt to hold a vote on Electoral College reform. This decision to filibuster (or, rather, to collectively commit themselves to the filibuster that was already under way) was ostensibly curious: if the opponents of reform had enough votes to sustain a filibuster (a two-thirds vote would be needed to end debate), they presumably also had the votes to prevent passage of a constitutional amendment. The southerners, however, did not want to run the risk of something going awry on a decisive, substantive vote. They feared that a series of floor votes on the various alternatives to direct elections might—as had happened in the House—create dynamics favorable to the passage of S.J. Res. 1. Ervin was particularly alert to that possibility, perhaps because many of North Carolina's House members had ended up voting for direct elections after their preferred options had been rejected. The southern opposition also worried that if the Senate voted on the substantive questions, the Griffin-Tydings amendment to S.J. Res. 1 might be approved (it needed only a simple majority vote), leading subsequently to the passage of a modified version of Bayh's resolution. Then too, a filibuster was a familiar tactic for Eastland, Ervin, and their southern colleagues; they had used it repeatedly over the years to impede civil rights legislation. They knew that cloture had been successfully enacted only eight times since World War I and that some senators would be reluctant to support cloture, even if they did not oppose electoral reform. A filibuster would also give opponents of reform two bites at the apple: if they failed to prevent cloture, they could then try to block S.J. Res. 1 in a vote on the amendment resolution itself.[97]

The strategy was uncompromising, but to be successful it needed help from Republicans: southern Democrats alone were not numerous enough to defeat a cloture vote. That help arrived at noontime when the Republican opponents of reform caucused and, despite considerable disagreement, decided not to agree to a timetable for voting and not to support any cloture motions. They reached that decision only after learning of the stance taken by the southern caucus.[98]

Shortly thereafter, Bayh rose on the Senate floor to announce that he was about to make a series of "unanimous consent requests to see if there is any common ground" that would permit the Senate to move forward. (A "unanimous consent" request was a conventional step, under Senate rules, to structure debate and move legislation forward; if no senator objected, the request was acted upon.) He then asked for the unanimous

consent of the Senate to vote the next day on the Griffin-Tydings amendment to S.J. Res. 1; if such a vote were successful, a final vote on S.J. Res. 1
would be held on September 18. Ervin objected. Bayh requested a vote on
a different pending amendment; Ervin objected again. Bayh then asked
for consent to consider all of the pending amendments to S.J. Res. 1, including four sponsored by Ervin, with two or four hours (or even an entire
day) of debate on each, followed by a vote. Ervin objected "especially with
reference to my own four amendments." Bayh, in the circuitous, overly po-
lite style of speech that characterized Senate debates of the era, then
voiced puzzlement about the efforts being made to prevent the senators
from standing up and voting "on the merits on an issue as vital as this."
Ervin responded that senators ought not "stand up and vote until they have
had time to exercise their intelligence in a deliberative fashion," especially
since there were "almost as many varieties of proposals as there are numbers of Heinz pickles." With all doubt removed that a filibuster was under
way, Mansfield filed a cloture motion, signed by himself and nineteen other
senators, including the two Republican leaders, Scott and Griffin. The cloture vote, under the senate's standing Rule XXII, would take place on
September 17. If it succeeded, the Senate would be limited to one hundred
hours of debate before voting on electoral reform.[99]

The two sides then continued sparring, less over the substance of different proposals than over the need for more debate. Ervin insisted that
he did not wish the Senate to be "hurried" by Bayh, observing that California had spent many weeks dealing with the sensational murder trial of
Charles Manson and that the Senate ought to give "at least as much consideration" to amending the Constitution. Republicans John Cooper of
Kentucky and John Williams of Delaware stated that they opposed cloture because the amendment needed full-time attention and the Senate
was occupied with too many other issues. Hruska complained that the
Senate had had only "seven skinny days" of debate and dodged Bayh's effort to get the Nebraska senator to commit to a vote after a longer and
more ample discussion. Charles Percy, a moderate from Illinois, responded
to his fellow Republicans by reminding them that it was the "dilatory tactics" of opponents of S.J. Res. 1 that had delayed the onset of the Senate
debate. He also noted, citing opinion polls, that "if the members of this
body have not had time to make their minds up, the American people

apparently have." In an important new development, Bayh read into the record a telegram that he had received from Clarence Mitchell and Joseph Rauh of the Leadership Conference on Civil Rights, strongly endorsing direct elections (a shift in Mitchell's stance) and insisting that the Senate vote on an issue that had been actively discussed in Washington since February 1966. "All of the arguments on both sides have been made, and there is no point in further talk—unless the Senate intends to strangle the measure by delay." "A vote against cloture," Mitchell and Rauh continued, "will be a vote to kill electoral reform without ever facing the question of its merits."[100]

Before the cloture vote was taken, Mansfield—a diplomatic, soft-spoken, and long-serving majority leader—took the rare step of publicly chastising some of his colleagues. "Using the filibuster device in this fashion to force a two-thirds vote," he declared, "when the question itself calls for two-thirds, abuses the clear purpose and intent of the Senate rules." He strongly urged that the Senate be "permitted to vote" on the substantive question.[101] To Mansfield's dismay—although not his surprise—the cloture vote did not succeed. Fifty-four senators voted in favor of ending debate, while thirty-six were opposed: Bayh and Mansfield were six votes short of the two-thirds vote that they needed. As Table 5.2 reveals, Democrats voted strongly in favor of cloture, while Republicans were fairly evenly split, with opposition most common among those from the plains and Rocky Mountain states. Nearly all senators from the largest states voted for cloture, and slight majorities of those from small and medium-sized states did the same. Notably, small-state Democrats strongly favored ending debate, while small-state Republicans went the other way. The most striking pattern in the vote was the contrast between southern and non-southern Democrats: the former voted sixteen to three against cloture, while the latter voted thirty to two in favor.[102]

The cloture vote was a blow to Bayh and his allies, but not a fatal one—in part because the outcome was anticipated, viewed as a test of strength rather than a final verdict. Although Mansfield was somewhat skeptical, both Bayh and Baker thought that it would be possible to win a second cloture vote after additional debate, in part because several senators who favored reform had been absent on September 17. Baker and Bayh also be-

TABLE 5.2: FIRST CLOTURE VOTE IN THE SENATE, SEPTEMBER 17, 1970

	Yea	Nay	Not voting
All senators	54	36	10
Democrats	33	18	6
Republicans	21	18	4
South[a]			
Democrats	3	16	0
Republicans	3	4	0
Total	6	20	0
Non-South			
Democrats	30	2	6
Republicans	18	14	4
Total	48	16	10
Large states[b]			
Democrats	5	0	0
Republicans	8	1	2
Total	13	1	2
Medium-sized states[b]			
Democrats	16	15	2
Republicans	6	5	0
Total	22	20	2
Small states[b]			
Democrats	12	3	4
Republicans	7	12	2
Total	19	15	6

Source: 116 Cong. Rec. 32357 (1970).

a. South includes FL, GA, SC, NC, VA, KY, TN, AL, MS, AR, LA, OK, TX. See Chapter 5, note 57.

b. "Large" includes all states that had fifteen or more electoral votes in the 1968 presidential election; "medium-sized" includes all states that had between seven and fourteen electoral votes in the 1968 presidential election; and "small" includes those with six or fewer electoral votes in the 1968 presidential election.

lieved that a direct election amendment could still be enacted, if they reached a substantive vote, because they were aware of senators who were pro-reform but reluctant to invoke cloture. Meanwhile, the filibuster was widely criticized in the press. On September 18, not only the *New York Times* and the *Washington Post*, but the *Atlanta Constitution*, a politically moderate southern voice, published editorials calling for an end to the stalling. "Talk should not block such an important change," wrote the venerable and influential Atlanta paper.[103]

With neither side surrendering, the debate sputtered on, with Bayh indicating that he and his allies would refrain from lengthy speeches in order to give opponents ample floor time to make their case.[104] Ervin responded with a disquisition about what had occurred in the elections of 1824 and 1876, followed by a series of his trademark homespun stories, a challenge to the integrity of the ABA panel on electoral reform, and the claim (often made before) that Hitler had come to power thanks to Germany's adoption of a national popular vote. Ervin also introduced a letter from former congressman Ed Gossett maintaining that the Chamber of Commerce's endorsement of direct elections was "completely false," based on a poll that was "dishonest and misleading." (A subsequent letter from the Chamber of Commerce dismissed Gossett's assertions as unfounded.)[105] Ervin, moreover, did not carry the ball alone: between September 17 and September 29, opposition to direct elections and / or to ending debate was also voiced by Thurmond, Hruska, Holland, Herman Talmadge of Georgia, Edward Gurney of Florida, Clifford Hansen of Wyoming, William Fulbright of Arkansas, John Stennis of Mississippi, and the two senators from Alabama, John Sparkman and James Allen (the latter of whom engaged in a long, drawn-out colloquy with Ervin). Nothing was said in these speeches that had not been heard many times before, although numerous speakers insisted that the subject was complicated, requiring more time for discussion and consideration. Carl Curtis offered evidence of the dangers of direct elections with runoffs in an erudite discourse about the instability of French governments, entering into the record a list of every president and prime minister of France from 1870 to 1940.[106]

Supporters of direct elections also spoke out, although far more briefly. Pastore declared that the issue was in fact "very simple" (as it had been when he first debated it in 1956), but "we come here and talk . . . and we keep repeating the same thing over and over again, and we never come to a vote." Fred Harris of Oklahoma and Joseph Montoya of New Mexico both affirmed their support of S.J. Res. 1, and Michigan's Philip Hart, known as the "conscience of the Senate," commended Bayh for his patience while endorsing the amendment. Bayh himself peppered his adversaries with challenges to their assertions and arguments, often annoying them in the process. He also tried to advance the process by signaling his openness to the Griffin-Tydings amendment or other alternatives to the oft-criticized runoff provision of S.J. Res. 1. He even offered to amend S.J. Res. 1 himself to incorporate the Griffin-Tydings plan and simplify the way forward, if there were no objections. To no one's surprise, Ervin announced that he would object.[107]

In a last-ditch effort to force a vote on S.J. Res. 1, Bayh turned, on September 24, to a version of the maneuver that he had successfully deployed in the Judiciary Committee. Once again fighting fire with fire, he announced that he would object to all unanimous consent requests to proceed with any business other than electoral reform or to permit committees to meet while the Senate was in session. He would, in effect, force the filibusterers to live with the consequences of a genuine filibuster—shutting down the workings of the Senate—rather than permitting them to kill electoral reform without sacrificing other legislation. (The *Washington Post* called Bayh's strategy "poetic justice.") Bayh justified this effort, on the floor and in a letter to his colleagues, by chronicling the delaying tactics that opponents of electoral reform had engaged in since the House vote a year earlier; he even singled out Thurmond by name as a particularly important culprit. Mansfield, always the conciliator (and aware in advance of Bayh's undertaking), then took the floor to voice his sympathies with Bayh, agreeing that one or two members of the Judiciary Committee had engaged in a regrettable "deliberate delay." He also explained that he, as majority leader, had "responsibilities" that went beyond S.J. Res. 1. He consequently urged committees to meet in the early morning before the Senate went into session and proceeded, the next day, to file a second cloture motion with a vote to be held on September 29.[108]

Bayh's strategy did not cause his opponents to blink. With the Senate now fully focused on electoral reform for a few days, the attacks on S.J. Res. 1 continued unabated, complete with more quotations from newspapers and magazines as well as repetitions of the (by now very familiar) minority report.[109] The criticism also became more personal, with Alabama's James Allen, in particular, attacking Bayh for taking up so much floor time and being the real "filibusterer." On Tuesday, September 29, during the final hours of debate before the second cloture vote, Ervin declared that the Senate should not attempt "to solve this problem in the closing days of a hurried and harried session." Mansfield once again decried the misuse of Senate rules to prevent a vote on a constitutional amendment, even suggesting that Rule XXII itself (already unpopular among liberals) might need to be revisited. He also maintained that a vote against cloture "must be considered a vote to protect the antiquated status quo of national elections." (That characterization was resisted by Fulbright and Hruska, who claimed that the vote was only about the need for more time to examine the issue.) Bayh repeated his readiness to alter the runoff provision and pledged, if cloture succeeded, to confer with the authors of all pending amendments to devise an acceptable procedure to consider each one. A morsel of perspective was injected into the debate by Jennings Randolph of West Virginia, who had first served in Congress during the early New Deal. He reminded his colleagues that under cloture rules the Senate would still be allowed 100 hours of debate; 8 hours a day for twelve and a half days seemed to Randolph to be ample time "to come to grips" with the issue.[110]

The words spoken had little impact on the vote, which the *New York Times* had dubbed the "last call for electoral reform." The final tally was fifty-three in favor of ending debate, thirty-four opposed: Bayh and his allies were still five votes short. Only two senators who had opposed cloture on the first vote supported it the second time; the absences were different, and more numerous, than on September 17, but they were not decisive.[111] As Table 5.3 makes clear, the voting patterns on September 29 were similar to those twelve days earlier. Shutting off debate was supported by 61 percent of all senators who were present and voting; Democrats were strongly in favor, while Republicans were evenly divided. Eighty percent of southerners opposed cloture, while 73 percent of senators from other regions voted favorably. Senators from the largest states, both Democrats and Republicans, supported cloture, their views apparently immune to claims that large states were advantaged by the Electoral College. In contrast, small-state senators tended to vote along party lines, with Democrats favoring cloture while Republicans voted negatively. If there was small-state resistance to an NPV, it was present only among Republicans! Boiled down to the essentials, reform was blocked by a coalition of southern Democrats and small-state conservative Republicans. The thirty-four senators who voted "nay" came from states with 27 percent of the nation's population.[112]

TABLE 5.3: SECOND CLOTURE VOTE IN THE SENATE, SEPTEMBER 29, 1970

	Yea	Nay	Not voting
All senators	53	34	13
Democrats	34	15	8
Republicans	19	19	5
South[a]			
Democrats	2	13	4
Republicans	2	3	2
Total	4	16	6
Non-South			
Democrats	32	2	4
Republicans	17	16	3
Total	49	18	7
Large states[b]			
Democrats	3	0	2
Republicans	9	0	2
Total	12	0	4
Medium-sized states[b]			
Democrats	19	11	3
Republicans	5	5	1
Total	24	16	4
Small states[b]			
Democrats	12	4	3
Republicans	5	14	2
Total	17	18	5

Source: 116 Cong. Rec. 34034 (1970).

a. South includes FL, GA, SC, NC, VA, KY, TN, AL, MS, AR, LA, OK, TX. See Chapter 5, note 57.

b. "Large" includes all states that had fifteen or more electoral votes in the 1968 presidential election; "medium-sized" includes all states that had between seven and fourteen electoral votes in the 1968 presidential election; and "small" includes those with six or fewer electoral votes in the 1968 presidential election.

That the Senate effort fell short after reformers had won such a decisive victory in the House can be traced to two key factors. One was that the large urban states, whose elected representatives tended to be liberal Democrats and moderate Republicans, wielded considerably less power in the Senate than they had in the House: the eight largest states (six of which were in the Northeast or Midwest) accounted for nearly half of all House seats but only sixteen senators. Both the senators and the representatives from those states were overwhelmingly in favor of an NPV, but their preferences carried less weight in the Senate. On the other hand, 40 percent of all senators, but only 10 percent of House members, came from small states, and Republicans from those states tended to be considerably more conservative than their large-state colleagues. The contrast between the 83 percent positive vote in the House and the 61 percent vote (for cloture) in the Senate was, in part, a consequence of the differences in composition of the two chambers.[113]

The second key factor was that the South was more united in opposition to an NPV in the Senate than it had been in the House a year earlier. In September 1969 a majority of representatives from Arkansas, Florida, North Carolina, and Virginia had voted in favor of the NPV amendment; twelve months later, all of the senators from those states voted against ending debate on Bayh's amendment.[114] One source of this divergence was the presence of geographic pockets of liberalism or moderation that elected House members (such as Florida's Claude Pepper, or Jack Edwards, an Alabama Republican) who were receptive to the reform of political institutions. Such moderates, however, were scarce in the Senate, where seats had to be won in statewide elections.[115] Even in the House, moreover, much of the southern support for direct elections was less than enthusiastic: it came from representatives who had initially supported district or proportional plans but voted for an NPV when it became the only alternative to preserving the Electoral College.[116] After H.J. Res. 681 had passed, those votes were criticized in the regional press, suggesting that opposition was hardening amid mounting apprehensions that an NPV might actually be adopted. Ervin accordingly made it clear to North Carolina newspapers as early as October 1969 that he had no intention of following in the path of the state's representatives who had first supported district elections and later voted for H.J. Res. 681.[117] Indeed, the filibuster strategy that he advocated was designed to prevent a replay of the legislative dynamics that had unfolded in the House.

After the second cloture vote was tallied, Bayh announced that he would no longer object to unanimous consent requests, thereby permitting the Senate to turn to its regular business. His decision was welcomed even by allies, many of whom had chafed at their inability to deal with other legislation. He also pledged to consult with other senators individually in search of a solution to the electoral reform impasse.[118] Several days later, on October 2, Mansfield filed a third cloture petition (Bayh's resolution was still a pending item of business), with a vote to be held on October 6. What Mansfield sought to achieve remains unclear, but his action led to a meeting in his office on October 5. Present were Bayh, Baker, Griffin, Hruska, and Ervin, as well as Bob Dole and Virginia Democrat William Spong, both of whom had put forward alternative reform measures. If Mansfield hoped to forge a compromise, to finally hold a substantive vote and bring years of legislative labor to a conclusion more satisfactory than a pair of defeated cloture petitions, he was disappointed. Hruska, according to sparse firsthand accounts, was taciturn and negative about possible compromises; Ervin objected to them on behalf of the southern caucus; the tone of the gathering became less than cordial, particularly between Bayh and Ervin. After an hour the meeting broke up, and the cloture petition was withdrawn.[119] More than a month later, after the election recess, a few final efforts were made to revive the issue, centering on Spong's hybrid scheme that would have required a successful candidate to win a majority of the electoral vote (without electors) as well as a plurality of the popular vote. But that proposal never generated much enthusiasm, among either supporters or opponents of direct elections.[120]

The second cloture vote had, in fact, brought to a halt the years-long campaign for direct elections. The Associated Press declared the reform effort to have been "all but killed" by the cloture decision, while United Press International agreed that it was "a probable fatal blow." Ervin himself pronounced S.J. Res. 1 to be dead and pledged to make a major effort to bring about "genuine reform" in the next Congress.[121] The conservative newspaper *Human Events* celebrated the outcome, giving credit to the recently founded American Conservative Union for its lobbying effort and to Attorney General Mitchell for persuading Nixon not to actively support Bayh's amendment. *Newsweek,* which had been lukewarm about direct elections, was fatalistic, concluding that the reformers simply did not have the votes to get the amendment passed. *Time,* favoring reform but skeptical about S.J. Res. 1, offered a quotation from Lord Falkland that John Kennedy had invoked during the 1956 debates: "When it is not necessary to change, it is necessary not to change."[122]

Newspapers sympathetic to direct elections conceded that nothing further could be done in the Ninety-First Congress or in time for the 1972 election, but they expressed guarded hope for the future. The *New York Times* urged congressional reformers to "regroup their forces for yet another try later on." It also urged them not to settle for "halfway" measures that would perpetuate some of the flaws of the existing system by, for example, retaining electoral votes or congressional participation. The *Los Angeles Times* echoed that advice. The *Washington Post,* on the other hand, urged Bayh and his allies to return to the issue in the next Congress and to develop alternatives to the runoff plan, such as the Griffin-Tydings proposal. It also denounced the filibuster and the "stubborn minority" that had prevented a vote on a measure with widespread support. Perhaps the most heated response in the national press came from *New York Times* columnist Tom Wicker, a native North Carolinian who was particularly incensed at the numerous "inconsistencies" in the arguments put forward by his fellow Tar Heel, Sam Ervin. On the morning of the second cloture vote, Wicker described the filibuster as "a blatant case of a little band of willful men who fear, and are therefore thwarting, both popular will and the political process that they extol."[123]

The Rise and Fall of Direct Election

In 1969–1970 the United States came closer to adopting a national popular vote for presidential elections than it ever had—or has—in its history. This moment also marked the closest the nation had come to any significant reform of the Electoral College since 1821, when the House fell a few votes short of endorsing a district elections amendment already passed by the Senate. In the twelve months beginning in September 1969, a constitutional amendment calling for direct popular election was approved by an overwhelming margin in the House and attained majority support in the Senate. Had an additional handful of senators been more favorable to reform or less reluctant to invoke cloture, the Senate too might have passed that amendment or a slightly modified version of it. Whether such an amendment would have been ratified by the requisite thirty-eight states is uncertain, but the prospects were reasonable and the momentum for change was strong. Although little remembered a half-century later and rarely mentioned in chronicles of the 1960s, this was a political juncture of no small consequence. Had the "Bayh amendment" become the law of the land, presidential elections since the early 1970s would have been conducted according to new rules and possibly with different outcomes.[124]

A full grasp of this episode requires not simply an understanding of why reform was thwarted (more on that soon) but also how it managed to come so near to success. The drive to replace the Electoral College with an NPV attracted stunningly widespread support for a proposal that had only scattered adherents in the political arena fifteen years earlier, or fifty years before that. For those citizens of the twenty-first century who regard a national popular vote as the most natural and democratic way to choose a president, this surge of support for the idea may seem to have been inevitable, even belated. But historians are rightly taught to be skeptical of explanations that rely heavily on presumptions about the direction of historical change. What needs to be explained is why the sharp rise in congressional support for direct elections occurred in a particular period, under particular conditions—not twenty years earlier, and not twenty years later. That Congress has never come close to adopting a national popular vote since 1970 only underscores the presence of historically specific factors in the 1960s.

One of these factors was ideological: the rise of support for an NPV had roots in a broader *zeitgeist*—in the strengthened embrace of democratic values that was widespread, if not quite global, after World War II and especially in the 1960s. It was during these years that "one person, one vote" became the principle undergirding representation in legislatures and the House of Representatives, while numerous restrictions on the franchise were eliminated by Congress and the courts. Equality, political and social, was celebrated as never before; measures promoting civil rights were passed by Congress; and long-standing discriminatory laws—laws that treated some groups and individuals differently than others—were newly found to violate the Constitution. For men and women who believed in, or came to respect, these democratic principles, it required no great leap of logic or imagination to see the Electoral College as a flawed institution and to conclude that direct national elections were a better fit with the nation's values.

It is not surprising, then, that popular support for a national vote rose in the late 1960s and into the early 1970s, reaching 78 to 80 percent. (See Appendix A.) This was a noticeable, although not a dramatic, shift from the 1940s when the first reliable opinion polls found that roughly two-thirds of adults favored adopting a national popular vote. Importantly, those polls from the 1940s had also revealed that the nation's citizens were far more receptive to the idea than were members of Congress. What this suggests is that the critical shifts in opinion that took place between the 1940s and the late 1960s occurred less in the population at large than among political elites, including members of Congress.

Senators and House members, of course, were themselves affected by the shifting *zeitgeist*, as evidenced by the legislation they passed (such as Lyndon Johnson's Great Society program) and by the stated views of liberals and moderates in both parties. As political actors, moreover, they were also influenced by events and developments in the electoral arena to which they were compelled to pay close, professional attention. Among these was the recurrent appearance of actual or threatened faithless electors, most commonly among southern Democrats who objected to their party's candidate or policies. The incidents of faithlessness never amounted to much, but they pointed a finger at the havoc that intermediaries could wreak. In addition, the close elections of 1948, 1960, and 1968 served as disturbing reminders that a candidate who lost the popular vote could still become president, an outcome that would violate prevailing conceptions of democracy and might, as Richard Nixon observed, make the country ungovernable.[125] The four-candidate contest in 1948 also brought into focus the potential hazards of a contingent election mechanism that seemed not only undemocratic but all too subject to partisan or factional manipulation. Twenty years later, George Wallace's candidacy drove that same point home, prompting both Republicans and northern Democrats to accelerate their efforts to change the system. In their own way, both Strom Thurmond and George Wallace contributed substantially to the cause of Electoral College reform.

These electoral events propelled political leaders from both major parties to search for alternatives to the existing system, yet they did not immediately generate significant support for a national popular vote. In the early postwar years, the reform proposals that had the widest backing were for proportional or district elections. But the decisive defeat of the Lodge-Gossett amendment in the House in 1950 made clear—despite later attempts to revive it—that northern liberal Democrats, as well as some Republicans, would block any proportional election scheme, at least as long as the South remained a one-party region with a disenfranchised minority. Hearings in Congress in the mid-1950s and the early 1960s made it equally clear that district election schemes would have great difficulty gaining the endorsement of two-thirds of Congress—in part because of apprehensions about their political consequences and in part because they would not actually solve the "wrong winner" problem. Proposals for the modest "automatic plan," which would end the threat of faithless electors while locking winner-take-all into the Constitution, also fell by the wayside, without ever gaining many adherents.[126]

By the early 1960s, thus, the reform ideas that had been most prominent for a century and a half had been rejected or so politically weakened that they likely could not be adopted by Congress. Meanwhile, the idea of an NPV was gaining adherents, in part because of its straightforward appeal to democratic principles, and in part because the forceful testimonies of Langer, Pastore, and other small-state politicians were gradually undermining the long-standing objection that a direct election amendment could never be approved. What then followed was a snowball effect—even if, at times, the snowball seemed to be rolling uphill! As other options faded, politicians who were determined to reform the Electoral College gave direct elections a closer look, and the erosion of the small-state argument made the passage of an NPV amendment seem more realistic, a perspective buttressed by opinion polls as well as by endorsements from mainstream organizations like the ABA and the Chamber of Commerce. The stance that had been voiced by men like Lodge and Kefauver—that they preferred an NPV in principle but doubted its prospects—began to melt away in the later 1960s. The key symbolic moment in that transition was Birch Bayh's announcement in 1966 that his views had changed and he had come to favor a national vote.

Bayh's consequential public shift also points to a cluster of contingent, although not entirely fortuitous, factors that contributed to the almost-successful drive for direct elections: the presence of reform advocates in key institutional positions in the Ninety-First Congress. Bayh, of course, was the most prominent, and his chairmanship of the Subcommittee on Constitutional Amendments, after Kefauver's sudden death at the age of sixty, positioned him as a gatekeeper for electoral reform proposals and as the point man for direct elections in the Senate. Similarly, passage of the amendment resolution in the House was facilitated by the powerful chairmanship of its Judiciary Committee being in the hands of Emanuel Celler, a New York liberal with seniority dating back to the Harding administration. It helped too that John McCormack, a Massachusetts Democrat, was Speaker of the House, that Mike Mansfield was the majority leader of the Senate, and that the Republican leaders of the Senate, Hugh Scott and Robert Griffin, were both pro-reform moderates.[127]

One other, more structural, factor warrants mention: the party system and the two national political parties themselves were in flux in the 1960s. Most critically, the tensions between the southern and northern wings of the Democratic Party were reaching a breaking point, with the latter wing becoming increasingly liberal while southern conservatives, led by Thurmond, were beginning their long and permanent migration to the Republican Party. What this meant was that the United States did not have a coherent two-party system in the 1960s. The nation's political forces were divided into three (or arguably four) key factions: northern Democrats, southern Democrats, and a Republican Party that had both conservative and moderate branches. As a consequence, the political responses to electoral reform proposals did not bifurcate along national party lines, as might have happened in a more ideologically stable two-party environment. Instead, the jaggedness and fluidity of the party structure opened up the political space for dramatic reform to receive serious consideration. Politicized responses were factional, rather than partisan, and there were no indications that either national party would be advantaged or disadvantaged by the adoption of direct elections. From the beginning (and at the end), support for reform was bipartisan—as was the opposition.[128]

If a diverse set of circumstances made it possible for an NPV amendment to rise from the political hinterlands to near-passage, an equally varied set of factors contributed to its defeat by slightly more than a third of the Senate. One of these, of course, was structural: the difficulty not only of gaining a two-thirds majority but of doing so through an amendment process that involved multiple committees and numerous veto points. The process, particularly in the Senate, permitted determined minorities to rule. A second factor was simply fear of change—apprehensions about shifting from a flawed but familiar institution to an untried system that might operate in unforeseen ways. "The idea is somewhat new to them," observed Henry Bellmon as he tried to explain why some of his colleagues declined to endorse direct elections. "It will be far wiser" for the country "to stick to the devil it knows," advised the *Wall Street Journal.* A third factor sprang from the limits of the postwar *zeitgeist:* although the impulse to democratize American society and American political institutions was widespread, it was not universal. There was ferocious opposition, largely in the South, to civil rights legislation and the Voting Rights Act, and the Supreme Court's apportionment decisions were denounced by many conservatives nationwide. In some quarters these legal changes were perceived not as democratic advances but as unwelcome intrusions by a too-powerful federal government into local and customary ways of ordering society and politics.[129]

Such perceptions permeated the opposition to direct elections. The conservative Republicans who broke with their own party leadership to vote against cloture were not, for the most part, averse to electoral reform or to amending the Constitution. Mundt, Hruska, and many of their allies were outspoken proponents of replacing winner-take-all with district elections.[130] But they were wary of federal power, and they worried that a national popular vote would invite the federal government to take control of the electoral process and thereby diminish the power of state officials. As importantly, these senators, many from predominantly rural states, feared being dominated by the rapidly growing, and increasingly liberal, urban centers to their east and west. Hruska, for example, lamented that "we who come from States comprising the farm bloc no longer have the power we used to have." He was joined in opposition to an NPV by the American Farm Bureau (which lobbied fiercely on the issue), as well as the National Grange and the National Cotton Council. Peering into the future and imagining that prevailing trends would also lead to the abolition of the Senate, Hruska envisioned a nation in which there would be "dominance of the national picture by the populous States. . . . The rest of the States can resign themselves to the proposition of taking a highly inferior role."[131]

Such sentiments went beyond the purported small-state reluctance to give up the two "senatorial" electoral votes. Hruska, of course, did not want to surrender those votes, and he viewed Nebraska's five electoral votes as a slight check on the "excesses" that large states might perpetrate. But his worries, and those of his Republican colleagues from the western plains and the Rockies, were focused more on broader power shifts, as well as on the sheer number of voters—liberal, Democratic voters—who might be mobilized in the major metropolitan centers. In a similar vein, the predictably conservative *Human Events* forecast that the major beneficiary of a national popular vote would be the "megalopolis," the band of high-population states running from southern New England and the mid-Atlantic to the industrial states of the Great Lakes.[132] What was at issue was less state size than ideology, party, and demographic change in an era of ascendant urban liberalism.[133] Small-state Democrats, notably, voiced no similar fears and strongly favored a national popular vote.

Southern opponents of S.J. Res. 1 shared many of these apprehensions about the growth of federal power and the increasing influence of northern liberals. They felt beleaguered and threatened by Washington, and they worried, with reason, that a national popular vote would invite the federal government to impose national suffrage laws or intrude further into the conduct of elections. As representatives of mostly medium-sized states, southern senators were reluctant to surrender their two "senatorial" electoral votes, and they were concerned that their region would lose even more influence because turnout (among whites) had long been significantly lower in the South than elsewhere. (That fact may have helped fuel Ervin's repeated, and curious, complaint that a popularly elected president would only "represent those who happen to vote on the particular election day.")[134] Southern Democrats, moreover, feared that a national popular vote would diminish the power of state parties and further the domination of their party by its northern wing. In their eyes, other reform options—such as district or proportional schemes—did not possess the same defects.[135]

The southern opposition to direct elections also had gnarlier roots, irretrievably entangled in the region's history of white supremacy and racial exclusion. As recounted in Chapter 4, the South had long rejected, and fiercely attacked, the idea of a national vote because it would directly diminish the electoral power of white southerners while also creating pressure to enfranchise African-Americans throughout the region. Such a prospect was anathema to many white southerners, as Richmond Hobson had discovered in 1914. In addition, numerous southern leaders in the late 1940s and 1950s had come to embrace the view, spelled out in Charles W. Collins's widely read Dixiecrat treatise *Whither Solid South?* (1947), that the Electoral College gave the South the ability to form a regional bloc that could successfully resist northern pressure to end segregation and the disenfranchisement of blacks. Collins, whose book was highly recommended—and freely distributed—by James Eastland, urged southerners to resist "any attempt to do away with the College because it alone can enable the Southern States to preserve their rights within the Union."[136]

That perspective endured into the 1960s, and the southern senators who spearheaded the fight against S.J. Res. 1 had been steeped in it for decades. "The Electoral College is one of the South's few remaining political safeguards," wrote Alabama senator James Allen in October 1969. "Let's keep it." The legal landscape, of course, had changed in the 1960s, thanks to the Voting Rights Act, the Twenty-Fourth Amendment, and numerous Supreme Court decisions: in 1968 three million African-Americans voted in the South. But the long-standing conviction that a national vote was inimical to the interests of white southerners did not dissipate overnight, and it remained the prism through which many of the region's leaders viewed presidential election reform. Its enduring presence helps to explain the animus, the intensity of commitment, that key southern senators brought to the fight against the Bayh amendment.[137] It also helps to explain why Ervin, among others, thought it more important to defeat S.J. Res. 1 than to advance any particular alternative proposal—despite his oft-repeated statements about the need for Electoral College reform.[138]

Ervin, Eastland, and Thurmond, the three primary architects of the filibuster, had, in fact, built their careers by fiercely opposing civil rights measures and by doing everything in their power to preserve the traditional racial order of the South. Thurmond, of course, had bolted the Democratic Party because of civil rights issues; all three had signed (and Ervin had helped to write) the Southern Manifesto in 1956; Eastland had denounced the *Brown* decision as "crap" and urged Mississippians to defy it. Ervin, a Harvard law graduate and former justice of the North Carolina Supreme Court, was appointed to the Judiciary Committee, as well as a key subcommittee, precisely because of his ability to deploy clever and high-sounding constitutional arguments to obstruct or slow civil rights legislation. ("Civil rights are constitutional wrongs," he once declared.) At the heart of many of these efforts was the belief that the federal government was exceeding its constitutional powers by interfering in matters (such as schooling, public accommodations, and voting rights) that had traditionally been controlled by state and local governments. A national popular vote amendment would deepen that trend, potentially weakening state control over elections and enhancing the power of Washington. "The name of this game," declared North Carolina television commentator, and later senator, Jesse Helms in the wake of the House vote, "is absolute centralization of political power in Washington."[139]

Although the handwriting of change was surely on the wall, these senators, and many of their colleagues, were not yet reconciled to the permanence of a new order in the South, to a world without segregation in which African-Americans voted freely and in large numbers. Thurmond would come around in the 1970s, hiring black staff and courting black voters, but in July 1970 he published an article in *Human Events* voicing the hope that recent legal challenges to the renewed Voting Rights Act ("a weapon to penalize the South") might be successful and lead to broader attacks on the law.[140] Ervin shared that hope, arguing not only in 1970 but into the 1980s that the Supreme Court decisions upholding the VRA were erroneously decided and should be reversed.[141] Ervin also maintained repeatedly that he was not aware of any "qualified" citizen having been denied the right to vote in North Carolina because of race. Not surprisingly, nearly all of the southerners who voted against cloture opposed the 1970 renewal of the Voting Rights Act.[142]

As long as Ervin, Thurmond, and others clung to the hope that black enfranchisement could be rolled back or even slowed down (only half of all African-Americans in the South voted in 1968), they did not want to see a national popular vote replace the Electoral College. Direct elections would only weaken, or further jeopardize, the fading political order that they were dedicated to preserving. If barriers to black voting, such as literacy tests, could somehow be preserved or reinstated, then white southerners would prefer to avoid the distasteful choices that would arise under a federally mandated popular vote regime. If such a rollback proved impossible and African-Americans were to be permanently enfranchised, an NPV could still have undesirable consequences, such as preventing the formation of an influential southern bloc of electoral votes or stimulating black turnout, which could impact local and state races in addition to the contest for the presidency.[143] The South's political future appeared uncertain in 1970, uncertain and difficult to read, and the Electoral College seemed far more likely than direct elections to help sustain the old order.

Then too, there was the Wallace factor. Southern senators were not, on the whole, great fans of the Alabama governor or his forays into presidential politics. Thurmond had abandoned third-party politics and campaigned for Nixon in 1968, while Democrats like Stennis, Talmadge, Richard Russell, Ervin, and Eastland remained publicly loyal to their party.[144] These senators knew well that the South was not a political monolith and that many white southerners rejected Wallace's loud racism and regretted his national prominence. At the same time, they were aware that Wallace enjoyed great popularity in some strata of southern society; he had won much of the deep South in 1968 and did well in other states, including North and South Carolina. They also recognized that the Bayh amendment was widely viewed as an effort to prevent Wallace, or any like-minded regional candidate, from wielding influence in a national election. (Ervin, in a draft speech, called it the "Bye-Bye Wallace" amendment.) Adamant opposition to Bayh's measure, thus, carried political benefits. All of the senators from states that Wallace had won voted against cloture on September 17; twelve days later, only Louisiana's Russell Long broke ranks.[145] Two days after that second cloture vote, the *Atlanta Constitution* editorialized that the defeat of reform in the Senate would benefit Wallace and harm Nixon's chances of being reelected. It also published a cartoon depicting Wallace speaking to Ervin and saying "Thanks, Senator. Things are LOOKING GOOD!"[146]

Although the filibuster against electoral reform would not have succeeded without the votes and voices of conservative Republicans, its animating energy and tactical sharpness came from the South, from men with abundant experience utilizing the rules of the Senate to thwart the will of majorities. It rightly belongs in the line of filibusters that southerners mounted to impede the adoption of democratizing reforms—both political and social—in the 1950s and 1960s. Convinced that direct elections constituted a grave threat to the South, and with the backing of most of their regional colleagues, Thurmond, Eastland, and Ervin took advantage of their strategic positions on the Judiciary Committee to stall consideration of electoral reform for a year after the House had endorsed it by an overwhelming vote. Once the issue finally reached the Senate floor, a determined southern caucus chose not to seriously debate or negotiate but rather to prevent the Senate from voting. It successfully induced the more-divided Republican opposition to follow its lead and, together, they shrewdly exploited the intricacies of Senate procedure to block a change that was clearly desired by a large majority of the American people.[147]

Although advocates of reform came tantalizingly close to achieving a goal that had been pursued since the early nineteenth century, the upshot of this dramatic episode was the preservation of an institution that had notably few contemporary defenders.[148] In the years of hearings and debates that unfolded between 1966 and 1970, almost no one argued that the Electoral College, with winner-take-all, was the best way to choose a president—or even a particularly good and reasonable way to do so. (The minority report of the Senate Judiciary Committee took a stab at such a claim, but its words rang hollow, coming from senators who had actively promoted other reforms.) Nor did opponents of direct elections openly reject the democratic principles that advocates of an NPV so strongly stressed: no member of Congress made the case that the votes of some people should count for more than the votes of others or that it was acceptable for a candidate other than the winner of the popular vote to be inaugurated as president. Opponents maintained instead that "arithmetic equality" was desirable but not of paramount importance and that the likelihood of a "wrong winner" was extremely low. As is often the case with electoral reform, the opposition to change was grounded less in principles or in differing visions of ideal electoral institutions than in apprehensions about the political consequences of doing things differently.[149] Those apprehensions, concentrated in three dozen members of the Senate, closed the window on the twentieth century's best opportunity to rid the nation of an institution that most citizens, and most political leaders, had come to regard as archaic, undemocratic, and dangerous.

SIX

LAST CALL FOR THE TWENTIETH CENTURY

The presidential election of 1976 was a cliff-hanger. The television networks waited until 3:30 in the morning to declare Jimmy Carter the winner, and even then, some uncertainty lingered. Carter had a lead of 1.7 million votes in the popular tally, but his margin in the Electoral College was precarious. He had won several states by razor-thin margins, and a switch of fewer than 4,000 votes in Hawaii and 6,000 in Ohio would have given President Gerald Ford an Electoral College victory.

Shortly after that long, tense election night, Birch Bayh placed a phone call to Senator Henry Bellmon, the Oklahoma Republican with whom he had worked closely in 1969–1970. "Henry, what do you think?" Bayh asked. "Do you think we ought to give it another try?" Bellmon replied that he had been intending to call Bayh. If the election "had backfired and Ford had been elected, it would have been good for the Republicans but it would have been bad for the Republic."[1]

Thus began the final chapter in the quest of Birch Bayh and his congressional colleagues to replace the Electoral College with direct presidential elections. This episode would unfold over two and a half years, beginning in January 1977 and reaching its anticlimactic conclusion in the summer of 1979. In many respects it was an echo, a rerun, of what had transpired in the late 1960s and 1970. Most of the arguments put forward by both advocates and opponents of reform were the same as they had been a decade earlier, and there were repeat performances by many of the *dramatis personae.* Once again the Senate was the decisive arena, with the legislative journey of the proposed constitutional amendment governed by that chamber's distinctive rules.

Yet there were also key differences, including the active support (at least for a time) of a Democratic occupant of the White House and the presence, by 1979, of sixty senators who had not engaged in the battles of 1970. (Twenty new senators, an unusually large number, were elected in 1978 alone.) Of equal importance, the political climate had shifted considerably between 1969–1970 and the late 1970s. The war in Vietnam had, at long last, come to an end, removing a bitterly divisive issue from the national agenda, but nagging economic problems had unsettled Washington and the nation for much of the decade. The Democratic Party retained its majorities in Congress, but its liberal wing had suffered stinging defeats in the presidential election of 1972 and the primary campaigns of 1976. The Republicans, meanwhile, were regrouping after the scandals of Watergate and the resignations of both a vice president and a president. In the South, white leaders were coming to accept the permanence of African-American enfranchisement and to accommodate a new electorate as well as shifting partisan lineups. The African-American community was flexing its muscles nationally and looking beyond the voting rights and civil rights victories of the 1960s. George Wallace was again governor of Alabama although, after surviving an assassination attempt in 1972, he had ceased to be a factor in presidential politics.

This last major reform attempt of the twentieth century, thus, unfolded with the country in a far different mood than it had been just a decade earlier. The renewed campaign to get rid of the Electoral College began auspiciously, with many participants and observers believing, well into 1979, that a national popular vote would finally be adopted. It ended in a decisive failure tinged with historical ironies.[2]

Chronology: The Winding Road Revisited

Although the failure to break the filibuster in 1970 had been a severe blow to the cause of electoral reform, its advocates in Congress had not abandoned hope. Proposals for constitutional amendments were introduced, by members of both parties, in every Congress in the early to mid-1970s, and in 1972 the platform of the Democratic Party—which had solid congressional majorities throughout the decade—called for the abolition of the Electoral College "to give every voter a direct and equal voice in Presidential elections." It was widely believed that the House would again endorse a direct election proposal, but its leadership understandably preferred to let the Senate act first.[3]

Before the 1976 election, however, there was little movement in the Senate. In September 1973, Bayh's Subcommittee on Constitutional Amendments held two days of hearings on his new proposal (S.J. Res. 1), which was transparently, if perhaps too ingeniously, designed to win over those who had objected to the runoff provision in 1970. It called for direct elections while retaining roles for both Congress and the existing electoral system: a popular vote winner with more than 40 percent of the vote would become president, as would a plurality winner with less than 40 percent who had been victorious in states with the equivalent of a majority of the nation's electoral votes. If no candidate reached either of those thresholds, the decision would be made by a joint session of Congress.[4] The proposal gained bipartisan support, including an endorsement from President Nixon's Justice Department, and was approved unanimously by Bayh's subcommittee, but the full Judiciary Committee gave it no further consideration. The hearings themselves attracted little attention, in or out of Congress—a sign both of diminished interest in electoral reform and the nation's growing preoccupation with the Watergate scandal and the brewing impeachment of a president.[5]

Two years later, in May 1975, Bayh's reconstituted subcommittee again endorsed a direct elections proposal, this time dropping the idea of electoral vote equivalents and handing the decision directly to a joint session of Congress if no candidate won more than 40 percent of the vote. Despite having forty-four co-sponsors, including a dozen Republicans, Bayh was unable to move the resolution through the Judiciary Committee, in part because of adamant southern opposition. The obstacles and veto points built into the amendment process remained as salient as they had been in 1970.[6]

Meanwhile, political scientists and other analysts set out to provide answers to some of the questions that had been hotly debated, and never fully resolved, in 1969–1970. Which states and social groups would gain or lose influence if the nation jettisoned the Electoral College and adopted direct elections? Small states, obviously, would surrender some electoral power, but would the same be true of large urban states that were also widely viewed as being advantaged by winner-take-all? (And if large states were to lose influence, who would gain?) Would direct elections harm the interests of African-Americans and other minorities (or urban liberals, as

Alex Bickel had repeatedly claimed)? Articles and books poured forth, some of them polemics, others serious empirical investigations, laced with statistics and often buttressed by mathematical models, many of them variants on John Banzhaf's celebrated model of "voting power."[7]

The upshot of these efforts was murky, at best. Some scholars maintained that the Electoral College enhanced the electoral clout of large states and metropolitan areas, whereas others maintained that only urban voters were advantaged. A strongly argued book by political scientist Harvey Zeidenstein concluded that the Electoral College did not "bestow special advantages" on either small states or urban residents of large states but that it did advantage "some southern states." Several scholars concluded that African-Americans did gain influence from their potentially pivotal role in large urban states; others found that to be untrue or argued that a national popular vote offered greater benefits to the black community as a whole, particularly given the large number of African-Americans still living in the South. In sum, the net effects of transforming the electoral system remained impossible to gauge with precision and seemed likely to vary as the partisan and demographic makeup of states and cities changed over time. Social science did not resolve the conflicts between competing political predictions, although as one carefully couched article pointed out, all of the studies made clear that biases and inequities abounded under the Electoral College.[8]

The 1976 election jolted Congress back into action. Birch Bayh and Henry Bellmon were hardly the only members who were shaken by the close call, which had been anticipated by some analysts before the election.[9] Not only was the election another "near miss" (in which the winner of the popular vote came within a whisker of not moving into the White House), but it was a close enough near miss that the losing ticket had contemplated a behind-the-scenes effort to see if they could reverse the outcome—much as critics of the Electoral College had long feared and predicted. As vice presidential candidate Robert (Bob) Dole affably acknowledged after the election, the Republicans, knowing that the Ohio vote would be subject to an automatic recount, began "shopping" for potentially faithless electors elsewhere who could get the Republicans over the top if they did end up winning Ohio. "We were looking around for electors," he acknowledged, naming a few states where they concentrated their efforts.[10] Politicians also knew that Jimmy Carter (and the Electoral College) had dodged a different bullet in New York. Eugene McCarthy, the iconoclastic liberal and former Democratic senator, had run as an independent candidate in thirty states, including New York. At the very last minute, however, the New York State Court of Appeals, responding to lawsuits launched by the state Democratic Party, decided to remove McCarthy's name from the ballot on highly technical grounds, involving the formatting of his signature petitions. Some observers believed that had he remained on the ballot, McCarthy might have attracted enough votes from liberals, who were lukewarm about Carter, to deliver New York and the presidency to Gerald Ford.[11]

In the weeks following the election, the nation's editorial (and op-ed) pages bristled with calls for the abolition of the Electoral College and the adoption of direct elections. The day after the election, the *Chicago Tribune* published a column by Jerald terHorst, Ford's former press secretary, demanding that Congress take action. The *Seattle Post-Intelligencer* declared that the "Electoral College System Must Go." "Abolish the College," insisted the *Rocky Mountain News*, only to be outdone in vehemence by the *Washington Post*'s call to "Demolish the College." The *Austin American-Statesman* urged Senator Bayh "to take up the cudgel again this year while the memory of . . . last November still is fresh."[12] Such views, to be sure, were not unanimous: the *Wall Street Journal*, for example, stressed the need to retain the Electoral College as one of the few remaining vestiges of federalism. Even some liberal newspapers, like the *Boston Globe*, urged caution—although within a few months the *Globe* would strongly back direct elections.[13] Perhaps the most surprising stance was that of the *New York Times*, which had been a strong advocate of direct elections in 1969–1970: two weeks after the 1976 election, the *Times* ran an editorial pointing to potential problems with a national vote and urging reformers to focus instead on eliminating electors and changing the contingent election system. The same issue of the newspaper contained a column by Tom Wicker favoring direct election.[14]

Meanwhile in Washington, Bayh, still chair of the Subcommittee on Constitutional Amendments, moved quickly, introducing Senate Joint Resolution 1 (S.J. Res. 1) on January 10, 1977; the resolution had forty-one co-sponsors. Reverting to the direct elections formula of 1969–1970, the resolution called for a national popular vote, with a runoff between the top two candidates if neither received 40 percent of the vote. Bayh made it clear that he and his allies strongly preferred a runoff to the alternative of a joint session of Congress because only a runoff could ensure that an incoming president had the backing of a majority of voters. He characterized his proposal as "the longest considered and most carefully debated constitutional amendment in the history of our country." A variety of companion resolutions were introduced in the House, although it was understood that the House would not move forward until after the Senate had acted.[15]

Less than three weeks later, hearings began under the auspices of the Judiciary Committee.[16] Bayh opened the proceedings on January 27 by underscoring the lessons of the recent election, observing that the "archaic electoral college came closer to defeating the popular will" than it had in either 1960 or 1968; a switch of "one-hundredth of 1 percent of the popular vote" would have kept Jimmy Carter from taking office. He also noted that the record of his subcommittee's hearings on Electoral College reform, beginning in 1966, was nearly 2,600 pages in length. The testimony of scores of witnesses added 600 pages to that total by the time the five days of hearings concluded in February; more than a few of the witnesses had testified in earlier years, and most of the testimony repeated arguments and viewpoints that had been put forward in the 1960s. "I admit to being somewhat hard pressed to find something new to say on this subject," observed Ruth Clusen, president of the League of Women Voters. "The American people have been ready for this for a long time," she added. "We hope that Congress is too."[17]

The most emotionally resonant testimony came from two men who had been candidates for national office, Senators Hubert Humphrey and Bob Dole. Humphrey, a former vice president who had returned to the Senate after his failed presidential bid in 1968, recalled that he had been testifying against the Electoral College for decades and urged Congress to act "while we have fresh in our memories the potential chaos of 1968 and 1976." A large and ebullient personality, Humphrey may have felt the press of time acutely because he had already been diagnosed with the cancer that would end his life a year later. The "present system," he insisted, "is a violation of democratic principle"; he also thought it regrettable that presidential candidates—himself included—ignored large sections of the country during election campaigns. Dole was characteristically more succinct but no less firm in his embrace of direct elections. There were simply "too many built-in pitfalls" in the current system, and he believed that, contrary to the claims of critics, direct elections would strengthen the two-party system and enhance the influence of small-state residents, without advantaging or disadvantaging either party. "The beauty of the direct election is its simplicity, its straightforwardness," he observed. "It's easily understood by the electorate, it's easily administered." "These characteristics are vitally important," he concluded, referring obliquely to the Watergate scandal, "if we're going to regain that public confidence or if we're going to restore that public confidence in the electoral system."[18]

A less well known witness who offered politically promising testimony to Bayh's committee was Representative Jack Edwards of Alabama. Edwards, whose career in the House had begun in 1965, was one of the first Republicans elected to Congress from the deep South since the nineteenth century; unlike some others in that cohort, he came from a longtime Republican family and was not an anti-civil-rights defector from the Democratic Party. A respected figure, Edwards sponsored one of the companion resolutions to S.J. Res. 1 and noted proudly that he had also voted for direct elections in 1969. That an Alabama representative was so actively supporting an NPV suggested to Bayh and others that it might be possible to crack the wall of southern opposition. In response to questions, Edwards indicated that several of the newspapers in his district "had concluded that I am right, I am happy to say." He also promised to promote the ratification of a direct elections amendment in Alabama, if the measure got that far. "I think if we take the time to explain it," he concluded, "the people will understand."[19]

Supporters of direct election received a boost in late March when President Jimmy Carter sent a message to Congress advocating an array of electoral reforms, including election-day voter registration, public financing of congressional elections, and a constitutional amendment to replace the Electoral College with a national popular vote. Carter, like many other leaders, was worried about declining electoral turnout as well as the loss of trust in government prompted by the Watergate scandal. Still, his unequivocal endorsement of direct elections was somewhat unexpected because he had in the past—even the recent past—appeared to favor more modest reforms. Vice President Walter Mondale, on the other hand, was known as a stalwart backer of direct elections, and Carter, according to some reports, relied on Mondale's judgment as he finalized his reform proposals. The president's views may also have been influenced by his own "near miss" in 1976 and by a strong pro-reform letter from the presidents of six major organizations, including the American Bar Association and the League of Women Voters. Whatever its sources, Carter's message meant that, for the first time, a sitting president—and a southerner at that—was publicly committed to a national popular vote.[20] "Mr. Carter's backing hopefully will provide the necessary impetus to move the Electoral College measure toward approval this time in both houses of Congress," predicted the *Denver Post*. The president's "endorsement is a shift in his position," noted the *Raleigh News and Observer*, signaling support for the measure among southern moderates, "and should hasten the end of a system designed for times when the electorate was regarded as an uneducated rabble and when the communication of information took weeks or months, not seconds."[21]

The drive for direct elections was buoyed by public opinion polls conducted during the first six months of 1977. A widely reported Gallup poll released in February found that 75 percent of the American people approved of replacing the Electoral College with a national vote, while only 15 percent disapproved; even in the South, where support was weakest, two-thirds of all respondents preferred direct elections. Seventy-nine percent of Republicans and 71 percent of Democrats favored a national popular vote, with support widespread across lines of gender, age, and levels of education. Only among two groups did support for direct elections fall below 60 percent: southern Democrats (57 percent) and nonwhites (48 percent).[22] At the end of May, Louis Harris released a poll with similar findings, including the notable gap between black and white preferences. The Harris poll also offered some breakdowns that Gallup had not included. Protestants, Catholics, and Jews (a remarkable 88 percent) all heavily favored direct election, as did residents of cities, suburbs, and rural areas; the same was true of executives, professionals, and blue-collar workers. Citizens who had voted for Ford and Carter preferred an NPV in roughly equal proportions (74 and 77 percent), while more than 70 percent of those who identified as conservative, liberal, or "middle of road" were on board with the proposed constitutional amendment.[23] As Birch Bayh observed in the Senate, all of the recent polling indicated that the preference for an NPV was "nation-wide and fairly even distributed throughout the country."[24]

Positive sentiment about direct elections, however, was less widespread in the Senate than among the nation's citizens—as had also been true in the late 1960s. Urban, liberal-leaning states were underrepresented in the chamber, many southern Democrats continued to oppose an NPV, and despite the presence of prominent Republican advocates (including Dole and minority leader Howard Baker), more conservative members of the GOP, who were numerous, displayed little interest in jettisoning the Electoral College. Indeed, in late April the Republican National Committee, increasingly reflecting the views of Ronald Reagan and his wing of the party, declared its opposition to President Carter's entire electoral reform package. (Reagan described Carter's reforms as an effort to destroy the Republican Party and "institutionalize one-party rule" in the United States; in barely coded language, he stated that eliminating the Electoral College "would almost certainly result in presidential elections being decided by swing votes in a handful of the largest cities.") In part because of this opposition, most of Carter's proposals were dead in the water by the end of the year, and the debate over Electoral College reform took on a more partisan cast than it had a decade earlier.[25] Congressional opponents of direct election, moreover, resorted once again to a strategy of delay, obliging Bayh and his allies to spend more than two years wrestling with an array of procedural obstacles that must have been all too reminiscent of 1969–1970.[26]

The opposition's tactical approach became apparent in June 1977 when Bayh, having spent the spring working to bring undecided colleagues on board, sought to bring the amendment to a vote in the Judiciary Committee, which was still chaired by James Eastland. As soon as the issue was brought forward, Bill Scott, the first Republican senator from Virginia since Reconstruction, immediately moved to recommit the measure to the subcommittee—which would effectively have killed it. Scott's motion was tabled by a narrow nine to eight margin, with the decisive vote cast over the phone by Robert Byrd of West Virginia, who had become majority leader after Mike Mansfield's retirement the previous January. Scott then began to filibuster Bayh's amendment within the Judiciary Committee, the same tactic that Strom Thurmond (still a committee member) had deployed for months in 1969–1970. Bayh, fearing that the momentum generated by the recent election would dissipate, responded with a threat to bypass the committee and have the resolution placed directly on the Senate calendar, an unusual stratagem that he had used successfully in 1971 to bring the Equal Rights Amendment to the floor. He also accused Scott of attempting to prevent the direct elections resolution from coming to any vote at all. "You're not willing to trust the will of the Senate or even the Judiciary Committee," he declared.[27] Scott may have been a newcomer to the Senate, but this was not Birch Bayh's first Electoral College rodeo.

The impasse was broken a month later when Scott ended his filibuster as part of a committee agreement promising a vote in September, to be preceded by additional hearings at which opponents of direct elections would have ample time to air their views. The hearings, held in late July and August, featured testimony from numerous defenders of the Electoral College, including academics Aaron Wildavsky, Herbert Storing, and Martin Diamond, an increasingly prominent conservative political scientist who was a sharp critic of direct elections and a forceful celebrant of the virtues of the Electoral College. The committee also heard from a few new advocates of direct elections, including Joseph Caudle, a member of West Virginia's House of Delegates, who reported that his state's legislature had, under Article V of the U.S. Constitution, passed a resolution calling for a constitutional convention to abolish the Electoral College and institute a national popular vote. Overall, the hearings attracted little attention and did not appear to change the minds of any Judiciary Committee members. What did draw attention was the sudden, tragic death of Diamond, who collapsed from a fatal heart attack shortly after completing his testimony.[28]

The Judiciary Committee finally voted on September 15, 1977. Replicating the dynamics of 1969–1970, southern opponents of direct elections put forward a series of substitute amendments (for district elections, proportional elections, and an "automatic" plan). All were narrowly defeated, as was a later proposal by James Allen of Alabama to replace the runoff election with a joint session of Congress. The committee then voted nine to eight to approve S.J. Res. 1. The favorable votes were cast by non-southern Democrats and by Republican Charles Mathias of Maryland. The opposition consisted of three southern Democrats, two southern Republicans, and three mountain-state Republicans.[29] A substantial committee report, offering majority, minority, and "additional" views, was submitted on December 6, 1977.[30]

Then nothing happened—for more than a year. (For Bayh, this must have felt like "déjà vu all over again," in the immortal words of New York Yankees catcher Yogi Berra.) Jimmy Carter, preoccupied with other issues, had gone silent on election reform; the Senate calendar was clogged with pressing business well into 1978; and Majority Leader Byrd was reluctant to schedule S.J. Res. 1 for a floor debate until Bayh could establish that he had the sixty votes needed to break the filibuster that loomed ahead.[31] (Thanks to a change made to Rule XXII in 1975, invoking cloture now required sixty votes rather than two-thirds of those voting. Bayh, among others, believed that this shift would make it easier to shut off debate and pass an amendment.) Although Bayh assured Byrd more than once that he had the votes to defeat a filibuster, Byrd chose to prioritize other issues and to not risk letting the Senate get bogged down, particularly in the busy final months of 1978. (One key item before Congress during those months was extending the time period for ratification of the Equal Rights Amendment, another cause important to Bayh.) The Ninety-Fifth Congress consequently adjourned without taking any further action on Electoral College reform, although the Senate leadership promised to bring the issue to the floor early in 1979, once a new Congress had been seated.[32]

While Bayh was waiting for the Senate leadership to place S.J. Res. 1 on the calendar in 1978, a new proposal had been thrust into the public arena, put forward by a prestigious task force of political analysts, strategists, and scholars assembled by the Twentieth Century Fund. The task force, which included both advocates and opponents of direct election, managed to unite its diverse factions behind a scheme called the National Bonus Plan. Under this plan, the Electoral College would continue to operate as it long had, but the winner of the national popular vote would be awarded an additional 102 electoral votes (two for each state and the District of Columbia). The plan's appeal was that it would effectively guarantee victory to the winner of the national vote, while appearing to preserve the role of states in presidential elections and to protect the major parties against incursions from splinter parties. Although he made clear that he still favored direct elections, Bayh took the strategic step in March 1978 of introducing an amendment resolution to implement the National Bonus Plan—to ensure that it would be discussed in the Senate. Despite its ingenuity and pedigree, the bonus plan proved inconsequential, never gaining much traction in or outside of Congress. Bayh was not alone in concluding that it was something of a "sham," a "direct election masquerading as the Electoral College."[33]

As the Senate leadership had directed, Bayh reintroduced the direct elections amendment, now relabeled Senate Joint Resolution 28 (S.J. Res. 28), on January 15, 1979. The passage of more than two years since the Carter-Ford election had, once again, slowed the momentum for reform and diminished the sense of urgency spawned by a close presidential election. It was also apparent that no action taken in the Ninety-Sixth Congress could be implemented in time for the 1980 election. The delays did, however, have one silver lining: changes in the membership of the Judiciary Committee rendered it far more sympathetic to direct elections. Scott and Eastland had retired at the end of the Ninety-Fifth Congress, and two other opponents of reform—John McClellan of Arkansas and James Allen—had died in 1978. (Sam Ervin, a particular thorn in Bayh's side in 1969–1970, was long gone, having decided not to seek reelection in 1974.) The new chair of the committee was Massachusetts senator Edward Kennedy, a committed backer of direct elections. Bayh's resolution had thirty-eight co-sponsors, including twelve Republicans.[34]

In light of both the long trail of procedural delays and the certainty of Judiciary Committee approval, Bayh attempted to speed things up by bypassing the committee and placing the issue directly on the Senate calendar. Orrin Hatch of Utah, the ranking Republican on Bayh's subcommittee, objected to this maneuver, pointing out that there were six new members of the Judiciary Committee who had not participated in its previous deliberations.[35] Nonetheless, Bayh brought his resolution to the Senate floor on March 14, opening the debate—in an almost empty Senate chamber, before the "half-shut eyes of twenty spectators"—with an impassioned review of both the resolution's history and the need for reform.[36] After "43 days of hearings, including 9 in the last Congress," he declared, it was time for the Senate "to come to grips with the issue on the merits." In response, Hatch, who was becoming the point man for the opposition, listed numerous substantive objections to direct elections and insisted that it was simply "wrong not to have committee hearings on this matter," given the presence of not only new committee members but also twenty new senators in the chamber (and a total of forty-eight who were in their first terms.) The next day a compromise was reached, with Bayh agreeing—again—to additional hearings in return for assurances that the amendment could be brought up on the Senate floor after June 1. Strategically, Bayh had little choice—he did not want to hand his adversaries a procedural club with which to attack the resolution—but the Indiana senator's annoyance was palpable. He could not resist pointing out that in 1977 senators Scott and Thurmond had demanded more hearings, but when the hearings were held, Scott attended for only part of one day and Thurmond never showed up at all.[37]

"I must admit to a certain sense of having been here before," Bayh acknowledged as he opened the hearings less than two weeks later. Indeed, many of the witnesses (including James Michener, Theodore White, Barry Goldwater, and Bob Dole) had testified at earlier hearings, and there was little said in the four days of hearings that Bayh and others had not heard before. The most notable development was the lengthy discussion sparked by the testimony of Vernon E. Jordan Jr., who was president of the National Urban League and chair of the Black Leadership Forum. Expanding on views that he had expressed often since the election of Jimmy Carter, Jordan sharply criticized the plan to replace the Electoral College with direct elections as being inimical to the interests of African-Americans. (More on that below.) The hearings also featured a deft exchange between Bayh and Jeane Kirkpatrick, a political science professor at Georgetown who warned of the possible harms that could come from direct elections. "Remedies produce ills, I think," she concluded. "But sometimes they save the patient," Bayh quickly retorted.[38]

After the hearings were completed on April 9, the Judiciary Committee, without a vote, reported S.J. Res. 28 back to the Senate floor, filing its written report early in May. The majority report was more extensive and more thoroughly argued than its earlier incarnations had been; in addition to making the affirmative case for direct elections, it also sought to rebut, one by one, the major objections that had been raised to an NPV. The "minority and additional views," authored by Hatch, Thurmond, and Republican Alan Simpson of Wyoming, were far more temperate in tone than the Ervin-inflected minority report of 1970 had been. Hatch and Simpson maintained that there was no need for Electoral College reform, while Thurmond, resurrecting the Lodge-Gossett proposal of 1950, argued that it was essential to eliminate winner-take-all and that the best way to do so would be through a proportional allocation of electoral votes. All three agreed that "direct election would create more problems than it would solve." The stage was set for the resolution to be debated on the Senate floor in June—and for the filibuster that everyone believed was coming.[39]

The Arguments

MOSTLY OLD

Much of the public debate between 1976 and 1979 rehashed arguments and claims that had been put forward a decade earlier (and in some cases, for decades before that). Advocates of an NPV insisted that there were "dangerous flaws" in the Electoral College system: the possibility of a "wrong winner," the hazards of faithless electors, the distortions wrought by winner-take-all, and a contingent election procedure that everyone prayed would never be set in motion. Bayh also stressed the danger of an election being brokered by a third-party candidate, citing a 1968 interview in which George Wallace indicated that if no candidate won an outright majority of the electoral votes, he expected to cut a deal with Nixon or Humphrey before the electors gathered to cast their votes. Alongside these criticisms of the Electoral College, proponents of S.J. Res. 28 reiterated, and emphasized, their core affirmative argument: that only a national popular vote, with a runoff election, was consistent with the "American principle of equal treatment under law." "Direct election," observed the majority report in 1979, "would insure that every vote counts, that all votes count the same, and that the candidate with the most votes wins." "It is time for every vote in the State of Arkansas to count just as much as it does in the state of Arizona or in the state of New York," declared Senator David Pryor, a moderate Arkansas Democrat who was sharply critical of efforts to gauge which states or populations benefited most from the Electoral College. The Electoral College, intoned Bob Dole, "is a perversion of democracy, which should demand victory for the candidate who receives the largest number of popular votes." That this perspective was shared by a large majority of the American people lent strength to its democratic pedigree.[40]

The opposition sounded equally familiar notes. An NPV would weaken federalism and reduce the power of the states.[41] It would vest too much power in large urban centers and diminish the influence of small states, leading to their being ignored during election campaigns. "I do not want to see a system," Thurmond declared in 1979, "where 12 big-city states can practically elect a President, where the candidates will have little inducement to go into the smaller states." An NPV, wrote John W. Scott of the farm organization, the National Grange, "would leave us with a voice but our words would never be heard."[42] Direct elections would encourage splinter parties and possibly destroy the two-party system; they could also yield a "sectionalist president" (presumably from the most populated regions of the country); they would likely lead to rampant fraud, as Theodore White had insisted in the 1960s; and they "will turn Presidential elections into centralized media ... events removed from the people of this country."[43] Runoffs, moreover, would be expensive and produce uncertainty, "which creates political intrigue and magnifies the likelihood of violence." A national ballot would also lead inescapably to Congress taking control over elections, further centralizing power in Washington.[44]

The rebuttals to these claims were also familiar, although they were pressed more strenuously in the 1970s than in earlier years. Federalism, in the oft-cited words of the venerated Mike Mansfield, was not strengthened "through an antiquated device which has not worked as it was intended to work." More combatively, Stephen Schlossberg, general counsel of the United Auto Workers and a member of the ABA commission on electoral reform, testified in 1977 that the federalism objections served as "a cloak to hide the refusal to allow people to elect their officeholders." (The ABA, in 1977, issued an updated version of its 1967 report endorsing direct elections.)[45] Small-state arguments were similarly dismissed. Howard Baker, Frank Church (Idaho), and Hawaii's Spark Matsunaga (among others) insisted that the small-state advantage in electoral votes was far outweighed by the advantages that accrued to large states under winner-take-all. "Coming from a small state," Church noted, "I am well aware of the argument of those who maintain that popular election ... would deprive the less populous states of the relative mathematical advantage they presently possess in the electoral college. In the real world, it simply does not work that way." Evidence was abundant, moreover, that candidates rarely visited small states during campaigns, and as Patrick Leahy (Vermont), Jake Garn (Utah), and John Chafee (Rhode Island) pointed out, most of the people residing in small states favored direct elections. Both Leahy, a Democrat, and Garn, a Republican, maintained that the small states would be better off under an NPV than they were with the Electoral College. Jack Edwards noted drily that "the large populous states could hardly have more leverage than they have now under the Electoral College system."[46]

Advocates of direct elections also discounted as conjecture the notion that an NPV would spawn splinter parties and destroy the two-party system. Dole, Leahy, and Douglas Bailey, the media manager of the Ford campaign, went further, maintaining that the two-party system would be strengthened by a national vote, in part because both parties would be encouraged to seek votes and build organizations in "safe" states.[47] Proponents also argued that election fraud was more likely to occur under the existing system than in a national election, because winner-take-all made it possible for a small number of fraudulent votes to deliver all of a state's electoral votes. Responding to concerns about runoffs, Bayh insisted that they would occur rarely, would be manageable if they did occur, and were preferable to any other arrangement, such as a joint session of Congress, that might lead to bargaining rather than the popular election of a president.[48] As had been true in the late 1960s, Bayh and his allies offered little resistance to the claim that an NPV might lead to congressional oversight of election rules and procedures.

A FEW THINGS NEW

A few new arguments made their way into the mix. Reform proponents, for example, maintained that an NPV would increase voter turnout, which had long been mediocre and had declined noticeably from 62 percent in 1964 to less than 54 percent in 1976. They attributed the low turnout, in part, to the "fact" that "people are smart enough to know that in the Electoral College their votes do not count in some circumstances."[49] The decline was also seen as a sign of deepening alienation from politics and government, spawned by the divisive war in Vietnam and the political scandals of the Watergate era. "It is hardly news that we are experiencing a crisis of confidence in our government institutions today," testified Lucy Wilson Benson of the League of Women Voters. "The credibility gap we have heard so much about in the Johnson years has become a chasm in the wake of Watergate."[50] A national popular vote, it was believed, would promote civic engagement and participation, giving citizens everywhere an incentive to show up at the polls. "Abolition of the Electoral College will be a large step in increasing each citizen's sense of participation in his government," emphasized Richard Schweiker, a Pennsylvania Republican, in 1977. Conversely, popular distrust of politicians and of government might be heightened if Congress declined to adopt a reform that was so heavily favored by the American people.[51]

Critics of direct elections made two important additions to their roster of arguments. The first was that there was simply no need for reform: the Electoral College "has served the country well," concluded John Stennis of Mississippi. A decade earlier most opponents of an NPV had accepted the premise that the Electoral College was seriously flawed while arguing that the flaws would best be remedied through district, proportional, or automatic plans. By the late 1970s such views were less prominent (although Thurmond stuck to his guns in support of a proportional plan). In their stead, opponents defended the Electoral College as "a more than workable system that has proven its effectiveness."[52]

Among the building blocks in the argument that the institution had worked "tolerably well" (as the *Wall Street Journal* put it) were denials that the ostensible defects of the Electoral College were, in fact, particularly important or dangerous.[53] "One wonders," wrote Orrin Hatch in 1977, "whether the 'faithless elector' is really a serious problem." After all, faithless electors were few in number and had never affected the outcome of an election. Although Hatch did favor changes to the contingent election procedure, the "meager" benefits of abolishing the office of elector "do not justify the effort to pass a constitutional amendment."[54]

"Equally chimerical" were fears that "the present system can elect a President who has fewer popular votes than his opponent." Hatch and his allies believed that the odds of such an event occurring were minuscule, and they reinterpreted the historical record (not altogether implausibly) to suggest that "wrong winner" elections had occurred less frequently than was commonly believed. The traditional narrative that Andrew Jackson had won the popular vote but not the presidency in 1824, thus, did not take into account that the legislatures of six states chose electors without holding a popular vote. In 1876 Samuel Tilden's ostensible popular vote victory over Rutherford Hayes came in an election in which "both parties engaged in widespread fraud," making it impossible to determine which candidate really had the most support. Even the 1888 election may not have been a clear-cut case of the popular vote winner (Grover Cleveland) losing the Electoral College, because the suppression of black votes in the South might have illegitimately reduced the totals for Benjamin Harrison. "Wrong winner" elections, in this telling, had been exceedingly rare in American history. Austin Ranney, a prominent political scientist then based at the conservative American Enterprise Institute, summed up the opposition perspective by testifying that the chances of a "wrong winner" "ever happening again are very slim." The minority report also dismissed concerns about the numerous "close call" elections, including those of recent vintage (1960, 1968, and 1976), as a "quadrennial parlor game."[55]

With twenty-first-century hindsight, it is all too evident that these confident predictions were sorely mistaken. That same hindsight, however, makes clear that opponents of reform were correct in one of their related claims: that there would be no major crisis even if a "runner-up President" were elected.[56] Advocates of an NPV had insisted, in the 1960s as well as the 1970s, that such an event would produce turmoil and have "potentially disastrous effects on the legitimacy" of an incoming president; it would surely generate "resentment, unrest, and public clamor," a "sense of shock and outrage."[57] Those dark worries were disputed by Hatch and other supporters of the Electoral College: no crisis had arisen in 1888, or when the unelected Gerald Ford assumed the presidency in 1974, and there was no reason to expect a crisis in the future. "The American people will not, on their own initiative, react with rage if one of the near-misses actually occurs," wrote Martin Diamond in 1977. "They will go about their business." Alan Simpson agreed, noting that a "wrong winner" would still have legitimacy and ample public support.[58] There was, in sum, no compelling reason to amend the Constitution to prevent an electoral mishap that was extremely unlikely to occur and that the nation could easily weather.

Defenders of the Electoral College also pushed back against the argument that the institution was inherently undemocratic, a claim that Martin Diamond disparaged as "populistic rhetoric." To do so, they offered a theoretical defense of the Electoral College as embodying "the American philosophy of democracy." Hatch, Diamond, and numerous others, including the learned Democratic senator from New York, Daniel P. Moynihan, insisted that the framers of the Constitution had expressly rejected the arithmetic conception of democracy championed by advocates of "one person, one vote" and direct elections. That conception was mere "majoritarianism," or "plebiscitary democracy," or "populism"; it "ignores political and historical realities," argued Nevada Democrat Howard Cannon. A national popular vote, declared Hatch, "would transform our Constitution into a document with all the depth and richness of an abacus." The "American idea of democracy," in contrast, had always interwoven the local with the national and blended "democratic considerations with all the other things that contribute to political well-being." It "channels and constrains democracy," Diamond asserted.[59]

American institutions, accordingly, were designed to generate or require a "reasonable" majority (a phrase from Thomas Jefferson's first inaugural address) or "concurrent" majorities rather than straightforward numerical ones. Invoking at some length the ideas of John C. Calhoun, the prominent nineteenth-century defender of states' rights and slavery, Moynihan, on the Senate floor, maintained that the success of the American experiment owed a great deal to the structures that required American governance to be built upon "concurrent majorities": federalism, bicameral legislatures, and the Electoral College, which obliged successful candidates to gain both state and national majorities. From this perspective, the Electoral College was neither "archaic" nor "undemocratic," as proponents of S.J. Res. 28 had insisted; it was, instead, a suitably complex mechanism for the "formation of consensus" in a large and diverse polity. "The Electoral College is easy to defend, once one gets the hang of it," Diamond insisted. "It is a paradigm of the American idea of democracy."[60] That a large majority of the American people preferred direct elections to "the American idea of democracy" was a potentially troublesome fact, but Simpson and other senators found it easy to dismiss. The "American people" simply did not understand the issues or "the full implications of a direct election system."[61]

This foray into American history and political theory did not go unchallenged. The report of the Judiciary Committee in 1979 noted that Jefferson's mention of a "reasonable" majority had nothing whatsoever to do with the presidential election system, and Bayh himself took Moynihan to task on the Senate floor for, among other things, ignoring the significance of slavery as an obstacle to the founders' adoption of direct elections in 1787.[62] The validity of the idea that there had always been a distinctively American conception of democracy was, however, beside the point. By asserting its existence, the opponents of an NPV were attempting to seize a portion of the high ground, to offer a plausibly principled reason for not applying the democratic value of "one person, one vote" to presidential elections. Although the drift toward conservatism in American politics was already under way in the late 1970s, the ideological resonance of the democratic surge of the 1960s—the civil rights movement, the reapportionment revolution, the expansion of voting rights—remained strong. Those who wished to preserve the Electoral College, particularly in the face of polls revealing that the people wanted to abolish it, needed to rescue, or insulate, the institution from the taint of being undemocratic. The "American idea of democracy" was one way of doing so.

MINORITIES

Believe it or not, Mr. Chairman, we are arguing here for the status quo.

—Vernon Jordan Jr.

The direct popular election of the President and Vice President is an idea whose time has not only come, but is long overdue.

—John Lewis

In the spring of 1977, soon after Jimmy Carter had put forward his electoral reform package, Louis E. Martin, one of the most influential African-Americans in Washington, predicted that "the abolition of the Electoral College is bound to stir up a lively debate with black leaders taking different sides of the issue." Martin knew whereof he spoke. A lively debate did indeed ensue among black leaders regarding the advantages and disadvantages, for African-Americans, of replacing the Electoral College with direct elections. Concerns about a national popular vote had, of course, been voiced in the late 1960s, by Clarence Mitchell among others, and the NAACP struggled with the issue in 1970, linking its worries about direct elections to the need to strengthen protections for voting rights in the South; its board finally endorsed direct elections in the early fall of that year. The issue then remained dormant in the early 1970s, receiving little attention from leaders or in the African-American press. After the 1976 election, however, the desirability of reform for minority groups became a prominent and consequential concern, not only in the African-American community but in the hearing rooms, and on the floor, of the Senate.[63]

As Louis Martin knew, African-American political leaders were deeply divided over Electoral College reform in the 1970s, as were black citizens nationwide. (See the polls cited earlier in this chapter.) The only African-American in the Senate, Edward Brooke, a Massachusetts Republican, was a co-sponsor of S.J. Res. 1 in 1977, although the failure of his reelection bid in 1978 meant that his voice would be absent from the final debates in 1979. Key black members of the House, including John Conyers, Augustus Hawkins, Shirley Chisholm, and Parren Mitchell (Clarence's brother), favored direct elections, as did the nationally known activist John Lewis, who would become a member of Congress in 1987. But the Congressional Black Caucus was too divided to take an official position, and the leaders of many important African-American organizations, including Benjamin Hooks of the NAACP and Vernon Jordan Jr. of the Urban League, lined up in staunch opposition to reform, insisting that "the precious, though limited, political influence of black Americans would be curtailed under direct elections."[64]

This opposing view—which lived in tension with the egalitarian ethos of the civil rights movement and the Voting Rights Act—was rooted in the perception that the Electoral College, with winner-take-all, encouraged presidential candidates to be responsive to the interests of African-Americans because they constituted a critical group of swing voters in large, northern states. Thanks to both their strategic geographic location and their tendency to vote as a bloc, African-Americans were able to wield power out of proportion to their numbers in presidential elections. According to the NAACP, that advantage was "justified and necessary" to offset the underrepresentation of blacks in Congress, and it would be lost in a national direct election that put no premium on gaining votes in large, pivotal states. This perspective echoed the arguments that African-American leaders and many white liberals had advanced in combating the Lodge-Gossett proportional plan in 1950.[65]

The virtues of the Electoral College seemed particularly salient to those black leaders who believed that the best political strategy for African-Americans was not to bind themselves too closely to the Democratic Party but to engage instead in "balance of power" politics—inviting Republicans, as well as Democrats, to address black issues and court black voters. Eddie Williams, the president of the Joint Center for Political Studies, a think tank in Washington, accordingly encouraged both the Ford and Reagan wings of the Republican Party to signal their support for civil rights issues at the 1976 convention. This effort bore little fruit: the party platform had little to say about civil rights, and Ford ended up winning only 8 percent of the African-American vote. But Williams and others continued to reach out to Republicans in the later 1970s, urging them to be attentive to African-American interests and not to write off the African-American vote. In 1978 Reverend Jesse Jackson, then the head of Operation PUSH, addressed a meeting of the Republican National Committee at which he declared that African-Americans needed the "Republican Party to compete for us" and assured his audience that blacks would vote for "Republicans who appeal to their vested interests." Vernon Jordan adopted a similar stance, suggesting ways the Republican Party could modify its policies to mesh well with the "black agenda." Republicans were responsive to these initiatives, particularly while former Tennessee senator Bill Brock was head of the RNC (1977–1981). The party did reach out to African-Americans and upped its share of the black vote to 14 percent in 1978 and to 15 percent in 1980.[66]

For Williams, Jordan, and many other African-Americans, the 1976 election validated the perception that blacks constituted a key group of swing voters who could play a decisive role in presidential elections, thanks to the Electoral College. Jimmy Carter, they were convinced, owed his narrow victory to the votes of African-Americans in key states like Ohio, as well as in the South, where the Georgia governor had (temporarily) rolled back the Republican tide that was transforming the region. The Joint Center for Political Studies determined that the black vote was responsible for Carter's margin of victory in seven states, leading Williams to conclude that the 1976 election marked "the first time in history that the black vote has played such a major role ... in the election of a president." More flamboyantly, Jesse Jackson declared that "hands that picked cotton in 1966 did pick the President in 1976, and could very well be the difference in 1980."[67]

Despite such celebratory declarations, the aftermath of the 1976 election seemed to affirm and encourage the need for a "balance of power" strategy and outreach to Republicans. Although black leaders and editorial writers were convinced that the election left Carter with a heavy debt to the African-American community, his early personnel appointments and policy choices, particularly with respect to the economy and jobs, indicated that the president's priorities were not their own.[68] All too quickly, the hope and excitement triggered by Carter's election soured into disappointment and a loss of confidence in his administration, sentiments that were sharpened by Carter's proposal to abolish the Electoral College. In July 1977, in a speech at the annual conference of the National Urban League, Jordan underscored his opposition to that proposal, insisting that it would have "undemocratic results." Direct elections "would weaken the political power of the cities and the poor, and it would unbalance our political system. Do away with the Electoral College," he warned, in a speech that caught Bayh and his staff by surprise, "and in 1980 the black vote will not make the difference it did in 1976." "It is unseemly," Jordan concluded, "for an administration that owes its existence to solid black electoral support to propose a new system whose effect would be to sabotage that support by diluting black voting power."[69]

A week after Jordan's speech, Williams testified before Bayh's subcommittee. Although he couched his statements tentatively, repeatedly citing the need for further research, Williams maintained that "abolition of the Electoral College at this time would probably have the effect of reducing the significance of the black vote." There were problems with the Electoral College, he acknowledged, but the likelihood of the popular vote loser becoming president was tiny and the faithless elector problem could be solved through other means. More pointedly, Williams believed that a switch to direct elections would redirect campaigns away from urban centers and dissipate the leverage that black voters gained from being "strategically concentrated in the metropolitan areas of key states." (When Bayh pointed out that many opponents of direct elections believed that precisely the reverse would be true—that metropolitan areas would gain clout—Williams equivocally responded that "one can argue in both ways.") Williams, who did not display a sure grasp of either the academic literature or previous testimony, also raised two other distinctive concerns. The first was that blacks, who had relatively low turnout rates, would be less likely than whites to "turn out to vote again in a runoff." The second, stemming from debates among activists, was that direct elections would encourage "special-interest" candidates, including African-Americans who made a "direct appeal to black interests." Such candidates would draw African-American voters away from the major parties and further lessen their influence. At the end of his testimony, Williams submitted as an exhibit a resolution passed by the NAACP a month earlier opposing the direct election of the president.[70]

This current of thought circulated widely among African-Americans in the late 1970s. The conservative *Atlanta Daily World,* the oldest black newspaper in Georgia, editorialized in defense of the Electoral College, emphasizing the critical role that African-Americans had played in the 1964 and 1976 elections; it also offered frequent reports that local notables and organizations preferred to keep the existing system. "Amendment Would Greatly Reduce Power of Negro Vote" ran the headline to one news story about Bayh's proposal. The Electoral College is "our last line of defense," claimed Roy Patterson, an influential journalist with ties to the Urban League; abolishing it would be "suicidal for black elected officials." "How can any black person in his right mind support the abolition of the Electoral College," he asked, referring to Congressman John Conyers, whose 1969 speech in favor of an NPV remained well known.[71] Farther north, the *Cleveland Call and Post,* also a conservative paper, ran guest columns about the Electoral College by Jordan, Williams, and Hooks in 1977, and the *Philadelphia Tribune* editorialized against direct election, pointing out that "this government never was intended to be the purist of all democracies."[72]

The most ample and focused articulation of these views came in Jordan's own testimony to Bayh's subcommittee during the last round of hearings in April 1979. Jordan appeared in his role as chair of the Black Leadership Forum (BLF), a recently created umbrella organization consisting of the heads of sixteen civil rights and political organizations.[73] His appearance had been preceded, six weeks earlier, by a controversial telegram from the BLF to Bayh, Thurmond, and others, opposing S.J. Res. 28 and demanding that Bayh not proceed without additional hearings.[74] Perhaps in response to Bayh's unhappiness with that telegram, Jordan opened his testimony with fulsome praise of the senator as "an old and dear personal friend" who "has long distinguished himself as a fighter for the rights of black people."[75]

Speaking on behalf of most, but not all, members of the BLF, Jordan, a powerful speaker, declared that "after much soul searching and weighing of available evidence . . . we must voice the strongest opposition to the proposal to abolish the Electoral College."[76] He then spelled out a full roster of objections to the proposed reform: there was no crisis that demanded action; the Electoral College was needed to preserve the two-party system; the Electoral College was "an essential balancing mechanism" that permitted large urban states to offset the advantages that small states held in Congress; and direct elections would diminish the influence of African-Americans by depriving them of their swing-vote status as well as their ability to form coalitions in the large industrial states in which they were concentrated. Such coalitions, he maintained, were most readily constructed in those states where "more white voters can be expected to empathize with the issues of major concern to blacks," and they would disappear in a direct-election environment in which "splinter parties and single issue candidates—black and white—would polarize voters." "Direct election," he noted, picking up a theme that Williams had introduced two years earlier, "would inevitably mean formation of black political parties, voting along racial lines and increasingly separated from the major parties, who would themselves be weakened and would be dependent on coalitions with splinter groups." As to the possibility of the Electoral College producing a "wrong winner," Jordan declared, "I am prepared to take my chances, based on history."[77]

Bayh, very respectfully, challenged not only Jordan's conclusions but also some of the claims he had put forward to make his case. Drawing on data prepared by his staff, the senator questioned whether African-Americans were really disproportionately concentrated in the large industrial states and whether election outcomes in those states had frequently been determined by close margins or by the black vote. Bayh also pointed out that much of the African-American population remained concentrated in the South, where blacks could not expect to remain as swing voters for very long—despite the unusual election results of 1976 when a former governor of Georgia was the Democratic candidate. Bayh's counterclaims were deftly presented, but they could not dislodge Jordan's conviction that the political well-being of the black community depended on maintaining a strong two-party system and the ability of African-American voters to serve as potentially decisive swing voters. The Electoral College served those aims well; direct elections, in contrast, offered a future "shrouded in uncertainty."[78]

Influential as the views of Jordan, Williams, and the BLF surely were, they were nonetheless challenged, publicly and strenuously, by other African-American leaders who favored direct elections and embraced the principle that all votes should count equally in presidential elections. Michigan representative John Conyers's speech on the floor of the House in September 1969 was often cited in the 1970s, including in the Judiciary Committee's 1977 report. Conyers, first elected in 1964 and one of the founders of the Congressional Black Caucus, had acknowledged that direct elections might "operate somewhat as a disadvantage" for African-Americans in the North, but he believed that this would be offset by the empowerment of blacks in the South. More important to Conyers, a progressive who would serve fifty years in Congress, were the inequalities in the weighting of votes in the existing system. Among the examples he cited was the contrast between Connecticut and South Carolina; each cast eight electoral votes in 1968, although 616,000 voters went to the polls in Connecticut while only 261,000 voters did so in South Carolina. The "sound" principle of "one man, one vote," he argued, "must be extended to our presidential elections just as it has been extended to the election of the House." Conyers stuck to those views in the 1970s.[79]

Civil rights leader and voting rights organizer John Lewis struck similar notes in a written statement delivered to Bayh's subcommittee in the spring of 1979. "It is based on the fundamental principle of 'one man, one vote' that I view the direct election of the President," Lewis wrote. "Its value is self evident: every person's vote counts, and every vote must count the same. It was on this principle that we suffered abuse, attack, and even death in the struggle for the right to vote for minorities." After sketching the substantial progress that had been made in the South since 1960, Lewis maintained that "one kind of major disfranchisement" remained, and "that is in the Electoral College system. . . . With the Electoral College and the 'winner-take-all' rule, you can be part of a minority—whether 5 percent or 49 percent—in a state and have your vote thrown away, or really, recast for the winner." He noted ruefully that it would have been "much easier . . . to register new people" in the South if they had believed that their votes would count in the final tally.[80]

Lewis, who was from Alabama and would later represent Georgia in Congress, acknowledged that some of his "friends in the black community maintain that they are in favor of the Electoral College because they believe it works to the advantage of blacks in the cities in the larger northern states." "But," he observed, "I have trouble understanding how they justify that belief—how can anyone explain to blacks in Chicago or Detroit or New York City that although they've turned out over 90 percent for one candidate, their state's electoral votes all go for another." Going a step further, Lewis insisted that the "temptation of temporary advantage" or partisan gain had to be put aside. "That every person's vote should count the same is one of the fundamental principles which is bedrock in this country. Having won the long and difficult and dangerous struggle to win the right to vote, we cannot now accept the proposition that any one person's vote can count more than another."[81]

Congressman Louis Stokes from Cleveland also seized the progressive baton, voicing a multipronged argument for direct elections in the spring of 1979. Testifying to Bayh's subcommittee, Stokes noted that he had voted for the NPV amendment in 1969 and had co-sponsored similar measures ever since. "The present system for choosing our Presidents is outdated, unsafe, and undemocratic," Stokes maintained, and "the only truly just alternative is direct election." Stokes, unlike Jordan, did worry that a winner of the popular vote could end up being denied the presidency, and he deplored the use of intermediaries to cast ballots for the nation's chief executive. The perpetuation of such an institution "is out of step with the trend of our history." Stokes believed that direct elections would encourage participation, particularly among southern blacks, and would "force the major parties to devote more attention to their non-centrist wings—thereby both making the parties more responsive to their memberships and also giving the voters a more meaningful choice at the polls." Stokes wanted the electoral system to challenge and stretch the two major parties, rather than simply protect the two-party system.[82]

The Ohio congressman also disputed, at length, the claim that the existing system was "advantageous to urban and minority voters." He was skeptical that political leaders in key states could actually deliver blocs of voters ("like great masses of cattle") or use them as "bargaining tools." At the same time, he thought that "black voting strength" was sufficiently transferable to the national level that candidates in a direct election were unlikely to ignore the interests of African-Americans. There was, therefore, no need to preserve an archaic institution in order to advance the interests of black people. Given the protections afforded by the Voting Rights Act, moreover, "there's no excuse for giving a voting advantage to some people and handicapping others. That's what we fought against in the reapportionment battles in the 1960s." (Stokes had played an important role in those battles in Ohio.) Direct election, in sum, was "essential to ensure both that the blacks have reason to go to the polls and that their votes do become a part of the national tally."[83]

The arguments put forward by Stokes and Lewis were, of course, implicitly critical of the stance taken by leaders of the major black organizations. Carl Rowan, a highly respected journalist and former official in the Kennedy and Johnson administrations, was more explicit. In June 1979, as the debate over the Bayh amendment neared its end, Rowan published a column attacking Jordan and Williams for being "hung up on the myth that black political power is concentrated in nine large states." Black political power, Rowan argued, was not concentrated in those northern states, and the Electoral College did not protect African-American interests. Indeed, thanks to the passage of the Voting Rights Act, it was the South that had become "the area of resurgent black political power," and "blacks in the South have really been shafted by the Electoral College"—generally casting their ballots for candidates who (except in 1976) never received any electoral votes. In a final jab, Rowan noted that conservatives like Thurmond were quoting black defenders of the Electoral College, and he cautioned Jordan and his allies to stop "letting the foes of electoral progress hide behind the pretense that they are looking out for 'those poor black folk.'"[84]

The sharply contrasting perspectives put forward by the two camps of black leaders were imported directly into the debates in the Senate and in the national press. As Rowan had angrily pointed out, this occurred partly because leading opponents of reform repeatedly and favorably cited African-American defenders of the Electoral College. "Direct election would endanger minority rights," declared the dissenting report authored by Eastland and Scott, among others, in 1977; its successor in 1979, written by Hatch, Thurmond, and Simpson, quoted Jordan at length.[85] In March 1979, from the floor of the Senate, Thurmond inserted into the record the telegram that he had received from the Black Leadership Forum arguing that direct elections would "result in the dilution of the votes of blacks and other minority groups." (Thurmond blithely ignored the fact that his own preferred plan, proportional elections, would have the same effect.) A day later, another former opponent of desegregation, Republican Jesse Helms of North Carolina, noted approvingly that under the Electoral College "minority groups within the heavily industrialized states can be decisive in the disposition of all of those states' electoral votes."[86] (No one appears to have remarked on the irony that this was precisely the reason Helms's southern predecessors and ideological kinsmen had sought to replace winner-take-all with proportional elections via the Lodge-Gossett amendment.) In the final rounds of debate, Hatch again cited Jordan's testimony, and Thurmond placed in the record an array of articles detailing black opposition to Bayh's proposed amendment. The opponents of electoral reform, thus, presented themselves as protectors of minority rights, and they had stronger evidence to back that claim than had been the case in 1970, when the same issue had briefly appeared.[87]

Unsurprisingly, Bayh and other advocates fought back strenuously, reaching out to African-American leaders outside the Senate and devoting substantial portions of both the 1977 and 1979 reports to countering the argument that direct elections would weaken black political influence. They mobilized academic studies and their own statistical breakdowns to challenge the notion that African-Americans had significant leverage in the large states; they emphasized that blacks in the South were seriously harmed by the Electoral College; and they underscored testimony from a well-regarded Republican campaign consultant that campaigns often "write off the black vote" because many states with sizable black populations were not competitive. (The consultant, Douglas Bailey, the media manager for the Ford-Dole campaign, had also testified that the black vote could not be ignored in a direct election and that consequently the "leverage of the minorities would increase.") The 1977 report cited Conyers's conclusion that "the direct election of our President will insure that a black man's vote will count in those states where it is currently ineffectual," and its successor in 1979 featured extensive quotations from Lewis and Stokes.[88] On the Senate floor, Edward Kennedy, a close friend of the civil rights movement, pointed out that in uncompetitive states like Massachusetts, neither African-Americans nor any other minority had any leverage in presidential elections. Bayh also reached beyond the confines of the Senate to put his perspective forward: in the spring of 1979 he sent a letter to the *Atlanta Daily World* (and presumably other newspapers as well) citing the opinions of well-known African-Americans who favored direct elections.[89]

Although the debate about the impact of reform on minorities was centered on African-Americans, some major Jewish organizations also weighed in. (In contrast to what might occur in the twenty-first century, there was scant mention of other ethnic or racial minorities.)[90] The American Jewish Congress (AJC) was the only Jewish organization that had voiced opposition to direct elections in 1969, and it reiterated its opposition in the late 1970s after difficult internal debates. Adopting a stance that paralleled Jordan's, Howard Squadron, a prominent New York lawyer serving as the president of the AJC, testified to Bayh's committee that his organization (and others) opposed direct elections because they would vitiate the influence of Jews in those urban states, including New York, where the Jewish population was concentrated. He also believed that the Electoral College helped to prevent "the nomination of candidates likely to be objectionable to sizable minority groups." Nathan Perlmutter, the national director of the Anti-Defamation League of B'nai B'rith, submitted a letter to Bayh making similar points. "The Electoral College provides minorities, be they of race, color, creed or political viewpoints, with the opportunity to be heard," he wrote. A national popular vote, in contrast, would destroy the two-party system and lead to "the formation of independent political parties by minority groups," which would yield presidents with "far less incentive" to consider "minority rights and needs." Neither Perlmutter nor Squadron believed that there was much chance that a candidate who lost the popular vote could become president, and both indicated that the "faithless" elector problem had less drastic solutions.[91] Notably, the views of both Squadron and Perlmutter were reported at length to the readers of the *Atlanta Daily World*.[92]

That Squadron and Perlmutter did not speak for the entire Jewish community was evident in the opinion polls indicating that Jews overwhelmingly favored direct election—polls that were downplayed by the executive director of the AJC.[93] It was underscored by Sherley Koteen, chair of the Washington Subcommittee of the National Council of Jewish Women. Testifying in favor of direct election in 1977 on behalf of the 100,000 members of her organization, she emphasized the importance of all votes counting equally and discounted claims that direct elections would damage federalism or destroy the two-party system. She also thought it important, at a time of declining trust in the political system, that reforms be enacted to promote fairness and equity. In a further challenge to Squadron and Perlmutter, Koteen took issue with the "premise" that there existed a Jewish "block vote," that all Jews in a state like New York could be expected to vote the same way. "We don't have a block vote even on this issue of the amendment among Jewish organizations and among Jewish individuals." Koteen's observations were on target: despite the prominence of organizations like the AJC and the Anti-Defamation League, five of the seven Jewish members of the Senate co-sponsored Bayh's amendment in 1979. New York's Jacob Javits, a liberal Republican who had served in the Senate since 1957, observed that "even if one believes that minorities can exercise disproportionate influence under the Electoral College, it seems to me to be contradictory to support the one-man, one-vote principle while at the same time opposing the direct election of the President."[94]

"In the foreground of the debate for the first time this year," reported the *New York Times* in 1979, "is an argument by minority groups that abolition of the Electoral College would deprive them of political influence." One remarkable, and deeply ironic, upshot of that foregrounding was that numerous black and Jewish leaders found themselves on the same side of the electoral reform debate as southern conservatives with whom they had little in common—and who had long defended the Electoral College as a means of protecting white supremacy. Still, the notion that the Electoral College protected minority interests gained some traction among liberals, who had been almost unanimous in their support for a national popular vote in the late 1960s. The Electoral College, wrote Curtis Gans, an activist and voting expert, "insures that the needs and desires of significant minorities will be taken into account." Most liberal members of Congress, to be sure, remained unpersuaded by the claim that a possible loss of influence by minority groups outweighed the manifold virtues of direct elections, yet even in the Senate, the argument made inroads. As Carl Rowan observed, "puzzled Senate liberals" were reluctant to "vote for anything that is construed as disenfranchising blacks."[95] The voices of those "puzzled" or unsettled liberals would be heard during the final weeks that S.J. Res. 28 remained before the Senate.

*   *   *

In retrospect, one of the more striking features of the debate among African-American leaders was the breadth of the gulf between the two camps. They disagreed about facts (whether or not black voters constituted a crucial bloc of swing voters in large northern states); about values (the sanctity or universality of the principle of "one person, one vote"); and about the relative importance of the North and the South to the black community's goal of influencing presidential politics. These disagreements emerged both from differing assessments of the historical record and from differences in ideology, temperament, and institutional agendas. The black community, as Jordan observed in his testimony to the Senate, was not "monolithic," and disagreements abounded about issues large and small.[96]

From the vantage point of the twenty-first century, the arguments in favor of keeping the Electoral College seem significantly less compelling than the "one person, one vote" vision advanced by men like Conyers, Stokes, and Lewis. As critics pointed out (at the time, and since), the notion that the Electoral College served the interests of minorities rested on a shaky, and shifting, factual foundation. African-Americans were not, in fact, disproportionately concentrated in the large industrial states of the North; those states were not necessarily close in presidential elections; and blacks, who had voted heavily Democratic since the mid-1960s, were not really swing voters, readily courted by both major parties.[97] In contrast, the position that all votes should count equally in a national popular election was grounded not in a political calculus but in a principle that had propelled the apportionment revolution and was at the heart of the civil and voting rights movements. That principle endured, while the estimations of electoral influence changed over time, not only for African-Americans but for all minority groups.[98]

The breadth of African-American support for the position taken by Jordan and his colleagues, thus, should be understood as the product of a particular historical moment during which it seemed plausible that the Electoral College could serve black Americans well. The Republican Party retained a strong moderate wing in the mid-1970s, and it was not unrealistic to believe that the GOP might seek to revitalize its historic ties to the African-American community and compete for black votes. Decades of large-scale migration out of the South, which intensified after World War II, had significantly enhanced African-American electoral power in the North, leading many to conclude that the key nodes of black political life and power would remain in cities like Detroit, Cleveland, Chicago, New York, and Washington. (In fact, the Great Migration northward was already coming to an end, but that was not yet clear in 1975.) Meanwhile, in the South, the political prospects of African-Americans were laced with uncertainty as newly enfranchised voters mobilized while facing a rapidly shifting partisan landscape. Above all, perhaps, the 1976 election appeared to demonstrate the truth of the proposition that the black vote could be decisive in the Electoral College: Carter's victory margin was narrow and an unusual number of states (including sizable ones like Ohio and Pennsylvania) were won by margins small enough to be attributable to the African-American vote. This backdrop lent credence to arguments for preserving the Electoral College despite its inegalitarian and problematic features—although those arguments, in the end, failed to persuade many black leaders and citizens.

Postscript. In subsequent decades, African-American support for the Electoral College faded. While Vernon Jordan's 1979 testimony continued to be cited, primarily by white conservatives, well into the twenty-first century, African-American leaders and organizations recalibrated their views.[99] Reverend Jesse Jackson, influenced in part by the outcome of the

2000 election, publicly called for abolition of the Electoral College in 2004; his son, Congressman Jesse Jackson Jr., introduced amendment resolutions calling for a national popular vote on numerous occasions between 2004 and 2012.[100] A more telling signal of change came in 2008 when the annual convention of the NAACP and the organization's board of directors approved a resolution expressing the organization's support for a national popular vote and "a constitutional amendment abolishing the Electoral College." The lengthy resolution repudiated, point by point, many of the claims that had undergirded the NAACP's support for the Electoral College in the 1970s. Relatively few African-Americans, the resolution noted, lived in the thirteen most competitive states, and even fewer lived "in states where the African American voting population is likely to determine the outcome of that state's election." Reflecting the indisputable fact that blacks voted overwhelmingly Democratic (and thus were not swing voters), "the interests of most African American voters are increasingly discounted by the platforms of both dominant political parties." Finally, the resolution proclaimed, "the NAACP supports the ideal of one person, one vote." Louis Stokes and John Conyers had, belatedly, won the day.[101]

Finale

For a decade, polls have shown that more than seventy-five percent of the American people want to elect their Presidents by popular vote.

The Senate does not.

—Seattle Times, July 11, 1979

The long-awaited final floor debate on Senate Joint Resolution 28 opened on June 21, 1979. The debate was expected to be lengthy, pausing for the weeklong July 4 recess, and resuming after senators returned to Washington. Both advocates and opponents of the resolution signaled publicly that the outcome was uncertain, and the threat of a filibuster loomed large. Alternatives to a national popular vote, such as district or proportional plans, might still be brought up for consideration, and Orrin Hatch himself had filed twenty-four amendments to S.J. Res. 28. Bayh and his allies believed that they had the requisite sixty votes to invoke cloture, but they were far less sure that they could muster the sixty-seven votes needed to approve the amendment. (The *New York Times* reported that they had an "outside chance" of reaching sixty-seven.) Their best hope was that the dynamics of the debate, including a successful cloture vote, might generate enough momentum to sway a large proportion of the dozen senators who were undecided.[102]

Bayh opened the debate with remarks emphasizing the impressive breadth of support for the amendment. Not only did national polls indicate that "in every region of the country . . . a large majority of the people favored" direct elections, but a recent poll conducted by the *Salt Lake Tribune,* Hatch's hometown newspaper, found that 80 percent of the citizens of the Rocky Mountain states expressed the same preference. (Many senators from those states had opposed the measure in 1970.) The people, Bayh declared, wanted to put "the election of the President on a truly democratic basis." Bayh also listed the major organizations that supported the amendment, including the Chamber of Commerce, the AFL-CIO, the Farmers Union, and the American Bar Association. He noted too that three different polls of state legislatures indicated that a majority "would vote to ratify an amendment for direct popular vote." (That a majority would be insufficient was not mentioned.) Finally, in an effort to preempt the small-state objection to a national popular vote, Bayh entered into the record the names of twenty-one co-sponsors who came from states with fewer than ten electoral votes.[103]

Hatch was more combative in his opening remarks, citing Yale Law professor Charles Black's 1970 observation that the proposal, if passed, would be "the most deeply radical amendment which has ever entered the Constitution of the United States." S.J. Res. 28, Hatch maintained, subordinated all other values to the goal of achieving "political equality" and reduced the "complex idea" of democracy "into a simple-minded arithmetic majoritarianism." He then extolled the virtues of both the Electoral College and of winner-take-all while itemizing the defects and hazards of a national popular vote. Along the way, he entered into the record articles and excerpts from testimony in support of his position.[104]

The debate then limped on for several days, with senators on both sides stating their positions and repeating well-worn arguments about (among other things) small and large states, minorities, the preservation of the two-party system, the likelihood of fraud, the dangers of runoff elections, and the intentions of the founding fathers. Despite numerous pointed exchanges between the two sides, there was far less rancor and edginess to the debate than there had been in 1970, as well as less drama, urgency, and public attention. A potentially significant detour, however, appeared on June 26 when Senator Harry Byrd of Virginia proposed to amend S.J. Res. 28 with his own long-sought amendment mandating a balanced budget for the federal government. According to Senate rules, Byrd's proposal had to be addressed before S.J. Res. 28 could be brought up for a vote. Partly in response, and fearing the introduction of other "non-germane" amendments as a delaying tactic, Bayh and seventeen other senators filed a cloture motion shortly before Congress recessed on June 27.[105]

When the debate resumed on July 9, Bayh and his allies were anticipating a cloture vote the next day or perhaps two cloture votes over the course of several days. If cloture were successfully invoked, and if Byrd's balanced budget amendment could be shelved, the Senate would turn to a time-limited debate on the merits of S.J. Res. 28, followed by a vote. But to Bayh's surprise, Hatch and Thurmond, on the Senate floor, proposed a different path forward: to forego or "vitiate" the cloture vote and proceed on July 10 to an "up or down" vote on the direct election amendment. "Everybody has made up his or her mind at this point," Hatch insisted, and it would be best to avoid "the charade of continued debate." "Why have a cloture vote?" asked the frequent filibusterer Thurmond, without a hint of irony. "That is going through a ceremony that is unnecessary." Bayh was caught off balance. He had been working for more than a decade to get the Senate to vote "up or down" on direct elections, yet he had been counting on several additional days of substantive debate and personal meetings to address issues of concern to uncommitted senators. He also quickly recognized, and acknowledged, that Hatch and Thurmond's tactical move meant that they were confident that "we do not have 67 votes." Clearly, Hatch and Thurmond, as well as Bayh, had been counting heads and making phone calls during the recess. After Harry Byrd was persuaded to withdraw his amendment (in exchange for commitments from Bayh to give it full consideration in his subcommittee), Bayh was left with little choice: he agreed to hold the vote at 5 P.M. on July 10.[106]

The final two days of debate were listless, with the Senate chamber often half-empty and leaders on both sides finding it difficult to round up enough speakers to fill the allotted time.[107] Still, the floor debate, before and after the recess, offered glimpses of two limited but noteworthy political shifts that had occurred since the showdown of 1970. The first was that a handful of southern Democrats actively supported a national popular vote: all of these men were new to the Senate in the 1970s, younger than their predecessors, less steeped in the conviction that the Electoral College was essential to protecting the southern way of life. David Pryor of Arkansas, for example, spoke out frequently in behalf of the principle of "one person, one vote," playing a role not unlike that of Howard Baker in 1970. (Baker, now the Republican minority leader, was less active in the debate but remained a steadfast advocate.) Pryor was joined by both senators from Kentucky, Wendell Ford and Walter Huddleston, who discoursed eloquently about the defects of the Electoral College. Support was quietly voiced by Donald Stewart of Alabama, who had been elected to fill the unexpired term of James Allen (and had been denounced by Allen's widow as a "flaming liberal.")[108] Some of the region's newspapers also endorsed reform.[109]

In the most compelling floor speech given by a southerner who favored direct election, Louisiana Democrat J. Bennett Johnston directly linked his embrace of a national popular vote to changes taking place in the South. He acknowledged that "in the past . . . southern senators have been associated with opposition to direct election," but there was, he maintained, a "new mood in the South today." What Johnston surely knew, but did not expressly state, was that behind that new mood were new political realities. By 1979 there could no longer be any doubt that the enfranchisement of African-Americans was permanent and that consequently one of the traditional southern arguments against a national popular vote (that it would create pressures to enfranchise blacks) had become obsolete. It was equally clear that the Republican Party was rapidly gaining strength in the region, making elections more competitive and winner-take-all a less sure-fire mechanism for delivering support to Democratic presidential candidates. Taking full note of these far-reaching changes, Johnston announced that one key reason that he supported direct election was to advance the interests of Louisiana's sizable black population: with the "political process" now opened up to minority groups, his state had many black local officials, yet in presidential elections African-Americans routinely had their votes cast for candidates that they did not support. Winner-take-all, he concluded, "disadvantages the minority community in my state enormously." (It also, of course, could disadvantage Louisiana Democrats in general.) After quoting John Lewis at length, Johnston declared that he was "proud to cosponsor direct election as the final step in our continuing effort to make certain that all Americans have the right to vote and that all votes are counted equally." These were extraordinary words from a senator whose predecessor, Allen Ellender, was a segregationist who had opposed not only direct elections but the Voting Rights Act.[110]

The second political shift revealed in the debates was the departure of some moderate-to-liberal northern senators from the cause of direct elections. Moynihan (at the conservative end of that spectrum) led the way with his lengthy historical disquisition of late June, urging his colleagues to resist a "radical transformation" of the political system in one of the world's only durable democracies. (Moynihan's seat during the 1970 debates had been occupied by Republican moderate, Charles Goodell, who supported abolition of the Electoral College.) Richard Schweiker, a Pennsylvania Republican who had endorsed a national popular vote as recently as 1977, announced on the Senate floor that he had changed his mind and preferred a "proven system" that "has worked reasonably well" to "a theory about what might be better." Schweiker's fellow Republican, Charles Percy of Illinois, who had voted for direct elections in 1970, explained that he was shifting his position largely in response to the concerns voiced by minority leaders like Jordan and officials of the American Jewish Congress. Bill Bradley, an independent-minded New Jersey Democrat, also cited concerns about minority "political strength" in detailing his reasons for opposing direct elections. Although "one person, one vote" was a "worthy and necessary goal," he explained, democracy entailed "attention to the rights and needs of the minority." (Bradley also worried that New Jersey—pinioned between New York and Philadelphia—"would disappear from the thoughts of candidates" in a direct national election.) If any further evidence were required that a once-solid wall of liberal support for a national popular vote had cracked, it was provided by the *New York Times,* which published an editorial on July 9 criticizing S.J. Res. 28. It concluded with the question: "Why change what works?" In what may well have been an historical first (and last!), the *Times'* editorial was entered into the Congressional Record by the archconservative Jesse Helms of North Carolina.[111]

The outcome of the vote was not a surprise, but the margin of defeat was wider than most observers had anticipated. Fifty-one senators, a slim majority of the Senate, voted in favor of S.J. Res. 28, and forty-eight were opposed. With ninety-nine senators voting, sixty-six favorable votes were needed for passage of an amendment resolution. The proponents of direct election were fifteen votes short.

The lineups on both sides of the issue were heterogeneous, composed of senators from states of diverse sizes, different regions, both parties, and varied points on the ideological spectrum. Supporters of S.J. Res. 28 included prominent liberals like Carl Levin (Michigan) and George McGovern (South Dakota) as well as moderates like Howard Baker and the conservative Jake Garn, a Utah Republican. Arrayed on the other side were conservative southern Democrats (such as Stennis of Mississippi and Herman Talmadge of Georgia), conservative Republicans (such as Hatch and Goldwater), and moderately liberal Democrats, including Edmund Muskie of Maine, Paul Sarbanes of Maryland, and Joe Biden of Delaware. Notably, the senatorial delegations from nearly half the states (twenty-two) were divided, with one senator voting favorably and the other opposed.[112]

Still, as Table 6.1 indicates, there were patterns. Most visibly, both party affiliation and region shaped the final tally. More than two-thirds of all Democrats supported direct elections, while a similar percentage of Republicans voted negatively. (In 1970 Republicans had been evenly divided.) There was also a discernible contrast between the South and the rest of the country: although the resolution had majority support (56 percent) outside the South, more than 60 percent of southern senators voted against it. As Bennett Johnston had predicted, more southerners voted favorably than in 1970, but the gain was relatively modest. It was also offset by an increase in the number of negative votes cast by Democrats from other regions.[113] State size, on the whole, bore little relation to the distribution of votes: senators from small, large, and medium-sized states split their votes fairly evenly. As had been true in 1970, small-state Democrats strongly

TABLE 6.1: SENATE VOTE ON S.J. RES. 28, JULY 10, 1979

	Yea	Nay	Not voting
All senators[a]	51	48	1
Democrats	39	19	0
Republicans	12	28	1
Independent[b]	0	1	0
South[c]			
Democrats	8	10	0
Republicans	2	5	0
Independent	0	1	0
Total	10	16	0
Non-South			
Democrats	31	9	0
Republicans	10	23	1
Total	41	32	1
Large states[d]			
Democrats	8	4	0
Republicans	1	5	0
Total	9	9	0
Medium-sized states[d]			
Democrats	16	9	0
Republicans	7	9	0
Independent	0	1	0
Total	23	19	0
Small states[d]			
Democrats	15	6	0
Republicans	4	14	1
Total	19	20	1

Source: 125 Cong. Rec. 17766 (1979).

a. Packwood (R-OR) did not vote but indicated he would have voted yea.

b. Harry F. Byrd Jr. (I-VA) caucused with the Democrats.

c. South includes FL, GA, SC, NC, VA, KY, TN, AL, MS, AR, LA, OK, TX. See Chapter 5, note 57.

d. "Large" includes all states that had fifteen or more electoral votes in the 1976 presidential election; "medium-sized" includes all states that had between seven and fourteen electoral votes in the 1976 presidential election; and "small" includes those with six or fewer electoral votes in the 1976 presidential election.

favored direct elections while their Republican counterparts tilted just as strongly in the opposite direction. Unlike 1970, however, large-state senators were also divided in 1979, primarily on party lines; nine years earlier, large-state senators, many of them Republican, had been almost unanimously supportive of the two motions to invoke cloture.[114]

What caught the attention of contemporary commentators was the opposition of roughly a dozen northern liberals and moderates from both parties, men who had generally sided with Bayh and other liberal leaders on constitutional and voting rights issues.[115] Four of them had voted in favor of direct elections in earlier years, and six of the dissenting Democrats were from the East Coast.[116] In the immediate aftermath of the vote, Bayh maintained that some of these "defections" came from "those who believed the large states would lose" influence if there were direct elections. The Indiana senator offered no evidence to support that conclusion—nor is much visible in the public record—but Moynihan, Schweiker, Percy, and perhaps Bradley were the obvious cases in point. Whether state size also played a role in the defections of some small-state liberals, like Biden and Muskie, was equally a matter of conjecture.[117]

Of greater significance, Bayh, as well as more detached observers, attributed the drop in liberal support to the lobbying of black and Jewish organizations, including the Urban League and the AJC.[118] As Carl Rowan had pointed out, many liberals were, in fact, hesitant to vote against the stated preferences of black and Jewish leaders. Most overcame that hesitance and cast their ballots in favor of direct elections, but some, like Percy and Bradley, were apparently persuaded by the argument that abolition of the Electoral College would harm minorities. For still others, the opinions voiced by black and Jewish leaders likely constituted one reason among several to part ways with their customary allies. Liberals too had concerns about the runoff mechanism, the possible proliferation of parties, and the potentially unforeseen consequences of changing electoral systems.[119] Indeed, just such a confluence of factors appears to have undergirded the remarkable shift in editorial posture by the *New York Times*.[120]

Although the liberal defections were important and revealing, their significance ought not be exaggerated. Even if every Democrat from outside the South had voted favorably, S.J. Res. 28 would still have been defeated; that would also have been true had Percy, Schweiker, and liberal Republican

Lowell Weicker of Connecticut joined the bandwagon.[121] The opposition needed only thirty-four votes to block the resolution, and it reached that total with the votes of southerners and conservative-leaning Republicans. The presence of liberal opposition to direct elections significantly enlarged the margin of defeat, making the outcome more politically decisive, but it did not determine the fate of Bayh's resolution. The *Atlanta Daily World* was somewhat off the mark when it declared the outcome in the Senate to be "a victory for Black and Jewish leaders."[122]

In effect, the same coalition that had blocked a national popular vote in 1970 triumphed again in 1979. Although Bennett Johnston believed that the "new mood" in the South would lead many of his fellow southerners to announce their support for direct elections, only a minority did so. The South, although not as solid as it had been, remained a center of opposition, despite the shifts in racial and party politics that, in theory, might have undercut the midcentury rationales for opposing direct elections. (Jack Edwards was apparently on target when he wryly observed that "my people have a tendency to keep things like they are.") The growth in southern support for a national vote, moreover, was counterbalanced, even outweighed, by declining support among Republicans generally: although they held only forty-one seats (compared to forty-three in 1970), Republicans cast twenty-eight negative votes, nine more than they had in 1970.[123]

Several factors, in addition to the defection of a few moderates, contributed to the strengthening of Republican opposition. The first was an increase in the number of Senate Republicans who identified ideologically with the conservative wing of their party. These men did not want to tinker with existing institutions or the Constitution; they wanted to roll back many of the federal initiatives of the 1960s; they feared increased involvement of the federal government in elections; and they disliked the majoritarianism that was embodied in S.J. Res. 28.[124] In addition, some Republicans had come to believe that the Electoral College favored their party in presidential elections, that there existed what would soon be called a Republican "lock" on the Electoral College. The source of this belief was demographic: the regions of the country that were gaining population, and thus electoral votes, were the West and the South, where the Republican Party was already strong or making strides. In contrast, reliably Democratic states in the Northeast and parts of the Midwest were gradually shedding electoral votes. The Republicans, moreover, were likely to win more states than the Democrats and would consequently benefit more from the two "senatorial" votes granted to each state. The combination of these two factors seemed to suggest that the Electoral College stood to advantage Republicans for some time to come.[125] In his 1977 testimony, Bob Dole had alluded to this belief, while making clear that he did not buy it. "Retention of the Electoral College," he wrote in a prepared statement, "does not inherently favor either of the two major parties." As his testimony implied, not all of his colleagues agreed.[126]

The opposition to reform was also buttressed, even encouraged, by the waning of public interest in the issue. The flare-up of concern about the Electoral College that had surfaced after the 1976 election had greatly subsided by the spring of 1979, pointing once again to the opposition's tactical wisdom in delaying the journey of Bayh's resolution through Congress. Both Washington and the country, moreover, were preoccupied with more compelling issues in the latter years of the 1970s: rampant inflation, an energy crisis, revolutionary turmoil in Iran and Nicaragua, and the SALT II arms reduction accord with the Soviet Union. Only a few days before the final Senate debate began in June 1979, President Jimmy Carter—who had gone silent about electoral reform after 1977—signed the controversial (and never-ratified) SALT II treaty with Leonid Brezhnev. A week after the Senate vote, Carter delivered his famous, or infamous, "malaise" speech in which he asserted that the nation was suffering a profound and pervasive "crisis of confidence." Confronted with these realities, it is little wonder that Birch Bayh himself, near the end of the floor debates, acknowledged that electoral reform "is not the most important issue facing the nation today." "As strongly as I have pursued this proposal for 10 years," he reflected, "I must say that if anybody while I was back home on July 4 had come up and talked to me about direct election instead of inflation, gas rationing, or SALT, I would have thought he was out of his mind."[127]

Even in the best of times, electoral reform was not an issue that readily galvanized many voters—and these were not the best of times. Although opinion polls indicated that a large majority of the populace favored direct elections (as did a majority of southerners and Republicans), there were no public demonstrations in favor of abolishing the Electoral College and no reports of mail deluging congressional offices. "In contrast to other years," observed the *Atlanta Constitution,* "the issue aroused little interest and no emotion." With little pressure coming from their constituents and public attention focused on the long lines at gas stations, senators on both sides of the aisle had no difficulty deciding to ignore the opinion polls and to vote based on their own judgments and concerns as professional politicians. A few even indicated that they inclined against S.J. Res. 28 in part because there were too many other problems demanding "our urgent attention" to add a new method of electing presidents to the national agenda. As had happened on more than one occasion in the past, the issue of electoral reform—which became salient at most every four years—had been eclipsed by more urgent matters.[128]

The contours of the Senate vote were also a sign, a reflection, of the declining fortunes of American liberalism in the 1970s. The effort to replace the Electoral College with a national popular vote had gained steam in the mid-1960s in tandem with an energetic and confident liberalism that promoted a host of other democratizing reforms as well as the pathbreaking social programs of Lyndon Johnson's Great Society. Both the energy and the confidence, however, were eroding in the 1970s, buffeted by persistent economic problems, ideological divisions within the Democratic Party, and backlash against civil rights, affirmative action, and feminism. The Democrats still controlled the presidency and both branches of Congress from 1977 to 1979, but the country was unmistakably moving in a conservative direction, drawn more toward deregulation and "law and order" than to further democratic innovation.[129] Sixteen months after the Senate vote on direct elections, Ronald Reagan, no friend of electoral reform, would be elected to the presidency, and Republicans gained control of the Senate for the first time since 1949. One of the nine Democratic incumbents defeated in the general election was Birch Bayh, who lost decisively to Representative, and future vice president, Dan Quayle.

"The large margin of defeat in 1979," concluded *Congressional Quarterly* in the wake of the Senate verdict on direct elections, "could postpone for years any further effort to revamp the presidential election system."[130] That somber assessment was widely shared. In contrast to what had occurred in 1970, there could be no second-guessing in 1979 about filibusters and procedural unfairness, about what the outcome might have been if the amendment resolution reached the floor of the Senate for an up-or-down vote. The vote on S.J. Res. 28 was conclusive, and the recognition that support for direct elections in the Senate had diminished since 1970 was more than a little sobering. That a sizable handful of liberals had joined the opposition only deepened the sense of finality. Birch Bayh's long and determined effort to amend the Constitution to provide for the direct election of presidents had come to an end, and his many allies in and outside the Senate knew it, even before the 1980 election. "Supporters of the electoral change," reported the *New York Times*, "conceded privately that they stood little chance of reviving the issue in the future unless a President was elected with a minority of the popular vote or the nation came disturbingly close to such a result."[131]

PART IV

Partisan Stalemate and Electoral Misfires

SEVEN

PESSIMISM AND INNOVATION, 1980–2020

In March 2001, former president Jimmy Carter, speaking as the co-chair of a new commission on federal election reform, publicly declared, "It is a waste of time to talk about changing the Electoral College. I would predict that 200 years from now, we will still have the Electoral College."[1] The former president's pessimism was surely shaped by his own frustrating experience in the late 1970s. It was also widely shared among politicians and political analysts during the final decades of the twentieth century and the first decades of the twenty-first. Following the defeat of S.J. Res 28 on the floor of the Senate in 1979, an aura of resignation enveloped the issue in Washington: although a solid majority of the American people still favored replacing the Electoral College with direct elections, few political leaders believed that change was likely, or even possible, in the foreseeable future.[2] During the thirty years that ended in 1979, electoral reform had been a prominent, recurrent subject of congressional debate and consideration; over the next forty years, it was barely present. As the Congressional Research Service noted in 2017, "the question of Electoral College reform largely disappeared from . . . Congress' legislative agenda."[3]

This was so despite a remarkable cluster of events that vividly displayed the shortcomings of the electoral system. The most dramatic of these, of course, were the "wrong winner" elections that took place in 2000 and 2016. For many decades, defenders of the Electoral College had insisted that the possibility of such an outcome was remote, but by January 2017 the country had inaugurated two presidents who had finished second in the popular vote: George W. Bush and Donald J. Trump. (A third "misfire" nearly happened in 2004, when Bush captured the popular vote but came close to losing in the Electoral College.)[4] A different, but still serious, problem had reared its head in 1992 when independent candidate H. Ross Perot seemed poised to win enough votes to prevent either major-party candidate from gaining a majority in the Electoral College. The election would then have been decided in the House of Representatives, with each state delegation getting one vote—an outcome that nearly everyone regarded as unpalatable. Anyone who had witnessed or read the congressional debates of the 1960s and 1970s might have expected these three episodes (alongside the usual run of faithless electors) to spark a concerted legislative effort to amend the Constitution and abolish the Electoral College. But no such effort materialized.

There were, as always, multiple reasons for the dearth of congressional activity, but the most salient factor in this period was the increasingly partisan cast that the issue acquired. Although Democrats, even liberal Democrats, were not of one mind about abolishing the Electoral College, initiatives for reform after 1980 almost invariably came from their side of the aisle. Republican politicians opposed any shift to direct elections (with fewer dissenters than there had been in the 1970s), and they displayed only sporadic interest in other options.[5] Republicans, moreover, wielded far more influence in Congress between 1980 and 2020 than they had between 1950 and 1980. The Democrats were the majority party in the House from 1955 until 1995, but thereafter Republicans held sway until 2019, except for a brief period from 2007 to 2011. In the Senate, Republicans broke a twenty-five year drought in the 1980 elections; from that "wave" election until 2020 each party had control roughly half the time.

The Republican Party was also changing in ways that made it less receptive to electoral reform. The moderate Republicans from the Northeast, parts of the Midwest, and a smattering of other states—legislators who had sometimes favored direct election—lost influence within the party beginning in the late 1970s, and their numbers in Congress gradually declined. By 2010, if not earlier, they were on the road to extinction. The ideological conservatives who were ascendant in the party had less sympathy for the egalitarian or majoritarian arguments that undergirded reform initiatives, and they were more inclined to perceive federal measures to democratize elections as a threat to the rights and prerogatives of the states. Conservative Republicans were also vocal about the dangers of voter fraud, particularly after the turn of the century, and they had long claimed that a national popular election would greatly increase its likelihood.[6]

The GOP also moved south. After the passage of civil and voting rights legislation in the mid-1960s, white southerners, in ever-growing numbers, abandoned the Democratic Party and voted Republican—first in presidential elections and then, gradually, in all elections; conservative politicians quickly followed suit (and occasionally led the way). By the mid-1990s, most southern representatives in Congress were Republican, and the party's leadership in the House was both southern and unflinchingly conservative. Indeed, the mushrooming growth of southern Republicanism solidified the conservatism of the party and helped to usher in an ideologically defined two-party system of a type that had not existed in the mid-twentieth century. The partisan migration of southern whites also gave Republicans a regional stronghold that had been a traditional bastion of opposition to replacing the Electoral College with a national vote.[7] The South, to be sure, was a different place in 1990 or 2010 than it had been in 1960. African-Americans went to the polls in large numbers, and few white citizens regarded the Electoral College as a critical bulwark against racial equality. But race remained a key issue, and dividing line, in the region's politics: large majorities of African-Americans supported the Democratic Party, whereas most whites voted Republican.[8] This racially polarized voting, coupled with winner-take-all, meant that in much of the South black votes did not translate into electoral votes. In 2004 the online periodical *The Black Commentator* lamented "black southern impotence" in presidential politics, arguing that winner-take-all in the region reduced by half the influence of black Americans in presidential elections.[9]

Meanwhile, national opinion polls revealed a growing, if erratic, partisan divide over Electoral College reform among the nation's citizens. In the 1970s and early 1980s, sizable majorities (more than 60 percent) of both Democrats and Republicans had favored replacing the institution with a national popular vote. In subsequent decades, however, Democratic support for direct election remained strong while Republican support declined, gradually at first and then sharply (to below 50 percent) in the wake of the 2000 election. The proportion of Republicans preferring an NPV later rebounded, exceeding 50 percent by 2011. The bipartisan consensus, however, was shattered by the 2016 election, after which only 20 to 30 percent of

Republicans favored reform while 65 percent preferred to keep the Electoral College. The gap between Democratic and Republican views on this issue, as on so many others, was larger than it ever had been.[10]

Republican resistance to reform was also informed by the belief, or at least the hunch, that the Electoral College benefited the GOP's presidential candidates. Party leaders rarely alluded to this notion in public because they did not want to suggest that the playing field was tilted or that their opposition to change had partisan sources. But in the 1980s, talk of a "Republican lock" on the Electoral College was widespread, as the party's candidates scored three decisive victories, giving Republicans a streak of five victories in the six elections held from 1968 to 1988. Although challenged by analysts as untrue or impermanent, the presence of a "lock"—or at least a competitive advantage—was treated, in some circles, as conventional wisdom.[11]

The notion that the Electoral College gave an edge to Republicans was, of course, reinvigorated by the 2000 election. Not only did Bush win the presidency while losing the popular vote, but his margin of victory in the Electoral College could be traced to his having won most of the small states that had electoral weight out of proportion to their populations. To be sure, generalizations drawn from the 2000 election could easily have been called into question after 2004, when Bush performed better in the popular vote than in the electoral tally, but one close call did not reorient Republican thinking.[12] In 2012 the national platform of the Republican Party, breaking decades of official silence on the subject, contained a provision emphasizing "the continuing importance of protecting the Electoral College," a stance that it reiterated in the summer of 2016.[13] The GOP's position was vindicated at the polls by Donald Trump's winning the Electoral College despite losing the popular vote to Hillary Clinton by nearly three million votes. That Republican voters, for the second time in sixteen years, responded to such an outcome by reducing their support for direct elections made it clear that partisan considerations played a strong role in their preference for keeping the Electoral College. In 2011, 54 percent of Republicans (and Republican-leaning independents) had favored a national popular vote; after the 2016 election, that figure plummeted to 19 percent.[14]

Against this political backdrop, it was hardly surprising that even committed critics of the Electoral College were not sanguine about the chances of passing a constitutional amendment to abolish, or significantly reform, the institution. Although proponents of reform periodically introduced resolutions in Congress, they did so largely as a matter of principle: action on their proposals was unlikely, and there was little point in a member of Congress spending much time or political capital promoting a measure that was doomed from the outset.[15] Inertia, however, did not prevail everywhere and at all times. The persistent stalemate in Congress led to bursts of activity in the states and to creative thinking about how to remedy the major defects of the electoral system. It also, and most consequentially, spawned an innovative, energetic, and well-funded movement to promote and achieve a national popular vote without any congressional action at all.

On the Back Burner, 1980–2000

Congressional advocates of Electoral College reform did not immediately abandon the cause after their chastening defeat in the Senate in 1979. Amendment resolutions, most of them calling for direct election, were introduced throughout the 1980s, although their numbers declined sharply after 1982 and remained low for a decade. A majority of these proposals came from Democrats, but a few Republicans, including Senator Charles Mathias of Maryland and Jack Edwards of Alabama, continued to promote reform despite opposition from their party's leadership.[16] None of these measures received any consideration beyond routine referrals to the appropriate committees. Nor was the subject of electoral reform much discussed in the press—although Wisconsin's electors in 1988 attracted some notice when they voted overwhelmingly in favor of abolishing the Electoral College, insisting that "the election of President was too important to be left to people like us."[17]

STIRRINGS IN THE STATES

With electoral reform becalmed in Washington, advocates of change, mostly Democrats, turned their attention to the states, focusing on one reform that state governments could enact by themselves: eliminating winner-take-all. Their singular success unfolded in Nebraska in 1991 when a coalition of Democrats and a handful of Republicans in the unicameral (and officially nonpartisan) legislature voted to adopt a district system for electoral votes. Each of the state's three congressional districts would choose one elector, with two additional electors awarded to the winner of the statewide popular vote. Democratic governor Ben Nelson signed the narrowly passed legislation into law and later vetoed two attempts to repeal it. The impetus for the shift was not altogether partisan—although it gave Democrats a chance to win an electoral vote in a state that had voted overwhelmingly Republican in the six previous presidential elections. What motivated many Nebraska lawmakers, and its major newspaper, was the hope that the new configuration would lure candidates, attention, and campaign expenditures to a state that had been routinely ignored by both parties. Those hopes went unrealized until 2008, when both John McCain and Sarah Palin visited the state and Barack Obama's campaign energetically manned two offices in Omaha; for the first time, the state ended up splitting its electoral votes, with one district going to Obama. (The only other state to choose electors by district, Maine, did not divide its votes until 2016.) Republicans thereafter redoubled their attempts to reinstate winner-take-all, but the Democrats, and the district system, hung on through the 2016 election.[18]

Similar district plans were also pursued in more than a dozen other states, many of them in the South, between 1989 and 1992. These efforts were promoted by a tiny Washington-based nonprofit called the Electoral Fairness Project (EFP), created in 1989. Its founder, George "Skip" Roberts, an experienced Democratic activist and organizer, readily admitted that the project had partisan origins. After Democratic defeats in three presidential elections in the 1980s, Roberts worried that Republican dominance in the South, as well as parts of the Midwest and West, had indeed given Republicans a "lock" on the Electoral College, thanks to winner-take-all. Operating on a shoestring budget, with little backing from the Democratic National Committee, Roberts and a handful of allies set out to pick that lock. In so doing, they argued with conviction that district elections would also serve broader, nonpartisan goals: stimulating popular participation, bringing the electoral vote into closer alignment with the popular vote (thereby making a "wrong winner" less likely), and changing the shape of campaigns by drawing candidates to more states. Support for district elections had a long, bipartisan pedigree, as conservative columnist George Will acknowledged in an ambivalent column about Roberts's effort; their leading champion in the 1950s and 1960s had been Republican Karl Mundt. Curtis Gans, director of the nonpartisan Committee for the Study of the American Electorate, commended the EFP for addressing "many of the serious ills of the modern campaign."[19]

Much of the energy of the EFP was aimed at the South. Six targeted states (Florida, Virginia, Georgia, Louisiana, North Carolina, and South Carolina) had slid into the reliably Republican column in presidential contests although Democrats retained majorities in their legislatures. (The shift toward the Republican Party in state and local elections lagged the swing in presidential politics.) Many Democratic legislators in these states believed that district elections would be more "fair" than winner-take-all; they would also, of course, permit their party to salvage some electoral votes in a region that was slipping from its grasp. Unsurprisingly, Republicans opposed these efforts, despite their own occasional expressions of interest in discarding winner-take-all. A GOP official in Florida claimed that Democrats were "cherry-picking, going after the Sun Belt States they haven't been able to win in recent years."[20]

The Democrats came close to success in Florida, the nation's fourth largest state. Backed by Democratic governor Lawton Chiles, the lower house of the legislature endorsed a district elections bill early in 1992, and the Democrats held a slim majority in the state senate. Republicans fought the measure as a blatantly partisan attempt to grab electoral votes for the Democratic candidate in the coming election. They also put forward amendments that would have delayed implementation of the bill until 1996 or until thirty-five states had taken similar action. After the Democrats rejected those amendments, the bill ended up in weeks of procedural limbo in the senate.[21] Republican interest in the measure surged briefly in June 1992, as Ross Perot's candidacy began to scramble partisan calculations, but the proposal died at the end of the legislature's special June session.[22]

In North Carolina (1989–1990) and Virginia (1992), district plans also won approval in one branch of the legislature but failed to pass in the other. A similar result was obtained in Connecticut (1990), which had a Democratic legislature but had favored the Republican presidential candidate every year since 1968.[23] In each of these states, as well as in others where the proposals fared less well, many Democrats endorsed the district elections bills, but they were not sufficiently united to overcome Republican opposition.[24] (That the Democratic National Committee took no formal position did not help the cause.) In North Carolina, Democratic Party chair E. Lawrence Davis was scornful of the proposal, arguing that it reflected a "defeatist attitude" and that ending winner-take-all would make it more difficult for Democrats to win national elections.[25] Connecticut's Democratic governor, William A. O'Neill, threatened to veto the bill if it reached his desk, because dividing up electoral votes would discourage candidates from visiting the state. Julia H. Tashjian, the Democratic secretary of state, agreed: in an op-ed published in the *Hartford Courant,* she described the proposal as one that "might make some sense as a halfway reform measure, but only if every other state did the same thing."[26] The concern that states would lose influence if they divided their votes was widespread. So too were worries about the risk of unforeseen consequences: as *Washington Post* columnist David Broder put it, "when you start screwing around, you can't predict who is going to benefit." Then too, the fruits of victory might prove to be minimal. Michael Dukakis had carried only one congressional district in North Carolina and Connecticut in 1988.[27]

Although the specific obstacles to the success of the EFP varied from place to place, two overarching problems loomed large. The first was the tension, the contradiction, between the partisan origins of the project and its claim to be pursuing nonpartisan objectives. Skip Roberts and his allies were surely correct that the virtues of district elections were potentially bipartisan, that Republicans in reliably Democratic states like Massachusetts could also benefit from abolishing winner-take-all. It was also true, as Connecticut legislator Miles Rapoport argued, that district elections could "help avert" the crisis of a "wrong-winner" election, a goal that was in the national interest.[28] But in fact there was no reform effort under way in Massachusetts or any other predominantly Democratic state. "Why aren't they doing it in New York?" asked one skeptical Republican. In the absence of a national reform campaign, the partisan aura—indeed, the taint of hypocrisy—was inescapable, which made it nearly impossible to enlist Republican supporters.[29] The second problem, which troubled legislators of both parties, was that there were, in fact, potential downsides to being an early adopter. Candidates might well pay less attention to a state if only a few electoral votes were in play. "I wouldn't want to see Florida do it and every other state hold on to winner-take-all," noted a state senator. The competitive logic that had led states to implement winner-take-all in the early decades of the nineteenth century could not be shifted into reverse.[30]

ROSS PEROT AND THE CONTINGENT ELECTION SYSTEM

The pattern of congressional silence regarding the electoral system was briefly interrupted in 1992 when H. Ross Perot, an outspoken Texas billionaire with a mix of conservative and liberal views, launched an independent campaign for the presidency. To the shock of most observers, Perot's candidacy caught fire, and polls conducted in the spring indicated that he might win 25 to 40 percent of the vote in a three-way race against incumbent president George H. W. Bush and the probable Democratic challenger, Arkansas governor Bill Clinton.[31] Those numbers raised the specter of an election in which no candidate received an electoral vote majority; that possibility had arisen before, as recently as 1980, but in the late spring of 1992, in the eyes of many observers, it appeared *likely* to occur.[32] Such an outcome would lead either to unseemly horse-trading over electoral votes or to the election being decided in the House of Representatives, where each state delegation would cast one vote. (The rules governing an election in the House would have to be concocted by the chamber itself.)[33] This prospect of a president being chosen through procedures that seemed neither fair nor democratic—and that had been in mothballs since 1824—generated alarm among politicians and political observers.[34] The House minority leader, Republican Robert Michel, declared that it would be an "utter disaster" if the election went to the House, that it would be an "outrage to the whole concept of popular sovereignty." His Democratic colleague Dan Glickman saw it as a "recipe for, at a minimum, chaos, and at a maximum, disaster."[35] The long-running failure of Congress to reform the electoral system—or at least the much-derided contingent procedure—might have finally come home to roost.

Perot quieted the alarms in mid-July when he abruptly announced that he was ending his campaign because he did not want to toss the election into the House and thereby make it difficult for the winner of the election to form an administration in time to take office. (Whether that was Perot's real reason was unclear: his announcement followed weeks of turmoil within his campaign; he later offered different—and more bizarre—explanations; and even as he stepped back, he encouraged supporters to continue trying to get his name on the ballot in all fifty states.)[36] Then, in early October, Perot changed his mind and re-entered the race, just in time to participate in the presidential debates. Although his popularity had plummeted after he dropped out, he performed well in the debates, thanks in part to a plainspoken style and punchy one-liners. On Election Day, Perot garnered 19 percent of the popular vote, more than any independent since Theodore Roosevelt in 1912. But he won no electoral votes, permitting the nation once again to avoid the trials of a contingent election.[37]

Not surprisingly, Perot's candidacy—particularly before his July withdrawal—caught the attention of Congress. Nearly a dozen measures were introduced to transform the electoral system, and House Speaker Tom Foley, a Washington Democrat, instructed the Rules and Judiciary committees to conduct a review of the procedures that the chamber would need to choose a president.[38] The Senate meanwhile scheduled the first hearing on electoral reform since 1979. Convened by Illinois Democrat Paul Simon, chair of the Senate Judiciary Committee's Subcommittee on the Constitution, the hearing focused on three joint resolutions: two, sponsored by Democrats James Exon (Nebraska) and David Pryor (Arkansas), offered plans for direct election, while the third, promoted by Republicans Slade Gorton (Washington) and Mitch McConnell (Kentucky), proposed a runoff election to replace the contingent process in the House. As fate would have it, the hearing ended up taking place several days after Perot's withdrawal, a fact that diminished both the urgency of the subject and the attendance of committee members.[39]

Still, the testimony at the hearing was revealing. Exon observed that "millions of Americans" had been awakened "to the ticking time bomb in our Constitution" and that Congress should seize the moment to take action. Pryor, quoting Thomas Jefferson's statement that the contingent procedure was "the most dangerous blot on our Constitution," urged the committee and the Senate to "not let this matter fade away. The end of Ross Perot's third party candidacy did absolutely nothing to solve the problems inherent in our electoral process, it just pushed off the final day of reckoning." Pryor, who had worked closely with Bayh in the late 1970s, proposed to solve these problems with a resolution identical to the one debated in the

Senate in 1979. Exon offered a new variant: a direct election that would deliver the presidency to a candidate who won 50 percent of the popular vote and at least one-third of the states. If no candidate reached that threshold, a runoff would be held within sixty days. This plan, Exon noted, would guarantee that the president had a popular mandate while guarding "against regionalism and the domination of large-population states." Both proposals would remove Congress from any role in the selection of presidents and vice presidents.[40]

Senators Gorton and McConnell took a different tack, urging the committee to retain the Electoral College but fix the contingent process. "Almost no one," Gorton noted, believed that presidential elections should be decided by the House. "It is nonsense," echoed McConnell, "to have the House of Representatives choose the president." (The House, it should be noted, had a Democratic majority, and Democrats in 1992 controlled thirty-one of the fifty state delegations.) What they proposed instead was a runoff election between the two candidates who received the most electoral votes, to be conducted according to the same rules (with electoral votes) as the initial balloting. Their plan, which would take effect in 1996, also contained language that would ban faithless electors. While making their case, Gorton and McConnell voiced strong opposition to the more extensive reforms championed by Pryor and Exon, insisting that the Electoral College "has served us well," direct elections were undesirable (for the usual reasons), and there was little chance that any proposal for a national vote could be approved by Congress. McConnell also claimed—perhaps protesting too much—that there were "no particular partisan implications" to his stance, pointing to the 1979 Senate vote as evidence that Democrats also opposed direct elections. The Kentucky senator went out of his way to sing the praises of Sam Ervin, who in 1970 had persuaded him—then a senate staffer—of the virtues of the Electoral College.[41]

Outside witnesses at the hearing, many of whom had testified in the 1970s, had predictably diverse views. Direct elections were endorsed by the League of Women Voters; Americans for Democratic Action; the San Juan, Puerto Rico, city council (which also promoted presidential voting rights for inhabitants of the island); and Lawrence Longley, a seasoned expert who attempted to inject the findings of recent scholarship into the discussion. Strenuous opposition was voiced by Henry Siegman of the American

Jewish Congress and by longtime opponent Judith Best ("the direct election movement is . . . a part of a centralizing plebiscitizing constitutional heresy"). More temperate concerns were shared by Thomas Mann of the Brookings Institute and Norman Ornstein of the American Enterprise Institute, both of whom favored the Gorton-McConnell resolution while recommending that any constitutional amendment also address problems with the Electoral College itself. A far more radical, if backward-looking, idea was offered by the iconoclastic former senator Eugene McCarthy, who suggested that the Electoral College be given a chance to work as the framers had originally intended—as a deliberative body. He proposed the creation of a body of 2,500 electors, each chosen by a small district, who would remain in office for four years, giving "responsible, trusted persons" the responsibility of choosing a president. Former campaign consultant Douglas Bailey, now the editor of *Hotwire,* a political newsletter, took a step even further back in history by advocating that members of Congress serve as electors, a concept that the framers had expressly rejected in 1787.[42]

The hearing adjourned after one day, and no further action was taken. Perot's withdrawal had taken the heat off, and—as had happened so many times in the past—the absence of an imminent threat permitted Congress to avoid wrestling with the issue. The episode also underscored the ongoing absence of consensus about a path forward. That the Gorton-McConnell resolution had five co-sponsors, all Republican, sent a message that the GOP had little interest in instituting direct elections; notably there were also Democrats, including Speaker Foley, who shared their reservations. At the same time, reformers like Pryor were loath to endorse an amendment such as Gorton's that would fix only the contingent process and affirm the perpetuation of the Electoral College. The upshot, despite the anxieties that had been so palpable in the spring of 1992, was that things remained at a standstill. After Perot re-entered the race, and even after the election itself, there were occasional calls for action, but these were easy to ignore. Despite the "hue and cry" about the "arcane" Electoral College, observed a reader of the *Milwaukee Journal Sentinel* in December, the issue had all too quickly become "moot." Indeed, the fact that Perot had won a large percentage of the popular vote without gaining a single electoral vote may have eased apprehensions about the risk of an election ending up in Congress.[43]

FIN DE SIÈCLE

After 1992 the issue of Electoral College reform again dropped from public view. Ross Perot mounted a second presidential campaign in 1996, but his diminished candidacy set off few alarms (he won 8.4 percent of the vote), and Bill Clinton's decisive victory over Bob Dole raised no questions about the electoral system. Still, the concerns voiced since the middle of the twentieth century did not melt away, to the chagrin of conservatives who believed that each passing election offered new evidence of the soundness of the system.[44]

The persistent criticism led to the introduction of more than a dozen amendment resolutions in Congress between 1993 and 2000 and to the twentieth century's final congressional hearing on the subject. That hearing was convened in September 1997 by the chair of the House Subcommittee on the Constitution, Charles T. Canady, a Florida Republican. Canady, a Yale Law School graduate who would later become chief justice of the Florida Supreme Court, opened the one-day hearing by stating that the existing system "seems to have served the nation fairly well" but that "there are indeed potential problems with the current manner in which we elect our President." One was that "the person who actually wins the electoral vote may receive fewer popular votes than his opponent." A second was that "a strong third-party candidate" could lead to a decision by the House of Representatives. Canady noted that many past discussions of reform had taken place either just before or just after "the heated political atmosphere of a Presidential election." The present moment, in contrast, offered the House a chance to examine the issue in a calmer "environment."[45]

The formal objective of the hearing was to consider two resolutions that called for replacing the Electoral College with direct popular elections. The first (H.J. Res. 28) was modeled on Bayh's resolutions of the 1960s and 1970s, calling for a runoff election if no candidate won 40 percent of the popular vote. It was sponsored by Bob Wise, a seasoned liberal Democrat from West Virginia (who would later serve as governor), and by Ray LaHood, a moderate Republican from Illinois (who would later serve as secretary of transportation under Barack Obama). The second resolution (H.J. Res. 43), which required a candidate to win 50 percent of the vote to avoid a runoff, was introduced by California Republican Tom Campbell, a moderate with a libertarian streak.[46] The testimony for and against these proposals, from a short roster of outside experts, was perfunctory: well-known advocates and opponents of direct election reiterated arguments that had been circulating for years.[47]

Still, the hearing had two noteworthy features. The first was that three Republican members of the subcommittee, including Canady, expressed some interest in altering the system. Bob Barr of Georgia, who would become the Libertarian candidate for president in 2008, observed that there was nothing "sacrosanct" about the Electoral College and that "probably" it was worth "amending in favor of something that is somewhat more direct." Edward Bryant, a solid conservative from Tennessee, worried at length that a candidate could win the popular vote but not the electoral vote. Canady himself opined that he had "difficulty understanding why it is that someone is better who is chosen through this particular mechanism than a person who is chosen by a majority of the people." Henry Hyde of Illinois, the chair of the powerful Judiciary Committee, offered a strong conventional defense of the Electoral College, but it was evident that there were at least a few Republicans, of various stripes, who were receptive to reform ideas.[48]

The second distinctive feature of the 1997 hearing was its preoccupation with the possibility of a "wrong winner," a phrase that became common only in the final decade of the century. Canady had raised the issue in his opening comments, and LaHood argued that his proposal "would hopefully rectify a potentially huge, looming political crisis, an election that results in a President being elected without winning the popular vote." Akhil Amar, an expert witness from Yale Law School, offered a vivid metaphor and a probing question:

> The dreaded specter of a clear popular loser becoming the Electoral College winner has not happened in this century. Why worry? But that's what someone might say after three trigger pulls in Russian roulette. One day we will end up with a clear loser President, clear beyond any quibbles about uncertain ballots. The question is, will this loser/winner be seen as legitimate at home and abroad?

Bryant picked up the theme, noting that his constituents often asked about it; if the loser of the popular vote were to be elected, he wondered, "how are we going to explain this to the American people"? Canady also believed "that the American public would not understand the election of a President who had not received the most votes in the election." "What implications," he asked, "does that have for the effectiveness of government if such a scenario develops?" The Florida congressman found the prospect "troubling." Nonetheless, he concluded the hearing on a pessimistic note.

> I will be very candid with you. I do not think this proposal is going anywhere. I do not know that we are going to spend a lot of energy on it or any more energy on it. I am not sure that this would pass the House, but I do not think it would pass the Senate. So there we are.[49]

Election 2000: Crisis and Aftermath

The long-awaited and long-dreaded event—the "coming debacle" as two political scientists called it in 1991—finally occurred in the autumn of 2000. Although it took weeks of legal wrangling for the outcome of the November 7 election to be settled, George W. Bush emerged as the winner of the electoral vote and the presidency; his principal opponent, Vice President Al Gore, won the popular tally by half a million votes. For the first time since 1888, the candidate who won the most votes nationwide did not occupy the White House.[50]

Predictions that this might occur were plentiful in the weeks before the election. Former candidate John Anderson published an op-ed piece in early November suggesting that this might be the year for a "wrong winner" and sketching out the case for abolition of the Electoral College. A few days earlier, Jeff Greenfield, a respected commentator, described the Electoral College as a "time bomb, buried in the parchment of the Constitution—and this year, the time bomb could blow up in our faces." What seemed to be the most likely scenario was a Bush victory in the popular vote coupled with a Gore win in the Electoral College. Most of the polls taken in the final weeks of the campaign showed that Bush had a small but consistent lead nationally but that Gore stood a good chance of snagging a majority of the electoral votes.[51]

Both campaigns prepared for the possibility of a split verdict. Bush's advisers are "not only thinking the unthinkable, they're planning for it," reported the *New York Daily News*. They devised a strategy to utilize talk-radio and ads to stoke public sentiment against the Electoral College for having thwarted "the will of the people," and they even hoped to get principled Democrats to join their cause. The goal would be to convince a sufficient number of Gore's electors to cast their votes instead for the popular vote winner. Gore's team had not gone as far in its preparations, but in the final days of the campaign key staff members were asked to research the historical record, contact scholars, and prepare talking points affirming the legitimacy of the Electoral College verdict. "You play by the rules in force at the time" of the election, observed one aide. Both camps were willing to switch their rhetorical positions in the event that the outcome was the reverse of what had been anticipated.[52]

In the immediate aftermath of the election, there were, predictably, numerous calls for the abolition or reform of the Electoral College. On November 10, three days after the ballots were cast, Massachusetts congressman William Delahunt, a Democratic member of the Judiciary Committee, wrote in the *Boston Globe* that "the collision between the electoral vote and the popular vote is no longer just a historical curiosity." It was time, he declared, for direct elections, and the country should act "while the sting of the contradiction is still fresh." "If the Electoral College merely echoes the election results, then it is superfluous," he argued succinctly. "If it contradicts the voting majority, then why tolerate it?" Ray LaHood and Illinois senator Richard Durbin urged support for a direct election resolution that they had introduced before the election. Less than a week after the balloting, Senator-elect Hillary Clinton, on a victory tour in upstate New York, declared that she had long believed that the Electoral College was an "anachronism" and promised to promote passage of an amendment resolution in the Senate. Op-ed columns calling for reform sprouted up quickly.[53]

Nonetheless, the great public clamor that had been predicted for decades did not materialize. Newspaper editorial pages were more often cautious than outraged, although both the *Boston Globe* and the *Atlanta Journal-Constitution* did call for replacement of the Electoral College within a week of the election. ("The thing is an inflamed appendix, useless and occasionally dangerous," wrote the *Journal-Constitution*.) The *Washington Post*, in contrast, acknowledged that there were "legitimate questions" to be asked but insisted that "this is no time for reform." The *New York Times* editorialized that the institution "has enough benefits to justify its survival," while both the *Los Angeles Times* and the *Chicago Tribune* put forward strong defenses of the system. Meanwhile, relatively few Democratic politicians were outspoken on the issue (House minority leader Richard Gephardt was an exception), and Republican critics like LaHood were a rarity; the "wrong" winner had turned out to be their winner. Most importantly, perhaps, the American people did not pour into the streets to demand that the electoral system be changed. The protests that did occur in Washington on the cold rainy day of President Bush's inauguration challenged the president's legitimacy ("Hail to the Thief" was a widespread sign), and Reverend Al Sharpton pointed out that Bush "was not elected by the people," but there were few explicit allusions to the Electoral College.[54]

This relatively muted response stemmed, at least in part, from the dynamics and sequencing of the political drama that engulfed the nation after ballots had been cast on November 7. It took five weeks for the outcome of the election to be finalized: not until the Supreme Court issued its verdict on December 12, halting the Florida recount that might have made Al Gore president, did anyone know with certainty that the Electoral College had indeed yielded a "contradiction" between the popular and electoral votes. In the course of those five weeks, the nation discovered a host of other problems with its electoral processes: unreliable and antiquated technology, poorly designed ballots, high rates of ballot spoilage or machine failure in minority precincts, the administration of elections by overtly partisan officials (such as Florida's secretary of state, Katherine Harris), election laws that varied considerably from one state to the next, the draconian lifetime disenfranchisement of felons in a handful of states, and the purging from the voter rolls of law-abiding citizens whose names were identical to those of felons.[55] Then too there was the remarkable news from Tallahassee, in the midst of the legal skirmishing, that the Republican-dominated state legislature was making plans to choose a slate of electors by itself if the dispute was not settled in a timely or acceptable fashion. According to the Constitution, the nation was reminded (and the Supreme Court confirmed), state legislatures—not voters—had the power to appoint electors, and they could assert that power even after having authorized a popular election.[56] The long list of problems outraged many citizens, as did the Supreme Court itself when it handed down an opaque final decision that could not escape the aroma of partisanship.

Although the Electoral College was always at the heart of the dispute (without winner-take-all, Florida would not have been on the hot seat), the utterly unforeseeable manner in which the 2000 election unfolded—the distended, conflict-ridden, back-and-forth journey through recounts and courts—drew attention away from the institution itself and toward a succession of other issues. As long as the outcome hung in the balance, the spotlight was on vote counting and legal maneuvers. After the verdict had been issued, those who were critical of the outcome aimed their ire at the Supreme Court: lingering questions about the legitimacy of Bush's election centered more on the Court's decision to halt the Florida recount than on the undisputed fact that Gore had won the national popular vote. By the time that the long drama had come to an end, moreover, there was a widespread sense of exhaustion and relief. The nation's electoral systems were unmistakably flawed, but the dispute was finally over—and it had at least ended peacefully. If there was a latent potential for an enormous public outcry over a "wrong winner," it was unlikely to have been realized in the unique circumstances of the 2000 election.[57]

There were other threads to the story as well. If the public clamor was muted, the silence in Congress was deafening. Nearly a dozen resolutions were introduced in the six months following the election, some calling for direct election and others offering district or proportional plans. Almost all were put forward by Democrats: Ray LaHood and Jim Leach, a respected moderate from Iowa, were the only Republicans to sponsor reforms.[58] But with a GOP majority in the House and control of the Senate teetering between the two parties, no action was taken on any of these measures, beyond referring them to committees.[59] The tone of the Republican stance was set early by Orrin Hatch, the chair of the Senate Judiciary Committee and a longtime adversary of direct election. (The chair of the Subcommittee on the Constitution was Strom Thurmond.) One day after the Supreme Court decision, Hatch praised the Electoral College, declaring that "it basically worked very, very well." "Even the smallest state made the difference in the election," he observed. "We ought to be very proud of our electoral system."[60] Faced with Republican opposition and recognizing that Democrats themselves were not unified in support of change, advocates concluded that pursuing Electoral College reform would be an exercise in futility.[61] As a senator, Hillary Clinton took no official steps to promote the adoption of direct elections, and neither did most of her Democratic colleagues. The discontents spawned by the 2000 election were channeled instead into a prolonged, multiyear effort to improve both voting technology and the administration of elections.[62]

The Electoral College was also given short shrift by the National Commission on Federal Election Reform, a blue-ribbon, bipartisan panel formed by the Century Foundation and the University of Virginia's Miller Center of Public Affairs. With former presidents Carter and Ford as its honorary co-chairs, the commission was tasked with gathering information, holding hearings, and making policy recommendations that would address the manifold issues that had arisen in the course of the 2000 election. Early in its internal deliberations, however, the commission decided to take the Electoral College off the table and "not make recommendations about whether or how the Constitution should be amended in order to do away with or refashion the choice of presidential electors." When Jack Rakove, a Stanford historian and constitutional scholar, urged the commission to take a serious look at the institution's shortcomings, Carter responded with his comment that it would be a "waste of time" to talk about Electoral College reform. The former president, who was the driving force behind the commission's work, later explained that he "was just talking about the almost inherent impossibility, in my opinion, of getting two-thirds of the House and Senate and three-fourths of the states to ratify." That sober-minded assessment meant that the principal nongovernmental body charged with devising remedies for the problems that had surfaced during the election remained silent about the electoral system that had yielded the crisis in the first place.[63] The final report of the commission, delivered to Congress in August 2001, focused instead on recommendations for improving turnout, registration systems, election administration, and voting machines.[64]

Washington's lack of interest in change did not, of course, put an end to public debate about the flaws and virtues of the Electoral College. Opinions on both sides remained strongly held, and for the next decade and a half they were aired frequently (especially in election years) at public gatherings, on radio and television, and in newspapers, magazines, scholarly publications, and social media.[65] In 2004, as another close contest brought the electoral system back into sharp focus, *Business Week* issued a detailed editorial in favor of a national popular vote: "The candidate with the most votes wins—no ifs, ands, or buts," its editors declared. In August 2004 the *New York Times,* in a rare public reversal, declared that "we were wrong" to have supported the Electoral College in 2000 and strongly endorsed a national popular vote (as it had also done in 1969–1970). A week later, perhaps in response, the *Wall Street Journal* announced that it was sticking with its long-standing position: "We're inclined to think the Founders got it right."[66] In November the country experienced another "near miss," as Democrat John Kerry came close to winning the Electoral College while decisively losing the popular vote.

The year 2004 also witnessed the publication of two notable books inspired by the 2000 election and its aftermath. *Enlightened Democracy: The Case for the Electoral College,* by Tara Ross, with a forward by columnist George Will, was a brief for the institution, a fluent, skillfully presented recitation of traditional arguments. Stressing that the United States was designed to be a federal Republic and not a democracy, the book touted the "successful results" that the Electoral College had obtained over the years and pointed to the hazards of direct election. Ross, a conservative writer and lawyer based in Texas, penned the book in response to what she believed to be the misguided and ill-informed criticism that had flooded the media after the 2000 election. It was the first of several volumes that she would write on the subject, as she became a prominent popular defender of the Electoral College.[67]

The second book, *Why the Electoral College Is Bad for America,* by George C. Edwards III, was a more scholarly endeavor. Edwards, a distinguished political scientist and editor of *Presidential Studies Quarterly,* was dismayed by the election of a president who had lost the popular vote and troubled by the claims commonly put forward to defend the Electoral College. He set out to test those claims conceptually and empirically and found them to be "faulty" or "contrary to fact." Edwards concluded that no coherent set of political principles undergirded the framers' design, nor were there important state or minority interests that were protected by the Electoral College. Small states, in fact, received little attention from presidential candidates, and the system did not oblige candidates to build broad national coalitions. The Electoral College, furthermore, was "not essential" to the maintenance of a two-party system and did not "safeguard" federalism either. Edwards's critique had ample precedents, but his unusually comprehensive book offered the most rigorous analysis and up-to-date evidence that had appeared in decades.[68]

Although much of the debate after 2000 followed well-trodden paths, the election did give rise to a few noteworthy twists in the arguments. Defenders of the Electoral College could no longer claim that the prospect of a divergence between the popular and electoral votes was merely hypothetical or extremely unlikely; gone was the refrain that no such outcome had occurred since the nineteenth century. In its place was a renewed emphasis on the institution as embodying a federalist conception of majorities—or, alternatively, on the claim that the United States was never intended to be a democracy in the first place.[69] Advocates of direct election, in contrast, found grist for their mill in the inauguration of a "wrong winner," but they were obliged to surrender the jeremiad that such an outcome would produce a popular upheaval or a crisis of legitimacy. The details of the Florida dispute provided new ammunition for both sides. Conservatives like Mitch McConnell repeatedly warned that the prolonged, messy recount in Florida was a harbinger of much worse horrors to come if direct elections were adopted—because recounts like Florida's might then have to be conducted simultaneously in multiple states.[70] Reformers, in turn, pointed to the actions of Florida's legislature as evidence of a significant democracy gap in the constitutional architecture: if state legislatures could indeed choose electors by themselves without regard to the preferences of the people, what would prevent them from doing so in future elections? Reformers also questioned the rationality of a system that delivered all of a state's electoral votes to one candidate when the outcome of the popular vote in that state was a statistical tie.[71]

One other shift in public discourse after 2000 warrants mention. This was the resuscitation of the notion that the small states were the principal beneficiaries of the Electoral College and that they consequently constituted a major roadblock to direct elections. From the late 1960s into the 1990s, a consensus had emerged, fostered in part by scholarly analyses, that both large and small states were advantaged by the Electoral College and that large states likely had the better deal. It was also known that some of the foremost congressional advocates of an NPV came from small states and that most residents of small states, according to polls, favored direct election. After the 2000 election—which George Bush won in part because of the small-state advantage—this consensus receded from view.[72] The large-state advantage began to receive far less public mention, and the presumption that small states would oppose (and likely prevent) abolition of the Electoral College became more widespread, even among those sympathetic to reform.[73] Historian Arthur Schlesinger Jr. commented in 2002 that some reformers seemed "intimidated" by the prospect of small-state opposition; he found this to be "odd" in light of the expert view that large states possessed an even greater advantage. Few participants in the post-2000 debates seemed to remember that small-state leaders like William Langer, Margaret Chase Smith, John Pastore, and Mike Mansfield had energetically favored a national vote.[74]

The posture of Congress in the immediate wake of the 2000 election set a pattern that would prevail for a decade. Amendment resolutions calling for direct, district, or proportional elections were introduced in the House in most years through 2011, almost invariably by Democrats. (No resolutions calling for direct election were introduced in either chamber between February 2011 and November 2016.)[75] Among the sponsors of these resolutions were Eliot Engel (NY), William Delahunt (MA), Gene Green (TX), Jesse Jackson Jr. (IL), and Zoe Lofgren (CA). In 2005, California's Democratic senators, Dianne Feinstein and Barbara Boxer, sponsored a direct election amendment in the upper chamber, and Florida Democrat Bill Nelson did the same in 2009. (Boxer acted again soon after the 2016 election.) No hearings were held on any of these proposals; indeed, no action of any type was taken.[76] As the Congressional Research Service concluded in 2016, the resolutions "experienced the fate of the vast majority of proposed amendments: assignment to the appropriate committee, and, then, oblivion."[77]

Notably, this was true even between 2007 and 2011 when the Democrats held majorities in the House and the Senate, and the judiciary committees were chaired by John Conyers of Michigan and Patrick Leahy of Vermont, both of whom had supported direct election in earlier decades. Leahy and Conyers had long experience in the workings of Congress, and they surely knew not only that Republican leaders adamantly opposed reform but that support among Democrats was far from unanimous: as recently as 2004, Democratic leader Harry Reid had defended the institution on the senate floor.[78] In addition, there was little pressure from within Congress or from organized outside groups to take up the issue in committees that already had full agendas.[79] Under these circumstances, even sympathetic politicians chose not to press the issue. Former representative William Delahunt explained in a retrospective interview that he never believed that the resolutions he sponsored would go very far. He had introduced them as a statement of principle, prompted by the 2000 election and his own commitment to the ideal of "one person, one vote." To be successful with electoral reform, he noted, there had to be dedicated and well-positioned congressional champions, willing to devote years to battling the "innate inertia" that enveloped such issues. The timing also had to be right, which meant, among other things, that Washington could not be preoccupied with pressing concerns like the Iraq war or a financial crisis.[80]

There was, in sum, even less activity in Washington after Bush's inauguration than there had been from 1980 to 2000—and dramatically less than there had been between 1960 and 1980. The 2000 election did not prod Congress into seriously considering reform, nor did Congress seem particularly moved by polls indicating that more than 60 percent of Americans continued to favor a shift to direct elections. A week before the balloting in 2000, Jeff Greenfield, speaking for many political analysts, had predicted that a split between the electoral and popular votes would have "one consequence" that was certain: "at long last, the Electoral College would either be abolished or radically altered."[81] But Greenfield, and those who shared his view, turned out to be mistaken. Denying the presidency to a candidate who had won the popular vote ended up having no systemic repercussions: the nation weathered the small storm kicked up by the split verdict, and Congress felt no obligation to prevent such an event from recurring. Although the policy consequences of George Bush, rather than Al Gore, having become president were of major significance, the electoral source of Bush's presidency faded from view—particularly as the nation became preoccupied with terrorist attacks on its own soil, followed by wars in Afghanistan and Iraq. For many in Washington, the quiescent aftermath of the 2000 election was proof of the resilience of the nation's political institutions, further evidence that there was no compelling need to alter the system. Committed advocates of change, in contrast, found themselves once more looking outside of Washington for ways to gain traction.

BACK TO THE STATES

In January 2001 state senator Ron Tupa introduced a bill in the Colorado legislature calling for a referendum that would ask the state's voters to decide whether to replace the winner-take-all allocation of electoral votes with district elections. Undaunted by the earlier failures of the Electoral Fairness Project, Tupa, a Boulder Democrat, was responding directly to the 2000 election. Despite winning only 51 percent of the state's popular vote, George Bush had received all eight of Colorado's electoral votes; if Al Gore had received three of those votes, he would have been president. The state senate, with a narrow Democratic majority, passed Tupa's measure, but it died in the Republican-controlled house.[82] Colorado had voted Republican in every recent presidential election except that of 1992, when, thanks to Ross Perot, Bill Clinton won the state with only 40 percent of the vote.

Three years later the effort to jettison winner-take-all was revived in altered form: an initiative to amend the state constitution so that electoral votes would be allocated according to the proportion of the popular vote each candidate received. As an initiative, Amendment 36, which was placed on the ballot after a petition drive, did not require approval from the politically divided legislature.[83] The campaign to win passage was spearheaded by Democratic consultant Rick Ridder, who regarded the measure as "a first step to reforming the Electoral College." Proportional elections, he maintained, would yield an electoral vote that would more closely mirror the popular vote and help prevent a repeat of the 2000 election. Much as Skip Roberts had in the early 1990s, Ridder's team insisted that the proposal was nonpartisan. "Make Your Vote Count," the organization formed to mobilize support for Amendment 36, had no direct ties to the Democratic Party, and the state party took no official position on the referendum.[84]

But a hotly contested presidential election campaign was under way in 2004, and Amendment 36 was embroiled in partisanship from the outset—in part because the amendment was designed to take effect immediately. If approved on Election Day, it would determine the distribution of electoral votes between President Bush and his Democratic rival, John Kerry. As the campaign entered its final months, Bush was leading in the polls, but Democrats had been gaining ground in Colorado, and Kerry was projected to run well; his state campaign director declared that she was less interested in the referendum than in winning the state. Still, Republican opponents characterized the amendment as an attempt to change the rules of the election in midstream (or even retroactively) in order to snag four electoral votes for Kerry in a tight national contest. Katy Atkinson, a Republican consultant who led an anti-amendment organization called Coloradans Against a Really Stupid Idea, acknowledged that the country needed to have a debate about the Electoral College but claimed that the issue at hand was whether "Colorado is going to be the lone state to try an untested system that could put us at a disadvantage."[85]

The state's leading newspapers and its Republican governor, Bill Owens, also criticized the measure. A proportional system, they argued, would diminish the incentive for a candidate to visit or pay attention to Colorado's interests. Opponents further charged that passage of Amendment 36 would encourage third parties, giving power to the likes of Ross Perot; it would increase the odds of an election going to the House of Representatives; and it could potentially land Colorado in a legal and constitutional crisis that would make it the "Florida" of 2004.[86] Whether it was constitutional for a popular initiative, rather than the state legislature, to determine the manner in which electors were chosen was a question that was surely headed to court if Amendment 36 were approved. At issue also was the legality of applying the amendment to the results of an election campaign conducted before the adoption of the proportional system.[87]

Amendment 36 attracted attention from the national press as well as funding from outside the state.[88] With the presidential contest expected to be close and September polls indicating that most Coloradans favored the proposal, the amendment appeared to be setting the stage for another November drama. It might also, as was widely observed, become a model for reform in other states. "It could set a dramatic and amazing precedent," declared a political scientist interviewed by the *New York Times*.[89] Members of both parties had voiced displeasure with winner-take-all (often linked to the state where they lived), and a state-by-state approach to reform seemed relatively promising given the stalemate in Washington. Proportional elections did not raise the federalism objections that arose in opposition to a national popular vote; nor did they arouse the concerns about gerrymandering that invariably greeted proposals for district elections. The idea, in brief, seemed potentially contagious. "Colorado gives new breath to an idea that is irrefutably democratic," opined the *Los Angeles Times*.[90]

Amendment 36, however, failed to win the approval of Colorado's voters. Republican opponents hammered the proposal with a barrage of ads during the fall while the state's leading Democrats steered clear of the issue; polls registered a steady decline in support for the measure.[91] Meanwhile, the race between Kerry and Bush tightened, leading some Democrats to believe that Kerry could win and thereby capture all nine of the state's electoral votes. On November 2, roughly 700,000 Coloradans voted in favor of the amendment while 1.3 million were opposed. The margin was substantially greater than the 100,000 votes by which Bush bested Kerry— which meant that many of Kerry's supporters had cast their ballots against Amendment 36.[92]

The defeat in Colorado did not deter groups elsewhere from pursuing similar objectives. For politicians and activists whose party had a strong presence in a state but relatively little chance of winning its presidential contest, the prospect of dividing up the state's electoral votes remained alluring. State campaigns to eliminate winner-take-all could serve partisan interests while being plausibly framed as attempts to make the system more democratic. As Colorado's experience made clear, however, such efforts could potentially create awkward tensions between the goals of local actors and the objectives of national parties and campaigns.

North Carolina was a key case in point. As early as 2001, Democrats, with majorities in both branches of the General Assembly, promoted a plan to choose electors by district. That plan was approved by the state senate but never came to a vote in the lower chamber.[93] The idea was revived in 2007 when the Democrats had a larger majority in the house of representatives; by then Republican candidates had won seven straight presidential races in the state. Democrats hailed their proposal (SB 353) as fairer than winner-take-all and likely to increase the engagement of voters, particularly among African-Americans, who, year after year, were having no impact on the electoral vote tally. Democrats further argued that a district system would lead national candidates to campaign in the state because at least some districts would be in play. Republicans countered that such a system would instead make the state "irrelevant" and that the effort was simply a partisan maneuver to pick up a half dozen electoral votes for the

Democrats. The districting proposal was passed by a narrow margin in the senate, and it also won approval, along party lines, in a key house committee. All that remained was a final vote on the floor of the house and the signature of Governor Mike Easley, a Democrat who supported the measure. But then something unusual happened: Howard Dean, the chair of the Democratic National Committee, placed a phone call to state senator Doug Berger, the lead sponsor of SB 353, and asked him to withdraw, or table, the measure for the remainder of the legislative session. Berger obliged, North Carolina ended up sticking with winner-take-all, and in November 2008 the state went to Barack Obama by a very slim margin.[94]

Dean's phone call was not prompted by clairvoyance about voting trends in North Carolina. What was on his mind was an unsettling development across the country, in California. There, a group of well-connected Republicans was attempting to put a district elections initiative on the ballot in June 2008. California had been voting Democratic in presidential elections since 1992, but roughly twenty of its fifty-three congressional districts were reliably Republican, and a gain of twenty electoral votes (a net shift of forty) would be an enormous boon for the GOP. Dean and other national Democrats believed that this Republican initiative had to be exposed as an illegitimate partisan maneuver or "dirty trick," but Democrats would have no rhetorical legs to stand on if they were embracing the same legislation in North Carolina. As one commentator in the Tar Heel state noted, gaining a maximum of seven electoral votes in his state while losing twenty-two in California was "not a very good trade."[95]

The idea of discarding winner-take-all had been circulating among California Republicans since at least 2000, but the effort began in earnest in July 2007 when attorney Thomas Hiltachk filed the papers for an initiative entitled the "Presidential Election Reform Act." Based in Sacramento, Hiltachk was Governor Arnold Schwarzenegger's personal lawyer for election matters, and his firm, which specialized in ballot initiatives, also represented the California Republican Party. Backers of the proposal then began to raise the needed funds—estimated to be $2 million—to collect the 434,000 signatures needed to put the initiative on the ballot.[96] Advocates predictably maintained that district elections would "benefit all Californians" because they would compel candidates to compete for their votes and address the state's issues. Kevin Eckery, a Republican consultant, argued that "winner take all" could not possibly "reflect California's diversity." "If five million voters decide to vote for the Republican nominee," asked another Republican, "why should that vote not be counted?" In late August, according to the *San Francisco Chronicle,* a Field poll indicated that voters were "inclined to support the initiative" but were not yet "sold on the idea."[97]

Democrats fought back fiercely. Chris Lehane, a strategist closely allied with Hillary Clinton's presidential campaign, declared that the proposal was "all about rigging the system . . . under the pretense of being a reform." It would dilute California's political power, he claimed, and lead to a continuation of the war in Iraq. Senators Dianne Feinstein and Barbara Boxer condemned the initiative as "a power grab orchestrated by the Republicans" and announced the formation of an opposition group called "Californians for Fair Election Reform."[98] Hollywood producer Stephen Bing and hedge fund director Thomas Steyer pledged to bankroll the opposition campaign, which began running radio ads against the proposal early in September.[99] Meanwhile, other Democrats asserted that the measure was unconstitutional because the power to change electoral vote systems rested exclusively with state legislatures.[100] Without a touch of hesitation or embarrassment, prominent figures in both parties were voicing precisely the arguments that the other party had put forward in Colorado and North Carolina. Ideological convictions and claims about principles were totally eclipsed by partisan interest.

Despite the attention that greeted its launch, the initiative campaign had trouble gaining momentum. Although 100,000 signatures were gathered in the first weeks, polling suggested a lack of enthusiasm for the idea, and fund-raising was slow. Schwarzenegger, the most popular Republican in the state, was noncommittal, publicly worrying about changing the rules of an election in midstream and privately commenting that the proposal seemed to reflect "a loser's mentality."[101] Then, in late September, the campaign took a serious hit when two of its leaders, Hiltachk and Eckery, resigned. They did so upon learning that its one large contribution ($175,000) came from a Missouri-based entity called Take Initiative America, that had been founded just one day before it made that contribution; the small-town attorney who had created TIA refused to disclose the identity of its donors. "I am not willing to proceed under such circumstances," Hiltachk wrote. Within days it was revealed that the secret donor was

Paul Singer, a billionaire confidant of Republican presidential aspirant Rudolph Giuliani. (Giuliani denied knowing about the contribution, and Singer stated that he acted because he believed in "proportional voting in the electoral college.") That the money came from out of state and was possibly illegal—as a violation of federal campaign finance laws—seriously tainted the campaign. Rubbing salt in the wounds, Democratic activists filed a complaint with the Federal Elections Commission.[102]

After floundering for weeks, the initiative was revived, thanks in part to Darrell Issa, a wealthy conservative representative from Southern California. Issa contributed his own funds, rallied other donors, and brought in experienced operatives to manage the effort. The reinvigorated campaign collected 700,000 signatures but failed to obtain and verify the requisite number in time to get on the ballot. Some activists vowed to try again, but in 2008 all of the state's electoral votes—more than a fifth of the number needed for national victory—went to a Democrat.[103]

The campaigns to jettison winner-take-all in Colorado, North Carolina, and California offered sobering lessons to proponents of state-level reform. All three were undertaken by experienced political actors who ended up with nothing to show for their efforts. If the Colorado campaign demonstrated the complexity of ending winner-take-all in a state where the two parties were fairly evenly matched, its counterpart in California made clear—once again—that an outnumbered minority party would face strong headwinds if it sought to carve off some electoral votes for itself. The most sobering lesson of all came from North Carolina, where Democratic legislators had succeeded in navigating a bill through both chambers of the General Assembly only to have victory snatched from their hands by their own national party. Understandable as it may have been, the Democratic Party's opposition to change in California, coupled with its willingness to sacrifice reform in North Carolina to protect electoral votes in California, sent a strongly discouraging message to state-level activists around the country: partisan advantage trumped long-simmering discontents with the workings of the Electoral College. The Democratic Party had, in effect, signaled that it would not support the elimination of winner-take-all in individual states because doing so could jeopardize the party's interest in retaining blocs of electoral votes from large, Democratic-leaning states like California. The logic that applied to North Carolina would surely apply elsewhere as well. If winner-take-all were to be abolished, it would have to be done everywhere at the same time—which seemed ineluctably to toss the ball back to Washington.[104]

Some ideas, however, just refuse to die, and the possibility of ending winner-take-all in individual states was revived a few years later—this time by Republicans.[105] In the wake of Mitt Romney's decisive Electoral College loss to President Barack Obama in 2012, Republicans in a handful of states began to seriously contemplate the prospect of replacing winner-take-all with district or proportional elections. These were states that Obama had won but where Republicans controlled both the legislature and the governor's office: Michigan, Ohio, Wisconsin, Pennsylvania, Virginia, and Florida. Anticipating that these states might remain in the Democratic column in presidential elections, some Republicans urged that steps be taken to prevent Democratic candidates from reaping the rewards of winner-take-all. "This is a concept that's got a lot of possibility and a lot of potential," declared a Washington-based Republican strategist. The Republican leader of Pennsylvania's state senate, Dominic Pileggi, put forward a proportional plan early in 2013; its goal, explained a spokesman, is "to more closely align the electoral vote in Pennsylvania with the popular vote." Similarly, Michigan Republican Saul Anuzis maintained that either district or proportional elections would be "more fair" than winner-take-all and that Republicans would have a "righteous argument" on behalf of such changes. Reince Priebus, head of the Republican National Committee, endorsed the concept, quickly adding that it was a decision to be made by individual states and not by the RNC. Democrats, of course, denounced these proposals as "nothing more than election-rigging"; a state senator in Pennsylvania found it "difficult to find the words to describe just how evil this plan is." Democrats were particularly incensed at the prospect of choosing electors by district in states that had been heavily gerrymandered by Republicans after the 2010 census.[106]

As it turned out, many Republicans, including key governors, were reluctant to end winner-take-all, in part because they—like their Democratic counterparts elsewhere—feared that their states would attract less attention if blocs of electoral votes were no longer at stake. None of the six legislatures, consequently, ended up taking action.[107] This proved to be fortunate for the GOP because in 2016 its candidate won five of the six states, several of them by small margins. Had winner-take-all not been in operation in these states, the collapse of the Democratic "blue wall" in 2016 would have brought fewer electoral votes into the Republican column.[108]

The National Popular Vote Interstate Compact

On February 23, 2006, a new approach to Electoral College reform was unveiled at a press conference in Washington. The Campaign for a National Popular Vote called for individual states to join an interstate compact through which they agreed to award their electoral votes to the presidential candidate who won the national popular vote; the compact would take effect only when states with a majority (270) of all electoral votes had signed on. Among those present at the press conference and endorsing the endeavor were Birch Bayh; Chellie Pingree, the president of Common Cause; Rob Richie, executive director of FairVote; and two former Republican congressmen, John Anderson (once an independent presidential candidate) and John Buchanan of Alabama. The organization promoting this reform, a newly formed nonprofit called National Popular Vote, announced that it planned to introduce the necessary legislation in all fifty states and that a bipartisan team of sponsors had already done so in Illinois. Coinciding with the press conference was the publication of *Every Vote Equal: A State-Based Plan for Electing the President by National Popular Vote,* a 600-page tome explaining and advocating this new strategy "to assure that the nationwide will of the people elects the President."[109]

In their prepared remarks at the press conference, Anderson, Bayh, and other speakers stressed three themes that would become hallmarks of the National Popular Vote campaign. The first consisted of traditional reasons for preferring a popular vote to the existing Electoral College system: all votes would count equally, and there would be no chance of a second-place finisher occupying the White House. The second focused on the legitimacy of states taking action to determine the shape of a national election. Winner-take-all, Buchanan pointed out, had become the norm thanks to the actions of individual states, and the states retained the power to reverse those decisions and adopt a different system. The third theme was that most states—red and blue, small and large—were ignored in presidential campaigns, attracting neither candidate visits nor campaign expenditures.

The action was entirely in the battleground states, and these had been declining in number. If state legislators of either party wished to give their states a more active and participatory role in choosing a president, they ought to seriously consider the idea of a national vote.[110]

The National Popular Vote Interstate Compact (NPVIC) was the creation of John Koza, a computer scientist who had co-invented the scratch-off lottery ticket, a venture that had earned him substantial wealth. A former Democratic presidential elector and a donor to Democratic candidates, Koza was a longtime critic of the Electoral College and—like many others—was deeply frustrated by the refusal of Congress to address the issue. Indeed, the movement for the NPVIC, both in its origins and in its gradual embrace by legislators in numerous states, can best be understood as a response to the frustrations felt by advocates of reform. For at least sixty years, a majority of the American people had favored replacing the Electoral College with a national popular vote, but Congress seemed inert, the obstacles to a constitutional amendment looked nearly insurmountable, and single-state approaches to reform had generally been stymied. The NPVIC offered a strategy for changing the electoral system without mustering the multiple supermajorities needed to amend the Constitution, and it promised to preserve the basic structure of the Electoral College (including the small-state advantage in electoral votes per capita) while transforming it into a mechanism for guaranteeing that the winner of the national popular vote would go to the White House. In addition, it would bring presidential campaigns into all (not just battleground) states and eliminate the troublesome contingent election procedure. Importantly, the NPVIC offered a strategy for state-by-state action that could eventually result in national change. In the eyes of some advocates, it was a mechanism for building political support for a national popular vote, in the hope that widespread adoption of the compact might eventually culminate in the adoption of a constitutional amendment.[111]

The idea of utilizing state legislative action to promote a national popular vote did not originate with Koza. In 2001 two provocative articles had appeared, written by law professors, suggesting that there might be paths to a national popular vote that did not include a constitutional amendment.[112] The first, by Northwestern University professor Robert W. Bennett, began by voicing concern that public debate about the Electoral College in the wake of the 2000 election might be "stifled" by the presumption that change could be achieved only through an almost-impossible-to-achieve constitutional amendment. He pointed out that the Seventeenth Amendment (for the popular election of senators) had gained congressional approval only after a number of states had taken unilateral steps to incorporate popular balloting into the process through which legislatures chose senators.[113] Bennett suggested that states could similarly put pressure on Congress by acting in concert with one another to pledge their electoral votes to the winner of the national popular vote. Even a handful of states (or two large states like California and Texas) might turn the trick: the popular vote winner would be guaranteed a sizable number of electoral votes, and candidates would acquire an incentive to campaign not just in battleground states but in any states where they could augment their national vote totals.[114]

A few months later, Akhil Amar of Yale Law School and his brother, Vikram Amar, a professor at the University of California Hastings School of Law, presented similar ideas, while toying creatively with the possibility of states generating reform by coordinating their efforts. A state like New Jersey, they proposed, could commit its electoral votes to the national vote winner "if and only if enough other states follow suit." Going one concrete step further, a state could pass a law promising to cast its electoral votes for the national popular vote winner "if and only if" states with 270 electoral votes had agreed to do the same. In a final flight of fancy, the Amar brothers imagined an even simpler mechanism: candidates for president and vice president could pledge that, if they lost the popular vote, they would ask their electors to cast ballots for the popular vote winner instead. Changing the electoral system might not be so difficult after all![115]

The core concepts at the heart of this new initiative, thus, were floating in the *zeitgeist* within a year after the 2000 election. What Koza added to the mix was the idea that the actions of individual states could be linked and unified through the architecture of a formal interstate compact. By joining the "Agreement among the States to Elect the President by Popular Vote," a state would be making a legally binding commitment to cast its electoral votes for the national popular vote winner once states with 270 electoral votes had signed on to the compact. Koza and attorney

Barry Fadem—a specialist in election law who became president of National Popular Vote—were familiar with interstate compacts from their experience promoting multistate lotteries (like the Tri-State Lotto Compact); compacts of this type—commonly covering issues like water rights, ports, and nuclear waste—had long had a place in the legal landscape. Such a compact, they believed, could provide a framework for building support one state at a time as well as a legal mechanism for enforcing states' commitments after the threshold of 270 had been reached. (The NPVIC made it clear that states could withdraw from the compact but had to adhere to it in the next election if the withdrawal had not occurred at least six months before the expiration of a presidential term.) Koza and Fadem also brought to the table a great deal of energy, considerable organizational skill, and substantial funding.[116]

To many observers, the NPVIC looked initially to be an implausible, long-shot approach to reform, a Rube Goldberg contraption that had little chance of making much political headway.[117] But within months after the campaign's announcement, several major newspapers, including the *New York Times,* published favorable editorials: "It may be the only way to kill the anachronistic institution," opined the *Los Angeles Times.*[118] Bills supporting the NPVIC were introduced in five states in 2006, most with bipartisan support, while leaders of the campaign—like Koza, Anderson, former Republican senator Jake Garn, and Rob Richie of FairVote—testified to legislatures and worked to drum up support. In April 2006 the Colorado senate approved an NPVIC bill, and by the end of the summer the California senate and assembly had done the same. Governor Arnold Schwarzenegger vetoed the California measure, declaring that it ran counter to "the tradition of our great nation which honors states' rights and the unique pride and identity of each state." Nonetheless, the progress made by Koza and his allies was apparent. In October the *American Prospect* observed, with a hint of surprise, that "the campaign to reform the Electoral College actually gains ground."[119]

The pace of activity picked up in 2007–2008. (See Table 7.1.) In April 2007 Maryland became the first state to join the compact, thanks to the efforts of FairVote and to the energetic sponsorship of Jamin Raskin, a recently elected Democratic state senator and law professor with long-standing commitments to democratic reform. The bill was also approved

TABLE 7.1: TIMELINE: PASSAGE OF LEGISLATION TO JOIN THE NATIONAL
POPULAR VOTE INTERSTATE COMPACT

State[a]	House passed	Senate passed	Governor vetoed	Governor signed	Enacted
California	2006	2006	2006		
	2008	2008	2008		
	2011	2011		2011	2011
Colorado		2006, 2007			
	2009				
	2019	2019		2019	2019[b]
Hawaii	2007	2007	2007		2008[c]
Arkansas	2007, 2009				
North Carolina		2007			
Maryland	2007	2007		2007	2007
Illinois	2007	2007		2008	2008
New Jersey	2007	2008		2008	2008
Vermont	2008	2008	2008		
		2009			
	2011	2011		2011	2011
Rhode Island	2008	2008	2008		
		2009, 2011			
	2013	2013		2013	2013
Massachusetts	2008	2008			
	2010[d]	2010		2010	2010
Michigan	2008				
Maine		2008			
		2019[e]			
Washington	2009	2008		2009	2009
Oregon	2009, 2013, 2015, 2017				
	2019	2019		2019	2019
New Mexico	2009				
		2017			
	2019	2019		2019	2019
Nevada	2009				
	2019	2019	2019		
Connecticut	2009				
	2018	2018		2018	2018

(*continued*)

TABLE 7.1 (Continued)

State[a]	House passed	Senate passed	Governor vetoed	Governor signed	Enacted
Delaware	2009, 2011				
	2019	2019		2019	2019
D.C.	2010	2010		2010	2010
New York		2010, 2011			
	2013				
	2014	2014		2014	2014
	2016	2016		2016	2016[f]
Oklahoma		2014			
Arizona	2016				
Minnesota	2019				
Virginia	2020				

Sources: https://www.nationalpopularvote.com/news-history; http://leginfo.legislature
.ca.gov/faces/billHistoryClient.xhtml?bill_id=200720080SB37; https://olis.leg.state.or.us
/liz/2017R1/Measures/Overview/HB2927; https://legislature.vermont.gov/bill/status
/2010/S.34; http://status.rilin.state.ri.us/; https://nyassembly.gov/leg/?sh=advanced.

a. By year of first passage by a legislative branch.

b. Pending the outcome of a referendum in 2020.

c. In 2008, Hawaii's legislature overrode the governor's veto.

d. The 2008 legislative session adjourned before sending the bill to the governor.

e. Maine's house also initially passed the NPVIC in 2019 but then reversed itself.

f. The bill that was passed in 2014 included a provision stipulating that "New York be removed from the compact at the end of 2018 if the agreement had not been adopted nationally." The 2016 bill removed this provision. See "Gov. Cuomo Signs Legislation Securing New York State's Place in the National Popular Vote Compact," *US State News,* Nov. 7, 2016, https://www.governor.ny.gov/news/governor-cuomo-signs-legislation -securing-new-york-states-place-national-popular-vote-compact.

by Hawaii's legislature in 2007, although it was vetoed by Republican governor Linda Lingle, who worried that Hawaii might cast its electoral votes for a candidate who had not won the state. The following year the legislature overrode her veto, and both Illinois and New Jersey signed up. During this two-year period, one or more branches of the legislature in ten other states, including North Carolina and Arkansas, approved NPVIC bills, while chambers in both North Dakota and Montana voted against doing so. The campaign's strength was unmistakably centered in predominantly Democratic states, but its successes had given the movement both momentum and political legitimacy.[120]

By September 2009, NPVIC bills had been introduced in forty-eight states and adopted in five. Over the next five years, the compact was joined by the District of Columbia and one or two states per year, except in the election year of 2012. Additional victories were registered in legislative branches in a handful of other states, including New Mexico, Nevada, Oregon, Delaware, and Oklahoma, where the majority-Republican senate voted favorably. The most prominent successes came in two large states, California and New York, which together accounted for more than eighty electoral votes, almost a third of the total needed to activate the compact. In California, the key to victory was the election of a Democratic governor, Jerry Brown, who signed an NPVIC bill in 2011, seven months after taking office. In New York, a prolonged legislative journey came to an end in 2014 when large bipartisan majorities were mustered in both branches of the legislature, most notably in the Republican-controlled senate. Republican supporters emphasized that they no longer wanted their state to be taken for granted in presidential elections.[121]

In most states, success came only after multiyear legislative efforts that included testifying, lobbying, and networking by the leaders of the campaign and by individuals and organizations sympathetic to the cause (like FairVote, Common Cause, the League of Women Voters, and the NAACP). The campaign commissioned and publicized statewide opinion polls, which generally demonstrated strong public support for a national popular vote; its educational arm, the Institute for Research on Presidential Elections, organized seminars and gatherings for legislators and opinion makers. In addition, the campaign hired lobbyists in almost every state where bills were being seriously considered. The New York effort received invaluable assistance, including funding, from Tom Golisano, a billionaire three-time independent candidate for governor with a history of backing both Democrats and Republicans. Golisano signed on to become a spokesman for the movement nationally, meeting with legislative leaders, governors, and editorial boards around the country; he actively did so from 2010 to 2012.[122]

THE ARGUMENTS: PRO AND CON

The reasons offered by state legislators and local newspapers for supporting or opposing the NPVIC echoed the debates of the late 1960s and 1970s. Advocates focused on the virtues of a national election and the defects of winner-take-all; they made little mention of the compact itself, other than to assert that it was a perfectly legal and constitutional means of pursuing change. "If you think every voter is equal, then you support this," advised a state representative from Illinois. Advocates further maintained that the NPVIC had bipartisan support and would not predictably benefit or harm either major party or states of different sizes. They often pointed to state polls indicating that most Republicans, as well as Democrats and independents, favored a national vote.[123]

Above all, supporters emphasized the manifold ways that winner-take-all skewed presidential campaigns, turning the citizens of most states, small and large, into taken-for-granted spectators. "California should not be ignored in presidential elections," declared the bill's sponsor in the state assembly. His Republican counterpart in Arizona's house in 2016 wanted Arizona to cease being a "flyover state."[124] Not only did candidates rarely visit or spend money in non-battleground states, it was argued, but the distinctive concerns of their citizens were ignored. Legislators also maintained that swing states received preferential treatment from the federal government. Curt Bramble, a Republican state senator in Utah (and the president of the National Conference of State Legislatures in 2016), lamented that his state had been obliged to rebuild Interstate 15 entirely with state funds while the "battleground states . . . get all sorts of federal help for their infrastructure projects."[125]

The bystander status of most states, an issue that had potential appeal to Republicans, was given center stage in all four editions of *Every Vote Equal*, on the campaign's continuously updated website, and in public statements by Koza, Fadem, and other national advocates.[126] FairVote's Rob Richie, as well as other analysts, stressed that the problem had grown more severe in recent decades thanks to both a decline in the number of battleground states and to the increasing predictability of their identities. If winner-take-all persisted, thus, three-quarters of the states would be consigned to spectator status for the foreseeable future. Those states had something important to gain from the NPVIC, and their growing number was a source of optimism for the leaders of the campaign.[127]

Opponents of the compact, from both parties, often responded with traditional arguments against any kind of national popular vote. The Electoral College had worked well for two centuries, some maintained; it preserved federalism and protected small and rural states.[128] A national popular vote, in contrast, would permit the large population centers to swamp the votes and interests of small states and rural America. "If it were passed," observed a North Dakota Republican, "our presidential elections would be controlled by the vote in New York, Chicago, Los Angeles, and Houston."[129] Numerous critics invoked the "post-Florida" nightmare that a national vote could lead to a murky election result resolvable only through controversial multistate recounts.[130]

Opponents also objected to the mechanism of an interstate compact. Some insisted that the NPVIC was illegal or unconstitutional, an "end run around the Constitution," or a way "to amend the Constitution without amending the Constitution." (Both Koza and Raskin liked to counter that an end run was a legal play in football.)[131] More than a few questioned whether an interstate compact would be valid without congressional approval.[132] Critics from both parties argued strenuously that it would be morally unpalatable—even leading to "civil insurrection"—for a state to cast its electoral votes for a candidate who lacked majority support in the state. "How undemocratic is that?" asked a Republican legislator in Connecticut.[133] Some adversaries further maintained—not without reason—that the NPVIC, if implemented, would spawn multiple lawsuits and court battles that could result in chaos and a legitimacy crisis. "This is going to be such a legal train wreck that you can't imagine how incredible that's going to be," asserted one state senator.[134] A different line of criticism came from legislators who worried that the compact would award the presidency to a plurality, rather than majority, winner of the popular vote; a few indicated that they favored a national popular vote but only if it could be instituted through a constitutional amendment.[135]

Meanwhile, far outside the halls of state legislatures, a different—and only partially overlapping—set of debates unfolded among legal scholars and political analysts. Writing in law reviews and other journals, commentators wrestled over the legality of the NPVIC, pointed to possible flaws in its design, and questioned whether it could, in fact, deliver what it promised. On the campaign's website and in *Every Vote Equal*, backers of the NPVIC offered detailed ripostes to these challenges.[136]

One cluster of issues concerned the status or constitutionality of the NPVIC in the absence of congressional consent. Critics like Derek Muller, a conservative law professor at Pepperdine University, maintained that it would not pass muster because the Constitution (Article I, section 10, clause 3) required such compacts to be approved by Congress.[137] Other legal academics, including Bennett and Vikram Amar, disagreed, characterizing the NPVIC as the type of agreement that federal courts had long upheld as permissible without congressional consent. Jamin Raskin was agnostic, arguing that the NPVIC offered a promising path to reform even if the courts decided that Congress did have to assent.[138] A different issue was whether state legislatures possessed an unalloyed right to decide the basis on which their electoral votes would be cast. Supporters of the NPVIC, including Raskin, believed that they did, but others, including law professor Norman R. Williams, argued that the discretion of the states was not absolute and that the NPVIC violated the intent of the presidential elections clause (Article II, section 1).[139] An additional legal, but not constitutional, question was whether the NPVIC came into conflict with the Voting Rights Act.[140] The detailed analyses presented in the legal literature did not settle any of these issues, but they made it abundantly clear that the NPVIC, if approved by the requisite number of states, would face multiple challenges in the courts. The answers to key questions could not be known until the NPVIC was implemented.

A second group of issues was more normative, with critics—some of whom favored a national popular vote—questioning whether the compact, as designed, could fully achieve its democratic objectives. The NPVIC, they argued, could all too easily elect a president who had the support of only a minority of the electorate—as little as 30 to 35 percent—if there were a multi-candidate contest. Because the framework of the Electoral College would remain in place under the compact, there could be no provision for a runoff election, and consequently the NPVIC had no mechanism for generating or requiring a popular vote (rather than electoral vote) majority. The compact, in effect, could guarantee that a plurality winner would take office, but it had no way of ensuring that a president would have majority or near-majority support.[141] In addition, the NPVIC did not call for national suffrage rules, leaving in place eligibility and procedural requirements that varied—sometimes substantially—from state to state. "Every vote" would therefore be "equal," but not all citizens would have an equal right to vote. There would be a national popular vote tally but not quite a national election.[142]

Finally there were questions about the feasibility, the workability, of the NPVIC. If a signatory state decided to abandon the compact after (or just before) the votes were counted, could the compact be enforced without protracted—and ill-timed—litigation? (It was not difficult to imagine scenarios in which state officials would come under enormous public pressure to take such a step.) Several scholars, including Williams, also worried about the ability of nonsignatory states to undermine or sabotage the compact: by not counting all of their own votes once the state winner had been clearly established, by declining to modify their state recount laws so that a close national vote would trigger a recount, or even by refusing to hold a popular election at all. Such problems were potentially soluble but only with careful state and federal legislation that might not be easily forthcoming.[143]

One additional problem had no legislative solution: the NPVIC created an inherently unstable electoral terrain. Even if the compact were successfully implemented for a particular presidential election, there was no guarantee that it would remain in force the next time around. Between elections, states could come and go as their legislatures wished. Presidential elections, consequently, might be conducted according to different sets of rules in different elections, as parties, states, and factions altered their views or maneuvered to game the system. Such a development might, of course, lead to a constitutional amendment that would abolish the Electoral College and put an end to the uncertainty, but it nonetheless had disturbing echoes of the political jockeying, between 1800 and 1830, that had eventuated in the widespread adoption of the "general ticket" in the first place.[144]

THE POLITICS OF PASSAGE

By the spring of 2014 the NPVIC had been endorsed by ten states and the District of Columbia, with a combined total of 165 electoral votes; it also had the declared support of more than 2,000 state legislators. Progress then slowed, with no new states signing up before the 2016 election. Although the gains made by the campaign were impressive, the pattern of victories and defeats suggested that there were still hills to climb. Numerous Republican legislators had voted in favor of NPVIC bills, but all of the jurisdictions that had joined the compact were reliably "blue" or Democratic. Many of the successful legislative votes, moreover, had closely followed party lines, and bills were stalled in a large handful of states where one chamber had given its approval between 2007 and 2009.[145] (See Table 7.1.) No solidly conservative "red" states had signed up nor had any states in the South; roughly a dozen had not even held hearings. Also missing were the battleground states in presidential elections, which seemed to enjoy the attention they received under the existing system.[146] A more long-run concern was that the compact did not "appear to have gained widespread awareness or support in the public at large." This was true even in states that had joined.[147]

The partisan pattern of responses to the NPVIC persisted despite the concerted efforts of the campaign's organizers. They worked assiduously to bring Republicans on board, dispatching Republican backers like public relations specialist Patrick Rosenstiel and former Michigan GOP chair Saul Anuzis to rustle up support in various states. Both the website and *Every Vote Equal* featured signs of progress in Republican legislative chambers as well as endorsements from prominent Republicans. Among the named Republicans (some of whom had well-known independent streaks) were former Speaker of the House Newt Gingrich; former senators Fred Thompson and Jake Garn; former congressmen Tom Campbell, Bob Barr, and Tom Tancredo; and a variety of other leaders, such as Joseph Griffo (NY), James Edgar (IL), and Rob Haynes (former chair of the American Legislative Exchange Council). Several wrote forewords to *Every Vote Equal*, including Minnesota conservative Laura Brod, who acknowledged that she had first had a reflexively partisan negative reaction to the proposal but had since embraced it. "The National Popular Vote bill is not a Democratic bill or a Republican bill," she wrote. "It is not even a liberal or conservative bill."[148]

Brod's assessment may have been correct, but many Republicans thought otherwise. During the early years of the NPVIC, conservatives voiced occasional criticism of the project, but, for the most part, they ignored it. As the campaign began to gain steam, however, a full-blown attack emerged among mainstream national Republicans. *Wall Street Journal* editor James Taranto derided the compact in 2010 as a "terrible idea," a "partisan protest masquerading as a high-minded reform."[149] The following year the Heritage Foundation convened a forum on the subject: five secretaries of state voiced concerns about particular features of the compact, and conservative activist Hans von Spakovsky condemned it as both unconstitutional and "bad public policy." Senate minority leader Mitch McConnell labeled the NPVIC "the most important issue in America nobody's talking about." "The proponents of this absurd and dangerous concept are trying to get this done while nobody notices," McConnell warned. "We need to kill it in the cradle before it grows up." The State Government Leadership Foundation (a nonprofit linked to the Republican State Leadership Committee) then announced that it would fight the NPVIC and defend the Electoral College throughout the nation. In both 2012 and 2016 the national platforms of the Republican Party denounced the compact while praising the Electoral College. Some state parties took similar steps.[150]

Despite the sharp attacks, there were cracks in the red wall of opposition. In addition to gaining endorsements by prominent figures, the project was attracting attention among Republican legislators who did not interpret the national party's stance as the last word on the subject. Leaders of the NPVIC campaign knew well that they needed Republican allies if they were to reach the 270-electoral-votes threshold, and they believed that those allies could be found in swing states or in red-leaning states where political leaders were tired of being taken for granted. Promising signs could be found in a handful of developments that unfolded between 2014 and November 2016. Not only did New York's Republicans rally around the NPVIC in 2014, but the Republican-controlled senate in Oklahoma passed a bill that same year. Two years later, Arizona's Republican-majority house voted to support the NPVIC by a margin of forty to sixteen. Meanwhile in Georgia a bill was reported favorably by a key committee in the house and had strong support in the senate. Bills with Republican sponsors were introduced in both chambers of Utah's legislature, leading to speculation that Utah might soon become the first Republican state to join the compact. (Utah's college Republicans had embraced the idea as early as 2012!) Opinion polls remained favorable, with clear majorities of both Democrats and Republicans favoring a national popular vote, even in states like Idaho, South Dakota, and Kentucky.[151] As the 2016 election approached, it appeared possible that the lineup of states endorsing the compact might soon shed its uniformly blue coloration.

November 2016

The 2016 presidential election delivered multiple shocks to the system. For the second time in less than two decades, the winner of the popular vote failed to win the electoral vote, and this time the gap between the two tallies was more sizable than it had been in 2000. Hillary Clinton received nearly three million more votes than Donald Trump, yet Trump won the Electoral College by a margin of 304 to 227. The institutional misfire of 2000 looked less like a fluke, and the notion that the Electoral College favored Republicans was strengthened. Democrats had won the popular vote in six of the seven elections since 1988, but on two of those occasions they ended up with nothing to show for it.[152]

The outcome of the election came as a surprise to most observers; nearly all of the polls and pundits had pointed to a Clinton victory. More importantly, Trump's election came as an unpleasant jolt to many on the left and center of the political spectrum who regarded him as frighteningly unqualified to hold the office of chief executive. Indeed, some who held such views, including Harvard Law professor Lawrence Lessig, sought to exploit the archaic mechanics of the Electoral College to deny Trump the presidency. Petitions, advertisements, op-eds, and news releases maintained that the founding fathers expected electors to use their own judgment and that it would be legal and legitimate for Republican electors to cast their ballots for someone other than Trump. Little came of these actions in the short run: two Republican electors defected from Trump, while five Democrats voted for candidates other than Clinton.[153] But after several states leveled sanctions against electors who were (or attempted to be) faithless, Lessig launched a set of lawsuits designed to clarify whether electors were—as the wording of the Constitution seemed to imply—free to cast their ballots for the candidates of their choice. In January 2020, the Supreme Court agreed to hear the case.[154]

Although mainstream newspapers and magazines had overwhelmingly favored Clinton during the campaign, the reaction to the Electoral College misfire was mixed, somewhat predictably so. The *New York Times* declared, once again, that it was time to be rid of an "antiquated mechanism" that could permit "the loser of the popular vote" to "wind up running the country." It endorsed national popular elections in general and the NPVIC in particular. The *Wall Street Journal*, in contrast, opined that Alexander Hamilton had been correct to pronounce the electoral system to be "at least excellent." The *Washington Post* ran dueling columns by conservative George Will and liberal E. J. Dionne, while the *Chicago Tribune* published an op-ed by Democrat William Daley, Barack Obama's former chief of staff, who recommended keeping the Electoral College despite its imperfections. *USA Today* acknowledged that the "current system is far from ideal" and urged states to consider replacing winner-take-all with a proportional system. The paper cautioned against holding national elections with plurality winners, pointing particularly at problems with the NPVIC; it simultaneously published a rebuttal by John Koza.[155]

For electoral reform advocates—and especially for progressives—the election of Donald Trump was one more compelling reason to abolish the Electoral College. A plurality of voters had preferred Hillary Clinton, but the nation's peculiar electoral system had installed a bombastic, ill-informed, extremely conservative real estate mogul in the White House. An archaic institution had, in effect, overridden the popular will and put the nation in jeopardy. A Gallup Poll conducted in late November 2016 reported that the proportion of Democratic (and Democratic-leaning) voters who favored replacing the Electoral College with a national vote rose sharply, to 81 percent (from 69 percent in 2012).[156]

Republicans, of course, drew different conclusions. Politicians interpreted the election results as evidence of their wisdom in opposing reform, and for the first time most Republican voters seemed to share their leaders' preference for the Electoral College.[157] According to Gallup, support for a national popular vote among Republicans and Republican-leaning independents plummeted with unprecedented speed and to unprecedented levels in the wake of Trump's election.[158] Republican interest in reform then rebounded slightly, but a Pew survey conducted in the spring of 2018 found that 65 percent still preferred the Electoral College.[159]

Among those whose views shifted during these years was Donald J. Trump. In 2012 he had tweeted that "the electoral college is a disaster for a democracy," but ten days after his election he declared it to be "actually genius." Eighteen months later, he reversed course again, declaring, "I would rather have the popular vote because . . . it's much easier to win the popular vote."[160]

With Republicans in control of both branches of Congress, the odds of electoral reform emanating from Washington were close to zero. Nonetheless, a handful of direct election amendments, differing in their details, were introduced in the House and the Senate by (among others) California senator Barbara Boxer, and Representatives Gene Green, Steve Cohen, and John Conyers. These proposals had no Republican co-sponsors and were referred to committees, which took no further action.[161] Conyers, as the ranking member of the House Judiciary Committee, also convened a forum on presidential election reform in December 2016, with experts presenting testimony focused on the shortcomings of the Electoral College as well as the comparative merits of the NPVIC and amending the Constitution. A few days later, Conyers published an op-ed, drawing on his own long experience, to counter the notion that the "obstacles to reform are insurmountable." In September 2017 Conyers and several colleagues put forward a "sense of Congress" resolution that Congress and the states should consider a constitutional amendment and also encourage reform "through such steps as the formation of an interstate compact." The resolution was referred to the Committee on the Judiciary (where no action was taken). Both Conyers and Boxer signaled that they were more hopeful about the interstate compact than they were about the possibility of securing an amendment.[162]

Yet things were not faring well with the NPVIC in the wake of Trump's election. Reflecting the anger spawned by the election's outcome, bills were introduced, or reintroduced, in at least seventeen states, but little progress was made. In February 2017, New Mexico's senate passed a bill, but its house of representatives (which had approved the legislation in 2009) failed to act.[163] Divisions among Democrats continued to prevent progress in Oregon, and swing states like Florida and Ohio displayed little interest. Nearly everywhere bills were stalled in committees, often without hearings, even in states where polling revealed a preference for a national vote.[164] The one positive note was struck in Connecticut, which joined the compact in May 2018 after a campaign that had lasted a decade. The votes in both legislative chambers followed party lines, with a few Republican exceptions. Connecticut was the only state to have approved the NPVIC since 2014, and like the other states in the compact, it had favored Hillary Clinton in 2016.[165]

The problem facing NPVIC advocates was that the 2016 election had administered a serious blow to their plan of inducing a few Republican-leaning states to join the compact and thereby create precedents that other red states could follow. Before November 2016, success had seemed within sight—if not quite within reach—in targeted states like Oklahoma, Arizona, Utah, and Georgia. If, as expected, Clinton had delivered a third straight victory for the Democrats, more Republicans, particularly in "flyover" states, might have defected from the official GOP position in the hope of bringing national campaigns into their own states. Had Clinton won the routine victory that most analysts anticipated, more Republicans might have given weight to the notion—current in some circles since 2012—that winner-take-all gave Democrats a "blue wall" of states that made it difficult for a Republican to win the presidency.[166]

As it turned out, however, the opposite happened: a key section of the "blue wall" crumbled, the Electoral College delivered the presidency to Trump, and Republican popular support for reform evaporated overnight. The political conditions that might have led to NPVIC victories in red states failed to materialize, and the post-election landscape suggested that it would be self-defeating, even foolish, for Republicans to discard a system that served them so well. Within weeks of the election, it was reported in Utah that the NPVIC was dead, despite having well-prepared Republican sponsors in both legislative chambers. The fatal blow, perhaps, was the recognition that, had the compact been in force, the Beehive State would have been obliged to cast its electoral votes for Hillary Clinton, who had received only 27 percent of Utah's popular vote.[167] The cracks in the red wall of opposition appeared to have been patched, and an NPVIC victory was receding from view. Some current and former backers of the compact, through a bipartisan organization called Making Every Vote Count, decided to pursue a streamlined strategy—focused on the state of Ohio—that they thought might work more expeditiously than the NPVIC.[168]

The prospects of the NPVIC brightened after the 2018 midterm elections. Democratic victories in state legislative and gubernatorial elections helped to pave the way for four new states to join the compact. Delaware, New Mexico, and Oregon passed the requisite legislation between March and June of 2019; Colorado did the same, although a subsequent petition campaign meant that the final decision would be made in a popular referendum in November 2020. A bill was also passed by both branches of Nevada's legislature, but it was vetoed by Democratic governor Steve Sisolak on the grounds that "it would diminish the role of smaller states like Nevada." In Maine an NPVIC measure passed by the senate was eventually rebuffed by the Democratic house after weeks of indecision. These successes, and near-successes, reinvigorated the campaign after a near-total drought that had lasted for almost five years. By the fall of 2019, the compact included fifteen states (plus the District of Columbia), representing 196 electoral votes; and in February 2020 Virginia's house approved an HPVIC bill. We are "inching closer and closer to victory," declared Common Cause in a mailing to its members.[169]

But the campaign had not yet demonstrated that Republican states could be drawn into the fold, and a poll conducted in April 2019 indicated that three-quarters of Republicans still preferred the Electoral College.[170] All of the states that had newly joined had voted for Clinton in 2016, and in Colorado, the most "purple" of these states, not a single Republican had endorsed the NPVIC. To reach the magic number of 270, pro-reform Democrats would have to gain control of additional state legislatures (the Republicans controlled thirty even after the 2018 elections), or Republican attachment to the Electoral College would somehow have to diminish. The latter option was surely preferable: the partisan imposition of a new electoral system seemed, at best, undesirable. Accordingly, NPVIC organizers again devoted substantial energy to red and purple states, widely circulating the views of Republicans who believed that a national vote could benefit their party and would definitely benefit residents of spectator states. Koza, who acknowledged that the project had been and would be "a long, hard haul," renewed his substantial financial commitment to the campaign and successfully secured new donors. The interstate compact would not be in place for the 2020 election, but the last chapter of the NPVIC story remained to be written.[171] In a thoughtful essay published in the spring of 2019, Vikram Amar argued that the campaign should aim to implement the compact only in 2032, thereby removing the issue from imminent presidential campaigns and giving Congress the opportunity to address the "dangerous gaps in the NPV design."[172]

WINNER-TAKE-ALL AND THE CONSTITUTION

For reform advocates who had less patience for the long haul, a new front was opened in February 2018: lawsuits were filed in four states challenging the constitutionality of their winner-take-all laws. The suits were brought by a coalition of law firms, led by David Boies, a well-known litigator, and the League of United Latin American Citizens (LULAC), a Latinx civil rights organization. Backed by prominent legal academics and a crowd-funding campaign organized by Lawrence Lessig, the lawsuits targeted two reliably Republican states, South Carolina and Texas, and two equally reliable Democratic ones, California and Massachusetts. Supporters of the losing presidential candidate in all four states, it was argued, were denied the right to an equal vote in presidential elections because their votes were effectively discarded and then converted into electoral votes for the victorious candidate in each state. The votes of Republicans in California carried no weight in the national election because all of the state's electoral votes were cast for the Democratic candidate; the same was true for Texas Democrats. This system violated the principle of "one person, one vote" embedded in the Fourteenth Amendment as well as citizens' First Amendment rights of political expression and association. The lawsuit reiterated long-standing criticisms of winner-take-all and added a new post-2016 claim that by concentrating the presidential campaign into a handful of battleground states, winner-take-all made the country more vulnerable to manipulation by foreign nations.[173] In both South Carolina and Texas, the lawsuits had an additional prong: the charge that winner-take-all provisions violated the Voting Rights Act of 1964 by effectively disenfranchising minority voters. The core evidence for this claim was that the presidential candidates preferred by minority voters had not received a single electoral vote in either state since 1976. The solution proposed to remedy all of these ills was to oblige states to allocate their electoral votes on a proportional basis.[174]

Federal district judges in all four states, however, dismissed the cases, concluding that there were no violations of either the First or the Fourteenth Amendments; in Texas and South Carolina, the courts also found that winner-take-all did not violate the Voting Rights Act. These decisions were appealed in the hope of convincing one or more circuit courts, and eventually the U.S. Supreme Court, that the winner-take-all practices that emerged in the early nineteenth century simply did not square with modern conceptions of voting rights and democracy. What would become of this legal initiative remained unclear in the winter of 2020. The district courts' decisions suggested that a judicial path to proportional elections was unlikely, and in February 2020 the Fifth Circuit Court of Appeals turned back the appeal of the Texas case. There was pushback as well from state officials, including Democrats. But Boies, Lessig, and other legal experts believed that innovative legal arguments coupled with advances in jurisprudence gave them a strong case, and the oral arguments in the First Circuit Court of Appeals (Boston) in September 2019 were promisingly robust. To some reform-minded observers, turning to the courts to overturn state laws that had been on the books for 200 years appeared to be a long shot, but even a long shot was better than no shot at all.[175]

THE PERSISTENCE OF RACE

Whatever their legal fate, the lawsuits in Texas and South Carolina once more put a spotlight on the relationship between race and the Electoral College. As we have seen in earlier chapters, the desire of white southerners to curb the political influence of African-Americans served as a powerful obstacle to Electoral College reform for much of the twentieth century. The 2018 lawsuits offered a disturbing update to that story, charging that even in the post-1960s, post–Voting Rights Act world in which blacks were enfranchised, the Electoral College continued to disadvantage the large African-American population that still resided in the South. In Texas, a state with thirty-eight electoral votes and a population that was 40 percent black or Hispanic, not a single electoral vote had been cast for the candidate preferred by minority voters from 1980 through 2016. In South Carolina, in this period, all of the state's electoral votes had been awarded to Republicans even though the state's population was 27 percent African-American and African-Americans voted heavily Democratic.[176]

The problem was not confined to Texas and South Carolina. Forty-eight percent of the nation's African-American population—roughly twenty million people—lived in the eleven states of the former Confederacy, and only one of those states (Virginia) had cast its electoral votes for the Democratic candidate in 2016. (National studies indicated that Clinton was the preferred candidate of 88 percent of African-Americans.) What this meant was that in a region whose population was 21 percent African-American, only 13 of 160 electoral votes (8 percent) were cast for the candidate favored by blacks.[177] This pattern had been in evidence since 1980. Mississippi and Alabama, like Texas and South Carolina, had never voted for a Democrat between 1976 and 2016, and only three southern states (Virginia, Florida, and North Carolina) had cast their electoral votes for a Democrat at any point after 1996.[178] In presidential elections, thus, the Electoral College greatly diminished or diluted the influence of the descendants of those African-Americans who had been enslaved before the Civil War and disenfranchised from the 1890s into the 1960s. Even more galling, perhaps, was that, thanks to winner-take-all, electoral votes that southern states possessed by virtue of their black populations were being cast for the candidates preferred by whites. Despite the inclusion of African-Americans in the electorate, a modified version of the three-fifths clause (or, more aptly, the five-fifths clause) remained in place in much of the South. It was not coincidental that southern legislatures that were dominated by white Republicans displayed little interest in the NPVIC, much as their forebearers had opposed a national popular vote in Congress in 1970 and 1979.

2020

As the second decade of the twenty-first century neared its end, the issue of Electoral College reform was spotlighted, overshadowed, and colored by the approach of the 2020 election and the mounting tumult of Donald Trump's presidency. Many observers believed that Trump might again triumph without winning the popular vote; despite his impeachment and high disapproval rates, the president seemed likely to win most, and perhaps all, of the states that had backed him in 2016. Depending on one's perspective, that was a reason either to deeply regret the failure of past reform attempts or to be grateful that the Electoral College was still in place.[179]

Looking forward, there were ample reasons for pessimism about the near- and middle-term prospects of reform. Although support for change was widespread among Democrats, Republican opposition was more staunch and reflexive than it had been even in the 1980s and 1990s, despite occasional spasms of interest in eliminating winner-take-all in states that had voted Democratic.[180] Many Republican politicians believed that the Electoral College had a favorable partisan tilt, their electoral base had embraced the institution, and their party controlled the Senate and most state legislatures. Forty years had passed since the last congressional vote on electoral reform, and no floor debates or formal hearings on the subject had been held in the twenty-first century. The innovative and unprecedented NPVIC campaign to alter the system without going through Congress had achieved impressive gains, but its progress was still checked by the same partisan forces that blocked action in Washington.[181] In addition, the political climate—overheated even before Trump's election—had become so fevered that it was difficult to imagine the kind of bipartisan cooperation that would be needed to produce durable change. A two-thirds vote in both branches of Congress seemed very far away.

Nonetheless, advocates of reform not only persisted but ramped up the intensity of their labors. Progressives and Democratic activists had refused to let the issue remain dormant during the early years of the century, and they redoubled their efforts after 2016, as part of a broad, multipronged movement to democratize American electoral rules and institutions. That movement, which had numerous concrete goals—such as reducing partisan gerrymandering and making it easier for less-well-off citizens to register and vote—was rooted in the conviction that more inclusive and egalitarian processes could yield different electoral outcomes and potentially more progressive policies. The Electoral College had become an important case in point: the elections of 2000 and 2016, by delivering the White House to conservatives who had won fewer votes than their liberal opponents, lent a felt urgency to the cause of presidential election reform.[182] Advocates of a national popular vote after 2000 and 2016 knew firsthand—not as a matter of nineteenth-century history—that candidates who lost the popular vote did sometimes become president and proceed to carry out controversial policies whose effects might endure for decades. George Bush's decision to go to war in Iraq was an obvious, sobering example, and Donald

Trump's presidency offered abundant sources of dismay, in both domestic and foreign affairs. Indeed, under Trump's leadership the nation's democratic norms and institutions seemed themselves to be under attack, and resistance to those attacks logically included abolition or reform of the Electoral College. Such concerns gave rise to popular mobilization as well as a steady stream of articles and columns in the mainstream press and in social media.

The salience of the issue was heightened when it was injected into the campaign for the Democratic nomination for president in 2019–2020. Numerous candidates, led by Massachusetts senator Elizabeth Warren, forcefully declared their support for a national popular vote, while only a few preferred to keep the existing institution. (The one candidate who had ever voted on an NPV proposal, former vice president Joe Biden, said little.) The pro-reform stances of leading candidates generated new attention in the press and raised the prospect of the 2020 Democratic Party platform calling for abolition of the Electoral College—something it had not done between 2000 and 2016.[183] Meanwhile John Koza and his colleagues plugged away relentlessly on behalf of the NPVIC, with significant support from major news outlets and reform organizations such as Common Cause. Activist lawyers pressed their case to have winner-take-all declared unconstitutional and to determine whether states could bind electors. Members of Congress, too, were taking more active steps to promote change. In October 2018 the Congressional Progressive Caucus, which had more than seventy-five members, distributed a mass email asking recipients to sign a petition calling for the abolition of the Electoral College and the adoption of a national popular vote. The following spring, a handful of senators, including Brian Schatz (HI), Richard Durbin (IL), and Kirsten Gillibrand (NY) introduced resolutions to amend the Constitution to replace the Electoral College with a national popular election.[184] Two hundred years after Abner Lacock had first put the idea forward on the floor of the Senate, the struggle to bring it to life was still ongoing.

CONCLUSION

Reforming an electoral system is almost always a serious challenge—and not just because people commonly disagree about the best way to elect leaders. Rules and procedures that have been in place for years create constituencies that have an interest, or a perceived interest, in preserving the status quo. Significant change promises to produce losers as well as winners. Legislators and citizens alike often prefer to stick with the "devil they know"—however flawed that devil might be—rather than experiment with new arrangements that might have unintended consequences. Reforming an electoral system is not the same thing as inventing one from scratch—and in the case of American presidential elections, inventing one from scratch was not so easy either, as the framers learned in Philadelphia in the summer of 1787.

These broad truths about electoral reform are relevant to the story told in these pages, but they do not go far toward answering the question that frames this book. For more than two centuries, the United States has elected its most powerful public official through a complex process that has been widely criticized and sometimes condemned outright, a process that does not conform to the democratic principles the nation has publicly championed—a process that is ill understood by many Americans, bewildering to nearly everyone abroad, and never imitated by another country or by any state of the United States. Many countries have struggled with the problem of electoral reform, but few, if any, have done so with such lack of success over so prolonged a period.

So why, after more than two centuries of reform efforts, do we still have this electoral system? A system that does not give equal weight to the votes of all citizens and does not always award the presidency to the candidate who wins the most votes? A system that relies on potentially "faithless" intermediaries and transforms most Americans into spectators of election campaigns that are actively conducted in only a handful of contested states? And why do we retain a contingent process—if no candidate wins a majority of electoral votes—that is so defective that no one has publicly defended it for two hundred years? Why, in sum, have all of the system's problematic features remained unchanged since the ratification of the Twelfth Amendment in 1804?

The history recounted here makes clear that there is no single or simple answer to these questions. Multiple factors have prevented reform or replacement of the Electoral College, and the lineup has shifted over time, with particular obstacles to change becoming more prominent at some moments than at others. The diverse factors, moreover, have often been layered, reinforcing or intersecting with one another in changing patterns and shapes. Broadly speaking, they can be thought of as structural, political, and historical—although the boundaries separating these categories are far from rigid.

The most prominent structural obstacle has always been the difficulty of amending the United States Constitution. Most, but not all, facets of the electoral system are set forth in the Constitution, and as a result they can be durably altered only by amending that document—which requires supermajorities in both branches of Congress and in the states.[1] On two occasions—in 1821–1822 and in 1970—that high bar directly blocked transformative measures that were approved by one branch of Congress and had majority support in the other; at other junctures, it contributed to the defeat of proposals or served as a deterrent to ongoing congressional pursuit of change. Supreme Court Justice Ruth Bader Ginsburg summed up the problem succinctly in a 2017 interview: "There are some things that I would like to change, one is the Electoral College," she observed, "but that would require a constitutional amendment and amending our Constitution is powerfully hard to do."[2] The arduous process of amending the Constitution has even inhibited action on limited modifications that likely had supermajority support, such as eliminating electors (and thus faithless electors). As Senator Sam Ervin, among others, noted, it was not worth the trouble of amending the Constitution just to solve the pesky but generally inconsequential problem of faithless electors.

The complicated design of the electoral system created additional structural impediments to change. As recounted in Part II, for example, the framers' decision to allow states to determine the "manner" in which electors would be appointed gave a power, or right, to the states that they could be reluctant to relinquish. This sometimes spawned resistance to any federally mandated method of appointment, such as district or proportional elections; state political leaders could and did construe such proposals as attempts to strip their states of a valuable prerogative. This same detail of the Constitution, by giving states the latitude to alter the manner of choosing electors, introduced an unintended bias in favor of winner-take-all. That bias encouraged the (sometimes reluctant) adoption of the general ticket as states competed to maximize their influence in the early nineteenth century, and it later helped to thwart attempts by individual states to distribute electoral votes in a different fashion. (Once instituted, winner-take-all also gave large states an incentive to resist changes that would prevent them from casting sizable blocs of electoral votes.) States have always had the constitutional authority to discard the general ticket, but they encounter a collective action problem if they try to do so: first movers would lose influence in comparison to states that clung to winner-take-all.

The presence of two distinct phases to the electoral process—the electoral colleges and the contingent mechanism—has posed additional problems, in part because the two phases are based on different principles of representation and were intended to counterbalance one another. (Electoral votes are roughly proportional to population, whereas each state gets one vote in the contingent process.) In the early nineteenth century, when the contingent mechanism seemed likely to be deployed often, proposals to reform the first (electoral) phase quickly led to questions about the second; and the political need to simultaneously reform both phases of the process—to satisfy states of different sizes—ended up preventing any change, despite more than a decade of serious effort. Many years later, when the candidacy of H. Ross Perot threatened to throw the election into the House, there was broad bipartisan agreement that the contingent process was unacceptable—yet many members of Congress were disinclined to pursue an amendment that would address only the contingent mechanism and, in so doing, tacitly assent to the perpetuation of the Electoral College.

This last dynamic, it should be noted, has impeded piecemeal reform more generally. From the era of Thomas Hart Benton into the 1970s, for example, reformers have proposed, even demanded, that electors be eliminated, and precious few voices have been raised in defense of that widely disparaged public office. But a constitutional amendment that dealt only with electors would inescapably appear to affirm the system's other, more controversial, features—a prospect that was always unpalatable to those members of Congress who sought broader changes. Ironically, the fact that the system has numerous problematic parts has made it more difficult to change any of them.

One other aspect of the system's design has also hindered reform: the decision of the framers not to give equal weight to the votes of all citizens. The Constitution granted more electoral votes per capita to small states than to larger ones, and it gave electoral votes to southern states on behalf of their nonvoting slaves. The advantage given to white southerners, of course, disappeared with the Civil War, but it was revived (and enlarged) in the late nineteenth century when African-Americans in the South were systematically disenfranchised. These inequalities had little impact on campaigns for district or proportional elections, both of which had supporters among small states and in the South. But the extra electoral influence granted by the Constitution did give both smaller and southern states an incentive to prevent the adoption of a national popular vote: they had something to lose if all votes counted equally. Although the role of small states in blocking an NPV has often been exaggerated, it is noteworthy, in light of the Constitution's original blueprint, that the coalition that blocked Birch Bayh's NPV amendment in the Senate in 1970 and 1979 consisted largely of southern and thinly populated western states.[3]

The Senate has posed further problems for a national popular vote—but not for other frequently proposed reforms.[4] The Senate, of course, gives equal representation to all states; it neither embodies nor reflects the majoritarian principles that undergird proposals for a national vote. In addition, its internal processes (particularly the difficulty of shutting off debate) can make it difficult to even hold a vote on measures that are supported by a majority—but not a supermajority—of senators. Bayh's amendment was defeated in 1970 on cloture votes after it had been approved by a large majority of the House. Support for an NPV was also stronger in the House than in the Senate in the late 1970s. In recent decades, too, the Senate has generally had a more conservative cast than the House, which has proportionally more members from large states and urban centers.

The temporal rhythms of electoral reform have also complicated matters. Presidential elections happen only once every four years, and most surges of interest in the Electoral College—from both politicians and the public— have come either in anticipation of, or in reaction to, troublesome elections. The 1800 election was the first such instance, but atypically it did lead to constitutional change, the Twelfth Amendment. In the 1820s, congressional pursuit of reform was propelled by the prospect of multi-candidate elections that might (and did) land in the House; in the 1960s, political leaders from both parties feared that George Wallace might emerge as a kingmaker. "Wrong winner" elections produced spikes of concern in 1824, 1876, 2000, and 2016, as did the "near misses" of 1916, 1960, 1968, and 1976.[5] Spurs to action have been episodic, rooted in crises, near crises, and potential crises.

Episodic disturbances, however, were not easily transformed into popular mobilization or even sustained congressional action. Public interest in electoral processes tended to fade between elections, and problems that came to the fore quadrennially (or less often) were unlikely to launch popular movements or prolonged legislative initiatives—particularly given the changes in congressional composition that occurred every two years. Opponents of change were well aware of these dynamics and often sought to delay action on proposals in Congress and legislatures, thereby allowing public concern to subside. As Oliver Morton in the 1870s and Price Daniel in the 1950s both learned, the window for action on amendment proposals could narrow quickly. Birch Bayh had to contend twice with the loss of momentum caused by prolonged delays.[6]

Electoral crises, moreover, could—and usually did—exacerbate partisan tensions, creating political climates that were far from conducive to the assembling of supermajorities. This was unmistakable after the 1824 election, when the Era of Good Feelings quickly segued into an era of intense partisan rancor; it was also true in the wake of the presidential elections of 1876 and 2000. "There's an awful lot of bad feelings that came out of that election," observed Leon Panetta, a former Democratic congressman and member of the Carter-Ford commission on federal election reform. "It's tough to see how both sides will put their differences aside."[7] Crises could also shift the focus of congressional and public concern away from the Electoral College itself and toward related problems that seemed more urgent or manageable. For a decade after 1876, consideration of all other reforms was suspended while Congress wrestled with the procedure for counting electoral votes. Similarly, the 2000 election ended up with the nation focusing on "hanging chads" and the need for modernized voting machines.

Crises, of course, were not the only moments when partisanship complicated the path to reform. Although rarely acknowledged in public, the stances taken by political leaders often reflected their assessments of the impact of a proposed reform on their party's electoral prospects. The pattern was established in the early 1800s, soon after parties had begun to form, when many Democratic-Republicans abandoned their support for district elections after gauging that winner-take-all would serve them better in coming elections. It was almost comically visible in Martin Van Buren's machinations on behalf of his faction in the mid-1820s. Partisan considerations were paramount in the Republican Party's preference for retaining winner-take-all (rather than district or proportional elections) from the late 1880s into the mid-twentieth century. They have also played a key role in the GOP's recent antipathy to a national popular vote—when it has been almost an article of faith that the Electoral College advantages Republican candidates. Partisan calculations undergirded Republican objections to district elections in North Carolina in 2007 as well as Democratic objections to district elections in California that same year. In each of these cases, the party seeking to preserve the status quo did so not to defend ideas or principles—although ideas and principles were abundantly invoked—but to enhance its chances of winning presidential elections.

Partisan interests, to be sure, have also fueled reform efforts, including the Democratic push for district elections in North Carolina and the analogous Republican campaign in California. Partisan factors loomed large in the decision of Democrats in the 1890s to institute district elections in Michigan and pursue them elsewhere in the Midwest; and they have been present in Democratic preferences for a national vote since the 2016 election. Still, the impact of partisan considerations has most visibly, and decisively, been in the direction of preserving the status quo, particularly with respect to action by the federal government: given the need for supermajorities in Congress, the opposition of either major party, or even a dominant wing of a party, has generally been sufficient to doom any proposed constitutional amendment. (Legislative drives in favor of reform, on the other hand, could advance only with bipartisan support.) Indeed, the presence of a recognized de facto partisan veto has often produced periods of congressional inactivity, punctuated by a trickle of proposals from advocates of change. That was the case from 1900 to 1940, when it was known that the Republican Party frowned on any reform that would jeopardize winner-take-all. Reform proponents during such periods—which include the first two decades of the twenty-first century—have introduced amendment resolutions simply as statements of principle, knowing well that the near-certain fate of their proposals was to die in committee. In 1997 everyone knew that Ray LaHood's proposal for a national popular vote would sooner or later be blocked by his colleague Henry Hyde.

The significance of partisan dynamics was indirectly revealed in another way as well: the two periods in which reform efforts came closest to success were ones when the party systems were unsettled. The first, of course, was the Era of Good Feelings (or, more precisely, the years between 1812 and 1824), when the Federalist Party was dwindling into insignificance and nearly all major political leaders called themselves Democrats or Democratic-Republicans. Partisan factors had little bearing on the debates of the era (despite the jockeying of men like Van Buren), as the Senate repeatedly approved district elections resolutions and the House came close to doing so. The second such period was in the 1960s and the 1970s, when both major parties were ideologically divided and southern Democrats were commencing their migration into an increasingly conservative Republican Party. The near success of a national popular vote amendment unfolded while the national parties were in flux and lacked unity.

Despite the periodic intrusions of partisanship, party interests have not consistently trumped other factors or shaped the history of attempts to transform the electoral system. Until recently, Electoral College reform was not an issue that clearly separated the two major national parties, and there have been no enduring claims that the Electoral College advantaged one party or the other. District and proportional schemes have long had both Republican and Democratic backers; the same has been true for a national popular vote. Similar arguments, for and against reform, have been heard from both sides of the aisle in Congress and state legislatures, as well as from newspapers with different leanings. Over the course of two centuries, many political leaders have taken positions on Electoral College reform not because of their parties' interests but because of their own ideas, principles, and temperaments. Numerous politicians and commentators, moreover, supported some reforms but not others, for reasons that had little to do with party. California representative Clarence Lea was a fervent and principled advocate of proportional elections in the 1930s, but he opposed a national popular vote.

The impact of partisanship was further restrained by the difficulty of gauging the political consequences of proposed reforms. For most of the nineteenth century, political leaders and commentators eschewed predictions that district or proportional election schemes would aid one party rather than another. (That changed only when the South became a one-party Democratic bastion, and the national consequences of ending winner-take-all became unmistakable.) Similarly, the prolonged public debate over a national popular vote, which stretched from the 1950s into the late 1970s, included few assertions in the press or in Congress that either major party would be harmed by replacing the Electoral College with an NPV. Local leaders commonly believed that they could foresee the consequences of reform in their own states, but the net partisan effect nationally was usually more opaque, particularly because—as everyone acknowledged—campaigns would be run differently if the rules changed.

The challenge of seeing into the future, however, did not always stop politicians and analysts from trying to predict the impact of a proposed reform. They did so almost reflexively, and on numerous occasions their predictions proved to be erroneous, often because they mistook recent developments for longer-term trends. In the 1820s, for example, political leaders reoriented their agendas to prioritize reform of the contingent process because they were convinced that most future elections would otherwise end up being decided by the House of Representatives. The era of multi-candidate elections and infrequent electoral vote majorities had arrived—or so they thought! Similar miscalculations were made by various political actors after the election of 1976, an election that would prove to be an outlier rather than a harbinger of patterns to come. Among them were African-American leaders who opposed a national popular vote because they mistakenly concluded that blacks would wield more influence if the Electoral College were retained. In other instances, faulty predictions were grounded in the presumption that the future would always resemble the past: in the late 1940s and early 1950s, for example, mainstream Republicans rejected their colleague Henry Cabot Lodge's proportional election scheme in part because they were convinced that their party would never win many votes in the South, whatever the electoral system. These mistaken forecasts (and others like them) provided ample evidence of the hazards of favoring or opposing reforms because of their anticipated political consequences. Nonetheless the practice has continued unabated.

The weight of history has also had profound effects on the evolution of Electoral College reform—and not just because the institution was created in the eighteenth century and the Constitution has been difficult to amend. Few factors have shaped the debates over the Electoral College as insistently as the presence and later the legacy of slavery; the politics of race and region have been closely tied to conflicts over reform for more than two centuries. The institution itself accommodated the interests of slave owners, and the slave states banished the idea of a national popular vote throughout the antebellum period. As James Barbour so delicately put it in 1816, direct elections were simply not compatible with the "population anomalous" that lived and worked in the South.

The impact of slavery did not end with emancipation. After Reconstruction, the South became a white-dominated, single-party region with a large, disenfranchised black minority in whose name white citizens cast electoral votes. Southern states and white political leaders augmented their national influence through this arrangement, and they once again became implacable foes of a national popular vote: it threatened to diminish the region's electoral weight and/or encourage the enfranchisement of African-Americans. That stance endured into the middle decades of the twentieth century, as southern politicians came to regard the Electoral College as a key political bulwark against the intrusions of a federal government that sought to end segregation and enfranchise African-Americans. The South's opposition helped to keep the idea of a national vote off the table for decades, and in 1970 the region's senators led the way in killing an NPV amendment that had been approved by the House and had majority support in the Senate. In the late 1970s, much of the senate debate over Birch Bayh's revived NPV proposal revolved around the benefits or harms that it would bring to African-Americans in the North and the South.

The politics of race and region were influential in other ways and episodes as well. The prolonged Republican defense of winner-take-all, beginning in the late nineteenth century, was a reaction to the South's having become a one-party region: many Republicans feared, with reason, that district or proportional elections would cost them electoral votes in the North without their making commensurate gains in the Democratic South. In the mid-twentieth century the mobilization of support for, and then opposition to, the Lodge-Gossett measure was deeply entangled in concerns about the civil and political rights of African-Americans. Congressman Ed Gossett and his southern allies saw proportional elections as a means of undercutting northern support for the civil rights movement, while northern liberals (belatedly) recognized that threat and blocked the amendment in the House. The mid-twentieth century also witnessed heightened concern about faithless electors, largely because some southern Democratic electors refused to cast their ballots for their party's presidential candidates, who were regarded as unduly sympathetic with the civil rights movement. Decades later, after blacks were enfranchised and partisan alignments reshuffled, Republican politicians in the South opposed reform in part because they had predictable, predominantly white majorities in most states and saw no reason to surrender the advantages of winner-take-all to the benefit of Democratic candidates backed by African-American voters.[8]

Issues linked to race, thus, have permeated the history of Electoral College reform, often intersecting with structural and partisan factors to compound the difficulties faced by proponents of alternative electoral methods. Slavery and its manifold legacies served to limit the options for change and, on some occasions, directly reduced the odds of reform campaigns succeeding. The shape, the configuration, of the story told in these pages would have been different—almost unimaginably different—had race not been such a penetrating presence in American political life. That is true, of course, of many strands of American history, and the evolution of Electoral College reform has been no exception.

*   *   *

The history recounted here has a Sisyphean air. For more than two centuries, advocates of change have pressed the case to modify or replace the presidential election system, and they have always fallen short, only occasionally coming within hailing distance of success. Dedicated and well-positioned members of Congress like Mahlon Dickerson, Oliver Morton, Henry Cabot Lodge, Emanuel Celler, and Birch Bayh labored for years to promote reform but came up empty-handed, leaving the country no closer to change when they finished than it had been when they started. For those citizens of the twenty-first century who believe that the Electoral College is a good and fair method of electing presidents, the headlines of this story may be reassuring: misguided reform ideas have repeatedly been rebuffed.[9] For the millions of Americans who are discontented with the system and hope for change, those same headlines could induce pessimism and inertia. The obstacles to change loom large, and the track record is largely one of failure.

Yet there are other themes and subplots in this story, facts and patterns that may be more encouraging to the reform-minded. The tale told here is a history of increasingly widespread democratic beliefs, of aspiration and striving, of determined efforts to make the process of presidential election conform to democratic norms that have grown broader and stronger over the last two centuries. Most nineteenth- and twentieth-century proposals for district and proportional elections were attempts to end the electoral distortions generated by winner-take-all, to enhance participation, and to bring electoral outcomes into closer harmony with the views of the voting public. Serious consideration of replacing the institution with a national popular vote, beginning in the mid-twentieth century, was another major step in that direction. All of these ideas have been supported, at one time or another, by most members of Congress and a majority of the American people. One can find signs of progress too in the unpopularity, indeed repudiation, of the contingent election system: the notion that each state, regardless of its population, should have an equal voice in deciding who becomes president has become politically and intellectually indefensible. Similarly, the consensus that electors are unnecessary reflects the conviction that the preferences of the people ought not be filtered through intermediaries. An undercurrent of democratic progress courses through the trail of legislative defeats.

Then, too, the history reminds us that the problematic practice of winner-take-all has frequently been criticized or even rejected by individual states and their leaders. In the early years of the republic, numerous states opted for district elections and only reluctantly—even grudgingly—shifted to the general ticket. Since that time, three states have voted to adopt district elections: Michigan's district elections experiment in the 1890s proved to be short-lived, but Maine and Nebraska have been faring well without committing all of their electoral votes to one candidate. Although the historical record indicates that decisions by individual states do not constitute a very promising path to national reform, the recent growth of support for the NPVIC reveals that many states would be happy to do away with winner-take-all as long as they have company in doing so.

Further glimmers of encouragement may be drawn from the important fact that Congress came very close to approving transformative constitutional amendments on two occasions, one of them within living memory. A few changed votes in 1821 or 1970, followed by effective ratification campaigns, would have permanently altered the conduct of presidential elections. A thought experiment can be valuable here: if Birch Bayh's amendment had become law in the early 1970s, it is unimaginable that the country would ever have seriously considered switching back to an electoral system as byzantine as the Electoral College.

Knowledge of the history beneath the stark headlines may also provide useful insights, demythologizing some claims, contextualizing the setbacks, distinguishing among the factors that have made the struggle for reform such an uphill climb. The historical record, for example, makes clear that the institution we now call the Electoral College was not inspired by surpassing wisdom and astute judgment on the part of the framers of the Constitution. It was an eleventh-hour compromise by gifted but tired men who had difficulty figuring out how to elect a president and had to bring their work to a close. The framers themselves did not regard the electoral system as their finest handiwork (whatever Alexander Hamilton might have written); it never really functioned as they intended; and in less than two decades it had misfired so badly that the Constitution had to be amended. By the 1810s and 1820s, a number of the framers, including James Madison, Thomas Jefferson, and Rufus King, were convinced that further changes were needed.

Attempts to modify or replace the system, moreover, have not been routinely vetoed by the small states, despite oft-repeated claims to the contrary. Nor have these numerous attempts been overwhelmed by persuasive arguments in favor of the status quo: although some of the arguments have warranted serious consideration, many of the claims commonly put forward by defenders of the Electoral College have tended to crumble when confronted with evidence.[10] Instead, the survival of the institution has been ensured by more mundane, more political, and, in some cases, more unseemly and disturbing factors. Majority preferences in favor of change have been denied by the need for supermajorities. Popular opinion has been ignored and overridden by professional politicians. The intricacy of the system's design—itself the result of eighteenth-century compromises—has made it difficult to remedy its flaws one at a time. Political parties and factions have repeatedly blocked reforms not because it was in the nation's interest but because they believed it to be in their own partisan interest. The desire to maintain white dominance in the South, often cloaked in disingenuous arguments about federalism and small states, suppressed debate about a national popular vote and later impeded the passage of an NPV amendment.

These obstacles have been formidable, but some of them, at least, have proved to be transient or contingent. Just as individual states have not always been "red" or "blue," the views of political parties and leading politicians have changed over time. Many prominent Republicans favored district elections before the party began to adamantly defend the general ticket in the late nineteenth century. There was substantial, even majority, GOP support for a national popular vote in the House in 1969 and the Senate in 1970; the Republican phalanx against change did not coalesce until after 1980. Most Democrats (outside the South) were sympathetic to reform in the twentieth century, but they favored different reforms at different junctures. Small-state representatives may have steadfastly opposed direct elections in the late nineteenth century (evidence is too sparse to be sure), but by the 1950s and 1960s more than a few of them were leaders in the fight for a national popular vote. African-American leaders were deeply divided over Electoral College reform in the 1970s, but by the twenty-first century nearly all had embraced an NPV. Meanwhile, politicians from both parties who embraced winner-take-all when their parties had predictable majorities in their home states have sometimes discovered the charms of district elections when their states became more competitive. In the South, long a bastion of opposition to an NPV, demographic and political shifts in recent years may portend an erosion of support for the Electoral College.[11]

The history tells us, in effect, that things change and that there is no necessary reason for the pattern of past defeats to recur indefinitely. Amending the Constitution to mandate direct popular elections to the Senate took decades. The movement to enfranchise women failed for nearly a century before it succeeded, and the effort to restore the voting rights of African-Americans in the South took almost as long. The historical record makes plain that successful reform can emerge only in particular historical and political circumstances, but it also reveals that favorable environments have existed in the past. In December 2016, shortly after the second Electoral College misfire of the twenty-first century, Michigan representative John Conyers published an op-ed essay reminding readers that in 1969 he had been "one of 338 members of the House of Representatives who voted on a bipartisan basis to amend the Constitution to eliminate the Electoral College." "Under the right circumstances," Conyers wrote, "the political will for reform can exist."[12]

*　　*　　*

Understanding why we still have the Electoral College does not tell us directly whether "we the people of the United States" *ought* to continue electing our presidents as we have thus far. A reader of this saga might well conclude that despite the institution's flaws, there is no compelling reason to discard it and replace it with something untried (or untried in the United States). The institution might be "clumsy," "archaic," and "cumbersome," but the nation has muddled through. Elections have been held every four years for more than two centuries, and even when the system has malfunctioned the official winners have taken office peacefully. All electoral designs have drawbacks, and the institution offers "enough benefits to justify its survival," as the *New York Times* once editorialized.[13]

Such conclusions would not be altogether unreasonable, but the history recounted here offers far stronger support for the view that significant changes to the electoral system are both warranted and long overdue. The recurrent efforts to replace or reform the Electoral College have reflected widespread and long-standing dissatisfaction with an institution that is central to the working of American democracy and, as such, ought to be broadly, even universally, respected. That the Electoral College does not command that respect has been evident for much of our history. Criticism of winner-take-all for its deforming effects on elections has been voiced in every decade since the nation's founding, by respected political leaders as varied as John Marshall, Andrew Jackson, Charles Sumner, Jimmy Carter, and Gerald Ford. Since the 1820s, electors have been regarded as useless at best and dangerous at worst. The contingent election system has been in bad odor since the early nineteenth century; that it is still with us, in its original form, has been a failure of governance fed by the quavering hope that it will never again be used.[14] Most importantly perhaps, the Electoral College is, and long has been, out of step with the nation's values—never more so than when it has elevated to the presidency candidates who did not win the popular vote. The nation has become more democratic since 1787 and more committed to political equality, but the Electoral College has not. Large segments of the population consequently doubt its fairness—which is no small matter at a time when the nation's institutions seem under more strain than they have been at any time since the Civil War.

The record of conflict over the electoral system further—and strongly—suggests that presidents ought to be chosen through processes that embody fundamental, broadly accepted, transparent, and hopefully durable principles. The Electoral College no longer matches that description—if it ever did. But a national popular vote would fit the bill: it would be grounded in the dual principles that all citizens have the right to vote for president and that all votes should count equally. The idea of electing a president through a national vote has a long American pedigree, stretching back to the Constitutional Convention in 1787; and as long as we have had opinion polls, it has been the plan preferred by a majority of the American people. It is attuned to the nation's proclaimed values—and to common sense. As Birch Bayh frequently pointed out, a national popular vote, unlike the Electoral College, would not provoke disputes about the advantages that accrued to large or small states, or urban versus rural voters; instead, "all our votes" will "count the same." That our nation has not adopted an NPV before now—despite the strenuous efforts of men like Bayh and William Langer—has been largely the consequence of political machinations and systemic inequalities that would best be consigned to the past.[15]

Whether the goal of implementing a national popular vote can be realized in the foreseeable future is an open question. No reader of this volume will underestimate the challenge. The political forces pressing for Electoral College reform are stronger now than they have been at any point since the 1970s, but the extreme polarization of the polity does not bode well for institutional changes that would have to be bipartisan and carefully reasoned. Knowledge of the past can help to free us from its constraints and to imagine different futures, but its predictive powers are limited, and for better or worse, we may now inhabit truly uncharted political terrain.

APPENDIX A

PUBLIC OPINION POLLS

APPENDIX TABLE A.1: THE ELECTORAL COLLEGE VERSUS A NATIONAL POPULAR VOTE

			Percentage of respondents who preferred		
Poll	Date	Sample population	Changing to a national popular vote	Keeping the Electoral College	No opinion[a]
Gallup[b]	Jun 1944	National adult	62	21	18
Gallup[b]	Mar 1947	National adult	70	19	11
Gallup[c]	May 1966	National adult	63	20	17
Gallup[b,c]	May 1967	National adult	58	22	20
Gallup[b]	Nov 1967	National adult	65	22	13
Gallup[b,c]	Sep 1968	National adult	66	19	15
Harris Survey[b,d]	Nov 1968	National adult	78	13	9
Gallup[b,c,e]	Nov 1968	National adult	80	12	7
Gallup[e]	Oct 1970	National adult	79	21	0
Gallup[b,f]	Feb 1977	National adult	73	15	12
Harris Survey[e]	May 1977	National adult	74	13	13
Cambridge Reports National Omnibus Survey[e]	Jul 1977	National adult	71	15	13
Civic Services Campaign Financing[e]	Mar 1978	National adult	64	31	5
Gallup[b,e,g]	Dec 1980	National adult	67	19	15
Harris Survey[e]	Jan 1981	National adult	77	21	2
CBS News/New York Times[e]	May 1987	National adult	61	33	6
ABC News/Washington Post[e]	Nov 1988	National likely registered voters	72	23	5
United We Stand America Political Reform Study[e]	Mar 1993	National adult	73	21	6
Newsweek[e]	Nov 2000	National adult	57	33	10
Time/CNN[e]	Nov 2000	National adult	63	29	8
Gallup/CNN/USA Today[b,e,h]	Nov 2000	National adult	61	35	4

(*continued*)

Poll	Date	Sample population	Percentage of respondents who preferred		
			Changing to a national popular vote	Keeping the Electoral College	No opinion[a]
CBS News/New York Times[e]	Nov 2000	National adult	60	31	9
ABC News/Washington Post[e]	Nov 2000	National adult	63	31	6
CBS News/New York Times Monthly[e]	Nov 2000	National adult	57	35	8
Gallup[b]	Dec 2000	National adult	63	33	4
NBC News/Wall Street Journal[e]	Dec 2000	National adult	50	44	6
CBS News/New York Times[e]	Dec 2000	National adult	57	39	4
Los Angeles Times[e]	Dec 2000	National adult	62	30	9
ABC News/Washington Post[e]	Dec 2000	National adult	62	33	5
Gallup/CNN/USA Today[e]	Jan 2001	National adult	59	37	4
Gallup[b,e]	Oct 2004	National adult	61	34	4
Time[e]	Oct 2004	National adult	56	37	7
Harris Survey[i]	Nov 2004	National likely voters	64	22	14
Washington Post/ Kaiser/Harvard University[e]	Jul 2007	National adult	72	23	4
Gallup[e]	Oct 2011	National adult	62	35	4
ABC News/Washington Post[e]	Oct 2012	National likely voters	56	37	7
CBS News[e]	Oct 2012	National adult	62	31	6
Quinnipiac University[e]	Dec 2012	National registered voters	60	29	11
Gallup[e]	Jan 2013	National adult	63	29	8
Civis Analytics[j]	Nov 2016	Registered voters	62	38	–
CNN/ORC[e]	Nov 2016	National adult	51	44	3

APPENDIX TABLE A.1 (Continued)

Poll	Date	Sample population	Changing to a national popular vote	Keeping the Electoral College	No opinion[a]
			Percentage of respondents who preferred		
Quinnipiac[c]	Nov 2016	National registered voters	53	39	8
Gallup[k]	Nov 2016	National adult	49	47	-
Bloomberg News[e]	Dec 2016	National adult	54	41	6
Marist Institute for Public Opinion[l]	Dec 2016	Registered voters	52	45	3
CBS News[m]	Dec 2016	National adult	54	41	5
Suffolk University/USA Today[e]	Dec 2016	National registered voters	42	50	8
Pew Research Center[n]	Mar 2018	National adult	55	41	4
Pew Research Center[o]	Apr 2018	National adult	55	41	-
PRRI/The Atlantic Voter Engagement Survey[e]	Jun 2018	National adult	65	32	3
Morning Consult/Politico[p]	Mar 2019	Registered voters	50	34	16
The Hill/HarrisX[q]	Mar 2019	Registered voters	44	37	19
Quinnipiac University[e]	Mar 2019	Registered voters	54	39	7
Fox News[e]	Apr 2019	Registered voters	52	41	7
Gallup[e]	Apr 2019	National adult	55	43	2
NBC/Wall St. Journal[e]	Apr 2019	National adult	53	43	4

a. "No opinion" includes results for respondents who did not have an opinion or did not provide an answer.

b. Gallup Analytics, https://www.gallup.com/analytics/213617/gallup-analytics.aspx.

c. George H. Gallup, *The Gallup Poll: Public Opinion, 1935–1971*, vols. 1–3 (Random House, 1972).

d. The Odum Institute for Research in Social Science, University of North Carolina at Chapel Hill, https://odum.unc.edu/.

e. The Roper Center for Public Opinion Research, Cornell University, https://ropercenter.cornell.edu/.

f. George H. Gallup, *The Gallup Poll: Public Opinion, 1972–1977*, vol. 2 (Scholarly Resources, 1978).

g. George H. Gallup, *The Gallup Poll: Public Opinion, 1980* (Scholarly Resources, 1981).

h. George Gallup, Jr., *The Gallup Poll: Public Opinion, 2000* (Scholarly Resources, 2001).

(continued)

APPENDIX TABLE A.1 (Continued)

i. Polling the Nations, http://www.orspub.com/.

j. Civis Analytics, Nov. 24, 2016, https://www.vox.com/policy-and-politics/2016/11/24/13731770/electoral -college-poll.

k. Gallup, Dec. 2, 2016, https://news-gallup-com.ezp-prod1.hul.harvard.edu/poll/198917/americans-support -electoral-college-rises-sharply.aspx.

l. Marist College Institute for Public Opinion, December 2016.

m. CBS News, Dec. 9–13, 2016, https://www.cbsnews.com/news/poll-more-americans-believe-popular -vote-should-decide-the-president/.

n. Pew Research Center, Mar. 7–14, 2018, http://www.people-press.org/question-search/?qid=19100408pid =51accid=51#top.

o. Pew Research Center, Apr. 26, 2018, http://www.people-press.org/2018/04/26/5-the-electoral-college -congress-and-representation/5_1-9/.

p. Morning Consult / Politico, Mar. 22–24, 2019, https://www.politico.com/f/?id=00000169-bbb5-dc6b -a96d-bfb5b0c50001.

q. The Hill / HarrisX, Mar. 23–24, 2019, https://thehill.com/hilltv/what-americas-thinking/435816-poll -republicans-support-electoral-college-while-democrats-want.

Poll	Date	Sample population	Percentage of respondents who preferred		
			Proportional division	Winner-take-all	No opinion[a]
Gallup	Aug 1948	National adult	58	15	27
Gallup	Mar 1950	National adult	56	22	22
Gallup	Sep 1951	National adult	57	21	22
Gallup	Feb 1955	National adult	52	29	19
Gallup	Mar 1956	National adult	60	28	12
Gallup	Mar 1960	National adult	50	28	22
Gallup	Dec 1960	National adult	56	26	18
Gallup	Sep 1961	National adult	61	21	18
Gallup	Jun 1965	National adult	57	28	15
Gonzales/Arscott Research & Communications[b]	Feb 2001	Maryland registered voters	33	55	12
Gallup/CNN/USA Today[c]	Oct 2004	Colorado adult	43	47	10

Sources: Gallup Analytics, https://www.gallup.com/analytics/213617/gallup-analytics.aspx;
George H. Gallup, *The Gallup Poll: Public Opinion, 1935–1971,* vols. 1–3 (New York, 1972); Polling the Nations, http://www.orspub.com/.

a. "No opinion" includes results for respondents who did not have an opinion or did not provide an answer.

b. This question referred to how Maryland should award electoral votes in presidential elections.

c. This question referred to how Colorado should award electoral votes in presidential elections.

APPENDIX B

CONSTITUTIONAL PROVISIONS FOR PRESIDENTIAL ELECTIONS

U.S. Constitution (Ratified 1788)

ARTICLE II, SECTION I

The Executive Branch

[1] The executive Power shall be vested in a President of the United States of America. He shall hold his Office during the Term of four Years, and, together with the Vice-President, chosen for the same Term, be elected, as follows.

[2] Each State shall appoint, in such Manner as the Legislature thereof may direct, a Number of Electors, equal to the whole Number of Senators and Representatives to which the State may be entitled in the Congress: but no Senator or Representative, or Person holding an Office of Trust or Profit under the United States, shall be appointed an Elector.

[3] [The Electors shall meet in their respective States, and vote by Ballot for two persons, of whom one at least shall not be an Inhabitant of the same State with themselves. And they shall make a List of all the Persons voted for, and of the Number of Votes for each; which List they shall sign and certify, and transmit sealed to the Seat of the Government of the United States, directed to the President of the Senate. The President of the Senate shall, in the Presence of the Senate and House of Representatives, open all the Certificates, and the Votes shall then be counted. The Person having the greatest Number of Votes shall be the President, if such Number be a Majority of the whole Number of Electors appointed; and if there be more than one who have such Majority, and have an equal Number of Votes, then the House of Representatives shall immediately chuse by Ballot one of them for President; and if no Person have a Majority, then from the five highest on the List the said House shall in like Manner chuse the

President. But in chusing the President, the Votes shall be taken by States, the Representation from each State have one Vote; a quorum for this Purpose shall consist of a Member or Members from two thirds of the States, and a Majority of all the States shall be necessary to a Choice. In every Case, after the Choice of the President, the Person having the greatest Number of Votes of the Electors shall be the Vice President. But if there should remain two or more who have equal Votes, the Senate shall chuse from them by Ballot the Vice-President.] (Note: Superseded by the Twelfth Amendment.)

[4] The Congress may determine the Time of chusing the Electors, and the Day on which they shall give their Votes; which Day shall be the same throughout the United States.

12th Amendment (Ratified 1804)

The Electors shall meet in their respective states, and vote by ballot for President and Vice-President, one of whom, at least, shall not be an inhabitant of the same state with themselves; they shall name in their ballots the person voted for as President and in distinct ballots the person voted for as Vice-President, and they shall make distinct lists of all persons voted for as President, and of all persons voted for as Vice-President, and of the number of votes for each, which lists they shall sign and certify, and transmit sealed to the seat of the government of the United States, directed to the President of the Senate;—The President of the Senate shall, in the presence of the Senate and House of Representatives, open all the certificates and the votes shall then be counted;—The person having the greatest number of votes for President, shall be the President, if such number be a majority of the whole number of Electors appointed; and if no person have such majority, then from the persons having the highest numbers not exceeding three on the list of those voted for as President, the House of Representatives shall choose immediately, by ballot, the President, the votes shall be taken by states, the representation from each state having one vote; a quorum for this purpose shall consist of a member or members from two-thirds of the states, and a majority of all the states shall be necessary to a choice. And if the House of Representatives shall not choose a President whenever the right of choice shall devolve upon them, before the fourth day of March next following, then the Vice-President shall act as President, as in the case of the death or other constitutional disability of the President.—The person having the greatest number of votes as Vice-President, shall be the Vice-President, if such number be a majority of the whole number of Electors appointed, and if no person have a majority, then from the two highest numbers on the list, the Senate shall choose the Vice-President; a quorum for the purpose shall consist of two-thirds of the whole number of Senators, and a majority of the whole number shall be necessary to a choice. But no person constitutionally ineligible to the office of President shall be eligible to that of Vice-President of the United States.

THE EVOLUTION OF THE TERM
ELECTORAL COLLEGE

For roughly half of our nation's history, the presidential election system was not called the "Electoral College." The phrase does not appear in the Constitution, and its modern usage was slow to emerge. During the first half of the nineteenth century, the term *electoral college* appeared in English primarily with reference to European (especially French) institutions. According to the *Oxford English Dictionary*, its debut in American English (referring to the U.S. presidential elections) occurred in congressional debates in 1800, although I have found one earlier instance of its use, in an Anti-Federalist pamphlet published in Pennsylvania in 1788: the pseudonymous author, Aristocrotis, referred to "the majority of the votes of the electoral college."[1]

In the first half of the nineteenth century, the term *Electoral College*—when deployed in an American context—generally referred to the group, or the gathering, of presidential electors who assembled separately in each state capital to cast electoral votes: for example, the Register of Pennsylvania reported that "the Electoral College" of that state convened in Harrisburg on December 3, 1828. More frequent were plural references to the *electoral colleges* of the states: the "majority received by General Jackson in the electoral colleges." Occasionally (and increasingly toward midcentury) the phrase referred not to the state gatherings but to the national total of electoral votes. ("The majority of General Pierce in the Electoral College is greater than that of any of his predecessors with the exception of Washington and Monroe.")[2]

The modern usage of the phrase—as a shorthand for the entire system of allocating electoral votes, choosing electors, and tabulating their ballots—appeared rarely before the Civil War, was more common in the 1870s, and became widespread only in the twentieth century. As late as 1906, J. Hampden Dougherty, a prominent legal scholar and attorney, published an entire book about the presidential election system, using the phrase *electoral college* only once, in a footnote. For the first half of the twentieth century, the two different usages—referring either to the national system or to the assembly of electors in a state—coexisted with one another. After World War II the systemic meaning became dominant, and, unsurprisingly, the plural *electoral colleges* disappeared.[3]

Abbreviations

AP	Associated Press
Bayh Papers	Birch Bayh Senatorial Papers, Modern Political Papers Collection, Indiana University Libraries, Bloomington
BG	*Boston Globe*
CDT	*Chicago Tribune* or *Chicago Daily Tribune*. The name of the newspaper has changed several times since 1847; most often it was *The Chicago Daily Tribune* or *The Chicago Tribune*. The abbreviation *CDT* is used throughout the notes.
CRS	Congressional Research Service
CSM	*Christian Science Monitor*
Ervin Papers	Sam J. Ervin Papers, Southern Historical Collection, Wilson Library, University of North Carolina at Chapel Hill
LAT	*Los Angeles Times*
NAR	*North American Review*
NWR	*Niles' Weekly Register*
NYT	*New York Times*
Papers of James Madison	*The Papers of James Madison*, ed. David B. Mattern, J. C. A. Stagg, Mary Parke Johnson, and Katherine E. Harbury (Charlottesville, 2016)
WP	*Washington Post*
WSJ	*Wall Street Journal*

Notes

1. Regarding the evolution of the term "Electoral College," see Appendix C. Regarding Madison's views, see Chapter 2.

2. The other four elections were in 1824, 1876, 1888, and 2000; as discussed later in this volume, there is some uncertainty or controversy regarding the popular vote totals in each of the three nineteenth-century elections. George Edwards argues that, contrary to the conventionally reported numbers, Richard Nixon defeated John Kennedy in the popular vote in 1960; he also provides a list of the "near misses." George C. Edwards III, *Why the Electoral College Is Bad for America*, 2nd ed. (New Haven, CT, 2011), 62–73. Polls indicate that most Americans regard it to be "unfair" that the winner of the popular vote could lose in the Electoral College and not become president; see Table A.1, as well as Gallup, Inc., "Election Wrap-Up," Field Date 12/15/2000–12/17/2000, question 14, https://institution-gallup-com.ezp-prod1.hul .harvard.edu/documents/question.aspx?QUESTION=71305.

3. The number of seats that each state has in the House of Representatives is proportional to its population—but that is not true of the Senate, where each state has two seats. The 2016 figures were calculated from U.S. Census Bureau Apportionment Tables, "Apportionment Population and Number of Representatives, by State: 2010 Census" (Washington, DC, 2010).

4. Edwards, *Electoral College*, 124–139.

5. In addition to Table A.1, see Chapter 7.

6. Quotation from Herman V. Ames, "The Proposed Amendments to the Constitution of the United States during the First Century of Its History," *Annual Report of the American Historical Association* 2 (1896). Regarding faithless electors, see Edwards, *Electoral College*, 49–60; and Robert Alexander, "Lobbying the Electoral College: The Potential for Chaos," in *Electoral College Reform: Challenges and Possibilities*, ed. Gary Bugh (Farnham, UK, 2010), 163–165. Regarding early discontents more generally, see Chapters 1 and 2.

7. The phrase "unit rule" was more common in the mid-twentieth century (and earlier) than it is today. It was applied both to Electoral College voting and to a similar practice in the national conventions of political parties.

8. *Republican Spy* 2, no. 69 (Oct. 16, 1804), 3. See Chapters 1 and 2.

9. Neal Peirce and Lawrence Longley, *The People's President: The Electoral College in American History and the Direct Vote Alternative*, rev. ed. (New Haven, CT, 1981), 146; U.S. Congress, House of Representatives, Committee on Election of President, Vice President, and Representatives in Congress, *Proposed Constitutional Amendment*

Providing for the Election of President and Vice President, Hearing, Mar. 14, 1930, on H.J. Res. 106, 71st Cong. 2nd Sess. 1930, 2–4, 14–41.

10. Thomas Jefferson to George Hay, Aug. 17, 1823, in *The Works of Thomas Jefferson,* ed. Paul Leicester Ford, 12 vols. (New York, 1904–1905), 12:302–304.

11. The events of 1948 and 1968 are described in Chapters 3 and 5. The 1992 episode, when H. Ross Perot ran as an independent candidate, is discussed in Chapter 7.

12. George W. Norris, *Fighting Liberal: The Autobiography of George W. Norris* (New York, 1945), 329.

13. Library of Congress, "A Century of Lawmaking for a New Nation: U.S. Congressional Documents and Debates, 1774–1875," preamble to S. Res. 7, 42nd Cong. (May 30 1872).

14. J. Hampden Dougherty, *The Electoral System of the United States* (New York, 1906), 348.

15. Some of the proposed changes would also have supplanted or altered the Twelfth Amendment. The texts of Article II, section 1, and the Twelfth Amendment are in Appendix B.

16. Regarding the National Popular Vote Interstate Compact, see Chapter 7.

17. The figure is an estimate and it is likely low. Tabulations have been prepared for different time periods by several scholars, as well as by the Congressional Research Service, but the different sets of figures do not mesh cleanly with one another. The only complete count for the years from 1787 to 1896 (224 proposals) comes from Ames's "Proposed Amendments," and that figure has been accepted as reasonable both by the Congressional Research Service (hereafter cited as CRS) and by Peirce and Longley, *The People's President,* 131. Peirce and Longley also found an additional 289 amendments for the years 1896–1966. More recently, Gary Bugh has concluded that between 1899 and 2010, 682 electoral reform measures were introduced. (Gary E. Bugh, "The Challenge of Contemporary Electoral College Reform," in Bugh, *Electoral College Reform,* 77–84.) The CRS, however, offers a slightly lower figure of 595 amendments between 1889 and 2004. (Paige Whitaker and Thomas H. Neale, "The Electoral College: An Overview and Analysis of Reform Proposals," CRS Report RL30804, Nov. 5, 2004, 17–24.) Adding Ames's tally to the CRS figure (plus those introduced since 2004) would yield a total of over 800; if Bugh is correct, the total would be greater than 900. Even higher figures have occasionally appeared in print, but they lacked verifiable sources. Whatever the exact tally, the import is the same: a great many amendment proposals have been introduced in Congress. I have relied here also on email correspondence with Thomas H. Neale, American National Government Specialist, CRS, Jan. 16, 2019.

18. Whitaker and Neale, "The Electoral College," 17; Robert W. Bennett, *Taming the Electoral College* (Stanford, CA, 2006), 48; Michael J. Korzi, "If the Manner of It Be Not Perfect," in Bugh, *Electoral College Reform,* 51; "Rethinking the Electoral College Debate: The Framers, Federalism, and One Person, One Vote," *Harvard Law Review* 114, no. 8 (June 2001): 2526; Donald Lutz et al., "The Electoral College in Historical

and Philosophical Perspective," in *Choosing a President*, ed. Paul D. Schumaker and Burdett A. Loomis (New York, 2002), 46.

19. Proposed amendments were approved (by a two-thirds vote) by the Senate in 1813, 1819, 1820, 1822, and 1950 and by the House in 1969. This tally does not include congressional action on the Twelfth Amendment. Since 1826 the House has voted on amendments only in 1950 and 1969, whereas the Senate did so in 1934, 1950, 1956, 1970, and 1979. Bugh, "Challenge," and Gary E. Bugh, "Representation in Congressional Efforts to Amend the Presidential Election System," in Bugh, *Electoral College Reform*, 9–10, 79–81.

20. The small alteration was a reduction, from five to three, in the number of candidates who would be considered by the House.

21. These "automatic plans," as they were often called, permitted states to decide how their electoral votes would be allocated (e.g., by district or by winner-take-all) but assigned those votes automatically, depending on the outcome of popular elections or the decisions of state legislatures.

22. The scholarly terrain has been left almost entirely to political scientists and legal scholars. The standard historical account is offered in one chapter of Peirce and Longley's *The People's President*, which is well executed but lacking in detail and analysis. Political scientist Gary Bugh has also explored portions of this history in various articles cited here. Several unpublished dissertations focusing on particular periods are cited in the chapters below. Questions regarding the survival of the Electoral College are raised but not broadly explored in Luis Fuentes-Rohwer and Guy-Uriel Charles, "The Electoral College, the Right to Vote, and Our Federalism: A Comment on a Lasting Institution," *Florida State Law Review* 29, no. 2 (2001): 881.

23. In recent decades the arguments in favor of retaining the Electoral College have tended to rely on factual assertions (e.g., that it serves the interests of small states) or on invocations of principle and political tradition (e.g., that it embodies the wisdom of the framers or that it preserves federalism). Another, perhaps stronger, line of defense for the Electoral College has been the claim that its defects are less severe or troublesome than the shortcomings (and potentially unforeseen consequences) of other methods of choosing a president. See, for examples, Judith A. Best, *The Choice of the People? Debating the Electoral College* (Lanham, MD, 1996); Best, *The Case against Direct Election of the President* (New York, 1975); Best, "Presidential Selection: Complex Problems and Simple Solutions," *Political Science Quarterly*, 119, no. 1 (Spring 2004): 39–59; Alexander Bickel, *Reform and Continuity: The Electoral College, the Convention, and the Party System* (New York, 1971); Tara Ross, *Enlightened Democracy: The Case for the Electoral College* (Dallas, 2004); Paul D. Schumaker, "The Good, the Better, the Best: Improving on the 'Acceptable' Electoral College," in Bugh, *Electoral College Reform*, 203–222; Schumaker, "Analyzing the Electoral College and Its Alternatives," in Schumaker and Loomis, *Choosing a President*, 10–30; and Lutz et al., "Electoral College." Critics, most recently George Edwards, have directly challenged the arguments about principle and assembled a great

deal of evidence indicating that the factual claims of the defenders are not valid. Edwards, *Electoral College*, 114–191. See also Jack N. Rakove, "The E-College in the E-Age," in *The Unfinished Election of 2000*, ed. Jack N. Rakove (New York, 2001), 201–234; and Akhil R. Amar and Vikram D. Amar, "Why Old and New Arguments for the Electoral College Are Not Compelling," in *After the People Vote*, 3rd ed., ed. John C. Fortier (Washington, DC, 2004), 55–65. The arguments from different periods, for and against Electoral College reform, are presented throughout this volume, and readers can judge their merits. My own views about the institution are briefly expressed in Alex Keyssar, "The Electoral College Flunks," *New York Review of Books*, Mar. 24, 2005.

24. Numerous examples of the assertion that small states would block efforts at reform are presented in Chapters 3–7; the appearance of this claim as conventional wisdom is discussed in Chapters 4 and 7. A small number of districting or proportional proposals did include provisions to change the allocation of electoral votes to the states (e.g., by making that allocation strictly dependent on population), but such provisions were unusual.

25. Senator Pastore (RI), 102 Cong. Rec. 5162 (Mar. 20, 1956); see the discussion in Chapter 4. See also Peirce and Longley, *The People's President*, 165.

26. Political scientists Lawrence D. Longley and Alan G. Braun concluded in 1972 that the roll call votes in the 1960s displayed "no consistent pattern corresponding to state size." Longley and Braun, *The Politics of Electoral College Reform* (New Haven, CT, 1972), 152, 175–176. More recently Mark McKenzie, using updated statistical methods and relying on a different definition of "small state," concluded that members of Congress from small states were somewhat (and sometimes) more likely to oppose a national popular vote but that state size did not have a decisive impact on the outcome of congressional votes between 1950 and 1979. Mark J. McKenzie, "Systemic Biases Affecting Congressional Voting on Electoral College Reform," in Bugh, *Electoral College Reform*, 95–112. See also Chapters 4–6 and the tables in those chapters. State size did play a role in reform debates in the first third of the nineteenth century, but not because of small-state resistance to a national vote. See Chapter 2.

27. Burdett A. Loomis, "Pipe Dream or Possibility? Amending the U.S. Constitution to Achieve Electoral Reform," in Bugh, *Electoral College Reform*, 226. See Chapters 5–7.

28. 102 Cong. Rec. 5149 (Mar. 20, 1956). As indicated in Chapter 2, it was widely believed in the early nineteenth century that large states were advantaged by the Electoral College itself, while small states benefited from the contingent election process. The weight of expert opinion in the 1960s and 1970s, from scholars versed in quantitative methods, was that the Electoral College conferred greater "voting power" (the likelihood of influencing the outcome of an election) on residents of large states than on inhabitants of small ones. See, for a key example, John Banzhaf, "One Man, 3,312 Votes: A Mathematical Analysis of the Electoral College," *Villanova Law Review* 13 (1968): 304–332. A 2001 law review article concluded, after surveying the literature, that the "empirical biases of the institution in favor of small or

large states are inherently unpredictable." "Rethinking the Electoral College Debate," 2527, 2533–2537. See also Chapter 5.

29. The amendments referred to here are the Twelfth, Fourteenth, Fifteenth, Seventeenth, Nineteenth, Twentieth, Twenty-Second, Twenty-Third, Twenty-Fourth, and Twenty-Sixth Amendments. Compare McKenzie, "Systemic Biases," 96–97. Peirce and Longley have argued that the difficulty of amending the Constitution meant that reform could not be accomplished without at least tacit support from "all the major political forces in the country." Peirce and Longley, *The People's President*, 179.

30. *Washington Post* (hereafter cited as *WP*), Nov. 14, 1916. Not surprisingly, the *Post* was anticipating that the South, in particular, would resist "national control of elections." For recent expressions of federalism concerns, see Chapters 6 and 7, as well as Derek T. Muller, "Invisible Federalism and the Electoral College," *Arizona State Law Journal* 44 (2012): 1237–1292; Muller, "The Compact Clause and the National Popular Vote Interstate Compact," *Election Law Journal* 6, no. 4 (Nov. 2007): 372–393. See also Fuentes-Rohwer and Charles, "The Electoral College," 879–922.

31. Many different districting schemes were put forward, but most of them called for one elector to be chosen in each congressional district and two electors to be selected at large. Such plans had the advantage of not requiring states to draw new district boundaries for presidential electors.

32. Peirce and Longley, *The People's President*, 137–138. The three Supreme Court cases that transformed districting were *Baker v. Carr*, 369 U.S. 186 (1962); *Reynolds v. Sims*, 377 U.S. 533 (1964); and *Wesberry v. Sanders*, 376 U.S. 1 (1964). Regarding the late nineteenth century, see Peter H. Argersinger, *Representation and Inequality in Late Nineteenth-Century America: The Politics of Apportionment* (New York, 2012).

33. *WP*, June 30, 1944; *New York Times* (hereafter cited as *NYT*), Nov. 9, 1936; Gary Wills, *"Negro President": Jefferson and the Slave Power* (New York, 2005), 111; Lucius Wilmerding Jr., *The Electoral College* (New Brunswick, NJ, 1958), 105; Peirce and Longley, *The People's President*, 166–168. See Chapters 4 and 5. The links between slavery and the origins of the Electoral College have been explored in numerous writings by Akhil Reed Amar, including *The Constitution Today: Timeless Lessons for the Issues of Our Era* (New York, 2016).

34. 96 Cong. Rec. 10416 (July 17, 1950); Peirce and Longley, *The People's President*, 161–206. See Chapters 3 and 5.

35. Bugh, "Challenge," 89–91. Peirce and Longley attributed the failure of reform to "the politics of each era" (*The People's President*, 179–180)—which is surely true but not very illuminating. As discussed in Chapter 7, Republicans have generally opposed Electoral College reform since the late 1970s, but there have been exceptions. After the 2012 and 2016 elections, for example, Republicans in some states proposed eliminating winner-take-all in favor of district or proportional systems. See Chapter 7.

36. James Madison to Thomas Jefferson, Oct. 24, 1787, in *The Papers of Thomas Jefferson*, 44 vols. (Princeton, NJ, 1955), 12:270–286.

37. Dougherty, *Electoral System*, 402.

I. FROM THE CONSTITUTION TO THE TWELFTH AMENDMENT

1. Max Farrand, ed., *Records of the Federal Convention of 1787* (New Haven, CT, 1966), 2:501. Volumes 1–3 were originally published New Haven, 1911; revised edition 1937. Volume 4, edited by James H. Hutson, a supplement to Farrand's work, was published in 1987 also by Yale University Press.

2. In late July 1787, Mason lamented that that "in every Stage of the Question relative to the Executive, the difficulty of the subject and the diversity of the opinions concerning it have appeared." Farrand, *Records,* 2:118. After the Convention had ended, Madison observed that "the right mode of election ... was found difficult in the convention, and will be found so by any Gentleman who will take the liberty of delineating a mode of electing the president, that would exclude those inconveniences which they apprehend." Madison, speaking to the Virginia Convention, June 18, 1788, Farrand, *Records,* 3:329; see also Madison to Thomas Jefferson, Oct. 24, 1787, Farrand, *Records,* 3:131–133.

3. Farrand, *Records,* 2:171, 185.

4. For an excellent account of ideas about executive power and the deliberations of the Constitutional Convention, see Jack N. Rakove, *Original Meanings: Politics and Ideas in the Making of the Constitution* (New York, 1996), 244–287. See also William G. Mayer, "What the Founders Intended: Another Look at the Origins of the American Presidential Selection Process," in *The Making of the Presidential Candidates 2008,* ed. William G. Mayer (Lanham, MD, 2008), 205; Jack Rakove, "The E-College in the E-Age," in *The Unfinished Election of 2000,* ed. Jack Rakove (New York, 2001); Shlomo Slonim, "The Electoral College at Philadelphia: The Evolution of an Ad Hoc Congress for the Selection of a President," *Journal of American History* 73, no. 1 (June 1986): 37. According to Slonim (37n), New Hampshire also elected its governor, but, as in Massachusetts, the legislature made the decision if no candidate won a clear majority of the popular vote.

5. Farrand, *Records,* 1:65; Mayer ("Founders," 203–232) contains an excellent chronology and analysis of the debates at the Convention regarding presidential selection; valuable accounts are also presented in George C. Edwards III, *Why the Electoral College Is Bad for America,* 2nd ed. (New Haven, CT, 2011), 98–113; and Richard P. McCormick, *The Presidential Game: The Origins of American Presidential Politics* (New York, 1982), 16–26. A less detailed description can be found in Rakove, *Original Meanings,* 256–275.

6. Farrand, *Records,* 2:31, 109, 500–501; see also Mayer, "Founders," 214–218; and Slonim, "Electoral College," 38–40. As Slonim observes, opinions regarding the desirability of legislative selection may have shifted between early June and mid-July as a result of the Convention's decision to grant each state an equal voice in the Senate while basing representation in the House on population.

7. Farrand, *Records,* 2:56.

8. The issue of "re-eligibility" was much discussed at the Convention and was often linked to the length of the executive's term of office. Most delegates seemed to agree that it was desirable for the executive to be eligible for reelection (because he would

have experience and because it would give him an incentive to govern well) but that re-eligibility would be problematic if the executive were chosen by the legislature—because it would encourage manipulation and scheming. The most commonly discussed alternative to re-eligibility was a single lengthy term (six years or more). For discussions of this issue, see Farrand, *Records*, 1:68–69, 2:32–36, 40, 51–57, 101–103, 111–112, 499, 501, 511; Madison to Jefferson, Oct. 24, 1787, in Farrand, *Records*, 3:132–133; Mayer, "Founders," 208–209. For some delegates (at some moments), the hazards of re-eligibility loomed as reasons to oppose congressional selection. Compare Slonim, "Electoral College," 42.

9. Farrand, *Records*, 1:69, 2:29.

10. In a report written for Maryland's legislature, delegate Luther Martin maintained that "those who wished as far as possible to establish a national instead of a federal government, made repeated attempts to have the President chosen by the people at large." Farrand, *Records*, 3:217; compare Slonim, "Electoral College," 56.

11. Farrand, *Records*, 2:56, 57, 109–111.

12. Farrand, *Records*, 2:57, 111. As this chapter implicitly indicates, I am less persuaded than some writers, Akhil R. Amar prominently among them, that slavery was the primary reason the founders rejected a national popular vote and created the Electoral College. The Electoral College surely protected the interests of slaveholders, but its adoption was determined by various factors in addition to the presence of slavery. For Amar's views, see his *The Constitution Today: Timeless Lessons for the Issues of Our Era* (New York, 2016), 333; "The Real Reason We Have an Electoral College: To Protect Slave States," interview by Sean Illing with Akhil Reed Amar, Vox, Nov. 12, 2016, https://www.vox.com/policy-and-politics/2016/11/12/13598316/donald-trump -electoral-college-slavery-akhil-reed-amar. Paul Finkelman takes a similar view in "The Proslavery Origins of the Electoral College," *Cardozo Law Review* 23, no. 4 (2001–2002): 1145–1157. For a different interpretation, more similar to my own, see Sean Wilentz, *No Property in Man: Slavery and Antislavery at the Nation's Founding* (Cambridge, MA, 2018), 70–71. For a recent exchange, see Sean Wilentz, "The Electoral College Was Not a Pro-Slavery Ploy," *NYT*, Apr. 4, 2019; and Akhil Reed Amar, "Actually, the Electoral College Was a Pro-Slavery Ploy," *NYT*, Apr. 6, 2019.

13. Farrand, *Records*, 2:29–31, 114. Regarding the stated fear of demagogues and its link to suffrage requirements, see Alexander Keyssar, *The Right to Vote: The Contested History of Democracy in the United States*, rev. ed. (New York, 2009), 7–20.

14. Both Mayer ("Founders," 211–214) and Slonim ("Electoral College," 35–36) discuss the Progressive interpretation of the Electoral College as a purposefully anti-democratic institution, as well as the alternative interpretation of political scientist John Roche that it was simply a "jerry-rigged" last-minute contrivance.

15. Farrand, *Records*, 2:32, 111; Pauline Maier, *Ratification: The People Debate the Constitution, 1787–1788* (New York, 2010), 114, 286; Mayer, "Founders," 207–208, 221–222; Rakove, "E-College," 210; Rakove, *Original Meanings*, 259; Edwards, *Electoral College*, 101–102, 108; Slonim, "Electoral College," 56. A proposal for a national popular vote was defeated by a vote of nine to one (with each state delegation getting one

vote) on July 17. Joshua Hawley observes that the delegates did not directly consider the issue of providing the president with "democratic legitimacy." Joshua D. Hawley, "The Transformative Twelfth Amendment," *William and Mary Law Review* 55, no. 4 (2014): 1515–1517.

16. Farrand, *Records*, 2:57, 98, 99, 101, 103–106, 112–115, 119; compare Slonim, "Electoral College," 47.

17. Farrand, *Records*, 1:80, 2:56–58, 100, 111, 119; Mayer, "Founders," 208–210.

18. Farrand, *Records*, 2:119; Mayer, "Founders," 206–211; Slonim, "Electoral College," 38.

19. Madison to Thomas Jefferson, Oct. 24, 1787, in Farrand, *Records*, 3:132.

20. Farrand, *Records*, 2:500. Having the electors meet in their own state capitals also satisfied the objection that the most qualified men would not want to travel a long distance to a national capital just to cast one set of votes. See Slonim, "Electoral College," 44; Mayer, "Founders," 209, 214.

21. If two candidates had a majority of the electoral votes and were tied, the Senate would choose between the two. The person with the second largest number of votes would become vice president; if there were a tie, the Senate would decide.

22. Farrand, *Records*, 2:500–502, 511.

23. Farrand, *Records*, 2:510.

24. Farrand, *Records*, 2:512–513; Rakove, *Original Meanings*, 264–265.

25. The decision to shift that power from the Senate to the House came almost immediately after the Convention had first (and reluctantly) agreed to let it remain in the Senate. Rakove, *Original Meanings*, 265. The Senate did retain the power to choose the vice president if two candidates tied in having the largest number of electoral votes after the president was chosen.

26. For the deliberations on the issues discussed in this paragraph as well as the wording of the committee's proposal (which differed in some respects from the text of the Constitution), see Farrand, *Records*, 2:500–524, 535–543.

27. Rakove, "E-College," 210–212; Edwards, *Electoral College*, 111–112. Mayer makes the important point that the compromises embedded in the final proposal were designed to retain certain core principles and ideas; they were not, as some earlier scholars have claimed, simply pragmatic patchwork. Mayer, "Founders," 211–229.

28. Two examples of such compromises and gestures are illustrative: (1) Permitting state legislatures to choose the manner in which electors would be selected was a gesture both to those who wished to retain power for the states and to those who sought popular electoral participation in the process. (2) Requiring electors to cast two ballots, one of which had to be for a person not from the elector's state, was a gesture to those who feared excessive influence by the large states. The apportionment of electoral votes among the states, of course, embodied the compromises over representation in Congress that aimed to satisfy both small and slave-owning states. Pauline Maier (*Ratification*, 33) has described the provision for presidential selection as "the most complex in the entire [Constitution]."

29. Slonim, "Electoral College," 41, 43, 51–56. As McCormick emphasizes, the system protected the small states against domination by the large states both through the

allocation of electoral votes and through the contingent election mechanism, in which each state would carry equal weight in choosing the president. *Presidential Game,* 22–26. See also Lucius Wilmerding Jr., *The Electoral College* (New Brunswick, NJ, 1958), 15–19.

30. Gary Wills, *"Negro President": Jefferson and the Slave Power* (Boston, 2003), 1–6. Regarding the 2000 election, see Alex Keyssar, "It Pays to Win the Small States," *NYT,* Nov. 20, 2000.

31. *The Federalist,* Modern Library ed. (New York, 1941), 68, 443–444; Farrand, *Records,* 2:500, 513; Rakove (*Original Meanings,* 265–266) concludes that most of the framers believed that the electors would end up simply nominating candidates.

32. See Rakove, "E-College," 213–215; Richard Hofstadter, *The Idea of a Party System: The Rise of Legitimate Opposition in the United States, 1780–1840* (Berkeley, 1970), 40–73. In 1802 Gouverneur Morris wrote that the Convention did foresee the possibility of problematic outcomes such as those that arose in 1800 but decided not to try to prevent them. Farrand, *Records,* 3:394.

33. Thirteen delegates had left the Convention before its end, some because of displeasure with its decisions. Three of those still present at the Convention's conclusion refused to sign the document. Regarding the views of the framers after the draft Constitution was completed, see Maier, *Ratification,* 35–49, 114. Maier cites, among others, Washington, who wrote to Benjamin Harrison, "I wish the Constitution . . . had been made more perfect, but I sincerely believe it is the best that could be obtained at this time." He was reassured by the presence of a "constitutional door . . . for amendment hereafter" (*Ratification,* 38). Madison, at the Virginia Convention, offered a similar observation, suggesting that, in at least one instance, the "mode which was judged most expedient was adopted, till experience should point out one more eligible." Madison, June 20, 1788, in Farrand, *Records,* 3:331.

34. *The Federalist,* 68, 441.

35. Gordon S. Wood, *The Creation of the American Republic, 1776–178* (Chapel Hill, NC, 1969), 519–543; Michael T. Rogers, "A Mere Deception—A Mere *Ignus Fatus* on the People of America: Lifting the Veil on the Electoral College," in *Electoral College Reform: Challenges and Possibilities,* ed. Gary Bugh (Farnham, UK, 2010), 19–41. At the Virginia ratifying convention, George Mason (who had refused to sign the draft Constitution in Philadelphia) denounced the system as a "mere deception" that gave the people only the illusion of being able to choose the president. Edwards, *Electoral College,* 107–108, 110–111. During the heated public debates over ratification in Pennsylvania, one pamphleteer sharply attacked the "mode of electing the president" as "calculated to render him the obsequious machine of congress." "Aristocrotis" maintained that the process would inevitably end up being decided by Congress. "The Government of Nature Delineated or an Exact Picture of the New Federal Constitution by Aristocrotis," in *The Complete Anti-Federalist,* ed. Herbert J. Storing (Chicago, 1981), 3:208.

36. This account of the first presidential election is drawn largely from William G. Mayer, "Theory Meets Practice: The Presidential Selection Process in the First Federal

Election, 1788–89," in *The Making of the Presidential Candidates, 2012,* ed. William G. Mayer and Jonathan Bernstein (Lanham, MD, 2012), 159–202. The Constitution was ratified on June 21, 1788, but the Congress under the Articles of Confederation did not pass an election ordinance until Sept. 13. States were required to choose their electors by Jan. 7, 1789; the electors were to cast ballots in their states on Feb. 4; and the votes were to be counted on Mar. 4.

37. Mayer, "Theory Meets Practice," 166, 178, 186; Tadahisa Kuroda, *The Origins of the Twelfth Amendment: The Electoral College in the Early Republic, 1787–1804* (Westport, CT, 1994), 28–37. The variety of methods was greater than a tabular presentation can reveal: e.g., in Maryland, five of the eight electors had to be from the western shore and three from the state's eastern shore. In New York the two branches of the state legislature could not agree on a method for choosing electors, and consequently New York did not participate in the election. In addition to selecting methods of choosing electors, the legislatures were also deciding how to choose senators and elect members of the new House of Representatives.

38. Mayer, "Theory Meets Practice," 172, 177–185; Kuroda, *Origins,* 28–37. Kuroda suggests that Federalists tended to favor statewide elections whereas Anti-Federalists preferred elections by district for both presidential electors and members of Congress.

39. Mayer, "Theory Meets Practice," 189–191.

40. Mayer, "Theory Meets Practice," 170–186. Anti-Federalist strength was also diminished by New York's failure to participate in the election (see note 37 above).

41. Mayer, "Theory Meets Practice," 186–189; Kuroda, *Origins,* 33; Jeffrey L. Pasley, *The First Presidential Contest: 1796 and the Founding of American Democracy* (Lawrence, KS, 2013), 26; John Ferling, *Adams vs. Jefferson: The Tumultuous Election of 1800* (Oxford, 2004), 58.

42. Pasley, *First Presidential Contest,* 8–9, 82–83; Ferling, *Adams,* 60–61. Pasley maintains that members of these clubs commonly referred to themselves as "Democrats" or "Republicans" and rarely as "Democratic-Republicans." See also Sean Wilentz, *The Rise of American Democracy: Jefferson to Lincoln* (New York, 2005), 40–41.

43. Pasley, *First Presidential Contest,* esp. 82–87, 277–291, 330–331; Ferling, *Adams,* 14, 16, 29, 48, 58–61, 81, 110–111, 127–129, 148–155; Wilentz, *Rise of American Democracy,* 32–37; Hawley, "Transformative Twelfth Amendment," 1529–1530; McCormick, *Presidential Game,* 49–50; Hofstadter, *Party System,* x–xi, 87–95.

44. Regarding the press and public debates, see Pasley, *First Presidential Contest,* 52–57, 329–340; Ferling, *Adams,* 53–55, 57, 87, 144–147; Joanne Freeman, "The Presidential Election of 1796," in *John Adams and the Founding of the Republic,* ed. Richard A. Ryerson (Boston, 2001), 150; regarding parties and partisanship, see Ferling, *Adams,* 55, 66; Pasley, *First Presidential Contest,* 1–3, 7, 9; Wilentz, *Rise of American Democracy,* 49–53, 60–68; Edward B. Foley, "The Founders' *Bush v. Gore:* The 1792 Election Dispute and Its Continuing Relevance," *Indiana Law Review* 44, no. 1 (2010): 23–84; Freeman, "Presidential Election," 146, 151, 156; see also "Address to the Electors and the Electors of the Electors of President and Vice President of the United States,"

by "No Foreigner," *Portland Gazette*, reprinted in *South-Carolina State Gazette and Timothy's Daily Adviser* 58, no. 6311 (June 28, 1800), 2, online at *Readex: America's Historical Newspapers*. Madison was among the first of the founders to conclude that a political party was necessary (largely to counter the machinations of Hamilton and those around him), yet Madison did not envision an enduring party system. There has been debate among scholars about whether the political organizations of this era ("the first party system") truly deserve to be called "parties," but that debate need not be engaged here: these organizations were doing many of the things that "parties" do. See Mayer, "Theory Meets Practice," 172.

45. Regarding the views of the framers, see Freeman, "Presidential Election," 143; Pasley, *First Presidential Contest*, 2–3, 383–384; Rakove, *Original Meanings*, 268; Hawley, "Transformative Twelfth Amendment," 1521, 1528; James W. Ceaser, *Presidential Selection: Theory and Development* (Princeton, NJ, 1979), 77, 94–95.

46. Ferling, *Adams*, 90–91.

47. On the electoral calendar, see Pasley, *First Presidential Contest*, 346–348; Ferling, *Adams*, 2, notes that "in 1800 people spoke of December 3 as Election Day," because it was the day when presidential electors assembled to cast their ballots. Regarding the importance of legislative elections, see, for example, Ferling, *Adams*, 127; and Kuroda, *Origins*, 84. On the campaign in 1796 more generally, see Pasley, *First Presidential Contest*, 348–406.

48. Pasley, *First Presidential Contest*, 354–358. Even in states that did not utilize district elections, it was often politically desirable (and, in some instances, legally mandated) that lists of electors include men from different parts of the state. For examples of such legal requirements, see Kuroda, *Origins*, 33 (regarding Maryland); and "An Act Providing for the Election of Electors to Elect a President and Vice President of the United States," passed on Aug. 8, 1796, in *Acts Passed at the Second Session of the First General Assembly of the State of Tennessee* (Knoxville, TN, 1796), 9–11.

49. Ferling, *Adams*, 85, 87, 130–131.

50. Rakove ("E-College," 207) concluded that "the original conception of 1787 was verging on obsolescence as early as 1796, and had certainly become an anachronism by 1800." Pasley, *First Presidential Contest*, 308, suggests that the election of 1796 ought to be seen as "marking a transition from one national political culture to another." See also McCormick, *Presidential Game*, 27–75.

51. Kuroda, *Origins*, 59. On the role of notables, see Pasley, *First Presidential Contest*, 307–348.

52. Andrew Busch, "The Development and Democratization of the Electoral College," in *Securing Democracy: Why We Have the Electoral College*, ed. Gary L. Gregg II (Wilmington, DE, 2001), 30.

53. Pasley, *First Presidential Contest*, 322–345. For examples of electors publicly pledging themselves to presidential candidates in 1796 and 1800, see Pasley, *Presidential*, 318–321; Kuroda, *Origins*, 89.

54. Freeman, "Presidential Election," 151.

55. "Franklin," *A Vindication of the General Ticket Law, Passed by the Legislature of Virginia, on the 18th day of January, 1800* (Richmond, VA, 1800), 17, online at *Readex: Early American Imprints, Series 1;* Freeman, "Presidential Election," 152; Kuroda, *Origins,* 59; Ferling, *Adams,* 166; Lucius Wilmerding Jr., *The Electoral College* (New Brunswick, NJ, 1958), 176–177; Busch, "Democratization of the Electoral College," 30. The concept of a "faithless" elector, of course, could arise only when electors were no longer expected to exercise their own judgment.

56. See Kuroda, *Origins,* 55–74, 66–69, 73–79, as well as Pasley, *First Presidential Contest,* 315–317, for the narrative details. In some states, in some years (e.g., New York in 1792), legislators were required to choose electors who came from different parts of the state.

57. For the complicated Pennsylvania narrative, see Pasley, *First Presidential Contest,* 351–363; Kuroda, *Origins,* 89–91; and Wilmerding, *The Electoral College,* 176–177. The Federalists got their comeuppance in 1796 when Republican political fortunes improved dramatically in the months just before the election, leading to a Republican electoral vote victory of thirteen to two. Although Pennsylvania was using the general ticket, the vote could be split because each voter had to list the names of fifteen individual electors. For an example of similar dynamics in New Jersey, see "Legislature of New-Jersey Debate," *Centinel of Freedom* 4, no. 8 (Nov. 19, 1799), 2, online at *Readex: America's Historical Newspapers.*

58. Ferling, *Adams,* 128–131, 157, 166–167; Jabez D. Hammond with General Erastus Root, *The History of Political Parties in the State of New York, from the Ratification of the Federal Constitution to December 1840,* 4th ed. (Buffalo, NY, 1850), 1:122–134, 144–145; Kuroda, *Origins,* 83–87, 199n11; Rakove, "E-College," 215–220. Edward Foley suggests that Jay may have been the last governor who would have made such a decision. Foley, "The Founders' *Bush v. Gore,*" 77–78. In Pennsylvania in 1800 when the house had a Republican majority and the state senate was controlled by Federalists, a prolonged battle over how to choose electors ended with a legislative compromise that gave the Republicans eight out of fifteen votes (Kuroda, *Origins,* 89–96). For a revealing set of developments in Maryland, in which a Federalist proposal to have the legislature select electors became a key issue in the legislative elections of 1800, see Edward J. Larsen, *A Magnificent Catastrophe: The Tumultuous Election of 1800, America's First Presidential Campaign* (New York, 2007), 201–203.

59. Kuroda, *Origins,* 74; Rakove, "E-College," 216–219; Ferling, *Adams,* 156–157; Neal R. Peirce and Lawrence D. Longley, *The People's President: The Electoral College in American History and the Direct Vote Alternative,* rev. ed. (New Haven, CT, 1981), 37–39; "Acts Passed at a General Assembly of the Commonwealth of Virginia" (Virginia, 1800), online at *Readex: Early American Imprints, Series 1.* For a detailed narrative of the changes made (and debated) in the methods of choosing electors in 1800, see Kuroda, *Origins,* 83–98.

60. "Legislature of New-Jersey Debate," 2. This interpretation of the Constitution was never accepted by federal courts; and it was implicitly rejected, two centuries later, in the majority decision in *Bush v. Gore,* 531 U.S. 98 (2000), 104. See also the discussion of Michigan's Miner Law in Chapter 3.

61. Kuroda, *Origins,* 54–59, 75–76, 82–84; Larsen, *Magnificent Catastrophe,* 203–204; Hammond and Root, *Political Parties in New York,* 1:133–134; Robert Goodloe Harper, *Bystander: A Series of Letters on the Subject of the "Legislative Choice" of Electors in Maryland* (Baltimore, 1800), 6, 17–20, online at *Readex: Early American Imprints, Series 1;* "Legislature of New-Jersey Debate," 2. Some states did consider choosing electors in congressional districts and then selecting the two additional electors by a different method.

62. Kuroda, *Origins,* 29–30, 36–37. For examples, see Pennsylvania laws 1792 and 1796 in *The Statutes at Large of Pennsylvania from 1682 to 1801,* ed. James T. Mitchell and Henry Flanders (Harrisburg, PA, 1909), 14:272–273, 15:428–429; as well as Tennessee law 1796, in *Acts Passed, State of Tennessee,* 9–11.

63. Jefferson to James Monroe, Jan. 12, 1800, in *The Papers of Thomas Jefferson,* 44 vols. (Princeton, NJ, 1950–2019), 31:300–301; James Madison to George Hay, Aug. 23, 1823, in James Madison, *The Writings of James Madison* (New York, 1900–1910), 9:168–175; Harper, *Bystander,* 2; "No Foreigner," "Address to the Electors"; Kuroda, *Origins,* 74, 113; "Franklin," *Vindication,* 10–11, 12.

64. "Franklin," *Vindication,* entire, esp. 6–8, 13, 18–19; Crito, *Considerations on the Propriety of Adopting a General Ticket in South Carolina* (Charleston, SC, 1801), 9:3–6, 11–12, 29, online at *Readex: Early American Imprints, Series 2;* "To the Honourable the Senate and House of Representatives of the Commonwealth of Pennsylvania," *The Constitutional Diary and Philadelphia Evening Advertiser* 1, no. 24 (Dec. 30, 1799), 3, online at *Readex: America's Historical Newspapers;* Kuroda, *Origins,* 90.

65. *Washington Federalist* 1, no. 28 (Oct. 1800), 14, online at *Readex: America's Historical Newspapers;* Kuroda, *Origins,* 90.

66. "Extract from a Letter to the Virginia Argus," *Constitutional Telegraph* 1, no. 43 (Feb. 26, 1800), 1, online at *Readex: America's Historical Newspapers;* Kuroda, *Origins,* 74, 110; Wilmerding, *Electoral College,* 61.

67. Jefferson to Monroe, Jan. 12, 1800, *Papers of Thomas Jefferson,* 31:300–301.

68. "To the Honourable Senate," 3; Harper, *Bystander,* 2, 8, 14, 22; "Franklin," *Vindication,* 7, 9.

69. Ferling, *Adams,* 83–112, 135–156; Wilentz, *Rise of American Democracy,* 79–83, 90. Hamilton, in a private letter, referred to Jefferson as an "atheist in religion, and a fanatic in politics." Peirce and Longley, *The People's President,* 38.

70. Ferling, *Adams,* 87–94; Kuroda, *Origins,* 66–67.

71. Ferling, *Adams,* 9–14, 140–143, 162–167, 199–200; Kuroda, *Origins,* 89–90; Larsen, *Magnificent Catastrophe,* 220–240, recounts a particularly complex chain of events in Maryland, Pennsylvania, and South Carolina.

72. Ferling, *Adams,* 174–176; Kuroda, *Origins,* 100–102. Kuroda, *Origins,* 99–105, surveys Federalist views regarding the choice between Burr or Jefferson. In contrast to the lame-duck House, the incoming House of Representatives, elected in 1800, had a solid Republican majority.

73. Ferling, *Adams,* 175–196; Kuroda, *Origins,* 99–108; Peirce and Longley, *The People's President,* 39–40; Wills, "*Negro President,*" 78–80; Wilentz, *Rise of American Democracy,*

93–94. Perhaps the strongest, and most detailed, characterization of the 1800 election as a severe crisis—one with potentially disastrous consequences—is put forward by Bruce Ackerman in *The Failure of the Founding Fathers: Jefferson, Marshall, and the Rise of Presidential Democracy* (Cambridge, MA, 2005), 3–4, 27–141. As the title of Ackerman's book suggests, he regards the original design of the electoral system as a significant "failure" on the part of the framers.

74. Ferling, *Adams*, 174, 185–195. Ferling concludes that Jefferson (and the people around him) may have given the Federalists assurances that he would not attack the Bank of the United States or remove Federalist officeholders. See also Wills, *"Negro President,"* 86–88.

75. Ackerman, *Failure*, 30–32. For evidence that Jefferson was widely viewed as the people's choice for president, see Kuroda, *Origins*, 100–102, and Ferling, *Adams*, 174.

76. For a detailed examination of the rationales for "designation" and the meaning of "majority" rule, see Edward B. Foley, *Presidential Elections and Majority Rule: The Rise, Demise, and Potential Restoration of the Jeffersonian Electoral College* (New York, 2019), 19–37.

77. 13 Annals of Cong. 422–423, 735 (1803–1804); Kuroda, *Origins*, 114, 118. See Jefferson to Albert Gallatin, Sept. 18, 1801, in *Papers of Thomas Jefferson*, 35:314–315.

78. Kuroda, *Origins*, 89, 113–114, 117–120; 11 Annals of Cong. 189–190 (1801–1802); Harper, *Bystander*, 2, 8, 14, 22; "Franklin," *Vindication*, 7; "Memorial to the Honorable the Senate and the House of Representatives," *Philadelphia Evening Advertiser*, Dec. 30, 1799. Harper relocated from South Carolina (where he had held a congressional seat) to Maryland in 1800. In Maryland in 1800 Republicans favored district elections while Federalists preferred selection by the legislature. Other Federalist supporters of district elections included Congressmen Benjamin Huger of South Carolina, Lewis Richard Morris of Vermont, and Benjamin Walker of New York. According to McCormick (*Presidential Game*, 82), Federalists in South Carolina and several New England states put forward amendments for district elections between 1796 and 1800.

79. 10 Annals of Cong. 617–618, 785 (1799–1801). The Federalists had a majority in the House until the new Congress was seated in March 1801. The three Federalists on the committee were Harper of South Carolina, Thomas Evans of Virginia, and the crusty conservative Roger Griswold of Connecticut. The other Republican, in addition to Nicholas, was Nathaniel Macon of North Carolina, who spent a long career opposing any growth in the power of the national government. Nicholas's proposed amendment would also have required members of the House of Representatives to be elected in districts—which was not required by the Constitution and was not always the practice in this period. Kuroda, *Origins*, 73–4, 110–112.

80. 10 Annals of Cong. 941–942 (1799–1801); Kuroda, *Origins*, 110–112.

81. 10 Annals of Cong. 941–942 (1799–1801); Kuroda, *Origins*, 110–112. The committee also rejected the second prong of the proposed amendment (requiring district elections for the House of Representatives) because it interfered with a power that Congress already possessed and was thus "superfluous." The tone of the report likely

reflected the views of the Federalist majority on the committee and in the House. Kuroda, *Origins,* 110–112, offers a different interpretation of this report.

82. Kuroda, *Origins,* 110, 117–120; *Newburyport Herald* 4, no. 36 (Feb. 20, 1801), 2; *Alexandria Advertiser and Commercial Intelligencer* 1, no. 158 (June 12, 1801), 3; 11 Annals of Cong. 189–190 (1801–1802). Maryland already held district elections and would continue to do so into the 1830s, longer than any other state. See the text of the Maryland resolution of Dec. 19, 1800 (Annapolis, MD, 1800), online at *Readex: Early American Imprints, Series 1.*

83. 11 Annals of Cong. 472 (1801–1802); see also 190–192, 263–264, 509–510, 602–603. See also Kuroda, *Origins,* 118–119; Jeremy D. Bailey, *Thomas Jefferson and Executive Power* (New York, 2007), 200–201; Albert Gallatin to Jefferson, Sept. 14, 1801, and Gallatin to Jefferson, Sept. 18, 1801, in *Papers of Thomas Jefferson,* 35:284–289, 314–315. Gallatin worried that, without reform, Republicans in 1804 would face a choice between fully supporting Burr for vice president (in which case the Federalists might try to vote him into the presidency) or scattering their second votes, in which case a Federalist could end up as vice president. Jefferson replied to Gallatin that their goal could also be achieved if elections were "by the people directly" and the general ticket were in use. Bailey characterizes the disagreements among Republicans on this issue as more about "Electoral College arithmetic" than principle. See also McCormick, *Presidential Game,* 82–83.

84. 6 Annals of Cong. 1823–1824 (1796–1797). Smith stated that he thought this the "proper time" for such an amendment because the issue was "fresh in people's minds" and the "period the most remote from an election." Regarding early interest in designation, by members of both parties, see Kuroda, *Origins,* 109, and Peirce and Longley, *The People's President,* 42.

85. Kuroda, *Origins,* 111–112, 118, 122–130, 159–160, 171. As McCormick (*Presidential Game,* 82) explains, Republicans also feared that they would have to allow a Federalist to win the vice presidency in order to guarantee the election of a Republican president.

86. U.S. House Journal, 7th Cong. 1st Sess. 104, 234–235 (1802); 11 Annals of Cong. 1285–1294 (1801–1802); Kuroda, *Origins,* 119–123. In the House, forty-five members (twenty-four Federalists and twenty-one Republicans) did not vote, presumably because they were absent, prompting a debate about whether an amendment needed a two-thirds vote of all members or just of those present.

87. 11 Annals of Cong. 259, 263–264, 303–304 (1801–1802); Kuroda, *Origins,* 119–123.

88. For a detailed account of the passage of the amendment through Congress and its subsequent ratification, see Kuroda, *Origins,* 127–161. Notably, much of the congressional debate focused on the number of candidates that would be considered by the House in the event of a contingent election. See, e.g., 13 Annals of Cong. 420–431 (1803–1804). Regarding the ongoing calls for district elections, see 11 Annals of Cong. 264 (1801–1802); 12 Annals of Cong. 449, 602–603 (1802–1803); 13 Annals of Cong. 380–381 (1803–1804); and Kuroda, *Origins,* 105, 120, 123, 128, 146, 159–160. One of the most insistent advocates of district elections was Benjamin Huger of South Carolina, a Federalist who had supported Jefferson in 1800. See also David P. Currie,

The Constitution in Congress: The Jeffersonians, 1801–1829 (Chicago, 2001), 40–41, 53–54. At the insistence of the Senate, the amendment also included a provision specifying that the vice president had to be constitutionally eligible to become president.

89. For an analysis of the debates in Congress regarding designation, see Hawley, "Transformative Twelfth Amendment," 1542–1555; see also Bailey's account (*Thomas Jefferson,* 25, 195–196, 201–211), which emphasizes the ways in which the debates were influenced by simultaneous congressional consideration of the Louisiana Purchase.

90. Currie, *Constitution in Congress,* 41; Kuroda, *Origins,* 124–126; 131; *Defense of the Legislature of Massachusetts, or The Right of New-England Vindicated* (Boston, 1804), 22–23; Wills, *"Negro President,"* 2, 110–112. John Quincy Adams claimed that the intention of the Twelfth Amendment was to prevent the election of a Federalist vice president in 1804. Wilmerding, *Electoral College,* 38.

91. 11 Annals of Cong. 1286 (1801–1802); 13 Annals of Cong. 380 (1803–1804); Kuroda, *Origins,* 158. Huger's trepidations did not, however, prevent him from supporting a district elections amendment.

92. One reason elections would be less likely to end up in the House was that it would no longer be arithmetically possible for more than one candidate to win a majority of electoral votes, as had happened in 1800. Designation was also expected to reduce the number of presidential candidates (heightening the chances of someone winning a majority), and it would diminish the use of strategic voting to block a candidate.

93. Currie, *Constitution in Congress,* 46–49; Peirce and Longley, *The People's President,* 43; Henry Adams, *History of the United States of America, during the First Administration of Thomas Jefferson* (New York, 1909), 2:132–134. Some members of Congress also argued that small states would be harmed by the reduction in the number of candidates in a contingent election from five to three. 13 Annals of Cong. 420–430 (1803–1804); Kuroda, *Origins,* 129–131, 136–138, 140–141, 157.

94. Currie, *Constitution in Congress,* 41–45, 51–52; Kuroda, *Origins,* 134, 172; 11 Annals of Cong. 1290 (1801–1802); Adams, *History,* 133; Mayer, "Theory Meets Practice," 163; Charles A. O'Neil, *The American Electoral System* (New York, 1889), 94; *Defense of the Legislature of Massachusetts,* 15; Hawley, "Transformative Twelfth Amendment," 1501, 1507; According to the 1829 edition of Noah Webster's dictionary, a gudgeon was a small fish, "easily caught, and hence: 1. A person easily cheated or ensnared; 2) a bait; allurement; something to be caught to a man's disadvantage." Noah Webster, *An American Dictionary of the English Language* (New York, 1828), 858.

95. Harper, *Bystander,* 8.

96. 11 Annals of Cong. 190 (1801–1802); 10 Annals of Cong. 943–944 (1799–1801); Kuroda, *Origins,* 110.

97. Kuroda, *Origins,* 118–120, 123, 159–160. In the congressional debates in 1802–1804, there were more Federalist expressions of support for district elections than for designation. Another option, of course, would have been to pass two amendments, one dealing with designation and the other with district elections. There is evidence that

even supporters of the two ideas preferred to keep them separate. 13 Annals of Cong. 1087–1088 (1803–1804).

98. Kuroda, *Origins*, 159–160, 163–169, 171–173. Jefferson's backing appears to have been tacit rather than explicit. Massachusetts, where Federalists retained a majority, also switched from legislative selection to a hybrid of the general ticket and district elections in 1804. Massachusetts Republicans favored district elections. For a sampling of public opinion in Massachusetts in 1804, see *National Aegis* 3, no. 133 (June 13, 1804), 3; *The Repertory* 1, no. 99 (June 26, 1804), 2; and *Republican Spy* 2, no. 69 (Oct. 16, 1804), 3: all online at *Readex: America's Historical Newspapers*.

99. 13 Annals of Congress 1087–1088 (1803–1804).

100. Kuroda, *Origins*, 172; Donald Lutz et al., "The Electoral College in Historical and Philosophical Perspective," in *Choosing a President*, ed. Paul D. Schumaker and Burdett A. Loomis (New York, 2002), 36–38; Ceaser, *Presidential Selection*, 105–106; Hawley, "Transformative Twelfth Amendment," 1501, 1507.

101. Two other alternatives to winner-take-all became prominent in the late nineteenth century and in the twentieth: a national popular vote and the awarding of a state's electoral votes in proportion to the percentage of the popular vote a candidate received. See Chapters 3–7.

102. Kuroda, *Origins*, 173; 15 Annals of Cong. 894–895 (1805–1806).

103. Wills, *"Negro President,"* 2; Kuroda, *Origins*, 125, 143; Wilentz, *Rise of American Democracy*, 78–83; Richard Hofstadter, *The Idea of a Party System: The Rise of Legitimate Opposition in the United States, 1780–1840* (Berkeley, 1970), 102–130; Ackerman, *Failure*, 155–156.

104. See Kuroda, *Origins*, 124–126; Wilentz, *Rise of American Democracy*, 90, 104–105. By 1804 the Federalists had their own litany of complaints about partisan conduct by the Republicans, including Jefferson's "war" on the judiciary, the removal of Federalists from federal offices, and the Louisiana Purchase—which was made with disputed constitutional authority and threatened to greatly enlarge the territory in which slavery was permitted. Issues related to slavery and sectional conflict were always lurking, often raising the political temperature. See Kuroda, *Origins*, 131; *Defense of the Legislature of Massachusetts*, 3, 8, 26–27; Wilentz, *Rise of American Democracy*, 104, 109, 114; Wills, *"Negro President,"* 90–101, 114–126; Hofstadter, *Party System*, 165–167.

PART II. THE LONG STRUGGLE TO ABOLISH WINNER-TAKE-ALL

Epigraph: 41 Annals of Cong. 1073 (1823–1824).

1. In Maine, legislation switching to the district system was approved in 1969 and first implemented in 1972; in Nebraska, the legislation was passed in 1991. In both Maine and Nebraska, one elector is chosen in each congressional district, while the statewide popular vote elects two at-large electors. See Chapter 7 regarding developments from the 1990s to the present.

2. Regarding the intentions of the framers, see Chapter 1; regarding Madison's later recollections of those intentions, see Chapter 2.

3. On the impact of the Electoral College on party strategies and policies, see Scott C. James and Brian L. Lawson, "The Political Economy of Voting Rights Enforcement in America's Gilded Age: Electoral College Competition, Partisan Commitment, and the Federal Election Law," *American Political Science Review* 93, no. 1 (Mar. 1999): 115–131; Scott C. James, *Presidents, Parties, and the State: A Party System Perspective on Democratic Regulatory Choice* (Cambridge, 2000), 6–7, 13–17, 44–51. Regarding the Electoral College and the formation of national parties, see Richard P. McCormick, *The Second American Party System: Party Formation in the Jacksonian Era* (New York, 1973), 13, 14, 20–21, 26, 169–171, 254, 329; Lisa Thomason, "Jacksonian Democracy and the Electoral College: Politics and Reform in the Method of Selecting Presidential Electors, 1824–1833" (PhD diss., University of North Texas, 2001), 18–19.

2. ELECTORAL REFORM IN THE ERA OF GOOD FEELINGS

Epigraph: James Madison to Thomas Jefferson, Jan. 14, 1824, in *The Papers of James Madison,* Retirement Series, vol. 3, Mar. 1, 1823–Feb. 24, 1826, ed. David B. Mattern, J. C. A. Stagg, Mary Parke Johnson, and Katherine E. Harbury (Charlottesville, 2016), 201–202 (hereafter cited as *Papers of James Madison*).

Epigraph: 2 Part 2 Reg. Deb. 1653–1654 (1826).

1. Jackson won a plurality of votes in the Electoral College and led in the popular vote as well. See the discussion of the 1824 election below.
2. For reasons similar to those that prompted the drive for presidential election reform, Congress was recurrently debating whether members of the House of Representatives should be elected by district or at large (by a "general ticket") within each state. Some states used each method, and it was not uncommon for methods to be changed for partisan reasons. Three amendments mandating district elections for both presidential electors and members of the House were approved by the Senate, in 1819, 1820, and 1822. In 1842 Congress passed legislation requiring district elections for the House. See Rosemarie Zagarri, *The Politics of Size: Representation in the United States, 1776–1850* (Ithaca, NY, 1987), 105–131, 154–157; Herman V. Ames, "The Proposed Amendments to the Constitution of the United States during the First Century of Its History," *Annual Report of the American Historical Association* 2 (1896): 90, 56–58. For an editorial explicitly linking the two issues, see "The Right and Power of Suffrage," *Niles' Weekly Register* (hereafter cited as *NWR*), Nov. 16, 1816, 178–179.
3. Ames, "Proposed Amendments," 80. There were two variants of the district elections resolutions. One called for all electors to be chosen in districts; the other permitted two electors in each state to be chosen by in a manner to be determined by the legislature. The latter approach would have permitted states to utilize congressional districts for presidential electors.
4. For a brief and witty account of these events, see David P. Currie, *The Constitution in Congress: The Jeffersonians, 1801–1829* (Chicago, 2001), 336–343.
5. After 1804 the Federalists never held more than 30 percent of the seats in the Senate or 37 percent in the House; in most years their totals were lower. Regarding their

enduring state and local strength, see Donald Ratcliffe, "Popular Preferences in the Presidential Election of 1824," *Journal of the Early Republic* 34 (Spring 2014), 48–51.

6. Richard Hofstadter, *The Idea of a Party System: The Rise of Legitimate Opposition in the United States, 1780–1840* (Berkeley, 1970), x, 188–208. The phrase "Era of Good Feelings" first appeared in the *Columbian Centinel,* July 12, 1817. By the early 1820s some Democratic-Republicans had begun calling themselves "Democratic" rather than "Republican." Donald Ratcliffe, *The One-Party Presidential Contest: Adams, Jackson, and 1824's Five Horse Race* (Lawrence, KS, 2015), 12. For a broader portrait of the politics of the era, see Sean Wilentz, *The Rise of American Democracy: Jefferson to Lincoln* (New York, 2005), 116–178.

7. Washington had warned "against the baneful effects of the spirit of party." Partisan conflict, he cautioned, "agitates the community with ill-founded jealousies and false alarms, kindles the animosity of one part against another," and "opens the door to foreign influence and corruption." George Washington, "Farewell Address," in *A Compilation of the Messages and Papers of the Presidents, 1789–1907,* ed. James D. Richardson (New York, 1908), 1:213–224.

8. Hofstadter, *The Idea,* x, 86, 123–124, 165, 173, 182–208; Michael Wallace, "Changing Concepts of Party in the United States: New York, 1815–1828," *American Historical Review* 74, no. 2 (Dec. 1968): 473–476; and Jeffrey S. Selinger, "Rethinking the Development of Legitimate Party Opposition in the United States, 1793–1828," *Political Science Quarterly* 127, no. 2 (Summer 2012): 263–288. On anti-partyism, see Nancy L. Rosenblum, *On the Side of the Angels: An Appreciation of Parties and Partisanship* (Princeton, NJ, 2008), 60–107.

9. Hofstadter, *The Idea,* 212–225, 237–238, 242–246, 249–252; Wallace, "Changing Concepts," 454, 456–460, 466–467; Selinger, "Rethinking," 283–286; Richard P. McCormick, *The Second American Party System: Party Formation in the Jacksonian Era* (New York, 1973), 333–348; Wallace, "Changing Concepts," 461–463; Selinger, "Rethinking," 286; Wilentz, *Rise of American Democracy,* 507, 516–517; Paul Frymer, *Uneasy Alliances: Race and Party Competition in America* (Princeton, NJ, 1999), 36–40. That a two-party system was functioning by the mid-1830s did not mean that anti-partyism had disappeared; the type of disciplined organization that Van Buren and others built had many detractors. Ronald P. Formisano, "Political Character, Antipartyism and the Second Party System," *American Quarterly* 21, no. 4 (Winter 1969): 686–700.

10. 30 Annals of Cong. 340 (1816–1817).

11. Charles A. O'Neil, *The American Electoral System* (New York, 1889), 104–106; Ames, "Proposed Amendments," 81–82; J. Hampden Dougherty, *The Electoral System of the United States* (New York, 1906), 39–40, 282, 289; 19 Annals of Cong. 1376 (1809). Notably the 1812 conflict over congressional districting in Massachusetts stemmed from the famous partisan map drawn by Republican governor Elbridge Gerry in 1811 that gave birth to the term "gerrymander." See also John B. McMaster, *A History of the People of the United States from the Revolution to the Civil War* (New York, 1895), 4:192–196 as well as the speech by Mahlon Dickerson of New Jersey, 31 Annals of Cong. 181–183 (1818).

12. "Constitution of the United States: Amendments Proposed," *Weekly Register,* Nov. 14, 1812, 174–175. Niles supported district elections both for electors and for members of the House.

13. Clark's "vindication of his vote" emphasized that it was not unconstitutional to permit the legislature to choose electors and that North Carolina had done so before. James W. Clark, "An Address to the Citizens of Edgcombe County" (Raleigh, NC, 1812). A similar justification, signed only by a "North Carolinian" but reportedly also authored by Clark, appeared a month later in "An Address to the Freemen of North Carolina, by a Member of Their Late General Assembly" (Raleigh, NC, 1812). Both documents were detailed, defensive in tone, and denied any partisan intent.

14. 25 Annals of Cong. 1848 (1812–1813); 26 Annals of Cong. 831, 836 (1813–1814); "Uniform Mode of Election," *NWR,* Jan. 20, 1816, 349. See also State of North Carolina, *Journal of the Senate,* Nov. 16–23, 1812, n.p. (labeled Nc U Copy). The district elections resolution specified that all persons who were qualified to vote for members of the House of Representatives could cast ballots for electors. According to the Constitution, all inhabitants who met the qualifications to vote for "the most numerous branch of the state legislature" could vote for members of the House.

15. 25 Annals of Cong. 57–58, 77, 85, 88–89, 90–91 (1812–1813). The records do not reveal why the provision regarding congressional elections was deleted, but many legislators believed that Congress already possessed the power to set the rules for elections to the House and thus that an amendment was unnecessary. Regarding efforts to mandate district elections for House members, see Zagarri, *The Politics of Size,* 106–144.

16. 25 Annals of Cong. 848, 1080, 1082 (1812–1813); 26 Annals of Cong. 790, 797–798 (1813–1814); 25 Annals of Cong. 828 (1812–1813). There is no comprehensive record of congressional debates during this period. The 42 volumes of the "History of Congress" (or Annals of the Congress of the United States) for the years 1789–1824 were assembled retrospectively (by two experienced congressional reporters) from newspapers, journals, and stenographic reports.

17. 25 Annals of Cong. 848–849 (1812–1813); J. Mills Thornton, "Pickens, Israel," *American National Biography Online,* http://anb.org/articles/03/03-00379.html.

18. 26 Annals of Cong. 828–835 (1814). It was common in many states for caucuses of the legislature to choose candidates for state offices as well as slates of electors. Regarding caucuses (and the antagonism to them) in one state, see Philip S. Klein, *Pennsylvania Politics, 1817–1832: A Game without Rules* (Philadelphia, 1940), 52–58, 77–84.

19. 26 Annals of Cong. 835–844 (1813–1814). William S. Powell, ed., *Dictionary of North Carolina Biography* (Chapel Hill, NC, 1979–1996). Gaston's speeches were widely reprinted and circulated. Regarding the "sanctity" of the Constitution, see also the speeches by Dickerson and Smith (of North Carolina), 33 Annals of Cong. 138 (1818–1819); 36 Annals of Cong. 1903–1904 (1820).

20. 26 Annals of Cong. 835–844 (1813–1814).

21. 26 Annals of Cong. 828–829, 835–844, 851 (1814); North Carolina, *Senate Journal,* Nov. 18–23, 1812.

22. 26 Annals of Cong. 835, 851, 852, 856 (1813–1814). The existing (incomplete) records do not provide the texts of the speeches by the handful of representatives who spoke against the resolution. Gaston's comment suggests that some representatives wished to retain the status quo but did not want to openly defend it.

23. 26 Annals of Cong. 1198–1199 (1813–1814). The House vote was technically a concurrence with the decision of the Committee of the Whole disapproving of the amendment by a vote of seventy to fifty-seven. 26 Annals of Cong. 848–849 (1813–1814).

24. The reasons that opposition to district elections was more common in large states than in small ones are discussed later in this chapter. Notably, this was not the case in the 1813 Senate vote, a fact not easily explained. In the House vote in 1814, but not in the Senate in 1813, northerners were less supportive of reform than were southerners; this was likely due to the stronger Federalist presence in the North.

25. 29 Annals of Cong. 158, 336, 1404 (1815–1816); 30 Annals of Cong. 74, 335, 340, 694 (1816–1817); 31 Annals of Cong. 65 (1817–1818); 32 Annals of Cong. 114 (1818); 33 Annals of Cong. 23–24, 42 (1818); 38 Annals of Cong. 35 (1821–1822).

26. 30 Annals of Cong. 256–257 (1816); William Plumer, "Legislature of New Hampshire, Governor's Speech," *NWR,* June 22, 1816, 380.

27. 29 Annals of Cong. 216 (1816).

28. 33 Annals of Cong. 147 (1819); 31 Annals of Cong. 179 (1818); 30 Annals of Cong. 302, 310, 340 (1816).

29. 30 Annals of Cong. 334, 340 (1816); 37 Annals of Cong. 962 (1821); 31 Annals of Cong. 183 (1818); 30 Annals of Cong. 138 (1816). Changes in the mode of choosing electors were less common between 1812 and 1820 than they had been between 1796 and 1804 or would be between 1820 and 1828. (See Table 1.1.)

30. 36 Annals of Cong. 1905 (1820).

31. 30 Annals of Cong. 308 (1816); 31 Annals of Cong. 183–184 (1818); 36 Annals of Cong. 1906 (1820).

32. 30 Annals of Cong. 329, 346 (1816).

33. 33 Annals of Cong. 145 (1819); 30 Annals of Cong. 340 (1816), see also 302–303, 335.

34. 31 Annals of Cong. 180 (1818); 33 Annals of Cong. 143 (1819); 37 Annals of Cong. 507 (1820).

35. 33 Annals of Cong. 143 (1819); 29 Annals of Cong. 219–220 (1816); 31 Annals of Cong. 180 (1818); 30 Annals of Cong. 311 (1816).

36. "Uniform Mode of Election," *NWR,* Jan. 20, 1816, 349; "Right and Power of Suffrage," *NWR,* Nov. 16, 1816, 178.

37. Jean E. Smith, *John Marshall: Definer of a Nation* (New York, 1996), 501. Marshall reportedly considered participating in the 1828 election in order to cast a ballot against Andrew Jackson; whether he did so is unclear.

38. 33 Annals of Cong. 139 (1819).

39. 29 Annals of Cong. 216 (1816). See 30 Annals of Cong. 327 (1816); 30 Annals of Cong. 333–335, 339–342 (1816).

40. 30 Annals of Cong. 340 (1816).

41. 36 Annals of Cong. 1909 (1819–1820). See also 30 Annals of Cong. 310–311, 328, 339–340, 352–356 (1816–1817); 29 Annals of Cong. 224 (1815–1816). Regarding the caucus system, see Wilentz, *Rise of American Democracy*, 246–247.

42. 29 Annals of Cong. 215 (1816); 30 Annals of Cong. 309, 351–352 (1816). Several speakers, in not-so-veiled reference to the "Virginia dynasty" and the 1816 election of James Monroe, maintained that the system had become so top-down that "the Executive finds no difficulty in designating his successor." Dickerson suggested that the system was so corrupt that a president could stay in office beyond two terms or secure the appointment of his son. 33 Annals of Cong. 147–148 (1819).

43. 33 Annals of Cong. 150 (1819).

44. 37 Annals of Cong. 508 (1820); 36 Annals of Cong. 1911 (1820); 30 Annals of Cong. 304 (1816).

45. 30 Annals of Cong. 307–310 (1816); 29 Annals of Cong. 215 (1816); 36 Annals of Cong. 1909 (1820).

46. 36 Annals of Cong. 1909 (1820). Smith, among others, voiced concern about low turnout and voter apathy. For expressions of the view that the two reforms were closely parallel to one another, see "Uniform Mode of Election," *NWR*, Jan. 20, 1816, 349, and "Right and Power of Suffrage," *NWR*, Nov. 16, 1816, 178–179.

47. 29 Annals of Cong. 218 (1815–1816); 33 Annals of Cong. 154 (1818–1819).

48. 30 Annals of Cong. 322–326 (1816–1817); David Johnson, *John Randolph of Roanoke* (Baton Rouge, 2012) is the most recent biography. Randolph freed his slaves at his death.

49. 30 Annals of Cong. 347–349 (1816–1817); 29 Annals of Cong. 219 (1815–1816); 34 Annals of Cong. 153–155 (1819); 37 Annals of Cong. 965–966 (1820–1821).

50. 30 Annals of Cong. 324–326 (1816–1817). See also 29 Annals of Cong. 219 (1815–1816) and 33 Annals of Cong. 154–155 (1818–1819).

51. 38 Annals of Cong. 117–118 (1821–1822). As early as January 1819, Barbour had sought to change the contingent election procedure, so that each member of the House (rather than each state) would get one vote. U.S. Senate Journal, 15th Cong. 2nd Sess. 156–157 (1818–1819); 33 Annals of Cong. 161–162 (1818–1819).

52. 30 Annals of Cong. 347–355 (1816–1817).

53. 30 Annals of Cong. 347–355 (1816–1817).

54. 30 Annals of Cong. 341–344, 347–355 (1816–1817).

55. 30 Annals of Cong. 308 (1816–1817). See 36 Annals of Cong. 1907–1908 (1819–1820); 37 Annals of Cong. 961 (1820–1821). See the statements of Senator John Pastore in Chapter 4.

56. 36 Annals of Cong. 1909–1910 (1819–1820); 37 Annals of Cong. 962 (1820–1821); 37 Annals of Cong. 507 (1820–1821).

57. 30 Annals of Cong. 306 (1816–1817). See also 329, 333–334, 338; 31 Annals of Cong. 185 (1817–1818); 34 Annals of Cong. 142, 155–156 (1819).

58. 34 Annals of Cong. 138 (1819); 38 Annals of Cong. 116 (1821–1822).

59. One such procedural vote took place on Mar. 20, 1816, after Barbour, who favored district elections for the House, moved to strike from the resolution the proposal to

choose electors by district: it was defeated twenty to twelve. 29 Annals of Cong. 226–227 (1815–1816). The resolutions passed by the Senate in 1819, 1820, and 1822 contained provisions mandating elections by district for the House. See Zagarri, *The Politics of Size*, 125–131.

60. 30 Annals of Cong. 355–356 (1816–1817). For examples of the legislative maneuvering, see U.S. House Journal, 15th Cong. 2nd Sess. 320 (1818–1819); U.S. House Journal, 16th Cong. 1st Sess. 436 (1819–1820); 33 Annals of Cong. 155 (1818–1819); 34 Annals of Cong. 1419–1421 (1819).

61. 37 Annals of Cong. 444–445, 459 (1820–1821). The previous April, Smith had told his House colleagues that it would be better to concur with the Senate resolution than to reject a popular proposal, which might lead the states to call for a constitutional convention. 36 Annals of Cong. 1911–1912 (1820).

62. The final weeks of debate included extensive discussion of the provision that would require states to choose members of the House by district. Most of the critics of this provision believed that Congress already had the power to require district elections for the House. 37 Annals of Cong. 444–445, 459–460, 504–508, 960–968 (1820–1821).

63. There were sixteen fewer votes (eleven fewer positive votes) on Jan. 25 than there had been on Dec. 5. At least one representative who had publicly declared his support for district elections for presidential electors, Richard Anderson of Kentucky, did not vote in January. Anderson had expressed reservations regarding the wisdom of amending the Constitution for House elections. See 37 Annals of Cong. 444–445, 459–460, 504–508, 960–968 (1820–1821).

64. I have no explanation for the relatively low levels of northern support in 1814 and 1818.

65. Based on an empirical analysis of the roll call votes utilizing the same sources as those underlying Tables 2.1–2.3, as well as *Historical Statistics of the United States* (New York, 2006). Across the time period (1813–1822), the differences among states with different methods of choosing electors were not statistically significant, largely because of the small sample size of votes coming from states that already held district elections.

66. State size was the only consistently significant variable ($p > 0.05$) to emerge from a logistic regression modeling the probability of an individual member of Congress voting in the affirmative across the time period from 1813 to 1822. (Results are available from the author upon request.) The other explanatory variables included in the estimated regression model were party affiliation, region, and the method of allocating electors in the state that a member of Congress was from. My thanks to Nicholas Lillios for these analyses.

67. See David P. Currie, "Choosing the Pilot: Proposed Amendments to the Presidential Selection Process, 1809–29," *Green Bag* 4 (Winter 2001): 143.

68. State size could be a proxy for other state-level characteristics that could not be analyzed because of the small sample size and the absence of data.

69. Voting against the resolution were Pennsylvania (eighteen to three) and Virginia (thirteen to seven); voting in favor of the resolution were Massachusetts (eleven to

three), North Carolina (ten to zero), and New York (thirteen to seven). Seven members of both the Massachusetts and New York delegations did not vote. The party lineups do not help to explain the disparities; the few remaining Federalists in each state delegation voted similarly to the Republicans. (Roll call data from Howard Rosenthal and Keith T. Poole, *United States Congressional Roll Call Voting Records, 1789–1990* (Pittsburgh, PA, 2000), http://doi.org/10.3886/ICPSR09822.v2.) Virginia and Pennsylvania utilized the general ticket to choose electors, as did Massachusetts after 1820. In New York, electors were still chosen by the legislature, leading to conflict among different political factions, as described later in this chapter. The split vote of New York's representatives on this resolution was linked to those conflicts. Regarding New York, see Evan Cornog, *The Birth of Empire: DeWitt Clinton and the American Experience, 1769–1828* (Oxford, 1998), 143; Robert Remini, "The Early Political Career of Martin Van Buren, 1782–1828" (PhD diss., Columbia University, 1951), 262; Steven E. Siry, *DeWitt Clinton and the American Political Economy: Sectionalism, Politics, and Republican Ideology, 1787–1828* (New York, 1990), 251–253. Zagarri's *The Politics of Size* (131–133) offers insights into the political dynamics in other states—although I disagree with her interpretation of the struggle over modes of selecting electors.

70. 33 Annals of Cong. 138 (1818–1819).

71. 33 Annals of Cong. 138 (1818–1819).

72. See note 63 above. See also Zagarri, *The Politics of Size*, 125–131.

73. 37 Annals of Cong. 965 (1820–1821).

74. 38 Annals of Cong. 551 (1821–1822); 38 Annals of Cong. 33, 283 (1821–1822); 39 Annals of Cong. 1249–1250, 1269 (1822); U.S. House Journal, 17th Cong., 1st Sess. 341 (1821–1822).

75. A detailed account of the 1824 election can be found in Ratcliffe, *One-Party Presidential Contest.*

76. 40 Annals of Cong. 158–159 (1822–1823); 40 Annals of Cong. 195 (1822–1823). Taylor's plan provided that if no candidate received a majority in the first congressional ballot, the president would be chosen by a plurality vote in a second round. See Currie, "Choosing the Pilot," 143–146.

77. 40 Annals of Cong. 176–177, 208 (1822–1823). Dickerson's proposal called for the names of the top three vote-getters to be sent to Congress; a president would be elected by a majority vote on the first congressional ballot or by a plurality thereafter.

78. 40 Annals of Cong. 206–223, 230 (1822–1823); 41 Annals of Cong. 850–865 (1823–1824). In 1810 the most populous state was roughly thirteen times larger than the smallest state, and only two states had fewer than five representatives in the House; a decade later, that ratio had nearly doubled and there were seven states with fewer than five representatives.

79. 41 Annals of Cong. 32–33 (1823–1824); 41 Annals of Cong. 178–204 (1823–1824).

80. 41 Annals of Cong. 169 (1823–1824).

81. 41 Annals of Cong. 178, 179, 189 (1823–1824).

82. 41 Annals of Cong. 178–204 (1823–1824). None of the proposals seriously considered by Congress would have eliminated the three-fifths clause. Regarding the idea of a national popular vote in this period, see Chapter 4.

83. 41 Annals of Cong. 39–40, 59–74 (1823–1824); 40 Annals of Cong. 228–234 (1822–1823); 41 Annals of Cong. 1179–1181 (1823–1824); "Presidential Election," *NWR*, Dec. 20, 1823, 241–242. Livingston's plan specified that electors would choose among the top two vote-getters.

84. Madison to George Hay, Aug. 23, 1823, in *Papers of James Madison*, 201–202, 108–111. See also Donald O. Dewey, "Madison's Views on Electoral Reform," *Western Political Quarterly* 15, no. 1 (Mar. 1962): 140–145.

85. Madison to George Hay, Aug. 23, 1823; and Madison to George McDuffie, Jan. 3, 1824, in *Papers of James Madison*, 108–111, 195–198.

86. Madison sent a sketch of this scheme to Jefferson. Madison to Thomas Jefferson, Jan. 14, 1824, in *Papers of James Madison*, 201–202. See also Madison to George Hay, Aug. 23, 1823, 108–111; Madison to George McDuffie, Jan. 3, 1824, 195–198; and Madison to Robert Taylor, Jan. 30, 1826, 677–679.

87. 42 Annals of Cong. 378–379 (1824); 40 Annals of Cong. 215–216 (1822–1823).

88. 42 Annals of Cong. 327, 373 (1824); 41 Annals of Cong. 850–866 (1823–1824); 41 Annals of Cong. 1067, 1179–1181 (1823–1824).

89. Dickerson's proposal provided that a candidate had to be elected by a majority in the first round of congressional voting; in subsequent rounds, a plurality would suffice. 41 Annals of Cong. 100–101 (1824); 42 Annals of Cong. 365–367, 376–378 (1824). The proposal for term limits received no attention in the debates.

90. 41 Annals of Cong. 1080 (1823–1824); 42 Annals of Cong. 365 (1824); 42 Annals of Cong. 379 (1824); 42 Annals of Cong. 403 (1824).

91. 42 Annals of Cong. 326–327, 355–362 (1824); "Presidential Election," *NWR*, Dec. 20, 1823, 241–242; "Election of President," *NWR*, Dec. 27, 1823, 260; "Presidential," *NWR*, Jan. 3, 1824, 273–274. Ratcliffe, *One-Party Presidential Contest*, 5. Regarding the rules of the Senate, I rely on the authority of (and give thanks to) Alan Frumin, for many years the parliamentarian of the Senate, personal correspondence, Oct. 2, 2015.

92. Robert V. Remini, *Martin Van Buren and the Making of the Democratic Party* (New York, 1959), 27, 37, 40, 43–50. Van Buren's role in blocking district elections for electors in New York that same winter may have contributed to King's anger. See Donald Cole, *Martin Van Buren and the American Political System* (Princeton, NJ, 1984), 128–130. Notably, Mahlon Dickerson was an ally of Van Buren's in mustering a caucus in February 1824. Jabez D. Hammond, *The History of Political Parties in the State of New-York from the Ratification of the Federal Constitution to December 1840*, 4th ed., with notes by Gen. Erastus Root (Cooperstown, NY, 1846), 2:148–149.

93. 41 Annals of Cong. 399–400, 417 (1824).

94. Had the conflict in New York played out differently, Henry Clay (rather than William Crawford) would have finished third in the Electoral College balloting; his name would then have been forwarded to the House of Representatives, where he

might have triumphed. Wilentz, *Rise of American Democracy,* 249–250. For a different perspective, see Ratcliffe, *One-Party Presidential Contest,* 237.

95. For a detailed chronicle of the events in New York, see Ratcliffe, *One-Party Presidential Contest,* 216–228

96. Remini, *Van Buren,* 30–36.

97. Remini, *Van Buren,* 35–41; Hammond, *History of Parties,* 2:130–113.

98. Remini, *Van Buren,* 41–42; Hammond, *History of Parties,* 2:130–132; Wilentz, *Rise of American Democracy,* 249, 851; Martin Van Buren, *The Autobiography of Martin Van Buren,* ed. John C. Fitzpatrick, in *Annual Report of the American Historical Association* 2 (1918), 142; Craig Hanyan, with Mary L. Hanyan, *DeWitt Clinton and the Rise of the People's Men* (Montreal, 1996), 13–20, 105–106. The strength of antislavery sentiment in New York made it unlikely that Crawford would garner much popular support.

99. Hammond, *History of Parties,* 2:140–142, 154; Remini, *Van Buren,* 45–46; Van Buren, *Autobiography,* 146–147; Cole, *Van Buren and the Political System,* 129.

100. Hammond, *History of Parties,* 2:140–147; Hammond, *History of Parties,* vol. 3, *Political History of the State of New-York, from Jan. 1, 1841 to Jan. 1, 1847, Including the Life of Silas Wright,* 4th ed., with notes by Gen. Root (Syracuse, 1852), 49–51; 42 Annals of Cong. 327, 366 (1824). In the assembly, proposals to permit electors to be chosen by a plurality vote were rebuffed by the Regency out of fear that doing so might boost Clinton's presidential candidacy. Reform forces were weaker in the senate because fewer members had been chosen in the recent elections.

101. Hammond, *History of Parties,* 2:153–165, Remini, *Van Buren,* 56–57; Hammond, *History of Parties,* 2:184–187.

102. Wilentz, *Rise of American Democracy,* 249; Remini, 70–71, 72–73; Cole, *Van Buren and the Political System,* 130, 133; Hammond, *History of Parties,* 2:160–166, 173, 175; Van Buren, *Autobiography,* 144.

103. Remini, *Van Buren,* 73, 63–70; Cole, *Van Buren and the Political System,* 133–134; Hammond, *History of Parties,* 2:177–178.

104. Wilentz, *Rise of American Democracy,* 250; Remini, *Van Buren,* 73–83; Hammond, *History of Parties,* 2:176–178; "Presidential Election," *NWR,* Nov. 20, 1824, 185–187; "Presidential Election," *NWR,* Nov. 27, 1824, 193–194. Van Buren continued scheming even after the election went to the House, hoping that if he prevented Adams from winning on the first ballot, there might then be a shift toward Crawford. Remini, *Van Buren,* 86–90; Van Buren, *Autobiography,* 149–152.

105. Remini, *Van Buren,* 93–94, 191–196; Hammond, *History of Parties,* 2:306; Cole, *Van Buren and the Political System,* 173–174. For the debates over methods of selecting electors in another state where the legislature clung to its power, see H. Clay Reed, "Presidential Electors in Delaware, 1789–1829," *Delaware History* 13 (1970–1971): 1–21.

106. Lisa Thomason, "Jacksonian Democracy and the Electoral College: Politics and Reform in the Method of Selecting Presidential Electors, 1824–1833" (PhD diss., University of North Texas, 2001), 49–53, 71–73.

107. Ratcliffe, *One-Party Presidential Contest,* 227–268, 280–281. Ratcliffe is skeptical that a "corrupt bargain" ever occurred. He also points out that the claim that Jackson "won"

the popular vote is dubious because there was no popular vote in six states—including New York, which strongly supported Adams. See also James C. Klotter, *Henry Clay: The Man Who Would Be President* (New York, 2018); and H. W. Brands, *Heirs of the Founders: The Epic Rivalry of Henry Clay, John Calhoun and Daniel Webster, the Second Generation of American Giants* (New York, 2018). For a recent summary of the historiography by a well-informed journalist, see Bonnie K. Goodman, "Corrupt Bargain?," https://medium.com/@BonnieKGoodman/corrupt-bargain-1824-john-quincy -adamss-election-as-president-henry-clay-as-secretary-of-state-7bb8ab7ebcd3.

108. For examples of messages from state legislatures to Congress, see Thomason, "Jacksonian Democracy," 82–83; see also Florence Watson, *The Presidential Election of 1828* (Washington, DC, 1938), 126–144.

109. 2 Part 1 Reg. Deb. 1365 (1825–1826); 2 Part 1 Reg. Deb. 16–19 (1825–1826); Dougherty, *Electoral System*, 332.

110. S. Report No. 22–19, at 2, 9–11, and *passim* (1826). The assertion that the committee was unanimous was made by Benton in his autobiography. Thomas H. Benton, *Thirty Years' View; or a History of the Working of the American Government for Thirty Years, from 1820 to 1850* (New York, 1854), 79. Judging from their comments, however, neither Dickerson nor Van Buren was fully on board with all of the recommendations. 2 Part 1 Reg. Deb. 692–694 (1825–1826).

111. S. Report No. 22–19, at 20–26 (1826); Thomason, "Jacksonian Democracy," 53.

112. 2 Part 1 Reg. Deb. 1388, 1466, 1551 (1825–1826); 2 Part 2 Reg. Deb. 1639 (1826).

113. 2 Part 1 Reg. Deb. 1376, 1378 (1825–1826), see also 1473; 2 Part 2 Reg. Deb. 1747 (1826); as well as *Speech of Mr. Saunders, on the Proposition to Amend the Constitution of the United States, respecting the Election of the President and Vice President* (Washington, DC, 1826), 14; Churchill C. Cambreleng, *Speech of Mr. Cambreleng, in Reply to Mr. McDuffie and Mr. Storrs, on the Proposition to Amend the Constitution of the United States* (Washington, DC, 1826), 12–14. Mitchell of Tennessee gave voice to a viewpoint that was shared by others: that he favored McDuffie's package but would be fine with any plan that got the election out of the House. 2 Part 2 Reg. Deb. 1747 (1826).

114. 2 Part 1 Reg. Deb. 1363, 1365–1366, 1378–1379, 1417–1418, 1419, 1462–1475 (1825–1826); U.S. House Journal, 19th Cong. 1st Sess. 115, 281, 319–320, 409–410 (1825–1826). According to McCormick, there were twenty-one amendments offered to McDuffie's resolution. Richard P. McCormick, *The Presidential Game: The Origins of American Presidential Politics* (New York, 1982), 157.

115. 2 Part 2 Reg. Deb. 1987–1990 (1826); 2 Part 1 Reg. Deb. 1570–1596, 1625 (1825–1826); Thomason, "Jacksonian Democracy," 83; Ratcliffe, *One-Party Presidential Contest*, 229, 237, 254–257.

116. 2 Part 1 Reg. Deb. 1570–1596, 1625 (1825–1826).

117. "Our Electoral Machinery," *North American Review* (hereafter cited as *NAR*), Oct. 1873, 384.

118. 2 Part 1 Reg. Deb. 1388–1390 (1825–1826); 2 Part 2 Reg. Deb. 1639–1640, 1740, 1744 (1826); 2 Part 1 Reg. Deb. 1473 (1825–1826); 2 Part 1 Reg. Deb. 17–18 (1825–1826); 2

Part 1 Reg. Deb. 1570–1596, 1625 (1825–1826). See also, regarding the corruption issue, *Speech of Mr. Cambreleng,* 12–14; William Drayton, *Speech of Mr. Drayton, on the Proposition to Amend the Constitution of the United States, Respecting the Election of the President and Vice President* (Washington, DC, 1826).

119. 2 Part 1 Reg. Deb. 1397–1402, 1406–1407 (1825–1826). Although Storrs opposed McDuffie's proposals, he did agree that electors should not be chosen by legislatures. Regarding the 1828 election, see Daniel Howe, *What God Hath Wrought: The Transformation of America* (New York, 2007), 280–283.

120. The growth of the slave population had gradually increased the number of electoral votes derived from slavery. Garry Wills, *"Negro" President: Jefferson and the Slave Power* (Boston, 2003), 6.

121. 2 Part 2 Reg. Deb. 1918–1919, 1827–1829, 1848–1849 (1826); see also 1664–6166, 1961–1962; 2 Part 1 Reg. Deb. 1469–1470 (1825–1826); and Dougherty, *Electoral System,* 297–298.

122. 2 Part 1 Reg. Deb. 1494, 1540 (1825–1826).

123. 2 Part 1 Reg. Deb. 1578–1580 (1825–1826); 2 Part 2 Reg. Deb. 1648–1649, 1735–1736 (1826); "The Constitution," *NWR,* June 3, 1826, 233.

124. 2 Part 2 Reg. Deb. 2004–2005 (1826).

125. The figures regarding party affiliation in Table 2.4 ought to be regarded as approximate. Party identifications were taken from Rosenthal and Poole, *Congressional Roll Call Records,* and from the Congressional Biographical Dictionary. The labeling of representatives as Adams or Jackson supporters in 1826 was based largely on whom they supported in 1828. Thirteen representatives were identified as neither Adams nor Jackson supporters.

126. Most members (70 percent) of the House appeared to regard the two reforms as parts of a single package; 45 percent voted favorably on both (including 60 percent of all Jacksonians), while 25 percent opposed both (including 45 percent of all Adams supporters). Fifty-eight members split their votes, with fifty-three voting against district elections but in favor of removing the contingent election from Congress. Half were from the North and half from the South; almost two-thirds (64 percent) were Jacksonians. Based on data from Rosenthal and Poole, *Congressional Roll Call Records.*

127. Once again, large-state delegations were not of one mind. New York (where the vote was twenty-seven to five in favor of reform) had recently adopted district elections, and North Carolina's representatives were just as staunch in their preference for district elections (thirteen to zero) as they had been in 1821. Pennsylvania (four in favor, eighteen opposed) and Virginia (eight to eleven) also voted much as they had in 1821. Massachusetts, however, (three to nine) reversed its 1821 preference. Ohio's delegation voted eleven to two against the resolution, and the vote from Kentucky was a six to six tie. The partisan breakdowns within these states also varied. In New York, for example, Adams supporters strongly supported the resolution; in North Carolina, all eleven Jacksonians did so. The opposition to districts in Pennsylvania and Virginia was dominated by Jacksonians. Rosenthal and Poole, *Congressional Roll*

Call Records. As Table 2.4 indicates, most representatives from small and medium-sized states also opposed district elections, presumably for reasons that had little to do with state size.

128. 2 Part 1 Reg. Deb. 1493 (1825–1826); 2 Part 1 Reg. Deb. 692–696 (1825–1826); 2 Part 1 Reg. Deb. 1848–1856 (1826); McCormick, *Presidential Game,* 157–161; Dougherty, *Electoral System,* 297–298. After the vote, Macon attributed the resolution's defeat to the Adams administration's opposition to mandatory district elections; whether the administration believed that such a change would disadvantage their candidate in 1828 is unclear—particularly given that a third of Adams supporters favored the resolution. Niles saw the tensions between the South and the North as one of the core obstacles to electoral reform. "The Constitution," *NWR,* June 3, 1826, 233.

129. 2 Part 1 Reg. Deb. 692–696 (1825–1826).

130. 2 Part 2 Reg. Deb. 2659 (1826).

131. "The Constitution," *NWR,* June 3, 1826, 233. See also *Salem Gazette,* Apr. 11, 1826, 2.

132. The same objections would have applied to a runoff procedure that involved a second round of balloting by the electors.

133. 2 Part 1 Reg. Deb. 694 (1825–1826). Niles concluded that he was "nearly certain" that electoral reform "cannot be brought about" because of the array of obstacles in its path. "The Constitution," *NWR,* June 3, 1826, 233.

134. 2 Part 1 Reg. Deb. 692–695 (1825–1826); U.S. House Journal, 20th Cong. 1st Sess. 71–72 (1827–1828). Cong. Globe, 23rd Cong. 1st Sess. 20, 439 (1833–1834); Cong. Globe, 23rd Cong. 2nd Sess. 129 (1834–1835); Cong. Globe, 25th Cong. 2nd Sess. 25–26 (1837–1838); Cong. Globe, 28th Cong. 1st Sess. 686–687 (1843–1844); Cong. Globe, 31st Cong. 2nd Sess. 627 (1850–1851); Cong. Globe, 32nd Cong. 2nd Sess. 443 (1852–1853); Cong. Globe, 33rd Cong. 1st Sess. 188–189, 202, 238, 283–284, 1372 (1853–1854); Cong. Globe, 33rd Cong. 2nd Sess. 527 (1854–1855); Cong. Globe, 33rd Cong. 1st Sess. 228, 252 (1853–1854); Ames, "Proposed Amendments," 91; Cong. Globe, 30th Cong. 2nd Sess. 25 (1848–1849). Some of these proposals were reported out of their committees. For other proposals, on various dimensions of presidential electoral reform, see 9 Part 1 Reg. Deb. 940–942 (1832–1833); U.S. House Journal, 24th Cong. 1st Sess. 347–349 (1835–1836); 12 Part 3 Reg. Deb. 3015–3017 (1836).

135. The change in public opinion regarding the desirability of district elections was noted on the floor of Congress by John Wright of Ohio in February 1829. 5 Reg. Deb. 362–363 (1828–1829).

136. For examples of popular pressure in the states to end legislative selection of electors, see Thomason, "Jacksonian Democracy," 102–106, 135–136; "Presidential Election," *NWR,* Dec. 20, 1823, 241–242; "Presidential Election," *NWR,* Nov. 27, 1824, 193–194. See also Ratcliffe, *One-Party Presidential Contest,* 267. South Carolina's legislature continued to choose electors until the Civil War.

137. Clement Dorsey, *The General Public Statutory Law and Public Local Law of the State of Maryland, from the Year 1692 to 1839* (Baltimore, 1840), 1126.

138. Thomason, "Jacksonian Democracy," 107–113, 117, 120, 130–139, 146–148, 149, 150–152; Dougherty, *Electoral System,* 299–300. Thomason concludes that six of the seven

states that changed their mode of selection for the 1828 election did so for "purely political reasons." In Illinois the switch stemmed from the difficulties encountered in attempts to translate a divided district vote into support for a candidate in the contingent election of 1824–1825.

139. 8 Part 2 Reg. Deb. 2164 (1831–1832); 8 Part 3 Reg. Deb. 3104 (1831–1832); 9 Part 1 Reg. Deb. 940–941 (1832–1833).

140. This would occur, presumably, only if (a) a political party controlled the legislature but did not think its candidate would win a majority of the popular vote; or (b) the parties in a state agreed to switch to district elections so that each could be assured of winning some electoral votes.

141. 2 Part 1 Reg. Deb. 1575 (1825–1826).

142. 2 Part 1 Reg. Deb. 1371 (1825–1826).

143. Andrew Jackson, "First Annual Message," in Richardson, *A Compilation*, 2:442–462.

144. See Jackson's other annual messages in the compilation cited above. He also, on occasion, proposed limiting presidents to one term of four to six years. 5 Reg. Deb. 119–125, 320–322, 337, 361–369 (1828–1829); 7 Reg. Deb. 23, 379 (1830–1831).

145. U.S. House Journal, 20th Cong. 1st Sess. 70–71 (1827–1828); Ames, "Proposed Amendments," 343; U.S. Senate Journal, 20th Cong. 1st Sess. 1828, 134; U.S. Senate Journal, 21st Cong. 1st Sess. 98–99 (1829–1830); U.S. House Journal, 21st Cong. 1st Sess. 237 (1829–1830); U.S. Senate Journal, 21st Cong. 1st Sess. 187 (1829–1830); 10 Part 1 Reg. Deb. 29 (1833–1834); 10 Part 2 Reg. Deb. 1813–1814 (1813–1814); *Resolutions of the Legislature of the State of Indiana*, H.R. Doc. No. 171–24 (1837); *Journal of the House of Representatives of the State of Ohio*, 25 (Dec. 4, 1826), 328–332, and 28 (Dec. 7, 1829), 74–75; U.S. House Journal, 25th Cong. 2nd Sess. 475–477 (1837–1838).

146. 8 Part 2 Reg. Deb. 1963–1964, 2164–2165 (1831–1832); 8 Part 3 Reg. Deb. 3102–3103 (1832); 9 Part 1 Reg. Deb. 940–942 (1832–1833); U.S. House Journal, 23rd Cong. 2nd Sess. 297–299 (1835); U.S. House Journal, 24th Cong. 2nd Sess. 50–52 (1836–1837); U.S. House Journal, 25th Cong. 2nd Sess. 4754–77 (1837–1838).

147. In 1844 the Massachusetts legislature took a stand against the three-fifths clause by forwarding to Congress an amendment resolution that would base each state's congressional representation (and thus its electoral votes) on its free population alone. U.S. Senate Journal, 28th Cong. 1st Sess. 85 (1843–1844). The resolution was so controversial that the Senate declined to have it printed.

148. U.S. House Journal, 19th Cong. 2nd Sess. 317 (1826–1827); U.S. House Journal, 20th Cong. 1st Sess. 246 (1827–1828); *Resolutions of the Legislature of the State of Indiana*, H.R. Doc. No. 171–1724 (1837).

149. U.S. House Journal, 20th Cong. 1st Sess. 71 (1827–1828); 8 Part 2 Reg. Deb. 1964 (1831–1832); 10 Part 2 Reg. Deb. 1813–1814 (1833–1834); U.S. House Journal, 23rd Cong. 2nd Sess. 298 (1834–1835); U.S. House Journal, 24th Cong. 2nd Sess. 50–52 (1836–1837).

150. The legislature of Indiana was more specific than most, advocating a runoff, as well as direct elections, a single term for presidents, and a ban on executive branch appointments of members of Congress. U.S. House Journal, 24th Cong. 2nd Sess. 520 (1836–1837).

3. THREE UNEASY PIECES, 1870–1960

1. Charles R. Buckalew, "The Electoral Commission and Its Bearings," *NAR*, Mar.–Apr. 1877, 162.
2. Regarding representation systems and gerrymandering, see Peter H. Argersinger, "The Value of the Vote: Political Representation in the Gilded Age," *Journal of American History* 76, no. 1 (June 1989): 66–67, 82.
3. See Roger Pryor's section of F. A. P. Barnard, William Purcell, H. L. Dawes, Roger A. Pryor, and Z. B. Vance, "How Shall the President Be Elected?," *NAR*, Feb. 1885, 121. Compare also the statement in the Southard committee report that "the people have been educated to the principle that the greater vote shall control." H. Report No. 819–45 at 11 (1878).
4. S. Report No. 395–43, at 7 (1874); see also George C. Edwards III, *Why the Electoral College Is Bad for America,* 2nd ed. (New Haven, CT, 2011), 82. The victorious candidates in 1844, 1848, and 1856 also lacked a majority of the popular vote.
5. For a discussion of a national popular vote and its advocates after the Civil War, see Chapter 4.
6. *NYT,* July 20, 1868; Cong. Globe, 39th Cong. 1st Sess. 349 (1865–1866); U.S. House Journal, 39th Cong. 1st Sess. 174, 207–213 (1866); Cong. Globe, 40th Cong. 2nd Sess. 2713–2716 (1868); Cong. Globe, 40th Cong. 3rd Sess. 1107–1108 (1869); see also Herman V. Ames, "The Proposed Amendments to the Constitution of the United States during the First Century of Its History," *Annual Report of the American Historical Association* 2 (1896).
7. Cong. Globe, 42nd Cong. 3rd Sess. 632 (1873); S.J. Res. 7, 42nd Cong. 2nd Sess. (1872); text of resolution is S.J. Res. 7, 42nd Cong. (1872). Other ideas were also put forward during the late 1860s and early 1870s. For a listing of proposed amendments relating to presidential elections during this period (through 1896), see Ames, "Proposed Amendments," 75–123, and appendix A. My own research into congressional and other primary sources suggests that Ames's listings, although extensive, are not exhaustive.
8. Cong. Globe, 42nd Cong. 3rd Sess. 364–368 (1873). For a detailed account of the vote-counting arguments before 1875, see J. Hampden Dougherty, *The Electoral System of the United States* (New York, 1906), 75–104.
9. S. Report No. 395-43, at 1–21 (1874). The report criticized the existing contingent process as corruptible and "manifestly" unjust to the larger states.
10. S. Report No. 395-43, at 1–21 (1874).
11. S. Report No. 395-43, at 3–5, 8, 19 (1874). The first year in which the new Republican Party fielded a presidential candidate was 1856. Views similar to Morton's were expressed by an unnamed author (who might have been Richard H. Dana Jr.) in "Our Electoral Machinery," *NAR*, Oct. 1873, 383–401. The recently founded magazine *The Nation,* an important voice of northeastern liberals, was supportive of Morton. "The 'Situation' for Senator Morton's Committee," *The Nation,* Aug. 1873, 124–126. Regarding fraud and the weakness of state electoral laws, see George W. McCrary, "Our Election Laws," *NAR*, May 1879, 449–461.

12. Cong. Globe, 42nd Cong. 3rd Sess. 1284–1294 (1873); Dougherty, *The Electoral System*, 4, 75–104.

13. The Twelfth Amendment stated only that "the President of the Senate shall, in the Presence of the Senate and House of Representatives, open all the certificates and the votes shall then be counted." Whether this language gave either the president of the Senate or Congress itself a mandate to judge the validity of electoral returns was hotly debated and would continue to be into the 1880s. It was often noted that the president of the Senate would likely have partisan loyalties and, on six occasions, had been one of the candidates for president. On the other hand, if Congress as a whole had the power to reject a state's electoral votes, then it could effectively decide any presidential contest by itself—which ran counter to the intent of the Constitution. S. Report No. 395-43, at 12–13, 15 (1874).

14. S. Report No. 395-43, at 10, 14–15, 20–21 (1874).

15. Dougherty, *The Electoral System*, 91–95, 344–348; for the debates on the counting bill, see 3 Cong. Rec. 1692–1695, 1759–1786 (1875). The report from the House Committee on Elections was never brought to a vote because the House too was preoccupied with vote-counting issues. *NYT*, Jan. 27, 1875; Ames, "Proposed Amendments," 93.

16. Paul L. Haworth, *The Hayes-Tilden Election* (Indianapolis, 1927), 340–341, concludes that Tilden's popular vote majority would have evaporated had African-Americans been allowed to vote freely in the South.

17. This brief narrative, which does not begin to capture the intricacies of the story, is drawn largely from the two most recent accounts of this election: Michael F. Holt, *By One Vote: The Disputed Election of 1876* (Lawrence, KS, 2008), and Roy Morris Jr., *Fraud of the Century: Rutherford B. Hayes, Samuel Tilden, and the Stolen Election of 1876* (New York, 2003). Older but still valuable is Haworth, *The Hayes-Tilden Election*. An excellent short narrative, coupled with a cogent analysis of the legal issues, can be found in Edward B. Foley, *Ballot Battles: The History of Disputed Elections in the United States* (New York, 2016), 117–149, 411. The debates in Congress about the best way to resolve the crisis can be found in 5 Cong. Rec. 1–1051 (Dec. 4 1876–Jan. 26, 1877).

18. Fueling this bitter legacy, as historians have pointed out, was the fact that each party could plausibly claim that the other had cheated. There is ample evidence that Republicans manipulated the vote counts in ways that benefited Hayes. It was also true that the Democrats engaged in widespread violence, among other methods, to suppress the votes of African-Americans. As Edward Foley has noted, the Democrats did not get a fair count, but the Republicans did not get a fair election. Haworth, *The Hayes-Tilden Election*, 341–342; Foley, *Ballot Battles*, 122. For an example of the post-election anger, see J. S. Black, "The Electoral Conspiracy," *NAR*, July–Aug. 1877, 1–34.

19. Morris, *Fraud*, 241–242.

20. Republican Party Platforms: "Republican Party Platform of 1884," June 3, 1884, at Gerhard Peters and John T. Woolley, eds., *The American Presidency Project*, http://www.presidency.ucsb.edu/ws/index.php?pid=29626.

21. The core of the Electoral Count Act was a provision leaving it to each state to determine and certify the winner of its electoral votes; this could be overridden only by a decision of both branches of Congress. For a cogent discussion of the origins and shortcomings of the act, see Foley, *Ballot Battles,* 157–160, 351–360; see also Nathan L. Colvin and Edward B. Foley, "Lost Opportunity: Learning the Wrong Lesson from the Hayes-Tilden Dispute," *Fordham Law Review* 79, no. 5 (Apr. 2011): 1043–1089; Dougherty, *The Electoral System,* 214–249. For examples of the congressional debates on the vote-counting issue, see 17 Cong. Rec. 815–820, 863–869 (1886).

22. *Atlanta Daily Constitution,* Nov. 15, 1876. The newspaper also noted that Tilden had won a large majority of the white vote.

23. *Harper's Weekly,* Apr. 28, 1877, 322–323; Buckalew, "Electoral Commission," 162; S. Report No. 395-43 (1874); 5 Cong. Rec. 124 (1877); see also Jurist, *The Electoral College* (Washington, DC, Dec. 1876).

24. *Chicago Daily Tribune* (hereafter cited as *CDT*), Feb. 8, 1877; see also Dec. 13, 1876. The paper voiced approval of a direct district elections plan without electors. Similar views were expressed in *The Independent,* Jan. 24, 1878, 16. *The Independent* (1828–1928) was an influential publication with ties to the Congregational Church; its editor in the 1870s was Henry C. Bowen, a businessman and Republican.

25. 5 Cong. Rec. 124, 144 (1876); Ames, "Proposed Amendments," 399; Dougherty, *The Electoral System,* 344–350.

26. "Address of Mr. McDonald of Indiana," 45th Cong. 2nd Sess. *Memorial Addresses on the Life and Character of Oliver P. Morton Delivered in the Senate and House of Representatives, January 17 and 18, 1878* (Washington, DC, 1878), 10–11.

27. Oliver P. Morton, "The American Constitution," *NAR,* May–June 1877, 341–346; "The American Constitution. II," *NAR,* July–Aug. 1877, 68–78; Dougherty, *The Electoral System,* 344–349.

28. For an account of Morton's role and the importance of his premature death, see Dougherty, *The Electoral System,* 344–349.

29. H. Report No. 819–845, at 8, 10, 11, 13–14 (1878); Ames, "Proposed Amendments," 96–97; Dougherty, *The Electoral System,* 354–363; Neal R. Peirce and Lawrence D. Longley, *The People's President: The Electoral College in American History and the Direct Vote Alternative,* rev. ed. (New Haven, CT, 1981), 144–146. According to Peirce and Longley (144), twenty proportional proposals were introduced between 1875 and 1889, most of them after 1877. Ames (96) suggests that the number may have been higher.

30. H. Report No. 819–45 at 2–13 (1878).

31. Buckalew, "Electoral Commission," 173.

32. Samuel T. Spear, "The Maish Amendment," *The Independent,* Oct. 4, 1877, 3–4. Regarding *The Independent,* see note 24 above. See also Dougherty, *The Electoral System,* 354–363.

33. The most comprehensive—but still incomplete—listing is in Ames, "Proposed Amendments," 75–123, and appendix A; see note 7 above.

34. Charles W. Calhoun, *Minority Victory: Gilded Age Politics and the Front Porch Campaign of 1888* (Lawrence, KS, 2008), 178–190. Democrats were well aware that

Cleveland's lead in the popular vote was attributable to the suppression of African-American votes in the South.

35. The reform proposals of this era typically provided for a plurality victor or a runoff election. Given that no election had devolved upon the House since 1824, the contingent mechanism received relatively little attention, although it was widely criticized as undemocratic. For examples, see H. L. Dawes, untitled, *NAR*, Feb. 1885, 113–118; "Our Electoral Machinery," 392; and Spear, "The Maish Amendment," which labeled the contingent system "wholly anti-republican" and "more objectionable" than the Electoral College. Spear, a Presbyterian minister, was a prolific and widely read author.

36. *NYT*, Feb. 12, 1881; *NYT*, Dec. 4, 1884. For Wallace's proposal and his defense of it, see 11 Cong. Rec. 1450–1459 (1881). Wallace included an impressively accurate history of earlier efforts to reform the electoral system. Regarding proposals and public opinion in the 1880s and early 1890s more generally, see *NYT*, Nov. 24, 1882; *NYT*, Dec. 4, 1884 (noting again that the electoral colleges are "not simply superfluous" but "liable to become mischievous"); *NYT*, Dec. 20, 1892 (supporting proportional elections); *CDT*, Feb. 27, 1885; *CDT*, Jan. 24, 1890; "The Electoral Count," *The Independent*, Jan. 29, 1885, 17–18. The *Washington Post* (Nov. 6, 1884) called for the abolition of the Electoral College and for a national popular vote with a plurality winner; see also *WP*, Dec. 21, 1885. Ongoing interest in the subject was also evident in the essays in Barnard et al., "How Shall the President Be Elected?"

37. A listing of the sources of dispute that had already arisen in presidential elections was presented in H. Report No. 819–45 at 5 (1878); see also p. 11 regarding "doubtful" states. The dispute over one of Oregon's electoral votes in 1876 focused on the eligibility of a Hayes elector who was also a postmaster—which was alleged, by Democrats, to have been a "position of trust or profit under the United States." That one vote could have turned the election. Foley, *Ballot Battles*, 124.

38. See, for example, *WP*, May 10, 1878, reporting on negotiations between House and Senate committees regarding possible reforms to the election system; the key source of disagreement concerned the role of Congress in settling electoral vote disputes.

39. 13 Cong. Rec. 5147–5149 (1882). Browne, as well as other reformers, held a view opposite to that expressed by Hewitt, arguing that Congress could not solve "the perplexing questions that may arise out of Presidential elections until we have cut that system up by the roots." 13 Cong. Rec. 5146 (1882). The House, in 1882, was not able to agree on either a dispute-resolution bill or substantive reform. See also Colvin and Foley, "Lost Opportunity," esp. 1053–1061. The authors, both legal scholars, have observed that the dispute resolution provision in the Southard committee report had "little chance of adoption" because it was attached to Electoral College reforms that were potentially controversial and would require two-thirds majorities. The reverse also seems to have been true: proposals for changing the mode of allocating electoral votes had little chance of receiving full consideration by Congress if they were tied to vote-counting measures that lacked consensus support.

40. The first political party to endorse reform was the Socialist Party, which in 1912 called for "a direct vote of the people." "The Socialist Party's Platform, 1912," accessed at Henry J. Sage, *Sage American History,* http://sageamericanhistory.net/progressive /docs/SocialistPlat1912.htm.

41. Other Democrats who encouraged reform well into the 1880s and 1890s included Richard Townshend and William Springer, both of Illinois. (*CDT,* Jan. 30, 1880; *CDT,* Dec. 26, 1892.) Springer introduced a proportional elections resolution in 1884 as well as in later years (H. Res 185, 48th Cong.), and Townshend proposed a national popular vote in 1886 (H. Res. 93, 49th Cong.).

42. Election results from David Leip, *Atlas of U.S. Presidential Elections* (uselectionatlas .org). Pennsylvania had twenty-nine electoral votes in 1876 and 1880, and thirty in 1884 and 1888.

43. Republican senator George Edmunds of Vermont maintained that the Democratic Party in Congress, on the whole, resisted legislation to implement the Fourteenth and Fifteenth Amendments and opposed federal laws trying to secure "fair and peaceful elections" to the House. George F. Edmunds, "Controlling Forces in American Politics," *NAR,* Jan. 1881, 26–27.

44. *The Independent,* Jan. 24, 1878, 16; H. Report No. 819–45 at 16–23 (1878); *Daily Constitution,* Apr. 9, 1878. See also the *Raleigh Observer,* Apr. 18, 1878. One exception to the southern Democratic pattern was Jordan E. Cravens of Arkansas, who responded to the 1876 election by introducing a proportional plan and arguing that no man should become the "Chief Magistrate" without having the "vote of a majority of the sovereign people of the States." In 1882 his party denied him renomination for his seat in Congress. Peirce and Longley, *The People's President,* 144; Jordan E. Cravens, "Address of Hon. Jordan E. Cravens to the Voters of the Third Congressional District," *Daily Arkansas Gazette* (Little Rock), Oct. 11, 1878.

45. Richard H. Dana Jr., "Points in American Politics," *NAR,* Jan. 1877, 6–7; see also "Our Electoral Machinery," 392–393; and "The 'Situation' for Senator Morton's Committee," *The Nation,* Aug. 21, 1873, 124–125. The "Mugwumps," largely from the Northeast, were a loose grouping of political leaders and intellectuals who were particularly concerned with ending corruption and promoting efficient government; originally Republicans, they bolted to the Democrats in 1884 because of the corruption linked to Republican nominee James Blaine.

46. "The Contributors' Club," *Atlantic Monthly,* Mar. 1889, 429; Calhoun, *Minority Victory,* 180; Vincent P. de Santis, "Republican Efforts to 'Crack' the Democratic South," *Review of Politics* 14, no. 2 (Apr. 1952): 244. De Santis (244–257) traces the complex evolution of Republican efforts to win votes and seats in the South from the Civil War into the early 1890s. The Republican Party platform of 1880 declared it to be a goal of the party to divide the "solid South." "Republican Party Platform of 1880," June 2, 1880, at Gerhard Peters and John T. Woolley, eds., *The American Presidency Project,* http://www.presidency.ucsb.edu/ws/?pid=29625.

47. The two-party system was less entrenched during this period than it would become in later decades. The Republican Party had been in existence for only two decades,

and the Greenback-Labor Party was a force in some states, as were the Knights of Labor and, of course, the Populists in the 1890s. At the same time, party commitments and identification were strong. For a broad portrait of politics in the 1880s, see Calhoun, *Minority Victory*.

48. De Santis, "Republican Efforts," 244–255. Argersinger, "Value of the Vote," 87, concludes that the Electoral College advantaged Republicans during this period, but his view is challenged in James C. Garand and T. Wayne Parent, "Representation, Swing, and Bias in U.S. Presidential Elections, 1872–1988," *American Journal of Political Science* 35, no. 4 (Nov. 1991): 1023–1024. They found a Democratic bias (meaning that Democrats received a higher proportion of the electoral vote than the popular vote) throughout the late nineteenth century, with the exception of 1896. Regarding the hardening of the Republican stance on the general ticket, see the next section of this chapter.

49. *NYT*, Jan. 27, 1875.

50. The popular vote margin in 1880 was less than 2,000 votes. The crisis of 1876–1877 generated several books about the electoral system: Charles O'Neil, *The American Electoral System* (New York, 1889); David A. McKnight, *The Electoral System of the United States* (Philadelphia, 1878); and, later, Dougherty, *The Electoral System*.

51. *CDT*, Feb. 27, 1885. Compare Ames, "Proposed Amendments," 114; *NYT*, Dec. 29, 1892.

52. Ames, "Proposed Amendments," 113.

53. Peter Argersinger, "Electoral Reform and Partisan Jugglery," *Political Science Quarterly* 119, no. 3 (2004): 506; *CDT*, Oct. 1, 1892. This account of the Miner Law relies heavily on Argersinger's work; he is the only historian to have explored the subject in any depth.

54. Peter Argersinger, *Representation and Inequality in Late Nineteenth-Century America: The Politics of Apportionment* (Cambridge, 2012), 8–19. Districting for congressional seats was constrained by an 1842 law requiring single-member districts with contiguous territory. In 1872 Congress further mandated that such districts contain "as near as practicable, an equal number of inhabitants." Congress, however, did not take steps to enforce these laws, and federal courts steered clear of districting issues until the 1960s. State apportionment laws were more complex and often had contradictory mandates. As I have discussed elsewhere, the South was not alone in trying to keep potential voters from the polls during this period: many northern states enacted laws aimed at immigrant workers. Alexander Keyssar, *The Right to Vote: The Contested History of Democracy in the United States* (New York, 2000), chap. 5.

55. Much of the Northeast and parts of the West were reliably Republican, whereas the South was predictably Democratic; meanwhile, third parties were gaining adherents, heralding the strong showings of the Populists in the 1890s.

56. Argersinger, "Partisan Jugglery," 512; Argersinger, *Representation*, 12–24.

57. Argersinger, "Partisan Jugglery," 504–506; Argersinger, *Representation*, 42–45, 53–59. The Democrats did engage in some high-handed maneuvers to ensure their control

of the state senate before redistricting. The congressional district boundaries were regarded as fair and were not challenged by Republicans.

58. Election statistics are from Leip, *Atlas of U.S. Presidential Elections*, http://uselectionatlas.org/. The official title of the Miner Law was Act 50 of the Public Acts of 1891 of the State of Michigan.

59. Argersinger "Partisan Jugglery," 502–503, 506–508, 515; Argersinger, *Representation*, 111–112; *WP*, Apr. 18, 1891; *NYT*, Dec. 29, 1892.

60. Argersinger, *Representation*, 109–121; Argersinger, "Partisan Jugglery," 507; *CDT*, June 20, 1892. Regarding the *Tribune*'s earlier views, see the previous section of this chapter.

61. Argersinger, *Representation*, 34–41; regarding Harrison and his rise to national power, see Calhoun, *Minority Victory*, 87–102.

62. Benjamin Harrison, "Third Annual Message," Dec. 9, 1891, at Gerhard Peters and John T. Woolley, eds., *The American Presidency Project*, http://www.presidency.ucsb.edu/ws/?pid=29532.

63. Stephen M. Merrill, "Our Electoral System," *NAR*, Oct. 1896, 411.

64. Argersinger, "Partisan Jugglery," 508.

65. Regarding the early nineteenth-century debates, see Chapter 2.

66. Edwin B. Winans, "Michigan's Presidential Electors," *NAR*, Apr. 1892, 439–445.

67. Argersinger, "Partisan Jugglery," 509–511; Argersinger, *Representation*, 109–125; *CDT*, May 20 and June 18, 1892; *WP*, June 18, 1892. For a detailed account of the legal proceedings (and the public debates that surrounded them), see Argersinger, *Representation*, 115–125.

68. Argersinger, "Partisan Jugglery," 512–514; Argersinger, *Representation*, 136–138; *NYT*, Oct. 18, 1892; *McPherson v. Blacker*, 146 U.S. 1 (1892).

69. *NYT*, Oct. 26, 1892; Argersinger, "Partisan Jugglery," 515; Argersinger, *Representation*, 139–140; *WP*, July 6, 1892; *CDT*, Oct. 1, 1892.

70. Argersinger, "Partisan Jugglery," 512–517; Argersinger, *Representation*; 141–143; *NYT*, Nov. 2, 1892. Two months later the *Times* editorialized in favor of proportional elections (*NYT*, Dec. 29, 1892).

71. Argersinger, "Partisan Jugglery," 517–519; Argersinger, *Representation*, 142–145, 281–282, 287–289; Keyssar, *Right to Vote*, 157; Michigan State Legislature, "Michigan Manual 2009–2010," 191–192 (https://www.legislature.mi.gov/documents/publications/MichiganManual/2009-2010/09-10_MM_III_pp_191-195_FormerState.pdf). Educational requirements for suffrage, aimed at immigrant workers, were enacted in many northern states in this period. Keyssar, *Right to Vote*, chap. 5.

72. Argersinger, "Partisan Jugglery," 506. Democrats had opposed these proposals in New York and New Jersey.

73. De Santis, "Republican Efforts," 244–253. The establishment of white one-party rule proceeded at different rates in different states, with the states of the upper South (North Carolina and Virginia, for example) remaining contested for a decade or more longer than Mississippi or Louisiana. The Populists made significant gains in

some southern states in the early 1890s, but their strength was greatly diminished by the end of that decade.

74. De Santis, "Republican Efforts," 253–257; Keyssar, *Right to Vote*, 108–116. The Republicans held majorities in both branches of Congress in 1890. The Federal Elections Bill was a precursor of (and model for) the Voting Rights Act of 1965. The bill was called a "force bill" by its opponents; it made little mention of the use of force, although the House version of the bill did authorize the president to deploy the army to protect elections.

75. Regarding both the content and the import of the Federal Elections Bill, see Richard M. Valelly, "Partisan Entrepreneurship and Policy Windows: George Frisbie Hoar and the 1890 Federal Elections Bill," in *Formative Acts: American Politics in the Making*, ed. Stephen Skowronek and Matthew Glassman (Philadelphia, 2007), 126–149. In 1900 the Republican presidential candidate polled less than 25 percent of the vote in four southern states; by 1904 this was true in seven states, with the Republican tally falling into single digits in Louisiana, Mississippi, and South Carolina. Election statistics from Leip, *Atlas of U.S. Presidential Elections*, http://uselectionatlas.org/.

76. *CDT*, Jan. 24, 1890. Reflecting a widespread view that southern elections were irretrievably corrupt, the *Tribune* claimed that a proportional system would "strengthen the temptation in the Southern States to count out and eliminate from the returns all Republican votes that found their way into the ballot box."

77. Winans, "Presidential Electors," 441–442.

78. This occurred in Wisconsin in the early 1890s when Democrats decided not to institute a version of the Miner Law. Argersinger, "Partisan Jugglery," 507.

79. Argersinger somberly concludes his study of the Miner episode with the observation that "in the end the partisans with effective political power over the electoral system used it ruthlessly to promote their own interests without regard to the rights of their opponents, their own expressed ideology, or the claims of democracy." *Representation*, 145.

80. James Melcher, "Electing to Reform: Maine and the District Plan for Selection of Presidential Electors" (paper presented at the 2004 Annual Meeting of the New England Political Science Association), 9–12. The district plan has been uncontroversial in Maine, and the state did not split its electoral votes between different candidates until 2016.

81. Alexander Burns, "Nebraska GOP: No Vote for Obama in '12," *Politico.com*, Sept. 19, 2011, http://www.politico.com/story/2011/09/neb-gop-no-vote-for-obama-in-12-063819; Paul Hammel, "Winner Take All Electoral Vote Bill Fails Again in Nebraska Legislature," *Omaha.com*, Mar. 17, 2015, http://www.omaha.com/news/legislature/winner-take-all-electoral-vote-bill-fails-again-in-nebraska/article_cbf16214-ccc3-11e4-8a03-8bc57b862824.html.

82. *CDT*, Dec. 26, 1892, Jan. 4, 9, 11, and 24, 1893; *WP*, Dec. 30, 1892. In February 1893 David De Armond, a Missouri Democrat, put forward, on behalf of a select committee, a report endorsing an amendment for proportional elections. The report included a brief section entitled "Partisan Objections Not Tenable." Taking clear aim

at Republicans' insistence on keeping winner-take-all, De Armond argued that "a constitutional amendment should hardly be treated as a matter of fleeting partisan policy." H. Report 2439 at 1–12 (1893).

83. John G. Carlisle, "Dangerous Defects of the Electoral System," *The Forum* 24 (Sept. 1897–Feb. 1898): 257–266; Norman T. Mason, "Should the Electoral System Be Abolished?," *American Journal of Politics* (Apr. 1893): 423. See also Neal Ewing, "A Defence of Our Electoral System," *NAR,* Nov. 1896, 637–640; Samuel M. Davis, "How Shall We Elect the President?," *American Magazine of Civics* 9, no. 5 (Nov. 1896); Merrill, "Our Electoral System."

84. *WP,* Sept. 12, 1904. See also Simon Newcomb, "Our Antiquated Method of Electing a President," *NAR,* Jan. 1905, 9–18.

85. According to Gary Bugh's thorough compilation, there were far fewer amendments introduced on this subject between 1899 and 1945 than there were between 1945 and 1981. Gary Bugh, ed., *Electoral College Reform: Challenges and Possibilities* (Farnham, UK, 2010), 239–253. A report prepared for the House of Representatives in 1929 found that fifty-three amendment resolutions appeared between 1889 and 1928, most of them favoring some type of proportional plan. H. Doc. No. 551-70, "Proposed Amendments to the Constitution," at 47–48 (1929). See also Marjorie Ann Smith, "The Movement to Abolish the Electoral College" (master's thesis, Stanford University, Aug. 1948), 84–108.

86. As discussed in Chapter 4, it was also widely known that southern Democrats in Congress opposed a national popular vote.

87. *WP,* Nov. 30, 1913. According to one of his biographers, Norris personally favored a national popular vote but did not think it politically feasible because both small and southern states would oppose it. Norman Zucker, *George W. Norris: Gentle Knight of American Democracy* (Urbana, IL, 1966), 36.

88. *WP,* Dec. 6, 1922; Feb. 16, 1923; Dec. 27, 1930; May 22, 1934; *NYT,* Nov. 19, Dec. 7, and Dec. 17, 1922; Mar. 22, 1933; Feb. 15 and 17, 1934; May 22, 23, and 27, 1934; Alfred Lief, *Democracy's Norris: The Biography of a Lonely Crusader* (New York, 1939), 433–434; Richard Lowitt, *George W. Norris: The Triumph of a Progressive, 1933–44* (Urbana, IL, 1978), 50–51; Richard L. Neuberger and Stephen B. Kahn, *Integrity: The Life of George W. Norris* (New York, 1937), 273–274; George W. Norris, *Fighting Liberal: The Autobiography of George W. Norris* (New York, 1945), 332–336; Zucker, *Norris: Gentle Knight,* 35–37; 78 Cong. Rec. 8937–8948 (1934); S.J. Res. 29, 73rd Cong. 1st Sess., Mar. 13, 1933. Norris's 1933 resolution was never voted on in the House.

89. Peirce and Longley, *The People's President,* 146; U.S. Congress, House of Representatives, Committee on Election of President, Vice President, and Representatives in Congress, *Proposed Constitutional Amendment Providing for the Election of President and Vice President, Hearing, March 14, 1930, on H.J. Res. 106,* 71st Cong. 2nd Sess. 2–4, 14–41 (1930); Bugh, *Electoral College Reform,* 240–241. According to Bugh, 63 percent of all amendments proposed for electoral reform from 1931 to 1960 were for a proportional system. Bugh, "The Challenge of Contemporary Electoral College Reform," in Bugh, *Electoral College Reform,* 88.

90. Marion D. Irish, "The Southern One-Party System and National Politics," *Journal of Politics* 4, no. 1 (Feb. 1942): 80–94. Garner had declared his candidacy before Roosevelt announced his desire for a third term. He was subsequently replaced as a vice presidential candidate by Henry Wallace, a stalwart of the party's liberal wing. There had not been a southerner in the White House since Andrew Johnson.

91. *NYT,* July 17, 1944; *WP,* June 14, July 22, and Aug. 7, 1944; *Chicago Defender,* June 17, 1944; Frank P. Huddle, "The Electoral College: Historical Review and Proposals for Reform," in *Editorial Research Reports 1944,* vol. 2 (Washington, DC, 1944), 97–114. Southerners were also mollified by the convention's decision to replace the left-liberal vice president, Henry Wallace, with Missouri senator Harry Truman. Kari Frederickson, *The Dixiecrat Revolt and the End of the Solid South, 1932–1968* (Chapel Hill, NC, 2001), 38–39.

92. Huddle, "The Electoral College," 99–114; 90 Cong. Rec. 6629–6636 (1944); *NYT,* Dec. 19, 1944. Some southerners, like Senator Claude Pepper of Florida, feared that the actions contemplated by Texas and several other states would lead to electoral reforms that would prove harmful to southern interests. In the Senate debate of June 23, 1944, several senators, including Pepper, seemed to confuse the Celler-Guffey proposal with William Langer's resolution calling for a national popular vote; the research report by Huddle, requested by Congress, repeated that confusion.

93. Frederickson, *Dixiecrat Revolt,* 67–186. For a colorful account of the 1948 rebellion, and its sources, see Glenn Feldman, *The Great Melding: War, the Dixiecrat Rebellion, and the Southern Model for America's New Conservatism* (Tuscaloosa, 2015), 188–278. The 1948 revolt was less an attempt to build a new party than to influence federal policy through a presidential election: the Dixiecrats did not run candidates for state or local offices. Their chances of success were increased by a rebellion of the left wing of the Democratic party, which nominated former vice president Henry Wallace as the candidate of the Progressive Party. Wallace won no electoral votes, although nationally he garnered nearly as many votes as Thurmond.

94. "Should Congress Adopt the Pending Plan for Direct Election of the President?," *Congressional Digest* 28, no. 8/9 (Aug.–Sept., 1949): 222.

95. Regarding Lodge, see Henry Cabot Lodge, *The Storm Has Many Eyes: A Personal Narrative* (New York, 1973), 68–69, 228–229; William J. Miller, *Henry Cabot Lodge: A Biography* (New York, 1967), esp. 187–208. Regarding Gossett, see Drew Pearson's syndicated column in the *Spokane Daily Chronicle,* Feb. 25, 1948; Jason M. Ward, *Defending White Democracy: The Making of a Segregationist Movement and the Remaking of Racial Politics, 1936–1965* (Chapel Hill, NC, 2011), 125; *CDT,* Apr. 3, 1946; *Southern Israelite,* May 6, 1949. Regarding Gossett's anti-Semitism, see also Ed Lee Gossett Papers, Accession no. 49, box 10, folders 48, 52, 56, Baylor Collections of Political Materials, W. R. Poage Legislative Library, Baylor University, Waco, TX.

96. *The Electoral "College" vs. The Will of the People: The Case for Reform (Statement of Hon. Henry Cabot Lodge, Jr. of Massachusetts in the Senate of the United States, January 1949)* (Washington, DC, 1949). Lodge's original proposal required that the presidency be awarded to the person who won the largest number of popular votes if there were

an electoral vote tie between the top candidates. The amended version provided that if no candidate reached 40 percent, a joint session of Congress would choose between the top two candidates. Regarding the 40 percent threshold, see 96 Cong. Rec. 1152–1155 (1950). See also Ruth C. Silva, "The Lodge-Gossett Resolution: A Critical Analysis," *American Political Science Review* 44, no. 1 (Mar. 1950): 88. The text of the original Lodge-Gossett bill can be found in *Congressional Digest* 28, no. 8/9 (Aug.–Sept. 1949): 199.

97. 95 Cong. Rec. 2891–2895 (1949).

98. Lodge, *The Electoral "College,"* 3–7, 10, 11; Peirce and Longley, *The People's President,* 146–147. Lodge reiterated many of these arguments in floor debates in January 1950. 96 Cong. Rec. 877–888 (1950). When first introduced in the Eightieth Congress, the resolution was S.J. Res. 200, but it became S.J. Res. 2 in 1949. New Jersey, Illinois, Wisconsin, and Michigan were also swing states in some years.

99. Lodge, *The Electoral "College,"* 4–5; 95 Cong. Rec. 2892 (1949); for another example of concerns about the left, see the statement of South Carolina senator Olin Johnston, 96 Cong. Rec. 1260 (1950). Regarding other minorities, see the discussion of Gossett's speech below as well as 96 Cong. Rec. 884 (1950) and the statement of Senator William Fulbright (Arkansas) in 96 Cong. Rec. 1162 (1950).

100. Lodge, *The Electoral "College,"* 4, 6; 95 Cong. Rec. 2895 (1949).

101. Lodge, *The Electoral "College,"* 6, 7, 18, 19; 96 Cong. Rec. 882–884 (1950). Estes Kefauver also alluded to the voting age in Georgia. 96 Cong. Rec. 1151 (1950). The voting age elsewhere in the United States was twenty-one. Lodge and other supporters of proportional elections repeatedly distinguished their plan from a national popular vote, which, they believed, would create inexorable pressures to have national suffrage requirements.

102. 96 Cong. Rec. 882 (1950); see also Lodge's letter to *NYT,* Jan. 18, 1949.

103. Lodge, *The Electoral "College,"* 12–26; Alexander Heard, *A Two-Party South?* (Chapel Hill, NC, 1952), 171. Only three of Lodge's co-sponsors were Republicans, one of whom (Wayne Morse of Oregon) would leave the party to become an independent in 1952. Several supportive newspapers, including the *Los Angeles Times* and the *Washington Post,* would have preferred a national popular vote but did not think that such a measure had a realistic chance of being enacted.

104. *Hearings before Subcommittee No. 1 of the Committee on the Judiciary, United States House of Representatives,* 81st Cong. 11–20 (1949). Gossett equated the "radical wing of organized labor" with the political action committee of the Congress of Industrial Organizations.

105. *Hearings before Subcommittee No. 1,* 17–18.

106. Both the majority and the minority reports are contained in H.R. Report 1011-81 (1949). A search for press coverage of Gossett's remarks yielded little. For one example, see *NYT,* Feb. 10, 1949.

107. 96 Cong. Rec. 1261–1263 (1950). Among those who shared Humphrey's views and backed Lodge's resolution was Matthew Neely, a long-serving liberal Democrat from West Virginia. See also Chapter 4.

108. Edward Sims, "Looking South," *Florence* (SC) *Morning News,* Feb. 15, 1949; *Dothan* (AL) *Eagle,* Mar. 12 and 30, 1948. For more critical southern perspectives, see the columns by John Temple Graves published in (among other places) the *Dothan Eagle,* Aug. 24 and Oct. 3, 1948. The first of these columns includes commentary by Charles W. Collins, author of the influential *Whither Solid South?,* who opposed Gossett's measure. Regarding Collins and his book, see also Chapter 5.
109. The fear that proportional representation would lead to extremism as it had in Europe in the interwar era surfaced frequently in public debate. See, for example, Lucius Wilmerding Jr., "Reform of the Electoral System," *Political Science Quarterly* 64, no. 1 (Mar. 1949): 1–23; Walter Lippmann, "Today and Tomorrow: Electing a President," *New York Herald-Tribune,* Mar. 6, 7, and 9, 1950. Lodge responded to Lippmann in a Mar. 25, 1950, letter to the editor of the *Boston Globe,* which published Lippmann's syndicated columns.
110. 96 Cong. Rec. 1064–1068, 1160 (1950). Ferguson illustrated his claim about federal control with the convoluted argument that S.J. Res. 2 would prevent the states from determining which candidates would be on the ballot because candidates would possess a constitutionally protected right to a certain share of each state's electoral votes.
111. 96 Cong. Rec. 1065–1066, 1069–1070, 1156–1157, 1267, 1269 (1950). Ferguson's alternative also specified that if no candidate obtained a majority of electoral votes, the decision would be made by a joint session of Congress. Kefauver's support for reform stemmed partly from his desire to avoid the type of chaos created by the southern revolts in 1944 and 1948. *Congressional Digest* 28, no. 8/9 (Aug.–Sept. 1949): 204–206.
112. 96 Cong. Rec. 1275–1278 (1950). For a multivariate analysis of the vote, see Mark J. McKenzie, "Systemic Biases Affecting Congressional Voting on Electoral College Reform," in Bugh, *Electoral College Reform,* 102–105. Only two southerners, both from Virginia, voted against S.J. Res. 2, and only one (the noted left-liberal, Claude Pepper of Florida) voted in favor of the national popular vote proposals. According to *New York Times* columnist Arthur Krock, the Virginians feared that minorities in the North would still retain power and believed that the resolution would contribute to a diminution of state power. Krock, "The Proposed Changes in Counting Electors," *NYT,* Feb. 3, 1950. Regarding the surprise of observers, see Krock, "Many Questions Raised by Electoral Reforms," *NYT,* Mar. 11, 1950.
113. In an unusual step, signaling the importance of the measure and the unusual divisions among liberals, the Rules Committee heard testimony from three senators (Lodge, Kefauver, and Humphrey) and from former representative Clarence Lea. 96 Cong. Rec. 877 (1950); *Congressional Quarterly Almanac, 81st Congress, 2nd Session 1950* (Washington, DC, 1951), D160; *Baltimore Afro-American,* Mar. 11, 1950; *NYT,* Mar. 10, 1950; Louis Lautier, "In the Nation's Capital," *Cleveland Call and Post,* Mar. 11, 1950; *WP,* Mar. 10, 1950; *WP,* Feb. 28, 1950; *Public Papers of the Presidents of the United States: Harry S. Truman, 1950* (Washington, DC, 1965), 194. Truman had opposed Lodge-Gossett in early 1949 but shifted his position after the Senate vote.

114. Krock, "Many Questions." In 1936 the Democratic Party had jettisoned its "two-thirds rule" for presidential nominations, effectively removing a southern veto of potential candidates. There was widespread concern that, under Lodge-Gossett, southerners would gain enough power within the party to reinstate the rule.

115. H.R. Report No. 1011-81, at 27–32 (1949).

116. Rather than acknowledge that the phrase was a shorthand used most often in reference to the South, the majority report defined "the solid states" as follows: "This term applies to those States whose people, for reasons satisfactory to themselves, repeatedly vote for the same party in successive elections pretty much in disregard of the changing issues that are involved." H.R. Report No. 1011-81, at 18–19 (1949).

117. H.R. Report No. 1011-81, at 28–32 (1949). Case mentioned that the Fourteenth Amendment contained a similar provision but that it had never been enforced; it specified that a state's representation in Congress would be reduced if the state denied the right to vote to adult male citizens aged twenty-one or older. Case acknowledged that his "suggested amendment would make the adoption of the Lodge-Gossett resolution more difficult." Case's political analysis of the potential consequences of Lodge-Gossett was given academic support in Silva, "The Lodge-Gossett Resolution," esp. 93–98.

118. WP, Feb. 17, 1950; letter to the editor from James Loeb Jr., WP, Feb. 19, 1950; WP, Mar. 10, 1950; NYT, July 13, 1950; NYT, July 23, 1950.

119. The African-American press in the South had expressed some cautious interest in the Lodge-Gossett measure because it would eliminate winner-take-all and encourage Republicans to compete for votes in the region, but as columnist Louis Lautier wrote early in 1950, "the effects of other provisions need careful study." Louis Lautier, "In the Nation's Capital," Norfolk (VA) Journal and Guide, Oct. 30, 1948, and Feb. 11, 1950; Atlanta Daily World, July 10, 1949, and Feb. 24, 1950.

120. Baltimore Afro-American, Feb. 11, 1950. The story was written from unattributed sources, and Mitchell had been a reporter at the newspaper early in his career.

121. Memorandum from John A. Davis to Clarence M. Mitchell, Feb. 28, 1950, in Denton L. Watson, ed., The Papers of Clarence Mitchell Jr., vol. 4 (Athens, GA, 2010), 597–602; Clarence Mitchell Jr., Monthly Report of the Labor Secretary (Mar. 3, 1950), in Papers of Clarence Mitchell Jr., 3:154, 157; Clarence Mitchell Jr., Monthly Report of the Labor Secretary (Aug. 31, 1950), in Papers of Clarence Mitchell Jr., 3:179–181; Denton L. Watson, Lion in the Lobby: Clarence Mitchell Jr.'s Struggle for the Passage of Civil Rights Laws (New York, 1990), 329–331; Cleveland Call and Post, July 29, 1950.

122. H.R. Report No. 1011-81, at 30–31 (1949); Gladstone Williams, "Facts behind the Lodge Amendment," Atlanta Constitution, Feb. 6, 1950. See also Ruth C. Silva, "Reform of the Electoral System," Review of Politics 14, no. 3 (July 1952): 394–407.

123. WP, Mar. 2, 1950. South Carolina senator Olin Johnston used language similar—and in places identical—to Gossett's in the Senate debates. 96 Cong. Rec. 1260 (1950). See also the language and political sentiments in Charles W. Collins, Whither Solid South? A Study in Politics and Race Relations (New Orleans, 1948).

124. *NYT*, Mar. 10, 1950; journal entry, May 5, 1950, Henry Cabot Lodge Jr., papers II, Confidential Journal, reel 17, Massachusetts Historical Society.

125. The Lodge-Gossett plan was viewed as a democratic advance not only because it would have instituted proportional elections but also because it would have eliminated electors and prevented elections from devolving on the House.

126. *NYT*, Nov. 5, 1940; Feb. 28, 1950; "Liberals and Electoral Reform," *The Nation*, Mar. 18, 1950, 244–245. Regarding disagreements among liberals, see also a letter to the editor from Lucy Waters Lonergan, *WP*, Feb. 24, 1950, as well as *WP*, Feb. 28, 1950. An example of liberals being charged with hypocrisy can be found in Gladstone Williams, "Pressure Groups Fight Vote Change," *Atlanta Constitution*, Feb. 23, 1950.

127. *New Republic*, Feb. 17, 1950, 5–7; *Hearings before Subcommittee No. 1 of the Committee on the Judiciary, United States House of Representatives*, 81st Cong. 305–306 (statement of James Loeb Jr.).

128. The *New York Times* referred to the procedure as a "take-it-or-leave-it showdown" and doubted that H.J. Res. 2 could get the two-thirds vote needed for passage. *NYT*, July 14, 1950.

129. The official record of this debate appears to contain a mix of speeches actually delivered on the floor and written statements submitted afterward. 96 Cong. Rec. 10413–10428 (1950). Midway through the debate (10421), Case asked for and received unanimous consent that all members be able "to extend their remarks at this point in the Record." As printed in the Congressional Record, Gossett's opening presentation seems far too long for him to have presented it orally, given the time limits set for debate; it also seems unlikely that he would have read aloud pages of his earlier testimony. Presumably, he summarized his views orally and extended his remarks with a written document. See Wm. Holmes Brown, Charles W. Johnson, and John V. Sullivan, *House Practice: A Guide to the Rules, Precedents, and Procedures of the House* (Washington, DC, 2011), 374–378; *Hearings before Subcommittee No. 1 of the Committee on the Judiciary, United States House of Representatives*, 81st Cong. (1949), 11–20.

130. 96 Cong. Rec. 10414–10417 (1950).

131. 96 Cong. Rec. 10416–10417 (1950).

132. 96 Cong. Rec. 10419 (1950). Herter invoked Lodge several times and mentioned Gossett hardly at all. Herter expressed doubts that the resolution would be approved but believed that something close to it would gain congressional endorsement in the future.

133. 96 Cong. Rec. 10417, 10420, 10422–10425 (1950).

134. *CQ Almanac*, 81st Congress, 2nd Sess., 389; 96 Cong. Rec. 10427–10428 (1950); Gary Bugh, "Representation in Congressional Efforts to Amend the Presidential Election System," in Bugh, *Electoral College Reform*, 12; McKenzie, "Systemic Biases," 105.

135. *Dallas Morning News*, July 18, 1950; *Cleveland Call and Post*, July 29, 1950.

136. *Hearings before Subcommittee No. 1 of the Committee on the Judiciary, United States House of Representatives*, 82nd Cong. 307 (1951).

137. "Electoral Reform," in *Congressional Quarterly Almanac, 84th Congress, 2nd Session, 1956* (Washington, DC, 1957), 2–3. Peirce and Longley, *The People's President,* 151–153. Kefauver was the Democratic candidate for vice president in 1956 and was one of only three southern senators who refused to sign the Southern Manifesto. Kefauver and Daniel reprised the political roles of Lodge and Gossett. Like Lodge, Kefauver personally favored a national popular vote, but he believed that it was a "political impossibility" because so many small states would lose influence; he was prepared to accept nationally "uniform qualifications" for voting. Daniel, in contrast, opposed uniform suffrage requirements and, in debate, raised—as had many others—the symbolic issue of the voting age in Georgia. 102 Cong. Rec. 5136–5139 (1956).

138. Regarding national popular vote proposals, see Chapter 4. Humphrey's compromise proposal would have given the plurality winner of each state two electoral votes; all other electoral votes (435 in total) would be divided among candidates according to the proportion of the national popular vote that each received. Humphrey made clear that his preference was for a national popular vote, but he did not think such a resolution could be passed. He was a co-sponsor of the Kefauver-Daniel proposal for proportional elections. 102 Cong. Rec. 2400–2402, 5365–5372 (1956).

139. "Electoral Reform," 3–4.

140. Wilmerding, "Reform of the Electoral System," 1–23; see also Lucius Wilmerding Jr., *The Electoral College* (New Brunswick, NJ, 1958); Lippmann, "Today and Tomorrow."

141. Mundt replied to objections about malapportioned districts by pointing out that Congress had the power to mandate that congressional districts be contiguous and of similar size. His critics noted that Congress had, in the past, enacted but not enforced such measures and that enforcement would depend on the willingness of majority parties to reject gerrymanders that worked to their advantage. 102 Cong. Rec. 5232–5234 (1956). For tabular data revealing how unequally populated congressional and legislative districts were in 1960, see J. Douglas Smith, *On Democracy's Doorstep: The Inside Story of How the Supreme Court Brought "One Person, One Vote" to the United States* (New York, 2014), 289–292.

142. Peirce and Longley, *The People's President,* 136–139. Mundt also advanced a more theoretical argument that Congress and the president should be elected by the same constituencies, which were geographically based districts.

143. 102 Cong. Rec. 5137–5138, 5146–5165, 5231–5254, 5332–5337, 5426–5440, 5569, 5573–5575, 5672–5674 (1956); *WP,* Mar. 21, 1956; *CDT,* Mar. 16, 1956; Peirce and Longley, *The People's President,* 138–139, 151–153. The hybrid plan included a provision requiring electors to vote as they had pledged to vote.

144. *WP,* Mar. 26 and 27, 1956; *CDT,* Mar. 16, 1956. For other opinions, see *NYT,* Mar. 25, 1956; *Austin Statesman,* Mar. 22, 1956; *Boston Globe* (hereafter cited as *BG*), Mar. 26, 1956.

145. 102 Cong. Rec. 5233–5234, 5245–5253 (1956); *WP,* Mar. 21, 1956; *NYT,* Mar. 25, 1956; Peirce and Longley, *The People's President,* 138–139, 151–153.

146. 102 Cong. Rec. 5243–5244 (1956). Ongoing African-American concern about proportional elections is discussed in Roy Wilkins, "The Future of the Negro Voter in the United States," *Journal of Negro Education* 26, no. 3 (Summer 1967): 429.

147. 102 Cong. Rec. 5159, 5254 (1956); Peirce and Longley, *The People's President*, 138–139, 151–153; "Electoral Reform," *CQ Almanac*, 84th Congress, 2nd Sess., 5. See also the letter opposing various district and proportional schemes, from ten prominent political scientists, including John A. Davis, Samuel H. Beer, and Arthur Schlesinger Jr., *NYT*, July 17, 1955, and inserted into the 102 Cong. Rec. Appendix A2779 (1956) by Sen. Paul Douglas (D-IL) on Mar. 29, 1956.

148. 102 Cong. Rec. 5574 (1956). Kennedy's stance was unusual among northern liberals. He displayed little interest in a national popular vote and, more broadly, claimed to see no compelling need to alter the system. 102 Cong. Rec. 5150, 5156, 5159–5160 (1956).

149. "Electoral Reform," 2–6; 102 Cong. Rec. 5148–5149 (1956); *NYT*, Mar. 25, 1956; Peirce and Longley, *The People's President*, 138–139, 143, 151–153; *CDT*, Mar. 28, 1956; Conrad Joyner and Ronald Pedderson, "The Electoral College Revisited," *Southwestern Social Science Quarterly* 45, no. 1 (June 1964): 32–34; Allan P. Sindler, "Presidential Election Methods and Urban-Ethnic Interests," *Law and Contemporary Problems* 27, no. 2 (Spring 1962): 228; McKenzie, "Systemic Biases," 105–106. Technically, the vote in 1956 was to substitute the hybrid plan for the proportional plan reported by the Judiciary Committee, but it served as an indicator of the strength of support for both measures.

150. Peirce and Longley, *The People's President*, 153–156. Kefauver died unexpectedly in 1963.

151. Peirce and Longley, *The People's President*, 139–144; *NYT*, Mar. 13, 1959; Mundt, letter to *NYT*, Nov. 22, 1964. Some observers during this period argued that Congress ought to limit its attention to reforms that were politically feasible, such as abolishing "the office of elector." See, for example, *WP*, Dec. 25, 1960.

152. Those beliefs were shared by many of the liberal and moderate senators who supported Lodge in 1949–1950. The progressive sentiments of Lodge, Kefauver, Humphrey, and several other supporters of S.J. Res. 2 were evident in their stated preference for a national popular vote.

153. To the consternation of the NAACP, some liberals, including Humphrey, Kefauver, Mike Mansfield, and Richard Neuberger, continued to support versions of the proportional elections proposal into the mid-1950s. Watson, *Lion in the Lobby*, 331–332.

154. Notably, the regional lineup among Democrats in the 1950s was the reverse of what it had been in the 1870s and 1880s. During the earlier period (as discussed in previous sections of this chapter), northern Democrats favored district or proportional elections while southerners opposed any reforms that involved federal mandates.

155. Humphrey, who supported S.J. Res. 31, nonetheless opposed the hybrid plan, stating that he could not endorse district elections; he noted that there had been no changes in the boundaries of Minnesota's state legislative districts since 1912. 102 Cong. Rec. 5371–5372 (1956). In testimony to the House Judiciary Committee in 1951, Clarence Lea also emphasized that widespread inequalities in the populations of different dis-

tricts undermined the promise of district elections. *Hearings before Subcommittee No. 1 of the Committee on the Judiciary, United States House of Representatives*, 82nd Cong. (1951), 17–18.

156. 113 Cong. Rec. 2042 (1967).

4. "A POPULATION ANOMALOUS" AND A NATIONAL POPULAR VOTE, 1800–1960

1. 29 Annals of Cong. 158, 164, 177 (1815–1816).
2. This tracked the suffrage requirement already in the Constitution for elections to the House.
3. 29 Annals of Cong. 213–219 (1815–1816). The Senate debate regarding Lacock's proposal also appeared under the title "Interesting Sketch of a Debate in the Senate," *Daily National Intelligencer* (Washington, DC), June 28, 1816.
4. 29 Annals of Cong. 220–221 (1815–1816). Lacock's original motion was to recommit the resolution "with instructions to report an amendment" providing for a popular election; he accepted Dana's suggestion that it be a motion for an "inquiry."
5. 29 Annals of Cong. 221–222 (1815–1816).
6. 29 Annals of Cong. 223–224 (1815–1816).
7. 29 Annals of Cong. 223–225 (1815–1816).
8. 29 Annals of Cong. 225 (1815–1816).
9. 29 Annals of Cong. 225 (1815–1816). Lacock's background offers little help in explaining his initiative on this issue. He had served as a justice of the peace as well as a member of the state legislature before entering the House in 1810 and the Senate in 1813. He was known as an advocate of public education, road construction, and war with Britain in 1812, and he later became an ardent promoter of canals and Henry Clay's American System. For biographical information, see J. M. S., "General Abner Lacock: United States Senator from Pennsylvania from 1813 to 1819," *Pennsylvania Magazine of History and Biography* 4, no. 2 (1880): 202; Harry Houtz, "Abner Lacock, Beaver County's Exponent of the American System," *Western Pennsylvania Historical Magazine* 22, no. 3 (1939): 177–187. James Kehl describes him as an ambitious, but not very adept, politician and as an unimpressive public speaker. James A. Kehl, *Ill Feeling in the Era of Good Feeling: Western Pennsylvania Political Battles, 1815–1825* (Pittsburgh, PA, 1956), 111–114.
10. 29 Annals of Cong. 225 (1815–1816).
11. 29 Annals of Cong. 226 (1815–1816).
12. 29 Annals of Cong. 226 (1815–1816).
13. Throughout this book, I have employed the phrase "national popular vote" to refer to an election in which the ballots cast by all voters, throughout the United States, would be counted to produce a single national tally. An NPV system could have either a majority or a plurality winner, and it could provide for either a runoff election or a resort to Congress if no candidate gained an outright majority. There would be no electors or electoral votes. Many other works about the Electoral College have used the phrase "direct vote" or "direct popular vote" to describe such proposals. The

"direct vote" language, however, can generate confusion—and often has done so—because it was also applied (in the nineteenth century and part of the twentieth) to proposals that attempted to eliminate electors while retaining electoral votes as well as the constitutional framework for allocating them among the states. Thomas Hart Benton, for example, always referred to his plan as calling for a "direct vote of the people," but in fact he was advocating district elections and leaving the state apportionment of electoral votes intact. (See Chapter 2.) The phrase "national popular vote" serves to clearly distinguish a true national plebiscite from numerous other "direct vote" alternatives. By the 1960s, "direct election" had come to refer only to an NPV, and I thus have used the terms interchangeably in my discussions of the 1960s and later periods (Chapters 5–7).

14. Quotation from Cong. Globe, 42nd Cong. 3rd Sess. 1602 (1873). Roughly eighty such proposals were introduced over this long span, but many were duplicates (introduced by the same person in different years) or companion resolutions (introduced in different branches of Congress during the same session). Herman Ames, in his compendium of proposed amendments to the Constitution, found thirty-seven NPV proposals from the nation's founding through 1889. Herman V. Ames, "The Proposed Amendments to the Constitution of the United States during the First Century of Its History," *Annual Report of the American Historical Association* 2 (1896): 87–89. My own research, however, has unearthed several possible nineteenth-century amendment proposals that were not included in Ames's listings while also determining that at least a few of those listed by Ames did not, in fact, call for a national popular vote. The errors in Ames have been imported into studies that have relied on his work, such as Neal R. Peirce and Lawrence D. Longley, *The People's President: The Electoral College in American History and the Direct Vote Alternative,* rev. ed. (New Haven, CT, 1981). These errors are often linked to the ambiguity of the phrase "direct popular vote," as discussed in the previous endnote. In addition, some proposals from the pre-1850 period were worded in such a way that it is difficult to ascertain what exactly was being proposed. Where possible, I have relied on congressional debates for clarification, but some proposals were never debated. A less helpful sequel to Ames's work is H. Doc. No. 551-70, "Proposed Amendments to the Constitution," (1929). For the twentieth century, I have relied primarily on the thorough, annual listing offered, for the years from 1899 through 2010, in Gary E. Bugh, ed., *Electoral College Reform: Challenges and Possibilities* (Farnham, UK, 2010), 239–253. Bugh finds twenty-four such proposals offered between 1900 and 1928, and another twenty-three between 1929 and 1960. Bugh offers additional details, as well as a careful discussion of the complexities of these listings, in "The Challenge of Contemporary Electoral College Reform," in Bugh, *Electoral College Reform,* 77–93.

15. The uncertainty here stems from ambiguities in the wording of some proposals, as discussed in the preceding endnotes. Ames, for example, identifies amendment proposals from Daniel Garnsey of New York as well as Jackson supporters Charles Kellogg of New York and Edward Livingston of Louisiana as favoring

a national popular vote. But my reading of the sources indicates that this was not true of either Garnsey's or Kellogg's proposals, and I have my doubts about Livingston's. 2 Part 1 Cong. Deb. 1377–1378, 1464, 1541 (1826) and 2 Part 2 Cong. Deb. 1839–1840, 1857–1859 (1826). Similarly, an Alabama resolution introduced in the House and the Senate on Feb. 4–5, 1828, proves, on close inspection, not to be proposing a national popular vote. U.S. House Journal, 20th Cong. 1st Sess. 246 (1828), U.S. Senate Journal, 20th Cong. 1st Sess. 134 (1828). I am uncertain too about the proposals of Jacksonians George Mortimer Bibb of Kentucky (1833) and Balie Peyton of Tennessee (1835). See Cong. Globe, 23rd Cong. 1st Sess. 20, 405 (1833–1834); 10 Part 1 Reg. Deb. 29–30 (1833–1834); 10 Part 2 Reg. Deb 1813–1814 (1834); Cong. Globe, 24th Cong. 1st Sess. 165 (1835–1836). For Ames's listings of proposals for a "general direct vote," see Ames, "Amendments," 87–88, 340–346.

16. U.S. House Journal, 19th Cong. 1st Sess. 115 (1825–1826). Although the wording contains some ambiguity, this proposal does appear to have been for an NPV.

17. 2 Part 1 Reg. Deb. 1463 (1825–1826).

18. U.S. House Journal, 19th Cong. 2nd Sess. 317 (1826–1827); 5 Reg. Deb. 362, 365 (1828–1829). For the text of the Ohio resolution that prompted Wright's proposal, see H.R. Doc. No. 109, "Resolutions of the Legislature of the State of Ohio on the Subject of Amending the Constitution" (1827). Wright did not identify himself as an Adams supporter, but he did join the National Republicans, a short-lived anti-Jackson party.

19. 5 Reg. Deb. 361–368 (1829). The reference to "political justice" also appears in the Ohio resolution cited above.

20. *Speech of Mr. Thomas Whipple, of New Hampshire, on the Proposition to Amend the Constitution of the United States, Delivered in the House of Representatives of the United States, Mar. 26, 1826* (Washington, DC, 1826), 12, 16.

21. 41 Annals of Cong. 18th Cong. 1st Sess. 181–182 (1823–1824).

22. Andrew Jackson, "First Annual Message," in *A Compilation of the Messages and Papers of the Presidents, 1789–1907,* ed. James D. Richardson (New York, 1908), 2:442–462.

23. 42 Annals of Cong. 1st Sess. 366–367 (1824); see also 40 Annals of Cong. 2nd Sess. 213 (1822–1823). It was notable that Dickerson did not allude to the interests of small states, although he had spent years grappling with state-size issues while promoting district elections. See Chapter 2.

24. Ames ("Amendments," 88–89) claims that there were twenty-five "direct" (and thus NPV) amendments proposed in the post–Civil War era, a number that is repeated in Peirce and Longley, *People's President,* 163. My examination of Ames's listings suggests that this figure is too high. Some of the resolutions listed are not for a national popular vote, whereas others are ambiguous in their wording (for instance, calling for a "direct vote"—meaning without electors—while not specifying that the votes be totaled nationally). Records clarifying the intent of some resolutions could not be located. See also notes 13 and 14 above. Peirce and Longley (163) repeat Ames's assertion that most of these proposals came from representatives from the "western

states." I find no evidence to support that claim; nor is it clear which states were considered "western."

25. It is possible that Ashley's was the second, and not the first, NPV proposal to appear after the Civil War. On Dec. 11, 1865, a month before Ashley made his proposal, Republican representative Thomas Jenckes of Rhode Island introduced a resolution calling for a direct vote for president and vice president, with a plurality winner; it guaranteed the right to vote in these elections to literate males, age twenty-one or older, without felony convictions. It is not clear whether this proposal was for an NPV or a direct election without electors. Cong. Globe, 39th Cong. 1st Sess. 18 (1865–1866); U.S. House Journal 39th Cong. 1st Sess. 38 (1865). Jenckes's proposal, like Ashley's, was referred to the Committee on the Judiciary.

26. Cong. Globe, 39th Cong. 1st Sess. 349 (1866); U.S. House Journal, 39th Cong. 1st Sess. 174, 207–213 (1866); Cong. Globe, 40th Cong. 2nd Sess. 2713–2716, 2722 (1868). Ashley's proposal did impose a one-year residency requirement for voting in any state or territory. Whether Ashley's equation of citizenship and suffrage meant that he favored enfranchising women is unclear, but the argument that citizenship brought with it the right to vote (and thus that women ought to be enfranchised) was a prominent one by the 1870s. It was not uncommon for NPV proposals of this era to limit presidents to a single term or to provide for a runoff election in the event that no candidate won a majority.

27. Cong. Globe, 40th Cong. 2nd Sess. 2713–2722 (1867–1868).

28. Cong. Globe, 40th Cong. 3rd Sess. 1107–1108 (1868–1869).

29. Cong. Globe, 39th Cong. 2nd Sess. 1185 (1867–1868); U.S. Senate Journal, 39th Cong. 2nd Sess. 246 (1867–1868); Charles Sumner, "A Single Term for the President, and Choice by Direct Vote of the People," Remarks in the Senate, Feb. 11, 1867, in *Charles Sumner: His Complete Works,* vol. 14 (Boston, 1909), 278–281; Cong. Globe, 42nd Cong. 2nd Sess. 4036 (1872); Cong. Globe, 42nd Cong. 3rd Sess. 632 (1872–1873); 2 Cong. Rec., 43rd Cong. 1st Sess. (1873–1874). Sumner's 1872 proposal also called for limiting presidents to a single four-year term and for elimination of the vice presidency. Sumner was actively engaged in numerous issues during these years, many of them international, and was not particularly focused on election reform. For a detailed account, see David H. Donald, *Charles Sumner* (New York, 1996), pt. 2, "Charles Sumner and the Rights of Man." Regarding conflicts within the Republican Party, see Heather Cox Richardson, *To Make Men Free: A History of the Republican Party* (New York, 2014), 79–126.

30. Cong. Globe, 42nd Cong. 3rd Sess. 82, 334, 353, 1425 (1872–1873).

31. Cong. Globe, 42nd Cong. 3rd Sess. 1601–1604 (1873).

32. 10 Cong. Rec. 391 (1880); 13 Cong. Rec. 241 (1882); 17 Cong. Rec. 884 (1886); 19 Cong. Rec. 209 (1888); *CDT,* Jan. 30, 1880; Peter H. Argersinger, "Electoral Reform and Partisan Jugglery," *Political Science Quarterly* 119 (2004): 502–503. Other proposals for a "direct vote of the people" were also brought forward in the mid- and late 1870s, but it is not clear whether they aimed to produce a national popular vote or simply

to eliminate the role of electors. For example, see 4 Cong. Rec. 756 (1876); 6 Cong. Rec. 233 (1877); U.S. House Journal, 45th Cong. 1st Sess. 128 (1877); 6 Cong. Rec. 250 (1877); 7 Cong. Rec. 737 (1878); U.S. House Journal, 45th Cong. 2nd Sess. 348 (1878). See also note 24 above.

33. *CDT,* Feb. 9, 1875; *CDT,* Jan. 30, 1880; *CDT,* Dec. 26, 1892; *WP,* Nov. 6, 1884, and Apr. 18, 1891; John A. Roebling, "Is Our Method of Electing the President Republican?," *American Journal of Politics* (Nov. 1892): 481–487 (Roebling was the grandson of the legendary engineer and bridge builder); *NYT,* Dec. 29, 1892. See also F. A. P. Barnard, William Purcell, H. L. Dawes, Roger A. Pryor and Z. B. Vance, "How Shall the President Be Elected?," *NAR,* Feb. 1885, 122; and Samuel T. Spear, "The Secondary Electoral College," *The Independent,* Mar. 15, 1877, 3.

34. 11 Cong. Rec. 1450–1459 (1881); "Our Electoral Machinery," *NAR,* Oct. 1873, 396–397; *WP,* Dec. 30, 1892; H. L. Dawes, "How Shall the President Be Elected?," *NAR,* Feb. 1885, 113–118.

35. Richard H. Dana Jr., "Points in American Politics," *NAR,* Jan. 1877, 10–11. The counterargument, as the *Chicago Daily Tribune* pointed out, was that winner-take-all was a greater stimulus to fraud because a few well-stuffed ballot boxes could alter the destination of all of a state's electoral votes. *CDT,* Jan. 30, 1880.

36. *WP,* Nov. 6, 1884.

37. "Our Electoral Machinery," 396–397; *WP,* Dec. 30, 1892; Dana, "Points," 10–11; *CDT,* Feb. 9, 1875, and Dec. 13, 1876. Regarding Oliver Morton, see Chapter 3 as well as *NYT,* June 8, 1877.

38. *NYT,* June 8, 1877; *WP,* Nov. 6, 1884.

39. Many of the reform proposals put forward after 1876 were referred to a joint commission, which ended up focusing almost exclusively on electoral count issues. *Proceedings of the Electoral Commission: Appointed under the Act of Congress Approved Jan. 29, 1877, Entitled "An act to provide for and regulate the counting of votes for President and Vice-President, and the decisions of questions arising thereon, for the term commencing Mar. 4, 1877,"* 44th Cong., 2nd Sess. (Washington, DC, 1877). See also Chapter 3.

40. See Chapter 3.

41. See Chapter 3 regarding the muted response to the 1888 election.

42. For a list of the resolutions introduced, see Bugh, *Electoral College Reform,* 239–243. According to a congressional study that includes a somewhat murky list of amendments from the 1890s to 1928, eight NPV resolutions were introduced between 1906 and 1928. H.R. Doc. "Proposed Amendments to the Constitution," 70th Cong. No. 551, 46–50 (1929); see also H.J. Res. No. 45, 63rd Cong. (1918). Barkley does not appear in Bugh's listing of resolution sponsors, but he did introduce H.J. Res. No. 45 favoring an NPV on Apr. 8, 1913. 50 Cong. Rec. 135 (1913). See also Barkley's autobiography, *That Reminds Me* (New York, 1954), 275–277; Peirce and Longley, *The People's President,* 163.

43. In 1916, after a delayed count, Wilson was declared the victor in California by a few thousand votes (out of a million cast), which gave him the Electoral College

victory. Nationally he won by half a million votes. Socialist and prohibitionist candidates won 4 percent of the vote. The *New York World* survey asked whether respondents would favor replacing the Electoral College with a "direct popular vote." A majority of the respondents from northern and western states said that they favored such a change, but some interpreted the question to mean a "direct vote" rather than an NPV. *New York World*, Nov. 23, 1916; *St. Louis Post-Dispatch*, Nov. 23, 1916; *Lexington Herald*, Dec. 2, 1916. The responses from northern political leaders and other public figures offered a wide range of views regarding Electoral College abolition. Harvard's president emeritus Charles W. Eliot believed that "the present method . . . is working fairly well," a view shared by Nicholas Murray Butler of Columbia University. In the early 1920s, progressive Republicans devoted energy to a modest "direct vote" amendment that would have eliminated electors but retained electoral votes (and presumably could have been proportional or winner-take-all). Although this reform at first looked promising, it quickly faltered. *NYT*, Dec. 7, 1922; *NYT*, Feb. 16, 1923; *WP*, Dec. 6, 1922.

44. Throughout this period, Republicans may have found an NPV more attractive than district or proportional schemes because it would have taken from southern Democrats the ability to cast electoral votes in the name of disenfranchised African-Americans. But the fact that it would have also eliminated winner-take-all apparently outweighed that consideration. In 1916 former president William Howard Taft, a respondent to the *New York World*'s inquiry, maintained that he opposed an NPV because of the disenfranchisement of blacks in the South, but his reasoning was obscure. *New York World*, Nov. 23, 1916; *St. Louis Post-Dispatch*, Nov. 23, 1916.

45. H.R. Doc. "Proposed Amendments to the Constitution," 70th Cong. No. 551, 46–50 (1929); *CDT*, Oct. 29, 1907; *BG*, June 25, 1932; 75 Cong. Rec. 13812 (1932). See also Chapter 3.

46. Roebling, "Our Method," 487–490; John Handiboe, "Presidential Elections by Direct Popular Vote," *NAR*, Aug. 1900, 281–288; *WP*, Sept. 12, 1904; *CDT*, Oct. 28, 1907. The quotations from the *World* and the *Herald* were reprinted, along with the views of other newspapers, in the *St. Louis Post-Dispatch*, Nov. 19, 1916.

47. James R. Doolittle and Paul L. Haworth, "The Electoral System," *Political Science Quarterly* 19, no. 3 (Sept. 1904): 369–370; "The Verdict of the People," *NAR*, Dec. 1916, 813–819.

48. Simon Newcomb, "Our Antiquated Method of Electing a President," *NAR*, Jan. 1905, 16; *Austin Statesman*, Aug. 25, 1924; Richard L. Neuberger and Stephen B. Kahn, *Integrity: The Life of George W. Norris* (New York, 1937), 273–274.

49. *St. Louis Post-Dispatch*, Nov. 23, 1916.

50. Walter Clark, "The Electoral College and Presidential Suffrage," *University of Pennsylvania Law Review* 65 (June 1917): 745–746; Joseph E. Kallenbach, "Recent Proposals to Reform the Electoral College System," *American Political Science Review* 30, no. 5 (Oct. 1936): 928; *WP*, Dec. 30, 1892; Statement of Clarence F. Lea, Hearings on H.J. Res. 181, Committee on Election of President and Vice President,

70th Cong. 1st Sess., Jan. 27, 1928, 1–19. In the late 1940s, Hubert Humphrey and Henry Cabot Lodge were among those who voiced concern that the small states would doom the chances of an NPV.

51. Lindsay Rogers, "Why Preserve a Dying Institution?," *Forum* 92, no. 1 (Jan. 1937): 18–19.

52. *Sioux Falls* (SD) *Argus Leader,* Jan. 10, 1931; Oct. 5, 1932; May 17 and Dec. 11, 1934.

53. J. Hampden Dougherty, *The Electoral System of the United States* (New York, 1906), 397; "The Verdict of the People," *NAR,* Dec. 1916, 818–819; *NYT,* Nov. 19, 1916. Dougherty was an advocate of proportional elections.

54. *WP,* Nov. 14, 1916; *NYT,* Nov. 19 and 26, 1916. The ownership of the *Post* changed hands after 1904. (See its editorial on Sept. 12, 1904.)

55. *NYT,* Nov. 9, 1936; statement of Clarence Lea, Hearings on H.J. Res. 106, Committee on Election of President and Vice President, 71st Cong., 2nd Sess., Mar. 14, 1930, 25–27; Kallenbach, "Recent Proposals," 928.

56. 78 Cong. Rec. 8939, 8946, 8948 (1934). Fess, a former professor, indicated that he had long desired to see the system changed so that the popular vote could not be overridden by the electoral vote, but the problem "cannot be cured . . . [i]f we are still to maintain the State as a unit; and I do not believe we will ever be willing to give up using the State as a unit."

57. Clark, "The Electoral College," 745–746; *WP,* Nov. 14, 1916; *St. Louis Post-Dispatch,* Nov. 19, 1916.

58. *NYT,* Nov. 26, 1916; Nov. 9, 1936; see also 78 Cong. Rec. 8939 (1934).

59. *NYT,* Nov. 26, 1916; Clark, "The Electoral College," 745–746; *New York World,* Nov. 23, 1916.

60. Henry E. Tremain, *Sectionalism Unmasked* (New York, 1907), 105.

61. Tremain, *Sectionalism Unmasked,* 50–51. For an appreciative review of the book, see *The Cambridge* (MA) *Chronicle,* Dec. 14, 1907. Statements for years other than 1904 are based on calculations by the author from census and election data. The inequalities in the number of votes cast per electoral vote were frequently noted in newspapers. See, for examples, the *Newport* (RI) *Mercury,* Oct. 11 and Nov. 22, 1924; Drew Pearson, "Merry-Go-Round," *WP,* June 30, 1944.

62. Tremain, *Sectionalism Unmasked,* 90–100, 223–228; *New York World,* Nov. 23, 1916; *Newport Mercury,* July 9, 1921. The provision of section 2 of the Fourteenth Amendment providing for a reduction in representation if a state disenfranchised eligible voters has never been enforced by Congress. See George D. Zuckerman, "A Consideration of the History and Present Status of Section 2 of the Fourteenth Amendment," *Fordham Law Review* 30, no. 1 (Oct. 1961): 93–120. For a more recent discussion, see Richard Kreitner, "This Long-Lost Constitutional Clause Could Save the Right to Vote," *The Nation,* Jan. 12, 2015, 10. For early twentieth-century views, see Emmet O'Neal, "The Power of Congress to Reduce Representation in the House of Representatives and in the Electoral College," *NAR,* Oct. 1905, 530–543; Joseph W. Keifer, "Power of Congress to Reduce Representation in Congress and in the Electoral College: A Reply," *NAR,* Feb. 1906, 228–238. One of the issues in the earlier

debate was whether the Fifteenth Amendment had effectively repealed section 2 of the Fourteenth.

63. *WP,* Dec. 6, 1916; *NYT,* Dec. 4, 1916.

64. *NYT,* Dec. 5, 1916; *St. Louis Post-Dispatch,* Nov. 23, 1916.

65. Clark, "Electoral College," 745–746. Clark was an advocate of women's suffrage and appears to have favored a proportional allocation of electoral votes. For biographical information on Clark, see William S. Powell, ed., *Dictionary of North Carolina Biography* (Chapel Hill, NC, 1979–1996); Willis P. Whichard, "Clark, Walter McKenzie," http://www.anb.org/articles/11/11-00166.html; *American National Biography Online,* Feb. 2000.

66. *WP,* Nov. 14, 1916.

67. *NYT,* Nov. 9, 1936. Southern opposition to pressure for a national suffrage requirement also surfaced in 1950 in debates about the Lodge-Gossett bill and the Langer alternative. See, for example, the statement of Sen. Olin Johnston, 96 Cong. Rec. 1261–1262 (1950).

68. Bugh, *Electoral College Reform,* 239–243. Two Oklahoma Democrats also introduced resolutions in 1916, but Oklahoma was not part the Confederacy. One of those Democrats, Charles D. Carter, was Native American.

69. Harvey Rosenfeld, *Richmond Pearson Hobson: Naval Hero of Magnolia Grove* (Las Cruces, NM, 2001), 27–95; Richard F. Snow, "Richmond Pearson Hobson," *American Heritage,* Aug./Sept. 1979; Daniel Okrent, *Last Call: The Rise and Fall of Prohibition* (New York, 2010), 67–75.

70. Rosenfeld, *Hobson,* 125–150, 162–172, 183–186; Richard N. Sheldon, "Richmond Pearson Hobson as a Progressive Reformer," *Alabama Review* 25 (Oct. 1972): 243–248, 252–260; Okrent, *Last Call,* 54, 67–75, 81.

71. Bugh, *Electoral College Reform,* 239–243; H.J. Res. 162, 62nd Cong. (1912); H.J. Res. 382, 62nd Cong. (1913); H.J. Res. 383, 62nd Cong. (1913); H.J. Res. 6, H.J. Res. 13; H.J. Res. 14, 63rd Cong. (1913).

72. Rosenfeld, *Hobson,* 186–193; *NYT,* Dec. 12, 1913, and Oct. 14, 1913; Sheldon, "Hobson," 252; Walter E. Pittman Jr., *Navalist and Progressive: The Life of Richmond P. Hobson* (Manhattan, KS, 1981), 150–152.

73. Underwood State Campaign Committee, "Democratic Senatorial Campaign: The Issues and the Facts," 24–26, Southern Pamphlet Collection, University of North Carolina, Chapel Hill, Wilson Library Special Collections.

74. Rosenfeld, *Hobson,* 192, 197–248; Okrent, *Last Call,* 57, 61, 67–74, 79–81, 87–89, 92, 104–105, 180, 240, 252. A prohibition amendment introduced by Hobson was a precursor of the Eighteenth Amendment. Pittman, *Navalist and Progressive,* 110–111, discusses Hobson's lack of identification as a southerner; regarding Hobson's later career, see 129–178.

75. *New York World,* Nov. 23, 1916; *St. Louis Post-Dispatch,* Nov. 23, 1916. Governor N. E. Harris of Georgia supported dispensing with electors and having a direct vote within each state, a method that would preserve the existing allocation of electoral votes and thus southern influence. *New York World,* Nov. 23, 1916; *St. Louis Post-Dispatch,* Nov. 23, 1916.

76. For examples, see *Atlanta Constitution,* Jan. 18, 1901, and June 6, 1944; *New Advocate* (Baton Rouge), June 27, 1912; *Lexington* (KY) *Herald,* Dec. 2, 1916; *New Orleans Times-Picayune,* Dec. 25, 1922; *Austin Statesman,* Aug. 25, 1924. The New Orleans *Herald,* Dec. 7, 1922, favored direct elections and a "national direct primary" to take elections out of the hands of urban bosses and restore power to "country America," but that was probably not an endorsement of an NPV. The *Austin Statesman,* Nov. 21, 1916, acknowledged that the existing system had "many flaws" and that an NPV would stimulate turnout, but it noted that change would not come quickly because political party leaders were resistant to it. In 1937 the conservative African-American newspaper the *Atlanta Daily World* cited approvingly the view of Harvard professor W. Y. Elliott that a national popular vote would rouse the "'sleeping dog' of the southern racial question" and force the issue "into national politics," which "would be most dangerous." *Atlanta Daily World,* Jan. 4, 1937. The conclusions regarding southern newspapers here are based upon searches of digitized or otherwise indexed newspapers for the years between 1900 and 1950. The evidence, thus, is fragmentary.

77. 96 Cong. Rec. 1276–1279 (1950).

78. The proportion of seats in Congress (and thus electoral votes) held by representatives from the South remained quite steady between 1876 and 1950. Akhil R. Amar has written extensively about the links between slavery and the creation of the Electoral College. As discussed in the endnotes to Chapter 1, I am not convinced that the Electoral College was created to protect the slave states, but there is no doubt that the slave states (and later the South) played a critical role in preserving the Electoral College and the advantages it gave to white southerners. See, among other writings, Akhil R. Amar, *The Constitution Today: Timeless Lessons for the Issues of Our Era* (New York, 2016), 332–352.

79. As discussed in Chapter 2, the disproportionate influence given to the small states if an election went to the House played a significant role in antebellum reform debates. By the twentieth century, however, that concern had receded from view, given that no election had gone to the House since 1824.

80. Unfortunately, evidence of any kind is sparse because there were no opinion polls (before 1944) and no occasions (such as legislative debates or roll call votes) that obliged politicians to express their views on the subject. Further probes into the political histories of individual states might yield different conclusions.

81. Bugh, *Electoral College Reform,* 240; S.J. Res. 175, 64th Cong. (1916); *Sioux Falls Argus Leader,* Oct. 5, 1932. The paper retained this perspective in subsequent decades; for examples, see Nov. 27, 1944; Dec. 14, 1948; Nov. 20, 1960; Jan. 7, 1961; Sept. 12, 1970.

82. *Burlington* (VT) *Free Press,* Mar. 28, 1947; the *Free Press* endorsed an NPV as early as July 30, 1924, as well as on May 16, 1967. Vermont in the 1940s was a solidly Republican state. Small-state newspapers with a mixed, equivocal, or changeable stance toward an NPV included the *Newport Daily Mercury,* Oct. 11 and Nov. 22, 1924; Nov. 23, 1928; Oct. 18, 1940; Feb. 14, 1969; *Great Falls* (MT) *Tribune,* Apr. 27, 1930; Nov. 22, 1940; Jan. 12, 1968; Nov. 9, 1968; Sept. 22, 1969; *Provo* (UT) *Daily Herald,* Dec. 26, 1940; June 27, 1944; Dec. 10, 1948; Jan. 17, 1949; Jan. 27, 1966; May 27, 1968;

Nov. 18, 1968; Oct. 11, 1970. The *Newport Daily News* supported an NPV in the late 1960s: May 15, 1967; Sept. 11, 1968. My (unscientific) sample was restricted to newspapers that could be searched digitally.

83. *Albuquerque Journal*, June 16, 1933; Nov. 11, 1940. The paper remained an NPV supporter into the 1970s: see May 22, 1967; Nov. 10, 1968; Apr. 26, 1970.

84. As noted in Chapter 3, the congressional debates of the late 1940s and 1950s contained many more references to the "solid states" than to "southern" states, although everyone knew where all (or nearly all) of the solid states were located. More strikingly, discussions of the unevenness of suffrage requirements almost invariably mentioned the exceptional voting age in Georgia (which was eighteen) rather than the disenfranchisement of millions of African-Americans.

85. Jay G. Hayden, Washington correspondent for the *Detroit News*, noted in a syndicated column in 1944 that "senators from the south and the little western states would combine to defeat a move for equal popular voting for president." *Decatur* (IL) *Daily Review*, Nov. 22, 1944.

86. Michael Lansing, *Insurgent Democracy: The Nonpartisan League in North American Politics* (Chicago, 2015), x–xi, 8–10, 33, 97; Brenda G. Plummer, *In Search of Power: African Americans in the Era of Decolonization, 1956–74* (Cambridge, 2013), 36–37; James Erwin, *Declarations of Independence: Encyclopedia of American Autonomous and Secessionist Movements* (Westport, CT, 2007), 130–131. The scandal originated in Langer's attempts to fund-raise by soliciting state employees to subscribe to a newspaper he had started. This was legal under North Dakota law, but after state highway employees began to be paid with New Deal funds, a U.S. attorney charged Langer with a federal crime. After Langer was convicted, the state supreme court ruled that he could no longer serve as governor. He initially responded by barricading himself in the governor's residence and declaring North Dakota to be an independent nation. Eventually he relented, and several trials later he was acquitted of the charges. Regarding Langer, see also Jim Newton, *Justice for All: Earl Warren and the Nation He Made* (New York, 2006), 281–283.

87. Bugh, *Electoral College Reform*, 239–253. Langer's 1947 resolution was co-sponsored by Glen H. Taylor of Idaho, who became the vice presidential candidate of the Progressive Party in 1948. The decades-long friendship and rivalry between Lemke and Langer is chronicled in Lansing, *Insurgent Democracy*.

88. 96 Cong. Rec. 949–951 (1950); *Congressional Digest* 32, no. 8/9 (Aug./Sept. 1953): 220–222; see also 102 Cong. Rec. 5161–5163 (1956).

89. There is no way to know whether similar opinions prevailed in earlier decades. Notably, there were no events in the 1930s or 1940s that would obviously have heightened support for an NPV.

90. In 1947 Langer and Taylor offered their amendment as a substitute to an amendment on presidential tenure, but it was rejected by a vote of sixty-six to fourteen. Joseph E. Kallenbach, "Pro: Should Congress Adopt the Pending Plan for Direct Election of the President," *Congressional Digest* 28, no. 8/9 (Aug./Sept. 1949): 212.

91. 96 Cong. Rec. 1261–1264 (1950). Matthew Neely, a prominent and long-serving liberal Democrat from West Virginia, briefly interrupted Humphrey's speech to announce that he agreed entirely with the Minnesota senator but feared that Humphrey's substitute amendment would be defeated in the states even if it were approved by Congress. Humphrey's simultaneous support for the Lodge-Gossett amendment is discussed in Chapter 3.

92. 96 Cong. Rec. 1276 (1950). If one expanded the definition of the South to include border states, then three other southern senators (in addition to Claude Pepper) voted for the Langer amendment. Two were from West Virginia, Harley Kilgore and Matthew Neely, and one, Garrett Withers, was from Kentucky. Withers had been appointed to the seat vacated by Alben Barkley when he became vice president; Barkley, as noted earlier, was a longtime advocate of a national popular vote.

93. There were thirty-four senators from small states.

94. Lehman's resolution was supported by seventeen senators, eight of whom were from small states. Both Langer's and Lehman's proposals were technically amendments to an amendment already proposed by Daniel.

95. It is unclear why the falloff in Republican support was so steep: five senators who had voted for NPV amendments in 1950 voted against them in 1956, and one (Margaret Chase Smith of Maine) voted for Langer's proposal but against Lehman's. Langer himself had little influence among his fellow Republicans, and the absence of Lodge (whose reelection bid had been thwarted by John Kennedy) deprived the debate of an important moderate Republican voice. Those Republicans who supported reform in 1956 tended to favor the hybrid plan and/or Karl Mundt's proposal for district elections. See Chapter 3.

96. For the roll call votes, see 102 Cong. Rec. 5637, 5657 (1956).

97. This argument, which was also applied to proportional elections, was stated forcefully by conservatives such as Homer Ferguson and Karl Mundt and echoed by some moderates like Kennedy. The concern that parties would proliferate contributed to decisions by backers of both an NPV and proportional schemes to require a candidate to receive at least 40 percent of the vote in order to be elected. 96 Cong. Rec. 1268, 1270, 1275 (1950); 102 Cong. Rec. 5156, 5159, 5248 (1956).

98. 96 Cong. Rec. 1270 (1950).

99. 102 Cong. Rec. 5156–5159, 5235, 5245 (1956).

100. 102 Cong. Rec. 5148–5149 (1956); John W. Byrnes, "Pro: Should the State Electoral Vote Be Cast in Ratio to Its Popular Vote," *Congressional Digest* 32, no. 8/9 (Aug./Sept. 1953): 212–214. In 1950 Henry Cabot Lodge was among those who made this case. *The Electoral "College" vs. The Will of the People: The Case for Reform (Statement of Hon. Henry Cabot Lodge, Jr. of Massachusetts in the Senate of the United States, January 1949)* (Washington, DC, 1949), 6, 7, 18, 19.

101. 96 Cong. Rec. 1261–1262, 1266–1269, 1273 (1950). For Ed Gossett's views of an NPV and its potential impact on suffrage laws, see the Hearings before Subcommittee No. 1 of the Committee on the Judiciary, U.S. House, 81st Congress (1949), 16–19; for an example of criticism coming from outside the South, see Walter Lippmann,

"The District System Should Be Restored," *BG,* Mar. 7, 1950. Lippmann, like members of Congress, referred to the voting age in Georgia and did not mention the disenfranchisement of African-Americans.

102. 102 Cong. Rec. 5245 (1956); 96 Cong. Rec. 10424 (1950) contains an example of opposition to national suffrage laws from a Wisconsin Republican; Kallenbach, "Pro: Should Congress Adopt," 212–217.

103. 96 Cong. Rec. 1266–1269, 1273 (1950).

104. 102 Cong. Rec. 5150, 5159 (1956). Late in the debates Kennedy did indicate a willingness to amend the Constitution to get rid of the apparatus of the Electoral College (while maintaining electoral votes and the unit rule) and to transfer the contingent election process to a joint meeting of the Senate and the House, with members voting as individuals. 102 Cong. Rec. 5574 (1956).

105. 96 Cong. Rec. 1263 (1950); 102 Cong. Rec. 5235 (1956); "Electoral College Reform," *New Republic,* Feb. 27, 1950, 5; see also Lippmann, "District System."

106. 102 Cong. Rec. 5138 (1956); see also Kennedy's statement at 5150.

107. Only three senators from the South did not sign the manifesto: the other two were Albert Gore (Tennessee) and Lyndon Johnson (Texas).

108. 102 Cong. Rec. 5162–5163 (1956); Kennedy's lengthy (and often interrupted) speech in favor of maintaining the status quo begins at 5156. His overall stance was that "no urgent necessity for immediate change has been proven," and that it would therefore be best to leave the electoral system alone and not experiment with "an unknown, untried" system.

109. 102 Cong. Rec. 5162–5163 (1956).

110. 102 Cong. Rec. 5162–5163 (1956).

111. 102 Cong. Rec. 5160–5163 (1956).

5. AN IDEA WHOSE TIME HAS COME

Epigraph: *Hearings on H.J. Res. 179, H.J. Res. 181 and Similar Proposals, before the Committee on the Judiciary,* 91st Cong. 5 (1969).

1. By the 1960s the label "direct election" had come to refer unambiguously to a "national popular vote," and consequently the two phrases will be used interchangeably in this and subsequent chapters. Regarding the hazards of equating the two terms in earlier periods, see Chapter 4, note 13.

2. George C. Edwards III, *Why the Electoral College Is Bad for America,* 2nd ed. (New Haven, CT, 2011), 55–56, 62–63, 67–71; Neal R. Peirce and Lawrence D. Longley, *The People's President: The Electoral College in American History and the Direct Vote Alternative,* rev. ed. (New Haven, CT, 1981), 63–71. As Cortez Ewing pointed out in 1962, the "faithless elector" issue in 1960 (and preceding elections) was grounded in the "contradiction between the two wings" of the Democratic Party. Cortez A. M. Ewing, "Constitutional Crisis in the American Party System," *Southwestern Social Science Quarterly* 43, no. 1 (June 1962): 8–18.

3. *Proposing Amendments to the Constitution Relating to the Method of Nomination and Election of the President and Vice President and Proposing Amendments to the Consti-*

tution Relating to Qualifications for Voting: Hearings before the Senate Subcommittee on Constitutional Amendments of the Committee on the Judiciary, 87th Cong. 1–2, 58–60, 31–33, 45, 58, 60–66 (1961).

4. *Hearings before the Senate Subcommittee on Constitutional Amendments of the Committee on the Judiciary*, 87th Cong. 108, 125, 171, 245–246, 338–339; Peirce and Longley, *The People's President*, 139–143, 153–156, 158–159, 166–167. As discussed below, scholarly arguments that the Electoral College benefited large (rather than small) states were to become prominent later in the 1960s.

5. Most of the testimony in 1961 rehashed arguments from the 1950s. Both proportional and district elections were advocated as methods of making the electoral vote align more closely with the popular vote while reducing the power of the large urban states. New York senator Kenneth Keating attacked both plans for failing to ensure that the winner of the popular vote would become president. Proportional elections were also criticized as playing into the hands of southern Democrats, and district elections were attacked as vulnerable to gerrymandering. Critics of the "automatic" plan noted that it was hardly worth the effort of a constitutional amendment to make such a minor change. *Hearings before the Senate Subcommittee on Constitutional Amendments*, 87th Cong. (1961), *passim;* for examples of Keating's interventions, 32, 33, 305; Peirce and Longley, *The People's President*, 138–143, 153–156, 158–160.

6. *Hearings before the Senate Subcommittee on Constitutional Amendments*, 87th Cong. 60–66 (1961).

7. Peirce and Longley, *The People's President*, 142, 157.

8. Lucas A. Powe Jr., *The Warren Court and American Politics* (Cambridge, MA, 2000), 239–245.

9. Powe, *The Warren Court*, 199–255; J. Douglas Smith, *On Democracy's Doorstep: The Inside Story of How the Supreme Court Brought "One Person, One Vote" to the United States* (New York, 2014), 218–280; Alexander Keyssar, *The Right to Vote: The Contested History of Democracy in the United States* (New York, 2000), 285–287.

10. *Albuquerque Journal*, May 22, 1967; Keyssar, *The Right to Vote*, 285–287. As discussed in Chapter 3, some advocates of district elections, like Mundt, maintained that the Court's decisions undercut one of the major arguments against selecting electors by district; although this was true, the apportionment rulings did not generate new support for district elections. Peirce and Longley, *The People's President*, 142–143.

11. Peirce and Longley, *The People's President*, 159, 167–168; *NYT*, Jan. 23, 1966. Regarding the democratic advances of the postwar period, see Keyssar, *The Right to Vote*, 256–257.

12. "Electing the President: Recommendations of the American Bar Association's Commission on Electoral College Reform," *American Bar Association Journal* 53, no. 3 (Mar. 1967): 219.

13. *Electing the President: A Report of the Commission on Electoral College Reform*, American Bar Association (Chicago, 1967), vi–vii; *NYT*, May 11, 1966.

14. "Electing the President," 220. In hearings held by the House Judiciary Committee in 1969, William Gossett, the president of the ABA, described the path that led the organization to endorse an NPV. *Hearings on H.J. Res. 179, H.J. Res. 181 and Similar Proposals, before the Committee on the Judiciary,* 91st Cong. 172–180 (1969).

15. "Electing the President," 219–224.

16. "Electing the President," 220–222; Peirce and Longley, *The People's President,* 170. The poll of state legislators had been initiated by North Dakota senator Quentin Burdick, who was William Langer's successor.

17. The Supreme Court of the United States, October Term, 1966; Motion for Leave to File Complaint, Complaint and Brief [at 2, 8, 10, 11, 12, 39, 91], *State of Delaware v. State of New York,* 385 U.S. 964 (1966) (No. 28 Original).

18. The Supreme Court of the United States, October Term, 1966; Brief in Opposition to Motion for Leave to File Complaint, Brief [at i–ii, 18–30], *State of Delaware v. State of New York,* 385 U.S. 964 (1966) (No. 28 Original).

19. Peirce and Longley, *The People's President,* 169.

20. According to New York's "Brief in Opposition," 2, the other states to join Delaware's motion (in addition to those already named) were Iowa, Kansas, Oklahoma, and Utah. *CQ Almanac* has a similar listing that also includes West Virginia; "Electoral Reform," *CQ Almanac 1966* 22 (1966): 496–500. Peirce and Longley, *The People's President,* 169, 326n.

21. Bayh had even offered to cover the subcommittee's expenses out of his own budget in order to keep the subcommittee alive. Birch Bayh, *One Heartbeat Away: Presidential Disability and Succession* (Indianapolis, 1968), 28–29; interview with Jason Berman, Mar. 8, 2017. Berman at the time was Bayh's legislative assistant. He became chief legislative assistant in 1969 and chief of staff in 1973.

22. Peirce and Longley, *The People's President,* 168; Lawrence D. Longley and Alan G. Braun, *The Politics of Electoral College Reform* (New Haven, CT, 1972), 135–136. Johnson had put forward his proposal in special messages to Congress early in 1965 and in 1966. Bayh had introduced the proposal in the Senate. It would have mandated the use of winner-take-all and called for a joint session of Congress to choose the president if no candidate garnered a majority of the electoral votes. "Action in the 89th and 90th Congresses," *Congressional Digest* 45, no. 11 (Nov. 1967): 264–267; *WP,* Jan. 29, 1965; *NYT,* Jan. 29, 1965; *Austin American-Statesman,* Mar. 5, 1965. Regarding Bayh's earlier endorsement of Johnson's proposal (and opposition to an NPV), see Press Release, Jan. 20, 1966, Subcommittee on Constitutional Amendments and Subcommittee on the Constitution, 1963–1980, Electoral Reform, 1963–1977, Hearings–Press Releases, box CA-23, in Birch Bayh Senatorial Papers, Modern Political Papers Collection, Indiana University Libraries, Bloomington (hereafter cited as Bayh Papers).

23. Kate Cruikshank, *The Art of Leadership: A Companion to an Exhibition from the Senatorial Papers of Birch Bayh, United States Senator from Indiana, 1963–1980* (Bloomington, IN, 2007), 35; Longley and Braun, *Politics,* 134. Bayh also spelled out the reasons for his change of views in his unsuccessful effort to persuade the Democratic

National Committee to include advocacy of direct elections in the party's 1968 platform. Statement to DNC Platform Committee, Aug. 23, 1968, Bayh Papers, box CA-23.

24. The Twenty-Fifth Amendment was ratified in 1967. Bayh had worked with the ABA in developing that amendment. He later authored the Twenty-Sixth Amendment, lowering the voting age to eighteen, becoming the first person since the framers to author two amendments to the Constitution. Bayh also played a key role in promoting the Equal Rights Amendment, which was approved by Congress but not ratified by the states.

25. Peirce and Longley, *The People's President*, 168; Longley and Braun, *Politics*, 136–138; "Action in the 89th and 90th Congresses," 94–96; *NYT*, Mar. 22, 1967. Bayh's reasons for preferring an NPV are spelled out in *Congressional Digest* 46, no. 11 (Nov. 1967): 274. Dirksen's support for direct elections diminished after the 1968 election. *Wall Street Journal* (hereafter cited as *WSJ*), Jan. 24, 1969, and Apr. 11, 1969. Dirksen died, after a short illness, in September 1969.

26. Several variants of each of these plans (NPV, district, and proportional) were also proposed for consideration by the committee. "The Major Proposals Now before Congress," *Congressional Digest* 46, no. 11 (Nov. 1967): 265–267. The "automatic" plan from the Johnson administration was not reintroduced in 1967.

27. Peirce and Longley, *The People's President*, 171–172; Longley and Braun, *Politics*, 136–138; "Electoral College Reform," *CQ Almanac 1967* 23 (1968): 575–577; *WP*, June 15, 1967.

28. John F. Banzhaf III, "One Man, 3312 Votes: A Mathematical Analysis of the Electoral College," *Villanova Law Review* 13 (Winter 1968): 304–332. Bayh wrote an approving comment in that same issue (at 333–335) expressly linking Banzhaf's work and the need for an NPV to Chief Justice Earl Warren and the apportionment cases. The key points in Banzhaf's article were also presented in his Senate testimony, which can be found in *Election of the President: Hearings before the Subcommittee on Constitutional Amendments*, 91st Cong. 362–370 (1969) (statement of John F. Banzhaf III).

29. Quotations are from the "comments" on Banzhaf's article by Neal R. Peirce, Karl Mundt, and John Sparkman, *Villanova Law Review* 13 (Winter 1968): 337, 339, 342.

30. Peirce and Longley, *The People's President*, 171; Longley and Braun, *Politics*, 104, 138–139; see also Joseph E. Kallenbach, "Our Electoral College Gerrymander," *Midwest Journal of Political Science* 4, no. 2 (May 1960): 162–191. Banzhaf's work led to a small wave of competing mathematical models developed by statisticians and political scientists.

31. *WP*, June 15, 1967; *NYT*, Mar. 22, 1967; Dan T. Carter, *The Politics of Rage: George Wallace, the Origins of the New Conservatism, and the Transformation of American Politics* (Baton Rouge, 1995), 299–323, 338–339, 358, 364, 369; Longley and Braun, *Politics*, 8, 13–17; Jason Berman, correspondence with the author, Mar. 16, 2017. On Thurmond, see Don Oberdorfer, "Ex-Democrat, Ex-Dixiecrat, Today's 'Nixiecrat,'" *NYT*, Oct. 6, 1968.

32. *WP,* June 15, 1967; Berman correspondence, Mar. 16, 2017. According to Berman, Bayh did not invite Wallace to testify because he wanted the focus to be on institutional reform and not on personalities or politics.

33. Carter, *Politics of Rage,* 356–364, 369, notes the negative impact on Wallace's campaign of his late selection of General Curtis LeMay as his running mate. Longley and Braun, *Politics,* 7–17, sketch the complex scenarios that might have arisen had the decision gone to the House, where most delegations were Democratic but many southern Democrats had indicated that they would not vote for Humphrey if their districts had favored Wallace or Nixon. The quotation is from Bayh's Senate speech, May 15, 1967, *Congressional Digest* 46, no. 11 (Nov. 1967): 274.

34. Longley and Braun, *Politics,* 140–141; "Reminder for Reform," *Time,* Jan. 17, 1969, 20. News articles and editorials in the *Charlotte Observer* (Jan. 4, 7, and 26, 1969) indicated that the demand for reform was strong in North and South Carolina.

35. Bickel maintained that the Electoral College favored urban areas, which he believed to be necessary to offset the rural bias in Congress even after the apportionment decisions. He also advanced the somewhat dubious argument (put forward by others as well) that the Electoral College often gave a significant margin of victory to candidates who only narrowly won the popular vote and that this enhanced the legitimacy of the outcome. Alexander M. Bickel, "Is Electoral Reform the Answer?," *Commentary,* Dec. 1968, 41–51; "Another Opinion for the Electoral College," *NYT,* Mar. 2, 1969; Alexander M. Bickel, *Reform and Continuity: The Electoral College, the Convention, and the Party System* (New York, 1971), 15–35.

36. Lucius Wilmerding, "What to Watch Out For," *National Review,* Jan. 28, 1969, 69–72; *WSJ,* Jan. 13, 1969; *Charlotte Observer,* Jan. 26, 1969.

37. *NYT,* Jan. 1, 1971; *CDT,* Jan. 4, 1969; *U.S. News & World Report,* Feb. 19, 1969, 41–43; Michael S. Martin, *Russell Long: A Life in Politics* (Jackson, MS, 2014), 159–160. An article in the *Charlotte Observer* (Jan. 6, 1969) characterized Kennedy's victory as a defeat for "the Senate's southern establishment." An attempt to get rid of Rule XXII, which required a two-thirds vote of the Senate to shut off debate, came close to passage in January 1969. "The Script That Failed," *Newsweek,* Jan. 27, 1969, 22–23. In September 1969, after Dirksen's death, Scott defeated Howard Baker to become minority leader in the Senate.

38. *Hearings on H.J. Res. 179, H.J. Res. 181 and Similar Proposals, before the Committee on the Judiciary,* 91st Cong. 2 (1969); Longley and Braun, *Politics,* 142–145; Peirce and Longley, *The People's President,* 182. For examples of committee members stating that they approached the hearings with open minds, see *Hearings on H.J. Res. 179, H.J. Res. 181 and Similar Proposals, before the Committee on the Judiciary,* 91st Cong. 10–35, 648–650 (1969).

39. *Hearings on H.J. Res. 179, H.J. Res. 181 and Similar Proposals, before the Committee on the Judiciary,* 91st Cong. 2–3, 5–7 (1969). H.J. Res. 181 was the proposal originally backed by Lyndon Johnson that would have kept electoral votes but dispensed with electors.

40. By the mid-1960s roughly a dozen states had passed laws requiring electors to formally pledge that they would vote for their party's nominees. The constitutionality of these pledge requirements had been upheld in 1952 by the Supreme Court in *Ray v. Blair*, a case brought by the Democratic Party of Alabama. (Alabama had enacted its law in the wake of the 1948 election.) The Court did not rule on the related issue of whether electors could be penalized for violating their pledges, and the enforceability of these laws therefore was open to doubt. Some state laws provided penalties for faithless electors; others did not. In a vigorous dissent from the Court's decision, Justice Robert Jackson argued that it was the clear intent of the framers to allow electors to be "free agents" and that the subsequent evolution of practice (in which electors routinely voted for their parties' candidates) did not override the language of the Twelfth Amendment. *Ray v. Blair*, 343 U.S. 214 (1952); Ronald Dubner, "The Electoral College: Proposed Changes," *SMU Law Review* 1, no. 21 (1967): 273–274n27; James A. Gardner and Guy-Uriel Charles, *Election Law in the American Political System*, 2nd ed. (New York, 2018), 53–55.

41. *Hearings on H.J. Res. 179, H.J. Res. 181 and Similar Proposals, before the Committee on the Judiciary*, 91st Cong. 517 (1969); see also the testimony on 30–31, 380–385, 410–428, 559–573, and 601–604 for examples of various witnesses discussing the shifts in political power that might result from different reforms.

42. Peirce and Longley, *The People's President*, 183. A list of the witnesses who appeared can be found in *Hearings on H.J. Res. 179, H.J. Res. 181 and Similar Proposals, before the Committee on the Judiciary*, 91st Cong. iii–vi (1969).

43. *Hearings on H.J. Res. 179, H.J. Res. 181 and Similar Proposals, before the Committee on the Judiciary*, 91st Cong. 153–158, 507–520 (1969); see also Celler's summary of these issues on 637–638.

44. *Hearings on H.J. Res. 179, H.J. Res. 181 and Similar Proposals, before the Committee on the Judiciary*, 91st Cong. 22–25, 72–81, 89–91, 113–125, 129–131, 136–138, 219–222, 227–229, 233–234, 297–299, 374–380, 432 (1969); Emanuel Celler, "Direct Popular Election of the President," H.R. Rep. No. 91-253 at 15–16, 19–20, 23 (1969).

45. *Hearings on H.J. Res. 179, H.J. Res. 181 and Similar Proposals, before the Committee on the Judiciary*, 91st Cong. 61, 69, 71, 162–165, 209–217, 223–227, 383–385, 395–396, 418, 429–433, 617–619 (1969). See also Peirce and Longley, *The People's President*, 183; and Tom Wicker's column in the *Charlotte Observer*, Feb. 1, 1969.

46. *Hearings on H.J. Res. 179, H.J. Res. 181 and Similar Proposals, before the Committee on the Judiciary*, 91st Cong. 172–187, 219–221, 306–374, 407–410 (1969). See also the testimony of representatives Margaret Heckler (153–158), Richard Ottinger (143–145), and James O'Hara (131).

47. Richard M. Nixon, "Special Message to the Congress on Electoral Reform, Feb. 20, 1969," *Public Papers of the Presidents of the United States, Richard Nixon, 1969* (Washington, DC, 1971), 121–122; *Hearings on H.J. Res. 179, H.J. Res. 181 and Similar Proposals, before the Committee on the Judiciary*, 91st Cong. 607–646 (1969); see also 510–511 (for George Meany's criticism of Nixon); *Congressional Digest* 49, no. 1

(1970): 8; Peirce and Longley, *The People's President*, 182–183; Longley and Braun, *Politics*, 142; *Atlanta Constitution*, Feb. 21, 1969; "Modest Reform," *Time*, Feb. 28, 1969, 26.

48. *Hearings on H.J. Res. 179, H.J. Res. 181 and Similar Proposals, before the Committee on the Judiciary*, 91st Cong. 286–297 (1969). Mitchell's views were shared by other—but not all—African-American leaders and civil rights activists. Roy Wilkins, also of the NAACP, had warned in 1961 that "any scheme" to alter the Electoral College could reduce the influence of African-Americans in northern cities. In contrast, the more progressive Bayard Rustin, writing soon after the 1968 election, strongly supported an NPV, in part because the Electoral College could give a segregationist like Wallace the opportunity to choose or influence the next president. Shortly before the House voted on September 18, 1969, John Conyers of Michigan delivered an eloquent floor speech in favor of a national popular vote. He acknowledged that this was "not an especially easy decision" because an NPV would deprive African-Americans of their swing-vote status in northern states, but he believed that it would greatly benefit African-Americans in the South. Above all, Conyers stressed the importance of all votes counting equally. He also introduced an amendment to give Congress "reserve power" to establish nationally uniform voting standards, but it was defeated. As indicated later in this chapter, Mitchell came around to supporting the Bayh amendment in 1970. Conrad Joyner and Ronald Pedderson, "The Electoral College Revisited," *Southwestern Social Science Quarterly* 45, no. 1 (June 1964): 26–36; Bayard Rustin, "Negroes and the 1968 Election," in *Down the Line: The Collected Writings of Bayard Rustin* (Chicago, 1971), 249; 115 Cong. Rec. 25997–25998 (1969).

49. The final affirmative vote was twenty-eight, rather than twenty-nine, because of an absence; it included sixteen Democrats and twelve Republicans. Among the six southerners on the Judiciary Committee, four voted negatively, one (Edwin Edwards of Louisiana) was absent, and Jack Brooks of Texas voted with the majority. The House resolution left suffrage issues to the states and provided that the amendment would have to be ratified by January 21, 1971, in order to take effect in 1972. Emanuel Celler, "Direct Popular Election of the President," H.R. Rep. No. 91-253 at 9 (1969); Longley and Braun, *Politics*, 148; *WP*, Apr. 30, 1969; *WSJ*, Apr. 30, 1969; *NYT*, Apr. 30, 1969.

50. Celler, "Direct Popular Election," 5.

51. *WSJ*, Apr. 11, 17, 18, 1969.

52. *NYT*, May 11, 1969; "Erasing the Blot, Slowly," *Time*, May 9, 1969, 30. James Michener, "Presidential Lottery: The Reckless Gamble in Our Electoral System," *Reader's Digest*, May 1969, 247–267; Michener's preferred reform was the "automatic plan," but an NPV was his second choice.

53. "Notes and Comment," *New Yorker*, Feb. 8, 1969, 24–26; "Comment," *New Republic*, Feb. 22, 1969, 9–10. Just before the vote in the House, the *New York Times* editorialized in favor of direct elections, as did *Life* magazine. *NYT*, Sept. 11, 1969; "A Better Way to Elect Presidents," *Life*, Sept. 26, 1969, 50B.

54. Longley and Braun, *Politics*, 148–149; *NYT*, July 25, 1969.

55. Peirce and Longley, *The People's President*, 185–187; Longley and Braun, *Politics*, 150–152; *NYT,* Sept. 11, 19, and 21, 1969. More than a third of House members had originally voted in favor of district elections, but most of those ended up supporting H.J. Res. 681. The House also rejected numerous other amendments that would have altered particular features of the resolution. For details, see *Congressional Digest* 49, no. 1 (1970): 8–9.

56. Richard Rovere, "Letter from Washington," *New Yorker,* Oct. 4, 1969, 128–132.

57. In the tables for this chapter (and Chapter 6), I have identified the "South" in accordance with the census definition of the region minus West Virginia, Maryland, and Delaware. The appropriate boundaries of the region have long been debated, but the political histories of those three states suggest that, on balance, they ought not be considered part of the South in the second half of the twentieth century. The broad voting patterns discussed here held true also for the census South and for the South defined as the states that had once belonged to the Confederacy. All the votes cast by representatives from Mississippi and South Carolina were negative, as were a majority of the votes from Alabama, Georgia, Louisiana, and (fitting less well with the pattern) Tennessee. In contrast, ten of eleven representatives from North Carolina voted positively, as did sizable majorities from Florida, Texas, and Virginia. All representatives from Arkansas as well as the border states of Kentucky, Maryland, and West Virginia voted in favor of the resolution. 115 Cong. Rec. 26007–26008 (1969).

58. 115 Cong. Rec. 26007–26008 (1969); Longley and Braun, *Politics*, 152–155; Peirce and Longley, *The People's President*, 186–187; Mark J. McKenzie, "Systemic Biases Affecting Congressional Voting on Electoral College Reform," in *Electoral College Reform: Challenges and Possibilities*, ed. Gary Bugh (Farnham, UK, 2010), 97–98, 106–108.

59. Longley and Braun, *Politics*, 155–157; *NYT,* Sept. 21, Oct. 8, and Nov. 23, 1969; Richard M. Nixon, "Special Message to the Congress on Legislative Reform," Oct. 13, 1969, *Public Papers of the Presidents of the United States, Richard Nixon, 1969* (Washington, DC, 1971), 788–796; Lyle Denniston, "Politics a Threat to Vote Reform," *Evening Star* (Washington, DC), Sept. 26, 1969. The *New York Times* found eight states solidly opposed to ratification and six leaning in that direction; the opposition was centered in the South and the mountain states. The Chamber of Commerce's magazine also conducted a survey revealing that "the popular vote is popular" among state legislators and concluding that the "small-state issue" had diminished in importance. *Nation's Business,* Sept. 1969, 29–30. The *Atlanta Constitution* surveyed the leaders of Georgia's legislature about ratification and concluded that the legislature was divided. One legislative leader observed that there were "good arguments on both sides," but "who the hell can argue with a popular vote?" *Atlanta Constitution,* Oct. 5, 1969.

60. *Electing the President: Hearings on S.J. Res. 1, et al., before the Subcommittee on Constitutional Amendments of the Committee on the Judiciary,* 91st Cong. 16–20, 25–29, 66 (1969). A list of witnesses and statements can be found on pp. iii–vii. Among the

more notable statements were those of Senators Barry Goldwater and Roman Hruska, and representatives from the Liberty Lobby, the National Cotton Council, and the American Jewish Congress. Ervin also advocated changing the contingent election procedure so that all members of Congress would vote. Regarding Ervin's views, see also *Wilson* (NC) *Daily Times,* Nov. 20, 1968; Ervin to Bayh, Nov. 19, 1968, Bayh Papers, Subcommittee on Constitutional Amendments, Electoral Reform 1963–1977, box CA-7, Correspondence–Congressional, 1968. Ervin, like Mundt, also argued that an NPV would have no chance of passage because of opposition from the smaller states. Mundt to Bayh, Dec. 20, 1968, Bayh Papers.

61. *Congressional Digest* 49, no. 1 (1970): 32; Longley and Braun, *Politics,* 149–150. The southern members referred to were Ervin, Thurmond, and Eastland.

62. *NYT,* Feb. 20, 1986; "James O. Eastland," *Mississippi History Now* (Apr. 2011), http://www.mshistorynow.mdah.ms.gov/articles/367/james-o-eastland; "Electoral College Reform Victim of Senate Filibuster," *CQ Almanac 1970* 26 (1971): 840–845.

63. "Senate Rejects Haynsworth Nomination to Court," *CQ Almanac 1969* 25 (1970): 337–349; Longley and Braun, *Politics,* 157–158; *NYT,* Aug. 19, Sept. 4, Oct. 19, and Nov. 4, 1969; "A Northern-Southern Strategy," *Time,* Aug. 3, 1970, 6–8.

64. "Senate Rejects Haynsworth"; *NYT,* Aug. 19 and 25, 1969; *NYT,* Sept. 26, 1969.

65. "Senate Rejects Haynsworth"; *NYT,* Aug. 19 and 25, 1969; *NYT,* Sept. 21, 25, and 26, 1969; *NYT,* Oct. 5, 9, 12, 19, and 21, 1969; *NYT,* Nov. 13 and 21, 1969.

66. "Senate Rejects Haynsworth"; *NYT,* Sept. 28, 1969; *NYT,* Oct. 3, 4, 10, and 15, 1969; *NYT,* Nov. 1, 14, and 22, 1969.

67. "Carswell Nomination to Court Rejected by Senate," *CQ Almanac 1970* 26 (1971): 154–162; for an analysis of the nomination and its failure, see Bruce H. Kalk, "The Carswell Affair: The Politics of a Supreme Court Nomination in the Nixon Administration," *American Journal of Legal History* 42, no. 3 (July 1998): 261–287.

68. "Carswell Nomination"; Kalk, "The Carswell Affair," 279–287; *NYT,* Mar. 17, 1970.

69. "Carswell Nomination"; Kalk, "The Carswell Affair," 284–287; *NYT,* Apr. 21, July 13, and Sept. 9, 1970; *U.S. News & World Report,* Sept. 7, 1970, 34.

70. *NYT,* Dec. 12, 13, and 19, 1969; "Congress Lowers Voting Age, Extends Voting Rights Act," *CQ Almanac 1970* 26 (1971): 192–199.

71. "Amendments to the Voting Rights Act of 1965," p. 6, speech by Sen. Samuel Ervin, Mar. 2, 1970, in Sam J. Ervin Papers, Southern Historical Collection, Wilson Library, University of North Carolina at Chapel Hill (hereafter cited as Ervin Papers), Subgroup A: Senate Records No. 3847A, folder 15142. See also Subgroup B: Private Papers, series 18.1 (folders 759–766), box 59.

72. Gary May, *Bending toward Justice: The Voting Rights Act and the Transformation of American Democracy* (New York, 2013), 204–208. As May explains, debate regarding the renewal was complicated by the inclusion of a provision, sponsored by Edward Kennedy, to lower the voting age to eighteen. See also Keyssar, *The Right to Vote,* 227–228.

73. *NYT,* Dec. 19, 1969; "Congress Lowers Voting Age." Some southerners were mollified by the nationalization of the literacy test ban as well as by changes to the cov-

erage formula that resulted in the inclusion of several northern counties, but the renewal was nonetheless perceived as hostile to the South.

74. Longley and Braun, *Politics,* 158–160; "Electoral College Reform Victim of Senate Filibuster."

75. *WSJ,* Apr. 22, 1970; *NYT,* Apr. 6, 19, 1970; *Charlotte Observer,* Apr. 16, 1970; U.S. Congress, Senate, Committee on the Judiciary, *Electoral College Reform,* 91st Cong., 2nd Sess., 1970, 77–101 (1970), including statement of Richard Goodwin, former assistant to Presidents Kennedy and Johnson. (For a list of those testifying at the hearings, see iii.) The quotation is from an op-ed by Goodwin (*WP,* Oct. 5, 1969) that he asked to have inserted into the record; for more on his views, see Richard Goodwin, "Electing the President: In Defense of the Electoral College," *Current* 113 (Dec. 1969): 33–35. For White's views, see also "Direct Elections: An Invitation to National Chaos," *Life,* Jan. 30, 1970, 4.

76. Paul R. Clancy, *Just a Country Lawyer: A Biography of Senator Sam Ervin* (Bloomington, IN, 1974), 237–238.

77. Longley and Braun, *Politics,* 158–160, 209–210; *WSJ,* Apr. 22 and 24, 1970; *NYT,* Apr. 6, 19, 24, and 25, 1970; *WP,* Apr. 26, 1970. Bayh and his allies deployed the same strategy in the Judiciary Committee that Celler had utilized in the House: bringing all of the other reform plans up for a vote first, defeating them, and then leaving members with a choice between direct elections or no reform at all. The only material difference between S.J. Res. 1 and the House resolution was that the Senate version called for a later date by which the amendment had to be ratified to take effect in 1972 (Apr. 15, 1971, rather than Jan. 21, 1971). Bayh indicated that leaders of the House had agreed to adopt the later date if the Senate approved the resolution.

78. *WP,* June 5, 1970; *NYT,* June 7, 1970; Carter, *Politics of Rage,* 381–396. Wallace ran behind Brewer in the first round of the Democratic primary but made up the ground in the runoff with an overtly racist campaign. Brewer, backed by a coalition of blacks and moderate whites, had assumed the governorship after the death of Wallace's wife, Lurleen.

79. *WP,* Sept. 6, 1970; Longley and Braun, *Politics,* 158–160, 209–210; Peirce and Longley, *The People's President,* 188–190.

80. "Abolition of the Electoral College Might Doom the Republican Party," American Conservative Union Papers, box 108, folder 15, Brigham Young University, Provo, Utah; "Direct Vote: Formula for Multi-Party Anarchy," *Human Events,* May 23, 1970. For an example of Ervin's efforts, see Ervin to Roman Hruska, Jan. 6, 1970, suggesting that all opponents of direct elections unite behind an automatic plan that would eliminate electors but not electoral votes. See also Ervin to J. Harvie Williams, July 8, 1970, regarding efforts to inform state legislative leaders about "the dangers of direct election," and J. Harvie Williams, "Memo to Defeat Senator Bayh's Direct Election Amendment in the Senate," all in Subgroup A: Senate Records No. 3847A, folder 9389, Ervin Papers. Williams led the Committee on Electoral College Reform of the American Good Government Society and was in regular contact with Ervin regarding strategies to block the Bayh amendment.

81. For opposition opinion in the spring of 1970, see Myron P. Curzan, "Voting for President," *New Republic,* Apr. 18, 1970, 14–16; Ronald Moe, "Let's Keep the Electoral College," *National Review,* Apr. 7, 1970, 356–359, 375; "Direct Vote: Formula for Multi-Party Anarchy"; "How Not to Elect a President," *Time,* May 4, 1970, 26–27; *U.S. News & World Report,* May 11, 1970, 26–29. The *Wall Street Journal* editorialized against direct elections in late April, arguing that a close, disputed vote would be a "recipe for strife, uncertainty, and bitterness." *WSJ,* Apr. 29, 1970.

82. Longley and Braun, *Politics,* 90–94, 137–138, 158–160, 209–210; Peirce and Longley, *The People's President,* 193; "How Not to Elect a President"; *NYT,* Apr. 19, 1970; Curzan, "Voting for President," 14–16; *U.S. News & World Report,* May 11, 1970, 26–29; 116 Cong. Rec. 31733–31734 (1970). The Dole-Eagleton plan was designed to encourage, or require, candidates in an NPV election to seek support from diverse geographic areas and not just in the large population centers. A candidate could become president if he won a plurality of the national vote as well as pluralities in more than 50 percent of the states (and DC) or pluralities in states that cast more than 50 percent of the votes in the election. If no candidate reached those thresholds, the election would be decided by electoral votes, cast automatically on a winner-take-all basis. If no candidate received a majority of the electoral votes, then the votes of states that had preferred third-party candidates would be distributed to the top two candidates in proportion to the votes they had received in those states. The Griffin-Tydings proposal is discussed below.

83. "Direct Popular Election of the President," S. Report No. 91-1123, at 1–14 (1970).

84. "Direct Popular Election," S. Report No. 91-1123, at 15–23. Griffin also maintained that his proposed provision regarding congressional control of voting qualifications would go a long way toward satisfying the concerns about direct elections expressed by Clarence Mitchell and by the American Jewish Congress. The arguments for and against a runoff election, and specifically regarding the alleged tendency of a runoff to lead to a proliferation of parties or an outcome perceived as illegitimate, are discussed at length, and critically, in Longley and Braun, *Politics,* 90–94, 137–138; and Harvey Zeidenstein, *Direct Election of the President* (Lexington, 1973), 12, 55–56, 71–73.

85. "Direct Popular Election," S. Report No. 91-1123, at 24–27, 34–46. To lend credibility to its predictions, the report quoted repeatedly from well-known critics of an NPV, including Bickel, Goodwin, and White. For sharp criticism of Bickel's views, see Gus Tyler, "The Electoral College," *Commentary,* Mar. 1969, 24.

86. "Direct Popular Election," S. Report No. 91-1123, 24–27, 34–46, 50–51, 58. James J. Kilpatrick, a conservative columnist who had encouraged "massive resistance" to school integration, praised the minority report as "truly brilliant" and "a superlative piece of work" (*BG,* Sept. 2, 1970); he extended the praise in "Excellent Minority Report Bares Direct Vote Perils," *Human Events,* Sept. 12, 1970.

87. "Direct Popular Election," S. Report No. 91-1123, at 41–42; *Electoral College Reform, Hearings before the Committee on the Judiciary, U.S. Senate,* 91st Cong. 67–70 (1970), statement of Honorable William L. Clay. Among the authors of the minority report, only Fong voted in favor of renewal of the VRA. 116 Cong. Rec. 7335–7336 (1970).

Regarding African-American opinions of H.J. Res. 681, see note 48 above; 115 Cong. Rec., 26007–26008 (1969); and Jennifer E. Manning and Colleen J. Shogan, "African American Members of the United States Congress: 1870–2012," CRS Report RL 30378, Mar. 6, 2012, 54. The only African-American senator, Ed Brooke of Massachusetts, voted for cloture in the Senate.

88. Longley and Braun, *Politics*, 165–166; *WP*, Sept. 10, 1970; *Atlanta Constitution*, Sept. 11 and Sept. 13, 1970; *BG*, Sept. 10, 1970; *NYT*, Sept. 10, 1970; Cato, "A Filibuster in the Works?," *National Review*, Sept. 22, 1970, 992.

89. Longley and Braun, *Politics*, 164–165; Cato, "Filibuster," 992.

90. 116 Cong. Rec. 30809–30840, 30838, 30981, 30988, 31003–31005, 31152 (1970); Longley and Braun, *Politics*, 164.

91. 116 Cong. Rec. 30892, 31139, 31144, 31147 (1970).

92. 116 Cong. Rec. 30834, 30839–30841, 30992, 31000, 31141, 31147, 31380 (1970).

93. 116 Cong. Rec. 31152–31153, 31361 (1970).

94. Longley and Braun, *Politics*, 164–169; *NYT*, Sept. 10 and 13, 1970. For examples of reading and inserting articles into the record, see 116 Cong. Rec. 30996–30997, 30999, 31001, 31361, 31375 (1970). A motion to invoke cloture, or end debate, required a two-thirds majority to be approved.

95. Longley and Braun, *Politics*, 161–164; *WP*, Sept. 12 and 17, 1970; 116 Cong. Rec. 31335–31338 (1970); "Bayh's Last Stand," *Newsweek*, Oct. 5, 1970, 29; *NYT*, Sept. 10 and 13, 1970; *Los Angeles Times* (hereafter cited as *LAT*), Sept. 12, 1970; *BG*, Sept. 13, 1970; Richard M. Nixon, "Special Message to the Congress on the Administration's Legislative Program," *Public Papers of the Presidents of the United States, Richard Nixon, 1969* (Washington, DC, 1971), 719–738. Nixon's stance was believed to have been influenced by his attorney general (and political strategist), John Mitchell. "ACU Instrumental in Electoral 'Reform' Defeat," *Human Events*, Oct. 17, 1970.

96. *WP*, July 13, Sept. 12, 1970; Kenneth Crawford, "Thurmond Threatens," *Newsweek*, Aug. 3, 1970, 25; Crawford, "The Hardy College Spirit," *Newsweek*, Sept. 21, 1970, 42; "Bayh's Last Stand"; *NYT*, July 18, Sept. 10 and 13, 1970; Longley and Braun, *Politics*, 161–164; Kevin P. Phillips, "Senator Strom Thurmond Worries the Administration," *Human Events*, Aug. 1, 1970; "Northern-Southern Strategy"; Berman, interview, Mar. 8, 2017, and correspondence, Mar. 9, 2017. Berman did not believe that Nixon's stance had a decisive impact. Regarding Nixon's preoccupation with Wallace, including his efforts to defeat Wallace in the 1970 Alabama primary, see Carter, *Politics of Rage*, 369–399.

97. Longley and Braun, *Politics*, 168–169; Cato, "Filibuster," 992; *NYT*, Sept. 17, 1970; Clancy, *Country Lawyer*, 238–239; clipping from *Winston-Salem Journal*, Oct. 1, 1969, Subgroup A: Senate Records No. 3847A, folder 8582, Ervin Papers.

98. Longley and Braun, *Politics*, 168–169.

99. 116 Cong. Rec. 31752–31754 (1970); *NYT*, Sept. 16, 1970; Longley and Braun, *Politics*, 170.

100. 116 Cong. Rec. 31757, 31762, 32348–32349, 32352–32355 (1970). Mitchell's concerns about direct elections, expressed in the House hearings of 1969, had presumably been lessened by the renewal of the Voting Rights Act.

101. 116 Cong. Rec. 32354 (1970); see *NYT,* Sept. 30, 1970. The *New York Times* offered similar views, both in an editorial and in a column by Tom Wicker (Sept. 17, 1970), as did the *Washington Post* (Sept. 17, 1970). The purpose of the Senate rule was to guarantee that issues would be amply considered and prevent the hasty adoption of legislation by a narrow majority vote. That procedural safeguard did not seem necessary for an amendment procedure that required a two-thirds majority in each chamber and then ratification by three-quarters of the states.

102. The voting patterns are also analyzed (with similar conclusions) in Longley and Braun, *Politics,* 170, 174–177; and, more formally, in Mark J. McKenzie, "Systemic Biases Affecting Congressional Voting on Electoral College Reform," in Bugh, *Electoral College Reform,* 98–99, 108–109. Longley and Braun apparently used a different definition of "South" than is used here (see note 57 above) and thus report slightly different numbers. Cutoff points for "small" and "large" states also vary across different studies but do not impact the conclusions here.

103. Longley and Braun, *Politics,* 170–171; *BG, LAT, NYT, WP, Atlanta Constitution,* all Sept. 18, 1970.

104. 116 Cong. Rec. 32869–32871 (1970).

105. 116 Cong. Rec. 2872, 33067, 33356–33367, 34377–34378 (1970).

106. 116 Cong. Rec. 33410–33452, 33554–33557, 33564–33581, 33958–33980, 33983–33987, 34029–34031, 33952–33956 (1970).

107. 116 Cong. Rec. 33068, 33071, 33444, 33586, 33854 (1970); Berman interview, Oct. 23, 2017.

108. 116 Cong. Rec. 33368–33371, 33583, 33403–33404, 33451 (1970); *WP,* Sept. 23, 1970; Longley and Braun, *Politics,* 171–172. One of the other items of business that concerned Mansfield was the Equal Rights Amendment, which was also before the Senate.

109. Opposition senators frequently quoted newspaper editorials from their own states, indicating that their position had significant local support. For examples, see 116 Cong. Rec. 31764, 33410, 33420, 33451–33452, 33962–33965, 33973 (1970).

110. 116 Cong. Rec. 33554–33582, 33827, 33952–33987, 34027–34031 (1970); "Bayh's Last Stand."

111. *NYT,* Sept. 29, 1970; 116 Cong. Rec. 34033–34034 (1970); Russell Long (Louisiana) and Robert Byrd (West Virginia) switched their votes in favor of cloture, while Gordon Allott (Colorado) went the other way. Longley and Braun, *Politics,* 173. According to the *Boston Globe* (Sept. 29, 1970), six of the absent senators were in Europe on official business, and others were campaigning.

112. Calculation based on the 1970 census. The contrast between the votes of small-state and large-state Republicans was likely ideological: Republicans from states like New York and Illinois were significantly less conservative than small-state Republicans from the plains and mountain states. Longley and Braun, *Politics* (168–173), reported that those favoring cloture tended to have more liberal voting records in 1970 than did those who opposed cloture. McKenzie, "Systemic Biases," did not analyze the second cloture vote.

113. The eight largest states were New York, California, Pennsylvania, Ohio, Illinois, Texas, Michigan, and New Jersey. A slight majority of House members from those

states were Democrats, but most senators were Republican. The presence of pro-portionately more conservative small-state Republicans in the Senate than in the House helps to explain the difference in overall Republican voting patterns in the House and the Senate. Southerners held roughly the same proportion of seats in the two chambers, as did the two parties.

114. A majority of representatives from Texas had also voted for reform, but in the Senate the Texas vote was split (and neither senator voted on September 29). Four of Georgia's ten representatives had voted for direct elections, but both of its senators voted against cloture. Regarding the definition of the "South" used here, see note 57 above. There were no African-Americans from the South in the House in 1969.

115. Regarding divisions within the South, see V. O. Key Jr., with the assistance of Alexander Heard, *Southern Politics in State and Nation* (Knoxville, TN, 1984), 668–675. Although there were moderate southern voices from the border states, the only southern progressive in the Senate in 1970 was Texan Ralph Yarborough, who was defeated for reelection later that year.

116. Thirty-nine of the sixty-six southern representatives who voted favorably on H.J. Res. 681 had initially supported district elections, and there were others who had voted for proportional and automatic plans. Their reasons for preferring those plans to the existing system varied. Richard Poff of Virginia, for example, believed that the Electoral College with winner-take-all gave too much power to large states and—echoing Ed Gossett from 1950—that it gave disproportionate influence to "tightly-organized . . . special interest groups in the large cities." *Radford* (VA) *News Journal,* Sept. 30, 1969.

117. Clipping from the *Winston-Salem Journal,* Oct. 1, 1969, in Subgroup A: Senate Records No. 3847A, folder 8582, Ervin Papers. On that same date, A. J. Fletcher, chairman of the board of WRAL-TV in Raleigh-Durham, North Carolina, delivered a "viewpoint" that was sharply critical of the state's congressmen who had voted for the direct elections amendment. According to Fletcher, those members of Congress mistakenly believed that voting against the amendment would have hurt their chances for reelection. Subgroup A: Senate Records No. 3847A, folder 9389, Ervin Papers. See also *Mobile Register,* Sept. 29, 1970; *Dallas Morning News,* Sept. 27, 1970, in which an editorial writer questioned "why a majority of our representatives voted last year for direct election and an end to state identity in presidential elections."

118. "Bayh's Last Stand"; 116 Cong. Rec. 34035 (1970).

119. Longley and Braun, *Politics,* 173–174; Berman correspondence, June 14, 2017.

120. Spong's plan would have retained winner-take-all for the electoral vote and called for the election to be decided by a joint session of Congress if no candidate won both the electoral vote and a plurality of the popular vote. This meant that the popular vote winner was not certain to take office; it also ran the risk of generating partisan maneuvers in Congress. Longley and Braun, *Politics,* 71–73, 213n125.

121. *BG,* Sept. 30, 1970.

122. "ACU Instrumental"; "Bayh's Last Stand"; "The Necessity Not to Change," *Time,* Oct. 12, 1970, 16.

123. *NYT,* Sept. 29 and 30, 1970; *LAT,* Oct. 2, 1970; *WP,* Oct. 2, 1970. The *New York Times* urged Bayh and his allies to stick to the runoff plan because it alone would guarantee that the winner of the popular vote would become president. The paper also maintained that having the decision made by Congress would give a dominant congressional party the opportunity to choose its own candidate rather than the person who had garnered the most votes.

124. If an NPV had replaced the Electoral College, all subsequent campaigns would, of course, have been conducted differently.

125. Longley and Braun, *Politics,* 1.

126. Some objected to the automatic system because it would reinforce the unit rule, while others believed that it was not worthwhile to go through the entire amendment process to make such a small change. Ervin quipped that "it would be almost like chasing a fly with an elephant gun." Peirce and Longley, *The People's President,* 160.

127. Longley and Braun, *Politics,* 134.

128. Neither party controlled the requisite supermajorities in Congress to pass an amendment. Democrats held fifty-seven seats in the Senate and 56 percent of the seats in the House. There was remarkably little discussion, and no consensus, regarding the potential partisan impact of direct elections. Some conservative groups (like the ACU; see note 133 below) believed that Republicans would be hurt by an NPV, but other observers believed that it would disadvantage Democrats. "How Not to Elect a President"; David W. Abbott and James P. Levine, *Wrong Winner: The Coming Debacle in the Electoral College* (New York, 1991), 38, 146.

129. Longley and Braun, *Politics,* 129–131; 116 Cong. Rec. 31005 (1970); *WSJ,* Apr. 29, 1970.

130. Mundt was not a presence in the 1970 Senate debates because he suffered a severe stroke late in 1969 and was subsequently unable to attend sessions of Congress; he remained in office until early 1973.

131. 116 Cong. Rec. 30834, 30839–30840, 30892 (1970); see also 33451–33452; "ACU Instrumental." Mundt had also voiced the fear that direct elections would lead to the abolition of the Senate. See his letter to James Allen of Alabama, dated Oct. 14, 1969, entered into the Congressional Record on Sept. 21, 1970, 116 Cong. Rec. 32864–32865 (1970).

132. 116 Cong. Rec. 30839 (1970); "Smaller States, South in Danger: Direct Popular Vote Battle Now Moves to Senate Floor," *Human Events,* Sept. 12, 1970.

133. An undated memo written after the 1968 election for the American Conservative Union, entitled "Abolition of the Electoral College Might Doom the Republican Party" (and forwarded to "Republican Party Leaders") argued that the Republican Party had been posting gains in small states and in the South and that those gains would be jeopardized by a national popular vote but not by district elections. "Abolition of the Electoral College," ACU Papers.

134. *WSJ,* Apr. 11, 1969; "How Not to Elect a President"; *U.S. News & World Report,* May 11, 1970, 26–29; "Smaller States, South in Danger"; "Abolition of the Electoral College," ACU Papers. For a penetrating discussion of the significance of low turnout in the South during the first half of the twentieth century, see V. O. Key Jr. and

Alexander Heard, *Southern Politics in State and Nation,* new ed. (Knoxville, TN, 1984), 502–508. Turnout in the South rose from 57 percent in 1964 to just over 60 percent in 1968, likely because of the addition of black voters. It remained roughly 10 percentage points lower than turnout in the North and the West; in South Carolina, turnout was 30 percentage points lower than it was in Minnesota in 1968. U.S. Department of Commerce, Bureau of the Census, "Voting and Registration in the Election of 1968," *Current Population Reports, Ser. P-20 Population Characteristics, no. 192* (Dec. 2, 1969), figs. 1 and 2.

135. Kevin Phillips, "Electoral College Politics," *WP,* Sept. 11, 1970; Kilpatrick, "Excellent Minority Report"; "Direct Popular Election," S. Report No. 91-1123, at 26–27; Zeidenstein, *Direct Election of the President,* 98–99. For a citizen's view of the South's beleaguered condition, see William L. Cox Sr. to Ervin, Sept. 21, 1970, Subgroup A: Senate Records No. 3847A, folder 9401, Ervin Papers.

136. Charles W. Collins, *Whither Solid South? A Study in Politics and Race Relations* (New Orleans, 1947), 279; Chris M. Asch, *The Senator and the Sharecropper: The Freedom Struggles of James O. Eastland and Fanny Lou Hamer* (New York, 2008), 123–124; Kari Frederickson, *The Dixiecrat Revolt and the End of the Solid South, 1932–68* (Chapel Hill, NC, 2003), 141; Stuart J. Little, "More than Race: Strom Thurmond, the States' Rights Democrats, and Postwar Political Ideology," *Southern Studies* 4, no. 2 (1993): 113–120; J. Lee Annis Jr., *Big Jim Eastland: The Godfather of Mississippi* (Jackson, MS, 2016), 81. See also, regarding Collins and his influence, Joseph E. Lowndes, *From the New Deal to the New Right: Race and the Southern Origins of Modern Conservatism* (New Haven, CT, 2008), 11–34; Matthew M. Hoffman, "The Illegitimate President: Minority Vote Dilution and the Electoral College," *Yale Law Journal* 105, no. 4 (Jan. 1996): 951–952.

137. Jim Allen, "Jim Allen Reports," *Athens* (AL) *News Courier,* Oct. 2, 1969.

138. Ervin advocated, at different moments in the late 1960s, district, proportional, and automatic plans (all to be followed by joint sessions of Congress if there were no Electoral College winner). He referred frequently in his correspondence to his opposition to the "unit rule" but ended up proposing to embed it in the Constitution if an automatic plan could be passed as an alternative to the Bayh amendment. It is evident from Ervin's papers that Ervin stood ready to support whatever proposal seemed to have the best chance of blocking an NPV. See, for examples, Ervin to Vann Donaldson, Aug. 19, 1970, folder 9401; Ervin to Brenda McCrimmon, Oct. 3, 1968, folder 7626; Ervin to members of the Senate, Nov. 19, 1968, folder 7627; Strom Thurmond to Ervin, Nov. 23, 1968, folder 7626; Ervin to C.J. Hyatt, Oct. 20, 1969, folder 8582; Ervin to Hruska, Jan. 6, 1970, folder 9389; copy of Ervin testimony in Senate, Apr. 7, 1970, folder 9388; all in Subgroup A: Senate Records No. 3847A, Ervin Papers. That this perspective on the Electoral College was shared by some of Ervin's constituents is indicated in their letters to him. See, for examples, Zeb Dickson to Ervin, Sept. 23, 1969, folder 8584, and Mrs. Mima Bland to Ervin, Feb. 11, 1970, folder 9389, Ervin Papers.

139. Little, "More than Race," 113–126; Tomiko Brown-Hall, "The Gentleman's White Supremacist: J. Strom Thurmond, the Dixiecrat Campaign, and the Evolution of

Southern Politics," *Southern Historian* 16 (Spring 1995): 61–86; Karl E. Campbell, "Claghorn's Hammurabi: Senator Sam Ervin and Civil Rights," *North Carolina Historical Review* 78, no. 4 (Oct. 2001): 431–456; Karl E. Campbell, *Senator Sam Ervin, Last of the Founding Fathers* (Chapel Hill, NC, 2007), 104–132; Clancy, *Country Lawyer,* 173–175, 201, 236–239; Jesse Helms, WRAL-TV, Viewpoint, Sept. 23, 1969, Subgroup A: Senate Records No. 3847A, folder 9389, Ervin Papers.

140. Strom Thurmond, "Court Tests Challenge Voting Rights Act," *Human Events,* July 11, 1970; *NYT,* June 27, 2003. By the 1970s, African-Americans constituted 30 percent of South Carolina's electorate.

141. Ervin, "Amendments to the Voting Rights Act of 1965," Mar. 2, 1970, Ervin Papers; Sam J. Ervin, "The Truth Respecting the Highly Praised and Constitutionally Devious Voting Rights Act," *Cumberland Law Review* 12, no. 2 (Spring 1982): 261–281; Campbell, "Claghorn's Hammurabi," 451; Campbell, *Ervin,* 141–144, 346n44. Although no longer in the Senate, Ervin sought to prevent the 1982 renewal of the VRA. See, for example, his letter to Henry Hyde, Aug. 4, 1981, folder 9074, Ervin Papers.

142. Clancy, *Country Lawyer,* 190; Campbell, *Ervin,* 132–160. Regarding Ervin's difficulty recognizing the changes taking place in the South, see Dick Dabney, *A Good Man: The Life of Sam J. Ervin* (Boston, 1976), 245. Among senators from the eleven ex-Confederate states who voted against cloture, only Fulbright (Arkansas) and Spong (Virginia) voted for the renewal of the VRA, although several others did not vote. 115 Cong. Rec. 3–4, 7335–7336, 32357, 34034 (1970). Most southern senators, including Ervin and Eastland, had also voted against the Voting Rights Act in 1965.

143. Longley and Braun, *Politics,* 166; Peirce and Longley, *The People's President,* 193.

144. See, for example, Campbell, *Ervin,* 214; and Annis, *Big Jim Eastland,* 224–225.

145. *Atlanta Constitution,* Sept. 17 and 18, 1970; "Wallace Wins," *Atlanta Constitution,* Oct. 1, 1970. See also, regarding Wallace and the House vote, Calvin Cox, "That Old College Spirit," *Atlanta Constitution,* Sept. 24, 1969. Ervin's draft speech was found in a folder labeled "Bills, S.J. Res. 1—Sam Ervin Opposition, 1969, Electoral Reform," Subcommittee on Constitutional Amendments and Subcommittee of the Constitution, Electoral Reform 1963–1977, Bayh Papers, box CA-23.

146. "Wallace Wins." The paper's editorial particularly chastised Republicans who had opposed cloture and S.J. Res. 1, thereby damaging their own candidate's chances in 1972. The editorial further argued that because Democrats controlled the House, a contingent election process, if set in motion by Wallace's candidacy, would lead to a Democrat's election.

147. For regional perspectives on the leading role played by southerners, see *Atlanta Constitution,* Sept. 16, 17, and 18, 1970.

148. The margin of defeat was sufficiently small that it is tempting to ask whether the outcome could have been different, particularly if less time had elapsed between the House and Senate votes. There is no doubt that momentum was lost during that year, but many of the delays were not fortuitous: they were part of the opposition's strategy and thus cannot be attributed to bad luck or unfortunate timing. That was not altogether the case, however, with the Haynsworth and Carswell nominations.

Nixon could have nominated other men or women who would have had smoother sailing through the Senate, leaving more time for consideration of S.J. Res. 1 outside the constraints of the fall election-season calendar. Whether the delays and acrimony generated by the Supreme Court nominations had an impact on the fate of the amendment is impossible to determine. Peirce and Longley, writing not long after the events, wondered whether "the ghosts of Haynsworth and Carswell were indirectly killing electoral reform" by contributing to Nixon's failure to actively support reform. But Jason Berman, then Bayh's legislative aide, believes that the debate would have been less "venomous" but the outcome the same. At the time the Senate opened debate in September 1970, most close observers believed that Bayh and his allies simply did not have the votes to pass S.J. Res. 1. Berman shares that view and thinks that the pro-reform forces never had the requisite number of votes. Longley and Braun, *Politics*, 165–166. Berman interviews, Mar. 8 and Oct. 23, 2017; Peirce and Longley, *The People's President*, 192

149. Berman recollects that Bayh and his allies were insistent that the design of any electoral institution had to be based on principles and not on an assessment of partisan consequences. They maintained that designing an institution to achieve a political outcome was inescapably shortsighted because conditions (political, demographic, etc.) would inevitably change—and so would the outcomes. In making the case for S.J. Res. 1, they attempted to maintain that stance, as is evident in the debates. Berman interview, Mar. 8, 2017. Bayh reiterated that position in the foreword he wrote to John R. Koza et al., *Every Vote Equal: A State-Based Plan for Electing the President by National Popular Vote*, 4th ed. (Los Altos, 2013), xxx–xxxi.

6. LAST CALL FOR THE TWENTIETH CENTURY

Epigraph: *The Electoral College and Direct Election: Hearings before the Committee on the Judiciary, United States Senate*, 95th Cong. 170, 407 (1977).

1. 125 Cong. Rec. 5102 (1979).
2. The *New York Times*, for example, reported on Apr. 13, 1977, that "its prospects for Congressional approval are probably stronger than they have ever been before." For optimistic assessments, see also Clayton Fritchey, "Stop the Presses! Electoral College May Be on Its Way Out," *Arizona Republic*, Nov. 19, 1976; *Rocky Mountain News*, Nov. 13, 1976; *Montgomery* (AL) *Journal*, Dec. 2, 1976; Gus Tyler, "Public Demands Direct Elections," *Newark Star Ledger*, Feb. 12, 1977. These articles were reprinted in *The Electoral College and Direct Election: Hearings before the Senate Subcommittee on the Constitution, United States Senate*, 95th Cong. 478–484, 495 (1977) (hereafter cited as *EC and DE, Sub.*). Note: There were two different sets of Senate hearings from 1977 that were printed with the title *The Electoral College and Direct Election*. One, cited here, was from the Subcommittee on the Constitution, and the other was from the full Senate Judiciary Committee: *The Electoral College and Direct Election: Hearings before the Committee on the Judiciary, United States Senate*, 95th Cong. (1977) (hereafter cited as *EC and DE, Judiciary*).

3. Thomas Durbin, *Proposals to Reform Our Presidential Electoral System: A Survey of the Historical Background and Development of the Electoral College and a Compilation of Proposals to Reform It, with Pro and Con Analysis, and a Selected Bibliography* (1980) (CRS-1980-AML-0027), 210–215; "Election Reforms: Delay and Defeat," *CQ Almanac 1977* (Washington, DC, 1978): 798–812, http://library.cqpress.com.ezp-prod1 .hul.harvard.edu/cqalmanac/document.php?id=cqal77-1201632; *Direct Popular Election of the President*, Senate Judiciary Committee, S. Report No. 94-94, at 37 (1975). There were 120 joint resolutions introduced in Congress between 1973 and 1979, three-quarters of them calling for some version of a national popular vote. One, in 1973, was sponsored by Rep. Gerald Ford, shortly before he became vice president. The NPV resolutions varied regarding the percentage of the vote required to win, what would happen if no candidate gained the required percentage (usually a runoff or a decision by a joint session of Congress), how voter qualifications would be regulated, and who would regulate the place, time, and manner of holding the elections.

4. S.J. Res. 1, 93rd Cong. (1973); the resolution specified that a candidate could become president with less than 40 percent of the popular vote if he / she won states that were entitled to a "majority of the whole number of Members of both Houses of the Congress."

5. Neal R. Peirce and Lawrence D. Longley, *The People's President: The Electoral College in American History and the Direct Vote Alternative*, rev. ed. (New Haven, CT, 1981), 197–198. Assistant Attorney General Robert Dixon testified in support of the principle of direct elections. *Electoral Reform: Hearings before the Subcommittee on Constitutional Amendments of the Committee on the Judiciary on S.J. Res. 1*, 93rd Cong. 33–53 (1973).

6. *WSJ*, May 22, 1975; *Chicago Daily Defender*, Aug. 25, 1975. The staff of Bayh's subcommittee drafted a report to be approved by the full Judiciary Committee, but it was never reported by that committee. *Direct Popular Election*, S. Report No. 94-94 (1975); S. Report No. 663, at 21 (1976); S. Report No. 1373, at 10 (1976). According to Jason Berman, who was Bayh's chief of staff beginning in 1973, Bayh did not expect his efforts in 1973 and 1975 to be successful, but he wanted to keep the issue under active consideration. Berman correspondence, May 15, 2019.

7. Seymour Spilerman and David Dickens, "Who Will Gain and Who Will Lose Influence under Different Electoral Rules," *American Journal of Sociology* 80, no. 2 (Sept. 1974): 444–448, contains a cogent summary of the literature, as does John Y. Yunker and Lawrence D. Longley, "The Biases of the Electoral College: Who Is Really Advantaged?," in *Perspectives on Presidential Selection*, ed. Donald R. Matthews (Washington, DC, 1973), 172–203. Partisan bias was analyzed in Michael C. Nelson, "Partisan Bias in the Electoral College," *Journal of Politics* 36, no. 4 (Nov. 1974): 1033–1048. The literature on these issues grew throughout the 1970s (and beyond) without reaching any consensus.

8. Spilerman and Dickens, "Who Will Gain," 443, 474; Yunker and Longley, "Biases," 174, 190–193, 203; John Y. Yunker and Lawrence D. Longley, "The Changing Biases of the Electoral College," printed in the appendix to *Hearings before the Senate Sub-*

committee on Constitutional Amendments of the Committee on the Judiciary, 93rd Cong. 187–212 (1973); Harvey Zeidenstein, *Direct Election of the President* (Lexington, MA, 1973), 25–54, 105. Bayh and his staff mobilized these studies to counter the notion that the Electoral College benefited African-Americans. Memo to Sen. Birch Bayh on "Comparative Voting Power of Black Voters" from Staff of the Subcommittee on the Constitution, Apr. 5, 1977, box CA-32, Staff Binders S.J. Res. 1, binder 4, pt. 2, Electoral Reform 1977–1980, Bayh Papers.

9. For examples, see op-eds by Neal Peirce, *WP,* Oct. 12, 1976, and David Rosenbaum, *NYT,* Nov. 2, 1976, reprinted in appendix 22 of *EC and DE, Sub., Supplement,* 95th Cong. 471–473 (1977).

10. *EC and DE, Judiciary,* 36–38 (1977). Dole later told reporters that President Ford had "effectively scotched" the attempt to flip electors by conceding to Carter the day after the election. *WP,* Feb. 1, 1977. See also Richard L. Strout, "Ford Still Could Take Presidency," *Christian Science Monitor* (hereafter cited as *CSM*), Dec. 3, 1976.

11. *NYT,* Aug. 14, 1976; Sept. 16, 1976; Oct. 9, 1976; Oct. 23, 1976; Oct. 30, 1976. The case was *Contessa v. McCarthy,* 40 N.Y.S. 2nd 308, 54 A.D. 2nd 781 (1976); *EC and DE, Judiciary* 61, 258, 315–316 (1977); Neal R. Peirce, "Electoral College: Its Time Has Run Out," *WP,* Dec. 3, 1976; Peirce and Longley, *The People's President,* 81–82. The 1976 election also included a faithless elector, a Republican who cast his ballot for Ronald Reagan.

12. *CDT,* Nov. 3, 1976; *Seattle Post-Intelligencer,* Nov. 8, 1976; *Rocky Mountain News,* Nov. 13, 1976; *WP,* Feb. 1, 1977; *Austin American-Statesman,* Dec. 23, 1976. These and dozens of other expressions of support for reform were reprinted in *EC and DE, Sub.,* 464–503 (1977).

13. *WSJ,* Jan. 11, 1977; *BG,* Nov. 19, 1976; Mar. 23, 1977.

14. *NYT,* Nov. 16, 1976. The reasons for the *Times'* shift are discussed below in note 120.

15. 123 Cong. Rec. 684–686 (1977); 123 Cong. Rec. 1100 (1977).

16. The Judiciary Committee in the new Congress had not yet met to organize its sub-committees, but Eastland permitted Bayh to convene (and chair) the hearings on behalf of the full Judiciary Committee. *EC and DE, Judiciary,* 1 (1977).

17. *EC and DE, Judiciary,* 1–3, 239–245 (1977); a list of the witnesses appears on iii–v.

18. *EC and DE, Judiciary,* 20–30, 33–41.

19. *EC and DE, Judiciary,* 358–362. Edwards's great-great-grandfather had also been a Republican representative in Congress, http://www.encyclopediaofalabama.org /article/h-3319; Biographical Directory of the United States Congress, http:// bioguide.congress.gov/scripts/biodisplay.pl?index=E000084. Two southern Democrats in the House—William Boner of Tennessee and Charles Bennett of Florida—also introduced resolutions in the 1970s calling for direct elections.

20. *NYT,* Mar. 23, 1977; Peirce and Longley, *The People's President,* 198–199, 333n94; Rick Perlstein, "How Jimmy Carter Pioneered Electoral Reform," *Newsweek,* Aug. 30, 2015; "Election Reforms: Delay and Defeat." A column by political commentators Jack Germond and Jules Witcover in March 1977 suggested that Carter may have initially misunderstood what was meant by "direct election" when he first signaled

approval to his staff and in public; he apparently (or allegedly) said that he did not want to alter the ratio of votes among the states, suggesting that he confused the "automatic plan" (no electors) with an NPV. According to Germond and Witcover, he left it to Mondale to study and sort out the confusion before his message to Congress was released. *Baltimore Sun,* Mar. 2, 1977. The other organizations whose leaders coauthored the letter to Carter were the United Auto Workers, Common Cause, the AFL-CIO, and the U.S. Chamber of Commerce.

21. *Denver Post,* Mar. 28, 1977; *Raleigh News and Observer,* Mar. 24, 1977; *EC and DE, Judiciary,* 498 (1977); see also, from the same hearings (464–469), a series of editorials from WSB-TV in Atlanta. In May 1977 the *Atlanta Constitution* published an op-ed by southerners Charles Morgan Jr. and Peggy Roberson, who quipped, in response to Carter's reform package, that "it looks now as though the country is about to enter a period of radical democracy in which people will find it incredibly easy to vote and each person's vote will count the same as the next person's." "It's High Time to Dismantle the Relic," *Atlanta Constitution,* May 14, 1977.

22. George H. Gallup, *The Gallup Poll: Public Opinion, 1972–1977,* vol. 2 (Wilmington, DE, 1978), 969–970. Three groups had notably high rates of "no opinion" responses: nonwhites (27 percent), southern Democrats (20 percent), and those with only a grade school education (23 percent). Regarding public opinion in the South, Morgan and Roberson (both from Birmingham) reported that Birmingham congressman John Buchanan had sent questionnaires to his constituents and learned that 76 percent favored a constitutional amendment to implement direct elections. "High Time to Dismantle."

23. Peirce and Longley, *The People's President,* 297–299; Louis Harris, "Abolish the Electoral College," *WP* (Harris Survey release) May 30, 1977. The Harris poll and the Gallup poll were entered as exhibits at the July–August hearings conducted by the Subcommittee on the Constitution. *EC and DE, Sub., Supplement,* 6–10 (1977). Unlike the Gallup poll, the Harris survey reported more support among Democrats than among Republicans, and it found support highest (81 percent) among independents. In the Harris poll, 37 percent of African-Americans reported that they were "not sure" if they supported the reform; the figure was 34 percent among all respondents with an eighth-grade education or less and 30 percent among those with an income under $5,000. These figures were considerably higher than they were for other groups.

24. 123 Cong. Rec. 685 (1977).

25. Perlstein, "Jimmy Carter"; *EC and DE, Sub.,* 454 (1977); "Election Reforms: Delay and Defeat." Regarding Reagan's opposition and Republican opposition more generally, see *Austin American-Statesman,* Mar. 26, 1977; *CSM,* Apr. 27, 1977; *LAT,* Apr. 16, 1977. In 1969 Reagan had criticized Nixon's qualified support for direct elections, insisting that they would be a "blow to our sovereign states." *Times-Picayune* (New Orleans), Oct. 1, 1969. Former president Ford, in contrast, repeatedly called for abolition of the Electoral College; see, for example, *LAT,* May 12, 1977; *Direct Popular Election of the President and Vice President of the United States: Hearings before the Senate Subcommittee on the Constitution of the Committee on the Judiciary,* 96th Cong.

308 (1979). Bayh's staff worried that the inclusion of direct elections in Carter's reform package had potentially undermined support among Republicans for an NPV. Nels Ackerson to Senator [Bayh], Apr. 26, 1977, Bayh Papers, box CA-32, Staff Binders S.J. Res. 1, binder 4, pt. 2, Electoral Reform 1977–1980.

26. Throughout these years, Bayh's staff periodically prepared memos indicating how senators were likely to vote. For example, see Marcia Thomas to Sen. Bayh, Mar. 1, 1977, Bayh Papers, box CA-9, Staff Binders S.J. Res. 1, binder 3, pt. 2, Electoral Reform 1977–1980.

27. *Congressional Quarterly Weekly Report* 35 (June 25, 1977): 1295; "Election Reforms: Delay and Defeat"; Peirce and Longley, *The People's President*, 199–200.

28. "Election Reforms: Delay and Defeat"; Peirce and Longley, *The People's President*, 199–200, 333n101; *NYT*, July 23, 1977. Diamond presented as his written testimony his publication *The Electoral College and the American Idea of Democracy* (Washington, DC, 1977). The record of the hearings can be found in *EC and DE, Sub.* (1977). A list of witnesses is on iii–v; Caudle's testimony, 186–189. Senator Scott was permitted to select some of the witnesses.

29. "Election Reforms: Delay and Defeat"; Peirce and Longley, *The People's President*, 200. The sponsors of the three (by this point traditional) substitutes were Allen, Thurmond, and Scott. The three western Republicans opposed to the measure were Orrin Hatch (UT), Malcolm Wallop (WY), and Paul Laxalt (NV).

30. S. Report No. 95-609 (1977).

31. Byrd had apparently been "burned" by relying on "bad head counts" for a previous bill. Bayh's staff closely tracked how senators would vote on a cloture motion. Memo from Nels Ackerson to BB, Jan. 18, 1978, and memo from Nels Ackerson to Marcia Thomas, Jan. 31, 1978, Bayh Papers, box CA-34, Electoral Reform 1977–1980, Staff Memos 1979 Jan.–Mar.

32. "Electoral College Revision," *CQ Almanac 1979* (Washington DC, 1980): 551–553, http://library.cqpress.com.ezp-prod1.hul.harvard.edu/cqalmanac/cqal79-1183818; Peirce and Longley, *The People's President*, 198, 200–201; *LAT*, Jan. 15, 1979. Bayh, as chair of the subcommittee on constitutional amendments, had played a major role in securing passage of the ERA.

33. Peirce and Longley, *The People's President*, 176–177, 334n34; Arthur Schlesinger Jr., "Bolster the Old System with Bonuses," *LAT*, Dec. 17, 2000; "Electoral College Revision"; 125 Cong. Rec. 5053–5054 (1979). Members of the task force included Arthur Schlesinger Jr., Jeane Kirkpatrick, Heinz Eulau, Patrick Caddell, Jules Witcover, and Jill Ruckelshaus. One senator who did express interest in the bonus plan was Russell Long of Louisiana. 125 Cong. Rec. 15872–15873 (1979).

34. Peirce and Longley, *The People's President*, 201; *Hartford Courant*, Mar. 18, 1979; *LAT*, Mar. 12, 1979. The Democrats had three fewer seats in the Senate after the 1978 midterms than in the previous Congress.

35. "Electoral College Revision"; Peirce and Longley, *The People's President*, 201–202.

36. There were three senators present: Bayh, Hatch, and Thurmond. *Newsday*, Mar. 15, 1979.

37. 125 Cong. Rec. 5002–5004, 5191; "Electoral College Revision"; Peirce and Longley, *The People's President*, 201–202. The compromise included a commitment by opponents of direct election not to filibuster a motion to take up the resolution in June, but it left open the possibility of a filibuster of the resolution itself.

38. *Direct Popular Election*, 96th Cong. 1, 104, 163ff. (1979); Peirce and Longley, *The People's President*, 202–203.

39. "Direct Popular Election of the President and Vice President of the United States," S. Report 96-111, at 4–43, 71–72 (1979). Thurmond pointed out that a proportional system would also eliminate electors (and thus faithless electors). The agreement forged on March 15 provided that the resolution would be reported back directly to the Senate without having to be debated and voted on by the Judiciary Committee. It did, however, require the committee to submit a written report. See also Peirce and Longley, *The People's President*, 202–203. Regarding the expectation of a filibuster, see *LAT,* Sept. 15, 1977; *WP,* July 8, 1979. On the increasing frequency of filibusters in the 1970s, see Christopher J. Bailey, *The Republican Party in the US Senate, 1974–85: Party Change and Institutional Development* (Manchester, UK, 1988), 11, 76–77.

40. S. Report 96-111, at 9–10, 13, 37 (1979); 125 Cong. Rec. 15902 (1979); 125 Cong. Rec. 5001 (1979); 125 Cong. Rec. 5183–5184 (1979). Here and in subsequent paragraphs, the citations offer examples of views that were expressed numerous times and by numerous speakers.

41. *EC and DE, Judiciary,* 227, 314, 493 (1977); *EC and DE, Sub.,* 115 (1977); *Direct Popular Election,* 96th Cong. 413 (1979).

42. 125 Cong. Rec. 5007 (1979); 5174; John Scott to Bayh, Bayh Papers, Electoral Reform 1977–1980, Staff Binders S.J. Res. 1, binder 3, pt. 1, Mar. 11, 1977. Columnist Tom Wicker pointed out in 1976 that two "contradictory arguments" were commonly "advanced against direct popular election. One is that such an amendment would disadvantage the small states. The other is that it would disadvantage the big urban states." *NYT,* Nov. 16, 1976.

43. S. Report No. 95-609, at 26–29 (1977); S. Report 96-111, at 61–64 (1979); 125 Cong. Rec. 16805, 16807 (1979); 5175; 17477. Malcolm Wallop of Wyoming, quoted here regarding "media events," further worried that direct elections, coupled with technological change, would lead to candidates who "will be beautiful, jelly-brained people who are capable of looking good on television." 125 Cong. Rec. 17477 (1979).

44. 125 Cong. Rec. 16805–16807 (1979); S. Report 96-111, at 63 (1979).

45. S. Report 96-111, at 6–7 (1979); *EC and DE, Judiciary,* 323–324 (1977). The revised ABA report, issued in 1977, was largely a reissue of the 1967 version, although it included several new appendices as well as italicized notes regarding developments since 1967. American Bar Association Special Committee on Election Reform, *Electing the President* (Chicago, 1977). See also John D. Feerick, "The Electoral College and the Election of 1976," *American Bar Association Journal* 63, no. 6 (June 1977): 757–758. Feerick was the chair of the ABA's committee on election reform.

46. 125 Cong. Rec. 5180–5182, 5196–5197, 5221 (1979); *EC and DE, Judiciary,* 360 (1977). The debate regarding the impact of changing electoral systems on states of different

sizes was informed by two reports submitted to the committee by Joseph B. Gorman of the Congressional Research Service. The first, widely cited by opponents of direct elections, concluded that the Electoral College advantaged small states. The second, from which Bayh quoted at length, concluded that there were two independent biases operating in the Electoral College: one (stemming from the allocation of electoral votes) benefited small states, while the other (linked to winner-take-all) "definitely favors the more populous states." The losers were the medium-sized states. The report also maintained that there was no way to "prove" which bias was "more significant" although the large states seemed to benefit more. Bayh and others argued that it was fruitless to try to determine which bias was more significant: the goal of direct elections was to eliminate all biases and have all votes count equally. 125 Cong. Rec. 5193–5196 (1979); *Direct Popular Election*, 96th Cong. 49–50 (1979); David W. Abbott and James P. Levine, *Wrong Winner: The Coming Debacle in the Electoral College* (New York, 1991), 149–150n2.

47. *EC and DE, Judiciary*, 38–41 (1977); S. Report No. 95-609, at 12–13 (1977).

48. S. Report No. 95-609, at 16–19 (1977); S. Report 96-111, at 31–34 (1979); *LAT*, May 29, 1977; 125 Cong. Rec. 16803 (1979).

49. *EC and DE, Judiciary*, 52, 307 (1977); 125 Cong. Rec. 5002 (1979); see also the editorial "Abolishing Electoral College Might Boost Voter Interest," *Louisville Courier-Journal*, Jan. 12, 1977. The turnout figures are those presented at the 1977 hearings by Clark MacGregor of the U.S. Chamber of Commerce, a supporter of direct elections. More recent statistical compilations, including that of the US Elections Project, are slightly different.

50. *Electoral Reform*, Senate Subcommittee on Constitutional Amendments, 93rd Cong. 18 (1973).

51. *Electoral Reform*, Senate Subcommittee on Constitutional Amendments, 93rd Cong. 53; 123 Cong. Rec. 689 (1977); 125 Cong. Rec. 16801–16802 (1979). By 1979 Schweiker had changed his mind, voting and speaking out against S.J. Res. 28, perhaps reflecting the growing influence of the anti-reform, pro-Reagan wing of his party. Although regarded as a liberal by conservative Republicans, Schweiker went on to serve in Reagan's cabinet. 125 Cong. Rec. 17527 (1979).

52. 125 Cong. Rec. 17451–17453 (1979); S. Report 96-111, at 44 (1979). Some other southern senators, like Herman Talmadge of Georgia, also favored a proportional system, as did Arizona senator Barry Goldwater, but there was little effort in the Senate to promote that reform. *EC and DE, Judiciary*, 402 (1977); 125 Cong. Rec. 17535 (1979).

53. *WSJ*, Jan. 6, 1977; the *Chicago Tribune* (Mar. 24, 1977) took a similar position. The view that the Electoral College had worked reasonably well was also expressed by Marvin Stone, "An Unworthy Idea," *U.S. News and World Report*, May 16, 1977, 100.

54. S. Report No. 95-609, at 37–38 (1977); *EC and DE, Judiciary*, 424 (1977).

55. S. Report No. 95-609, at 37–39 (1977); S. Report 96-111, at 47–48, 67–70 (1979); *EC and DE, Judiciary*, 263 (1977). This reinterpretation of the "wrong winner" elections

was accurate with respect to 1824, and it was true that the 1876 and 1888 elections were marred by fraud and chaos in some states.

56. S. Report 96-111, at 43 (1979).

57. S. Report 96-111, at 12 (1979); Feerick, "Electoral College and the Election of 1976," 757–758; *EC and DE, Judiciary,* 501–502 (1977); 125 Cong. Rec. 17527 (1979). Bayh, in a draft speech, predicted "that there would be a political crisis" if a "wrong winner" were elected, and that "the mandate of the President to lead would be severely, perhaps irreparably weakened." Speech draft, "Three Reasons to Adopt Direct Election," Bayh Papers, box CA-33, Electoral Reform 1977–1980, Speeches and Statements—Drafts 1978, July 14, 1978.

58. Martin Diamond, *The Electoral College and the American Idea of Democracy* (Washington, DC, 1977), 18; 125 Cong. Rec. 16552 (1979).

59. Diamond, *Electoral College,* 11, 21; S. Report No. 95-609, at 40 (1977); 125 Cong. Rec. 16547 (1979); 16547; 17757.

60. S. Report No. 95-609, at 25 (1977); Diamond, *Electoral College,* 1–14, 22; 125 Cong. Rec. 16547, 16808–16812 (1979); Gary E. Bugh, "Representation in Congressional Efforts to Amend the Presidential Election System," in *Electoral College Reform: Challenges and Possibilities,* ed. Gary Bugh (Farnham, UK, 2010), 16–17.

61. 125 Cong. Rec. 5175 (1979).

62. S. Report 96-111, at 17–18 (1979); 125 Cong. Rec. 16812–16814 (1979).

63. Louis Martin, "Look for New Black Power Debate," *New Pittsburgh Courier,* Apr. 16, 1977. Martin was a distinguished newspaperman who had served as an adviser in the Kennedy, Johnson, and Carter administrations. He was sometimes referred to as the "godfather of black politics." Regarding the NAACP, see Chapter 5 as well as *New York Amsterdam News,* Apr. 19, 1969; Baltimore *Afro-American,* Oct. 3, 1970; *Oakland Post,* Oct. 1, 1970; see also *NYT,* Oct. 8, 1969, regarding black opposition to reform among state legislators.

64. 123 Cong. Rec. 684 (1977); *Direct Popular Election,* 96th Cong. 165, 169 (1979); testimony of Eddie N. Williams, *EC and DE, Sub.,* 251 (1977); Carl Rowan, "Electoral College Doesn't Help Blacks," *Atlanta Constitution,* June 29, 1979, 4A. Bayh's office was in frequent contact with members of the Congressional Black Caucus on these issues. See, for examples, memo to Sen. Bayh from staff, "Comparative Voting Power of Black Voters," April 5, 1977; "Draft letters to Black Caucus," June 1, 1977; and memo to Senator Bayh from Fred [Nation]; in Bayh Papers, box CA-35, Electoral Reform-Topical Files 1977–1980, Black Caucus 1977–1979, Mar. 20, 1979.

65. For one iteration of this perspective, see the testimony of Eddie N. Williams, *EC and DE, Sub.,* 243–256 (1977); the quotation is from a resolution approved by the NAACP convention in 1977, entered as Exhibit 20 of Williams's testimony. As discussed in Chapter 3, a similar analysis of African-American influence, from a different political perspective, had been put forward in 1950 by segregationists like Ed Gossett who sought to eliminate winner-take-all in part to diminish the influence of minorities in northern states.

66. Leah Wright Rigueur, *The Loneliness of the Black Republican: Pragmatic Politics and the Pursuit of Power* (Princeton, NJ, 2015), 245–249, 256, 270–279, 280, 283–291.

67. Ronald W. Walters, *Black Presidential Politics in America: A Strategic Approach* (Albany, 1988), 34; Wright Rigueur, *Loneliness,* 262–263; Vernon E. Jordan Jr., "To Be Equal," *Oakland Post,* Nov. 17, 1976; Frances Fox Piven and Richard Cloward, *Why Americans Still Don't Vote and Why Politicians Want It That Way* (Boston, 2000), 132. Some observers believed that John Kennedy's victory in 1960 could also be attributed to the black vote in key northern states.

68. Walters, *Politics,* 35–36; Wright Rigueur, *Loneliness,* 276–283; Vernon E. Jordan Jr. with Annette Gordon-Reed, *Vernon Can Read! A Memoir* (New York, 2002), 273–275.

69. Vernon E. Jordan Jr., with Lee A. Daniels, *Making It Plain: Standing Up and Speaking Out* (New York, 2008), 54–55. As late as May 1977, Bayh's staff had hoped to enlist Jordan's support; the staff subsequently prepared memos providing Bayh with data to refute Jordan's arguments. Memos to Bayh from Nels [Ackerson], May 12, 1977, and July 25, 1977; Marcia [Thomas] to Bayh, Aug. 4, 1977, Bayh Papers, box CA-35, Electoral Reform—Topical Files 1977–1980, Black Vote 1977–1979.

70. *EC and DE, Sub.,* 250, 253, 255–256, and Exhibit 20 (1977). Williams mentioned that there was scholarly support for his position from the Brookings Institution; he was presumably referring to Wallace Sayre and Judith Parris, *Voting for President: The Electoral College and the American Political System* (Washington, DC, 1970). Alexander Bickel's work was often cited in support of the claim that the Electoral College protected urban minorities. Williams published a preliminary version of his arguments in the *Washington Post,* Apr. 14, 1977.

71. *Atlanta Daily World,* Mar. 29, 1977; Aug. 4, 1977; Apr. 3, 5, 6, 15, and 22, 1979. Regarding Roy Patterson, see Michelle E. Shaw's obituary of Patterson, *Atlanta Journal-Constitution,* Apr. 26, 2012. The *Tri-State Defender* (Memphis) also published columns and articles opposing abolition of the Electoral College (e.g., June 16, 1979). Regarding Conyers's speech, see also Chapter 5, note 48.

72. *Cleveland Call and Post,* Apr. 23, Sept. 17, and Nov. 12, 1977; *Philadelphia Tribune,* Oct. 8, 1977; see also an article entitled "An Attack on Black Power!" in the *Bay State Banner* (Boston), Sept. 29, 1977; *Atlanta Daily News,* https://issuu.com/adwnews/docs/adw_12-27.

73. Testimony of Vernon E. Jordan Jr., *Direct Popular Election,* 96th Cong. 163 (1979).

74. According to documents prepared by Williams in late February 1979, Bayh was angered by the telegram and maintained that it was sent by Williams over the signatures of some BLF members who knew nothing about it. Bayh also accused Williams of having inaccurately claimed that he had not been permitted to testify at earlier hearings. Bayh then refused to allow Williams to join a meeting he was holding (about direct elections) with Will Maslow and Howard Squadron of the American Jewish Congress. Eddie N. Williams to Vernon Jordan, Feb. 28, 1979; Memorandum of Conversation, from Eddie Williams, Feb. 27, 1979; Williams to Betty Carter, Feb. 15, 1979; all in Papers of the Assistant for Black Affairs (Louis E. Martin Jr.), Section D, 63–66, Civil Rights During the Carter Administration,

1977–1981, box 92, part 1, Jimmy Carter Library, Atlanta, GA, microfilm publication by University Publications of America, 2006. Allusions to uncertainty regarding the views held by the signatories to the telegram also appear in Jordan's testimony, *Direct Popular Election,* 96th Cong. 178–179 (1979), and in 125 Cong. Rec. 5007–5009 (1979). Nels Ackerson, who was Bayh's chief legislative aide, recollects being present at a meeting with Williams in Bayh's office, during which Bayh expressed disappointment with the stance taken by Williams and several other civil rights leaders regarding direct elections. Williams's response was to demand that Bayh withdraw his proposed amendment, at which point the meeting came to an end (Ackerson correspondence with the author, Apr. 5, 2018).

75. *Direct Popular Election,* 96th Cong. 163–164 (1979); Thurmond had circulated the telegram to all members of the Senate. Thurmond to "colleague," Bayh Papers, box CA-35, Electoral Reform—Topical Files 1977–1980, Black Leadership Forum Telegrams 1979, Feb. 23, 1979.

76. Among those whom Jordan named as sharing his views were: Williams; Julius Chambers of the NAACP Legal Defense Fund; Benjamin Hooks, executive director of the NAACP; Dorothy Height, president of the National Coalition of Negro Women; Joseph Lowery of the Southern Christian Leadership Conference; Richard Hatcher, the mayor of Gary, IN; and Jesse Jackson of Operation PUSH. *Direct Popular Election,* 96th Cong. 164 (1979). Bayard Rustin of the A. Philip Randolph Institute was also listed as supportive of Jordan's position (which contrasted with his earlier views), yet by most accounts Rustin was isolated and little involved in domestic political issues by the late 1970s. See David Levine, *Bayard Rustin and the Civil Rights Movement* (New Brunswick, NJ, 2000), 227–228; John D'Emilio, *The Life and Times of Bayard Rustin* (New York, 2003), 475–480.

77. *Direct Popular Election,* 96th Cong. 164–168, 172 (1979).

78. *Direct Popular Election,* 96th Cong. 168, 173–183 (1979). Bayh had raised similar concerns during the testimony of Eddie Williams. *EC and DE, Sub.,* 253 (1977).

79. 115 Cong. Rec. 25997–25998 (1969); S. Report No. 95-609, at 22–23 (1977). See Chapter 5, note 48.

80. Prepared Statement of John Lewis, *Direct Popular Election,* 96th Cong. 405–406 (1979).

81. *Direct Popular Election,* 96th Cong. 405–407 (1979).

82. Testimony of Hon. Louis Stokes, *Direct Popular Election,* 96th Cong. 83–90 (1979); the statement was also inserted into the record by Senator Warren Magnuson. 125 Cong. Rec. 15906 (1979).

83. *Direct Popular Election,* 96th Cong. 83–90 (1979).

84. Rowan, "Electoral College."

85. S. Report No. 95-609, at 30 (1977); S. Report 96-111, at 57–58 (1979).

86. 125 Cong. Rec. 5007–5009, 5186 (1979); see also *Newsday,* Mar. 15, 1979.

87. 125 Cong. Rec. 15879–15880, 16543–16547 (1979). Regarding 1970, see Chapter 5.

88. S. Report No. 95-609, at 20–23 (1977); S. Report 96-111, at 28–30 (1979). Bayh's papers contain numerous memos and letters addressing these issues; see, for example,

Bayh to John Conyers, Bayh Papers, Electoral Reform 1977–1980, Correspondence-House of Rep. 1978, Apr. 26, 1978.

89. 125 Cong. Rec. 15906, 16540–16541 (1979); *Atlanta Daily World*, Apr. 3, 1979. A letter from Bayh in support of the direct elections amendment was also published in the *Norfolk Journal and Guide*, Jan. 14, 1978.

90. One exception was the prepared statement submitted to Bayh's committee in 1977 by Claude Lenehan, a Franciscan friar and social justice activist. "It is possible that there will be little concern for the Black vote in the South, the Puerto Rican vote in New York, or the Chicano vote in the Southwest if the Electoral College is completely eliminated. A candidate might view the poor minority vote not as a key to a state's electoral votes but only as a few million scattered among the nationwide hundred and fifty million votes." *EC and DE, Judiciary*, 486 (1977). Sherley Koteen also mentioned Puerto Rican and Hispanic minorities in her testimony cited below.

91. *NYT*, May 19, 1969; *Direct Popular Election*, 96th Cong. 83–90, 190–195, 376–381 (1979); Louise Milone to Bayh, "Direct Election and the Jewish Community," Bayh Papers, box CA-34, Electoral Reform 1977–1980, Staff Memos 1979 Jan.–Mar., Apr. 3, 1978. See also the exchange between Bayh and Hatch about Squadron's testimony, 125 Cong. Rec. 15879–15880 (1979). There is some evidence that the New York office of the AJC, and Squadron in particular, were significantly more hostile to reform than were other branches and officials of the organization. Peirce and Longley, *The People's President*, 335n124, 335n126.

92. *Atlanta Daily World*, Apr. 12 and 17, 1979; equally notable was the reporting of Vernon Jordan's testimony in *New York Jewish Week*, Apr. 29, 1979, 2.

93. Naomi Levine to Bayh, Bayh Papers, box CA-35, Electoral Reform—Topical Files 1977–1980, Jewish Organizations—Correspondence 1977–1979, Aug. 25, 1977. Levine also maintained (letter to Bayh, Oct. 17, 1977) that most Jewish organizations opposed direct elections.

94. *EC and DE, Sub.*, 283–288 (1977); *Direct Popular Election*, 96th Cong. 405 (1979); *Newsday*, Mar. 15, 1979. Further evidence regarding divisions within the Jewish community, and within the American Jewish Congress, can be found in Peirce and Longley, *The People's President*, 335nn124–126.

95. *NYT*, July 4, 1979; Curtis B. Gans, "Four Reasons to Keep the Electoral College," *WP*, July 2, 1978; Gans, "Electoral College Rates a Little Rah-Rah," *LAT*, Mar. 14, 1979; Rowan, "Electoral College." For a critique of Gans's views, see the column by Thomas Hayes in *Newsday*, July 26, 1978. See also Bruce Cain and Daniel Kevles, "Why Should Our Republic Have Democratic Elections?," *LAT*, Apr. 3, 1979.

96. *Direct Popular Election*, 96th Cong. 169 (1979). Jordan also noted that the disagreements among African-American leaders were "healthy." Louis Martin ("New Black Power Debate," 1977) characterized the debate among African-American leaders as between those who "fear change" and those who "see in the direct popular election system a fresh opportunity to inspire the rank and file to participate in the political process." In a later recollection, Bayh attributed Jordan's

stance, at least in part, to his desire to retain the personal (and organizational) "clout" that came with the ability to help deliver blocs of electoral votes to presidential candidates. Brian Howey, "Birch Bayh and the Enduring Electoral College," WTHR-TV, Mar. 22, 2019, https://www.wthr.com/article/howey-birch -bayh-and-enduring-electoral-college.

97. George C. Edwards III, *Why the Electoral College Is Bad for America*, 2nd ed. (New Haven, CT, 2011), 140–144; see also a succinct summary of these arguments in Tom Wicker, "Black Voting Power," *NYT*, Sept. 16, 1977. By the 1990s a consensus had formed in the scholarly literature that the Electoral College, in fact, disadvantaged African-American voters. For example, see Lawrence D. Longley and James D. Dana Jr., "The Biases of the EC in the 1990s," *Polity* 25, no. 1 (Autumn 1992): 140–145; Luis F. Rowher and Guy-Uriel Charles, "The Electoral College, the Right to Vote, and Our Federalism: A Comment on a Lasting Institution," *Florida State University Law Review* 29, no. 2 (2001): 905–906.

98. In the 1970s the argument for preserving the Electoral College may have been stronger for Jews because they were potentially swing voters in a very small number of states; it may apply now to Cuban-Americans in Florida. For a survey of Jewish views just after the 2000 election, see "Abolishing the Electoral College: Could It Really Be Bad for Jews?," *Jewish News of Northern California*, Dec. 1, 2000. In recent decades the absence of a national debate about Electoral College reform has meant that organizations representing Hispanics and other minorities have had little occasion to register their views.

99. See, for example, Jim Riley and Robert Hardaway, "Hands Off Electoral College," *Denver Post*, Feb. 8, 2007.

100. For examples of Reverend Jackson's views, see *New York Daily News*, Aug. 9, 2004; *LAT*, Aug. 20, 2017. In an interview with the author, Reverend Jackson suggested that he and other black leaders who had defended the Electoral College in the 1970s had not fully grasped the workings of the institution at that time. He indicated that the 2000 election (as well as the efforts of his son) had played a role in shifting his own views, and he stressed that the principle undergirding presidential elections ought to be "one person, one vote." (Interview with Reverend Jesse Jackson, Mar. 7, 2018.) Regarding Congressman Jackson's efforts, see U.S. Library of Congress, Congressional Research Service, *The Electoral College: Reform Proposals in the 108th Congress*, by Thomas H. Neale, RL32612 (2005).

101. *The Crisis* 115, no. 4 (Fall 2008): 55–56; "Presidential Elections Reform Program," FairVote, http://archive.fairvote.org/index.php?page=2332.

102. "Electoral College Revision"; *WP*, July 8, 1979; *NYT*, July 4 and 9, 1979; *Congressional Quarterly Weekly Report* 37, no. 26 (June 30, 1979): 1299–1300.

103. 125 Cong. Rec. 15871–15875 (1979). Bayh and his staff had also attempted privately to provide information to senators who were concerned about the small-states issue, like John Melcher from Montana. Staff memo, Bayh Papers, box CA-34, Electoral Reform 1977–1980, Staff Memos Jan.–Mar. 1979, Feb. 22, 1978.

104. 125 Cong. Rec. 15864–15900, 17695 (1979). Hatch, later in the debate, listed the organizations that backed his position, including the NAACP, the American Farm Bureau, and the National Association of Manufacturers. Black's statement, originally made in testimony to the Senate Judiciary Committee in April 1970, was frequently cited by opponents of an NPV.

105. 125 Cong. Rec. 16542 (1979); 16799–16800, 16826–16827; Peirce and Longley, *The People's President*, 204; "Electoral College Revision." Filibusters and cloture votes occurred far more frequently in the 1970s than they had earlier. Bailey, *The Republican Party*, 11.

106. 125 Cong. Rec. 17421–17427, 17454–17456 (1979); "Electoral College Revision"; Peirce and Longley, *The People's President*, 204–205; Marcia [Thomas] to Bayh, "Direct Election," June 18, 1979, and "DE Calls and Contacts," June 20, 1979, Bayh Papers, box CA-34, Electoral Reform 1977–1980, Staff Memos 1979, April–June.

107. *NYT*, July 11, 1979; *Atlanta Constitution*, July 11, 1979.

108. 125 Cong. Rec. 15901–15902, 16548–16549, 16804, 17697–17698, 17756 (1979); *Congressional Quarterly Weekly Report* 37, no. 26 (June 30, 1979): 1299–1300.

109. Among the southern newspapers that voiced support were *Montgomery* (AL) *Journal*, Nov. 19, 24, and Dec. 2, 1976; *Louisville Courier-Journal*, Jan. 12, 1977, and July 14, 1979; *Kingsport* (TN) *Times News*, Mar. 28, 1977; *Raleigh News and Observer*, Mar. 24, 1977; *Atlanta Constitution*, May 14, 1977; and the *Austin American-Statesman*, Apr. 4, 1977. As noted earlier, Alabama representative Jack Edwards testified that several newspapers in his district had come around to supporting direct elections.

110. 125 Cong. Rec. 16540–16541 (1979).

111. 125 Cong. Rec. 16809–16812, 17527, 17702–17703, 17744, 17755–17756; *NYT*, July 9, 1979. That same day, the *Washington Post* editorialized in favor of direct elections. Regarding the *New York Times*, see note 120 below.

112. Journalist Thomas Edsall noted that one reason "for the absence of a clear regional or geographic split was the fact that there was no agreement on what the political consequences of a shift to direct election would be." *Baltimore Sun*, July 11, 1979.

113. I have identified the "South" here (as in Tables 5.1 through 5.3) utilizing the census definition of the region, minus West Virginia, Maryland, and Delaware. The reasons for doing so are spelled out in Chapter 5, note 57. The general patterns evident in the 1979 roll call would also hold true utilizing broader or narrower definitions of the South. For additional analyses of the vote, see Peirce and Longley, *The People's President*, 205–206; "Electoral College Revision"; *Congressional Quarterly Weekly Report* 37, no. 28 (July 14, 1979): 1407–1408; Abbott and Levine, *Wrong Winner*, 140–145; and Mark J. McKenzie, "Systemic Biases Affecting Congressional Voting on Electoral College Reform," in Bugh, *Electoral College Reform*, 96–99, 108–110. McKenzie concluded that "southern opposition" played a key role in the defeat of the resolution, and Abbot and Levine determined that in 1979 "the South continued to be a formidable barrier to direct election." McKenzie defined the South as the states of the Confederacy; Abbot and Levine did not specify their definition. The region that voted most strongly in favor of the resolution (sixteen to eight) was

the Midwest. The pattern of liberal defections resulted in a majority of senators from the five Mid-Atlantic states voting negatively; a majority of New England senators voted favorably.

114. The category of "large states" (fifteen or more electoral votes) in 1979 included Florida plus the same eight states that had constituted that category in the 1970 tables. Judgments regarding the role played by state size in the vote have varied somewhat among analysts. Peirce and Longley, *The People's President*, 191–206, discounted the role of state size in both 1970 and 1979. McKenzie ("Systemic Biases," 108) concluded that small-state opposition (as well as ideology and region) played a role in the defeat of the amendment. His criteria for identifying a "small state," however, were not specified, although he argued that Peirce and Longley's definition of a small state (eight or fewer electoral votes) was too encompassing. Abbott and Levine (*Wrong Winner*, 140–145) maintained that senators from both the ten largest and especially the ten smallest states were more likely to vote negatively than were senators from middle-sized states. They also noted, however, that the senatorial delegations from many states (including the largest and the smallest) were divided, "suggesting that for a good number of senators the main factor was what they thought about direct election on the merits of the issue" (143). That explanation seems relevant to the differences in the voting patterns of large-state senators in 1970 and 1979. Regarding the 1970 cloture votes, see Tables 5.2 and 5.3.

115. The northern Democrats who voted negatively were Moynihan, Bradley, Sarbanes, Eagleton, Muskie, Biden, John Durkin (NH), and John Melcher (MT). Although they occupied different points on the Democratic ideological spectrum, most were moderates rather than left-liberals. The Republican moderate-liberals who voted negatively were Schweiker, Percy, Lowell Weicker (CT), and William Cohen (ME).

116. The four who had earlier supported direct election were Percy, Schweiker, Muskie, and Thomas Eagleton of Missouri. "Electoral College Revision."

117. "Electoral College Revision"; Peirce and Longley, *The People's President*, 205. Mark Gitenstein, a staff aide to Biden in 1979, believed that Biden may have been influenced both by Delaware's status as a small state and by Eddie Williams's argument that the Electoral College protected minorities. Gitenstein also recalled that Biden was not particularly engaged in the issue of electoral reform. (Interview with the author, Oct. 24, 2017.)

118. *NYT*, July 10, 1979; *Baltimore Sun*, July 11, 1979; *WP*, July 11, 1979; "Electoral College Revision."

119. See, for example, Sarbanes's statement, 125 Cong. Rec. 17475 (1979). Such concerns were also voiced by the generally liberal *New Republic* in an editorial entitled "A Bad Idea Whose Time Has Come" (May 7, 1977). Reflecting the divisions of opinion among liberals, the managing editor of the *New Republic*, Michael Kinsley, wrote a column six weeks later sharply attacking the magazine's editorial (June 25, 1977). See also Marcia [Thomas] to Bayh, "Direct Election," June 18, 1979 and "DE Calls and Contacts," June 20, 1979, Bayh Papers, box CA-34, Electoral Reform 1977–1980, Staff Memos 1979, Apr.–June.

120. There were three *NYT* editorials (Nov. 6, 1976; Feb. 7, 1977; and July 9, 1979) regarding Electoral College reform during these years. All three supported modest reforms, such as eliminating electors, and the latter two expressly opposed a national popular vote. Max Frankel, who became the editorial page editor at the end of 1976, indicated in correspondence with the author that the editorial board had several concerns about direct election, including possible problems with "chaos and corruption" in the vote count, the risk of promoting ideological third and fourth parties, and the desire to maintain the moderating influence of the two-party system. Frankel also recalled as influential the arguments against reform put forward by the leaders of black and Jewish organizations. (Correspondence with the author, Feb. 27 and 28, 2018.) The editorial board of the *Times* was undergoing something of an ideological shift during this period; Frankel's predecessor, John Oakes, had been a more predictable and consistent supporter of liberal causes. Max Frankel, *The Times of My Life and My Life with the Times* (New York, 1999), 370–387; Godfrey Hodgson, *The Gentleman from New York, Daniel Patrick Moynihan: A Biography* (Boston, 2000), 266–280.

121. Robert Packwood, a liberal Oregon Republican, missed the vote but had been expected to vote favorably.

122. *Atlanta Daily World,* July 20, 1979.

123. There were eighteen negative Republican votes on the first cloture vote in 1970 and nineteen on the second. Edwards's statement is in *EC and DE, Judiciary,* 361 (1977).

124. Bailey, *Republican Party,* 1–2, 4–5, 54–55, 65–67, 70–75. See, for an example of these conservative views, the statement of Malcolm Wallop of Wyoming, 125 Cong. Rec. 17478 (1979). A more psychological dimension was invoked by journalists Jack Germond and Jules Witcover, who observed that there existed "a fear among both politicians and academics of sailing into unknown, uncharted water. The Electoral College may be a monster, but it's their monster." *CDT,* Dec. 21, 1977.

125. The phrase "electoral lock" or "Republican lock" was coined (or at least popularized) in 1980 by Horace Busby, a longtime aide to Lyndon Johnson, who correctly predicted a Reagan landslide against Jimmy Carter. The belief that Republicans held an intrinsic advantage in the Electoral College was already present in some circles in the 1970s; it remained current at least through the 1980s and has resurfaced in the twenty-first century. I. M. Destler, "The Myth of the 'Electoral Lock,'" *PS: Political Science and Politics* 29, no. 3 (Sept. 1996): 491–494; Steven Taylor, "Whatever Happened to the Republican 'Lock' on the Electoral College?" *New England Journal of Political Science* 7, no. 1 (Spring 2013): 26–58; Abbott and Levine, *Wrong Winner,* 40–41; *CSM,* Sept. 13, 1984; *NYT,* July 8, 1988, and June 1 and 3, 2000. Abbott and Levine argued in 1991 that the notion of a "Republican lock" on the Electoral College was misleading. They maintained that the "lock" was not on the Electoral College but on the voters, and they predicted that Republicans were likely to lose the presidency only if a Democratic candidate proved to be a "wrong winner" thanks to the Electoral College. So much for prognostication!

126. *EC and DE, Judiciary,* 38–39 (1977).

127. 125 Cong. Rec. 17424 (1979); Judith Stein, *Pivotal Decade: How the United States Traded Factories for Finance in the Seventies* (New Haven, CT, 2010), 205–224.

128. *Atlanta Constitution,* July 11, 1979; "Electoral College Revision." On July 9, 1979, the *Dallas Morning News* criticized the Senate for wasting time talking about election reform rather than focusing on "gasoline lines, nuclear missiles, and rampaging revolutionaries in Nicaragua. . . . The Electoral College won't destroy the Republic. Running out of energy will."

129. Among numerous recent studies of the 1970s, see Stein, *Pivotal Decade,* and Jefferson Cowie, *Stayin' Alive: The 1970s and the Last Days of the Working Class* (New York, 2010).

130. "Electoral College Revision."

131. *NYT,* July 11, 1979. The *LAT* (July 15, 1979), which was almost alone in urging Bayh to keep fighting for direct elections, nonetheless concluded that "it will probably take another loser-take-all fiasco to convince the Senate that the Electoral College must go." The *Louisville Courier-Journal* (July 14, 1979) agreed and encouraged more modest reforms to the electoral system. For other press reactions, see *WP,* July 11, 1979; *CDT,* July 16, 1979; *Seattle Times,* July 11, 1979; *WSJ,* July 11, 1979.

7. PESSIMISM AND INNOVATION, 1980–2020

1. National Commission on Federal Election Reform, Transcript, Hearing 1, Panel 4, Mar. 26, 2001, available from The Century Foundation, http://web1.millercenter.org /commissions/comm_2001.pdf.

2. The only point at which overall support for direct elections dropped below 50 percent (to 49 percent) in Gallup polls was in December 2016. Art Swift, "Americans' Support for Electoral College Rises Sharply," *Gallup News,* Dec. 2, 2016, https://news .gallup.com/poll/198917/americans-support-electoral-college-rises-sharply.aspx; Lydia Saad, "Americans Would Swap Electoral College for Popular Vote," in *The Gallup Poll: Public Opinion 2011,* ed. Frank Newport (Lanham, MD, 2013), 376–377; Lydia Saad, "Americans Call for Term Limits, End to Electoral College," in Newport, *The Gallup Poll: Public Opinion 2013* (Lanham, MD, 2015), 23–24.

3. CRS, *Electoral College Reform: Contemporary Issues for Congress,* by Thomas H. Neale, R43824 (2017), 4.

4. The phrase "wrong winner" became current in the 1990s; after the 2000 election, "Electoral College misfire" appeared repeatedly as a way of referring to "wrong winner" elections. See, for example, CRS, *The Electoral College: Reform Proposals in the 114th and 115th Congress,* by Thomas H. Neale, R44928 (2017), 1.

5. Regarding the partisan lineups after 1980, see Gary E. Bugh, "The Challenge of Contemporary Electoral College Reform," in *Electoral College Reform: Challenges and Possibilities,* ed. Gary E. Bugh (Farnham, UK, 2010), 89–91.

6. Geoffrey Kabaservice, *Rule and Ruin: The Downfall of Moderation and the Destruction of the Republican Party from Eisenhower to the Tea Party* (New York, 2012), 326–388, 392; Donald T. Critchlow, *The Conservative Ascendancy: How the GOP Right Made Political History* (Cambridge, MA, 2007), 162–219; "Republican Views on the Electoral College," Republican Views, Mar. 26, 2018, https://www.republicanviews

.org/republican-views-on-the-electoral-college/; Alexander Keyssar, *The Right to Vote: The Contested History of Democracy in the United States,* rev. ed. (New York, 2009), 264, 277–287.

7. Kabaservice, *Rule and Ruin,* 375–378.

8. These patterns were evident in presidential elections as early as the 1980s, although the Democrats held on to statehouses in some states into the 2000s.

9. Matthew M. Hoffman, "The Illegitimate President: Minority Vote Dilution and the Electoral College," *Yale Law Journal* 105, no. 4 (Jan. 1996): 937–939, 959–960, 1001–1009; "Black Vote Smothered by Electoral College," *Black Commentator,* Oct. 28, 2004, http://www.blackcommentator.com/111/111_electoral_college.html.

10. "Americans Have Long Questioned Electoral College," *Gallup News,* Nov. 16, 2000, https://news.gallup.com/poll/2305/americans-long-questioned-electoral-college .aspx; Darren K. Carlson, "Public Flunks Electoral College System," *Gallup News,* Nov. 2, 2004, https://news.gallup.com/poll/13918/public-flunks-electoral-college -system.aspx; Saad, "Americans Call," 23–24; Saad, "Americans Would Swap," 376–377; "The Electoral College, Congress, and Representation," in Pew Research Center, *The Public, the Political System and American Democracy* (Washington, DC, Apr. 2018), 55–63; Swift, "Americans' Support for Electoral College Rises Sharply"; Carl Bialik, "The Electoral College Has Become Another Partisan Issue," *FiveThirtyEight,* Dec. 19, 2016, https://fivethirtyeight.com/features/the-electoral-college-has-become -another-partisan-issue/; see Appendix Table A.1.

11. See Chapter 6, endnote 125, regarding the origins of the phrase "Republican lock," which referred to a Republican advantage rather than a guarantee of winning. See Robert L. Dudley and Alan R. Gitelson, *American Elections: The Rules Matter* (New York, 2002), 144; William Schneider, "An Insider's View," *Atlantic Monthly,* July 1988, 29–57; James C. Garand and T. Wayne Parent, "Representation, Swing, and Bias," *American Journal of Political Science* 35, no. 4 (Nov. 1991): 1011–1031; E. J. Dionne Jr., "Analyzing the Electoral Vote: Does the GOP Have a 'Lock'?," *NYT,* Oct. 12, 1988; Barney Warf, "The U.S. Electoral College and Spatial Biases in Voter Power," *Annals of the Association of American Geographers* 99, no. 1 (2009): 197–198; Hoffman, "Illegitimate President," 960. In the 1980s (and occasionally later), some observers believed that a key source of the "Republican lock" was the presence of a "solid West" that voted heavily Republican. *WP,* Feb. 19, 1984; Gerald R. Webster, "Presidential Voting in the West," *Social Science Journal* 25, no. 2 (1988): 211–232; Frederick D. Schwartz, "The Electoral College: How It Got That Way and Why We're Stuck with It," *American Heritage,* February / March 2001, 43–50.

12. Alex Keyssar, "It Pays to Win the Small States," *NYT,* Nov. 20, 2000. In 2004 a switch of 60,000 votes in Ohio would have made John Kerry president, although George Bush won three million more votes nationally.

13. The immediate target of the platform statements appears to have been the National Popular Vote Interstate Compact, as discussed later in this chapter. But the party emphasized that it opposed "any other scheme to abolish or distort the procedures of the Electoral College." Gerhard Peters and John T. Wooley, "2012 Republican

Party Platform," American Presidency Project, Aug. 27, 2012, https://www.presidency
.ucsb.edu/node/302338; and Peters and Wooley, "2016 Republican Party Platform,"
American Presidency Project, July 18, 2016, https://www.presidency.ucsb.edu/node
/318311.

14. Swift, "Americans' Support for Electoral College Rises Sharply."
15. William Delahunt, interview with the author, Mar. 1, 2018.
16. Bugh, "The Challenge," 85–86; Bugh, *Electoral College Reform,* 251–252. Proposals for
district elections were introduced by John Ashbrook, an Ohio Republican, and Don
Fuqua, a Florida Democrat.
17. U.S. Congress, Senate, Committee on the Judiciary, Subcommittee on the Constitution, *Electoral College and Direct Election of the President,* 102nd Congress, 2nd Sess.,
113 (1992).
18. *WP,* Apr. 7, 1991; *Omaha World-Herald,* Apr. 24, 2017; James P. Melcher, "Exploring
the Difficulties of Electoral College Reform at the State Level: Maine and Nebraska
Lead the Way," in Bugh, *Electoral College Reform,* 133–139. Maine adopted a district
system in 1969. See Chapter 3.
19. Curtis Gans, "A Better Way to Elect a President," *WP,* June 26, 1990; testimony of
Curtis Gans, Subcommittee on the Constitution, *Electoral College and Direct Election,* 125, 131–132 (1992); *NYT,* June 7, 1992; George Will, "Electoral College's Campus
Radical," *WP,* June 3, 1990; Martin Dyckman, "Let's Make Florida Count Again in
Presidential Elections," *St. Petersburg Times,* Mar. 10, 1991; "Electoral College Unfair to Some States," Morning Edition, NPR, July 3, 1992; George "Skip" Roberts,
interview with the author, June 19, 2018. In that interview and in correspondence
(June 15 and 22, 2018), Roberts indicated that he attempted to develop legislative
support in as many as twenty states; most newspaper listings mention only eight or
nine in which the project made some headway. His project also played a role in Nebraska through his contact with state senator DiAnna Schimek, who spearheaded
the effort in the legislature. Roberts stated that the EFP received no direct funding
from the Democratic National Committee.
20. *NYT,* June 7, 1992; Jill Lawrence, "Democrat-Led Group Pushing for Changes in
Electoral College," Associated Press (hereafter cited as AP), July 16, 1990, Nexis Uni;
CNN Inside Politics, June 26, 1992, Nexis Uni; William M. Welch, "Proposal Could
Change Electoral System," AP, June 10, 1992, Nexis Uni; Roberts, interview and
correspondence, June 15, 19, 22, 2018; *Philadelphia Inquirer,* July 29, 1990; *Richmond
Times-Dispatch,* Feb. 8, 1992; *Charlotte Observer,* July 15, 1990.
21. *NYT,* June 7, 1992; Lawrence, "Democrat-Led Group"; CNN Inside Politics, June 26,
1992, Nexis Uni; Welch, "Proposal Could Change Electoral System"; *Orlando Sentinel,*
Feb. 25, 1992; Bill Kaczor, "Democrats in Senate Committee OK Electoral Vote," AP,
Feb. 20, 1992, Factiva; *St. Petersburg Times,* Feb. 26, 1992; *Panama City News Herald,*
Feb. 28, 1992; "Still No Action on Electoral Votes Bill," AP, Mar. 3, 1992, Factiva;
Journal of the Senate, State of Florida, 24th Sess., no. 11 (Feb. 25, 1992), 440, 442, 459;
no. 13 (Mar. 3, 1992), 507. The bill appears to have been stalled initially on a technicality
and then by its sponsors' inability to win a two-thirds vote to waive a ruling requiring

a third reading. Roberts believed that some softness in Democratic support contributed to its failure in the Florida senate. Roberts, interview, June 19, 2018.

22. George Will, "Divvy Up Electoral Votes? Be Careful," *Trenton Evening Times,* June 22, 1992; Will, "Campus Radical"; Bill Bergstrom, "Perot Strength Could Revive Electoral Proposal," AP, June 7, 1992, Factiva. Some observers believed that Perot's candidacy might shift the partisan balance in a state like Florida, making district elections more attractive to the GOP. There were also worries that the 1992 election might be more likely to end up in the House of Representatives if some states replaced winner-take-all with district elections.

23. *Richmond Times-Dispatch,* Feb. 8, 1992; Welch, "Proposal Could Change Electoral System."

24. In addition to the southern states noted earlier, district proposals were also put forward in New Jersey, Arizona, and Indiana. In New Jersey, the idea received tepid support from Democrats and vigorous opposition from Republicans. *Star Ledger* (Newark), Aug. 11, 1991.

25. *Richmond Times-Dispatch,* July 27, 1990; *Charlotte Observer,* July 15, 1990.

26. *Hartford Courant,* Apr. 3 and 24, 1990. The *Courant* editorialized against the bill while expressing support for a national popular vote. Mar. 19, 1990.

27. *Fayetteville* (NC) *Observer,* July 30, 1990; *Bradenton* (FL) *Herald,* Mar. 19, 1991; *Charlotte Observer,* Aug. 10, 1989, and July 15, 1990; *Richmond Times-Dispatch,* July 27, 1990; *Hartford Courant,* Apr. 11 and 24, 1990.

28. Dyckman, "Let's Make Florida Count Again"; *New Haven Register,* Apr. 11, 1990.

29. Dyckman, "Let's Make Florida Count Again"; Will, "Divvy Up Electoral Votes?"; *Palm Beach Post,* Mar. 20, 1992; "Changes in the Electoral College discussed," CNN Inside Politics, June 26, 1992, Nexis Uni. The eight states (plus Nebraska) cited by the *New York Times* as having had bills formally introduced in the legislatures had all voted Republican in 1988. *NYT,* June 7, 1992. Roberts believed that the national Democratic Party had no serious interest in a national reform campaign or in pressing for district elections in states where Democrats held solid majorities; he also thought that the Clinton campaign was ambivalent about promoting district elections in the South because one argument in favor of Clinton's candidacy was that only he could win the South for the Democrats. Roberts, interview, June 19, 2018.

30. Dyckman, "Let's Make Florida Count Again"; *Palm Beach Post,* Mar. 20, 1992. The fear of losing influence in the national election may have mattered less in small states like Maine and Nebraska that had little influence to lose.

31. "Gallup Presidential Election Trial-Heat Trends, 1936–2008," *Gallup News,* https://news.gallup.com/poll/110548/gallup-presidential-election-trialheat-trends-19362004.aspx#4; *NYT,* Apr. 24, 26, and June 11, 1992; *Minneapolis Star Tribune,* May 24, 1992.

32. Perot's candidacy brought more attention to these issues because his poll numbers were far higher than any that Anderson attained. Even in 1980, however, the possibility that no candidate would win a majority of the electoral votes had given rise

to a lengthy analysis of the problematic scenarios that could arise. Lawrence Tribe and Thomas Rollins, "Deadlock: What Happens if Nobody Wins," *Atlantic Monthly*, Oct. 1980, 49–62. In addition, Texas representative Martin Frost had prepared a memo for the House Rules Committee regarding the rules the House would have to adopt if it had to decide the outcome of the election. *NYT*, June 11, 1992. See also Elizabeth McCaughey, "Democracy at Risk: The Dangerous Flaws in the Electoral College," *Policy Review* 63 (Winter 1993): 79–82.

33. The Constitution specified that each state would cast one vote in the House, choosing among the top three recipients of electoral votes; it also required a candidate to receive a majority of the votes cast in the House to become president. The Constitution, however, said nothing about the rules or procedures that would govern the balloting, including whether a state's vote should be determined by a majority or a plurality of its representatives. Nor did it indicate whether the incumbents in the House or those newly elected would choose the president. The House itself would make those determinations. The need for early action on these issues was spelled out in an article in *NYT*, June 11, 1992; see also *Newsday*, May 10, 1992. In May, Representative Dan Glickman wrote to the House Speaker and to the Senate majority leader urging Congress to update its procedures in the event of a deadlocked election. *Baltimore Sun*, May 23, 1992. The Senate's procedure for choosing the vice president would be simpler: each senator would vote for one of the top two candidates. A detailed CRS report, issued on May 20, 1992, explored what one newspaper called the "constitutional chaos and uncharted waters" that might lie ahead. CRS, *Contingent Election: Congress Elects the President and Vice President*, by L. Paige Whitaker and Thomas H. Neale, 92–453 GOV (1992); *Daily Oklahoman*, May 31, 1992.

34. For examples, see James J. Kilpatrick, "Just Imagine if . . . ," *Trenton Evening Times*, Apr. 4, 1992; Bill Sellers, "Ross Perot Could Flunk Electoral College Exams," *Mobile* (AL) *Register*, Apr. 26, 1992; *Augusta* (GA) *Chronicle*, June 6, 1992; *WP*, June 21 and July 15, 1992; Lloyd Cutler, "Electoral College Dramas," *WP*, June 22, 1992; Doug Bailey, "1993—The Year Congress May Pick a President," *WSJ*, Apr. 22, 1992; *LAT*, May 16, 1992; *Hartford Courant*, June 4, 1992; *NYT*, May 10, June 4, 1992; *Minneapolis Star Tribune*, May 24, 1992.

35. David Broder, "Root of the Crisis: Divided Government," *Trenton Evening Times*, May 27, 1992; *Baltimore Sun*, May 23, 1992. Many Republicans were concerned that the Democratic House would select Clinton regardless of the popular vote.

36. *NYT*, July 17 and Oct. 26, 1992; *LAT*, Oct. 26, 1992. In October, Perot announced that he had withdrawn from the campaign in order to thwart a plot to disrupt his daughter's wedding.

37. *NYT*, Sept. 26, Oct. 2, 25, and 26, 1992.

38. *Roll Call*, July 13, 1992; *St. Louis Post-Dispatch*, May 24, 1992.

39. *Roll Call*, July 13, 1992; Subcommittee on the Constitution, *Electoral College and Direct Election*, 113 (1992). Each of the Senate resolutions had counterparts in the House. One of the committee members who did not attend was Orrin Hatch, who had led the fight against reform in 1979.

40. Subcommittee on the Constitution, *Electoral College and Direct Election*, 1–8 (1992).
41. Subcommittee on the Constitution, *Electoral College and Direct Election*, 8–18 (1992). Gorton indicated that if the vice presidential decision ended up in the Senate in 1992, he would cast his ballot for the candidate who had won the national popular vote rather than the candidate he personally preferred or for whom his state had voted. This idea foreshadowed the National Popular Vote Interstate Compact, as discussed below. Conservative columnist Charles Krauthammer endorsed Gorton's view. Charles Krauthammer, "Avoiding the Electoral Train Wreck," *WP*, May 29, 1992.
42. Subcommittee on the Constitution, *Electoral College and Direct Election*, 18–161 (1992). Bailey had been a Republican political consultant and in the 1970s had testified regarding the Electoral College.
43. *Milwaukee Journal Sentinel*, Dec. 8, 1992; Edward T. McHugh, "Electoral College Is an Anachronism Today," *Worcester* (MA) *Telegram and Gazette*, Oct. 18, 1992; *Mobile Register*, Nov. 8 and 14, 1992; *Roll Call*, July 13, 1992; for examples of post-election calls for reform, see *St. Louis Post-Dispatch*, Nov. 16 and Dec. 18, 1992.
44. *Proposals for Electoral College Reform: Hearing before the House Subcommittee on the Constitution of the Committee on the Judiciary*, 105th Cong. 37–40 (1997). A sharply critical portrait of the Electoral College was published in 1991 by political scientists David W. Abbott and James P. Levine: *Wrong Winner: The Coming Debacle in the Electoral College* (New York, 1991). A lengthy defense of the institution was offered in Robert M. Hardaway, *The Electoral College and the Constitution: The Case for Preserving Federalism* (New York, 1994). Both Walter Berns (whose testimony is cited below) and Hardaway (*The Electoral College*, 10–11) attributed anti–Electoral College public opinion to the "popular annual deluges" of criticism of the institution.
45. *Proposals for Electoral College Reform*, 105th Cong. 1–2 (1997); Bugh, *Electoral College Reform*, 252–253. Nearly all of the resolutions introduced between 1993 and 2000 were sponsored by Democrats. Canady himself had been a Democrat until 1989. Several years later a CBS news report mentioned that Henry Hyde, chair of the Judiciary Committee, had authorized this hearing as a favor to Ray LaHood, a fellow Illinoisan. "Hillary Calls for End to Electoral College," *CBS News*, Nov. 11, 2000, https://www.cbsnews.com/news/hillary-calls-for-end-to-electoral-college/.
46. *Proposals for Electoral College Reform*, 105th Cong. 3–8 (1997).
47. Akhil Amar, Becky Cain from the League of Women Voters, and Ray LaHood spoke in favor of direct elections; Judith Best, Curtis Gans, and Walter Berns of the American Enterprise Institute were opposed.
48. *Proposals for Electoral College Reform*, 105th Cong. 12–16, 40–41, 45–46, 53 (1997). A Democratic defender of the Electoral College at the hearing was subcommittee member Robert C. Scott of Virginia (9–12).
49. *Proposals for Electoral College Reform*, 105th Cong. 14, 31, 46, 53–54 (1997). Berns, an opponent of reform, nonetheless believed that a "wrong winner" would produce a crisis. Judith Best dismissed the issue, maintaining that such an outcome could be

explained to the American people in the same way that Gerald Ford's ascension to the presidency after Nixon's resignation had been explained (37, 46). Canady surely knew that Hyde had already decided that the full Judiciary Committee would hold no hearings on the resolutions, as was reported in *BG*, Sept. 5, 1997, and the *St. Louis Post-Dispatch*, Sept. 7, 1997.

50. Abbott and Levine, *Wrong Winner: The Coming Debacle in the Electoral College.*

51. John Anderson, "Electoral College Outlives Usefulness," *USA Today*, Nov. 2, 2000; *USA Today*, Oct. 30, 2000; Jeff Greenfield, "A Time Bomb in Parchment," *CNN*, Oct. 31, 2000, http://www.cnn.com/2000/ALLPOLITICS/stories/10/31/greenfield .column/; *Time*, Oct. 23, 2000; Steven Hill, "Perils of the Electoral College," *CSM*, Nov. 2, 2000; Jack N. Rakove, "The E-College in the E-Age," in *The Unfinished Election*, ed. Jack N. Rakove (New York, 2001), 202.

52. *New York Daily News*, Nov. 1, 2000; Jason Furman, interview with the author, June 25, 2018; *WP*, Nov 13, 2000; Charles Krauthammer, "Democracy and Legitimacy," *WP*, Nov. 10, 2000.

53. *BG*, Nov. 10, 2001; *WP*, Nov. 17, 2000; *NYT*, Nov. 11, 2001; *CBS News*, "Hillary Calls for End"; Akhil Amar, "The Electoral College, Unfair from Day One," *NYT*, Nov. 9, 2000; E. J. Dionne Jr., "Scrap This System," *WP*, Nov. 9, 2000; *CSM*, Dec. 4, 2000; Ronald Dworkin, "A Badly Flawed Election," *New York Review of Books*, Jan. 11, 2001.

54. *WP*, Nov. 13, 2000; *NYT*, Dec. 19, 2000, and Jan. 21, 2001; *BG*, Nov. 8, 12, 26, and Dec. 23, 2000; *Atlanta Journal-Constitution*, Nov. 12, 2000; *LAT*, Nov. 11, Dec. 17, 2000; *CDT*, Nov. 9, 28, 2000; Daryl Lindsey, "Thousands Protest Bush's Inauguration," *Salon*, Jan. 21, 2001, https://www.salon.com/2001/01/21/protests_8/. Another Republican exception was Representative Jim Leach of Iowa, a moderate who later co-sponsored a reform amendment. *WP*, Nov. 17, 2000.

55. *WP*, Nov. 17, 2000; Keyssar, *Right to Vote*, 258–262.

56. *LAT*, Nov 29, 2000; *WP*, Nov. 18, 2000; *CDT*, Nov 30, 2000. The Supreme Court majority, in the case that decided the election, wrote that "the individual citizen has no federal constitutional right to vote for electors for the President of the United States unless and until the state legislature chooses a statewide election as the means to implement its power to appoint members of the Electoral College. . . . [T]he State . . . after granting the franchise . . . can take back the power to appoint electors." Keyssar, *Right to Vote*, 262; see also Keyssar, "Shoring Up the Right to Vote: A Modest Proposal," *Political Science Quarterly* 118, no. 2 (Summer 2003): 181–203.

57. "Remembering Florida," *WP*, Dec. 17, 2000; see Rakove, "The E-College," 202–203.

58. Bugh, *Electoral College Reform*, 253.

59. Control of the Senate changed hands several times in 2000–2001. The Republicans held 55 seats during the final weeks of 2000, but in the 107th Congress, which was sworn in on January 3, 2001, there was initially a 50–50 split. From January 3 to January 20, Vice President Gore held the tie-breaking vote, giving the Democrats a majority. That changed on January 20, when Vice President Dick Cheney took of-

fice; it changed again on May 24, when Republican moderate James Jeffords of Vermont announced that he had become an independent and would henceforth caucus with Democrats.

60. Earle Geoff, "Hatch Defends Electoral College, Others Want Changes," *Congress Daily*, Dec. 13, 2000, 6; 147 Cong. Rec. 2109 (2001).

61. Among the Democrats who were not convinced that the Electoral College should be abolished were Al Gore and Bill Clinton. Mario Trujillo, "After Bush v. Gore, Obama, Clinton Wanted Electoral College Scrapped," *The Hill*, Oct. 27, 2012 (the title of the article refers to Hillary Clinton). Senate minority leader Tom Daschle also opposed reform. Mark J. McKenzie, "Systemic Biases Affecting Congressional Voting on Electoral College Reform," in Bugh, *Electoral College Reform*, 111. See Rakove, "E-College," 202–203.

62. In her 2003 memoir *Living History* (New York, 2003), Hillary Clinton sharply criticized the Supreme Court for its role in the 2000 election but made no mention of the Electoral College (524). She did, however, reiterate her criticism of the Electoral College as "profoundly undemocratic" in her 2017 volume *What Happened* (New York, 2017), 386–387.

63. Jimmy Carter, Gerald R. Ford, Lloyd N. Cutler, Robert H. Michel, and Philip D. Zelikow, *To Assure Pride and Confidence in the Electoral Process: Report of the National Commission on Federal Election Reform* (Washington, DC, 2002), 22–23; The Commission on Federal Election Reform, Hearing 1, Citizen Participation—Panel 4: The Federal Election System: Historical Perspectives, Mar. 26, 2001. The commission's final report (p. 23) contained statements suggesting that the virtues of the Electoral College outweighed its defects; it also indicated that members of the commission held "different views" on the subject. In a statement included in the final report (p. 94), commission member John Seigenthaler chided the commission for having "so obviously taken sides on a matter we agreed to avoid."

64. Carter et al., *To Assure Pride*, 5–14. Some of the commission's recommendations were imported into the Help America Vote Act of 2002.

65. Among many examples, see Michael Nelson, "Flunking the Electoral College," roundtable with Representative James Clyburn, Walter Berns, Representative William Delahunt, and James R. Whitson, *American Prospect*, Dec. 19, 2001, https://prospect.org/article/flunking-electoral-college/; Dworkin, "A Badly Flawed Election"; and an excellent four-part series in *Slate* by Timothy Noah titled "America's Worst College" (Aug. 22 and 27, Sept. 9, and Oct. 19, 2004). Numerous later examples can be found in the citations below.

66. *NYT*, Aug. 29, 2004; *WSJ*, Sept. 8, 2004; Richard S. Dunham, Lee Walczak, Paula Dwyer, Mike McNamee, and Alexandra Starr, "The Few Decide for the Many," *Business Week*, June 14, 2004, 62–65.

67. Tara Ross, *Enlightened Democracy: The Case for the Electoral College* (Los Angeles, 2004), 5–13, 31–75, 149–162, 153–173. See also Ross's more recent book, *The Indispensable Electoral College: How the Founders' Plan Saves Our Country from Mob Rule* (Washington, DC, 2017).

68. George C. Edwards III, *Why the Electoral College Is Bad for America*, 2nd ed. (New Haven, CT, 2011), x, 192–194; Edwards also made a strong affirmative case for a national popular vote.

69. William N. Grigg, "Save the Electoral College," *New American*, Jan. 1, 2001; Ross, *Enlightened Democracy*, 17–59; Gary L. Gregg II, "The Origins and Meaning of the Electoral College," in *Securing Democracy: Why We Have an Electoral College*, ed. Gary L. Gregg II (Wilmington, DE, 2001), 13–17.

70. Norman Ornstein, "No Need to Repeal the Electoral College," *State Legislatures* 27, no. 2 (Feb. 2001): 12–13; *LAT*, Dec. 17, 2000; Noah, "America's Worst College," pt. 2, Aug. 27, 2004; Mitch McConnell, "Introduction," in Gregg, *Securing Democracy*, xv; Edwards, *Electoral College*, 148.

71. See note 56 above regarding the Supreme Court's affirmation that legislatures could, by themselves, choose electors. CRS, *Electoral College Reform: Contemporary Issues*, R43824 (2017), 6. The Florida outcome was widely viewed as a statistical tie because the margin of error of the vote-counting apparatus was clearly larger than the margin of victory for either candidate. Rakove, "E-College," 221.

72. Bush won 19 of the 26 states that had fewer than ten electoral votes. The net "senatorial" electoral votes that they conferred were larger than his margin of victory in the Electoral College. Alex Keyssar, "It Pays to Win the Small States," *NYT*, Nov. 20, 2000; *NYT*, Dec. 19, 2016.

73. Ornstein, "No Need," 14–16; *LAT*, Nov. 9, 2000. A study of newspaper articles from Sept. 1, 2000 to Apr. 2, 2001 found frequent mention of the small-state advantage yet much less mention of the large-state bias than had appeared during the preceding fifteen years. "Rethinking the Electoral College Debate: The Framers, Federalism, and One Person, One Vote," *Harvard Law Review* 114, no. 8 (June 2001): 2533–2549. Jamin Raskin has described the claim that the Electoral College benefits small states as a "tenacious myth." Jamin B. Raskin, "Neither the Red States nor the Blue States but the United States: The National Popular Vote and American Political Democracy," *Election Law Journal* 7, no. 3 (2008): 188–195. For a scholarly synthesis of the view that prevailed into the 1990s, see Lawrence D. Longley and James D. Dana Jr., "The Biases of the Electoral College in the 1990s," *Polity* 25, no. 1 (Autumn 1992): 140.

74. Arthur Schlesinger Jr., "Not the People's Choice: How to Democratize American Democracy," *American Prospect*, Mar. 6, 2002, 23–27; Noah, "America's Worst College," pt. 1, Aug. 11, 2004, also commented on the "fatalism" of commentators who were sympathetic to reform, apparently unaware of the large-state advantage and convinced that small states would inescapably oppose direct elections. (For an example, see Katha Pollitt, "Let's Not Devalue Ourselves," *The Nation*, July 29, 2004.) See also the mistaken reading back of this perspective into history in a 2012 *NYT* editorial that erroneously ascribed the 1970 filibuster to senators from small states. *NYT*, Nov. 15, 2012.

75. Bugh, *Electoral College Reform*. 253; CRS, *The Electoral College: Reform Proposals in the 107th Congress*, by Thomas H. Neale, RL30844 (2001), 5–9; CRS, *Electoral College Reform: Contemporary Issues*, R43824 (2017); CRS, *The Electoral College: How It Works*

in Contemporary Presidential Elections, by Thomas H. Neale, RL32611 (2017), 18. The sole Republican initiative came from a conservative Virginia representative, Virgil H. Goode, who introduced a proposal in the 110th Congress that would have reformed the contingent election procedure but retained the Electoral College. CRS, *Contingent Election of the President and Vice President by Congress: Perspectives and Contemporary Analysis,* by Thomas H. Neale, R40504 (2016), 15.

76. CRS, *The Electoral College: An Overview and Analysis of Reform Proposals,* by L. Paige Whitaker and Thomas H. Neale, RL30804 (2004); CRS, *The Electoral College: Reform Proposals in the 108th Congress,* by Thomas H. Neale, RL32612 (2004); CRS, *The Electoral College: Reform Proposals in the 109th Congress,* by Thomas H. Neale, RL32831 (2006); CRS, *Electoral College Reform: 111th Congress, Proposals and Other Current Developments,* by Thomas H. Neale, R40895 (2009).

77. CRS, *Contingent Election,* R40504 (2016), 16.

78. 150 Cong. Rec. 5360 (2004); Representative Robert C. Scott, interview with the author, July 27, 2018.

79. Perry Apelbaum and James Park, House Judiciary Committee staff, interview with the author, Apr. 7, 2018.

80. Delahunt, interview, Mar. 1, 2018. Delahunt noted that he could have spent years working on this issue but chose not to—both because there was little chance of victory and because other issues, like the Iraq war, took precedence.

81. Greenfield, "A Time Bomb in Parchment"; for polling data, see Appendix A. A 2013 Gallup poll found that more than 60 percent of Republicans, Democrats, and independents favored "doing away" with the Electoral College. Saad, "Americans Call," 23–24; Saad, "Americans Would Swap," 376–377.

82. Tom Curry, "Split Colorado's Electoral Votes?," *NBC News,* Sept. 27, 2004, http://www.nbcnews.com/id/6106804/ns/politics-tom_curry/t/split-colorados-electoral-votes/#.XaaDHyMrIWJ; *WSJ,* Aug. 16, 2004, and Sept. 13, 2004; Jeff Milchen, "Equal Protection for Voters," *Denver Post,* Mar. 15, 2001, http://extras.denverpost.com/opinion/guest0315.htm.

83. After the 2000 census, Colorado had nine electoral votes.

84. *NYT,* Sept. 19, 2004; David Kuhn, "Is Colorado the Next Florida?," *CBS News,* Oct. 11, 2004, https://www.cbsnews.com/news/is-colorado-the-next-florida/; Curry, "Split Colorado's Electoral Votes?"; *Rocky Mountain News,* Sept. 18, 2004.

85. *NYT,* Sept. 19, 2004; "Our View: Vote No on Amendment 36," *Steamboat Pilot and Today,* Oct. 12, 2004, https://www.steamboatpilot.com/news/our-view-vote-no-on-amendment-36/; *Rocky Mountain News,* Sept. 18, 2004; *WSJ,* Sept. 12, 2004; Curry, "Split Colorado's Electoral Votes?"

86. *CSM,* Oct. 18, 2004; *WSJ,* Sept. 13, 2004; Kuhn, "The Next Florida"; *CDT,* Oct. 29, 2004; "Colorado Selection of Presidential Electors Initiative 36 (2004)," Ballotpedia, https://ballotpedia.org/Colorado_Selection_of_Presidential_Electors,_Initiative_36_(2004).

87. *BG,* Sept. 21, 2004; *WSJ,* Aug. 16, 2004; *WP,* Sept. 18, Oct. 4, 2004; Bryan Curtis, "Colorado: How Kerry Could Win It and Still Lose It, or Lose It and Still Win

It," *Slate,* Oct. 22, 2004, https://slate.com/news-and-politics/2004/10/how-kerry
-could-lose-and-win-it.html; Richard L. Hasen, "When 'Legislature' May Mean
More than 'Legislature': Initiated Electoral College Reform and the Ghost of Bush
v. Gore," 35 *Hastings Constitutional Law Quarterly* 599 (2007–2008).

88. The largest donor to groups favoring the amendment was a Phoenix- and California-
based businessman, Jorge Klor de Alva. The two largest contributors to the opposition campaign were Sheldon Adelson and Alice Louise Walton, an heir to the
Walmart fortune. John Harwood, "Challenge to Electoral College in Colorado
Could Have Big Impact," *WSJ,* Sept. 13, 2004.

89. *NYT,* Sept. 19, 2004; *BG,* Sept. 21, 2004; for a conservative view, see *WSJ,* Sept. 8, 2004.

90. Bill Whalen, "Colorado Dreamin'," *Weekly Standard,* Aug. 17, 2004; *CSM,* Oct. 18,
2004; *LAT,* Oct. 24, 2004; *St. Petersburg Times,* Oct. 26, 2004; *WSJ,* Sept. 13, 2004;
USA Today, Sept. 20, 2004; "Black Vote Smothered by Electoral College," *Black
Commentator,* Oct. 28, 2004; Curry, "Split Colorado's Electoral Votes?" For a more
skeptical view of the idea's promise, see *WP,* Oct. 4, 2004.

91. *St. Petersburg Times,* Oct. 26, 2004; Curtis, "Colorado"; *WSJ,* Sept. 12, 2004.

92. *NYT,* Sept. 29, 2004; Colorado Secretary of State, *Official Publication of the Abstract
of Votes Cast in the 2004 General Election* (Denver, State of Colorado, 2005), 138–139.

93. Gary D. Robertson, "N.C. Electoral Vote Distribution Change Moving Closer to
Passage," AP State and Local Wire, July 25, 2007, Nexis Uni.

94. *NYT,* Aug. 11, 2007; "North Carolina: This Is Why Controlling State Legislatures Is
Important," *The Hotline,* July 26, 2007, Nexis Uni; *News and Observer* (Raleigh), Aug. 1,
2007; Gary D. Robertson, "House, Senate Considering Dozens of Bills to Beat Dead-
line," AP State and Local Wire, May 24, 2007, Nexis Uni; Robertson, "N.C. Electoral Vote Distribution"; AP State and Local Wire, May 24, 2007, Nexis Uni; Ken
Rudin, "Parties Tussle over Electoral Votes," *NPR,* Sept. 26, 2007, https://www.npr
.org/templates/story/story.php?storyId=14728940; General Assembly of North Carolina, Sess. 2007, Senate Bill 353, "Presidential Electors by District," introduced
Feb. 27, 2007, https://www.ncleg.net/sessions/2007/bills/senate/pdf/s353v1.pdf;
"NC May Change Process for Selecting State's Electors," *Frontrunner,* July 31, 2007;
"Wed. July 25 at the NC General Assembly," AP, July 26, 2007, Nexis Uni.

95. Scott Shepard, "California Ballot Initiative Could Throw 2008 Presidential Election in Turmoil," Cox News Service, Aug. 16, 2007, Nexis Uni; Hendrik Hertzberg,
"Votescam: California's 'Presidential Reform Act,'" *New Yorker,* Aug. 6, 2007,
https://www.newyorker.com/magazine/2007/08/06/votescam; *NYT,* Aug. 11, 2007.

96. *LAT,* Aug. 6, 2007; Hertzberg, "Votescam"; *Inland Valley Daily Bulletin* (On-
tario, CA), Sept. 2, 2007; Peter Dreier, "GOP Dirty Tricks Campaign Seeks to
Divide California's Electoral Votes," *Huffington Post,* Nov. 4, 2007, https://www
.huffingtonpost.com/entry/gop-dirty-tricks-campaign_b_71065. The June election
was expected to have low turnout, which would likely have favored supporters of
the measure.

97. *LAT,* Aug. 6 and Sept. 3, 2007; *CSM,* Aug. 13, 2007; William Schneider, "California
(2/5 Primary): Doin' the Splits?," *National Journal,* Sept. 8, 2007, https://www

.nationaljournal.com/s/276849/california-2-5-primary-doin-splits?; Bill Berkowitz, "Republicans Trying to Split California Electoral Vote," Media Transparency, Sept. 12, 2007, http://web.archive.org/web/20071008181331/http://www.mediatransparency .org/story.php?storyID=211.

98. *LAT,* Aug. 6, 2007; *North County Times* (San Diego and Riverside Counties, CA), Sept. 18, 2007; *USA Today,* Aug. 17, 2007.

99. *LAT,* Sept. 3, 2007; *North County Times,* Sept. 18, 2007; *Sacramento Bee,* Sept. 29, 2007.

100. Bob Herbert, "In 2008, Bush v. Gore Redux?," *NYT,* Sept. 22, 2007; Doug Kendall, "The Legislature Thereof," *Slate,* Sept. 13, 2007, https://slate.com/news-and-politics /2007/09/california-voters-can-t-change-the-2008-election-rules-on-their-own .html.

101. *NYT,* Sept. 29, 2007; *LAT,* Sept. 27, 2007; *Contra Costa Times,* Sept. 29, 2007; Dreier, "GOP Dirty Tricks Campaign."

102. *LAT,* Sept. 28 and 29, 2007; *San Francisco Chronicle,* Oct. 1 and 2, 2007; *Contra Costa Times,* Oct. 2, 2007. Donors were permitted to make unlimited contributions to initiative campaigns, but donations designed to benefit individual candidates were limited by federal law.

103. Michael R. Blood, "Calif. Republican Attempts to Revive Electoral-Vote Plan," AP State and Local Wire, Oct. 4, 2007, Nexis Uni; *NYT,* Oct. 4, 2007; *Contra Costa Times,* Sept. 29, 2007; Dreier, "GOP Dirty Tricks Campaign"; *WP,* Nov. 4, 2007; *San Gabriel Valley Tribune,* Dec. 8, 2007; *San Jose Mercury News,* Feb. 6, 2008; "Calif. Electoral Plan in Trouble," UPI, Dec. 2, 2007, https://www.upi.com/Top_News/2007 /12/02/Calif-electoral-plan-in-trouble/69121196578340/; *Inland Valley Daily Bulletin,* Sept. 29, 2007.

104. In theory, all states could simply agree to abolish winner-take-all, without congressional involvement, but no one found that scenario to be plausible. The need for national change was stressed in editorials in the *NYT* (Aug. 22, 2007) and the *San Francisco Chronicle* (Aug. 20, 2007).

105. Some Republicans had proposed state-level changes earlier in the twenty-first century. After the 2000 election, for example, Grover Norquist had recommended that Republicans end winner-take-all in New Jersey and Pennsylvania; Republican leaders were uninterested. *WSJ,* Sept. 13, 2004.

106. *Harrisburg* (PA) *Inquirer,* Dec. 4, 2012; *Detroit Free Press,* Nov. 23, 2014; *Lansing* (MI) *State Journal,* Dec. 7, 2014; *Milwaukee Journal Sentinel,* Jan. 13, 2013; John Nichols, "RNC's Priebus Proposes to Rig Electoral College So Losing Republicans Can 'Win,'" *The Nation,* Jan. 14, 2013, https://www.thenation.com/article/rncs-priebus -proposes-rig-electoral-college-so-losing-republicans-can-win/; Reid Wilson, "Republicans Want to Reform the Electoral College to Help Themselves," *The Atlantic,* Dec. 17, 2012, https://www.theatlantic.com/politics/archive/2012/12/republicans-want -to-reform-the-electoral-college-to-help-themselves/266355/; Alan Greenblatt, "Some in GOP Want New Electoral Rules," NPR, Jan. 25, 2013, https://www.npr .org/sections/itsallpolitics/2013/01/25/170276794/some-in-gop-want-new -electoral-college-rules; Ed Garvey, "The GOP's Latest Scheme to Grab the

Presidency," *Capital Times and Wisconsin State Journal,* Dec. 26, 2012; Jonathan Oosting, "Winner Won't Take All?," *MLive,* Jan. 29, 2013, https://www.mlive.com /politics/index.ssf/2013/01/winner_wont_take_all_michigan.html; Dana Liebelson, "The GOP's Plan to Rig the Electoral College, Explained," *Mother Jones,* Jan. 31, 2013, https://www.motherjones.com/politics/2013/01/gops-election-rigging-plan -explained/.

107. Richard L. Hasen, "Democrats, Don't Freak Out! Why Fears that Republicans Will Gerrymander the Electoral College Are Overblown," *Slate,* Jan. 25, 2013, http://www.slate.com/articles/news_and_politics/politics/2013/01/republican _plans_for_electoral_college_reform_democrats_shouldn_t_worry.html; Claire Daviss, "Virginia Bill Would Allocate Electoral Vote Proportionally," FairVote, Jan. 29, 2015, http://www.fairvote.org/virginia_bill_would_allocate_electoral_votes _proportionally; "Virginia Kills Electoral College Reform Bill," UPI, Jan. 29, 2013, https://www.upi.com/Va-kills-Electoral-College-reform-bill/73501359507844/; *Lansing State Journal,* Dec. 3, 2014; *Philadelphia Inquirer,* Feb. 8, 2013.

108. A back-of-the-envelope calculation suggests that if these states had distributed their votes in some proportional manner, Trump would likely still have won the election but by a significantly reduced margin. The outcome might, in fact, have depended on whether those states chose a proportional system or an allocation by gerrymandered districts. To be sure, had winner-take-all not been in place, the campaigning would also have been different. See *WP,* Jan. 25, 2017.

109. "Press Release for Initial Press Conference," and "Prepared Remarks from Press Conference," National Popular Vote, Feb. 23, 2006, http://archive.nationalpopularvote .com/pages/releases/20060223.php. The quotation is from Buchanan's remarks. See also *Pittsburgh Post Gazette,* Feb. 26, 2006. For an excellent summary of the historical backdrop to the NPVIC and its progress from 2006 through 2014, see CRS, *The National Popular Vote Initiative: Direct Election of the President by Interstate Compact,* by Thomas H. Neale and Andrew Nolan, R43823 (2014).

110. National Popular Vote, "Prepared Remarks," Feb. 23, 2006.

111. *NYT,* Sept. 22, 2006; CRS, *Electoral College Reform: 111th Congress,* R40895 (2009), 19–20.

112. Similar ideas had appeared before 2001 but had garnered little attention. The foremost example was Dale Read Jr., "Direct Election of the President without a Constitutional Amendment: A Call for State Action," *Washington Law Review* 51, no. 2 (Mar. 1976): 321–360.

113. Robert W. Bennett, "Popular Election of the President without a Constitutional Amendment," *Green Bag* (Spring 2001): 241–245. In the late nineteenth and early twentieth centuries, proposals to amend the Constitution to require the popular election of senators encountered substantial resistance in Congress. Many states responded by holding "unofficial" popular elections that guided the decisions of their legislatures. After these de facto popular elections had been instituted in numerous states, Congress approved the Seventeenth Amendment. See Todd J. Zywicki, "Beyond the Shell and Husk of History: The History of the Seventeenth Amendment

and Its Implications for Current Reform Proposals," *Cleveland State Law Review* 45 (1997): 165.

114. Bennett, "Popular Election," 241–246. Bennett developed his ideas more amply in his 2006 book, *Taming the Electoral College* (Stanford, CA, 2006), esp. 45–73, 161–190. He was also concerned about the failure of Congress to alter features of the electoral system that were almost unanimously seen as problematic, such as faithless electors and the contingent election procedure.

115. Akhil Amar and Vikram Amar, "How to Achieve Direct National Election without Amending the Constitution," FindLaw, Dec. 28, 2001, https://supreme.findlaw.com /legal-commentary/how-to-achieve-direct-national-election-of-the-president -without-amending-the-constitution.html. See also Jennings "Jay" Wilson, "Bloc Voting in the Electoral College: How the Ignored States Can Become Relevant and Implement Popular Election Along the Way," *Election Law Journal* 5, no. 4 (2006): 384–409.

116. *NYT,* Sept. 22, 2006; CRS, *Electoral College Reform: 111th Congress,* R40895 (2009), 17; correspondence with John Koza, Dec. 22, 2018. The text of the compact can be found in John Koza et al., *Every Vote Equal: A State-Based Plan for Electing the President by National Popular Vote,* 4th ed. (Los Altos, CA, 2013), 259–260. The wording regarding withdrawal is in Article IV-2: "Any member state may withdraw from this agreement, except that a withdrawal occurring six months or less before the end of a President's term shall not become effective until a President or Vice President shall have been qualified to serve the next term."

117. For example, Tim Storey of the National Conference of State Legislators characterized the NPVIC as a "non-starter" and "tilting at windmills." Louis Jacobson, "Electoral Vote Reform: Is It an Idea Whose Time Has Come?," *Roll Call,* May 10, 2006.

118. *LAT,* June 5, 2006; *NYT,* Mar. 14, 2006. See also *NYT* editorials on Oct. 20, 2008, Nov. 15, 2012, and Nov. 8, 2017. Endorsements also came from the *Minneapolis Star Tribune, Denver Post,* and *Chicago Sun-Times.*

119. Jacobson, "Electoral Vote Reform"; *St. Louis Post-Dispatch,* May 11, 2006; *NYT,* Oct. 3, 2006; "News History," National Popular Vote, https://www.nationalpopu larvote.com/news-history; Shane Johnson, "College Drop Out," *Salt Lake City Weekly,* Aug. 31, 2006, 20; Brendan Mackie and Ben Weyl, "College Dropouts: The Campaign to Reform the Electoral College Actually Gains Ground," *American Prospect,* Oct. 2006, 15.

120. "News History," National Popular Vote; Raskin, "Neither the Red States nor the Blue States," 188–195; *Ottumwa* (IA) *Courier,* Apr. 10, 2007; *NYT,* Apr. 14 and Aug. 11, 2007; "Hawaii Governor Vetoes Popular Plan for President," AP State and Local Wire, Apr. 24, 2007, Nexis Uni; Mark Niesse, "Hawaii Joins Drive for Presidential Popular Vote," AP, May 2, 2008, Nexis Uni; *Daily Herald Suburban* (Chicago), Apr. 7, 2008; "North Dakota, Montana, Reject Plan to Alter US Pres Elections," *Dow Jones International News,* Feb. 8, 2007, Factiva; Ernest Dumas, "One Man, One Vote," *Arkansas Times,* Feb. 12, 2009.

121. "News History," National Popular Vote; CRS, *Electoral College Reform: 111th Congress,* R40895 (2009), 15–18; Randy Dotinga, "A Backdoor Plan to Thwart the Electoral College: Some States Try to Ensure That the Winner of Popular Vote Becomes President," *CSM,* June 16, 2006; Rob Richie and Andrea Levien, "Big New York Win for National Popular Vote Drive to Reform (Not Abolish) Electoral College," *Huffington Post,* June 4, 2014, https://www.huffingtonpost.com/entry/big-new-york -win-for-nati_b_5093548; *Orange County* (CA) *Register,* Nov. 5, 2012. The bill approved in New York in 2014 stipulated that the state would be removed from the compact if it had not become binding by 2018. In 2016 the legislation was modified to eliminate that sunset date. "Gov. Cuomo Signs Legislation Securing New York State's Place in the NPV Compact," Nov. 7, 2016, https://www.governor.ny.gov/news /governor-cuomo-signs-legislation-securing-new-york-states-place-national -popular-vote-compact.

122. Koza, correspondence, Dec. 22, 2018; Michael Beckel, "National Popular Vote Plan Pushers Hire New Lobbyists, Bring on Deep-Pocketed Help," Center for Responsive Politics, Feb. 23, 2011, https://www.opensecrets.org/news/2011/02/national -popular-vote-plan-pushers-hire-new-lobbyists/; Lynn Morski, "League of Women Voters Keeps National Popular Vote Movement Alive in Colorado," *Independent Voter News,* July 17, 2017, https://ivn.us/2017/07/17/league-women-voters-keeps -national-popular-vote-movement-alive-colorado/; Tim Alberta, "Is the Electoral College Doomed?," *Politico Magazine,* Sept./Oct. 2017, https://www.politico.com /magazine/story/2017/09/05/electoral-college-national-popular-vote-compact -215541; John Miller, "Idaho Latest Venue for Presidential Election Reform," AP State and Local Wire, Oct. 7, 2009, Nexis Uni; *Philadelphia Tribune,* Oct. 7, 2011. In Oklahoma, some Republicans publicly objected to the hiring of lobbyists from out of state. Michael Bates, "National Popular Vote's Ray Haynes Lobbying Oklahoma Grassroots Conservatives," *BatesLine,* Sept. 10, 2014, http://www.batesline.com /archives/2014/09/ray-haynes-national-popular-vote.html; and "Betrayal: Oklahoma Senate Passes National Popular Vote Bill," *BatesLine,* Feb. 13, 2014, http://www .batesline.com/archives/2014/02/national-popular-vote-oklahoma.html. The results of the polls conducted in each state can be found at www.nationalpopularvote.com.

123. David Klamann, "Colorado Should Join National Popular Vote Interstate Compact," *Daily Camera* (Boulder), Nov. 14, 2016; *Santa Fe New Mexican,* Feb. 21, 2009; Dennis Ferguson, "No More College," *Memphis Flyer,* June 16, 2011; *St. Louis Post-Dispatch,* Feb. 22, 2007; Maine Legis. Rec. H-1014 (Feb. 2, 2010), http://lldc.mainelegislature .org/Open/LegRec/124/House/LegRec_2010-02-02_HP_pH1011-1030.pdf; Richie and Levien, "Big New York Win," July 12, 2015; "Rep. Mimi Stewart to Intro National Popular Vote Bill," *Democracy for New Mexico,* Dec. 29, 2008, Nexis Uni; *Cedar Rapids* (IA) *Gazette,* Oct. 18, 2011.

124. Dumas, "One Man, One Vote"; *Times Reporter* (New Philadelphia, OH), Feb. 10, 2008; John Curran, "Douglas Vetoes Bill to Bypass Electoral College System," AP State and Local Wire, May 16, 2008, Nexis Uni; Ainsley Shea, "Correcting and Replacing: California State Senate Passes National Popular Vote Law," *Business*

Wire, July 14, 2011, https://www.businesswire.com/news/home/20110714006438/en /CORRECTING-REPLACING-California-State-Senate-Passes-National; "Gov. Cuomo Signs Legislation"; *Arizona Daily Star* (Tucson), Feb. 2, 2016.

125. *Salt Lake Tribune,* Oct. 22, 2016. Bramble had initially been an opponent of the compact but became a strong advocate after "learning more about the pros and cons." Regarding the ability of swing states to attract federal funds and grants, see also Robert Richie and Andrew Levien, "How the 2012 Presidential Election Has Strengthened the Movement for the National Popular Vote Plan," *Presidential Studies Quarterly* 43, no. 2 (June 2013): 355; Connecticut Gen. Assembly, Senate, transcript of debate on HB5421, May 5, 2018, 3; Nebraska Leg., Government, Military and Veterans Affairs Comm. Hearing transcript, Jan. 23, 2015, 67, https://www.nebraskalegislature.gov /FloorDocs/104/PDF/Transcripts/Government/2015-01-23.pdf.

126. The most recent edition of *Every Vote Equal* was published in 2013; the website can be found at www.nationalpopularvote.com. See also *The Record* (northern NJ), Dec. 15, 2008; Mackie and Weyl, "College Dropouts," 15. For examples of this argument's appeal to Republicans, see the *Journal Record* (Oklahoma City), July 30, 2013; *Salt Lake Tribune,* Oct. 22, 2016.

127. Richie and Levien, "2012 Presidential Election," 353–376; Adam Liptak, "The Vanishing Battleground," *NYT,* Nov. 3, 2012. The number of swing states declined from more than twenty in the 1970s to fewer than a dozen in 2012. The number of electoral votes cast by swing states also declined, in part because few large states remained contested.

128. Tara Servatius, "By Popular Demand?," *Creative Loafing* (Charlotte, NC), June 13, 2007; Paul Greenberg, "Electoral College Worth Saving," *Arkansas Democrat-Gazette* (Little Rock), Apr. 5, 2007; Bob Katzen, "Beacon Hill Roll Call," *Lowell* (MA) *Sun,* June 6, 2010; "Editorial: Still Ill-Conceived," *Pueblo* (CO) *Chieftain,* Jan. 28, 2007; Connecticut Gen. Assembly, House of Representatives, transcript of proceedings, Apr. 26, 2018, 26. Nearly all of the objections to the NPVIC mentioned here were responded to at length in Koza et al., *Every Vote Equal,* chap. 9.

129. "North Dakota, Montana Reject Plan," Dow Jones International News, Feb. 8, 2007, Factiva. This point was made often in less-populated areas. For examples, see "They're Still Sore about Bush v. Gore," *Victorville* (CA) *Press Dispatch,* Aug. 21, 2011, Nexis Uni; Steven K. Paulson, "Colorado Lawmakers Debate Plan to Dilute Electoral College," AP State and Local Wire, Apr. 11, 2006, B4; *Register-Guard* (Eugene, OR), Mar. 15, 2017; *Charleston* (WV) *Gazette,* Oct. 23, 2008; *St. Louis Post-Dispatch,* May 11, 2006: Maine Legis. Rec. H-1017 (Feb. 2, 2010). It was also emphasized in the veto message delivered by Vermont governor Jim Douglas in 2008. Curran, "Douglas Vetoes."

130. For examples, see *Daily Herald Suburban* (Chicago), Apr. 7, 2008; *WSJ,* Mar. 28, 2009; *Santa Fe New Mexican,* Feb. 21, 2009; Jan Ting, "It Still Has Its Place: Electoral College," *San Marcos* (TX) *Daily Record,* Aug. 25, 2011; Maine Legis. Rec. H-1021 (Feb. 2, 2010).

131. Dotinga, "A Backdoor Plan"; David Gram, "Vt. Senate Advanced National Popular Vote Measure," AP State and Local Wire, Feb. 22, 2011, Nexis Uni; "Editorial:

Lawmakers Wrong for Attempting to Go around the Electoral College," *Walla Walla* (WA) *Union-Bulletin,* Apr. 23, 2009; *Gazette* (Colorado Springs), Mar. 9, 2007; *Daily Reflector* (Greenville, NC), May 29, 2008; *Oregonian* (Portland), Mar. 12, 2009; Raskin, "Neither the Red States nor the Blue States," 193.

132. Martin G. Evans, "Picking a President—Through the Constitution," *BG,* Jan. 22, 2008; Benjamin Israel, "Efforts to Change Presidential Voting," *St. Louis Journalism Review,* Sept. 1, 2008, 6. When the issue was raised in Nebraska in 2015, Patrick Rosenstiel replied that "the time to talk about congressional consent would be after states totaling 270 or more electoral votes pass the bill." Patrick Borchers, a legislator, pointed out the hazards of such an approach. Nebraska Leg., Hearing transcript, Jan. 23, 2015, 70, 80.

133. *Annapolis Capital-Gazette,* Feb. 17, 2009; Gary D. Robertson, "Exciting Vote Leads to Talk about How NC Picks a President," AP, May 18, 2008, Nexis Uni; *Hartford Courant,* May 13, 2009; *Santa Fe New Mexican,* Feb. 21, 2009; Connecticut Gen. Assembly, Senate, May 5, 2018, 43; Israel, "Efforts to Change," 6. This issue became prominent in Oregon, where an NPVIC bill was passed by the house several times but blocked by the president of the senate, Democrat Peter Courtney, who argued that Oregon's electoral votes should never be cast for a candidate who had not been endorsed by the state's voters. In 2018 Koza donated $30,000 to Courtney's primary opponent and to his Republican opponent in an unsuccessful effort to block his reelection. Shawn M. Griffiths, "Democratic Leaders Block National Popular Vote in Oregon," *Independent Voter News,* July 7, 2017, https://ivn.us/2017/07/07/democratic -leaders-block-national-popular-vote-bill-oregon/; *Willamette* (OR) *Week,* Apr. 14, 2018; *Statesman Journal* (Salem, OR), Apr. 26, 2018.

134. Connecticut Gen. Assembly, Senate, May 5, 2018, 32; Connecticut Gen. Assembly, House, Apr. 26, 2018, 47. See also *The Record* (North Jersey), Dec. 15, 2008; "Editorial: Still Ill-Conceived," *Pueblo Chieftain,* Jan. 28, 2007; "Attorney General Suthers," *US States News,* Jan. 25, 2007, Nexis Uni.

135. Evans, "Picking a President"; Steve Haycox, "Electoral College Is Overdue for the Dustbin," *Alaska Dispatch News* (Anchorage), Dec. 4, 2016, https://www.adn.com /opinions/2016/12/03/electoral-college-is-overdue-for-the-dustbin/; Michael Bates, "2019 OKGOP Convention Thoughts," *BatesLine,* Apr. 5, 2019, http://www.batesline .com/archives/2019/04/2019-okgop-convention-thoughts.html; Maine Legis. Rec. H-1015 (Feb. 2, 2010); Connecticut Gen. Assembly, Senate, May 5, 2018, 38. A cogent summary of the arguments for and against the NPVIC can be found in CRS, *National Popular Vote Initiative,* R43823 (2014), 11–27.

136. Koza et al., *Every Vote Equal,* 4th ed. (2013) contained more than 400 pages of "responses to myths about the National Popular Vote Compact." It surveyed the legal and political objections to the compact (including those noted in this chapter) and concluded that they were all without merit.

137. Derek T. Muller, "The Compact Clause and the National Popular Vote Interstate Compact," *Election Law Journal* 6, no. 4 (2007): 372–393; Muller, "More Thoughts on the Compact Clause and the National Popular Vote," *Election Law Journal* 7, no. 3

(2008): 227–232. The compact clause of the Constitution specifies that "no state shall, without the Consent of Congress … enter into any agreement or compact with another state." Muller acknowledged that many interstate agreements that lacked congressional approval had been sanctioned by the courts, but he observed that these generally concerned matters like bridges, port authorities, and natural resources. He argued that the NPVIC, which would be the first interstate compact involving elections, required congressional assent because it would produce shifts of power among the states. Ian Drake went a step further than Muller, arguing that it would be unconstitutional for Congress to approve the NPVIC. Ian Drake, "Federal Roadblocks: The Constitution and the NPV Interstate Compact," *Publius: The Journal of Federalism* 44, no. 4 (2013): 681–701. For a digest of these constitutional issues, see CRS, *National Popular Vote Initiative*, R43823 (2019 update).

138. Jennifer S. Hendricks, "Popular Election of the President: Using or Abusing the Electoral College?," *Election Law Journal* 7, no. 3 (2008): 218–226; Bennett, *Taming the Electoral College,* 170–173; Vikram Amar, "The Case for Reforming Presidential Elections by Subconstitutional Means: The Electoral College, the NPVC, and Congressional Power," *Georgetown Law Review* 100, no. 1 (2011): 237–261; Raskin, "Neither the Red States nor the Blue States," 193; CRS, *National Popular Vote Initiative,* R43823 (2019 update), 18–27; Brian J. Gaines, "Compact Risk: Some Downsides to Establishing National Plurality Presidential Elections by Contingent Legislation," in Bugh, *Electoral College Reform,* 117–118; Robert W. Bennett, "Current Electoral College Reform Efforts among the States," in Bugh, *Electoral College Reform,* 192–201. Court rulings in the nineteenth century made it clear that interstate compacts that enhanced the power of states vis-à-vis the federal government would require congressional consent. Most legal commentators do not believe that the NPVIC belongs in this category. A second issue is whether the NPVIC would enhance the power of some states (e.g., those participating in the compact) in relation to others, and, if so, whether that would trigger the need for congressional approval. Discussions of these issues are presented in Koza et al., *Every Vote Equal,* 205–253.

139. The gist of Williams's argument was that states do not possess the right to cast their electoral votes based on votes cast in other states. The only constitutional route to direct elections, therefore, was through the amendment process. Norman R. Williams, "Why the National Popular Vote Compact Is Unconstitutional," *Brigham Young University Law Review* 2012, no. 5 (2012): 1523–1579 (see esp. 1526n12); Raskin, "Neither the Red States nor the Blue States," 188–195.

140. David Gringer, "Why the National Popular Vote Plan Is the Wrong Way to Abolish the Electoral College," *Columbia Law Review* 108, no. 1 (Jan. 2008): 182–230. The NPVIC did receive preclearance from the Justice Department in 2012 after it was adopted by California.

141. Sanford Levinson, "Is Moderation Sufficient When Addressing the Ills of the Electoral College?," *Election Law Journal* 6, no. 2 (2008): 222–225; Norman R. Williams, "Reforming the Electoral College: Federalism, Majoritarianism, and the Perils of Subconstitutional Change," *Georgetown Law Journal* 100 (2011): 203–204;

Curtis Gans, "Why National Popular Vote Is a Bad Idea," *Huffington Post,* Mar. 7, 2012, https://www.huffingtonpost.com/curtis-gans/national-popular-vote_b_1189390 .html; CRS, *National Popular Vote Initiative,* R43823 (2019 update), 15. In response to these concerns, there has been discussion of adding ranked choice voting to the NPV initiative to guarantee that the winning candidate would have majority support. See, for example, Lee Drutman, "If We're Abolishing the Electoral College, Let's Also Have Ranked Choice Voting," *Vox,* Mar. 21, 2019, https://www.vox.com /polyarchy/2019/3/21/18275785/electoral-college-ranked-choice-voting-president -democracy. For a critique of this approach (and the NPVIC's lack of majoritarianism more broadly), see Edward B. Foley, "Want to Fix Presidential Elections? Here's the Quickest Way," *Politico,* May 4, 2019, https://www.politico.com/magazine /story/2019/05/04/electoral-college-reform-2020-226792.

142. Amar and Amar, "How to Achieve Direct National Election"; Amar, "The Case for Reforming," 237–261; Vikram Amar, "The National Popular Vote Bill Proposal in California and Ultimately (Perhaps) in Washington, D.C.," *Verdict,* Justia, Aug. 5, 2011, https://verdict.justia.com/2011/08/05/the-national-popular-vote-bill-proposal -in-california-and-ultimately-perhaps-in-washington-d-c; Williams, "Reforming the Electoral College," 222–232. The Amar brothers, in their early proposal, had advocated uniform national suffrage rules and election procedures. Derek Muller raised questions, both normative and pragmatic, about any shift toward national standards for suffrage and electoral administration. Muller, "Invisible Federalism and the Electoral College," *Arizona State Law Journal* 44 (2012): 1238–1292.

143. Williams, "Reforming the Electoral College," 178–180, 208–219, 232; Bennett, *Taming the Electoral College,* 174–177; Robert W. Bennett, "Possibilities and Problems in the National Popular Vote Movement," *Election Law Journal* 7, no. 3 (2008), 183–185; Amar, "The Case for Reforming," 237–261; Gaines, "Compact Risk," 118–120, voiced concerns about the challenges of recounts even if states were cooperating. The debates in the Connecticut senate also touched on this issue. Connecticut Gen. Assembly, Senate, May 5, 2018, 17. See also Koza et al., *Every Vote Equal,* chap. 9.

144. Statement of Alexander Keyssar, forum on "The Electoral College and the Future of American Democracy," Judiciary Committee, United States House of Representatives, Dec. 6, 2016. My recollection is that Akhil Amar and Jack Rakove, both of whom were in attendance, concurred with this point. See also Gaines, "Compact Risk," 120–122. This issue was raised in debate in the Connecticut House, Apr. 26, 2018, 49. Koza, in correspondence with the author (Dec. 22, 2018), pointed out that states currently have the right to switch from winner-take-all to district or proportional elections every four years. The historical record, however, suggests that changes away from winner-take-all are unlikely to occur.

145. For an example of party-line voting in a state that approved the compact, see *The Record* (North Jersey), Dec. 15, 2008. When one branch of a legislature approved a bill, it remained "alive" only until the next legislative elections.

146. *WP,* Aug. 2, 2013; CRS, *National Popular Vote Initiative,* R43823 (2019 update), 10–12; Nate Silver, "Why a Plan to Circumvent the Electoral College Is Probably

Doomed," *FiveThirtyEight*, Apr. 17, 2014, https://fivethirtyeight.com/features/why
-a-plan-to-circumvent-the-electoral-college-is-probably-doomed/; Gaines, "Compact Risk," 123–124. Regarding the resistance of battleground states, see also *Tampa
Bay Times*, Jan. 1, 2017; Tim Alberta, "Is the Electoral College Doomed?"; *Cedar
Rapids (*IA) *Gazette*, Mar. 3, 2009, and Oct. 18, 2011. In 2009, a spokesman for Iowa's governor, Chet Culver, warned that a national popular vote would end Iowa's
status as "a battleground state and the opportunity to ensure that the ideas that are
important to Iowa's Main Streets remain important on both ends of Pennsylvania
Avenue." Two years later, however, Culver endorsed the NPVIC. "Fred Thompson,
Chet Culver, and Jim Edgar Endorse National Popular Vote Bill," National Popular
Vote, May 14, 2011, http://archive.nationalpopularvote.com/pages/misc/hl_20110514
_thompson-culver-edgar.php.

147. CRS, *National Popular Vote Initiative*, R43823 (2019 update), 28. In the author's experience, primarily in Massachusetts, relatively few citizens attending events sponsored by organizations like the League of Women Voters knew that their state had
joined the NPVIC.

148. Koza et al., *Every Vote Equal*, xxxviii; Rosenstiel identified himself as a "Steve Forbes
Republican." Nebraska Leg., Hearing transcript, Jan. 23, 2015, 68–70. In several states,
including Nebraska (Hearing transcript, 76–77), some legislators expressed annoyance (and suspicion) at the presence of out-of-state lobbyists working on behalf of
a bill promoted by a wealthy Californian.

149. David L. Schaefer, "Don't Mess with the Electoral College," *WSJ*, July 12, 2008;
George Detweiler, "Assault on the Electoral College," *New American*, June 26,
2006, 33–34; Patrick McIlheran, "The New Coke Voting Scheme," *Milwaukee
Journal Sentinel*, June 12, 2006; Jim Riley and Robert Hardaway, "Hands Off
Electoral College," *Denver Post*, Feb. 8, 2007; John Samples, "A Critique of the National Popular Vote," Cato Institute Policy Analysis 622, Oct. 13, 2008, https://www
.cato.org/sites/cato.org/files/pubs/pdf/pa-622.pdf; James Taranto, "Faithless Lawmakers: Why the National Popular Vote Interstate Compact Should Die," *WSJ*,
July 29, 2010.

150. Trujillo, "After Bush v. Gore"; CRS, *National Popular Vote Initiative*, R43823 (2019
update), 12–16; Eliza Carney, "GOP Nonprofit Backs Electoral College," *Roll Call*,
Dec. 7, 2011. Regarding the national party platforms, see note 13 above; regarding
state parties, see "SREC Approves Resolution Supporting the Electoral College,"
Republican Party of Texas, Apr. 12, 2018, https://www.texasgop.org/srec-approves
-resolution-supporting-the-electoral-college/; Bates, "Betrayal"; Nebraska Leg.,
Hearing transcript, Jan. 23, 2015, 86–87.

151. *Salt Lake Tribune*, Feb. 10, 11, Mar. 2, 2012, and Oct. 22, 2016; Alberta, "Is the Electoral College Doomed?"; *Arizona Capital Times* (Phoenix), Feb. 1 and 4, 2016; Pete
Aleshire, "Debating Popular Vote Change in Presidential Elections," *Payson* (AZ)
Roundup, Mar. 16, 2016, https://www.paysonroundup.com/government/arizona
_state/debating-popular-vote-change-in-presidential-elections/article_fe478005
-6be3-5678-86bf-45eefeaf4b18.html; Robert Richie, interview with the author,

Aug. 29, 2018. For an optimistic assessment of the compact's chances, see Richie and Levien, "Big New York Win." By the end of 2013 the compact had been introduced in all states and had been actively considered in twenty-six of them. CRS, *National Popular Vote Initiative,* R43823 (2014), 8–10.

152. These numbers represent the actual electoral votes cast; the figures would have been slightly different had there not been faithless electors. Trump, unlike Bush in 2000, did not benefit by winning a disproportionate number of small states. *NYT,* Dec. 29, 2016.

153. Three additional Democratic electors attempted to vote for someone other than Clinton but were prevented from doing so. The total number of faithless electors was the highest on record. Lawrence Lessig, "The Constitution Lets the Electoral College Choose the Winner: They Should Choose Clinton," *WP,* Nov. 24, 2016; Kyle Cheney, "Lessig, Lawyers to Offer Support to Anti-Trump Electors," *Politico,* Dec. 5, 2016, https://www.politico.com/story/2016/12/larry-lessig-electors-trump-232231. Some reform advocates publicly opposed the attempt to mobilize electors to vote for someone other than Trump. Ed Kilgore, "Trying to Deny Trump the Presidency in the Electoral College Is a Really Bad Idea," *New York Magazine,* Nov. 30, 2016, http://nymag.com/intelligencer/2016/11/electoral-college-plot-against-trump-will-fail-and-backfire.html; Paul Thornton, "Electoral College, Go Ahead and Make Trump President," *LAT,* Dec. 17, 2016.

154. One case originated in Colorado and the other in Washington State. In Colorado an elector was replaced (and his vote voided) after he attempted to vote for John Kasich rather than the popular vote winner, Hillary Clinton; in Washington, several electors were fined for voting for candidates to whom they were not pledged. Both punitive actions were in accordance with state law. By 2016 approximately thirty states had laws of this type, seeking to prevent electors from being faithless, but the constitutionality (and enforceability) of these laws had never been tested. (See Chapter 5, note 40.) The lawsuits filed by Lessig's legal team argued that such laws were not enforceable, that the Constitution gave electors the right to vote as they wished. Washington's Supreme Court disagreed, holding (by an eight to one vote) that the state had the authority to fine faithless electors. An appeal of a federal district court decision in Colorado, however, yielded a different result: in August 2019 the Tenth Circuit Court ruled that the state did not have the authority to remove an elector and cancel his vote. To resolve the conflict, petitions were filed, asking the U.S. Supreme Court to hear appeals of the two cases so that the issue could be settled outside the context of a heated or disputed election. For the legal documents relevant to these cases, see https://equalcitizens.us/legal-materials/. See also *NYT,* Aug. 22 and 30, 2019; Richard Hasen, "The Coming Reckoning over the Electoral College," *Slate,* Sept. 4, 2019; Wilfred U. Codrington III, "Can the Members of the Electoral College Choose Who They Vote For?," Brennan Center for Justice, Jan. 8, 2020, https://www.brennancenter.org/our-work/research-reports/can-members-electoral-college-choose-who-they-vote. Regarding the faithless elector issue more broadly and other strategies for dealing with it, see Bennett, "Current

Electoral Reform Efforts," in Bugh, *Electoral College Reform,* 197, 200; Bennett, *Taming the Electoral College,* 95–121.

155. *NYT,* Dec. 19, 2016; *WSJ,* Nov. 14, 2016; *WP,* Dec. 16 and 25, 2016; *CDT,* Dec. 5, 2016; *USA Today,* Nov. 10, 2016. For additional editorials calling for reform, see *Baltimore Sun,* Nov. 13, 2016; *Detroit News,* Apr. 28, 2018; *San Jose Mercury News,* Nov. 16, 2016.

156. CRS, *The Electoral College: How It Works,* RL32611 (2017), 3.

157. For a conservative jeremiad about California's potential impact in a national popular vote, see Michael Barone, "Ditching the Electoral College Would Allow California to Impose Imperial Rule on a Colonial America," *Washington Examiner,* Dec. 4, 2016, https://www.washingtonexaminer.com/ditching-electoral-college-would-allow -california-to-impose-imperial-rule-on-a-colonial-america.

158. CRS, *The Electoral College: How It Works,* RL32611 (2017), 3; Swift, "Americans' Support for Electoral College Rises Sharply."

159. Other polls also registered sharp increases in Republican support for the Electoral College. A Marist poll found that 29 percent of Republicans favored a popular vote while 67 percent preferred the Electoral College. David Goldstein, "So Should We Keep the Electoral College? Poll Finds Voters Divided," *McClatchy DC Bureau,* Dec. 19, 2016, https://www.mcclatchydc.com/news/politics-government/white -house/article121442557.html. See also "American Voters Support Abortion, Oppose the Wall, Quinnipiac University National Poll Finds; Voters Differ with Trump on Guns, Taxes, Other Issues," Quinnipiac University Poll, Nov. 23, 2016, https://poll .qu.edu/national/release-detail?ReleaseID=2406; "President Trump: Cause for Hope and Disgust in the Garden State," Fairleigh Dickinson University's Public Mind Poll, Dec. 15, 2016, http://publicmind.fdu.edu/2016/161215/final.pdf; Pew Research Center, "The Electoral College, Congress, and Representation," 55.

160. *WP,* Nov. 15, 2016; Marie Solis, "Trump Wants Presidential Elections to Be Decided by Popular Vote, Which He Lost," *Newsweek,* Apr. 26, 2018, https://www.newsweek .com/trump-presidential-election-popular-vote-902916.

161. CRS, *Electoral College: Reform Proposals in the 114th and 115th Congress,* R44928 (2017), 5–18.

162. John Conyers Jr., "Electoral College Belongs in 1787," *USA Today,* Dec. 19, 2016, https://www.usatoday.com/story/opinion/2016/12/19/electoral-college-trump -democracy-states-column/95587592/; H. Res. 79, 115th Cong. (2017); 162 Cong. Rec. 6532 (2016); 163 Cong. Rec. 1228.

163. Anthony Jackson, "Ski Passes, Newspaper Ads and Meals: A Look Inside Lobbyist Spending during the Session," *New Mexico in Depth,* Jan. 29, 2018, http://nmindepth .com/2018/01/29/ski-passes-newspaper-ads-and-meals-a-look-inside-lobbyist -spending-during-the-session/; Dan McKay, "Political Notebook: National Popular- Vote Initiative Targets NM," *Albuquerque Journal,* July 27, 2018.

164. "Florida Voters Support the National Popular Vote for President, Poll Finds," League of Women Voters of Florida, Jan. 17, 2018, https://www.lwvfl.org/florida-voters -support-national-popular-vote-presidential-elections-poll-finds/; *Tampa Bay Times,* Jan. 1, 2017, Oct. 23, 2017; *Willamette Week,* Apr. 13, 2018; see also note 133 above

regarding Oregon. For capsule histories of what transpired in other states during these years, see "News History," NationalPopularVote.com.

165. Mark Pazniokas and Clarice Silber, "Connecticut Commits to National Popular Vote for President," *Connecticut Mirror* (Hartford), May 5, 2018, https://ctmirror.org/2018 /05/05/connecticut-commits-national-popular-vote-president/. The final vote in the Connecticut House was seventy-seven to seventy-three. *Hartford Courant,* May 13, 2009. Brian J. Gaines, "The Electoral College and Prospects for Reform," *State Journal Register* (Springfield, IL), Dec. 7, 2016.

166. CRS, *Electoral College Reform: Contemporary Issues,* R43824 (2017), 15–16; Alberta, "Is the Electoral College Doomed?"

167. *Salt Lake Tribune,* Oct. 22 and Nov. 19, 2016; Alberta, "Is the Electoral College Doomed?" In Utah, independent candidate Evan McMullin received 22 percent of the vote. Advocates in Utah did continue to raise the issue in 2017 and 2018. *Deseret Morning News,* Nov. 18, 2017; *Salt Lake Tribune,* Feb. 4, 2018.

168. Thea Cohen, "The New Plan to Make Every Vote Count," Making Every Vote Count, Mar. 5, 2019, https://www.makingeveryvotecount.com/mevc/2019/3/5/the -new-plan-to-make-every-vote-count. The initial plan, which harkened back to ideas put forward by Bennett and the Amar brothers, focused on the idea of getting the state of Ohio to agree to cast its electoral votes for the winner of the national popular vote; that alone, it was believed, could likely ensure that the winner of the popular vote would become president. By the fall of 2019 the focus had shifted away from Ohio. Author's interviews with Richard Tedlow, Oct. 11, 2018, and Reed Hundt, Oct. 3, 2019. For another innovative approach, see Edward Foley, "Want to Fix Presidential Elections? Here's the Quickest Way"; and Foley, *Presidential Elections and Majority Rule* (New York, 2019).

169. Mike Rosen, "Colorado Voters Get Final Say on National Popular Vote," *Colorado Springs Gazette,* Sept. 13, 2019; George Will, "The Electoral College Is Here to Stay," *WP,* Aug. 28, 2019; *Corvallis Advocate,* June 10, 2019; Matt Ford, "The State that Liberal Dreams Are Made Of," *New Republic,* June 5, 2019; *NYT,* May 22, 2019; *Bangor* (ME) *Daily News,* June 17, 2019; Common Cause, email to supporters, Aug. 31, 2019.

170. See the NBC News / *Wall St. Journal* poll as well as other 2019 polls in Appendix Table A.1.

171. Alberta, "Is the Electoral College Doomed?"; Jillian Evans and Brian J. Gaines, "Little Momentum for NPVIC," *News-Gazette* (Champaign-Urbana, IL), June 3, 2018. For more optimistic views, see Scot Lehigh, "How to Bring About True Democracy," *BG,* Dec. 20, 2016; Benjamin Hart, "Connecticut Joins Effort to Overturn Electoral College," *New York Magazine,* May 6, 2018, http://nymag.com /intelligencer/2018/05/connecticut-joins-effort-to-overturn-electoral-college.html ?gtm=top&gtm=top; Zachary Wolf, "There's One Thing Democrats Need if They Want to Break the Electoral College," May 30, 2019, https://www.cnn.com/2019/05 /28/politics/interstate-vote-compact-electoral-college/index.html; "Rosenstiel: More than Election Outcomes, the Electoral College Has Pervasive Effects on American Life," *St. Pete* (FL) *Catalyst,* Sept. 20, 2019.

172. Vikram Amar, "Overcoming Partisan Objections to Electoral College Reform: How Red States Could (and Should) Adopt the National Popular Vote Interstate Compact but Defer Implementation until 2032," *Verdict,* Justia, Apr. 18, 2019, https:// verdict.justia.com/2019/04/18/overcoming-partisan-objections-to-electoral-college -reform. Among the gaps that Amar highlighted were the absence of uniform voting requirements and recount procedures.

173. Steve LeBlanc, "Winner Take All?," AP Newswires, Mar. 26 2018, https://www .apnews.com/e7bcc365bb354952912ea85dc28ac157; *BG,* Aug. 10, 2018. For the legal documents related to these cases, see https://equalvotes.us/legal-documents/. See also the website of EqualCitizens.us, https://equalcitizens.us/, as well as the documents and articles at https://www.nationalpopularvote.com/lawsuits-filed-invalidate -state-winner-take-all-laws. For Lessig's account of the origins of the lawsuit, see Lawrence Lessig, "The Challenge to 'Winner Take All' Launched," *Medium,* https:// medium.com/@lessig/the-challenge-to-winner-take-all-launched-35ff6865a1c6.

174. In addition to the sources cited in note 173, see Stephen Young, "Lulac Sues Texas, Three Other States over Winner-Take-All Electoral College," *Dallas Observer,* Feb. 22, 2018, https://www.dallasobserver.com/news/texas-sued-over-electoral -college-10396193; John Monk, "Lawsuit Challenges SC's System of Winner-Take-All Presidential Voting," *The State* (Columbia), Feb. 23, 2018; Schuyler Kropf, "South Carolina Democrats Join National Effort Challenging Electoral College," *Post and Courier* (Charleston), Feb. 23, 2018.

175. *BG,* Aug. 10, 2018; Lessig, "The Challenge"; Adam Eichen, "The Electoral College Reform Movement Made Great Strides This Month, but Is It Enough?," *Medium,* May 30, 2018, https://equalvotes.us/2018/05/31/adam-eichen-medium-the-electoral -college-reform-movement-made-great-strides-this-month-but-is-it-enough/; Lawrence Lessig, interview with the author, Oct. 18, 2018; email from Jason Harrow to Equal Citizens mailing list, Sept. 10, 2019; League of Latin American Citizens v. Abbott, No. 19-50214 (5th Cir. Feb. 26, 2020).

176. Young, "Lulac Sues Texas"; Nicholas Papantonis, "Group Sues South Carolina in Effort to Change How We Pick a President," *ABC15 News,* Mar. 29, 2018, https:// wpde.com/news/local/group-sues-south-carolina-in-effort-to-change-how-we-pick -a-president; League of United Latin American Citizens, Joseph C. Parker Jr., Hector Flores, et al., v. Governor of the State of Texas and Secretary of State of the State of Texas, 5:18-cv-0017 (TX 2018); Eugene Baten, Chester Willis, et al., v. Governor of the State of South Carolina, Secretary of State of the State of South Carolina, South Carolina Election Commission, 2:18-cv-00510-PMD (SC 2018).

177. Sonya Rastogi et al., "The Black Population: 2010," *Census Brief, Report C2010BR-06,* U.S. Census Bureau, Sept. 2011, https://www.census.gov/prod/cen2010/briefs/c2010br -06.pdf; *WP,* Sept. 25, 2017. Barack Obama received 95 and 93 percent of the black vote in his two election campaigns; John Kerry's level of support (88 percent) was the same as Clinton's.

178. North Carolina voted Democratic only once (in 2008) during this period. Virginia did so three times and Florida twice. "Elections 1840–2008," Voting America: United

States Politics, 1840–2008, University of Richmond Digital Scholarship Lab, https://dsl.richmond.edu/voting/elections.html.

179. E. J. Dionne, "The Electoral College Is in Trouble," *WP,* Aug. 28, 2019; Greg Sargent, "Trump Is Betting that the Electoral College—and the Courts—Will Save Him," *WP,* Apr. 17, 2019. Some analysts suggested that Trump might lose the popular vote by an even greater margin than he had in 2016 but still remain in office.

180. A Pew poll conducted in April 2018 found that 55 percent of adults preferred an NPV; the figure was 75 percent among Democrats but only 32 percent among Republicans. Pew Research Center, "The Electoral College, Congress and Representation," 55. In the wake of the 2016 election, Republicans in Virginia, Minnesota, and New Hampshire briefly explored the possibility of switching from winner-take-all to districts. *WP,* Jan. 24 and 25, 2017; "'Winner Takes All' Electoral System Will Stay in Virginia," WTKRNews3 (Richmond), Jan. 27, 2017, https://wtkr.com /2017/01/27/winner-takes-all-electoral-vote-system-will-stay-in-virginia/; James Pindell, "Changing the Electoral College Would Make NH Voters Less Powerful," *New Hampshire Magazine,* March 2017; Brian Bakst, "Minnesota Lawmakers Weigh Presidential Politics," *Capitol View,* Minnesota Public Radio, Jan. 26, 2017, https:// blogs.mprnews.org/capitol-view/2017/01/minnesota-lawmakers-weigh -presidential-politics/.

181. It also remained possible that the NPVIC, once joined by the requisite number of states, would need congressional consent.

182. *NYT,* Jan. 3, 2019. Some progressives, like Representative Alexandria Ocasio-Cortez of New York, have maintained that the Electoral College is biased against minorities and favors white rural voters. Mairead McArdle, "Ocasio-Cortez: The Electoral College Is a 'Scam,'" *National Review,* Aug. 20, 2019; see also Eric Levitz, "Here's Every Defense of the Electoral College and Why They're All Wrong," http://nymag .com/intelligencer/2019/03/why-every-argument-for-preserving-the-electoral -college-is-wrong-warren-cnn.html. Nate Cohn voiced skepticism of this view in "The Electoral College's Real Problem," *NYT,* Mar. 22, 2019.

183. Biden had voted against an NPV in 1979; he did not address the subject of Electoral College reform in the fall and winter of 2019–2020.

184. Email from the Congressional Progressive Caucus PAC, distributed by *The Nation,* Oct. 24, 2018; Li Zhou, "Senate Democrats Introduce a Constitutional Amendment to Abolish the Electoral College," *Vox,* Apr.3, 2019, https://www.vox.com/2019/4/3 /18292513/abolish-electoral-college-senate-brian-schatz-kirsten-gillibrand -elizabeth-warren. Schatz did not expect his proposal to come to fruition anytime soon. "I don't underestimate the difficulty here," he observed. Senator Jeff Merkley (Oregon) also introduced a resolution as part of a broader electoral reform package.

CONCLUSION

1. There have been two recent efforts to achieve reform without amending the Constitution: the National Popular Vote Interstate Compact and a set of lawsuits that aim to have winner-take-all declared unconstitutional. Whether either of these

strategies can yield durable change is an open question. See the discussions in Chapter 7.

2. Ariane de Vogue, "Ginsburg Talks Partisan Rancor, Electoral College, and Kale," CNN, Feb. 7, 2017, https://www.cnn.com/2017/02/07/politics/ruth-bader-ginsburg -electoral-college/index.html.

3. Regarding the validity (or lack thereof) of claims that small states have generally resisted an NPV, see the discussions in Chapters 4–6.

4. The Senate has never approved an NPV proposal by the requisite two-thirds majority. It did, however, approve district elections proposals between 1813 and 1822, and it passed the Lodge-Gossett proportional measure in 1950.

5. The notable exception to this pattern among "wrong-winner" elections was the election of 1888, which did not generate much of a stir.

6. A decline in the sense of urgency in the years following a crisis election also contributed to the failure of efforts to mandate district elections in 1801–1804. The most clear-cut instances of deliberate delays vitiating support for reform occurred in 1969–1970 and after the 1976 election.

7. *WSJ*, Aug. 1, 2001.

8. Racially polarized voting has been persistent in the South in recent decades. See Charles Stewart III, Nathaniel Persily, and Stephen Ansolabehere, "Regional Differences in Racial Polarization in the 2012 Presidential Election: Implications for the Constitutionality of Section 5 of the Voting Rights Act," *Harvard Law Review Forum* 126 (2013), 205–262; Matthew M. Hoffman, "The Illegitimate President: Minority Vote Dilution and the Electoral College," 105 Yale L.J. 935 (1996). For a thought-provoking perspective on race and the Republican Party, see Stuart Stevens, "Ex-Romney Strategist: Kill the Electoral College to Help America and, Yes, Republicans," *USA Today*, July 8, 2019.

9. For a recent example of this perspective, see Christopher Demuth, "The Man Who Saved the Electoral College," *National Affairs* 42 (Winter 2020), https://www .nationalaffairs.com/publications/detail/the-man-who-saved-the-electoral-college.

10. For rejoinders to the claims made on behalf of the Electoral College, over the course of two centuries, see the writings and debate records cited throughout this book. For a recent analysis of the arguments in defense of the Electoral College, see George C. Edwards III, *Why the Electoral College Is Bad for America*, 2nd ed. (New Haven, CT, 2011), 114–194. See also the discussion of Edwards's book in Chapter 7.

11. Virginia, for example, now has a Democratic state government, and its House recently voted to join the NPVIC. Democrats have also been making significant gains in Texas and Georgia.

12. John Conyers Jr., "Electoral College Belongs in 1787," *USA Today*, Dec. 19, 2016.

13. *NYT*, Dec. 19, 2000. The *Times* changed its position several years later.

14. See, for example, the discussion of congressional responses to Ross Perot's candidacy in Chapter 7.

15. *Direct Popular Election of the President and Vice President of the United States: Hearings before the Senate Subcommittee on the Constitution of the Committee on the*

Judiciary, 96th Cong. 2 (1979) (statement of Sen. Birch Bayh). As Bayh and his colleagues discussed at length in the late 1960s and the 1970s, there are different possible configurations of a national popular vote. The differences center on the procedure to be adopted in the (not-so-unlikely) event that a multi-candidate race eventuates in no candidate winning an outright majority of the vote in the initial balloting. A simple approach to this problem would be to award the presidency to the plurality winner, but numerous critics have pointed out that this could yield presidents who had the support of only a distinct minority of the electorate. Bayh's resolutions usually required a candidate to receive at least 40 percent of the vote in order to win election; otherwise a runoff election would be held between the top two candidates. Other NPV advocates have maintained that there should be a runoff if the leading candidate receives anything less than 50 percent of the vote. In recent years, there has been considerable discussion among reformers about the possibility of avoiding runoff elections (and their possible pitfalls) through the use of "ranked choice ballots" that would permit voters to indicate how favorably they regard each of the competing candidates. Such a mechanism, which modern technology makes feasible, could ensure that the candidate with the strongest support overall would be elected.

APPENDIX C. THE EVOLUTION OF THE TERM
ELECTORAL COLLEGE

1. Entry "electoral, adj. and n.," *OED Online,* accessed July 23, 2013, http://www.oed .com.ezp-prod1.hul.harvard.edu/view/Entry/60241; third quotation refers to Senator Abraham Baldwin (GA), *Annals of the Congress of the United States,* 6th Cong. 1st sess. (Jan. 23, 1800), 31 (Washington, DC, 1851). J. Hampden Dougherty, *The Electoral System of the United States* (New York, 1906), 74, also maintains that the phrase first appears in congressional debates in 1800. The 1788 quotation is from "The Government of Nature Delineated or an Exact Picture of the New Federal Constitution by Aristocrotis," Carlisle, [PA], 1788, reprinted in *The Complete Anti-Federalist,* ed. Herbert J. Storing (Chicago, 1981), 3:208.

2. "Electoral College of Pennsylvania: In the Senate," *Register of Pennsylvania,* 2, no. 23 (Dec. 20, 1828): 359; Joseph Blunt, ed., *The American Annual Register; for the Year 1832–33, or the Fifty-Seventh Year of American Independence* (New York, 1835), 17; "Political Portraits, No. XII: Silas Wright Jr.," *United States Magazine, and Democratic Review,* Apr. 1839, 413; "Maryland Election," *NWR,* Sept.–Mar 1817, 47. Fitzwilliam Byrdsall, *The History of the Loco-Foco or Equal Rights Party* (New York, 1842), 60, offers an early example of the systemic usage: "that clumsy aristocratic machinery, called the electoral college."

3. One author, in 1885, used the phrase *electoral college* in several different ways (referring to the electors of one state, to the national body of electors, and systemically) in a single short publication: F. A. P. Barnard, "How Shall the President Be Elected?," *NAR,* Feb. 1885, 97–108. General statements about the history of the phrase, and its

meaning and incidence, are based on analyses drawn from the following three sources: Analyses of Ngrams from Google for "electoral college" and "electoral colleges," Google Books Ngram Viewer, http://books.google.com/ngrams; entry "college, n.," *OED Online,* accessed July 25, 2012, http://www.oed.com.ezp-prod1.hul .harvard.edu/view/Entry/36298; and, perhaps most importantly, Mark Davies, *The Corpus of Historical American English: 400 Million Words, 1810–2009* (2010), http:// corpus.byu.edu/coha/. This last source, unfortunately, does not include newspapers before 1860.

Acknowledgments

During the years that this book has been in preparation, I have received support and assistance from many sources. It is a pleasure long anticipated to express my gratitude.

It has been my good fortune during this time to have had, first, Don Olander, and, then, Scott Stackpole working with me on an almost daily basis. During the first phases of this project, Don kept the research files organized, tracked down innumerable sources and loose ends, and wrestled expertly with often complicated citations. Even after he had ceased to officially work with me, he remained the go-to person for the endnotes. After Don moved on to another job at the Harvard Kennedy School, Scott took over these tasks and carried them out with patience and care. In the last year, his attention to detail and fine editorial instincts have been invaluable in readying the manuscript for publication. Both Scott and Don have often gone well beyond the call of nine-to-five duty to make sure things got done and got done right. Of equal importance, they have always been superb company.

This project has also benefited from the labors of a rotating team of student research assistants. Eduardo Canedo, Chase Foster, and Maya Brodziak made sustained contributions during the early years of this project; more recently, Madeline Alvendia and Carolyn Angius have done the same. Andrew Pope helped in numerous ways, not least with his knowledge of southern history and its sources. Justin Curtis has been an extraordinary assistant for several years, offering good-humored, efficient, and informed responses to scores, probably hundreds, of emails, many of them sent at odd hours of the night. Others who have contributed to the research include Keru Cai, Mary Chobanian, Mary Davis, Holger Droessler, Louis Gerdelan, Andrew Hecht, Tsin Yen Koh, Nicholas Lillios, Stephane de Messieres, Mircea Popa, Laura Ryan, Shirley Vargas, Emmet von Stackelberg, Jonathan Warsh, David Weinstein, Kenneth Weisbrode, and Katherine Williams. Funding to (modestly) remunerate these researchers has been provided by the Wiener, Ash, and Shorenstein Centers as well as the dean's office at the Harvard Kennedy School.

Friends and colleagues have read and commented on the manuscript, encouraging the author while improving the product. Jack Rakove applied his sharp editorial eye and knowledge of early American history to the eighteenth- and nineteenth-century portions of the manuscript; Ben Page did the same for the twentieth-century chapters while gently pressing me to think seriously about political science perspectives. Edward Foley took time away from his own insightful book on presidential elections to make thoughtful suggestions about mine. I also received valuable comments and criticism on parts of the manuscript from Sven Beckert, Dan Carpenter, John Demos, Robert Goldstein, Martin Miller, Tova Wang, and Lewis Wurgaft. Martina Viarengo generously and cheerfully guided me through terrains where she is expert and I am not. Douglas Myers gave a close reading to the entire manuscript (some chapters more than once), graciously urging me to sharpen my arguments and surrender some unfortunate stylistic habits. I benefited, too, from the questions raised by audience members at numerous universities and centers where I have presented portions of this book. My colleagues at the Kennedy School heard me out twice, productively challenging me on both occasions; my students have done so annually.

I am indebted also to the librarians and archivists who helped me to access and utilize sometimes obscure and complicated sources. Harvard's libraries are unparalleled, and the men and women who make them user-friendly are indispensable for historical researchers. Keely Wilczek and Daniel Becker, research librarians at the Kennedy School library, deserve special mention. Further afield, Tim Hodgdon at the Wilson Library, UNC-Chapel Hill, fielded numerous queries about Senator Sam Ervin's papers. Kate Cruikshank, Political Papers Specialist at Indiana University, helped me to access the papers of Senator Birch Bayh and generously arranged for the timely digitization of the parts of the collection most relevant to this study. She also introduced me to several former members of Bayh's staff.

I am grateful, too, for the conversations and correspondence that I have had with those who witnessed or participated in some of the more recent episodes in this story: Nels Ackerson; Perry Apelbaum; former representative William Delahunt; Max Frankel; Mark Gitenstein; John Koza; Rob Richie; George "Skip" Roberts; and my college roommate, Representative Robert C. Scott. Jason Berman has become a regular correspondent, providing numerous insights and facts to supplement the documentary record of the 1960s and 1970s as well as witty commentary about all that has happened since.

My agent, Andrew Wylie, and my editor, Kathleen McDermott, encouraged this project well before the 2016 election (when the topic suddenly seemed to become more timely), and they have stood by it through a series of unanticipated delays. Kathleen's good judgment has helped to shape some of the contours of the book. Melody Negron and her team at Westchester Publishing Services have superintended the book's production with professionalism and patience.

I would also like to acknowledge two communities that have contributed to my thinking about political institutions and electoral reform over the past two decades. Books are solitary ventures, but they emerge from and are influenced by communities of engagement and debate. One such community for me has consisted of colleagues at Havard (many of them, alas, now retired or departed to other universities) with whom I thought through the intersections among the social sciences, public policy, and the study of history. The other has been the broad, geographically dispersed community of scholars, activists, journalists, politicians, and filmmakers who have been striving to reinvigorate democratic institutions in the United States and elsewhere. I have learned a great deal from them.

Finally, I'd like to thank members of my family—who may have trouble believing that this book is actually done. My sister, Judith Redwing Keyssar, mobilized her unique healthcare talents to assist me through several difficult patches. My daughter, Natalie, while pursuing her own career in far-flung parts of the globe, has been a constant source of joy, sharing her own discoveries and understanding my frequent disappearances into my study—even when she is visiting. My wife, Rosabelli, to whom this volume is dedicated, has been there every day in innumerable ways.

Index

A page number followed by the letter f refers to a figure. A page number followed by the letter t indicates a table.

Madison, James (*continued*)
20–21, 22, 24, 171, 175; political parties
and, 64, 406n44; reform ideas in 1823,
89–91; on separation of powers, 19
Maine, district elections in, 1, 58, 142–143,
316, 376, 413n1, 434n80; and NPVIC,
345t, 358
Maish, Levi, 125, 127, 128
Mansfield, Mike: on federalism and
national popular vote, 277; 1956 vote
on national popular vote and, 201;
NPV resolution of 1967 and, 214;
NPV resolution of 1969 and, 240,
243, 244, 247–248, 251, 256; proposal
after 1960 election, 208; as small-state
leader, 332
Marshall, John, 73, 379
Martin, Louis E., 282, 283, 481n96
Mason, George, 18, 20, 22, 24, 74–75
Massachusetts, 18, 27, 35, 47, 66, 70, 82, 292,
318; winner-take-all lawsuit and, 359
McCarthy, Eugene, 267, 322
McConnell, Mitch, 320, 321, 322, 331, 353
McDuffie, George, 57, 87, 89, 90, 91, 92, 99,
100–104, 106–109, 111
Michigan, 12, 58, 117. *See also* Miner Law
Miner Law, 131–143, 163, 182, 370, 376
minorities: debates regarding impact of
NPV on, 236–237, 265–266, 282–296,
510n182; Lodge-Gossett proposal and,
149. *See also* African-American voters;
Hispanic voters; Jewish organizations
"misfire, Electoral College," 486n4
Mitchell, Clarence, Jr., 157–158, 223, 244,
283, 460n48
Monroe, James, 63, 64, 74, 93, 418n42
Morris, Gouverneur, 19, 20, 22, 23–24, 43,
48, 171
Morton, Oliver P., 119–124, 127, 129, 184,
369, 375
Moynihan, Daniel P., 281–282, 300, 303
Mugwumps, 129, 431n45
Mundt, Karl, 166–167, 169, 170, 208, 214,
215–216, 228, 257, 317, 440nn141–142,
453n97, 462n60
Mundt-Coudert proposal, 166–168

National Bonus Plan, 273–274
National Commission on Federal
Election Reform, 329
national popular vote (NPV): antebellum
proposals for, 101, 173–176, 177–179;
arguments against, 183–184, 187–189,
195–198, 221–222, 236–238, 277–278,
279–282, 297, 200–301, 330; arguments
for, 182–196, 199–205, 222, 276–277,
278–279, 297, 299–300, 326, 330–331,
378–379; Constitutional Convention
and, 19–22, 171; defined, 443n13;
Delaware's Supreme Court motion
of 1966 and, 212–213; during Reconstruction and late nineteenth century,
177, 180–185; entering mainstream of
public debate, 210–213; final hearing
of twentieth century dealing with,
323–325; Lacock proposal of 1816,
173–177; little progress from 1890 to
1945, 185–189; Lodge's preference for,
151; in 1940s and 1950s, 165, 199–205;
partial enfranchisement of women
and, 189; public opinion polls regarding,
7, 199–200, 236, 270–271, 383–386t; recent
partisan opposition to, 312–315, 370; roll
call votes on, 245t, 249t, 302t; slavery
and, 9–10, 21–22, 171, 373 (*see also* three-
fifths clause); small-state advantage and,
7–8, 175, 183–184, 187, 196–198, 221–222,
248, 250, 277, 368; southern opposition
to, 189–198, 208, 250, 258–262, 373, 377;
summary of history of, 171–172; Supreme
Court apportionment rulings and,
209–210; waves of resolutions favoring,
177. *See also* Bayh, Birch; public opinion
polls, on national popular vote; Langer,
William
National Popular Vote Interstate
Compact, 5, 341–353; arguments pro and
con, 348–351; conception of, 341–344;
continuing effort on behalf of, 362, 363;
after 2016 election, 354–358; after 2018
election, 357–358; issues regarding
design and workability of, 350–351; legal
issues regarding, 349–350, 502n137,